GALE
ENCYCLOPEDIA OF
MULTICULTURAL
AMERICA PRIMARY DOCUMENTS

GALE
ENCYCLOPEDIA OF
MULTICULTURAL
AMERICA PRIMARY DOCUMENTS

volume 1

Afghan Americans – Italian Americans

Edited by

JEFFREY LEHMAN

GALE GROUP

Detroit
San Francisco
London
Boston
Woodbridge, CT

Jeffrey Lehman, *Editor*
Elizabeth Shaw, *Associate Editor*
Gloria Lam, *Assistant Editor*
Linda S. Hubbard, *Managing Editor*

Contributing editors: Brian Koski, Ashyia N. Henderson,
Allison McClintic Marion, Mark F. Mikula, Joseph M. Palmisano, Patrick Politano

Maria Franklin, *Permissions Manager*
Edna Hedblad and Keryl Stanley, *Permissions Specialists*

Mary Beth Trimper, *Production Director*
Evi Seoud, *Assistant Production Manager*

Cynthia Baldwin, *Product Design Manager*
Martha Schiebold, *Art Director*

Barbara J. Yarrow, *Imaging and Multimedia Content Manager*
Randy Bassett, *Image Database Supervisor*
Pamela A. Reed, *Imaging Coordinator*
Mike Logusz, *Senior Imaging Specialist*

ISBN (set) 0-7876-3990-7
ISBN (Vol 1) 0-7876-3991-5
ISBN (Vol 2) 0-7876-3992-3

Library of Congress Cataloging-in-Publication Data

Gale encyclopedia of multicultural America. Primary documents / edited by Jeffrey Lehman.
p. cm.
Includes bibliographical references and index.
Summary: Primary documents, including letters, articles, cartoons, photos, and songs, illuminate the experience of culture groups in the U.S. from colonial times to the present.
ISBN 0-7876-3990-7 (set : alk. Paper) — ISBN 0-7876-3991-5 (v. 1) —ISBN 0-7876-3992-3 (v. 2)
1. Pluralism (Social sciences)—United States—History—Sources—Juvenile literature. 2. Minorities—United States—History—Sources—Juvenile literature. 3. Ethnology—United States—History—Sources—Juvenile literature. 4. United States—Ethnic relations—Sources—Juvenile literature. 5. United States—Race relations—Sources—Juvenile literature. [1. Ethnology. 2. Minorities. 3. United States—History—Sources.] I. Title: Encyclopedia of multicultural America. Primary documents. II. Lehman, Jeffrey, 1969-
E184.A1 G15 1999
305.8'00973–dc21   99-044219

CONTENTS

PREFACE

The *Gale Encyclopedia of Multicultural America: Primary Documents* was created as a companion to the award-winning *Gale Encyclopedia of Multicultural America*. Each ethnic group represented in *Primary Documents* has an essay in the second edition of *Gale Encyclopedia of Multicultural America*. The 210 primary documents included in this book bring history to life by providing insight into key events as well as the everyday lives of 90 different cultures. Students and teachers of U.S. history, social studies, and literature will find this book an indispensable tool for research projects, time period exploration, and independent analysis and critical thinking about historical evidence.

SCOPE

Unlike many compilations of primary documents, the *Gale Encyclopedia of Multicultural America: Primary Documents* is not limited to one type of document, one group of people, or a small period of time. We have chosen almost 20 document types, including letters, poems, oral histories, autobiographies, political cartoons, recipes, speeches, and photographs. They represent 90 national, ethnoreligious, and Native American groups. The documents originated throughout the history of North America, from transcriptions of Native American legends—which date from long before European arrival—to periodical articles from 1999.

Each item was chosen for one of the following reasons: it expands upon an individual's American experience or the general immigrant/minority experience in America; or it records the treatment of an entire group. The 198 text documents average a little more than 2,000 words each. The graphical documents have been enlarged to nearly full-page size to maximize legibility. With the exception of articles from scholarly journals, the majority of documents were created by members of the group being highlighted.

FORMAT

The *Gale Encyclopedia of Multicultural America: Primary Documents* is arranged alphabetically by group name. When a group has more than one item, they appear chronologically from oldest to newest date of creation. A commentary of about 800 words introduces each document to provide historical, literary, and/or biographical context.

For more information on the group's experiences in the United States—specifically in the areas of acculturation and assimilation; family and community; language; religion; employment and economics; politics and government; and significant contributions to American society—please consult the second edition of the *Gale Encyclopedia of Multicultural America*.

ADDITIONAL FEATURES

More than 80 photographs, maps, and other illustrations provide visual cues to the groups and their experiences. A two-level general index follows the last document in the second volume. It cites specific documents by title as well as ethnic groups, concepts, people, and places.

ACKNOWLEDGMENTS

This book would not have seen publication in as fine a form as it has without the intelligent guidance and unflagging persistence of Liz Shaw. See the separate "Credits" section for acknowledgment of the copyright holders when cooperation made this collection possible.

SUGGESTIONS ARE WELCOME

The editor welcomes your suggestions on any aspect of this work. Please mail comments and suggestions to: The Editor, *Gale Encyclopedia of Multicultural America: Primary Documents*, The Gale Group, 27500 Drake Road, Farmington Hills, MI 48331-3535; call 1-800-877-GALE [877-4253]; fax to (248) 699-8062; or e-mail galegroup.com.

CREDITS

The editors wish to thank the copyright holders of the excerpted criticism included in this volume and the permissions managers of many book and magazine publishing companies for assisting us in securing reproduction rights. We are also grateful to the staffs of the Detroit Public Library, the University of Detroit Mercy Library, Wayne State University Purdy/Kresge Library Complex, and the University of Michigan Libraries for making their resources available to us. Following is a list of the copyright holders who have granted us permission to reproduce material in these volumes of *Gale Encyclopedia of Multicultural America: Primary Documents*. Every effort has been made to trace copyright, but if omissions have been made, please let us know.

Copyrighted excerpts in the *Gale Encyclopedia of Multicultural America: Primary Documents*, were reproduced from the following periodicals:

Ethnicity, v. 2, September, 1975. Copyright © 1975 by Academic Press, Inc. Reproduced by permission.—*Indiana Folklore: Journal of the Hoosier Folklore Society,* v. III, 1970. Reproduced by permission. —*New York Folklore Quarterly,* v. XX, September, 1964; v. XXI, September, 1965. Both reproduced by permission of the publisher./ v. XXIV, December, 1968 for "Polish Customs in New York Mills, N.Y." by Robert Maziarz. Reproduced by permission of the publisher and the author. —*The Nation,* New York, v. 253, September 23, 1991; v. 259, December 12, 1994; v.264, February 3, 1997; v. 266, May 18, 1998. © 1991, 1994, 1997, 1998 *The Nation* magazine/ The Nation Company, Inc. All reproduced by permission. —*The New Republic,* v. 217, November 24, 1997. © 1997 The New Republic, Inc. Reproduced by permission of *The New Republic.* —*The New York Times,* April 3, 1998; June 26, 1998; February 10, 1999; April 4, 1999; April 7, 1999; May 2, 1999; May 10, 1999. Copyright © 1998, 1999 by The New York Times Company. All reproduced by permission. —*Society,* v. 14, September-October, 1977. Reproduced by permission. —*Utah Historical Quarterly,* v. 43, Winter, 1975. © Copyright 1975 Utah State Historical Society. Reproduced by permission. —*Vital Speeches of the Day,* v. XI, August 1, 1945. Reproduced by permission. —Zia, Helen. From a speech delivered on January 29, 1994 at the 6th Annual Gay Asian Pacific Alliance in San Francisco. Copyright © 1994 by Helen Zia. Reproduced by permission.

Copyrighted excerpts in the *Gale Encyclopedia of Multicultural America: Primary Documents*, were reproduced from the following books:

Adamic, Louis. From *Laughing in the Jungle.* Harper & Brothers, 1932. Copyright 1932 by Louis Adamic. Renewed 1959 by Stella Adamic. Reproduced by permission of Harper-Collins Publishers. —Alvarez, Jaime. From *American Mosaic: The Immigrant Experience in the Words of Those Who Lived It,* by Joan Morrison and Charlotte Fox Zabusky. E. P. Dutton, 1980. Copyright © 1980 by Joan Morrison and Charlotte Fox Zabusky. All rights reserved. Reproduced by permission of Joan Morrison and Charlotte Zabusky. —Ayobami, Tunde. From *American Mosaic: The Immigrant Experience in the Words of Those Who Lived It,* by Joan Morrison and Charlotte Fox Zabusky. E. P. Dutton, 1980. Copyright © 1980 by Joan Morrison and Charlotte Fox Zabusky. All rights reserved. Reproduced by permission of Joan Morrison and Charlotte Zabusky. —Bode, Janet. From *New Kids on the Block: Oral Histories of Immigrant Teens.* Franklin Watts, 1989. Copyright © 1989 by Janet Bode. All rights reserved. Reproduced by permission. —Bray, Bill. From *First Person, First Peoples.* Edited by Andrew Garrod and Colleen Larimore. Cornell University Press, 1997. Copyright © 1997 by Cornell University. Reproduced by permission of Cornell University Press. —Burns, Allan F. From *Maya in Exile: Guatemalans in Florida.* Temple University Press, 1993. Copyright © 1993 by Temple University Press. All rights reserved. Reproduced by permission. —Chawla, Sudershan S. From *Asian American Experience in the United States,* by Joann Faung Jean Lee. McFarland & Company, Inc., 1991. Copyright © 1991 by Joann Faung Jean Lee. All rights reserved. Reproduced by permission. —Criddle, Joan D. From *Bamboo & Butterflies: From Refugee to Citizen.* East/West Bridge Publishing House, 1992. Copyright © 1992 by Joan D. Criddle. All rights reserved. Reproduced by permission. —El Saadawi, Nawal. From *Memoirs from the Women's Prison.* Translated by Marilyn Booth. University of California Press, 1994. Copyright © Nawal El Saadawi 1983. Translation © Marilyn Booth 1986. Afterward for the American edition © 1994 by The Regents of the University of California. Reproduced by permission of the publisher and the author. —Espada, Martin. From *Trumpets from the Island of Their Eviction.* Bilingual Press/Editorial Bilingue, 1987, 1994. Copyright © 1987, 1994 by Martin Espada. All rights reserved. Reproduced by permission. —Flores, Rita. From *American Mosaic: The Immigrant Experience in the Words of Those Who Lived It,* by Joan Morrison and Charlotte Fox Zabusky. E. P. Dutton 1980. Copyright © 1980 by Joan Morrison and Charlotte Fox Zabusky. All rights reserved. Reproduced by permission of Joan Morrison and Charlotte Zabusky. —From "Birth Chant for Kau-I-ke-ao-uli" in *The Echo of Our Song: Chants & Poems of the Hawaiians.* Edited and translated by Mary Kawena Pukui and Alfons L. Korn. University Press of Hawaii, 1973. Copyright © 1973 by The University Press of Hawaii. All rights reserved. Reproduced by permission. —From "The Pearl" in *The Echo of Our Song: Chants & Poems of the Hawaiians.* Edited and translated by Mary Kawena Pukui and Alfons L. Korn. University Press of Hawaii, 1973. Copyright © 1973 by The University Press of Hawaii. All rights reserved. Reproduced by permission. —Hadley, Su-Chu. From *American Mosaic: The Immigrant Experience in the Words of Those Who Lived It,* by Joan Morrison and Charlotte Fox Zabusky. E. P. Dutton, 1980. Copyright © 1980 by Joan Morrison and Charlotte Fox Zabusky. All rights reserved. Reproduced by permission of Joan Morrison and Charlotte Zabusky. —Haney, Michael. From a speech delivered on March 30, 1991 on the International Indian Treaty Council before the United Nations Subcommission on the Prevention of Discrimination Against Minorities, at the American Indian Community House in New York, NY. Reproduced by permission of the author. —Hassan, Ibrahim. From *American Mosaic: The Immigrant Experience in the Words of Those Who Lived It,* by Joan Morrison and Charlotte Fox Zabusky. E. P. Dutton, 1980. Copyright © 1980 by Joan Morrison and Charlotte Fox Zabusky. All rights reserved. Reproduced by permission of Joan Morrison and Charlotte Zabusky. —Hernandez, Antonia. From a speech delivered on October 5, 1994, on "Are We Compassion Fatigued?" at the Temple Isaiah in Los Angeles, CA. Reproduced by permission of the author. —Johanson, Gunnar. From *American Mosaic: The Immigrant Experience in the Words of Those Who Lived It,* by Joan Morrison and Charlotte Fox Zabusky. E. P. Dutton, 1980. Copyright © 1980 by Joan Morrison and Charlotte Fox Zabusky. All rights reserved. Reproduced by permission of Joan Morrison and Charlotte Zabusky. —Jordan, Barbara. From *"A New Beginning: A New Dedication."* Reproduced by permission of the Estate of Barbara C. Jordan. —Kanosky, Stella. Excerpt from *"Case Study in Family Relationships,"* August, 1941. Reproduced by permission of Stella McDermott. —Karenga, Maulana. In an introduction to *"The Million Man March/Day of Absence Mission Statement."* Reproduced by permission. —Kiet, Kim Huot. From *Asian American Experiences in the United States,* by Joann Faung Jean Lee. McFarland & Company, Inc., 1991. Copyright © 1991 by Joann Faung Jean Lee. All rights reserved. Reproduced by permission. —Kochiyama, Yuri. From *Asian American Experiences in the United States,* by Joann Faung Jean Lee. McFarland & Company, Inc., 1991. Copyright © 1991 by Joann Faung Jean Lee. All rights reserved. Reproduced by permission. —Laxalt, Robert. From *Sweet Promised Land.* Harper & Brothers Publishers, 1957. Copyright 1957, renewed 1985 by Robert Laxalt. Reproduced by permission of HarperCollins Publishers. —Lee, Li-Young. From *The City in Which I Love You.* BOA Editions, Ltd., 1990. Copyright © 1990 by Li-Young Lee. All rights reserved. Reproduced by permission. —Liadis, Nikos. From *American Mosaic: The*

Santoli, Al with Tesfai Gebremariam and Lem Lem Gebremariam. From *New Americans, An Oral History: Immigrants and Refugees in the U.S. Today,* by Al Santoli. Viking Penguin, 1988. Copyright © Al Santoli, 1988. All rights reserved. Reproduced by permission of Penguin Putnam Inc. —Siu, Paul C. P. From *The Chinese Laundryman: A Study of Social Isolation.* Edited by John Kuo Wei Tchen. New York University Press, 1987. Copyright © 1987 by Paul C. Siu All rights reserved. Reproduced by permission. —Smith, Faith. From "I See an Incredible Force within Native People" in *Messengers of the Wind: Native American Women Tell Their Life Stories.* Edited by Jane Katz. Ballantine Books, 1995. Copyright © 1995 by Jane Katz. All rights reserved. Reproduced by permission of Random House, Inc. —Song, Cathy. From *Picture Bride.* Yale University Press, 1983. Copyright © 1983 by Cathy Song. All rights reserved. Reproduced by permission. —Stennett, Rennie. From *American Mosaic: The Immigrant Experience in the Words of Those Who Lived It,* by Joan Morrison and Charlotte Fox Zabusky. E. P. Dutton, 1980. Copyright © 1980 by Joan Morrison and Charlotte Fox Zabusky. All rights reserved. Reproduced by permission of Joan Morrison and Charlotte Zabusky. —Sue, Sam. From *Asian American Experiences in the United States,* by Joann Faung Jean Lee. McFarland & Company, Inc., 1991. Copyright © 1991 by Joann Faung Jean Lee. All rights reserved. Reproduced by permission. —Suettinger, Sue Jean Lee. From *Asian American Experiences in the United States,* by Joann Faung Jean Lee. McFarland & Company, Inc., 1991. Copyright © 1991 by Joann Faung Jean Lee. All rights reserved. Reproduced by permission. —Tracy, Deescheeny Nez. From "Deescheeny Nez Tracy" in *Stories of Traditional Navajo Life and Culture.* Edited by Broderick H. Johnson, translated by Casey Allison & others. Navajo Community College Press, 1977. Copyright © 1977 by Navajo Community College Press. All rights reserved. Reproduced by permission. —Valdez, Luis. From *Zoot Suit and Other Plays.* Copyright © 1992 by Luis Valdez. Arte Público Press—University of Houston. Reproduced by permission. — Whitehorse, Emmi. From "In My Family, The Women Ran Everything" in *Messengers of the Wind: Native American Women Tell Their Life Stories.* Edited by Jane Katz. Ballantine Books, 1995. Copyright © 1995 by Jane Katz. All rights reserved. Reproduced by permission of Random House, Inc. —Whiteman, Roberta Hill. From "Let Us Survive" in *Messengers of the Wind: Native American Women Tell Their Life Stories.* Edited by Jane Katz. Ballantine Books, 1995. Copyright © 1995 by Jane Katz. All rights reserved. Reproduced by permission of Random House, Inc. —Whiteman, Roberta Hill. From *Star Quilt.* Holy Cow Press, 1984. © 1984. Reproduced by permission. —Yamileth. From *Undocumented in L.A.: An Immigrant's Story.* Scholarly Resources Inc., 1997. © 1997 by Scholarly Resources Inc. Reproduced by permission. —Yau, Wong Chun. From *Asian American Experiences in the United States,* by Joann Faung Jean Lee. McFarland & Company, Inc., 1991. Copyright © 1991 by Joann Faung Jean Lee. All rights reserved. Reproduced by permission.

Photographs appearing in the *Gale Encyclopedia of Multicultural America: Primary Documents* were received from the following sources:

Albanian family waiting to board bus at McGuire Air Force Base, New Jersey, May 5, 1999, photograph by Charles Rex Arbogast. AP/Wide World Photos. Reproduced by permission. — Albanian refugee sitting on prayer rug, refugee village, Fort Dix, New Jersey, May 14, 1999, photograph by Charles Rex Arbogast. AP/Wide World Photos. Reproduced by permission. —Amish boys photograph. AP/Wide World Photos. Reproduced by permission. —Amish man in horse and buggy crossing traffic, Lancaster, Pennsylvania, July, 1998, photograph by Rusty Kennedy. AP/Wide World Photos. Reproduced by permission. —"Arapaho Ghost Dance," c. 1900, painting by Mary Irvin Wright based on photographs by James Mooney. National Archives and Records Administration. — Armenian immigrants on Ellis Island, photograph. Corbis-Bettmann. Reproduced by permission. —Barnes, Robert, II, hugs son at Million Man March, Washington, D.C., 1995, photograph. AP/Wide World Photos. Reproduced by permission. —Bates, Daisy, photograph. AP/Wide World Photos. Reproduced by permission. —Batik created in Djojakarta, Java, Indonesia, photograph by Charles Lenars. Corbis/Charles & Jossette Lenars.

Reproduced by permission. —Cherokee Indian scholar Sequoyah, holding his syllabary, lithograph. The Library of Congress. —Cherokee Syllabary, illustration. From *Beginning Cherokee*, by Ruth Bradley Holmes and Betty Sharp Smith. Second Edition. University of Oklahoma Press, 1977. Reproduced by permission. —Chief Joseph (Himaton-yalatk-it), 1877, photograph. National Archives. —Chinese launderer, woodcut, photograph. Corbis-Bettmann. Reproduced by permission. —Chisholm, Shirley, photograph. AP/Wide World Photos. Reproduced by permission. —Corner grocery store Japanese American owners interned ("I Am An American"), photograph. National Archives and Records Administration. —Cuban exiles using mirrors to signal shoreline, Florida Straits, July 18, 1998, photograph by Joe Cavaretta. AP/Wide World Photos. Reproduced by permission. —Cuban refugees aboard freighter "Red Diamond," Straits of Florida, June 2, 1980, photograph. UPI/Corbis-Bettmann. Reproduced by permission. —Cuban refugees, June 4, 1980, photograph. Corbis-Bettmann. Reproduced by permission. —Cuban-American children carrying crosses in Patriotic Reaffirmation. March, December 6, 1997, photograph by Joe Cavaretta. AP/Wide World Photos. Reproduced by permission. —Customers waiting in line for zeppole on St. Joseph's Day, Scialo Bros. Bakery, March 19, 1999, photograph by Paul Connors. AP/Wide World Photos. Reproduced by permission. —Dim Sum Dumplings served at Ocean Star Restaurant, Los Angeles, California, photograph by Nik Wheeler. Corbis/Nik Wheeler. Reproduced by permission. —Echford, Elizabeth, photograph. AP/Wide World Photos. Reproduced by permission. —Espada, Martin, photograph by Terry Pitzner. Reproduced by permission of Martin Espada. — Field hands picking Ginseng, photograph by Richard Hamilton Smith. Corbis/Richard Hamilton Smith. Reproduced by permission. —Filipino laborers, Hawaii, 1920's, photograph by George Bacon. Hawaii State Archives. Reproduced by permission of Mrs. George Bacon. —Filipino migrant workers, 1939, photograph by Dorothea Lange. Corbis. Reproduced by permission. —Four Korean Americans, photograph. Reproduced by permission of Jamie Lew. —Funeral for Jorge Mas Canosa, November 25, 1997, Miami, Florida, photograph by Joe Cavaretta. AP/Wide World Photos. Reproduced by permission. —Garcia, David, adding cream topping to zeppole on St. Joseph's Day, Scialo Bros. Bakery, Providence, Rhode Island, March 19, 1999, photograph by Paul Connors. AP/Wide World Photos. Reproduced by permission. —Gelmu Sherpa rubbing "singing bowl," May 20, 1998, photograph by Suzanne Plunkett. AP/Wide World Photos. Reproduced by permission. —Geronimo, 1887, photograph by Ben Wittick. The Library of Congress. —Greek women (five women standing on ship deck), photograph. UPI/Corbis-Bettmann. Reproduced by permission. —Group of Chinese American women doing morning Tai Chi exercises, Washington Square, San Francisco, photograph by Alison Wright. Alison Wright Photography. Reproduced by permission. —Group representing traditional Greek soldiers march in Boston, March 28, 1999, photograph by Patricia McDonnell. AP/Wide World Photos. Reproduced by permission. —Guatemalan Indian woman weaving, photograph by Nik Wheeler. Corbis/Nik Wheeler. Reproduced by permission. —Hayakawa, S.I., photograph. UPI/Corbis-Bettmann. Reproduced by permission. —Hernandez, Antonia, photograph by George Rodriguez. Reproduced by permission of Antonia Hernandez. —Him Mark Lai, reading poetry on Angel Island wall, photograph. AP/Wide World Photos. Reproduced by permission. —I'ini, Lei Ku'u, performing Hawaiian dance, May 24, 1996, photograph by Lennox McLendon. AP/Wide World Photos. Reproduced by permission. —Inouye, Daniel, photograph. UPI/Corbis-Bettmann. Reproduced by permission. —Italian family celebrating Ferragosto, 1947, photograph. UPI/Corbis-Bettmann. Reproduced by permission. —Italian family gathering, 1936, photograph. Corbis-Bettmann. Reproduced by permission. —Japanese American girl standing, holding U. S. flag, Japanese internment camp, photograph. The Library of Congress. —Japanese American relocation (mother and child) during WWII, photograph. Archive Photos, Inc. Reproduced by permission. —Japanese mother and daughter, near Guadeloupe, California, March, 1937, photograph. Corbis. Reproduced by permission. —Jewish Americans celebrating Seder, March 22, 1989, photograph by Roger Ressmeyer. Corbis/Roger Ressmeyer. Reproduced by permission. —Jordan, Barbara, photograph. AP/Wide World Photos. Reproduced by permission. —Kanosky Family, August, 1941. Reproduced by permission of Stella McDermott. —Korean bride in red silk with large bouquet, photograph by Leslye Borden. Leslye Borden/PhotoEdit. Reproduced by permission. —Letter written by members of the Blackfoot tribe to the Honorable Franklin K. Lane, February 23, 1915. The Library of Congress. —Lord, Bette Bao, photograph. AP/Wide World Photos. Reproduced by permission. —Man and woman with kolaches at Kolache Festival, photograph. Kolache Festival. —Mankiller, Wilma 1985, photograph. AP/Wide World Photos. Reproduced by permission. —Mardi Gras float from Krewe of Troth, February, 1994, photograph by Drew Story. Reuters/Drew Story/ Archive Photos, Inc. Reproduced by permission. —Marti, Jose, photograph. Corbis-Bettmann. Reproduced by permission. —Mas Canosa, Jorge, photograph. UPI/Corbis-Bettmann. Reproduced by permission. —Matachine Dancers, Christmas Eve, 1996, photograph by Tom Bean. Corbis/Tom Bean. Reproduced by permission. —Means, Russell, photograph. AP/Wide World Photos. Reproduced by permission. —Million Man March, photograph by Greg Newton. Reuters/Greg Newton/Archive Photos, Inc. Reproduced by permission. —Mormon family in front of log cabin, 1875, photograph. Corbis-Bettmann. Reproduced by permission. —"My Country 'Tis of Thee," cartoon, Life, 1918. —Natividad, Irene, photograph. AP/Wide World Photos. Reproduced by permission. —Nicoloso family at dinner, November 23, 1948, Rome, Italy, photograph. UPI/Corbis-Bettmann. Reproduced by permission. —"No Haitians Need Apply," 1994, political cartoon by Neil R. King. Reproduced by permission of Neil R. King. —Omaq-kat-tsa, Chief of Blackfoot tribe photograph. The Library of Congress. —Paths of Early Europeans, map. National Park Service, Department of the Interior. — Personnel record of Japanese American, featured in exhibit on Ellis Island, April 2, 1998, photograph by Bebeto Matthews. AP/Wide World Photos. Reproduced by permission. —Plantation workers, 1930, photograph. —Proprietor of Greek coffee shop, Aliquippa, Pennsylvania, 1938, photograph by Arthur Rothstein. The Library of Congress. —Protestors, marching to the El Conquistador Hotel July 14, 1996, Fajardo, Puerto Rico, photograph by John McConnico. AP/Wide World Photos. Reproduced by permission. —Roshetsky, Oksana, photograph. UPI/Corbis-Bettmann. Reproduced by permission. —Sadawi, Nawal, October 3, 1993, photograph by Robert Maass. Corbis/Robert Maass. Reproduced by permission. — Seguin, Juan Nepomuceno (in 19th century officer's uniform), painting. U.S. Department of Defense. —Spitzer, Jeff and Carol, holding trays of Kuchen, Eureka Bakery, Eureka, South Dakota, March 15, 1999, photograph by Jill Kokesh. AP/Wide World Photos. Reproduced by permission. —Supporters (Governor Pedro Rossello addresses the crowd in Guanica, Puerto Rico) photograph by Lynne Sladky. AP/Wide World Photos. Reproduced by permission. —"The Good for Nothing in Miss Columbia's School," political cartoon by Thomas Nast. Harper's Weekly, 1871. —"The Water Carriers," 1874, photograph by John K. Hillers. Copyright © 1995-1999 Denver Public Library. Reproduced by permission. —Valdez, Luis, poster of "Zoot Suit" in the background, photograph. AP/Wide World Photos. Reproduced by permission. —Warum, Jodi, directing preparations of Purim baskets with students, Ramaz Hebrew Day School, March 1, 1999, photograph by Tina Fineberg. AP/Wide World Photos. Reproduced by permission. —Williams, Janine Caubit, wearing French resistance armband, May 10, 1999, photograph by Berry Craig. AP/Wide World Photos. Reproduced by permission. —Winnemucca, Sarah, photograph. Nevada Historical Society. Reproduced by permission. —Women on Mulberry Street, Italian Market, New York, circa 1910, photograph. Gift of State Historical Society of Colorado, 1949. The Library of Congress. —Wovoka, or Jack Wilson, photograph. Nevada Historical Society. Reproduced by permission. —Yellow Bird (lying dead on Wounded Knee battlefield), 1891, photograph by George Trager. The Library of Congress. —Zia, Helen, photograph. Reproduced by permission.

AFGHAN AMERICANS

Afghan Americans are a small population group. Immigration from this nation-state has historically been by students seeking advanced degrees. Afghans were categorized as "other Asian" in early immigration records, so exact figures are not available. There are few statistics from the years prior to 1953. Records show that a group of about 200 Pushtuns, an ethnic group in Afghanistan, immigrated to the United States in 1920. The U.S. Immigration and Naturalization Service records show that 78 people from Afghanistan became U.S. citizens between 1953 and 1963. This figure doubled for the next ten years, with 155 naturalized citizens. Many of these individuals were students who stayed in the country after finishing their degree programs. These Afghan immigrant patterns are reflected in the individual experience of David Nasser, who describes his experience in the United States as a foreign-exchange student in this document. Nasser stayed with an American family during his senior year of high school and returned to Afghanistan in 1970, just before political upheavals began.

In this oral history, Nasser talks about his difficulties comprehending American family relationships, which allowed parents to pay their own children for work. Afghans are intensely loyal to the extended family and to the tribe. The concept of the self-determining individual does not exist. Afghans consider one's family needs to take priority over one's personal needs. Nasser also mentions that Afghanistan had a more demanding high school curriculum. In the 1960s in Afghanistan, elementary schooling was free and compulsory for children ages 5 through 11, but only 10 percent of the population aged 15 or more were literate. Roughly one out of every nine elementary students continued schooling in secondary schools, perhaps a reason for Nasser's comment that "Afghanistan was not a country that had many foreign-exchange students."

At the end of "My Brother's Way," after recounting his happiness at the prospect of seeing his family again, but the sadness with which he left his American friends, Nasser stated ominously that "None of us could imagine what was about to happen in my country." In 1973, military leaders overthrew the monarchy in Afghanistan and declared the nation-state a republic. Afghanistan is bordered by Turkmenustan, Uzbekistan, Taijikistan, China, Pakistan, and Iran. During the nineteenth century Britain and Russia had struggled for control over the area; Russia wanted an outlet to the Indian Ocean, and Britain wanted to protect interests in India. In 1978 a Socialist group took over the government and called for Soviet help. In 1979 the Soviets invaded Afghanistan and fought until 1989, when the last of the Soviets withdrew, leaving the Afghans to determine their own political future. Islamic factions who had united to fight the Soviets splintered over religious and political considerations in creating a strict Islamic state. Since that time, armed conflict between opposing political factions has devastated the country and turned its citizens into refugees, with as many as 6.2 million people displaced. By 1999, the Taliban, made up of Pashtun Islamic students lead by Mullah Mohammed Omor, controlled 90 percent of Afghanistan. They are resisted by the Northern Alliance, an opposi-

tion group of ethnic minorities led by Ahmed Shah Massou, the former Defense Minister of Afghanistan, and the former President Tijik Professor Burhanuddin Rabbani, who is still recognized by the United Nations as the head of state.

According to U.S. Census records, around 1,300 Afghans immigrated to the United States each year in the 1990s. From 1981 until 1990, 26,600 Afghans immigrated. During the same years, 8,080 Afghans were admitted as permanent residents under refugee acts. From 1981 until 1990, 22,946 Afghans were admitted as refugees. From 1990 until 1996, 13,600 Afghans immigrated, and another 9,065 were admitted as refugees. There are Afghans living in almost every state of the Union. The largest communities of Afghan Americans live in Los Angeles, Washington, D.C., and New York.

MY BROTHER'S WAY

M. David Nasser
Refugee from Kabul, Afghanistan
Medical Doctor
Eastham, Massachusetts

A very formative part of my high-school education was in Massachusetts, where I lived with an American family during my senior year. Afghanistan was not a country that had many foreign-exchange students. I entered a nationwide competition for a scholarship. We took a series of intensive exams and were interviewed by American and Afghan officials.

In August 1969, I was sent to Eastham, Massachusetts, a small working-class town on Cape Cod. It's very Americana, settled in the 1600s by the Pilgrims. The local people are very friendly.

Edward and Bernice Brown treated me like one of their three sons. Peter, was in the same class as me. We played soccer on the same team. David, who was in college out of the state, would visit once in a while on weekends at Christmas. The oldest son, Edward, was in his second or third year of medical school.

One of the first differences I noticed in America is the size of families. In Afghanistan, even the smallest family has five or six kids. And extended-family members are very close-knit; brothers-and-sisters-in-law, aunts and uncles, and grandparents all live together or nearby.

Only the father works and takes the responsibility to provide for the family. Even if he doesn't make a large amount of money, he shares whatever he earns with the extended family. Even in households where people are hungry most of the time, everybody shares what little food they have.

I saw in America that everyone in the family works to pay for his or her life. Even teenage children like my American brother worked part-time in the summer to pay for college and contribute some rent to his parents. Mom and Dad were teaching the children responsibility. From an American point of view, that's good. But from my cultural point of view, it was shocking and strange.

In Kabul, I knew families who had stores. Nephews and nieces worked for them, but none of them got paid. They believed that it was their duty to help the family business.

The first weeks that I lived with the Browns, while everyone in the family went out to their jobs, I stayed alone at home and felt kind of bored. One morning, while we were having breakfast, I asked my American mother if I could work in their grocery store.

What I meant by "work" was that I wanted to help them. I didn't know that there is a difference between "work" and "help" in this country. If you say "help," it means you don't expect to get paid. I said, "Mom, I'd like to work with my brothers in your store." She said, "I'm sorry, how much money do you want?"

My face got red. I was kind of embarrassed. I said, "Why is money being mentioned? I don't want money. I just want to help you, because I am a member of the family."

Mrs. Brown said okay. I worked in the store until school began at Nauset High, which was the only high school for three or four towns: Eastham, Orleans, Brewster, and Wellfleet. American high school was something really new. It was especially hard for me to see a boy and girl holding hands and kissing in school—I thought that I was dreaming. Having girlfriends, dating, and dances were something new to me. For a while I thought that it was not a nice way to behave in public. It was the sixties. To see girls dressed in short dresses, miniskirts, was strange and frustrating. But after a while I got used to it.

In Afghanistan, there is no such thing as dating, especially in high school. If a boy and a girl liked each other, they would try to keep it secret. Almost all marriages were arranged by the families. Even today, in the countryside, nobody can break the old rules. In the cities, traditions are changing. Some of the younger generation have their own way of life. But they are not as independent as children in this country. You cannot date or see each other without the parents' permission.

My marriage was arranged by our families, who are distant cousins. My wife, Aquela, and I were engaged from the time that she was two or three years old and I was six or seven. The reason for an early engagement is that families try to make their relationship stronger by sharing their children. My father worked in the Ministry of Finance, and Aquela's father was a schoolteacher. When I started high school, my parents told me that Aquela was going to be my wife.

Sometimes arranged marriages don't work. But divorces are very few, because in our culture and religion divorce is considered shameful. If a husband and wife are having problems, the family will try to discuss and resolve their differences.

Both sets of parents try to mediate, even if it means that the wife must spend some time away, in her father's house. I was very surprised, when I came to America, to find out the number of families that are broken and divorced.

When I left high school in Afghanistan, I was in the middle of my junior year. At Nauset High, I was placed in the senior class. I was confident that I wouldn't have any difficulty with English, because I had taken language classes in Kabul. But people were talking so fast, I couldn't understand the New England accent. And my vocabulary was limited. For a few months, I had a terrible time. I forced myself to listen carefully.

In my country it was required to take seventeen different subjects during junior year. Every one was compulsory, including geography, history, geology, literature, chemistry, religion, trigonometry, and others. If you failed one, you failed the whole year.

I found the American school system to be much easier—only a few compulsory subjects like English, physical education, and American history. When I registered at Nauset High, I had to go through a list of subjects that my counselor gave me. I picked out fifteen or sixteen subjects. The principal was amazed. He thought that I was kidding. I said, "This is the way that we do it in my country. The schedule is staggered so that we can take many courses."

The principal said, "Even if you are capable of taking that many courses, our curriculum couldn't fit you into our timetable." So I cut it down to five or six subjects, including advanced biology. There were only four Americans in the class, and one of them dropped out. In calculus, also, there were only three of us.

The examinations system is easier here, too— the multiple-choice questions. Even if you read through the textbook once, it's easy to get a passing grade. Afghanistan's system is like that of the French. You have to memorize a thick book, and for the exam you write a long essay. If you were tired and missed a few pages of the text, or didn't have time to read them, you could fail the test and consequently the whole term.

My second semester here, after my English improved, I made the honor role. I became a member of the National Honor Society. The advanced biology course was a tough one—I got a C+ in the first semester. So the next semester, when they gave me the Honor Society membership card, I was surprised. I doubted myself and thought that I didn't deserve it. I learned that the American system is very fair. In Afghanistan, you can be an excellent student all through the year, but the final examination can break you. I liked school in America, because there wasn't that much pressure and students have a wider choice of subjects that they could enjoy.

After I graduated from American high school, I went back to Afghanistan in July 1970. I was happy to be returning to my family. But I felt sad that I had to say goodbye to my American friends. None of us could imagine what was about to happen in my country.

Source:
New Americans: An Oral History, by Al Santoli.
New York: Viking Penguin Inc., 1988. pp. 13-41.

Afghanistan is an agricultural society in central Asia. The country's political development has been heavily influenced by its neighbors, the former Soviet Union. In 1978 the U.S.S.R. set up a government in Afghanistan that favored Russia. One year later the Soviet Union invaded Afghanistan in an effort to protect the infantile Marxist regime that was installed. Eight years of conflict ensued during which the Soviet-backed Afghan government contested for power with U.S.- and Pakistani-backed Afghan guerillas called the mujahidin. The Soviets withdrew from Afghanistan in 1988. During and after the war many Afghans escaped to the United States as refugees.

When people of different cultural backgrounds come to the United States they face the monumental task of making the transition into American society. For some ethnic groups the transition is facilitated by the presence of a large population of immigrants in the United States from their home land. However, other ethnic groups who have a relatively small communal population in the United States to rely on for support are essentially on their own. This is the case for Afghan Americans and other ethnic groups that come from a Muslim tradition. The majority of Afghanistan people subscribe to the Muslim faith. One of the tenets of Islam is the belief that Muslims should live wholesome and pure lives on earth which poses a challenge for their assimilation into America's indulgent society. Orthodox Muslims do not drink alcohol or eat pork; pray five times per day in the direction of their holy city, Mecca; fast during Ramadan; believe in one God and his prophet Muhammad; and pledge to make one pilgrimage to Mecca during their life.

For younger Muslims the transition is exacerbated by the socially competitive environment of American public schools. One particular Afghan boy named Abdul volunteered his experiences which provide an indication of just how difficult it is for a young Muslim trying to make the transition into American culture. Learning English was one of the most difficult aspects of the transition for Abdul. "If the teacher asked me a question and I knew the answer, when I said it, because I couldn't pronounce it well and I had the wrong accent, they [the American children] laughed at me. I felt very bad." Because of experiences such as this Abdul hated living in the United States and wanted to return to his homeland. However, he understood that this was not possible and resigned himself to his new home. After a few years Abdul learned how to adapt to the culture and as he grew more "American" he found less resistance to the transition.

Still there are obstacles for Abdul and others like him that prevent him from feeling at home in the United States. One of the most formidable challenges he faces is faithfully practicing his religion, which is dear to him. Many immigrants with an Islamic background compromise their religion in order to survive socially in the United States. For example, women are expected to wear a "chadoor" which covers their entire body. However, for fear of social ridicule, many go without. In addition, young adults are not allowed to date members of the opposite sex and marriages are arranged in accordance with the Islamic tradition. Many Muslim teens find values such as these difficult to honor in the United States where social interaction between the sexes is considered a normal part of adolescence. For Abdul, however, holding firmly to Islamic traditions is important for him and he goes out of his way to respect the Islamic way. He will refrain from dating, his marriage will be arranged, he will abstain from many of the decadent American foods his culture finds reprehensible, and he will continue to pray five times a day when he can.

ABDUL, AGE 17

Afghanistan is a landlocked Asian nation of bleak deserts, jagged mountain peaks, and the famed Khyber Pass. Surrounded by the Soviet Union, Pakistan, Iran and a sliver of China, this Muslim country has been vulnerable to its neighbors for thousands of years. In the fourth century B.C., Alexander the Great stormed across it on his way to India. The seventh century A.D. saw Islamic conquerors; the thirteenth, Genghis Khan. During the next centuries, Afghanistan was a battleground, then an independent nation and a kingdom ruled by an emir. In 1979, with Soviet troops rumored to be entering Afghanistan, Abdul's father decided that for his family's safety and future, they must leave the country. In 1989, after a war that created more than three million Afghan refugees, the Soviet troops withdrew. Today Abdul, who lives in Brooklyn, New York, thinks back to the land of his birth and worries about his homeland's future.

Suddenly at four in the morning my father and mother said, "Wake up. Be quiet! Hurry!" My brothers and sisters, we were very surprised. "Where are we going? Where are we going?" we said.

"We have to leave now," my mother said, and she helped us get dressed. I was very scared. I was just a little boy, seven years old. But I remember well. The smugglers, their trucks, the desert. I remember small things: I couldn't decide what to take and what not to take. My soccer ball? My science book? My mother said, "Don't take anything."

My father was always listening to the radio. He was very curious about the world. I think he suspected the Soviets were going to attack and he was scared. I didn't talk to any of my friends about this. It was just in my house with my family that we talked about the Soviets and that maybe we should go out of Afghanistan. Nobody else knew. It was our family secret.

In the darkness we waited for a car that would take us to the smugglers and their truck. By the time we met them the sun had come up and it was early morning.

There were three smugglers. These men live in the desert. That is their place. They were smuggling other things, too, but I don't know what. That was covered and under our feet and those of the two other families who were heading out. We were hiding in the back of the small truck, standing but with our heads down so you couldn't see us. The smugglers were driving very fast. We were bouncing around, almost falling down. They were scared of

the Afghan, the Pakistan, and the Iranian governments, that we would be caught up by one of them.

I had no idea where we were going. I thought we were going to die. We didn't know what was going to happen next. We were out there and there was nothing! Flat desert full of sand. Very hot. No food. No water. No other people. Suddenly we heard a noise; it sounded like a plane. The smugglers said, "Lie down! Lie down on the floor of the truck!" We lay down and my father and mother said, "Don't cry, children. It will be all right." The sound disappeared and again silence, only the sound of the truck.

At night it got very cold. We had a little food from my house, but soon that food was finished. We were drinking salt water that was mixed with oil. The smugglers did that on purpose. They didn't want us to drink too much, because there wasn't any more water in the desert. My parents and those guys tried to calm us. Each hour, they were telling us, "Nearby, there's a city. There's a lake. There's a lot of water." It was their way of telling us, "Be strong. Don't get sick. Don't die."

The second day we met a shepherd. We were very lucky. The smugglers bought a sheep from him and killed it. We all ate together. It was my last night in Afghanistan. By the light of the next day we crossed into Iran, to a town called Zahedan. We were safe. The smugglers took ten thousand Afghani money from my father for this trip. That's a lot of money, like a thousand dollars. Then we went to a motel where we stayed and rested for two or three days. Zahedan is not a good place to live because it's too near the border. Instead, we moved to Shiraz, a big city in Iran to live with relatives.

I was very sad to leave Afghanistan. I liked my life there in Kandahar. It is the second largest city after Kabul, the capital. There were no apartment buildings in Kandahar. We had our own house; it was big with all the rooms around a central courtyard, like having a backyard inside. But we all slept in one room, me, my parents, my four brothers, and two sisters. Afghan people don't like living in different rooms. They have large families and like to be together. My uncle lived on the other side of the house with his family. My father owned a small shop. My mother stayed home. Most women don't work in Afghanistan. My brothers and sisters and I went to the local school. I played outside with my friends. The weather was warm; we were near the desert. We didn't have snow the way they did in Kabul, to the north in the middle of many high mountains.

Two months after we came to Iran, my father heard the news: the Soviets had invaded Afghanistan. He had been right. "Now," he said, "it is time to enroll in school." For one week, two weeks, we went to school, but the teacher would say, "You need an Iranian birth certificate." We didn't have that. We were in the country illegally. My father was very worried. I thought the only scary part was leaving my country, and now it was scary again. The school found out we were Afghan and we were thrown out. My father said, "You must find a job in order to have a future. Staying home doesn't help."

I was a plumber's helper to a friend of my father's. I worked with pipes. He'd tell me what to do. He didn't pay much because I was just there to learn how to become a plumber. My brothers became tailors. My father worked in a shop. My sisters stayed home with my mother.

We were in Iran for six years. One day my father told us we were going to the United States to go to school, to have a future. There was no future for us in Iran. We didn't even have legal papers. And so, once again, we left. We had to go back to Zahedan, then we went south, illegally again, to Pakistan. There we would find an American Embassy.

I don't date. My religion forbids it. My marriage will be arranged.

The day we arrived my father went to the embassy and tried to get us here as refugees. We knew that the United States takes people to come here. We didn't know there would be a very long line wanting to go. When my father's turn came, they told him, "Come back to the embassy office with all your family, not just you." It was very hot there in Pakistan. We lived in a building with other people who waited in line. Days passed. Weeks passed. My father worried. Would we get to the United States? Would my sister we left in Iran be okay? Would his other children by okay? He got sick. I don't know what happened. In his sleep, he died. A heart attack?

For us, there was no turning back. We must go to the United States. We couldn't go back to Afghanistan because there was war. We didn't want to go back to Iran because we had no papers, and if we returned, our friends would say, "What a shame." America was our only future.

By then, it had been a few months, we had everything, all the papers. But when my father died, we had to go tell the embassy. They didn't believe that it was true. They thought it was a trick! They wanted proof of his death. Finally, finally, they accepted our papers; we got the airplane tickets and we came.

I was fourteen then. Within a month of arriving, I enrolled in a big public high school. I remember I was happy that I was coming to school again to learn something, to become someone. But I was scared, too. The school counselor just looked at me and said, "If you're fourteen, you're in the eighth grade." Getting used to studying after six years was hard. I had to learn English because my family didn't speak it and we couldn't talk to anyone.

One period a day they put me in ESL, English as a Second Language. The words began to become a little familiar to my ears. But the American kids gave me a hard time. They made fun of me. And the curse words! All day. Every day. If the teacher asked me a question and I knew the answer, when I said it, because I couldn't pronounce it well and I had the wrong accent, they laughed at me. I felt very bad.

I couldn't do anything about it. Even if I had wanted to get physical, fight with them, it wasn't good. I'm not an animal. I'm human being. I have a brain. I can talk. Why fight? Being peaceful, I think, is the best way. Some teachers knew what was going on, but they didn't care. I was a problem they didn't need.

I wanted to go back to Afghanistan. I hated this place. I didn't have any friends. I didn't have anyone to talk to. I still don't have a lot of friends, good friends, like best friends. My sister and brothers went to a different school. I was lonely, but I had to deal with it. I went through it. I went to school. I came home. And I had to study hard to learn English. Like in social studies I had to read, then I'd find a word where I didn't know the meaning and I had to look it up in the dictionary. It would take me a long time to do just one page.

Now I'm seventeen and the American kids don't always know that I'm a foreigner. They tease less. I found out that if you act the way they do, say the things they say, do the things they do, they will be calm. So I try not to act strange to them. I wear T-shirts and stone-washed jeans and aviator glasses. My hair looks like their hair. I'm about five feet ten inches. Clint Eastwood and Charles Bronson are my heroes. After school I watch TV—"Three's Company" and "Different Strokes"—to help me know what's going on in American families, what they do.

There are no others from Afghanistan in my school. Afghan people are spread all around. You can't find them too much. In each city you can find one or two. That's it. Sometimes I tell people where I'm from and I'm very surprised that they don't know Afghanistan. They are very weak in geography. They say, "Where's Afghanistan? Is it a town? Do they have cars? Do they have school?"

I always think about my country, going there one day, seeing it, practicing my religion with no problem. Religion is very important in my life. I am Muslim. We have a small mosque where we go on Saturdays. From eleven to three I go to religious school. I study Dari and Pashto, the two languages of my country. Then from eight to midnight, I go to mosque. I believe in Allah and his Prophet Muhammad. The Qur'an is the holy book.

There are rules, the Islamic rules, for everything, for daily life. But here I can't practice my religion when I should. Five times a day I should pray, the first time before sunrise. I can do that with my family, but at school I can't say to my teacher, "Please, teacher, I need to leave because I must pray." Also the food in school is a problem. I'm not allowed to eat all kinds of food; pork, for example. I just eat pizza because of the cheese, that's all right. Other things I don't eat, because I don't know how they make it. Or it's not right, the way it should be for a Muslim. So I do without.

I don't date. My religion forbids it. My marriage will be arranged. For a Muslim, your parents have to decide who you should marry. For me, my mother and my uncle will discuss it and decide.

Then they will say, "This girl is good for this son." That's fine with me. In fact, I think it's perfect. I know my mother; she went through it herself and she knows. I don't have to think about disease. I know I'm gong to marry someday, so why should I date girls? I listen to my mother. I don't want to change my culture and forget my language.

For me, for all Muslims, it's very unusual to be here. A Muslim woman should cover herself with what we call a chadoor. It is a long, black robe that covers everything, her body, her hair, her face. They have little holes for the eyes. My sister doesn't wear one. She says, "Here, other people don't, so I don't. People would laugh if I do that." My mother still wears her chadoor and in the home, too. I'm not supposed to talk to girls at certain times. I make a sin if I look at a lady without the chadoor. Looking at people who go to the beach, in their underwear, that's a sin for me. Other immigrants from different cultures who come here get used to the American habits. They date girls. They do what Americans do. But not so much us.

Ten years from now I hope to be married, have a career, a house, and children. I will raise them to be good Muslims. They are my face of the future.

Source:

Janet Bode, *New Kids on the Block: Oral Histories of Immigrant Teens*. New York: Franklin Watts, 1989. pp. 20-28.

AFRICAN AMERICANS

In 1843, Henry Highland Garnet attended the National Convention of Negro Citizens in Buffalo, New York, and on August 16 he delivered a militant oration calling for slave rebellions as the most assured means of ending slavery. It was perhaps the most radical speech by an African American during the period prior to the Civil War. The proposal moved the delegates and failed by a single vote of being adopted. After reading the speech, anti-slavery advocate John Brown had it published at his own expense in 1848.

Garnet's speech is, for all intents and purposes, addressed to an audience not present to receive it. He speaks to the enslaved on behalf of the assembled conventioneers. Apologizing for the softness and ineffectiveness of abolitionist efforts, Garnet encourages slaves to "Arise! Strike for your lives and liberties." For Garnet's immediate audience, his message is one of anger and exasperation, as well as a summons for heightened militancy.

HENRY HIGHLAND GARNET'S ADDRESS TO THE SLAVES OF THE UNITED STATES OF AMERICA (EXCERPT)

Brethren and fellow citizens: Your brethren of the North, East and West have been accustomed to meet together in national conventions, to sympathize with each other, and to weep over your unhappy condition. In these meetings we have addressed all classes of the free, but we have never, until this time, sent a word of consolation and advice to you. We have been contented in sitting still and mourning over your sorrows, earnestly hoping that before this day your sacred liberties would have been restored. But we have hoped in vain. Years have rolled on, and tens of thousands have been borne on streams of blood and tears to the shores of eternity. While you have been oppressed, we have also been partakers with you; nor can we be free while you are enslaved. We, therefore, write to you as being bound with you.

Many of you are bound to us, not only by the ties of a common humanity, but we are connected by the more tender relations of parents, wives, husbands and sisters and friends. As such we most affectionately address you.

Two hundred and twenty-seven years ago the first of our injured race were brought to the shores of America. They came not with glad spirits to select their homes in the New World. They came not with their own consent, to find an unmolested enjoyment of the blessings of this fruitful soil.. . . Neither did they come flying upon the wings of Liberty to a land of freedom. But they came with broken hearts from their beloved native land and were doomed to unrequited toil and deep degradation. Nor did the evil of their bondage end at their emancipation by death. Succeeding generations inherited their chains, and millions have come from eternity into time, and have returned again to the world of spirits, cursed and ruined by American Slavery.

[T]he time has come when you must act for yourselves. It is an old and true saying that, "if hereditary bondsmen would be free, they must

8

themselves strike the blow." You can plead your own cause and do the work of emancipation better than any others. The nations of the Old World are moving in the great cause of universal freedom, and some of them at least will, ere long, do you justice. The combined powers of Europe have placed their broad seal of disapprobation upon the African slave trade. But in the slaveholding parts of the United States the trade is as brisk as ever. They buy and sell you as though you were brute beasts. The North has done much; her opinion of slavery in the abstract is known. But in regard to the South, we adopt the opinion of the *New York Evangelist*— "We have advanced so far, that the cause apparently waits for a more effectual door to be thrown open that has been yet."

. . .[G]o to your lordly enslavers and tell them plainly that you are determined to be free. Appeal to their sense of justice and tell them that they have no more right to oppress you than you have to enslave them. Entreat them to remove the grievous burdens which they have imposed upon you, and to remunerate you for your labor. . . .Inform them that all you desire is freedom, and that nothing else will suffice. Do this, and forever after cease to toil for the heartless tyrants, who give you no other reward but stripes and abuse. If they then commence the work of death, they, and not you, will be responsible for the consequences. You had far better all die—die immediately—than live slaves and entail your wretchedness upon your posterity. If you would be free in this generation, here is your only hope. However much you and all of us may desire it, there is not much hope of redemption without the shedding of blood. If you must bleed, let it all come at once— rather die freemen than live to be slaves. It is impossible, like the children of Israel, to make a grand exodus from the land of bondage. The Pharaohs are on both sides of the blood—red waters!

Where is the blood of your fathers? Has it all run out of your veins? Awake, awake; millions of voices are calling you! Your dead fathers speak to you from their graves. Heaven, as with a voice of thunder, call on you to arise from the dust.

Let your motto be Resistance! Resistance! Resistance! No oppressed people have ever secured their liberty without resistance. What kind of resistance you had better make you must decide by the circumstances that surround you, and according to the suggestion of expediency. Brethren, adieu! Trust in the living God. Labor for the peace of the human race, and remember that you are three millions!

Source:

Lift Every Voice: African American Oratory, 1787-1900, edited by Philip S. Foner and Robert James Branham. Tuscaloosa: University of Alabama Press, 1998. pp. 198-205.

"The Heart of a Woman" appeared in Georgia Douglas Johnson's 1918 book of poems The Heart of a Woman and Other Poems. *It is especially interesting as a reworking of the "caged bird" theme, first sounded in Paul Laurence Dunbar's poem "Sympathy" and taken up by many subsequent African American writers. For Johnson, the figure of the caged bird, which sings of its imprisonment, becomes an apt image for the black woman poet, whose work must be accomplished within "sheltering bars" and amid "echoes the heart calls home."*

THE HEART OF A WOMAN
by Georgia Douglas Johnson

The heart of a woman goes forth with the dawn,
As a lone bird, soft winging, so restlessly on,
Afar o'er life's turrets and vales does it roam
In the wake of those echoes the heart calls home.

The heart of a woman falls back with the night,
And enters some alien cage in its plight,

And tries to forget it has dreamed of the stars,
While it breaks, breaks, breaks on the sheltering
    bars.

Source:
The Heart of a Woman, and Other Poems. Boston,
    The Cornhill Company, 1918. p. 1.

Daisy Bates, a journalist and newspaper publisher, took an active role in the campaign for desegregation in Little Rock, Arkansas, supporting and counseling the nine black students who enrolled at Central High School. Her memoir of the events of 1957-1958, The Long Shadow of Little Rock, *appeared in 1962. Chapter 5, "She Walked Alone," concerns an attack on Elizabeth Eckford, one of the "Little Rock Nine," and the education editor of the* New York Times, *Benjamin Fine. The story of their narrow escape from a violent mob is told mostly in their own words.*

THE LONG SHADOW OF LITTLE ROCK (EXCERPT)
by Daisy Bates

Chapter V: She Walked Alone

Dr. Benjamin Fine was then education editor of *The New York Times.* He had years before won for his newspaper a Pulitzer prize. He was among the first reporters on the scene to cover the Little Rock story.

A few days after the National Guard blocked the Negro children's entrance to the school, Ben showed up at my house. He paced the floor nervously, rubbing his hands together as he talked.

"Daisy, they spat in my face. They called me a 'dirty Jew.' I've been a marked man ever since the day Elizabeth tried to enter Central. I never told you what happened that day. I tried not to think about it. Maybe I was ashamed to admit to you or to myself that white men and women could be so beastly cruel.

"I was standing in front of the school that day. Suddenly there was a shout— 'they're here! The niggers are coming!' I saw a sweet little girl who looked

Elizabeth Echford of the Little Rock Nine.

about fifteen, walking alone. She tried several times to pass through the guards. The last time she tried, they put their bayonets in front of her. When they did this, she became panicky. For a moment she just stood there trembling. Then she seemed to calm down and started walking toward the bus stop with the mob baying at her heels like a pack of hounds. The women were shouting, 'Get her! Lynch her!' The men were yelling, 'Go home, you bastard of a black bitch!' She finally made it to the bus stop and sat down on the bench. I sat down beside her and said, 'I'm a reporter from *The New York Times*, may I have your name?' She just sat there, her head down. Tears were streaming down her cheeks from under her sun glasses. Daisy, I don't know what made me put my arm around her, lifting her chin, saying, 'don't let them see you cry.' Maybe she reminded me of my fifteen-year-old daughter, Jill.

"There must have been five hundred around us by this time. I vaguely remember someone hollering, 'Get a rope and drag her over to this tree.' Suddenly

I saw a white-haired, kind-faced woman fighting her way through the mob. She looked at Elizabeth, and then screamed at the mob, 'Leave this child alone! Why are you tormenting her? Six months from now, you will hang your heads in shame.' The mob shouted, 'Another nigger-lover. Get out of here!' The woman, who I found out later was Mrs. Grace Lorch, the wife of Dr. Lee Lorch, professor at Philander Smith College, turned to me and said, 'We have to do something. Let's try to get a cab.'

"We took Elizabeth across the street to the drugstore. I remained on the sidewalk with Elizabeth while Mrs. Lorch tried to enter the drugstore to call a cab. But the hoodlums slammed the door in her face and wouldn't let her in. She pleaded with them to call a cab for the child. They closed in on her saying, 'Get out of here, you bitch! Just then the city bus came. Mrs. Lorch and Elizabeth got on. Elizabeth must have been in a state of shock. She never uttered a word. When the bus pulled away, the mob closed in around me. 'We saw you put your arm

Daisy Bates

around that little bitch. Now it's your turn.' A drab, middle-aged woman said viciously, 'Grab him and kick him in the balls!' A girl I had seen hustling in one of the local bars screamed, 'A dirty New York Jew! Get him!' A man asked me, 'Are you a Jew?' I said, 'Yes.' He then said to the mob, 'Let him be! We'll take care of him later.'

"The irony of it all, Daisy, is that during all this time the national guardsmen made no effort to protect Elizabeth or to help me. Instead, they threatened to have me arrested—for inciting to riot."

"They moved closer and closer. Somebody started yelling, 'Lynch her! Lynch her!'"

Elizabeth, whose dignity and control in the face of jeering mobsters had been filmed by television cameras and recorded in pictures flashed to newspapers over the world, had over-night become a national heroine. During the next few days newspaper reporters besieged her home, wanting to talk to her. The first day that her parents agreed she might come out of seclusion, she came to my house where the reporters awaited her. Elizabeth was very quiet, speaking only when spoken to. I took her to my bedroom to talk before I let the reporters see her. I asked how she felt now. Suddenly all her pent-up emotion flared.

"Why am I here?" she said, turning blazing eyes on me. "Why are you so interested in my wel-

fare now? You didn't care enough to notify me of the change of plans—"

I walked over and reached out to her. Before she turned her back on me, I saw tears gathering in her eyes. My heart was breaking for this young girl who stood there trying to stifle her sobs. How could I explain that frantic early morning when at three o'clock my mind had gone on strike?

In the ensuing weeks Elizabeth took part in all the activities of the Nine—press conferences, attendance at court, studying with professors at nearby Philander Smith College. She was present, that is, but never really a part of things. The hurt had been too deep.

On the two nights she stayed at my home I was awakened by the screams in her sleep, as she relived in her dreams the terrifying mob scenes at Central. The only times Elizabeth showed real excitement were when Thurgood Marshall met the children and explained the meaning of what had happened in court. As he talked, she would listen raptly, a faint smile on her face. It was obvious he was her hero.

Little by little Elizabeth came out of her shell. Up to now she had never talked about what happened to her at Central. Once when we were alone in the downstairs recreation room of my house, I asked her simply, "Elizabeth, do you think you can talk about it now?"

She remained quiet for a long time. Then she began to speak.

"You remember the day before we were to go in, we met Superintendent Blossom at the school board office. He told us what the mob might say and do but he never told us we wouldn't have any protection. He told our parents not to come because he wouldn't be able to protect the children if they did.

"That night I was so excited I couldn't sleep. The next morning I was about the first one up. While I was pressing my black and white dress—I had made it to wear on the first day of school—my little brother turned on the TV set. They started telling about a large crowd gathered at the school. The man on TV said he wondered if we were going to show up that morning. Mother called from the kitchen, where she was fixing breakfast, 'turn that TV off!' She was so upset and worried. I wanted to comfort her, so I said, 'mother, don't worry.'

"Dad was walking back and forth, from room to room, with a sad expression. He was chewing on his pipe and he had a cigar in his hand, but he didn't light either one. It would have been funny, only he was so nervous.

"Before I left home Mother called us into the living-room. She said we should have a word of prayer. Then I caught the bus and got off a block from the school. I saw a large crowd of people standing across the street from the soldiers guarding Central. As I walked on, the crowd suddenly got very quiet. Superintendent Blossom had told us to enter by the front door. I looked at all the people and thought, 'maybe I will be safer if I walk down the block to the front entrance behind the guards.'

"At the corner I tried to pass through the long line of guards around the school so as to enter the grounds behind them. One of the guards pointed across the street. So I pointed in the same direction and asked whether he meant for me to cross the street and walk down. He nodded 'yes.' So, I walked across the street conscious of the crowd that stood there, but they moved away from me.

"For a moment all I could hear was the shuffling of their feet. Then someone shouted, 'Here she comes, get ready!' I moved away from the crowd on the sidewalk and into the street. If the mob came at me I could then cross back over so the guards could protect me.

"The crowd moved in closer and then began to follow me, calling me names. I still wasn't afraid. Just a little bit nervous. Then my knees started to shake all of a sudden and I wondered whether I could make it to the center entrance a block away. It was the longest block I ever walked in my whole life. Even so, I still wasn't too scared because all the time I kept thinking that the guards would protect me.

"When I got right in front of the school, I went up to a guard again. But this time he just looked straight ahead and didn't move to let me pass him. I didn't know what to do. Then I looked and saw that the path leading to the front entrance was a little further ahead. So I walked until I was right in front of the path to the front door.

"I stood looking at the school—it looked so big! Just then the guards let some white students go through.

"The crowd was quiet. I guess they were waiting to see what was going to happen. When I was able to steady my knees, I walked up to the guard who had let the white students in. He too didn't move. When I tried to squeeze past him, he raised his bayonet and then the other guards closed in and they raised their bayonets.

"They glared at me with a mean look and I was very frightened and didn't know what to do. I turned around and the crowd came toward me.

"They moved closer and closer. Somebody started yelling, 'Lynch her! Lynch her!'

"I tried to see a friendly face somewhere in the mob—someone who maybe would help. I looked into the face of an old woman and it seemed a kind face, but when I looked at her again, she spat on me.

"They came closer, shouting, 'No nigger bitch is going to get in our school. Get out of here!'

"I turned back to the guards but their faces told me I wouldn't get help from them. Then I looked down the block and saw a bench at the bus stop. I thought, 'If I can only get there I will be safe.' I don't know why the bench seemed a safe place to me, but I started walking toward it. I tried to close my mind to what they were shouting, and kept saying to myself, 'If I can only make it to the bench I will be safe.'

"When I finally got there, I don't think I could have gone another step. I sat down and the mob crowded up and began shouting all over again. Someone hollered, 'drag her over to this tree! Let's take care of the nigger.' Just then a white man sat down beside me, put his arm around me and patted my shoulder. He raised my chin and said, 'don't let them see you cry.'

"Then, a white lady—she was very nice—she came over to me on the bench. She spoke to me but I don't remember now what she said. She put me on the bus and sat next to me. She asked me my name and tried to talk to me but I don't think I answered. I can't remember much about the bus ride, but the next thing I remember I was standing in front of the School for the Blind, where Mother works.

"I thought, 'maybe she isn't here. But she has to be here!' So I ran upstairs, and I think some teachers tried to talk to me, but I kept running until I reached Mother's classroom. "Mother was standing at the window with her head bowed, but she must have sensed I was there because she turned around. She looked as if she had been crying, and I wanted to tell her I was all right. But I couldn't speak. She put her arms around me and I cried."

Source:
Daisy Bates. *The Long Shadow of Little Rock: A Memoir.* New York: David McKay Co., 1962.

Shirley Chisholm was the first African American woman to sit in Congress, a fact that she found appalling, considering that the nation was 192 years old at the time of her election. This is her first speech as a representative from Brooklyn.

"It Is Time for a Change" was delivered in March of 1969. The nation was still deeply embroiled in the Vietnam War, spending countless millions on the war effort at a time when programs were being cut back at home. Chisholm rose to assert her own priorities: "I intend to vote 'No' on every money bill that comes to the floor of this House that provides any funds for the Department of Defense. Any bill whatsoever, until the time comes when our values and priorities have been turned right side up again."

IT IS TIME FOR A CHANGE
by Shirley Chisholm

Mr. Speaker, on the same day President Nixon announced he had decided the United States will not be safe unless we start to build a defense system against missiles, the Headstart program in the District of Columbia was cut back for the lack of money.

As a teacher, and as a woman, I do not think I will ever understand what kind of values can be involved in spending nine billion dollars—and more, I am sure—on elaborate, unnecessary and impractical weapons when several thousand disadvantaged children in the nation's capital get nothing.

When the new administration took office, I was one of the many Americans who hoped it would mean that our country would benefit from the fresh perspectives, the new ideas, the different priorities of a leader who had no part in the mistakes of the past. Mr. Nixon had said things like this:

> If our cities are to be livable for the next generation, we can delay no longer in launching new approaches to the problems that beset them and to the tensions that tear them apart.

And he said, "When you cut expenditures for education, what you are doing is shortchanging the American future."

But frankly, I have never cared too much what people say. What I am interested in is what they do. We have waited to see what the new administration is going to do. The pattern now is becoming clear.

Apparently launching those new programs can be delayed for a while, after all. It seems we have to get some missiles launched first.

Recently the new Secretary of Commerce spelled it out. The Secretary, Mr. Stans, told a reporter that the new administration is "pretty well agreed it must take time out from major social objectives" until it can stop inflation.

The new Secretary of Health, Education and Welfare, Robert Finch, came to the Hill to tell the House Education and Labor Committee that he thinks we should spend more on education, particularly in city schools. But, he said unfortunately we cannot "afford" to, until we have reached some kind of honorable solution to the Vietnam war. I was glad to read that the distinguished Member from Oregon (Mrs. Green) asked Mr. Finch this:

> With the crisis we have in education, and the crisis in our cities, can we wait to settle the war? Shouldn't it be the other way around? Unless we can meet the crisis in education, we really can't afford the war.

Secretary of Defense Melvin Laird came to Capitol Hill, too. His mission was to sell the antiballistic-missile insanity to the Senate. He was asked what the new administration is doing about the war. To hear him, one would have thought it was 1968, that the former Secretary of State was defending the former policies, that nothing had ever happened—a President had never decided not to run because he knew the nation would reject him, in despair over this tragic war we have blundered into. Mr. Laird talked of being prepared to spend at least two more years in Vietnam.

Two more years, two more years of hunger for Americans, of death for our best young men, of children here at home suffering the lifelong handicap of not having a good education when they are young. Two more years of high taxes, collected to feel the cancerous growth of a Defense Department budget that now consumes two thirds of our federal income.

Two more years of too little being done to fight our greatest enemies, poverty, prejudice and neglect, here in our own country. Two more years of fantastic waste in the Defense Department and of penny pinching on social programs. Our country cannot survive two more years, or four, of these kinds of policies. It must stop—this year—now.

Now, I am not a pacifist. I am deeply, unalterably opposed to this war in Vietnam. Apart from all the other considerations—and they are many—the main fact is that we cannot squander there the lives, the money, the energy that we need desperately here, in our cities, in our schools.

I wonder whether we cannot reverse our whole approach to spending. For years, we have given the military, the defense industry, a blank check. New weapons systems are dreamed up, billions are spent, and many times they are found to be impractical, inefficient, unsatisfactory, even worthless. What do we do then? We spend more money on them. But with social programs, what do we do? Take the Job Corps. Its failure has been mercilessly exposed and criticized. If it had been a military research and development project, they would have been covered up or explained away, and Congress would have been ready to pour more billions after those that had been wasted on it.

The case of Pride, Inc., is interesting. This vigorous, successful black organization, here in Washington, conceived and built by young inner-city men, has been ruthlessly attacked by its enemies in the government, in this Congress. At least six auditors from the General Accounting Office were put to work investigating Pride. They worked seven months and spent more than $100,000. They uncovered a fraud. It was something less than $2,100. Meanwhile, millions of dollars—billions of dollars, in fact—were being spent by the Department of Defense, and how many auditors and investigators were checking into their negotiated contracts? Five.

We Americans have come to feel that it is our mission to make the world free. We believe that we are the good guys, everywhere—in Vietnam, in Latin America, wherever we go. We believe we are the good guys at home, too. When the Kerner Commission told white America what black America had always known, that prejudice and hatred built the nation's slums, maintain them and profit by them, white America would not believe it. But it is true. Unless we start to fight and defeat the enemies of poverty and racism in our own country and make our talk of equality and opportunity ring true, we are exposed as hypocrites in the eyes of the world when we talk about making other people free.

I am deeply disappointed at the clear evidence that the number-one priority of the new administra-

Shirley Chisholm

tion is to buy more and more weapons of war, to return to the era of the cold war, to ignore the war we must fight here—the war that is not optional. There is only one way, I believe, to turn these policies around. The Congress can respond to the mandate that the American people have clearly expressed. They have said, "End this war. Stop the waste. Stop the killing. Do something for your own people first." We must find the money to "launch the new approaches," as Mr. Nixon said. We must force the administration to rethink its distorted, unreal scale of priorities. Our children, our jobless men, our deprived, rejected and starving fellow citizens must come first.

For this reason, I intend to vote "No" on every money bill that comes to the floor of this House that provides any funds for the Department of Defense. Any bill whatsoever, until the time comes when our values and priorities have been turned right side up again, until the monstrous waste and the shocking profits in the defense budget have been eliminated and our country starts to use its strength, its tremendous resources, for people and peace, not for profits and war. It was Calvin Coolidge, I believe, who made the comment that "the Business of America is Business." We are now spending eighty billion dollars a year on defense—that is two-thirds of every tax dollar. At this time, gentlemen, the business of America is war, and it is time for a change.

Source:
Congressional Record, 91st Congress, 1st session,
U.S. Government Printing Office, 1969.

A native of Houston, Texas, Barbara Jordan was elected to the Texas Senate in 1966 and to the U.S. House of Representatives in 1972. She served on the House Judiciary Committee during the 1974 impeachment hearings concerning President Richard Nixon. On two occasions, in 1976 and again in 1992, Jordan was the keynote speaker at the Democratic National Convention.

Her 1976 speech, reprinted here, was a momentous event, the first time in the party's 140 years that the keynote address had been given by a black American. Jordan alludes to this fact in her opening, but then goes on to delineate a vision of community in which individuals work together responsibly to sustain a "government by the people." She warns against the nation's becoming "a collection of interest groups: city against suburb, region against region, individual against individual. Each seeking to satisfy private wants."

A NEW BEGINNING: A NEW DEDICATION
by Barbara C. Jordan

One hundred and forty-four years ago, members of the Democratic Party first met in convention to select a Presidential candidate. Since that time, Democrats have continued to convene once every four years and draft a party platform and nominate a Presidential candidate. And our meeting this week is a continuation of that tradition.

But there is something different about tonight. There is something special about tonight. What is different? What is special? I, Barbara Jordan, am a keynote speaker.

A lot of years passed since 1832, and during that time it would have been most unusual for any national political party to ask that a Barbara Jordan deliver a keynote address. . .but tonight here I am. And I feel that notwithstanding the past that my presence here is one additional bit of evidence that the American Dream need not forever be deferred.

Now that I have this grand distinction what in the world am I supposed to say?

I could easily spend this time praising the accomplishments of this party and attacking the Republicans but I don't choose to do that.

I could list the many problems which Americans have. I could list the problems which cause people to feel cynical, angry, frustrated; problems which include lack of integrity in government; the feeling that the individual no longer counts; the reality of material and spiritual poverty; the feeling that the grand American experiment is failing or has failed. I could recite these problems and then I could sit down and offer no solutions. But I don't choose to do that either.

The citizens of America expect more. They deserve and they want more than a recital of problems.

We are a people in a quandary about the present. We are a people in search of our future. We are a people in search of a national community.

We are a people trying not only to solve the problems of the present: unemployment, inflation. . .but we are attempting on a larger scale to fulfill the promise of America. We are attempting to fulfill our national purpose; to create and sustain a society in which all of us are equal.

Throughout our history, when people have looked for new ways to solve their problems, and to uphold the principles of this nation, many times they have turned to political parties. They have often turned to the Democratic Party.

What is it, what is it about the Democratic Party that makes it the instrument that people use when they search for ways to shape their future? Well I believe the answer to that question lies in our concept of governing. Our concept of governing is derived from our view of people. It is a concept deeply rooted in a set of beliefs firmly etched in the national conscience, of all of us.

Now what are these beliefs?

First, we believe in equality for all and privileges for none. This is a belief that each American regardless of background has equal standing in the public forum, all of us. Because we believe this idea so firmly, we are an inclusive rather than an exclusive party. Let everybody come.

I think it no accident that most of those emigrating to America in the nineteenth century identified with the Democratic Party. We are a heterogeneous party made up of Americans of diverse backgrounds.

We believe that the people are the source of all governmental power; that the authority of the people is to be extended, not restricted. This can be accomplished only by providing each citizen with every opportunity to participate in the management of the government. They must have that.

We believe that the government which represents the authority of all the people, not just one interest group, but all the people, has an obligation to actively underscore, actively seek to remove those obstacles which would block individual achievement obstacles emanating from race, sex, economic condition. The government must seek to remove them.

We are a party of innovation. We do not reject our traditions, but we are willing to adapt to changing circumstances, when change we must. We are willing to suffer the discomfort of change in order to achieve a better future.

We have a positive vision of the future founded on the belief that the gap between the promise and reality of America can one day be finally closed. We believe that.

This my friends, is the bedrock of our concept of governing. This is a part of the reason why Americans have turned to the Democratic Party. These are the foundations upon which a national community can be built.

Let's all understand that these guiding principles cannot be discarded for short-term political gains. They represent what this country is all about. They are indigenous to the American idea. And these are principles which are not negotiable.

In other times, I could stand here and give this kind of exposition on the beliefs of the Democratic

Barbara Jordan

Party and that would be enough. But today that is not enough. People want more. That is not sufficient reason for the majority of the people of this country to vote Democratic. We have made mistakes. In our haste to do all things for all people, we did not foresee the full consequences of our actions. And when the people raised their voices, we didn't hear. But our deafness was only a temporary condition, and not an irreversible condition.

Even as I stand here and admit that we have made mistakes I still believe that as the people of America sit in judgment on each party, they will recognize that our mistakes were mistakes of the heart. They'll recognize that.

And now we must look to the future. Let us heed the voice of the people and recognize their common sense. If we do not, we not only blaspheme our political heritage, we ignore the common ties that bind all Americans.

Many fear the future. Many are distrustful of their leaders, and believe that their voices are never heard. Many seek only to satisfy their private wants. To satisfy private interests.

But this is the great danger America faces. That we will cease to be one nation and become instead a collection of interest groups: city against suburb, region against region, individual against individual. Each seeking to satisfy private wants.

If that happens, who then will speak for America?

Who then will speak for the common good?

This is the question which must be answered in 1976.

Are we to be one people bound together by common spirit sharing in a common endeavor or will we become a divided nation?

For all of its uncertainty, we cannot flee the future. We must not become the new Puritans and reject our society. We must address and master the future together. It can be done if we restore the belief that we share a sense of national community, that we share a common national endeavor. It can be done.

There is no executive order; there is no law that can require the American people to form a national community. This we must do as individuals and if we do it as individuals, there is no President of the United States who can veto that decision.

As a first step, we must restore our belief in ourselves. We are a generous people so why can't we be generous with each other? We need to take to heart the words spoken by Thomas Jefferson: "Let us restore to social intercourse that harmony and that affection without which liberty and even life are but dreary things."

A nation is formed by the willingness of each of us to share in the responsibility for upholding the common good.

A government is invigorated when each of us is willing to participate in shaping the future of this nation.

In this election year we must define the common good and begin again to shape a common good and begin again to shape a common future. Let each person do his or her part. If one citizen is unwilling to participate, all of us are going to suffer. For the American idea, though it is shared by all of us, is realized in each one of us.

And now, what are those of us who are elected public officials supposed to do? We call ourselves public servants but I'll tell you this: we as public servants must set an example for the rest of the nation. It is hypocritical for the public official to admonish and exhort the people to uphold the common good if we are derelict in upholding the common good. More is required of public officials than slogans and handshakes and press releases.

More is required. We must hold ourselves strictly accountable. We must provide the people with a vision of the future.

If we promise as public officials, we must deliver. If we as public officials propose, we must produce. If we say to the American people it is time for you to be sacrificial; sacrifice. If the public official says that, we (public officials) must be the first to give. We must be. And again, if we make mistakes, we must be willing to admit them. We have to do that. What we have to do is strike a balance between the idea that government should do everything and the idea, the belief, that government ought to do nothing. Strike a balance.

Let there be no illusions about the difficulty of forming this kind of a national community. It's tough, difficult, not easy. But a spirit of harmony will survive in America only if each of us remembers that we share a common destiny. If each of us remembers when self-interest and bitterness seem to prevail, that we share a common destiny.

I have confidence that we can form this kind of national community.

I have confidence that the Democratic party can lead the way. I have that confidence. We cannot improve on the system of government handed down to us by the founders of the Republic, there is no way to improve upon that. But what we can do is to find new ways to implement that system and realize our destiny.

Now, I began this speech by commenting to you on the uniqueness of a Barbara Jordan making the keynote address. Well I am going to close my speech by quoting a Republican President and I ask you that as you listen to these words of Abraham Lincoln, relate them to the concept of a national community in which every last one of us participates: "As I would not be a slave, so I would not be a master."

This expresses my idea of democracy. Whatever differs from this, to the extent of the difference is no democracy.

Source:
Representative American Speeches: 1976-1977. New York: H.W. Wilson, 1977.

*T*he Million Man March and Day of Absence held in Washington, D.C., on October 16, 1995, was both a celebration of unity and a calling. The demonstration, organized by Nation of Islam leader Louis Farrakhan, celebrated the perseverance of the African American community and the strides made toward equality and challenged all people to commit to improving social, economic, and environmental conditions in the United States and the rest of the world.

The event was held at the peak of the 1996 presidential campaign. Political leaders such as President Bill Clinton, Bob Dole, Colin Powell, Jack Kemp, Richard Lugar, and Pat Buchanan, all of whom were entertaining presidential aspirations, were uncharacteristically reticent at the time of the demonstration. Because of the history of racial tensions in the United States, the presidential hopefuls believed that there was far too much more to lose than gain by aligning with a controversial figure such as Farrakhan. Farrakhan has been criticized for his public statements toward whites, and in particular the Jewish American community. Colin Powell, who was widely believed to be the first viable African American candidate for the presidency (although he ultimately decided not to run), declined an invitation to speak at the march.

Two important events surrounded the Million Man March that added fuel to an already explosive political atmosphere. The first issue was the recent verdict handed down on the O.J. Simpson trial which had held the nation captive for several months. The nation had mixed emotions over his acquittal and some saw the verdict as representative of current state of affairs in U.S. race relations. The second major issue was surrounding the Million Man March was the fate of affirmative action programs. The Supreme Court had begun handing down decisions that reflected a growing national sentiment of opposition to the programs.

Affirmative action programs, which are designed to redress past social injustices suffered by minorities, were being challenged in the courts by whites on the grounds of reverse discrimination. In Adarand Constructors, Inc. V. Pena (1995), for example, the Supreme Court curtailed the federal government's ability to privilege minorities in the allocation of federal contracts. Most leaders of the African American community believe the programs are warranted and serve to rectify social and economic disparities by opening up opportunities for minorities. In this environment, in the midst of a race for the White House, politicians were reluctant to speak out definitively in favor or against the programs. The ambivalence was captured in President Clinton's 1996 State of the Union address, in which he recommended the nation "mend but not end" the programs.

But the Million Man March was not about advocating one federal program or another; it was a "day of atonement" for African Americans and whites, according to Louis Farrakhan, who was the keynote speaker at the event. The Nation of Islam leader called on African Americans to take responsibility for themselves and for African Americans and whites to unify against hatred. An estimated 500,000 people took part in the event which was held between the Capitol building and Washington Monument. The peaceful demonstration accomplished its goal of drawing attention to the nation epidemic of racism that has plagued the United States since its inception.

Although the Thirteenth, Fourteenth, and Fifteenth Amendments to the Constitution were designed to guarantee equal rights to African Americans it was not unit the twentieth century that some measure of equality was achieved. African Americans have had to rely on the Supreme Court to protect fundamental rights such as *access to public schools, fair employment standards, and access to public facilities. Despite the 1960s civil rights movement, during which prominent figures such as Martin Luther King, Jr. and President John Kennedy made revolutionary strides toward improving racial tensions in America, discrimination persists. The Million Man March served as a reminder of the racial tensions that still exist and, more importantly, sent the message to African Americans that they cannot simply rely on the political system to look out for their interests; African Americans, according to Farrakhan, must rely on their own devices to overcome social injustices.*

THE MILLION MAN MARCH/DAY OF ABSENCE MISSION STATEMENT (EXCERPT)
by Dr. Maulana Karenga

I. Introduction

The Black men and women, the organizations and persons, participating in this historic Million Man March and Day of Absence held in Washington, DC, on October 16, 1995, on the eve of the 21st century, and supported by parallel activities in cities and towns throughout the country: *conscious* of the critical juncture of history in which we live and the challenges it poses for us; *concerned* about increasing racism and the continuing commitment to white supremacy in this country; deteriorating social conditions, degradation of the environment and the impact of these on our community, the larger society and the world; *committed* to the ongoing struggle for a free and empowered community, a just society and a better world; *recognizing* that the country and government have made a dangerous and regressive turn to the right and are producing policies with negative impact on people of color, the poor and the vulnerable; *realizing* that every man and woman and our community have both the right and responsibility to resist evil and contribute meaningfully to the creation of a just and good society; *reaffirming* the best values of our social justice tradition which require respect for the dignity and rights of the human person, economic justice, meaningful political participation, shared power, cultural integrity, mutual respect for all peoples, and uncompromising resistance to social forces and structures which deny or limit these; *declare* our commitment to assume a new and expanded responsibility in the struggle to build and sustain a free and empowered community, a just society and a better world. We are aware that we make this commitment in an era in which this is needed as never before and in which we cannot morally choose otherwise.

In doing this, we self-consciously emphasize the priority need of Black men to stand up and assume this new and expanded responsibility without denying or minimizing the equal rights, role and responsibility of Black women in the life and struggle of our people.

Our priority call to Black men to stand up and assume this new and expanded sense of responsibility is based on the realization that the strength and resourcefulness of the family and the liberation of the people require it;

that some of the most acute problems facing the Black community within are those posed by Black males who have not stood up; that the caring and responsible father in the home; the responsible and future-focused male youth; security in and of the community; the quality of male/female relations, and the family's capacity to avoid poverty and push the lives of its members forward all depend on Black men's standing up;

that in the context of a real and principled brotherhood, those of us who have stood up, must challenge others to stand also; and that unless and until Black men stand up, Black men and women cannot stand together and accomplish the awesome tasks before us.

II. The Historical Significance of the Project

This Million Man March, forming a joint project with its companion activity, The Day of Absence, speaks to who we are, where we stand and what we are compelled to do in this hour of meeting and posing challenges. Its significance lies in the fact that:

Hundreds of thousands of men gathered from across the United States during the Million Man March.

1. It is a timely and necessary state of challenge both to ourselves and the country in a time of increasing racism, attacks on hard won gains, and continually deteriorating conditions for the poor and vulnerable and thus an urgent time for transformative and progressive leadership;

Robert Barnes hugs his son before the Million Man March.

2. It is a declaration of the resolve of Black men, in particular and the Black community in general, to mobilize and struggle to maintain hard won gains, resist evil and wrong wherever we find it and to continue to push our lives and history forward;

3. It is a reaffirmation of our self-understanding as a people that we are our own liberators, that no matter how numerous or sincere our allies are, the greatest burdens to be borne and the most severe sacrifices to be made for liberation are essentially our own;

4. It is an effective way to refocus and expand discussion on critical issues confronting our people, this country and the world and put forth our positions on them;

5. It is both an example and encouragement of operational unity; unity in diversity, unity without uniformity, and unity on principle and in practice for the greater good;

6. It is a galvanizing and mobilizing process to raise consciousness, cultivate commitment and lay the groundwork for increased positive social, political and economic activity;

7. And finally, it is a necessary continuation of our ancient and living moral tradition of speaking truth to power and seeking power for the vulnerable, justice for the injured, right for the wronged and liberation for the oppressed. . . .

VII. Continuing Practice and Projects

38. The Million Man March and Day of Absence can only have lasting value if we continue to work and struggle beyond this day. Thus, our challenge is to take the spirit of this day, the process of mobilization and the possibilities of organization and turn them into ongoing structures and practices directed toward our liberation and flourishing as a people.

39. Central to sustaining and institutionalizing this process is:

   a. the follow-up development of an expanded Black political agenda and the holding of a Black Political Convention to forge this agenda for progressive political change;

   b. a massive and ongoing voter registration of Black people as independents; using our vote to insist and insure that candidates address the Black agenda; and creating and sustaining a progressive independent political movement;

   c. the building and strengthening of Black united fronts and collective leadership structures like the National African American Leadership Summit to practice and benefit from operational unity in our addressing local, national and international issues;

   d. the establishment of a Black Economic Development Fund to enhance economic development, cultivate economic discipline and cooperative practices and achieve economic self-determination;

   e. the reaffirmation and strengthening of family through quality male/female relations based on principles of equality, complementarity, mutual respect and shared responsibility in love, life and struggle; and through loving and responsible parenthood that insists on discipline and achievement, provides spiritual, moral and cultural grounding and through expanding rites of passage programs, mentorships and increasing adoptions;

   f. the ongoing struggle for reparations in the fullest sense, that is to say: public admission, apology and recognition of the Holocaust of African Enslavement and appropriate compensation by the government; and support for the Conyers Reparations Bill on the Holocaust;

   g. the continuing struggle against police abuse, government suppression, violations of civil and human rights and the industrialization of prisons; and in support of the freedom of all political prisoners, prisoners' rights and their efforts to transform themselves into worthy members of the community;

   h. the critical task of organizing the community as a solid wall in the struggle against drugs, crime and violence in the community which we see as interrelated and which must be joined with the struggle to reduce and end poverty, increase employment, strengthen fatherhood, motherhood and family, support parents, provide education and prevention programs, and expose and reject those who deal in death for the community.

   None of this denies external sources of drugs nor stops us from demanding uniform sentencing and penalties for those involved in the drug trade on the local, national and international level, but it compels us to stand up and take responsibility for the life we must live in spite of external impositions;

   i. continuing and expanding our support for African-centered independent schools through joining their boards, enrolling our children, being concerned and active parents, donating time, services and monies to them and working in various other ways to insure that they provide the highest level of culturally-rooted education; and intensifying and broadening the struggle for quality public education through heightened parental concern and involvement and social activism which insist on a responsible administration, professional and committed teachers, continuing faculty and staff development; safe pleasant, encouraging and fully-equipped campuses and an inclusive and culture-respecting curriculum which stresses mastery of knowledge as well as critical thinking, academic excellence, social responsibility and an expanded sense of human possibility;

   j. continuing and reinforced efforts to reduce and eliminate negative media approaches to and portrayals of Black life and culture; to organize a sustained and effective support for positive models, messages and works; to achieve adequate and dignified representation of Blacks in various media and in various positions in these media; to expand support for and development of independent Black media; and to challenge successful and notable African Americans in various media to support all these efforts;

   k. strengthening and supporting organizations and institutions of the Black community concerned with the uplifting and liberation of our people by joining as families and persons, volunteering service, giving donations and providing and insisting on the best leadership possible;

   l. building appropriate alliances with other peoples of color, supporting their liberation struggles and just demands and engaging in mutually supportive and mutually beneficial activities to create and sustain a just and good society;

m. standing in solidarity with other African peoples and other Third World peoples in their struggles to free themselves, harness their human and material resources and live full and meaningful lives;

n. reaffirming in the most positive ways the value and indispensability of the spiritual and ethical grounding of our people in accomplishing the historical tasks confronting us by freeing and renewing our minds and reaffirming our commitment to the good, the proper and the beneficial, by joining as families and persons the faith communities of our choice, supporting them, living the best of our traditions ourselves and challenging other members and the leadership to do likewise and constantly insisting that our faith communities give the best of what we have to offer to build the moral community and just society we struggle for as a people;

o. and finally, embracing and practicing a common set of principles that reaffirm and strengthen family, community and culture, The Nguzo Saba (The Seven Principles); Umoja (Unity); Kujichagulia (Self-Determination); Ujima (Collective Work and Responsibility); Ujamaa (Cooperative Economics); Nia (Purpose); Kuumba (Creativity); and Imani (Faith).

Source:

For full text of the Mission Statement, contact University of Sankore Press, 2560 W. 54th St., Los Angeles, CA 90043; phone (800) 997-2656; fax (213) 299-0261.

ALBANIAN AMERICANS

Albanians have immigrated to the United States for nearly one hundred years. Early in the 1900s, Albanians immigrated to increase their economic position or were refugees from the civil wars in Albania between 1904 and 1914. They settled primarily in the Boston area, and became merchants of fruit stores, grocery stores and restaurants. The immigration of Albanians was halted in 1939 because of World War II; then, Communist forces overtook Albania in 1944. Immigration to the United States did not resume until the late 1980s, when the Communist government collapsed.

With the fall of the Communist government, there was a tremendous amount of conflict in the area. Kosovo was a province of Serbia, and both were initially a part of the original Yugoslavia. Serbia claimed Kosovo as sacred ground to Christian Serbs, as it holds many ancient monasteries and a famous battlefield. Serbian troops have fought Kosovo's Albania Muslims since the late 1980s. In 1989, Slobodan Milosevic denied Kosovo's autonomy and established martial law over the province. Kosovo Albanians engaged in primarily pacifist resistance until military action began in 1998. Once hostilities broke out, Serbs tried to crush Kosovo, driving refugees primarily into the neighboring territories of Macedonia and Montenegro.

Between the spring and fall of 1998, the conflict in Kosovo resulted in hundreds of thousands of Albanian refugees and displaced persons. In 1999, hundreds of thousands more fled Kosovo, pursued by Serbian troops. Refugees' stories were terrifying — many described police squads coming to their houses and giving them five minutes to flee their homes before being shot. Refugees told tales of flight, and traveled to United Nations sponsored refugee camps in Macedonia, where food, tents, and medical attention were available. The living conditions in these camps were difficult at best. In 1999, many countries offered to take in thousands of Kosovo Albanian refugees. The United States offered to take 20,000 refugees, providing government benefits for these people and granting permanent residence in three years.

This article from the New York Times details the arrival of Sytkije Deva and her family in America. Sytkije Deva's sister, Lili Erebeli, sponsored Deva and her family's arrival in the United States. Erebeli and her husband, Rex, were active members of the Albanian Community in New York. They, too, were refugees, expelled in the late 1960s because they supported Albanian political causes. "Albanian nationalism survived across the generations" and their daughters supported Albanian nationalism, too. The Erebelis were among approximately 700 Albanian-Americans who applied to sponsor their extended families upon their arrival in the United States. The family welcomed 14 members of their extended family after filing papers to sponsor them with the International Rescue Committee. In this document, the mixed emotions and culture shock that the Devas feel are clearly conveyed, as they find relative safety after enduring a devastating war in their homeland.

IN BROOKLYN, A WARM REFUGE
FOR KOSOVO KIN

After six terrifying weeks fleeing war at home in Kosovo, Sytkije Deva and her family had finally arrived at Kennedy International Airport late Saturday night to great fanfare: they were showered with flowers and stuffed toys, surrounded by a gaggle of news reporters, and fussed over by politicians making speeches in a language they did not understand.

But when it was time to leave the airport and walk free into the streets of New York, Mrs. Deva, 67, looking bewildered and frail in an oversized navy blue suit, stared up at her sister Lili Erbeli and asked whether they were going to a refugee camp next.

Mrs. Erbeli, eyes brimming, bent over, took her eldest sister's hand and broke the good news in rapid-fire Albanian. "You're coming home with me," she said, and helped her rise from her seat.

That night, Mrs. Erbeli, 55, and her husband, Rex, 59, brought home to their three-bedroom duplex in Sheepshead Bay 14 of their Kosovo kin: Mrs. Deva and her husband, Musa, 72, their three grown children and their spouses, and six grandchildren, ages 11 to 2.

They were undoubtedly among the world's luckiest exiles of war. They were among a planeload of 102 who landed at Kennedy on Saturday night from Skopje, Macedonia, via London. They came as refugees into the United States, eligible for government benefits and permanent residence in a mere three years. Most of all, unlike those who had arrived at Fort Dix, N.J., last week, these refuges had relatives in New York to sponsor them and take them directly home.

So on Saturday night, three generations of Albanian-American Erbelis came to fetch three generations of their Kosovo cousins.

At a hangar set up as a welcoming hall, they waited breathlessly behind a line of Port Authority police officers. Lili Erbeli waited up front, dressed in red and black, the colors of the Albanian flag, and as soon as she spotted a familiar face, hurried past the officers. Her American-born daughter, Albana, 26, followed, and threw her arms around her eldest cousin, Bujar. Mr. Erbeli escorted the elderly Mr. Deva to a chair. Mrs. Erbeli covered her mouth and whispered, "Look, how skinny!"

One by one, the American Erbelis embraced their old-country kin, the grown-ups' faces streaked with tears, the children's cheeks covered with lipstick. The Erbelis' granddaughter, Brianna, 8, opened a bag of toys she had brought from her own collection. Their 12-year-old nephew Argjent began chatting with an 11-year-old cousin, Dren, whom he had never met, and they seemed to hit it off immediately—Dren telling his American cousin of a friend who had been shot and killed with his father in their hometown of Kosovska Mitrovica, and then, comparing notes on their favorite programs.

At home in sheepshead Bay it was a most unusual family reunion.

The extraordinary occasion was marked by a relatively quiet meal. Dinner was served in shifts, for there were too many to fit around the 10-seat dining table. In the kitchen, an efficient assembly line of Erbeli women cleared one set of plates and filled another with chicken cutlets, peas and spoonfuls of rice pilaf. Tiny cups of Turkish coffee were passed around, with bowls of flan that Mrs. Erbeli had prepared the night before.

Lili and Rex Erbeli seemed unfazed about making do with an extra 14 people. After all, they said, closets had already been cleared and the refrigerator stocked with giant jugs of juice and soda. Extra pillows and blankets had been found, and foam mattresses borrowed. Rex Erbeli joked that he would sleep on the balcony if he had to. Lili Erbeli said they would simply have to share.

"You help them now or never," she said.

Thirty years ago, Rexhap and Liriej Erbeli were themselves refugees. Both teachers in Yugoslavia and active in Albanian political causes, they were expelled, Mr. Erbeli said, for hoisting an Albanian flag in Serbian territory. The International Rescue Committee, the same relief agency that arranged to bring their relatives on Saturday, had arranged for their own passage to the United States.

Neither Rex nor Lili Erbeli knew a word of English when they first arrived with a 5-month-old daughter, Arberesa—now Betsy, 31. A friend of Mr. Erbeli's father met them at the airport, put them up in his apartment for a week, and from there began their typical immigrant's journey. He cleaned the presses at *The Daily News*, trimmed the hedges at a Manhattan park, drove a cab.

In 1999, the United States granted legal alien status to about 20,000 refugees fleeing conflict in Kosovo. Here, an ethnic Albanian family looks down a long line of fellow refugees boarding buses after arriving at an Air Force base in New Jersey.

Last year, Rex Erbeli retired as an office building manager in midtown Manhattan. Lili Erbeli still works as a teacher's assistant at a nearby elementary school.

They have been active in Albanian-American organizations. They sent their girls back to Kosovo every summer, so they would not forget who they were. Albanian nationalism survived across the generations. Albana, who is scheduled to graduate later this year from the Fashion Institute of Technology, has tattooed the eagle of the Albanian flag on the small of her back. For a while, she thought of fighting with the Kosovo Liberation Army. Betsy has given her daughter, Brianna, the middle name of Kosova.

When the NATO bombings began seven weeks ago, the Erbelis, like scores of Kosovars in New York, were on the phone nearly every day with family members in Kosovo. Mrs. Erbeli heard of the houses that had been torched in their neighborhood. She heard the children in the background asking Auntie Lili to send a helicopter to fetch them.

Shortly after the bombing started, Mrs. Erbeli lost contact. "That's it, I said, they are dead," she remembered. "I was crazy for a few days."

The family in Kosovo, it turned out, had hidden at home for eight days, leaving only when a neighbor, a Serb, offered to help them get away. If they did not leave, the neighbor told them, they would be killed. Two hours later, with a few bags packed with food and clothes for the children, cash and jewelry, they left. Remembering the advice of Bosnian refugees who came to their city some years ago, they also brought all the family photos they could.

Sitting in the Erbelis' living room, Bujar Deva, 38, and his wife, Njeldez, 35, quietly told this story early yesterday morning with the help of a cousin, Fatmir Kodra, who translated. Their faces looked weary, and repeatedly they spoke of how unreal it still seemed, being in New York.

After leaving their house in Kosovo, they spent several nights in an abandoned trailer near the Macedonian border, waiting for the authorities to let them cross. The women and children were separated from the men for a few days, but eventually, all ended up at the home of relatives in Skopje.

They said they thought they could return home in a few weeks, but then came the news that their house had been burned, along with the liquor store that Bujar ran nearby. Bujar whispered this, for he has yet to tell his parents.

While the Devas were considering their prospects in Macedonia, the Erbelis were rushing to the offices of the International Rescue Committee in New York. They were among some 700 Albanian-Americans who filed papers to sponsor their extended families. Last Wednesday, the call came in: all 14 of their relatives would be coming into Kennedy Airport on Saturday.

That night, before heading to the airport. Rex Erbeli was describing his plans to set them up here. "We're going to find an apartment for them, we're going to fix up the apartment for them, we're going to find them a job," he said with great confidence.

But would the Devas of Kosovka Mitrovica really want to stay?

"Who wants to go back?" Mr. Erbeli snapped, convinced that Slobodan Milosevic would never let the Albanians live peacefully in Kosovo. "They

stop now, O.K. Twenty years from now, they start again."

For his part, Bujar could not stop thinking about what he was leaving behind. When he boarded the plane at Skopje on Saturday, he said he was thinking only how quickly he could return.

"It's difficult to realize at this age," he said, "that you have to start everything."

Source:
Article by Somini Sengupta in the *New York Times*, May 10, 1999.

Albania is located in southeastern Europe, and it is a mountainous country, inhabited by over three million people. The majority of Albanian immigrants in the United States arrived during the twentieth century, and their numbers were relatively small. Before World War I, Albanians came to America because of political concerns in Albania, economic conditions or to avoid conscription in the Turkish army. More Albanians migrated to the United States after Albania fell under Communist control in 1944. Early Albanian Americans settled around Boston before moving to other parts of Massachusetts where there were many factory jobs.

Albanian immigrants are predominantly Orthodox Christians, Roman Catholics, or Muslims. Churches established by the Albanian Orthodox Church were first built in the early 1900s, while Roman Catholic Albanians arrived much later, in the 1960s and 1970s. Albanian Muslims arrived in the United States around 1913, and there are between 25,000 and 30,000 Albanian Muslims in the United States, primarily of the Sunni branch within Islam.

During 1998 and 1999 many Albanians fled their homes to escape the horrors that were being carried out in the name of "ethnic cleansing" by Slobodan Milosevic. In this picture, an ethnic Albanian refugee participates in a Muslim prayer service by praying while sitting on a prayer rug at the refugee village at Fort Dix, New Jersey in 1999. On this day, about 100 Albanian refugees placed prayer rugs outside of their mess hall on a grassy plain for an hour long community prayer service, or jumma, to celebrate their weekly sabbath.

ALBANIAN PRAYER SERVICE

Source:
Associated Press.

MISH

*T*he Amish are Anabaptists, believing that only adults can be baptized and adhere to the teachings of the New Testament. They believe that an individual can forge a personal relationship with God without an intermediary such as a priest. They also believe that all forms of violence is wrong. Each member of the Amish community agrees to live by an order called the "Ordnung." By agreeing to the code of conduct put forth in the Ordnung one agrees not to use self-propelled farm equipment and agree not to divorce their spouse. Those who break these rule are "put in the barn," or banned from all communal ties. The term "Amish" derives from the founder of the community, Jacob Amman. There are seven Amish sects throughout the United States with over 100 congregations (each of which contain roughly 150 people). The primary concentrations of Amish are in Pennsylvania, Ohio, and Indiana. In 1995 the population of Amish in the United States was estimated at 150,000.

Lancaster County, Pennsylvania, is home to the oldest generation of the Amish of Pennsylvania Dutch. The ancestral roots of the Pennsylvania Dutch are tied to the Swiss who, advocated a complete separation of church and state. The Amish represented the extreme case as adherents of this principle which was exemplified in a dispute between residents of an Amish community in Maryland and public officials over sewage disposal technology in Amish schools. The Amish community in Maryland wanted to maintain out houses in their schools while policy makers wanted to force the community to use electronically operated plumbing for sanitation purposes. The Amish are well known for their staunch position against the introduction of modern conveniences into their daily lives. Leaders of the Amish community contend that such conveniences potentially undermine one's relationship with God. The extent to which the Amish incorporate this principle into their lives is essentially what distinguishes one Amish community from another. While some communities hold firmly to traditional Amish values of asceticism, others have grown more progressive.

The community in general, however, is finding it more and more difficult to hold to their principles and remain competitive in the marketplace at the same time. There are different grades of conservatism among the Amish communities in the United States. Lancaster County Amish in Pennsylvania allow tourists to visit their relatively technology-free lifestyle, albeit from a comfortable distance. Some members of the Amish community in Maryland even use battery operated tools. The most conservative group among the Amish reside in the Kishacoquillen Valley in the center of Pennsylvania. The Amish categorize their communities according to a "high/low" scale which is used in reference to their churches. A "low" church is one that has managed to retain much of the original conservative traditions inherent to the Amish while a "high" church has "compromised" (according to some) some of its values in an effort to adapt to changing times.

The Amish in general have moved away from relying on agriculture to support their communities. Many Amish supplement income through the sale of arts and crafts, baked goods, and carpentry. Although the communities vary in their rela-

tionship to "worldly" conveniences, they are unified in their position of privileging community over economics. As long as the fundamental values and faith in God are strong, they will flourish. The Amish are also unified in their view of what they call the "English," which refers to all non-Pennsylvania Dutch peoples. They are cautious not to get too close to English ways for fear of losing their grip on tradition.

IN AMISH LAND, WITNESSES TO OLD AND NEW

To visit Pennsylvania's Amish country is to drive 150 miles from New York City and feel like an outsider in your own land. I have lived in New Delhi and Tokyo, but I felt almost as foreign in Bird in Hand and Intercourse, two villages at the historic center of the Amish settlement, where my family and I spent a recent weekend. Although I found much to love in the area— the honest food, the impressive quilts, the plain, verdant esthetic—there were uncomfortable moments over the two days.

When my husband asked our Amish buggy driver about the attitude of the traditional Old Order Amish toward the more modern groups, the driver sternly replied: "There aren't any attitudes. The Bible tells us not to judge others." A sign at Hannah Stoltzfoos Quilts and Handmades warned, "No photographs, no tourists beyond this gate." In a museum slide documentary, an Amish farmer recounted how a tourist once asked him, "Hey, are you for real?" The farmer, disdainful, replied: "No, we're the fake ones. The real ones live down the road."

The Amish clearly have a complicated relationship with the tourists who make their roads as impassable in summer as the Montauk Highway yet spend $400 million a year in Lancaster County, much of it on Amish-made products. As Donald B. Kraybill writes in *The Riddle of Amish Culture* (Johns Hopkins University Press, 1989), one of the books on the community, "To discard the buggy, for instance, would not only break Amish tradition but also shatter powerful expectations placed upon them by the outside world." In this way, Dr. Kraybill says, tourism may be inadvertently strengthening, not diluting, Amish life. The Amish of Lancaster County are, after all, thriving; they numbered around 1,000 at the turn of the century, compared with 22,000 today.

So there is more than ever to see, and to stew about. How can you understand a culture whose essence is not letting outsiders in?

Our weekend began in Times Square late on a Friday afternoon. The four of us—my husband and me and our children, Madeleine, 8, and Teddy, 4—drove for three and a half hours, then checked into the Village Inn of Bird in Hand, a restored nineteenth century red brick building on the main street of town. Local lore has it that the original inn, built in the eighteenth century, and the village got their names when two road surveyors of the Old Philadelphia Pike couldn't decide whether to stay at the inn that was in front of them or go on to Lancaster. One of them said, "A bird in hand, etc.," and so the inn was named.

Though we heard the passing klopklop of horses' hooves through the night, the noise seemed surreal, until the next morning. Despite all the pictures, despite the movie *Witness* starring Harrison Ford, which angered the Lancaster County Amish and put them in a big way on the tourist maps, it was still startling to see for the first time a black Amish buggy driven by men in dark suits, long beards and straw hats. They looked like part of a stage set, but turned out to be some of the most authentic sights we saw all day.

No Cars, No War

Our first stop on Saturday morning was the People's Place, an "interpretation center" in Intercourse, where we arrived just behind a tour bus and saw the slide documentary "Who Are the Amish?" The photographs were lush, the narration intelligent. We were told that the Amish struggle between seeking humility and perfection, and that their lives are hardly idyllic. Like all families, they have problems with the temptations of modern life. This week, in fact, two Lancaster County Old Order Amish men in their 20's were indicted on charges of buying cocaine and distributing it to young members of the community.

Upstairs we walked through "Amish World," a child-friendly exhibition. There was an Amish

The Amish may appear to be a homogenous group, but they vary in many respects. One common thread among the Amish, however, is their use of horse-and-buggy transportion.

buggy, Amish clothes for dress up and a display of 12 months in the life of Amos and Susie, two hypothetical Amish children. Some of the adult exhibits were a little dense.

Here is what I think is important to know, culled from Dr. Kraybill's book:

The Amish do not drive cars, use electricity from public utilities, accept Social Security or Medicare benefits, or go to war. They trace their roots to the religious upheavals of sixteenth-century Europe, when a group of renegades in Zurich became impatient with the pace of the Protestant Reformation, and critical of the continuing baptism of infants. In their view, only adults able to choose obedience to Christ deserved baptism.

The rebels were called Anabaptists, meaning "re-baptizers," because they had already been baptized as infants in the Roman Catholic church. Adult baptism became the symbol of the new movement, although Dr. Kraybill writes that the real issue was one of the control: were the Protes-

tant and Catholic civil authorities the interpreters of Christian faith, or was it the Bible?

The Swiss radicals illegally re-baptized themselves in January 1525, an intolerable challenge to the state authorities who controlled the church. Over the next 200 years, thousands of Anabaptists were executed by civil and religious authorities; Anabaptist hunters were commissioned to torture, burn, drown or dismember them.

Meanwhile, a Dutch Anabaptist, Menno Simons, became such a powerful leader that his followers were soon calling themselves Mennonites. The Amish emerged a century and a half later, in 1693, after a split with the Mennonites led by Jacob Amman, a leader in Alsace.

The first large group of Amish to settle in Lancaster County arrived in Philadelphia in 1737, on the ship the *Charming Nancy*. The centuries of bloody persecution led in part to their decision to separate themselves from the outside world.

Today Lancaster County is a complex mix of Amish sects and the generally more modern Mennonites, lumped together under the term Pennsylvania Dutch, which refers to the many groups that fled southern Germany for Pennsylvania. ("Dutch" is believed to be a corruption of "Deutsch.")

More progressive Amish groups have splintered off; today most of Lancaster County's Amish are Old Order Amish, the most distinct in their customs and the fastest growing and one of the largest groups of Amish in the United States. They have worked as farmers traditionally, but in recent years more than half the adults have become entrepreneurs in small businesses like farm machinery, furniture and crafts.

Steel Wheels

Next stop after the museum was Aaron and Jessica's Buggy Rides, billed by the guidebooks as the only buggy business owned and run by the Amish. Our buggy was a sedate gray, but unlike the enclosed boxes that the Amish really drive, ours had big side windows for a better view and rubber around the wheels for a smoother ride. The Amish use steel, believing that rubber will lead to mobility and the car.

For half an hour, under a brilliant sky, our horse pulled past alfalfa fields and orchards of pear, peach and apple trees. It was quiet, bountiful and orderly, a landscape molded with thought and discipline. Our guide pointed out a windmill, the house of a bishop—the main religious authority for the surrounding district—and a one-room school house. A 1972 Supreme Court decision gave the Amish the right to take their children out of school after the eighth grade; the Amish believe that a high school education separates children from their parents and values.

On the way back, our guide pulled the buggy into the driveway of a small farmhouse, calling out to two children in Pennsylvania German. The kids ran into the house and came back shyly offering us a red horseshoe, which we bought for $2. "You've made them very happy," our guide said.

We had lunch in nearby Smoketown at Good 'n' Plenty. From the roadside billboards, I could see it was a big tour-bus magnet and I did not have high hopes. But inside at communal tables we were served an amazingly delicious array of Pennsylvania Dutch food, crisp, succulent fried chicken, creamy mashed potatoes, buttered noodles, forever-cooked green beans (mushy and wonderful), rhubarb sauce, Jell-O and shoofly pie. We waddled out an hour later.

In the afternoon, we drove off Route 30, the attraction-glutted main highway, and into the countryside. We took Route 772 out of Intercourse and turned left on Cattail Road, bounding past teams of horses in the fields. That was nice. Then we headed over the gentle hills to Lapp Valley Farm in New Holland, where the children got homemade ice cream from a little shop and wandered around looking at the cows, a bloody-necked ostrich that had lost a fight and a peacock that insisted on opening its fan out of picture range in the garage. That was nice, too.

Then we looped back to Bird in Hand, stopped at the disappointing farmer's market—more tour buses parked outside—and Hannah Stoltzfoos Quilts, where I bought two potholders. We had dinner in Mount Joy at Groff's Farm Restaurant, a sunny country club golfer-type, place, not Amish, with Betty Groff's creamed chicken Stoltzfus in pastry shells and Betty herself making a fuss over the children.

How Real Is It?

When I returned to New York, I called Dr. Kraybill, now the provost of Messiah College, a liberal arts college in Grantham, Pa., founded by the Brethren in Christ Church, a pacifist denomination similar to the Mennonites. Was it possible, I asked, to have an authentic Amish experience for a weekend in Lancaster County?

"It's mostly hopeless," said Dr. Kraybill, who is a Mennonite. He called the tourist sites "front-stage replicas," and said the backstage reality was largely inaccessible. "You need to be there probably two weeks. If you really want to plunge in, you need to stay on a farm for two to three months."

Dr. Kraybill said the only real way for weekend tourists to interact with the Amish was to visit their farm stands and shops, which we had done. He also suggested arranging for dinner in an Amish home through the Mennonite Information Center in Lancaster.

The director of the center, Wesley Newswanger, acknowledged that most Old Order Amish want to be let alone, but said that there are some who find tourists as fascinating as they are irritating. Some Amish, he said, might take in small groups for dinner, and then for prayers and singing afterward. The expected "donation" is around $12.50 a person. If I had it to do over again, Mr. Newswanger would be my first call.

Was the weekend pointless then?

"There's nothing wrong with a two-day visit," Dr. Kraybill said, reasonably. "It's a prelude. It's just enough to get you curious."

Source:
Article by Elisabeth Bumiller in the *New York Times*, June 26, 1998.

APACHES

The word "extermination," as applied to human beings, is most commonly associated with the twentieth century. Yet long before the Turkish-Armenian genocide, not to mention the Soviet-Ukrainian and Nazi-Jewish, it was already being used to describe U.S. government policy with regard to Native Americans. Not only had the term come into use by 1866, the date of this New York Times editorial, but thoughtful individuals such as the editorial's author had come to question the practice.

The date is telling: on May 16, 1866, the Civil War had been over for 13 months, and the commander of the Union forces who won the war, General Ulysses S. Grant (1822-85), was the man of the hour. In 1866 he had been promoted to the highest of all ranks, the newly created General of the Army. Hence the occasion for this piece, a letter from an unnamed "gentleman" offering his unpaid services to Grant for the purpose of "clear[ing] Arizona of Apaches in twelve months."

Up to the end of the Civil War more than two generations later, Americans had been preoccupied with the question of preserving the Union. Once the war put an end to that question, however, a new phase of American history began: the settling of the western frontier, which necessarily (in the eyes of many citizens, at least) involved the removal of tribes such as the Apaches.

The editorial writer questioned this policy. He noted that the government was certainly capable of removing all Indian tribes, and that the settlers would be happy for it to do so. At the very least, they would be happy for federal troops to remove the Native Americans nearest to them, whether they be Sioux, Cheyenne, or Apache. Few Americans had the stomach for the full-scale extermination of the native tribes; on the other hand, the writer seemed to suggest, they could endure it on a piecemeal basis.

Of course, something close to full-scale extermination is indeed what ensued during the generation between the end of the Civil War and the end of the nineteenth century. The trickle alluded to by the editorial writer as "white settlements. . .planted here and there all over the Plains, and on both sides of the Rocky Mountains," was about to become a flood.

In such an environment, spirits were high. The writer's use of the word sanguinary is interesting: the term means "bloody," but is also related to the word sanguine, which can be used to describe a cheerful, optimistic disposition. This optimism on the part of the settlers spelled doom for the Apaches and other nations.

Having presented the fact that any number of whites would readily dispatch the Native Americans to the fabled "hunting grounds," the native religion's Afterworld, the writer goes on to a defense of the Indians. First, he notes that they are rapidly becoming settled, or "exchanging the soil for the sod," which is one of the prerequisites of civilization.

Whites of the mid-1800s were accustomed to using the term civilization *as a form of judgment, almost as a moral yardstick, but in fact it has a distinct meaning quite apart from any value judgments. Among the defining aspects of civilization are a settled, or non-nomadic, way of life, which the Apaches were developing, along with cities and a written language. Written language, in fact, could have helped the Apaches make a case for themselves, as the author goes on to note.*

Thus the second aspect of the writer's defense: because the Apache do not have a newspaper or any other means of disseminating information to the world at large, "we only hear one side" of the story. Though certainly true, this was a remarkably liberal attitude to adopt at the outset of the conquest of Indian territories in the West.

The editorial's concluding paragraph offers a plan for future policy with regard to the Apache and other tribes. First, the writer suggests, the federal government should bring all native peoples together in one area, which would presumably remain Indian territory thenceforth; second, this policy should be carried out by fair-minded and just military commanders.

Of course, what ensued was far less orderly than suggested, and certainly less humane. The Spanish and later the Mexican government, which had controlled much of what is now the southwestern United States up until the end of the Mexican War in 1848, had pursued its Indian policy with finesse, avoiding bloodshed once it had established its power over the Apaches in the 1780s. The United States conducted its Apache relations with considerably less care and skill—and considerably more bloodshed. The issue would not be fully decided until the surrender of the Apache leader Geronimo (1829-1909) to U.S. troops in 1886.

THE POLICY OF EXTERMINATION AS APPLIED TO THE INDIANS

A gentleman somewhat known in connection with adventure and speculation in our Southwestern Territories, has written a letter to Gen. GRANT, proposing to take command of a regiment of cavalry, for the purpose of punishing the Apaches of Arizona. He says: "I desire neither rank nor pay, only the absolute handling of this force without restrictions. I will then undertake to clear Arizona of Apaches in twelve months."

We do not suppose that Gen. GRANT would ever entertain the least thought of acceding to any such proposition, any more than we doubt that, if he did, it would lead to the extermination of this wildest of all the wild tribes of the Western plains.

It is now unquestionably in the power of our Government to exterminate not only one obnoxious tribe of Indians, but the whole Indian race, from the savage Sioux of the far North to the untamable Apaches of the far South, from the wild Arapajos and Cheyennes of the central regions to the wretched tribes on the Pacific coast. And such a policy of extermination would receive almost universal support from the white settlers on the Western plains. At all events, those living within range of the Sioux would like *that* tribe extirpated, those living within range of the Apaches would like *that* tribe extirpated, those living within range of the Cheyennes would like *their* extermination, and so on. The white settlements that are now planted here and there all over the Plains, and on both sides of the Rocky Mountains, would eagerly cooperate with the military forces in the work of extermination; and these settlements are so numerous, so widely scattered, and so advantageously located, that they could operate to most sanguinary purpose. They would not be rendered the more averse to do so, in that they would acquire the coveted lands and the "plunder" of the Indians, and would secure the expenditure among themselves of vast sums of Government money. Under this policy, the red man, once so powerful and populous on this continent, now so lean and circumscribed in numbers and domain, would quickly be relegated forever to those shadowy "hunting grounds" where the "pale face" will never dispute his possession.

We think, however, that even those most covetous of the Indian's heritage might be satisfied at the rate with which he is exchanging the soil for the sod. Looking at the restricted and disconnected territorial allotments now left him, at the tenure of his possession and the conditions of his toleration—looking at the rapidity and the steadiness with which his range is ever being limited, and the swiftness with which he himself is fading away, one might think that such furious desires of extermination as are expressed in the aforementioned letter to Gen. GRANT, and which, as we have said, are so widely entertained in the far West, might well be somewhat modified.

As for the Indian "outrages" of which we are continually hearing and of which the Apaches in Arizona furnish the latest illustration, it must be said that we only hear one side. The Apaches print no newspapers, and have no means of communicating to the world a knowledge of the outrages committed upon *them*. But it is on record, as the experience of all those most familiar with Indian affairs, that the aggressors in nearly all quarrels, and the beginners of nearly all outrages, are the whites— rarely indeed the Indians.

Our permanent policy toward the Indians should be, in brief and comprehensive terms, to exercise a steady pressure and influence toward securing the *aggregation* of the entire race and all the scattered tribes as far as possible; and secondly, to appoint military officers to the various Western posts who have a deep appreciation of justice, and who will be more anxious to avoid a quarrel than secure a fight; in the meantime spurning with proper contempt, as inhuman and unchristian, any and all propositions for exterminating any tribe in twelve months "with a regiment of cavalry."

May 16, 1866

Source:
Ethnic Groups in American Life, edited by Gene Brown. New York: Arno Press and the *New York Times*, 1978. p. 3.

*T*he Chiricahua Apache chief Geronimo (1829-1909) remains one of the great enduring symbols of Indian pride, independence, and courage in the face of overwhelming odds. As a young man, he fought alongside such chiefs as Cochise (1812-1874) and Victorio (1820-1880). In 1876, when the U.S. government closed down the Chiricahua reservation in Arizona and moved the tribe to the San Carlos Agency in New Mexico, Geronimo headed to Mexico with a band but was apprehended and brought back to San Carlos.

In 1881 he escaped again, this time with a group of warriors including one of Cochise's sons. They began a series of raids in Arizona and New Mexico. After two years, he surrendered to the famous Indian fighter General George Crook (1829-1890) and was returned to San Carlos. Geronimo escaped again in 1885. After evading the Mexican Army and 5,000 U.S. soldiers for eighteen months, Geronimo surrendered his band of 144, including 101 women and children. Considered prisoners of war this time, they and approximately 250 other Chiricahua Apaches who had stayed at San Carlos were sent to a fort in Florida, where they were imprisoned. Many of them died. The children were forcibly removed to the Indian School at Carlisle, Pennsylvania. Geronimo was later taken to Fort Sill, Oklahoma, where he lived until 1909, still considered a prisoner of war.

In 1906, well into his seventies, the former warrior dictated his autobiography to S.M. Barret, an educator who lived near Fort Sill. Although some objected to *the publicity this gave to an "outlaw" Indian, President Theodore Roosevelt (1858-1919), who had been a cowboy in the Far West, gave his permission for the project to go forward. In the portion reproduced here, Geronimo speaks of the massacre of "Kaskiyeh," in 1858, in which his mother, wife, and children were killed by Mexicans. He also describes his first contacts with the United States and his efforts to keep his people alive and his tribe intact.*

GERONIMO: THE STORY OF HIS LIFE (EXCERPT)

About the time of the massacre of "Kaskiyeh" (1858) we heard that some white men were measuring land to the south of us. In company with a number of other warriors, I went to visit them. We could not understand them very well, for we had no interpreter, but we made a treaty with them by shaking hands and promising to be brothers. Then we made our camp near their camp, and they came to trade with us. We gave them buckskin, blankets, and ponies in exchange for shirts and provisions. We also brought them game, for which they gave us some money. We did not know the value of this money, but we kept it and later learned from the Navajo Indians that it was very valuable.

Every day they measured land with curious instruments and put down marks which we could not understand. They were good men, and we were sorry when they had gone on into the west. They were not soldiers. These were the first white men I ever saw.

About ten years later some more white men came. These were all warriors. They made their camp on the Gila River south of Hot Springs. At first they were friendly and we did not dislike them, but they were not as good as those who came first.

After about a year some trouble arose between them and the Indians, and I took the warpath as a warrior, not as a chief. I had not been wronged, but some of my people had been, and I fought with my tribe; for the soldiers and not the Indians were at fault.

Not long after this some of the officers of the United States troops invited our leaders to hold a conference at Apache Pass (Fort Bowie). Just before noon the Indians were shown into a tent and told that they would be given something to eat. When in the tent they were attacked by soldiers. Our chief, Mangus Colorado, and several other

warriors, by cutting through the tent, escaped; but most of the warriors were killed or captured. Among the Bedonkohe Apaches killed at this time were Sanza, Kladetahe, Niyokahe, and Gopi. After this treachery the Indians went back to the mountains and left the fort entirely alone. I do not think that the agent had anything to do with planning this, for he had always treated us well. I believe it was entirely planned by the soldiers.

From the very first the soldiers sent out to our western country, and the officers in charge of them, did not hesitate to wrong the Indians. They never explained to the Government when an Indian was wronged, but always reported the misdeeds of the Indians. Much that was done by mean white men was reported at Washington as the deeds of my people.

The Indians always tried to live peaceably with the white soldiers and settlers. One day during the time that the soldiers were stationed at Apache Pass I made a treaty with the post. This was done by shaking hands and promising to be brothers. Cochise and Mangus-Colorado did likewise. I do not know the name of the officer in command, but this was the first regiment that ever came to Apache Pass. This treaty was made about a year before we were attacked in a tent, as above related. In a few days after the attack at Apache Pass we organized in the mountains and returned to fight the soldiers. There were two tribes—the Bedonkohe and the Chokonen Apaches, both commanded by Cochise. After a few days' skirmishing we attacked a freight train that was coming in with supplies for the Fort. We killed some of the men and captured the others. These prisoners our chief offered to trade for the Indians whom the soldiers had captured at the massacre in the tent. This the officers refused, so we killed our prisoners, disbanded, and went into hiding in the mountains. Of

Geronimo (Goyathlay)

those who took part in this affair I am the only one now living.

In a few days troops were sent out to search for us, but as we were disbanded, it was, of course, impossible for them to locate any hostile camp. During the time they were searching for us many of our warriors (who were thought by the soldiers to be peaceable Indians) talked to the officers and men, advising them where they might find the camp they sought, and while they searched we watched them from our hiding places and laughed at their failures.

After this trouble all of the Indians agreed not to be friendly with the white men any more. There was no general engagement, but a long struggle followed. Sometimes we attacked the white men—sometimes they attacked us. First a few Indians would be killed and then a few soldiers. I think the killing was about equal on each side. The number killed in these troubles did not amount to much, but this treachery on the part of the soldiers had angered the Indians and revived memories of other wrongs, so that we never again trusted the United States troops.

Perhaps the greatest wrong ever done to the Indians was the treatment received by our tribe from the United States troops about 1863. The chief of our tribe, Mangus-Colorado, went to make a treaty of peace for our people with the white settlement at Apache Tejo, New Mexico. It had been reported to us that the white men in this settlement were more friendly and more reliable than those in Arizona, that they would live up to their treaties and would not wrong the Indians.

Mangus-Colorado, with three other warriors, went to Apache Tejo and held a council with these citizens and soldiers. They told him that if he would come with his tribe and live near them, they would issue to him, from the Government, blankets, flour, provisions, beef, and all manner of supplies. Our chief promised to return to Apache Tejo within two weeks. When he came back to our settlement he assembled the whole tribe in council. I did not believe that the people at Apache Tejo would do as they said and therefore I opposed the plan, but it was decided that with part of the tribe Mangus-Colorado should return to Apache Tejo and receive an issue of rations and supplies. If they were as represented, and if these white men would keep the treaty faithfully, the remainder of the tribe would join him and we would make our permanent home at Apache Tejo. I was to remain in charge of that portion of the tribe which stayed in Arizona. We gave almost all of our arms and ammunition to the party going to Apache Tejo, so that in case there should be treachery they would be prepared for any surprise. Mangus-Colorado and about half of our people went to New Mexico, happy that now they had found white men who would be kind to them, and with whom they could live in peace and plenty.

No word ever came to us from them. From other sources, however, we heard that they had been treacherously captured and slain. In this dilemma we did not know just exactly what to do, but fearing that the troops who had captured them would attack us, we retreated into the mountains near Apache Pass.

During the weeks that followed the departure of our people we had been in suspense, and failing to provide more supplies, had exhausted all of our store of provisions. This was another reason for moving camp. On this retreat, while passing through the mountains, we discovered four men with a herd of cattle. Two of the men were in front in a buggy and two were behind on horseback. We killed all four, but did not scalp them; they were not warriors. We drove the cattle back into the mountains, made a camp, and began to kill the cattle and pack the meat.

Before we had finished this work we were surprised and attacked by United States troops, who killed in all seven Indians—one warrior, three women, and three children. The Government troops were mounted and so were we, but we were poorly armed, having given most of our weapons to the division of our tribe that had gone to Apache Tejo, so we fought mainly with spears, bows, and arrows. At first I had a spear, a bow, and a few arrows; but in a short time my spear and all my arrows were gone. Once I was surrounded, but by dodging from side to side of my horse as he ran I escaped. It was necessary during this fight for many of the warriors to leave their horses and escape on foot. But my horse was trained to come at call, and as soon as I reached a safe place, if not too closely pursued, I would call him to me. During this fight we scattered in all directions and two days later reassembled at our appointed place of rendezvous, about fifty miles from the scene of this battle.

About ten days later the same United States troops attacked our new camp at sunrise. The fight lasted all day, but our arrows and spears were all gone before ten o'clock, and for the remainder of the day we had only rocks and clubs with which to fight. We could do little damage with these weapons, and at night we moved our camp about four miles back into the mountains where it would be hard for the cavalry to follow us. The next day our scouts, who had been left behind to observe the movements of the soldiers, returned, saying that the troops had gone back toward San Carlos Reservation.

A few days after this we were again attacked by another company of United States troops. Just before this fight we had been joined by a band of Chokonen Indians under Cochise, who took command of both divisions. We were repulsed, and decided to disband.

After we had disbanded our tribe the Bedonkohe Apaches reassembled near their old camp vainly waiting for the return of Mangus-Colorado and our kinsmen. No tidings came save that they had all been treacherously slain. Then a council was held, and as it was believed that Mangus-Colorado was dead, I was elected Tribal Chief.

For a long time we had no trouble with anyone. It was more than a year after I had been made Tribal Chief that United States troops surprised and attacked our camp. They killed seven children, five women, and four warriors, captured all our supplies, blankets, horses, and clothing, and destroyed our tepees. We had nothing left; winter was beginning, and it was the coldest winter I ever knew. After the soldiers withdrew I took three warriors and trailed them. Their trail led back toward San Carlos.

After this trouble all of the Indians agreed not to be friendly with the white men any more. There was no general engagement, but a long struggle followed.

While returning from trailing the Government troops we saw two men, a Mexican and a white man, and shot them off their horses. With these two horses we returned and moved our camp. My people were suffering much and it was deemed advisable to go where we could get more provisions. Game was scarce in our range then, and since I had been Tribal Chief I had not asked for rations from the Government, nor did I care to do so, but we did not wish to starve.

We had heard that Chief Victoria of the Chi-henne (Oje Caliente) Apaches was holding a council with the white men near Hot Springs in New Mexico, and that he had plenty of provisions. We had always been on friendly terms with this tribe, and Victoria was especially kind to my people. With the help of the two horses we had captured, to carry our sick with us, we went to Hot Springs. We easily found Victoria and his band, and they gave us supplies for the winter. We stayed with them for about a year, and during this stay we had perfect peace. We had not the least trouble with Mexicans, white men, or Indians. When we had stayed as long as we should, and had again accumulated some supplies, we decided to leave Victoria's band. When I told him that we were going to leave he said that we should have a feast and dance before we separated.

The festivities were held about two miles above Hot Springs, and lasted for four days. There were about four hundred Indians at this celebration. I do not think we ever spent a more pleasant time than upon this occasion. No one ever treated our tribe more kindly than Victoria and his band.

We are still proud to say that he and his people were our friends.

When I went to Apache Pass (Fort Bowie) I found General Howard in command, and made a treaty with him. This treaty lasted until long after General Howard had left our country. He always kept his word with us and treated us as brothers. We never had so good a friend among the United States officers as General Howard. We could have lived forever at peace with him. If there is any pure, honest white man in the United States army, that man is General Howard. All the Indians respect him, and even to this day frequently talk of the happy times when General Howard was in command of our Post. After he went away he placed an agent at Apache Pass who issued to us from the Government clothing, rations, and supplies, as General Howard directed. When beef was issued to the Indians I got twelve steers for my tribe, and Cochise got twelve steers for his tribe. Rations were issued about once a month, but if we ran out we only had to ask and we were supplied. Now, as prisoners of war in this Reservation, we do not get such good rations.

Out on the prairie away from Apache Pass a man kept a store and saloon. Some time after General Howard went away a band of outlawed Indians killed this man, and took away many of the supplies from his store. On the very next day after this some Indians at the Post were drunk on "tiswin," which they had made from corn. They fought among themselves and four of them were killed. There had been quarrels and feuds among them for some time, and after this trouble we deemed it impossible to keep the different bands together in peace. Therefore we separated, each leader taking his own band. Some of them went to San Carlos and some to Old Mexico, but I took my tribe back to Hot Springs and rejoined Victoria's band.

Soon after we arrived in New Mexico two companies of scouts were sent from San Carlos. When they came to Hot Springs they sent word for me and Victoria to come to town. The messengers did not say what they wanted with us, but as they seemed friendly we thought they wanted a council, and rode in to meet the officers. As soon as we arrived in town soldiers met us, disarmed us, and took us both to headquarters where we were tried by court-martial. They asked us only a few questions and then Victoria was released and I was sentenced to the guardhouse. Scouts conducted me to the guardhouse and put me in chains. When I asked them why they did this they said it was because I had left Apache Pass.

I do not think that I ever belonged to those soldiers at Apache Pass, or that I should have asked them where I might go. Our bands could no longer live in peace together, and so we had quietly withdrawn, expecting to live with Victoria's band, where we thought we would not be molested. They also sentenced seven other Apaches to chains in the guardhouse.

I do not know why this was done, for these Indians had simply followed me from Apache Pass to Hot Springs. If it was wrong (and I do not think it was wrong) for us to go to Hot Springs, I alone was to blame. They asked the soldiers in charge why they were imprisoned and chained, but received no answer.

I was kept a prisoner for four months, during which time I was transferred to San Carlos. Then I think I had another trial, although I was not present. In fact I do not know that I had another trial, but I was told that I had, and at any rate I was released.

After this we had no more trouble with the soldiers, but I never felt at ease any longer at the Post. We were allowed to live above San Carlos at a place now called Geronimo. A man whom the Indians called "Nick Golee" was agent at this place. All went well here for a period of two years, but we were not satisfied.

In the summer of 1883 a rumor was current that the officers were again planning to imprison our leaders. This rumor served to revive the memory of all our past wrongs—the massacre in the tent at Apache Pass, the fate of Mangus-Colorado, and my own unjust imprisonment, which might easily have been death to me. Just at this time we told that the officers wanted us to come up the river above Geronimo to a fort (Fort Thomas) to hold a council with them. We did not believe that any good would come of this conference, or that there was any need of it; so we held a council ourselves, and fearing treachery, decided to leave the reservation. We thought it more manly to die on the warpath than to be killed in prison.

There were in all about 250 Indians, chiefly the Bedonkohe and Nedni Apaches, led by myself and Whoa. We went through Apache Pass and just west of there had a fight with the United States troops. In this battle we killed three soldiers and lost none.

We went on toward Old Mexico, but on the second day after this United States soldiers overtook us about three o'clock in the afternoon and we fought until dark. The ground where we were attacked was very rough, which was to our advantage, for the troops were compelled to dismount in order to fight us. I do not know how many soldiers

we killed, but we lost only one warrior and three children. We had plenty of guns and ammunition at this time. Many of the guns and much ammunition we had accumulated while living in the reservation, and the remainder we had obtained from the White Mountain Apaches when we left the reservation.

Troops did not follow us any longer, so we went south almost to Casa Grande and camped in the Sierra de Sahuaripa Mountains. We ranged in the mountains of Old Mexico for about a year, then returned to San Carlos, taking with us a herd of cattle and horses.

Soon after we arrived at San Carlos the officer in charge, General Crook, took the horses and cattle away from us. I told him that these were not white men's cattle, but belonged to us, for we had taken them from the Mexicans during our wars. I also told him that we did not intend to kill these animals, but that we wished to keep them and raise stock on our range. He would not listen to me, but took the stock. I went up near Forth Apache and General Crook ordered officers, soldiers, and scouts to see that I was arrested; if I offered resistance they were instructed to kill me.

This information was brought to me by the Indians. When I learned of this proposed action I left for Old Mexico, and about four hundred Indians went with me. They were the Bedonkohe, Chokonen, and Nedni Apaches. At this time Whoa was dead, and Naiche was the only chief with me. We went south into Sonora and camped in the mountains. Troops followed us, but did not attack us until we were camped in the mountains west of Casa Grande. Here we were attacked by Government Indian scouts. One boy was killed and nearly all of our women and children were captured.

After this battle we went south of Casa Grande and made a camp, but within a few days this camp was attacked by Mexican soldiers. We skirmished with them all day, killing a few Mexicans, but sustaining no loss ourselves.

That night we went east into the foothills of the Sierra Madre Mountains and made another camp. Mexican troops trailed us, and after a few days attacked our camp again. This time the Mexicans had a very large army, and we avoided a general engagement. It is senseless to fight when you cannot hope to win.

That night we held a council of war; our scouts had reported bands of United States and Mexican troops at many points in the mountains. We estimated that about two thousand soldiers were ranging these mountains seeking to capture us.

General Crook had come down into Mexico with the United States troops. They were camped in the Sierra de Antunez Mountains. Scouts told me that General Crook wished to see me and I went to his camp. When I arrived General Crook said to me, "Why did you leave the reservation?" I said: "You told me that I might live in the reservation the same as white people lived. One year I raised a crop of corn, and gathered and stored it, and the next year I put in a crop of oats, and when the crop was almost ready to harvest, you told your soldiers to put me in prison, and if I resisted to kill me. If I had been let alone I would now have been in good circumstances, but instead of that you and the Mexicans are hunting me with soldiers." He said: "I never gave any such orders; the troops at Fort Apache, who spread this report, knew that it was untrue." Then I agreed to go back with him to San Carlos.

It was hard for me to believe him at that time. Now I know that what he said was untrue, and I firmly believe that he did issue the orders for me to be put in prison, or to be killed in case I offered resistance.

We started with all our tribe to go with General Crook back to the United States, but I feared treachery and decided to remain in Mexico. We were not under any guard at this time. The United States troops marched in front and the Indians followed, and when we became suspicious, we turned back. I do not know how far the United States army went after myself, and some warriors turned back before we were missed, and I do not care.

I have suffered much from such unjust orders as those of General Crook. Such acts have caused much distress to my people. I think that General Crook's death was sent by the Almighty as a punishment for the many evil deeds he committed.

Soon General Miles was made commander of all the western posts, and troops trailed us continually. They were led by Captain Lawton, who had good scouts. The Mexican soldiers also became more active and more numerous. We had skirmishes almost every day, and so we finally decided to break up into small bands. With six men and four women I made for the range of mountains near Hot Springs, New Mexico. We passed many cattle ranches, but had no trouble with the cowboys. We killed cattle to eat whenever we were in need of food, but we frequently suffered greatly for water. At one time we had no water for two days and nights and our horses almost died from thirst. We ranged in the mountains of New Mexico for some time, then thinking that perhaps the troops had left Mexico, we returned. On our return through Old

Mexico we attacked every Mexican found, even if for no other reason than to kill. We believed they had asked the United States troops to come down to Mexico to fight us.

South of Casa Grande, near a place called by the Indians Gosoda, there was a road leading out from the town. There was much freighting carried on by the Mexicans over this road. Where the road ran through a mountain pass we stayed in hiding, and whenever Mexican freighters passed we killed them, took what supplies we wanted, and destroyed the remainder. We were reckless of our lives, because we felt that every man's hand was against us. If we returned to the reservation we would be put in prison and killed; if we stayed in Mexico they would continue to send soldiers to fight us; so we gave no quarter to anyone and asked no favors.

After some time we left Gosoda and soon were reunited with our tribe in the Sierra de Antunez Mountains.

Contrary to our expectations the United States soldiers had not left the mountains in Mexico, and were soon trailing us and skirmishing with us almost every day. Four or five times they surprised our camp. One time they surprised us about nine o'clock in the morning, and captured all our horses (nineteen in number) and secured our store of dried meats. We also lost three Indians in this encounter. About the middle of the afternoon of the same day we attacked them from the rear as they were passing through a prairie—killed one soldier, but lost none ourselves. In this skirmish we recovered all our horses except three that belonged to me. The three horses that we did not recover were the best riding horses we had.

Soon after this we made a treaty with the Mexican troops. They told us that the United States troops were the real cause of these wars, and agreed not to fight any more with us provided we would return to the United States. This we agreed to do, and resumed our march, expecting to try to make a treaty with the United States soldiers and return to Arizona. There seemed to be no other course to pursue.

Soon after this scouts from Captain Lawton's troops told us that he wished to make a treaty with us; but I knew that General Miles was the chief of the American troops, and I decided to treat with him.

We continued to move our camp northward, and the American troops also moved northward, keeping at no great distance from us, but not attacking us.

I sent my brother Porico (White Horse) with Mr. George Wratton on to Fort Bowie to see General Miles, and to tell him that we wished to return to Arizona; but before these messengers returned I met two Indian scouts—Kayitah, a Chokonen Apache, and Marteen, a Nedni Apache. They were serving as scouts for Captain Lawton's troops. They told me that General Miles had come and had sent them to ask me to meet him. So I went to the camp of the United States troops to meet General Miles.

When I arrived at their camp I went directly to General Miles and told him how I had been wronged, and that I wanted to return to the United States with my people, as we wished to see our families, who had been captured and taken away from us.

General Miles said to me: "The President of the United States has sent me to speak to you. He has heard of your trouble with the white men, and says that if you will agree to a few words of treaty we need have no more trouble. Geronimo, if you will agree to a few words of treaty all will be satisfactorily arranged."

So General Miles told me how we could be brothers to each other. We raised our hands to heaven and said that the treaty was not to be broken. We took an oath not to do any wrong to each other or to scheme against each other.

Then he talked with me for a long time and told me what he would do for me in the future if I would agree to the treaty. I did not greatly believe General Miles, but because the President of the United States had sent me word I agreed to make the treaty, and to keep it. General Miles said to me: "I will take you under Government protection; I will build you a house; I will fence you much land; I will give you cattle, horses, mules, and farming implements. You will be furnished with men to work the farm, for you yourself will not have to work. In the fall I will send you blankets and clothing so that you will not suffer from cold in the winter time.

"There is plenty of timber, water, and grass in the land to which I will send you. You will live with your tribe and with your family. If you agree to this treaty you shall see your family within five days."

I said to General Miles: "All the officers that have been in charge of the Indians have talked that way, and it sounds like a story to me; I hardly believe you."

He said: "This time it is the truth."

I said: "General Miles, I do not know the laws of the white man, nor of this new country where you are to send me, and I might break their laws."

He said: "While I live you will not be arrested."

Then I agreed to make the treaty. (Since I have been a prisoner of war I have been arrested and placed in the guardhouse twice for drinking whisky.)

We stood between his troopers and my warriors. We placed a large stone on the blanket before us. Our treaty was made by this stone, and it was to last until the stone should crumble to dust; so we made the treaty, and bound each other with an oath.

I do not believe that I have ever violated that treaty; but General Miles never fulfilled his promises.

When we had made the treaty General Miles said to me: "My brother, you have in your mind how you are going to kill men, and other thoughts of war; I want you to put that out of your mind, and change your thoughts to peace."

Then I agreed and gave up my arms. I said: "I will quit the warpath and live at peace hereafter."

Then General Miles swept a spot of ground clear with his hand, and said: "Your past deeds shall be wiped out like this and you will start a new life."

Source:

Geronimo's Story of His Life, by Geronimo. Taken down and edited by S. M. Barrett. New York: Duffield & Company, 1906. pp. 113-147.

ARGENTINEAN AMERICANS

The Marta Ramirez family story reflects the relatively late arrival of Argentinean immigrants in U.S. history. In a brief interview, Marta related her hopes of a new life in the United States. Like almost 90 percent of native Argentineans, Marta was raised a Roman Catholic. Her husband was a government worker under Argentinean leader Juan Domingo Perón. As with many Argentineans caught in a politically unstable environment of repeated military takeovers through much of the twentieth century, Marta's husband lost his job in 1955 when Perón was overthrown and forced into exile.

After a brief futile job search, the Ramirezes sold their home and moved to a small community in New Jersey where many other Argentinean Americans settled. Marta seemed relieved to leave and avoid possible political persecution from anti-Perón factions. She was pleased to find a beautician's job and tried hard to become an American.

Marta's interview relates well the wonderment over American holiday traditions not found in Argentina, including the arrival of a gift-bearing Santa Claus at Christmastime. As Marta described it, "We arrive here in December. I go down to the town center to buy some things, and I see all the Christmas stuff and I say, 'What is this Santa Claus?' and the lady in the store tell me, and I go home and I tell my daughter Angela, she was six then, 'In this country Santa Claus brings you presents.'" Though the Ramirezes enjoyed the new holiday form of celebration, like many Argentinean American Catholics, they still continued to celebrate the Day of the Three Wise Men, Argentina's version of the Epiphany in early January.

Argentinean immigrants, like the Ramirezes, were more educated than the general Argentinean populace. They held a strong desire to join mainstream American society and make all the opportunities in America available for their children. The Ramirezes expressed considerable pleasure with their new home, and clearly did not miss the socio-political instability of their former home.

MARTA RAMIREZ: FROM ARGENTINA, 1963

My husband had a job as a government worker under Perón—not an important worker, just a clerk. When Perón was overthrown—zat!—he loses his job and can't get no other. He looked three months, and then we say, "The hell with it," and we sell the house—we didn't get much for it neither—and take the money to come to the U.S.

We arrive here in December. I go down to the town center to buy some things, and I see all the Christmas stuff and I say, "What is this Santa Claus?" and the lady in the store tell me, and I go home and I tell my daughter Angela, she was six then, "In this country Santa Claus brings you presents."

"Good," she says, and I take her to see Santa Claus in that little house they have in the shopping center.

On Christmas Eve she hangs up her stockings and we put some stuff in them and a nice doll besides—one of those dolls that says words. And the next day my daughter is very happy. We want to be Americans, that is why we do it that way.

Then on the Feast of the Epiphany, January 6, we go to church, and on the way home my daughter says, "Tonight the Three Kings will come."

"Angela," I say, "Santa Claus comes in the United States, the Three Kings don't come here."

"They come all over the world," she says, "you told me so yourself."

"No," I say, and my husband says "No, no," but she gets out her shoes anyway and puts them by the window. That is what we do in Argentina for the Three Kings.

I clean up the kitchen and wash the dishes and then I go in to cover up Angela, because it is cold. She is sleeping, so sweet, like a real angel, and the shoes are by the window. I call my husband and he looks at her and goes out and buys a—what you go on the snow with?—a sled.

In the morning Angela comes in to us and says, "You see, I told you the Three Kings come to New Jersey."

Source:

American Mosaic: The Immigrant Experience in the Words of Those Who Lived It, compiled by Joan Morrison and Charlotte Fox Zabusky. Pittsburgh: University of Pittsburgh Press, 1993. p. 352.

Armenian Americans

An interview with Armenian American Araxi Chorbajian Ayvasian in the 1970s recounted the violent history of the Armenian people of Eastern Europe. Araxi's Armenian ancestors attained important social standing during four centuries of Ottoman Turkish rule only to suffer mass genocide under the newly formed Turkish government during World War I. Mass murders of Armenians in the region had begun earlier, at the end of the nineteenth century, about the time of her birth. Araxi was born in Marash, Turkey, in the region of the former Armenian kingdom. Her Armenian heritage is evident in part by the "ian" ending to her surname, as is the case with most Armenians.

In the interview, Araxi recalled the turbulent period's impacts on her family beginning in 1904 when her father was injured by acid tossed at him. Forced to flee in 1915 due to Turkish actions against Armenians, the Araxi family left their home and family business behind for another part of the region. Benefitting from her grandfather's connections as a lawyer and representative in the Turkish parliament in Aleppo, they were able to evade the locations of mass murders. The world war's conclusion seemingly brought safety for Araxi's people, but the persistent political instability in Turkey forced occupational French troops to withdraw leaving the Armenians again at the mercy of the Turks.

Consequently, millions of surviving Armenians scattered throughout the world shortly after World War I, including Araxi who was among some 30,000 Armenians seeking to escape the resurgent bloodshed by immigrating to the United States. Araxi was part of a second wave of Armenian immigrants to the United States, the first being a surge prior to World War I. Like many Armenian Americans at the time, Araxi settled in the Northeast working for a small Armenian-owned business, a Hairenik Press bookstore. Given her strong educational background, the transition to American society seemed relatively easy.

In her interview, Araxi reminisced about Armenian family traditions, "We always liked large families. Armenian families lived together. The son would get married and they lived together in one part of the parent's house. There was no such thing as going away." She fondly described the role of Armenian mothers in educating their young. But, Araxi remained disturbed over Armenian population losses earlier in the twentieth century and the seeming lack of official recognition of the Armenian plight by the United States government, likening it somewhat to the plight of Indians and blacks in the United States.

ARAXI CHORBAJIAN AYVASIAN— DEPORTED FROM ARMENIA

May 13, 1975, and June 3, 1976
Arlington, Massachusetts

I was born in Turkey. We used to have an Armenian kingdom there. Of course, after the Turks occupied those places, the Armenian kingdom came to an end.

In the town of Marash there were thirty thousand people where I was born, and we were under the domination of the Turks. Five hundred years since their occupation they have always subdued and massacred and tortured and confiscated property, no matter whose it was, even though we were citizens and we accepted them as our government. The worst came for mass murders starting in 1890—even 1880s—starting in the upper Armenia, and then in the Cilician Armenia 1894, 1895. There was a massacre in 1904 in Marash. In 1907 there was the one in Adana where they killed all the priests and all men of religion and culture—three thousand.

I remember the massacre in 1904, I think it was. Even though I was four years old, there were certain events I remember. One thing, my father had closed his fabric shop. As he was coming home they had thrown a bottle of acid on him. Fortunately, it was not to his face. It was his leg that was bad. It was all skinned off. They killed about three thousand people in one day in Marash.

Of course, the worst came in 1915, during the First World War. They just herded the cream, the top—all cultural, professional, and church people. And they said they were going to take them to a certain part of Turkey, but they never got there.

Zeytoun was a village. My hometown was on one side of the mountains and Zeytoun was on the other side. It was a *purely* Armenian village. It was mountainous, it was a summer resort, as well. They had hot springs there. These Zeytoun people had twice fought against the Turks. They lost a lot of men at Zeytoun.

My grandfather, my mother's father, was a representative in the Turkish parliament in Aleppo. He had come to the Aleppo "congress," let's say. He was there two years, I think. In the month of the harvest he was asked, with a clergyman and another layman, to go to Zeytoun and persuade the Zeytounists to give their arms up. He refused. Those three people were the first ones to be deported.

The Zeytoun people were finally disarmed, and they were brought to Marash. After a few weeks they sent them down, to Syria. The first stop was Aleppo. The first station was Meskéné, Raqqa, Dayr az Zawr, which was the biggest tomb along the Euphrates. People used to walk for days and days and months and months. Of course, we couldn't take much when we left.

I was born at the turn of the century, so I was about fourteen years old then.

In 1915, after the Zeytoun people were banished down toward the Euphrates, then it was our turn. Out of the thirty thousand there were left only a few hundred old people in Marash. The rest of them were all sent out.

Everyone was drafted up to age forty. Later on we found they were building roads, and as they were building roads, they were being shot until every one of them was killed. Nobody came back. You could either give a certain amount of money or go to the army. For that once, it was fifty Turkish pounds. First they drafted; then those who paid were deported six months later. My father paid money and stayed. They took the money, mules, donkeys, our horses; they took them all. Then, six months later, we were deported. My father was drafted.

My family was a hundred people. My father's family was five brothers. We were the least, five children. There were three generations. My mother's family was with us, too, but they were a small family. We had a mule. We couldn't take anything much. We left everything, the homes, the shops, to their mercy. We reached about two miles down. They started killing people already. We found out later one of my cousins was beheaded. It was at night when we went. The group had to rest for a while; you couldn't walk at night.

On the first night, the Turkish gendarmes, they were supposed to protect us—but they were the ones who attacked young girls. They raped them, and some of them were never returned, if they wanted to take them elsewhere.

Every day, every other day the deportations, a group of five hundred, four hundred, three hundred, that way. In a couple of months everybody was out. So we came to Aleppo. It took us about ten days.

Fortunately, my grandfather in the senate had some friends, and instead of deporting us all the way down to Dayr az Zawr, we were taken off a train and to a hideout. When we were deported, my grandfather was already in Aleppo. Through bribery he had found a way to take us into the city. They never let the Armenians go to the city. It would be about three miles out of the proper city, where they'd stay for the night, and the next morning they have to move again.

The night we had reached Aleppo some soldiers came and looked for my father. We didn't know what was happening. They singled us out. My grandfather's family is six daughters, one boy. He was not with us. My grandmother had another member of the family, and us.

These Turkish gendarmes took us from the group. They took us to some interior part of the city. My grandfather was in a hideout, so we went there. We were saved at this first hurdle.

One man, an Arab, also a representative and friend of my grandfather, owned a whole village. He said, "I'll take your family to my own village," because he knew what was going to happen to all the people who were going to Dayr az Zawr. In that village we stayed about six months, safe, sound. We thought we were free. And at the end of six months, an order came that we had to be deported. They had found out where we were.

My grandfather was a lawyer and was an educated man. They really wanted to kill him. So at the end of six months, we were deported again from Maara. My mother was pregnant. It was very difficult. It was *too* hot in the summer. We were still walking. My family, and there were a couple of other families also, whom my grandfather had brought after we had settled there. Most Armenians had already been deported, from Aleppo station down to Meskéné or Ragga, Dayr az Zawr. The fact is that these Turkish gendarmes loved Turkish gold pounds. They'll take your money. They'll say they'll save you—one month, two months—and then the final station is Dayr az Zawr. You will finally be sent to Dayr az Zawr no matter what. At Dayr az Zawr they were all put into ditches. They were all shot in groups and thrown into the Euphrates River. How many *thousands*, hundred and thousands of Armenians, were killed in that Euphrates River! They were bound and thrown, all in groups. And some Armenian girls killed themselves there. They were pressured by the gendarmes. Rather than get raped, they threw themselves in the river.

Finally we went to Meskéné. There were a lot of people living in tents with four sticks and a sheet or something. We were held there for a while, and my grandfather had friends in the government who were responsible for organizing from station to station. They had a small house there, and my grandfather did some work for this fellow. He helped us again; we stayed there, but finally the order came for us. He said, "I can't keep you anymore. You have to go."

The next morning, we found my grandfather wasn't moving. He had a shock He couldn't talk. He couldn't walk. He was in bed. He couldn't get up. We were supposed to leave, but he was paralyzed. They permitted us to stay a few days and find out what the situation was.

By this time my mother had her last child. She was not able to walk. We hired a camel to take care of her. The baby was delivered by itself. There were no doctors, no midwives, nothing. My grandmother helped her. The baby lived, but for worse days.

My grandfather died within the same week. Two gendarmes came and they took him near the river where there were a lot of people. They buried him in a mass grave in the sand, as if it was a cemetery or something. Every day hundreds would die of starvation. They would all take them and *dump* them.

In the time that we were detained there for six months, my father became an army soldier. He had two horse-drawn carts, and he was working for the government. By then we had a visitor, my aunt's husband. He quit the army and he was deported. It was a surprise. He was there—young, strong, a very courageous man. He had seen the world.

Now we are trying to flee because the baby was born, my grandfather dead. We either fled or we would be dead. You can't believe the story, but this is how it happened. My father gave him one of the carts. He started going back and forth, bringing supplies to the Turkish army. Each time he took one of us with him. One of us would ride under the army supplies, wheat, lentils, thing like that. My mother, myself, and the baby were together. The baby cried. Finally the whole family was transferred to Aleppo, one by one, by this brother-in-law, my aunt's husband. We would ride with him; then about one hour from the city, he would drop us off. He's give us directions as to where to go. It lasted about two months. Everybody was in Aleppo.

There were so many millions of people there. My uncles died there of diseases; typhus was prevalent. We lost quite a few of the family.

This was 1917 when we came back to Aleppo. After we stayed there my father was still a soldier, and they transferred him. My mother started working, to make clothing for the army. With the armistice, November 11, 1918, the Allies occupied Aleppo. First the British came, then the French. The French went to occupy Cilicia, where my hometown was. So back and forth letters came. "Marash is beautiful now. The French have occupied. Everybody's free."

We had orange groves, olive orchards, vineyards. So we thought, "All right." We'd been out of the country three years now. We *had* to go back—like fools! This time there were only half the people who were deported that were alive.

We hired a truck, and the whole family rode in the truck. It took us about four days to go back. My father wanted to go back because there wasn't enough for us in Aleppo. We had no home, we had no house, we had no place to be. We were in a rented room, two families—my grandmother's family and my family. We thought if we went there we could at least get the fruits of our land. My father was quite a well-to-do person. With all his brothers they had three clothing stores, and a lot of property. So, we went there.

They vacated the house when we went. Some of them were burned. Most of the houses they had destroyed. Four years was too long a time for anything to stay intact by the Turks. The churches were all ruined. But it was nice. When we went the occupation was by the English. And then somehow there was an agreement between the English and the French. The English withdraw and the French came, and after the French came Armenian legionnaires in the French army.

Everything was beautiful, but the empire was deteriorating. A lot of the territory was taken by the Allies. There was no more Turkish government in Marash. Turkey, it was decimated. They didn't even have twenty-five percent of the Old Ottoman Empire. We left again at the end of 1918; this was about a year after we went back, because we had harvested one harvest of rice and vineyards.

The war started between the Turks. This time it was the Kemalists from the north. They had come to fight. Kemal, Ataturk, Mustafa Kemal Pasha, they called them. First the Sultan abdicated, and then the Young Turks took over. During the war the Young Turks were in charge, but when the war was over and they had lost everything, the Young Turks disappeared. And now, Mustafa Kemal, who was against the Young Turks, took over this time.

There were about ten thousand Armenians by this time in Marash. Of the thirty thousand, two-thirds were killed or died, and of the ten thousand, the shooting was going on, the homes were being burned. The Turkish soldiers were coming, advancing every night, one street to the other. When the turn came to our house to be burned, we had to flee.

My father wasn't home on Christmas Day. He had gone to visit his brothers.

We had made holes in the walls of the homes so that we could go from one to the other. Our home was on the street, so it was very easy to get to. There were about five hundred people 'way at the end of the street. They had to move out—all of us.

We ran out of the house. It was a *bleak*, snowy night, in the middle of the night. We left that other child who was born in the desert, in Meskéné. She was left behind. There was one man who took charge of things, and he refused to take any smaller children. We thought that they would not do anything to the children and the old people. There were a lot of old women and other children that were left there. This Armenian—U.S. citizen guided us to the street and told us, "From now on you're on your own. Run!"

The Armenian mother is very different from any other mother. The man has always been the head of the family. The mother has always been there for the children; to educate them, to clothe them.

A lot of us fell on the street because the Turkish army was shooting from the citadel, from the minarets. It was a very light night on account of the snow and ice, a full moon, beautiful night. We were seeing the people just dropping as the bullets were coming. But we all got to where my father was, a big Jesuit monastery. When we went there it was, oh [sighing], just a mess. There is no room to sit, even leave alone lying or anything. There was about three, four thousand people in that one church.

The French and the Turks fought for three weeks exactly. At the end of twenty-one days there were rumors that the French people were going to withdraw, leave the town to the mercy of the Kemalists. And, of course, it happened. The Armenian fellows were fighting for the French. The Armenians in the church knew that the French were up to something. They said, "You're not going to go unless you take the young people with you." The French refused. There was a skirmish between the French soldiers stationed here in the church and the Armenian young people. Anyway, that night the church was almost emptied of men and young boys. They followed the French army who were withdrawing, whereas they could have won the war if they'd stayed.

It snowed twenty-four hours. They were all frozen on the road to Islahie, where they could get a train. Turkish gendarmes came, two days after the French withdrew. They told us we can go back to our homes. They brought some food and rice. By this time there were some Americans. There was an American girls' college, and there were a lot of orphanages, American orphanages. They went around the city. They collected all these children who were left in the homes and they put them in the orphanages.

We got out child again. She was three or four years old. She suffered from diarrhea because she didn't have enough shelter or the proper food or anything. She was sick for quite a long time, and then I think about six months later, one afternoon, she complained of some pain in her neck. She died in twenty-four hours of the complaints. We couldn't get to a doctor then, you know. No hospital, no medication she got. Those three weeks killed her. She died a natural death, you would call it; but I'm sure if she didn't go through that, she wouldn't die.

Life started again, on rice and olive oil. People were all sick because they were hungry. They all had diarrhea, and it took another couple of years to find themselves, but soon enough they wanted to leave. No matter where, it would be better than Marash.

People in groups left. They were again killed on the road. If five people started, one of them reached Aleppo. Of the ten thousand I don't think two thousand survived.

This time my father didn't go, because, well, we were all young people, girls mostly. My brother left with the French. He was only about thirteen years old. My uncle, my cousins, they all left. Some of them perished. The brother-in-law that transferred us from Meskéné from the desert to Aleppo saw my brother on the road there, and he carried my brother all the way to Islahie. His toes were frozen; he couldn't walk. They were later taken care of in Adana, where the French had a government.

My father had some Turkish friends, and those people who had taken care of our lands and property when we were away, they were nice enough to give a truck to my father. We filled in the truck again; my grandfather, my brother, and my uncle were off. The family was *all* women. Nobody. Grandfather died, my uncle had left with the French soldiers, my brother left, my cousins. But we

came back to Aleppo our second time; this was our second deportation.

[Some years after I came to the United States] I became a bookkeeper by profession. I was in charge of a small bookstore that we had at the Hairenik Press.

You didn't have any children?

No. I couldn't have children. I was in my fifties when I got married. He waited twenty years.

What effect was there on the relationship between men and women as result of Armenian persecution?

The Armenian mother is very different from any other mother. The man has always been the head of the family. The mother has always been there for the children; to educate them, to clothe them. "Family education" is what you give and what the children take with them all their lives. They learn a lot in school, but we call it the "family education," *undanegan dagtiaragoutune*, which is something more than what any school can give. Mothers have been very, very tender, yet very strict with their children, both ways.

I'd like to read you something. It's a very short epic poem. "The Mother's Heart." He says that there is a legend that a boy loved a girl. And this girl asked the boy to prove that he really loves her. And it says in order to prove, he should go and bring his mother's heart to her. Kill the mother and bring the heart. So the boy is sorry and sad, crying, and the girl was very angry and said, "Don't show your face to me unless you come with your mother's heart!" The boy goes and kills a goat and brings the goat's heart, and the girl recognizes that it's not the mother's heart, so she's even angrier. And then the fellow goes again. He's so sad and he's lost himself. He kills his mother and he's bringing his mother's heart to the girl. On the way he falls, and he hears the voice of the mother, even though it's only a heart; the mother's heart says, "Oh, my boy, did you *hurt* yourself?"

See? This is a legend, but it shows the Armenian mother. Even though taken out of the physical body, just a heart, the heart speaks to the boy, in tenderness, and says, "Oh, my boy, did you hurt yourself?" So the Armenian mother is something very different. It's actually the truth about every mother.

In the last hundred years, the Armenian men had a difficult time. They had to compete to get someplace. While they were doing that, to provide for the family, the mother was doing everything in the home, to serve the husband and to serve the children. And mind you, every Armenian mother, six was the average, six children, at least. My grandmother had eleven, plus two or three that died. My mother had eight. And she was one of the modernistic ones. If it wasn't for deportations and so on and so forth, maybe she would've had more. We always liked large families. Armenian families lived together. The son would get married and they lived together in one part of the parent's house. There was no such thing as going away. The bride would come right to her in-laws' home and live there, as long as it was possible, as long as they had three, four, five children. Now, after fifty years, we have the fiftieth anniversary of the deportation, of the genocide. We applied to the House of Representatives. We made a petition that April 24 should be set as a day of men's inhumanity to men. We didn't even *mention* Armenians. But even that was denied to us.

I don't know why the U.S. doesn't sign. Maybe because they have experienced genocide with the Indians and also the blacks. Some Turk may come and say, "Look what you did to your native Indians! Look what you have been doing after Proclamation freeing the Negroes by Lincoln, a hundred years."

We should have learned a lot from the Negroes, you know, what they did. A lot of them were imprisoned, a lot of things happened to them, but they are getting there. The TV screen comes on. What do you see? All blacks. They are getting there, and in business, everywhere. They have bet-

ter houses. In a short span of life, only a decade and a half. I hope we do something ourselves.

Where is that [pause] old, beautiful trustworthy U.S.A.? Where is it now? Half the government was indicted, for God's sake. They were all found guilty, even your president, even this president. Four weeks after the country made its president resign, the other one gets up and pardons him. Let him suffer a little bit. Well, they thought, "He might get sick; he might get breakdown." So what? He deserves to get breakdown. He deserved it. Look what *he* did.

No one person is permanent in this world. We all have our ups and downs. But if we are guilty, we should *suffer* [bangs her hand down on the table] the consequences. They should enforce the law, be it on the president, or on the state secretary, or on the community. If parents punish their children for their little mistakes, they will learn to grow better. From children to their parents to the representatives to their government to their president. It starts from top to bottom.

Source:

First Generation: In the Words of Twentieth Century American Immigrants, compiled by June Namias. Revised edition. Urbana: University of Illinois Press, 1992. pp. 82-92.

*G*enocide is the systematic murder of a whole group of people on the basis of race, class, or nationality. It is largely a twentieth-century phenomenon, because prior to that time, governments did not have the means—or, with a few exceptions, the desire—to carry it out. The Nazis in Germany set out to destroy the Jews, and killed some 6 million in carefully planned and designed camps. Likewise the Soviet Union under Josef Stalin in the 1930s methodically eliminated millions of "class enemies," as did the Chinese Communist government under Mao Zedong several decades later. Similarly, between 1975 and 1979, Communist forces in Cambodia slaughtered some 2 million people in an act of genocide planned by a group of Cambodian intellectuals. On a much smaller scale in the 1990s, Serbian forces in the former nation of Yugoslavia undertook "ethnic cleansing," which involved the systematic murder of thousands.

Much has been written about genocide, including its psychological effects on survivors. This is particularly true of the Nazi Holocaust, and many survivors later reported feelings of guilt precisely because they survived. It seemed unfair that they should have lived, some said, while loved ones went to their deaths in the gas chambers.

Despite the many words written on genocide and its effects, however, little attention has been devoted to the first act of genocide in history. This occurred in

1915, when Hitler was still a German army corporal and Stalin a minor functionary in an insignificant political party, yet it established a pattern for much of what was to come.

The nation that perpetrated this massacre was the Ottoman Empire, as Turkey was called from the 1300s until the end of World War I; and the victims were the Armenians. Once a vast realm that stretched across much of the Middle East, the Ottoman Empire was in a rapid state of decline by that time. It still included Armenia, however, but the latter had begun agitating for independence, and Ottoman leaders perceived it as a threat.

Between 1894 and 1896, the Ottoman sultan or king massacred a quarter-million Armenians. He was later deposed by a group of Turkish army officers collectively called the Young Turks. Led by Enver Pasha, Mehmet Talaat Pasha, and Ahmed Djemal Pasha, the Young Turks allied their country with Germany in World War I, and proceeded to undertake the full-scale extermination of the Armenians.

As with later instances of genocide, this one was inspired by an intellectual, in this case Ziya Gökalp, who promoted a philosophy called "Pan-Turkism." Though the expression "ethnic cleansing" had yet to be coined, Pan-Turkism called for exactly that: the elimination of the Armenian minority in order to "purify" Turkey. The genocide was a planned affair, having been outlined in 1913, but as with the later Nazi Holocaust, the leaders waited until they could carry it out under the cover of war.

The Armenians declared their loyalty to the Ottoman Empire in the war, but after a major defeat of Ottoman forces by Russians in January 1915, the Young Turks decided to begin the killings as a way to take attention off their wartime troubles. The genocide began on April 24, 1915, in Constantinople, and continued until the early 1920s. In a particularly cynical move, Ottoman authorities used another national minority, the Kurds, to carry out many of the killings.

In the end, between 1 and 1.5 million Armenians died. When the rest of the world learned about the killings, there was a massive outcry, but little in the way of direct action. With Turkey's defeat in the war, the three leaders of the Young Turks were all killed, but by assassination or in battle, not by execution. Twenty years later, as Adolf Hitler prepared to invade Poland, he asked his advisors the rhetorical question, "Who still talks nowadays of the extermination of the Armenians?"

Few did, and many who remembered, such as Leo Hamalian's father, were silent. He was overcome by the all-too-common guilt of the survivor, in his case compounded by his feeling that he had simply run away while his loved ones were dying. His son's essay is a touching tribute on both a personal and political level.

AMID BOUNTY, LONGING

My father, like most Armenian survivors of the Turkish genocide, was a man who never wanted to leave home. Until he was forced to flee, he loved the place where he had been born and brought up. It was a milieu alien to the American mentality, and as a result my father never really adapted to the customs of this country. As I look back upon his memory, more in sadness then in the anger I used to feel flaring so often in his presence, I think that his life was about the damage done to the human spirit by exile.

From the time that he set foot in the New World in 1911, an early victim of the Turkish pogroms against Christians, to the day of his lonely death in 1939, neither the chimera of the American Dream nor the bounty of material rewards could numb the pain of a refugee who found himself uprooted in a strange land where he was forced to flourish or founder. He all those things that transformed other transplanted Armenians into lovers of this land.

Yet I remember him as a ghost who gestures, talks, but utters no words, not even the smallest murmur, of that interior grief that I now realize he had held within like a stone for 25 years.

He must have left recognizing the grim shadow that the future threw before him. Of a large family of prosperous peasants in the Lake Van area, only he and his sister got out of Turkey before the Turks got them, he to America, she to Egypt, where she lived out her days as a stateless person. But not even a futile reality is easily replaced not the wounds of separation quickly healed.

He tried to be a good American as he understood the idea. He became a photoengraver, took his family to picnics in Hudson Park, argued politics while he played backgammon with his cronies, attended church on 34th street, and perhaps hoped that he Big Dream would materialize, as it did for so many other Armenians. Instead, I suspect, it only emphasized his sense of loss. His emotional attachment to the place that had treated him like dirt was so massive, so monumental that he was almost blind to the bounty he had reaped in his new homeland.

Why did he resist resurrection when other Armenians were rising out of the ashes of the Turkish tragedy? I am not sure I know, but I think that the stone of sorrow in his guts may simply have stayed stone. Nothing softened it, and his stonified sorrow showed itself in excessive sternness with his children. The more American we became, the more infuriated he became. We couldn't tell whether his anger was directed against America or against us. We felt that we had somehow misbehaved by becoming what we had to become in face of the heavy claims made upon out malleable natures.

I think my father believed that he could regain, magically, some part of his past, even alleviate the pain of his exile if he could keep his children Armenian. Thus, he would triumph over the Turk, who had sought to destroy his Armenian identity. So we spoke only Armenian at home, ate only Armenian food, and saw mainly Armenian friends. In those days, the nativist elements used the public schools to disparage the cultural origins of foreigners; I must confess that I was an innocent but willing collaborator. I had no notion that my childish gestures of rebellion might have been torture to my father.

Now I think I know what was eating like acid at my father. Did he deserve the bounty and safety that the New World offered for the earning? Were those signs of success in reality the fruits of his failure as a man? Should he have stayed behind with his parents? Should he have left his sister? Should he have had the courage to confront his enemies, no matter what the cost to him?

I think my father felt guilty that he had escaped the fate of his family. Though he knew that he had avoided terror and even death, in one part of himself he became persuaded that he had betrayed his family by not sharing their destiny, that he had—this will sound irrational to all those but the survivors of concentration camps—survived at their expense.

Thus far his insight took him, but no further. The act of sorting out and comprehending these ambivalent feelings proved too much for this uneducated though intelligent immigrant. And indeed why should he have been proud that he had had to run away, even to save his life? This frame of mind was made doubly difficult to endure by obtuse neighbors and America-firsters. He was in America. He was safe. He was prospering. His children had opportunities. What more did he want? Let the dead bury the dead. But my stubborn father could not bring himself to congratulate himself for what he considered to be an act of betrayal.

Fortunately, our society no longer puts pressure on immigrants to forget their former associa-

Driven by pogroms in Turkey, Armenians emigrated in mass to the United States in the early twentieth century.

tions, or to deny anything dear left behind. We deplore the bitterness of a destiny that displaces people from their homes, that uproots and deracinates, that creates a league of dislocated persons. Such people are no longer debarred from the ranks of "good and true" Americans by virtue of their tragic sense of life. We can be thankful that we have developed this dimension of spiritual toler-

ance. I prize it and my father, were he alive, would have prized it.

December 1, 1976

Source:

Ethnic Groups in American Life, edited by Gene Brown. New York: Arno Press and the *New York Times*, 1978. pp. 332-333.

ASIAN INDIAN AMERICANS

The anonymous scientific researcher who gave the following interview grew up in Allahabad, India, and came to the United States with his wife and child in 1969 to study for a doctoral degree in electrical engineering. After completing his degree, he accepted a job with a large corporation just west of Boston.

He and his family are part of the "new immigration" to the United States after 1965, when national quotas were dropped in favor of promoting family reunification and the immigration of skilled labor. More than 24,000 Indians arrived between 1966 and 1970, one-third of them being classified as "professional, technical, or kindred workers."

However, even if many of the new Asian Indian immigrants come from the professional class, and even if many, like the researcher, find employment in their fields of specialization, many cannot find work commensurate with their training. Many college-educated Asian Indian professionals in the United States run travel agencies, sari shops, and fast food restaurants. Many drive taxis in America's major cities. They also can be found operating motels, where they occupy a particular niche: about 20 percent of the nation's hotels and motels are operated by Asian Indians.

In the following interview, conducted in 1977, the researcher comments on his reasons for coming to the United States and on his generally positive experiences in American society. His only apprehension seems to be the growing cultural differences he notices between himself and his young son. (A. L. Sarkar is a pseudonym.)

INDIAN RESEARCHER
April 8, 1977
Waltham, Massachusetts

After a year of working I wanted to go for higher studies and I really wanted to go to an advanced country just to look around and see how the things are. I got this admission and assitantship, but at that point my father died, in '63, early '64 I had some family responsibilities.

The structure in India is somewhat different than what you have here. I had my sisters who were not married, and marriage is a big deal there. I decided that I could not leave the responsibility I had for the family. So I completely cooled the idea of going for several years.

Then in '68 it occurred to me that maybe I should go out, maybe write to this university and see what they say now. I wrote back to them. They provided assistance. I said, "I'll go and study there two or three years and see how things go." In fact I came on a study visa. You could arrange five years.

Naturally I talked it over with the family. In my own family it really was no problem. My brother was really no problem; he quickly agreed. My mother was somewhat skeptical about it; she did not think I should go, but knowing that I had waited for so many years, and she is very negotiable, she

55

really didn't object that much. My wife's parents were quite strong on this. They did not want us to go away and forget India completely. They had a feeling that we would not come back—come back in the sense of living there permanently. But we talked it over with them and basically they understood that I am going to fulfill my ambition—I'll not stay for long. And there was no main difficulty in convincing my wife; we had good communication. The child was only three years old, so we didn't have to ask him.

In the beginning, somehow it didn't look like to me a great step. The only difference was that I would be that much further away from home. I think if I had a choice that I had to come on my own money there is no way I could have come, because the money gets divided by a factor of eight or nine between there and here. That is one aspect of it. The other aspect is that you can't get that kind of foreign exchange released from the government. They just don't want to do that. So on my money I wouldn't have come.

How come you stayed here after you got your degree?

My feeling was that going to school was good—it gave me a certificate, gave me some background, all right. But I didn't get any idea about how the industry's operating. I planned to be in the area of research for the rest of my life. I really thought for me to take advantage of my stay here I really ought to work, really to get the firsthand experience. And then we decided I would work about three, four years and then go back.

I thought that three years is a long period originally. But you know, three years really gets you started and that's the reason we really have to postpone it. If it's '80 it gives me six, seven, eight years of working there. To a certain extent financial is one thing but more than that I think gives me enough experience. Really I feel I should be satisfied by then and if I'm not satisfied then, forget it. I'll never be. This is the lower limit.

Upper limit comes from the consideration that we have two children now. One is ten, the other is two and a half. So, I don't think I would like to impose my decision on my child. At sixteen, having been brought up here, he's at the age where he thinks what he's doing, at least he thinks that. He becomes completely Americanized. I am not saying that he is not now. He still has some habits because we try to inject on him. We observe the festivals, we observe the values, we have fairly good, in fact very good, interaction with the community from back home. Being a large group here we get together almost every weekend or so. So he does get pret-

ty good exposure to our culture, our values. [But] my son now is roughly ten years old and he does not think the way I do. Our fairy tales are different. Our stories are different and our songs, poems are different. I am not saying that he will not be a misfit if he goes at twelve, but certainly he'll be a bigger misfit if he goes at sixteen.

I am saying we are planning to go back in '80, '81. I am not saying that we have got a plane ticket and we will go. We will probably review at that time. But I think if we decide not to go at that time then we are here for good.

Have there been any kinds of discrimination against you?

No. That is something, I really appreciate that very much. I never felt that I was discriminated against. In fact, I always felt that I got my share and more. I have heard people talk about it. Discrimination is something which has a very tight link with the economy of the country and I guess that that is one of the reasons that it is happening in Canada and why it is very severe in England. I am not saying it does not exist here, but to my knowledge I haven't seen any, at least in my life that's the only one you can comment on. Everybody's circumstances are different. Maybe I am just lucky I met the right people.

Earlier I used to worry about my accent, which I have and I live with. Earlier I used to feel that maybe it's bad, maybe I should work on it. Very quickly I decided that's not the way to work. You can't change these things. You really can't. I'm sure that if you went to another country, you can't be one of those. We can be compatible. We can live happily, very friendly, but you don't have to be one of them to live there. I may be wrong.

Would you say from the point of view of India, the Indian economy, they have lost a great deal?

I feel that the point that the country has been losing a lot has been overemphasized. First of all, the way I think, I don't think the country has lost a heck of a lot if I stay away eight years and come back with better training. In fact they may come out winner. That's one aspect of it. Another aspect is I have already worked there. It's not a total waste. The other facet is our education is more or less completely subsidized by the government, so the number of people who go to colleges is much higher and some people feel that, I don't feel that, if I go back I will be displacing somebody. It's not there's a dearth of trained people there. There are people available. If I can get enough training, that can be useful. But for the point of view that the country has spent on me, I agree that they lost some. But part of it is very well paid for, for my work earlier, and maybe if I go back, it's paid for.

But many students leave at nineteen and they are never heard from again.

True. I think that is a total loss as far as India is concerned. If I did that I would feel guilty, in a way—guilty not in the sense that I am not doing the right thing. If I really look from a very broad point of view, after all, I am contributing to the good of the society. Why should it be for the country that I lived in? But I feel strongly that if the education is subsidized by the government, I think they have a point in expecting me to do something

for them. Otherwise they have lost the money. Another aspect is, if I didn't go to school they might have trained somebody else. I think it's a valid point. But I don't believe that if I went to school there, I am bound to work the rest of my life without doing any betterment to myself, or without really doing what I want to do. I work on compromises, as you can very well tell.

Source:

First Generation: In the Words of Twentieth-Century American Immigrants, compiled by June Namias. Revised edition. Urbana: University of Illinois Press, 1992. pp. 183-186.

*S*udershan S. Chawla, a first-generation immigrant from India, maintains the strong beliefs that were shaped by her native culture. She continues to wear Indian dress, although other people may mock it; she was brought up with a belief that women should not expose their legs, so she never wears short pants or skirts. In addition, Chawla "lives clean" no smoking, drinking, or cursing. Here she also relates Indian marriage customs and the significance of the red dot that women receive when they marry.

Chawla also works hard as a nurse. She is frugal with her earnings, trying to save money and avoid being wasteful. She says that her thrifty lifestyle is guided by her beliefs.

DIFFERENT BY CHOICE
by Sudershan S. Chawla

"We wear our Indian dress because of our culture, and because we are proud of it. But there are people who say, 'this is like a curtain.' They embarrass us. 'You wrapping around a curtain?' They don't even know the value. They don't know the culture. They don't know that we want to cover up our bodies, that we don't show our bodies to people, to have them look at us, to give us remarks. In India, we don't use the clothes people in this country use, like bikinis or shorts or clothes that show the body. We cover it up. Pants suits and long skirts aren't bad because you can't see the legs. But if anyone sits and shows her legs, that is not good. It is not right to show a man my legs. We don't like it because we were raised like that. The whole coun-

try is like that, not just myself. That's why these people shout their remarks but we don't care. We don't say anything about their dress. My dress is mine, yours is yours. I don't care.

"We don't drink, we don't smoke. One person in a thousand might do it, like film stars. We don't curse like here. Here, every single minute they curse. And we like peace, no fighting, no cursing, no arguments or hitting between husband and wife. We will fight a little inside, but not like here. Today the marriage, tomorrow's the fighting, the next day go to court and get a divorce.

"In our country we stay with our parents until marriage. And they spend the money for our education. We don't work until we finish our education. And we are dependent on our parents for everything. And we don't go outside to boyfriends, and we don't have children before marriage. If a woman has a child before marriage, she is like a prostitute, and the people would hate her and throw her out. Here, if a teenager has a child, the parents seem proud. They say, 'my daughter has a boyfriend. My daughter is pregnant.' They talk openly. We don't talk openly, that is the difference. Everything like that is secret. But here, nothing is secret."

The Red Dot: "When a girl gets married she gets the red dot. At eighteen or nineteen, she is married off. It is an arranged marriage by her parents. My father gave me a ring for me to give to my husband and he also gave a ring to my husband to give to me. Then the red dot is put on the forehead as a symbol of marriage, to say you're a wife. After the ceremony the woman wears the dot until she becomes a widow. The earrings on the nose are for fashion. The girl, especially after she marries, can decorate herself with jewelry and rings. Five hundred years ago, our culture did not allow a woman to wear makeup or jewelry until she was married. But today, we can decorate ourselves with any color jewelry we like. Even my elevenyearold daughter can wear jewelry.

"I'm a nurse. My friends have stores, restaurants or motels. We work hard. We cook at home all the time. We don't spend too much money. We don't take the check, cash it, and sit in a restaurant to eat. We bring everything home. We cook and everyone eats together, so we save money. When we save money, then we invest. We have to study to get a good job.

"Some people don't like us, because we come from another country, and they have their own way. They look to us, and want to change themselves, but they can't because they have troubles. They take drugs, or smoke dope, for instance. If I'm smoking, I can't tell my daughter not to smoke. So these problems make it hard for them to make money, and they go to welfare. They steal. We feel something, but we don't get involved. Let them do what they want.

"But the killing, that is no good. If we killed one of them, everyone would come after us. But they killed an Indian, and we had to go to the court and talk to the politicians to get them to listen.

"'Hindu, Hindu, Hindu, Indian girl with the sari,' sometimes blacks call us that, sometimes Spanish, sometimes white. You can't say it is only one particular group. The Filipinos, the Chinese, the Japanese, they are good ones, no trouble.

"If we move to another area you know what they will think: 'these people are scared of us' so they will go scare the others. We don't move. We have to stay here, and we face the people. If we move, they could do the same thing in another area to scare us. So where do we go? That means we go home, that's it. Right? So we don't move."

Source:

Joann Faung Jean Lee. *Asian American Experiences in the United States: Oral Histories of First to Fourth Generation Americans from China, the Philippines, Japan, India, the Pacific Islands, Vietnam and Cambodia.* Jefferson, NC: McFarland & Co., 1991. pp. 118-120.

AUSTRIAN AMERICANS

*T*he hard working, agrarian lifestyle of many Austrian Americans is chronicled in *a 1938 interview with immigrant Joe Poeffel. Joe was born on a small farm in Deutchausen, Austria in 1866 on the eve of the formation of the Austro-Hungarian Empire in 1867. Joe proudly recounted that by ten years of age he was a steady worker on the farm, herding cattle, hauling wood, and plowing fields with oxen. However, increasing industrialization began displacing agrarian workers causing many Austrian peasants and farmers to relocate to the American Midwest. The earliest Austrian immigrants in search of land settled in Illinois and Iowa.*

In 1877, Joe's father was one of many to take advantage of relaxed Austrian emigration policies designed to relieve overpopulation problems arising in some areas. He established a homestead in Platte County, Nebraska, and in 1879 Joe with his mother, brother, and two sisters joined him. The Poeffels arrived just ahead of massive 1880s European immigration to the United States and before an intensive Austrian immigration of skilled laborers during the first decade of the twentieth century. Most Austrians, like the Poeffels were Roman Catholic. Consequently, the family's adaptation to their new home was smoothed by the nineteenth century Austrian policy of sending many Roman Catholic missionaries and priests to America's Midwest frontier to both serve Austrian immigrants and convert natives.

The Poeffels were a tight, self-sufficient Austrian nuclear family in contrast to the extended families of other European traditions. As with many Austrians accustomed to the multi-ethnic populations of the Austro-Hungarians, Joe and his family seemed to experience few socialization problems in their new home. Despite the harshness of farming on the Midwest prairies with seasonal floods and blizzards. Regarding his own process of becoming economically self-sufficient, Joe related, "I herded cattle away from home for two summers for which I was paid $18 for the season; worked as a hired man on the farm for three years and helped at home until I was twenty-nine years old when I got married." In European tradition, at marriage Joe received 80 acres of land from his father to begin his own farm which he tended until retirement years later.

JOE POEFFEL—AUSTRIAN AMERICAN

FORM A: Circumstances of Interview

NAME OF WORKER: Eilert Mohlman.

ADDRESS: Columbus, Neb.

DATE: Nov. 30, 1938. SUBJECT: Folklore

l. Name and address of informant: Joe Poeffel , Columbus, Nebr.

2. Date and time of interview: Nov. 29, 1938 10-12 A.M.

3. Place of interview: At his home

4. Name and address of person, if any, who put you in touch with informant: No one.

5. Name and address of person, if any, accompanying you: No one

6. Description of room, house surroundings, etc.: Kitchen, house moderately furnished and located on edge of town, surroundings neatly kept— with garden space.

FORM B: Personal History of Informant

NAME AND ADDRESS OF INFORMANT: Joe Poeffel , Columbus, Nebr.

1. Ancestry: German-Austrian.

2. Place and date of birth: Deutchausen, Austria, June 24, 1866.

3. Family: Wife — 6 children.

4. Place lived in, with dates: Austria 1866-1879; Platto Co. farm, 1879-1918; City of Columbus 1918 to date.

5. Education, with dates: Country schools 1872-1881.

6. Occupations and accomplishments, with dates: Farm hand and farmer 1884-1918[?].

7. Special skills and interests: General farming and stock raising.

8. Community and religious activities: Member Catholic Church; School director for a number of years.

9. Description of informant: Medium build; height 5' 8/9"; 160#.

10. Other points gained in interview: Now retired and enjoys his daily visits among old friends. One daughter still living with them at home.

FORM C: Text of Interview (Unedited)

Nov. 30, 1938.

We had a small farm near Deutchausen, in Austria, and when I was about ten years old I had to help with the farm work, herd cattle, haul wood out of the timber. We farmed with oxen those days, and when there was a lot of field work to do we used to hitch up a cow with them but it was slow work. We did not raise very much small grain and we did our threshing with a "flail", which is a long stick with another stick or club fastened on the end, the grain was loose and was laid on boards and with the flail we pounded out the grain.

My father was anxious to come to America, but he did not want to take my mother or any of us along, saying that it would be too wild a country and that there were too many Indians here that we might get killed.

He then started out alone to this country in 1877, he worked as a hired farm hand and also did some carpenter work around, and bought a homestead from another man, paying $1.00 an acre for it and he proved up on it. He then sent for us in 1879, my mother, one brother and two sisters. We came direct to Columbus and I remember my father met us at the train with a pair of oxen hitched to a lumber wagon and we kids sat on a board in the wagon box, and it took us a long time to get home from Columbus.

We lived in three different sod houses for about ten years. The first one was near a creek and one time a big rain storm came up and the water got so high that it came through the door and windows of our sod house, the furniture that we had was swimming around in the house; we had to run to the granary and there was high water on both sides of it so we could not get out and had to stay there until the water went down the next afternoon. We lost a lot of chickens and sixteen head of hogs that weighed 200 pounds a piece. The water had ruined our sod house so that it caved in the next day and then we had to build a new one, which we made of square blocks of prairie laid together like our cement blocks are now and smoothed on the inside with mortar that was made of sticky mud, we would whitewash the inside walls to make it look nice; it was warm in the house in winter time and pretty cool in the summer time.

When I was still at home we did not have much money, we would make our own coffee by roasting barley in the oven; we used this kind of coffee for about ten years. Coffee cost about sixty cents a pound and when we used it, it would be as a special treat on Sundays.

I herded cattle away from home for two summers for which I was paid $18 for the season;

worked as a hired man on the farm for three years and helped at home until I was twenty-nine years old when I got married. Then got 80 acres of land from my father and started farming for myself.

In the year of 1880, about the middle of October, we had one of the worst blizzards that I remember of, it lasted for three days and three nights. I was working out at that time; our barn was just about under, we had to start shoveling snow on the roof so that we could get into the barn to milk the cows. We would have to hitch four mules to the hayrack to get half a load of hay for the cattle. We had a blizzard about three times a week that winter and it got to 35 below zero.

The next spring about the middle of April, when the wheat and oats were all sowed, we had another three day blizzard and everything froze. It was one of the coldest winters I ever went through.

Source:

Library of Congress. *American Life Histories: Manuscripts from the Federal Writers' Project, 1936-1940* from the American Memory website (http://memory.loc.gov/ammem/wpaintro/wpa-home.html).

BELGIAN AMERICANS

A wealth of different ethnic groups have migrated to the United States, each of whom at one time brought with them a rich cultural heritage. The United States is by far the most heterogenous society in the world. However, many groups undergo a transformation shortly after arriving in the United States. The transformation is called "Americanization" and involves adapting to a rigorous work ethic, fast paced cities, changes in diet and recreation, and often times learning a new language. The demands of an energized advanced capitalist society often causes ethnic groups to lose their connection to traditions inherited from their homelands. Although many groups often make a conscious effort to pass on old customs and values, out of necessity, their assimilation into American society inevitably results in some cultural casualties.

The Belgian American community is somewhat of an exception to this trend. According to Joseph Amato, author of Servants of the Land: God, Family, and Farm, the early Belgian Americans persevered by constructing strong communal ties based on the traditional values of their homeland. The Belgians are an enterprising group of people who value small agricultural operations, religion, and large cooperative family units. Amato attributed the success of early Belgian Americans to their ability to construct interdependent agricultural communities which enabled them to create a thriving economic foundation for subsequent generations of Belgian immigrants. Belgian Americans relied on their strong religious ties as well as their agricultural heritage to fortify their community in the United States. In addition, the Belgians imported some recreational activities which helps them maintain a close relationship to their roots. A game often seen being played in Belgian American communities is called "rolle bolle" (pronounced ROE-lee BOE-lee). The game features a beveled wheel that teams of three roll between stakes that are arranged thirty feet apart.

In Omaha, Nebraska, which is home to a high concentration of Belgian Americans who came to the United States between the 1890s and the early 1900s, an organization called the Belgian American Society was established. The society organized events for the community including a Thanksgiving parade every year. Although the procession organized by the Belgian American Society is all male, female Belgian Americans have countered with an organization called the Ladies' Belgian American Club which organizes events for women. The Omaha community of Belgian Americans was elated when the King of Belgium visited the region in 1959.

Although the Belgian American community represents a group which has managed to retain a unique measure of cohesiveness and close ties to the past some of the old traditions are fading. Evidence of this is the difficulties folklore researchers have trying to substantial data to inform projects on Flemish traditions. S.J. Sackett, who conducted folklore research on Belgian Americans in Kansas, suggests that there is a sense of urgency to capture the Belgian traditions in America before they fade. Sackett had difficulty finding candidates to inform his project forcing him to conclude that, "[t]he very paucity of results from my efforts in St. Mary's should *be a warning that unless the lore of these colonies or enclaves is recorded and preserved now, it will soon be too late." Among Sackett's findings on Belgian American folklore was a recipe for fruitcake and hearty meat dishes; the Belgian art of lace-making which was used in embroidering sheets; and the custom of taffy pulling at Christmas time.*

FLEMISH FOLKLORE IN KANSAS

Dorson has pointed out that one of the most urgent folklore-collecting projects in the United States is to record the traditions of the many immigrant groups that have come here, most of them during the last century. The task is made more urgent by the rapid attrition of these traditions in the new country. As an example of this attrition, I should like to cite my experience in collecting Flemish folklore in St. Marys, Kansas.

Having become interested in Flemish language, literature, and culture, I asked J. Neale Carman, chairman of the Department of Romance Languages at the University of Kansas and authority on the distribution of foreign language groups in the state, if there were any Flemish enclaves in Kansas. He wrote that there were two: the larger between Lenexa and Kansas City, Kansas, with highest concentration at Kinney Heights (a district of Kansas City, Kansas); the smaller at St. Marys. I could not locate any Flemings at Kinney Heights, but with the help of the archivist of St. Mary's College and of a former student of mine who had once taught in the town of St. Marys I compiled a list of potential informants to whom I wrote. To those who did not reply I sent follow-up letters. Three were too old and infirm to be interviewed; three had no recollection of any traditions; one who did not reply to my letters was, I was told, not intelligent enough to help. Only one, Mrs. Clara Verschelden Keefe, proved to be a good informant. I interviewed her on November 6, 1959, at her home in St. Marys. She is an intelligent woman and was extraordinarily helpful. Most of what she told me she had heard from her mother, who had been born Marie DeMerhier in Grammont, Belgium, in 1868.

Mrs. Keefe's father, Dr. Oscar Verschelden, was a veterinarian and the mayor of St. Marys from 1909 to 1914. Born in Belgium, he traced his descent according to family tradition from a Lady Zageman, a noblewoman whose property was confiscated by Napoleon. The family lived in Renaix, Belgium, for generations, and Dr. Verschelden was born there the son of August Verschelden, a well-to-do farmer. Hoping for wealth and social status in the New World, and frightened by anti-Catholic demonstrations in Belgium, August Verschelden and his family emigrated from Volkeghem, near Audenarde, in 1883. According to Achille A. Ronsse of St. Marys, whose parents traveled with the Verscheldens and who was seven at the time, they were attracted to St. Marys by the Catholic St. Mary's College and by the fame of Father DeSmet, a Belgian priest in the town. With the Verscheldens and Ronsses in the party were the DeDonders, the Loberts, the Crieses, and the Pessemirs. Of these the descendants of the first and last are still in the St. Marys area. Other families joined them later, planning to form a Flemish colony. Of the original immigrants only two are still alive, Achille Ronsse in St. Marys and Sister Mary Christopher (an aunt of Mrs. Keefe's) in Ghent, Belgium. Most of the children are scattered, and St. Marys is now predominantly German in family background. Though most individual Flemings were successful, the effort to found a Flemish colony at St. Marys must be ruled a failure.

Two of the Verschelden daughters remained in Belgium and became nuns; the rest of the family, including six children, migrated to this country. Two of the girls returned to Belgium in 1891 and 1892 and became nuns. Mary, now Sister Mary Christopher, is at the Visitation Convent in Ghent. Oscar returned to Belgium in 1897, married Mary DeMerhier of Grammont the following year, and returned to St. Marys with his bride. In 1898 Mr. and Mrs. August Verschelden returned to Gavere, Belgium, where they are now buried.

Despite Mrs. Keefe's unusual willingness, she was able to give me very little information about the traditions of her people. The fact that so little could be obtained from a superior informant underlines my point: collecting materials from immigrant groups is already desperately difficult; to delay further would be to risk collecting nothing at all. What Mrs. Keefe told me I have arranged under the headings of Food, Folk Arts, Customs, Games, and Cures.

Foods. The only one of her mother's recipes that Mrs. Keefe currently uses is one for Belgian fruitcake:

Take one pound small raisins, one pound pitted dates, one cup chopped English walnuts and a one pound jar of Dromedary cut fruit cake mix [the use of a mix is obviously a recent adaptation]. Wash raisins in warm water. Cut dates in small pieces. Combine and pour two glasses of port wine, rum, or whiskey [Mrs. Keefe recommends rum] over fruit and let stand overnight. Next day pour off liquid that has not soaked in. Cream one pound butter and one pound sugar. Whip seven eggs and add two at a time. Add two and one-half cups browned flour (brown flour in skillet over low flames), one tablespoon cinnamon, one tablespoon nutmeg, two teaspoons vanilla, and one teaspoon soda dissolved in one tablespoon warm water. Add liquid from fruit (if any). Bake one hour in slow oven (275). Makes two angel-food-size cakes and one loaf.

This was always served with wine made at home by Mr. Verschelden.

But, though Mrs. Keefe prepares only this recipe, she remembers many other dishes her mother used to fix. Once a year, when the bishop came to St. Marys for confirmation, Mrs. Verschelden would roast a pig with an ear of corn in its mouth. For this occasion she would begin the meal with a soup course, a bouillon; and for this and all other special occasions she would serve asparagus as a treat.

Other dishes that Mrs. Verschelden prepared included pickled tongue and pickled pigs' feet, as well as cream peas in individual cups, about the size of those in muffin tins or the paper cups used in making cupcakes, called timbales. If I understood correctly, the peas were cooked by placing these timbales in deep hot fat.

Two of her mother's meat dishes were also recalled by Mrs. Keefe. One was rabbit, fried and then put in the oven with a sauce made like a white sauce but with wine. The other was sweetbreads mixed with ground veal and cooked in a cream sauce with lemon. She also remembers that her mother often served mutton, and that her father's favorite bedtime snack was limburger cheese on rye bread.

Folk arts. Lace-making is of course a famous Belgian folk art, and Mrs. Keefe's mother was an adept, having learned the skill at the convent where she was educated. Mrs. Keefe showed me lovely linen sheets to which her mother had attached handmade lace borders and had beautifully embroidered with the initials VDM (Verschelden DeMerhier).

Customs. Mrs. Keefe still had in her possession a very artistic scrapbook which her mother had made for the Verschelden children, containing many pictures of the Belgian St. Niklaas, a much slimmer gentleman than our Santa Claus. But she recalls that it was not he but the American Santa who filled their long, above-the-knee stockings. One traditional feature of the Verschelden family Christmas was the taffy pull. At Christmas, too, Mrs. Verschelden would make pink and green peppermint candy of powdered sugar, cream, and butter, not cooked. Half an almond was pressed into the center of each round, flat wafer.

Every Lent Mrs. Verschelden pickled a keg of herring, enough to last the entire six weeks. Mrs. Keefe no longer remembers the components, but believes they included peppers, onions, and vinegar. The roe and liver were pickled along with the rest; Mrs. Keefe recalls liking the former but not the latter.

All seven of the Verschelden children had the same baptismal dress, a long handmade one in which Mrs. Verschelden herself had been christened. There was always a big dinner to celebrate a christening.

Mrs. Keefe recalled two of her mother's customs: visiting newcomers to St. Marys (she took along engraved calling cards), and letting her husband pick a new hat for her from five or six she would bring home from the milliner's.

Mrs. Verschelden kept house on a definite schedule, her daughter recalls Monday was always washday, rain or shine, and days were set aside for ironing, mending, cleaning house, and visiting.

Games. Mrs. Keefe could not recollect ever having learned any Flemish children's games. She does remember her parents' favorite games were high-five and whist.

Cures. Mrs. Keefe remembers that once her Grandmother DeMerhier visited them and spent much time rolling pills. These were, she believes, made of cascara; at any rate, they were a laxative, very bitter, and given for any childhood complaint.

Mrs. Keefe was emphatic that the Belgians did not have any superstitions and spoke scornfully of her late husband's parents for such common folk practices as carrying potatoes or wearing copper chains round their wrists for curing arthritis.

Conclusions. Ideally a study of this type should compare the folklore collected with that of the country of origin to determine whether New World conditions have affected the lore in any way; if so, conclusions should be drawn as to how the way of life of the national group has been changed by its experiences in the United States, and if not, an explanation should be offered, probably that its cultural isolation has led the group to maintain its traditions in pure form. As the footnotes indicate, I have compared what I collected from Mrs. Keefe with two of the standard collections of Flemish folklore, all that were available to me, but I did not find enough points of comparison to reach any conclusions. Obviously, however, the use of Dromedary cut fruitcake mix in the fruitcake indicates one way in which the customs of immigrant groups have been affected by life in the United States. American technology has enabled them to substitute packaged preparations for materials that previously had to be prepared by hand.

But although I was not able to reach any conclusions about the effects which American life had a Flemish folklore, I was able to come to one conclusion which I believe is worth calling to the attention of all American folklorists; and that is that the folklore of immigrant groups in American life is rapidly disappearing. The very paucity of results from my efforts in St. Marys should be a warning that unless the lore of these colonies or enclaves is recorded and preserved now, it will soon be too late.

Source:

"Flemish Folklore in Kansas," by S. J. Sackett. In *Western Folklore*, vol. XX, 1961. pp. 175-178.

BLACKFOOT

The Blackfoot Indians were affiliated with the Algonquian linguistic group which included the Siksika, Piegan, and Blood tribes. The tribal name "blackfoot," according to legend, originates from one of the early chiefs of the tribe. The chief dreamt that he sent his sons to hunt buffalo and to encourage them against the ferocious beasts he provided black medicine to be applied to their feet. According to folklore magic medicine helped the sons hunt buffalo successfully which enabled the tribe to flourish. The Blackfoot Indians were hunters and trappers until firearms were introduced into the community which strengthened their position against white settlers in Montana. A series of encounters with the white man as well as the virtual extinction of the Bison and outbreaks of disease nearly eliminated the tribe. The majority of Blackfoot Indians in the United States now reside on reservations in Montana.

Historians believe that the Blackfoot originally settled in the Great Lakes region. Disputes over fur pelt trading with other tribes drove the tribe westward in the 18th century causing the Blackfoot to settle in Montana. Peak of the Blackfoot tribal community was in the late 17th century to the early 19th century when guns were acquired and there were plenty of buffalo to hunt. A small pox epidemic in 1837 that killed 6,000 Blackfoot nearly wiped out the community. During the winter of 1883-1884 600 Blackfoot starved to death as the staple of their community, the buffalo, suddenly disappeared. In 1896 the Blackfoot agreed to sell a large portion of their land to the U.S. government for $1.5 million; the land would be used to create Glacier National Park. The Blackfoot had difficulty surviving as a community after the white man virtually eliminated their supply of buffalo. In the early part of the 20th century (1907-1912) the Blackfoot reservation was converted from collective ownership of their land to privately run 320 acre blocks of land.

THE DISAPPEARANCE OF THE BUFFALO

IT WAS, INDEED, A GLORIOUS COUNTRY WHICH THE BLACKFEET HAD WRESTED from their southern enemies. Here nature has reared great mountains and spread out broad prairies. Along the western border of this region, the Rocky Mountains lift their snow-clad peaks above the clouds. Here and there, from north to south, and from east to west, lie minor ranges, black with pine forests if seen near at hand, or in the distance mere gray silhouettes against a sky of blue. Between these mountain ranges lies everywhere the great prairie; a monotonous waste to the stranger's eye, but not without its charm. It is brown and bare; for, except during a few short weeks in spring, the sparse bunch-grass is sear and yellow, and the silver gray of the wormwood lends an added dreariness to the landscape. Yet this seemingly desert waste has a beauty of its own. At intervals it is marked with green winding river valleys, and everywhere it is gashed with deep ravines, their sides painted in strange colors of red and gray and brown, and their perpendicular walls crowned with fantastic columns and figures of stone or clay, carved out by the winds and the rains of ages. Here and there, rising out of the plain, are curious sharp ridges, or square-topped buttes with vertical sides, sometimes bare, and sometimes dotted with pines,—short, sturdy trees, whose gnarled trunks and thick, knotted branches have been twisted and wrung into curious forms by the winds which blow unceasingly, hour after hour, day after day, and month after month, over mountain range and prairie, through gorge and coulee.

These prairies now seem bare of life, but it was not always so. Not very long ago, they were trodden by multitudinous herds of buffalo and antelope; then, along the wooded river valleys and on the pine-clad slopes of the mountains, elk, deer, and wild sheep fed in great numbers. They are all gone now. The winter's wind still whistles over Montana prairies, but nature's shaggy-headed wild cattle no longer feel its biting blasts. Where once the scorching breath of summer stirred only the short stems of the buffalo-grass, it now billows the fields of the white man's grain. Half-hidden by the scanty herbage, a few bleached skeletons alone remain to tell us of the buffalo; and the broad, deep trails, over which the dark herds passed by thousands, are now grass-grown and fast disappearing under the effacing hand of time. The buffalo have disappeared, and the fate of the buffalo has almost overtaken the Blackfeet.

As known to the whites, the Blackfeet were true prairie Indians, seldom venturing into the mountains, except when they crossed them to war with the Kutenais, the Flatheads, or the Snakes. They subsisted almost wholly on the flesh of the buffalo. They were hardy, untiring, brave, ferocious. Swift to move, whether on foot or horseback, they made long journeys to war, and with telling force struck their enemies. They had conquered and driven out from the territory which they occupied the tribes who once inhabited it, and maintained a desultory and successful warfare against all invaders, fighting with the Crees on the north, the Assinaboines on the east, the Crows on the south, and the Snakes, Kalispels, and Kutenais on the southwest and west. In those days the Blackfeet were rich and powerful. The buffalo fed and clothed them, and they needed nothing beyond what nature supplied. This was their time of success and happiness.

Crowded into a little corner of the great territory which they once dominated, and holding this corner by an uncertain tenure, a few Blackfeet still exist, the pitiful remnant of a once mighty people.

Omaq-kat-tsa, Chief of the Blackfoot tribe.

Huddled together about their agencies, they are facing the problem before them, striving, helplessly but bravely, to accommodate themselves to the new order of things; trying in the face of adverse surroundings to wrench themselves loose from their accustomed ways of life; to give up inherited habits and form new ones; to break away from all that is natural to them, from all that they have been taught—to reverse their whole mode of existence. They are striving to earn their living, as the white man earns his, by toil. The struggle is hard and slow, and in carrying it on they are wasting away and growing fewer in numbers. But though unused to labor, ignorant of agriculture, unacquainted with tools or seeds or soils, knowing nothing of the ways of life in permanent houses or of the laws of health, scantily fed, often utterly discouraged by failure, they are still making a noble fight for existence.

Only within a few years—since the buffalo disappeared—has this change been going on; so recently has it come that the old order and the new meet face to face. In the trees along the river valleys, still quietly resting on their aerial sepulchres, sleep the forms of the ancient hunter-warrior who conquered and held this broad land; while, not far away, Blackfoot farmers now rudely cultivate their little crops, and gather scanty harvests from narrow fields.

It is the meeting of the past and the present, of savagery and civilization. The issue cannot be doubtful. Old methods must pass away. The Blackfeet will become civilized, but at a terrible cost. To me there is an interest, profound and pathetic, in watching the progress of the struggle.

Source:

Blackfoot Lodge Tales: The Story of a Prairie People, by George Bird Grinnell. New York: Scribner, 1892. Reprinted. Lincoln: University of Nebraska Press, 1962.

BLACKFOOT LETTER TO SECRETARY OF THE INTERIOR

*T*he difficulty the Blackfoot suffered trying to make the transition from a hunting to an agricultural community prompted the tribal leaders to appeal to the federal government to help them learn contemporary farming techniques. In a 1915 letter to Secretary of Interior Frank K. Lane, the Blackfoot asked government officials to send Martin Bentley, whom they trusted, to the reservation to teach them how to cultivate the land. The letter is indicative of how the Blackfoot Nation, a once vibrant flourishing community, was reduced to dependency on the white man's way when the pillar upon which their community was founded, was eliminated.

Browning, Montana.
February 23rd, 1915.

Honorable Franklin K. Lane,
Secretary of the Interior,
Washington, D.C.

Dear Sir:
        We, the Blackfeet Indians are now look-
ing to you to help us a little more. You helped us
once when you took Agent McFatridge away from here.
Now we ask you to help us again, when you send us
a new Agent.

        Two years ago Chief Curly Bear and many
of our other Chiefs and Coundilmen and head men went
to Washington and told you about our troubles. While
in your City we met a good white man, his name is
Martin J. Bentley, and we had a long talk with him.
What he said to us and what we said to him we have
told our people. We are thinking about that yet. We
know that the Great Spirit does not want us to set
down and let trouble catch us. He wants us to work
and push until we get what is right. We know that
when we work right we sleep well. The earth is our
mother. She holds a plenty for us all. We must find
the way to get it. We can't get it now in the old
Indian way. The game is gone. We must dig it out of
the ground. We think Mr. Bentley can show us how.
We have made a lot of noise about our bad Agents.
Send us this man because we know a good man when we
see him. We know him in a different way from the
White man's way. We may be mistaken about Mr. Bentley but if we are xxxxx we will kick ourselves and
not kick you.

                Respectfully submitted,

                1   Robt J. Hamilton
                2   Chief Curly Bear
                3   Chief Wolf Plume
                4   White Antelope
                5   Black Weasel
                6   Chas. Dustybull
                7   White Quiver

Source:
Library of Congress.

BRAZILIAN AMERICANS

*T*his article, "Newcomers" documents a positive aspect of the American immigrant story in the late 1990s. Recently immigrated Brazilian Americans are transforming a decayed Framingham suburb by purchasing real estate in an area that other citizens have fled. Immigrant stories in the press have often stereotypically suggested the loss of American jobs or the burden to other Americans imposed by welfare benefits extended to newcomers. Immigrant neighborhood enclaves were also cast in a negative perspective. One negative aspect that is suggested in this report is the description of the non-taxed "off-the-books" immigrant business. However, problems with non-taxed business activity is common for most communities. For example, millions of untaxed dollars are spent at yard sales held in every suburb in the country. Additionally, in the 1980s and 1990s a barter system among businesses that avoided taxes was also addressed in many communities. Untaxed economic activity among Brazilian Americans in Framingham was not the most serious problem for the community. Instead, the larger problem was the conflict was between the town's social services providers and the immigrants who were competing for space in this town.

Brazilian Americans have a long history in the United States. The first Brazilian immigrants were said to have arrived in 1654, but records are not definitive. Brazilian immigrants were counted as South Americans until 1960, so patterns of Brazilian immigration can only be suggested by data encompassing an entire continent. Data from 1960 shows that about 2,000 Brazilian immigrated each year from 1960 until 1980. In the 1980s, Brazil's economy began to falter and citizens lost confidence in their political leadership. As a result, immigration to the United States as well as to Japan, Europe and other South American countries rose to about 1.4 million departures. U.S. Census records show that between 1987 and 1991, 20,800 Brazilians came to the United States, and 8,133 of those came during 1991. The 1990 U.S. Census shows that there are about 60,000 Brazilians living in the United States. However, even this figure is misleading because of some confusion brought about by the "Hispanic" category listed on the census form. In order to be counted as Brazilian, census takers had to write Brazilian in the "Other Hispanics" category. This was misleading because Brazilians are not Hispanic. The term Hispanic refers to people of Spanish or Spanish-speaking origin from South America, Central America, and the Caribbean. Brazilians are of Portuguese descent.

NEWCOMERS

Not long ago, the South Side of Framingham, Massachusetts, looked much like the old industrial quarters of other dying New England mill towns. The factories were closed and the downtown real estate had been ceded to the homeless, the addicts, and the prostitutes. Inner-city Framingham was the kind of place middle-class people wouldn't want to visit, much less inhabit. But that has all changed now. On a recent Sunday morning, I walked along the South Side's Hollis Street, following the aroma of fresh bread. The scent led to the newly opened Padaria Brasil, where about 20 customers were waiting in line to buy bread and rolls. All along Hollis Street, in fact, broken glass, vomit, and trash have given way to a thriving scene of new beauty parlors, lingerie stores, and magazine shops, almost all of them established by immigrants from Brazil. Even the few surviving old-line businesses have Brazilian flags draped in their windows, in recognition of the immigrant revival.

Framingham, of course, is not alone. Its immigrant-led inner-city boom is an increasingly familiar pattern in the industrial Northeast, another example of the complex ways in which immigrant workers and entrepreneurs have helped propel economic growth in '90s America. Yet, even as many in Framingham celebrate the South Side's comeback, others say the town has to spend too much on bilingual education and other services for poor, undocumented aliens whose underground economic activity generates no local tax revenue. Critics say the homes and businesses of immigrants are taking up real estate needed by social service agencies that minister to the needs of low-income citizens who were in Framingham first. Thus, Framingham's experience encapsulates an issue at the heart of the immigration debate: Who, exactly, are the "deserving" poor?

It's certainly true that while Framingham allows immigrants to profit from their labor, it has not yet found an efficient way to tap that wealth for public use. Much of the Brazilians' economic activity takes place on a cash-only—that is, untaxed—basis. Upstairs, off the street, all over town, Brazilians are selling one another soft drinks, magazines, and cookies imported from home, or renting bootlegged videos of Portuguese-language soap operas. Other businesses help newer immigrants prepare taxes, study for driving tests, or handle the naturalization process. Often these entrepreneurs send their earnings back home to relatives in Brazil.

Meanwhile, tensions mount between the immigrants and the town's social service providers, led by the federally funded South Middlesex Opportunity Council (SMOC). When the city bottomed out years ago, nonprofit social service agencies set up shop downtown to take care of those who were unable or, in some cases, unwilling to care for themselves. Today the immigrants want to buy up the buildings where the agencies operate, on the tacit assumption that, when the agencies leave, their clients will, too. "They're in conflict," Lew Colten, the town's building inspector, says of the two poor communities, immigrant and welfare. "SMOC, the Department of Mental Health, all these programs, they pick up houses at fire-sale prices and fix them up. But a lot of [that] housing stock could be part and parcel of the ethnic community."

Of course, as Colten notes, property owned by nonprofit organizations doesn't yield any more tax revenue for the city than an off-the-books immigrant business does. SMOC, for example, has a $30 million annual budget and employs over 500 people. Since 1985, SMOC has also purchased more than 50 downtown buildings. Although by its own accounting SMOC has pumped millions of dollars into downtown by renovating neglected property, some townspeople complain that it negates those benefits by turning the same buildings into permanent outposts of society's most troubled elements. Once a federally funded poverty agency buys property, complains Kathleen Pendergast, who chairs Framingham's board of selectmen, "the neighborhood never has a chance to gentrify."

And the demand for property from rising Brazilians keeps on growing. On the books or off, immigrant businesses are allowing hundreds of immigrants to pull themselves up from poverty and form the nucleus of a new working-class ethnic community. Even while the South Side's factories were closing—and its white middle class was fleeing—the Brazilians kept coming, and working. "Of my customers, I guess maybe two hundred have already bought homes," says Fernando Castro, himself an immigrant who operates the One Stop Income Tax service on Concord Street. "Almost all of them are downtown." Castro, like many of his clients, earned his start-up capital vacuuming carpets, grouting bathroom tile, and washing clothes in suburban homes. Without help from people like Mr. Castro, many a suburban mom would not have been free to take a job—and earn her own family a second income.

Thus, in the contest between the untaxed social service agencies and their largely voiceless clientele, on one side, and the untaxed but economically rising Brazilians on the other, the town's officials have tilted subtly toward the latter. Colten, for example, has earned a modest national reputation with Operation Red—boarding up derelict real estate with plywood panels spray-painted bright crimson. The practice, known locally as "red-boarding," is a kind of Scarlet Letter for landlords. Some old properties had become crack houses, and appeared beyond redemption. Then the city red-boarded them—and sold two of them off to Brazilian immigrants.

"Fifty Freeman Street, that was one of the worst," Colten recalls. "Crack house, typical abandoned property. Prostitution, the works. We red-taped the doors, boarded it up, then levied a tremendous amount of fines." After a brief court challenge, the original owner dropped his claim and let the town auction it off. The buyers were Tony and Marcus Quintela, two Brazilian brothers who have been bottom-fishing for houses in the neighborhood. It was their fourth buy in the past two years. The Quintelas started out cleaning homes—then added offices and the multi-screen cinemas at the shopping malls along Route 9, the major thoroughfare through the western suburbs of Boston. All told, some 30 members of their extended family are employed in seven different cleaning businesses.

Active members of the local Roman Catholic parish, St. Tarcisius's Church, the Quintelas became homebuyers as soon as Tony became a citizen; they acquired their first home, a rundown two-family duplex after the local Framingham Savings Bank foreclosed on the previous owner's mortgage.

By becoming citizens they broke the cycle of repatriating dollars to Brazil. Thus, when they're not cleaning someone else's castle, they're on Torrey Street, putting sweat equity into one of their own. "We pay less to own than we would to rent," Marcus explained to me, shouting over the buzz of his power saw. In a few hours Marcus would be cleaning an empty movie theater, but right now he was squeezing in a few minutes of work on the new floor boards of his restored front porch. After making a modest down payment, the Quintelas leveraged their home-cleaning earnings with a mortgage, whose terms—$300 a month—are easy by almost anyone's standards.

The Quintela experience suggests that, as the good news about citizenship spreads through their community, more Brazilian families will buy property and move from the informal economy to taxpayer status. Already, the town's registry of new homeowners reads like a Rio de Janeiro telephone book: Almeida, Amaral, Soares Batista, Carvalho, Dias, Fernandes, Pereira, Oliveira. But the list is also a roll call of urban ethnic-group assimilation. This age-old American process has its costs; but in Framingham, the town fathers seem to have decided that the benefits are even greater. Immigrants, Colten says, "are the solution, not the problem."

Source:

Article by Joel Millman in *The New Republic*, November 24, 1997. Vol. 217, no. 21, pp. 16(2).

CAMBODIAN AMERICANS

Kim Huot Kiet, an officer in the air force of the Khmer Rouge, escaped Cambodia before the regime of Pol Pot launched its genocidal campaign in the late 1970s. Kiet left behind his wife and four children, who were killed.

After settling in the United States, he reclaimed Cambodian culture through art by reproducing the traditional garb worn by Cambodian dancers. "In Cambodia, there is traditional and classical dance with mask and crown and costume," Kiet says, but until he found a book in the Library of Congress, he did not know what the masks looked like.

Kiet began sketching and painting art masks, and with the help of friends he helped bring from Cambodia, one of whom knew how to perform Cambodian dances, he also makes costumes and headdresses. Kiet's work has been exhibited from New York to Florida, insuring that Cambodian culture endures in America.

KHMER MASKS
Kim Huot Kiet

Kim Huot Kiet is in his mid-fifties. He is Cambodian and fled to the United States from Thailand in 1975. I visited him in his home in New York. Three walls of his cramped living room are lined to the ceiling with golden faces, some haunting, others angry, a few smiling. All are frozen symbols of Cambodian culture. There are over thirty Khmer dance masks, all made by him. Their presence is a soothing reminder of happier days in Cambodia.

"In 1975, while on mission in Thailand, there was very heavy fighting in Cambodia. I heard the president of the Republic of Khmer, Pot Pol had escaped from Cambodia, and there was a really serious problem there. I had no way of going back because airplanes and transport by land had been banned, and there was heavy fighting. There was no way for me to go back, and no way to keep in touch with my family. I never saw them again—not my wife, nor my four children. They all got killed. But I don't know how.

"When I was in Cambodia, I was an officer in the Air Force. This was thirty years ago when it was still the Kingdom of Cambodia. The prince, Sianouk, would go around the country to inaugurate hospitals and schools, and I flew escort planes for the royal party. In 1970, I was assigned to Thailand by the Khmer Air Force to train as an airplane commander. I had flown for fourteen years already. I flew mostly light planes to patrol and observe our country in air space, and also a transporter plane. That year, there was a coup. The communists started to invade Cambodia. The uprising lasted five years. The communists finally took over.

"After a few months in Thailand, I decided to come to the United States. I was stationed in the American air base in Thailand at the time. I did not want to stay in Thailand, and could not go back to Cambodia because I was not sure what fate I would suffer. Because of my past position, I felt I would be in danger. But it was hard for me to decide to leave my country. At the time, the United States helped Cambodians who wanted to come here. It was a temporary decision. I decided to come here and wait and see what happened in my country in the next few weeks, the next few months, the next few years. It's been fourteen years since I arrived, and although I didn't plan to stay here this long, I have no choice. My country is still communist, and I can't take a chance on returning.

"In 1979, the Vietnamese invaded Cambodia, and after that the people could return home and look for their family. When my brother found out I was in the United States, he sent me a letter from Cambodia. He told me that only he and my sister were alive. I wrote and asked him about my family. He didn't know how they died. Both my sister and brother are married and have families in Cambodia. They are alive. My father had five children, including me, from our mother. I also have two half sisters, and three half brothers. They are all either dead or missing. I don't know what happened to them. I think they got killed. I don't know how my children and wife died. But I can only imagine that it must have been terrible. At that time, there was no food, no shelter. You had to move along the street, and there were purges. But what can you do? It was the transfer of one regime to another. Everything was in turmoil. Everything was mixed up. It was just terrible. People had no choice, no human rights, no freedom. But what can you do?

"I don't think things are much better today. Our country still remains in the control of Vietnam. So how can things be better? I feel the Vietnamese are terrible. They tried to swallow up the land of Southeast Asia. The Vietnamese have been traditional enemy of Cambodia since the eighteenth century, when the former lowlands of Cambodia was taken over as part of Vietnam. So most Cambodians in Cambodia dislike the Vietnamese.

"It is very hard for me to talk about the camps today very hard. You escape from Cambodia. Along the road there are mine fields. When you've crossed the mine fields, there are thieves. And you get to the camps. But you have to struggle to get into the camps. And once inside the camps it is controlled by the Thai authorities. And they are terrible, the camps. Then the Cambodians come to the United States a strange place and they put them in neighborhoods they don't know anything about, and some neighborhoods in New York are very bad. I think this is terrible, even to think about.

"There are still a lot of people waiting in camps in Thailand and the Philippines. I know of one lady who just got into a camp in Thailand. She arrived in the Thai camp in November 1988. She has a family of five. She came by boat, and fortunately, she landed safely in Thailand. As you know, many people have had bad luck, met some sea pirates, and refugees got raped. It's hard to talk about this. I don't want to think about it too much. But as long as they survive. I try to help them when they come here.

"Who do you blame for what happened in Cambodia? I cannot blame anybody. The only thing I can blame is the Vietnamese and Thailand, because my country is located between the two. As our country is a Buddhist society, we don't like to have violence. We don't fight much. I think war is terrible the revenge, the hate. I am still a Buddhist. I am not bitter. I think what happened to me happened because my country got into a war. I miss my country; I miss my legacies; I miss my family, my people. I can't compare this feeling with anything in the world. Since the communist takeover. I feel everything's changed. It's not that all the culture is lost. I hope someday there will be a good leader to restore the country to the peace there was before. I would like to go back when that happens. If I could live there, I would, because it is my country and I love it very much."

Looking Back: "When I was young, we used to sing a song, 'Kampuchea Is a Golden Land.' (Kampuchea is the original name. The English called it Cambodia.) So I feel Cambodia was rich in everything, and it hadn't been exploited yet. I was the son of a merchant my father was an officer of the census bureau not of people but of rice. He used to go from town to town to survey the rice, to see how much was produced during the year. And my mother was a sales woman. She sold cake. So I grew up not very rich, not very poor. I felt I was very sociable. I had a lot of classmates who loved to play together in their spare time. And I felt happy. I didn't think of anything else but being happy. In my hometown there was a river nearby where I could go swimming. My hometown once a year would be flooded, so we would have to make bridges to our houses. Sometimes we would make a small boat to take people back and forth to their houses. I felt very happy. My experience in my childhood was very nice. I try not to think too much about my life in Cambodia anymore. I just remember that when I was growing up, things were very good there."

Life in the U.S.: "Now, here, my life has changed. I have remarried. But I cannot get a pilot's job anymore. I only have a private license so it is difficult to find a job. I tried for about a year. I tried to start from ground school again. Finally, I couldn't get any further because you had to pay more money to go commercial. I miss flying.

"In this country, I worked on a Khmer art project for three years. I made over thirty figures, headdresses and masks of Cambodian dancers. In Cambodia, there is traditional and classical dance with the mask and crown and costume. The dancing is not for everyday life, but for special occasions and celebrations. Once there was an Empire of Cambodia, then later, it became the Kingdom of Cambodia, where there was a king. During the Kingdom period, there was a group of dancers who performed in the palace for receptions, and once a year, they used to play for the population when the water went down. There are rivers stretching through Cambodia, and the capitol of Cambodia was along the border of one of the rivers. So when the water went down, they celebrated what was called the Water Festival. So I learned how to make these masks and headdresses here. I went to the Library of Congress to find a book, and I used to read the art books. I read how to paint and sketch these masks. I went to the stores to see the tools to use. In 1980, I had a friend in the camps in Thailand. He was in the Khmer Air Force, and served on the Royal Air Force. He has six children. His wife knew how to perform the Cambodian dances. So when I knew he was in the camp, I filed an affidavit for them to come to New York. In 1981, when the Cambodian community wanted to celebrate Cambodian New Year, I didn't know what material to use to sew the costumes. So she said she knew how

to sew the costumes, but didn't have the material. She knew how to make the costumes, but she didn't know how to make the headdress. She had some pictures and showed me the form. And I made the handmaiden headdress for her to perform with.

"I didn't know how to do any of this before I came to this country, but I learned. I taught myself to do it. I want to preserve the culture. I want my culture to be alive in this country, not to die out. We've already had many exhibitions here in the United States, from New York to Florida. A lot of people are interested. They say, 'Oh, these are Khmer masks.' It was lost, so that is why I had to learn how to make it to make it survive again. That's the most important thing: to keep the culture alive. I know they are still dancing in the camps in Thailand, Cambodia, Florida, New York and California. There are people dancing, and keeping the culture alive."

Source:

Joann Faung Jean Lee. *Asian American Experiences in the United States: Oral Histories of First to Fourth Generation Americans from China, the Philippines, Japan, India, the Pacific Islands, Vietnam and Cambodia.* Jefferson, NC: McFarland & Co., 1991. pp. 57-61.

CHEROKEES

The Cherokee Nation is a North American Indian tribe affiliated with the Iroquois linguistic group. The tribe flourished in southern states such as Georgia, North and South Carolina, and Tennessee until their destruction by small pox and disputes with settlers in the 1830s. Andrew Jackson was instrumental in driving the Cherokee out of Georgia in response to which many Cherokee began migrating west. The journey west nearly eliminated the Cherokees and was appropriately named the "Trail of Tears."

The expulsion of the Cherokee Nation is one of the most regrettable chapters in American history. At the peak of their communal development the Cherokee Nation devised their own syllabary language, constructed a capital which was modeled after Washington, D.C., established a democratic government with a bicameral legislature, and set the groundwork for a supreme court building, post office, museum, and academy. Threatened by the growth of the nation, the governor of Georgia petitioned the Georgia legislature to pass laws that would undermine the Cherokees. The laws banned Cherokee council meetings and revoked the Cherokee's property rights. The Cherokee Nation appealed the discriminatory laws to the U.S. Supreme Court which handed down a ruling in their favor. However, President Jackson refused to adhere to the Court's ruling supporting Georgia in their efforts to drive out the Cherokees. In May of 1838 the Cherokees were rounded up in a campaign led by General Winfield Scott and put in "collection camps." An estimated one fourth of the Cherokees placed in the camps died because of overcrowding and disease. The final stage of the expulsion involved leading the Indians on a trail westward during which many Cherokees perished figuratively and literally leaving a "trail of tears."

One of the most notable legacies passed on by the Cherokee nation is the 84-character syllabary created by Sequoyah in 1821. Sequoyah's ingeniously crafted syllabary enabled the Cherokees to publish a newspaper in their own language which contributed to their early formation. The Cherokee language is one of the few elements that remain of their rich cultural heritage. According to Kay Bannon, professor at Gordon College, the Cherokee language is on the verge of extinction. One of the reasons the language has had difficulty surviving is that the Cherokee were forbidden from speaking it after Jackson's campaign to drive the nation west. Bannon wrote a children's book called "Yonder Mountain," that uses both English and Cherokee in an effort to revive interest in the language. A syllabary is a list of characters each of which represents a syllable. In Sequoyah's syllabary a character represents a consonant and a vowel.

The Cherokee Nation is now centered in Northeast Oklahoma. In 1993 the school districts in Oklahoma began offering the Cherokee language (along with the Creek, Choctaw, and Seminole) in public schools. The program is designed to salvage what remains of one of the most cherished legacies of the Cherokee Nation— the syllabary language system.

SEQUOYAH'S CHEROKEE SYLLABARY

Sequoyah, holding his syllabary.

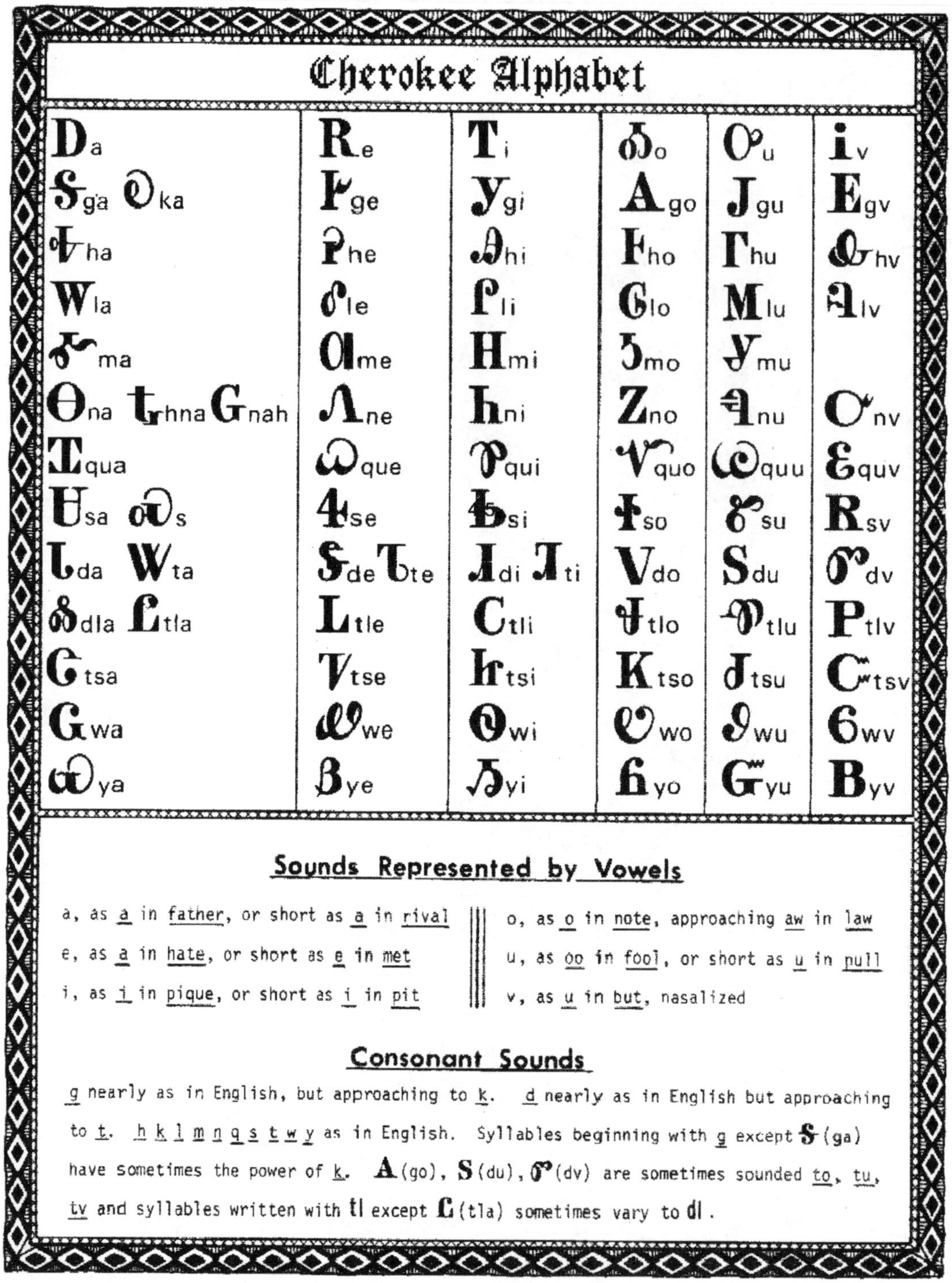

Cherokee Alphabet

D a	R e	T i	Ꮼ o	O u	i v
Ꮝ ga Ꮖ ka	F ge	� gi	A go	J gu	E gv
Ꮲ ha	Ꮅ he	Ꮴ hi	F ho	Ꮁ hu	Ꮾ hv
W la	Ꮈ le	P li	Ꮁ lo	M lu	Ꮑ lv
Ꮪ ma	Ꮧ me	H mi	Ꮥ mo	Ꮩ mu	
Ꮎ na Ꮏ hna G nah	Ꮑ ne	Ꮒ ni	Z no	Ꮠ nu	O nv
Ꮖ qua	Ꮖ que	Ꮖ qui	Ꮖ quo	Ꮖ quu	Ꮾ quv
U sa Ꮝ s	Ꮞ se	Ꮟ si	Ꮢ so	Ꮧ su	R sv
Ꮪ da W ta	Ꮥ de Ꮦ te	Ꮧ di Ꮨ ti	V do	S du	Ꮪ dv
Ꮬ dla Ꮭ tla	L tle	C tli	Ꮷ tlo	Ꮸ tlu	P tlv
Ꮳ tsa	Ꮴ tse	Ꮵ tsi	K tso	Ꮷ tsu	Ꮳ tsv
G wa	Ꮺ we	Ꮻ wi	Ꮼ wo	Ꮽ wu	Ꮾ wv
Ꮿ ya	Ᏸ ye	Ᏹ yi	Ᏺ yo	G yu	B yv

Sounds Represented by Vowels

a, as _a_ in _father_, or short as _a_ in _rival_   o, as _o_ in _note_, approaching _aw_ in _law_

e, as _a_ in _hate_, or short as _e_ in _met_   u, as _oo_ in _fool_, or short as _u_ in _pull_

i, as _i_ in _pique_, or short as _i_ in _pit_   v, as _u_ in _but_, nasalized

Consonant Sounds

_g_ nearly as in English, but approaching to _k_.   _d_ nearly as in English but approaching to _t_. _h k l m n q s t w y_ as in English. Syllables beginning with _g_ except Ꮝ (ga) have sometimes the power of _k_. A (go), S (du), Ꮪ (dv) are sometimes sounded _to_, _tu_, _tv_ and syllables written with tl except Ꮭ (tla) sometimes vary to dl.

Source:

Beginning Cherokee, by Ruth Bradley Holmes and
    Betty Sharp Smith. 2nd edition. Norman:
    University of Oklahoma Press, 1977.

The Indian Removal Act was passed by the U.S. Senate on April 23, 1830, by a vote of 28 to 19. The House of Representatives voted on May 24 and passed it, 102 to 97. President Andrew Jackson (1767–1845) quickly signed the bill, and forced removal of Native Americans from their lands in the Southeast now had the full force of the federal government. The State of Georgia moved three days later to assert its jurisdiction over 192,000 acres of Creek land and more than four and a half million acres of the Cherokee Nation.

The legislation had been hotly debated. Southern votes ensured its passage. In the Senate, New Englanders voted against it 11 to 1, but all 18 southern votes supported it. In the lower chamber, New England's representatives split 28 to 9 against, while southern members voted 60 to 15 for the bill.

The act gave the president the power to exchange lands in the West, beyond the Mississippi River, for the Indian homelands and appropriated $500,000 to carry out the forced emigration process. It also authorized the chief executive "solemnly to assure the tribe or nation with which exchange is made, that the United States will forever secure and guaranty to them. . .the country so exchanged."

INDIAN REMOVAL ACT

An Act to Provide for an Exchange of Lands with the Indians Residing in any of the States or Territories, and for their Removal West of the River Mississippi.

Be it enacted by the Senate and House of Representatives of the United States of America, in Congress assembled, That it shall and may be lawful for the President of the United States to cause so much of any territory belonging to the United States, west of the river Mississippi, not included in any state or organized territory, and to which the Indian title has been extinguished, as he may judge necessary, to be divided into a suitable number of districts, for the reception of such tribes or nations of Indians as may choose to exchange the lands where they now reside, and remove there; and to cause each of said districts to be so described by natural or artificial marks, as to be easily distinguished from every other.

SECTION II

And be it further enacted, That it shall and may be lawful for the President to exchange any or all of such districts, so to be laid off and described, with any tribe or nation of Indians now residing within the limits of any of the states or territories, and with which the United States have existing treaties, for the whole or any part or portion of the territory claimed and occupied by such tribe or nation, within the bounds of any one or more of the states or territories, where the land claimed and occupied by the Indians, is owned by the United States, or the United States are bound to the state within which it lies to extinguish the Indian claim thereto.

SECTION III

And be it further enacted, That in the making of any such exchange or exchanges, it shall and may be lawful for the President solemnly to assure the tribe or nation with which the exchange is made, that the United States will forever secure and guaranty to them, and their heirs or successors, the country so exchanged with them; and if they prefer it, that the United States will cause a patent or grant to be made and executed to them for the same: Provided always, That such lands shall revert to the United States, if the Indians become extinct, or abandon the same.

SECTION IV

And be it further enacted, That if, upon any of the lands now occupied by the Indians, and to be exchanged for, there should be such improvements as add value to the land claimed by any individual or individuals of such tribes or nations, it shall and may be lawful for the President to cause such value to be ascertained by appraisement or otherwise, and to cause such ascertained value to be paid to the person or persons rightfully claiming such improvements. And upon the payment of such valuation, the improvements so valued and paid for, shall pass to the United States, and possession shall not afterwards be permitted to any of the same tribe.

SECTION V

And be it further enacted, That upon the making of any such exchange as is contemplated by this act, it shall and may be lawful for the President to cause such aid and assistance to be furnished to the emigrants as may be necessary and proper to enable them to remove to, and settle in, the country for which they may have exchanged; and also, to give them such aid and assistance as may be necessary for their support and subsistence for the first year after their removal.

SECTION VI

And be it further enacted, That it shall and may be lawful for the President to cause such tribe or nation to be protected, at their new residence, against all interruption or disturbance from any other tribe or nation of Indians, or from any other person or persons whatever.

SECTION VII

And be it further enacted, That it shall and may be lawful for the President to have the same superintendence and care over any tribe or nation in the country to which they may remove, as contemplated by this act, that he is now authorized to have over them at their present places of residence: Provided, That nothing in this act contained shall be construed as authorizing or directing the violation of any existing treaty between the United States and any of the Indian tribes.

SECTION VIII

And be it further enacted, That for the purpose of giving effect to the provisions of this act, the sum of five hundred thousand dollars is hereby appropriated, to be paid out of any money in the treasury, not otherwise appropriated.

Approved, May 28, 1830.

Source:
U.S. Statutes at Large, 4:411-12.

In 1987, Wilma Mankiller made history when she became the first woman elected chief of a major Native American tribe. Her victory capped a life plagued by poverty, racism, sexism, and several close brushes with death—heavy burdens even for a person whose family name harks back to an old Indian military title meaning "one who safeguards the village." As leader of the Cherokee Nation, which is second in size only to the Navajo Nation, Mankiller has worked tirelessly to bring economic prosperity to her people while seeing to their many social and cultural needs as well. In the process, she has become a near-legend in the Native American community for her dedication and compassion.

Born in Tahlequah, Oklahoma (the capital of the Cherokee Nation), to a Cherokee father and a mother of Dutch and Irish descent, Mankiller was one of eleven children. She spent the first decade of her life not far from her birthplace, happily close to her family but barely getting by on what meager crops her father was able to raise and sell. When the struggle finally proved too great, the Mankillers accepted the federal government's offer to move them to California, where they settled in a San Francisco ghetto as part of a Bureau of Indian Affairs program to "urbanize" Native Americans. Life did not improve, however; the children were desperately homesick and cringed at the racist insults of their classmates, and Charlie Mankiller, Wilma's father, had trouble landing steady employment.

Eventually, however, the Mankillers adjusted to living in the city. Wilma finished high school and went on to college at San Francisco State, where throughout the 1960s she pursued studies in sociology with an eye toward becoming a social worker. It was during this same period that she arrived at a new appreciation of her heritage when she began associating with a group of young Native American activists. In 1969, some of them occupied Alcatraz Island in San Francisco Bay to protest the U.S. government's mistreatment of Indian people and reassert their treaty rights. Mankiller's subsequent efforts to round up support for the demonstrators led her into the fledgling American Indian Movement, and by 1975 she had left California to return to Oklahoma and what she hoped would be an opportunity to work on behalf of the Cherokee people.

Mankiller spent the next few years developing and implementing a number of economic and social self-help programs in the community under the auspices of the Cherokee Nation. She also resumed her education, this time at the University of Arkansas in Fayetteville. While driving back home after class one morning in late 1979, she was involved in a car accident that killed her best friend and left Mankiller critically injured. Not long afterward, she was diagnosed with a serious muscle disease, myasthenia gravis. All of this was in addition to the kidney problems she had been suffering from since the early 1970s—problems severe enough that she would later undergo surgery and eventually a transplant.

Mankiller struggled for nearly a year to overcome the physical and emotional trauma of the accident and its aftermath. Once she was able to work again, she took up where she had left off, setting up programs to help her people help themselves (primarily in the areas of health care and housing) as director of the Cherokee Nation Community Development Department. Her success soon attracted the attention of tribal leaders, including Principal Chief Ross Swimmer, who asked her to be his running mate (for the post of deputy chief) in his 1983 re-election campaign. Despite facing opposition from some male members of the tribe who felt that a woman had no business being in the race, Swimmer and Mankiller managed to win by a narrow margin. Two years later, when Swimmer resigned to accept a job with the administration of President Ronald Reagan, Mankiller assumed the role of principal chief, making her the first woman ever to hold the position.

In 1987, Mankiller decided to seek election as principal chief in her own right. Once again, she faced some resistance; not all of the men were convinced that a woman was suited for the post. Also, Mankiller's continuing health problems were of concern. But with the encouragement and support of her husband, Charlie Soap, who works on rural development projects for the Cherokee Nation, she was able to summon the strength and the will to prevail over her opponent.

WILMA MANKILLER'S INAUGURAL ADDRESS

Good afternoon. I'd like to tell you how truly delighted I am to be here today. There's no greater honor I've ever had than to be chosen by my own people to lead them and I think that feeling is shared by Deputy Chief John Ketcher and members of the Tribal Council.

I heard someone say this week, "How are all these 'ordinary' people elected to the tribal council going to make the weighty decisions for the Cherokee Nation?" I can tell you quite frankly that "ordinary" people take very seriously the responsibility and trust that has been given them. I think you'll see a change in these people who have been elected to make decisions for you, merely from the weight of that responsibility. People say that crisis changes people and turns ordinary people into wiser or more responsible ones. As crises develop within the Cherokee Nation and we begin to resolve those crises, you will see many changes.

"I think I can say without the tiniest bit of false pride that we are one of the most progressive tribes in the U.S. today."

I'd like to talk just a little about the Cherokee Nation, where I see us today and where I see us going in the future. I think I can say without the tiniest bit of false pride that we are one of the most progressive tribes in the U.S. today. That progress we enjoy today, the Cherokee Nation that you see today—a very progressive, large, diverse organization—is not the result of the work of one person. It's the work of many, many people. There are a lot of people who laid the foundation for the work we're doing today, beginning principally in this latest revitalization, with Chief Milam, moving to Chief Keeler, to Chief Swimmer, who was my immediate predecessor, and myself.

The tribal council members who have become more active and assumed more responsibility within the tribal government are responsible for much of that work. I don't ever forget that much of the good work at the Cherokee Nation and much of our success can be attributed directly to the hundreds of tribal citizens who become involved in our work, as well as the tribal employees who carry out the policies established by the tribal government. Many people only see the employees. They rarely get to see the inner workings of the tribal government, so I

would also like to thank all the tribal employees who make our government what it is today.

We've grown very rapidly in the past fifteen years, just in the past ten years that I've been associated with the tribe. That growth has been phenomenal, and the manifestation of the growth over the past fifteen years is all around you. You can see the new Hastings Hospital, Cherokee Nation Industries, Cherokee Gardens, rural health clinics, the Head Start centers and many other examples of this growth. When I came to the Cherokee Nation ten years ago, there were two hundred or three hundred tribal employees. There are now well over seven hundred permanent employees, and several hundred more have seasonal employment.

That growth has not occurred without problems. Growth is a painful process. I'd like everybody to remember that we're still growing, we're still young. In the totality of Cherokee history, fifteen years isn't very long. And we've got many more painful processes to work through before we reach a point where we will level off.

Our overall goal determined by the last tribal council and the last chief and deputy chief was a goal of self-sufficiency as total independence from federal aid. That's not at all what we mean. I personally think that the U.S. government owes us much in federal aid. We paid for much of what we receive today in lost lives and lost land. Our interpretation of self-sufficiency could simply be described as capability—the capability to do things for ourselves. . .the capability to do things with some assistance from the BIA [Bureau of Indian Affairs], but basically running the tribe ourselves. . .with some assistance from the IHS [Indian Health Service], but making the decisions ourselves. If you'll look where we are today, we're well on our way to self-sufficiency. Many people talk about self-sufficiency, self-reliance and self-determination in a rhetorical sense, but to translate that into reality is a very difficult task that I think the Cherokee Nation is doing fairly well.

We have an excellent group of elected officials, a very diverse group of people from various areas throughout the Cherokee Nation, from various backgrounds. We have some very serious challenges ahead of us. I will talk very briefly about one related to the constitution. Because the rest of the

United States is talking about the U.S. Constitution, I'm going to talk about the Cherokee constitution.

In this election of 1987, the Cherokee voters overwhelmingly passed an amendment to our Constitution which would allow the council members to be elected by districts. One of the major tasks of this newly elected tribal council, the legislative body of the tribe, is to develop a plan for districting. That is a monumental undertaking. The voters have said "we want districting," but the details have to be worked out during the next four years.

I also think there's a need for a constitutional convention. In fact, our constitution requires us to have one within the next fifteen years. The reason we review our constitution is the same reason the U.S. government reviews its Constitution—it should reflect the collective values of the Cherokee people. As time changes our values and needs, the constitution needs a new look and some amendments. This amendment we just passed is the first to our constitution, but I certainly don't think it's the last. The Cherokee constitution, as you heard in our oaths, basically provides a legal infrastructure for our government. That's our Bible, everything we do follows that so that's one of the very important challenges we have to undertake in the next four years. It's principally the task of the tribal council.

Another important task we face is that of protecting tribal rights. By tribal rights, I mean the protection of those rights that are afforded us because we are tribal government. This is something that I, the deputy chief, and the tribal council are going to have to spend a great deal of time on. There are powerful anti-Indian lobbyists who are constantly trying to diminish tribal rights, and I think that what we have to do is constantly protect our tribal rights. Many of the services and programs we enjoy today are a direct result of the special government-to-government relationship with the U.S. government that has to be protected.

I also believe that we need to concentrate on the stimulation and development of the economy in this area. As I've told many of you before, we can't do economic development in a vacuum. We don't have the resources to do that by ourselves. We have to work in a team effort with the Oklahoma Chamber of Commerce, state government, local bankers, and the business community to develop the economy of this area. Oklahoma in general is suffering from a depressed economy. I believe the Cherokees are suffering even more. Our people are very hardworking. That's a well known fact. You can look at Cherokee Gardens, Cherokee

Wilma Mankiller

Nation Industries, many of the industries in Arkansas that recruit and bus Cherokees across the border into Arkansas because they are good workers. We have hardworking people, but many of them don't have a place to work. One of our priorities is searching for ways to develop the economy of this area. That's critical.

We also must continue to move our health care system outward. When we proposed this eight or nine years ago, it seemed like a radical idea. At that time we didn't have rural health clinics and we were only developing a tribal-specific health plan and talking about moving services closer to the people. Today that's a reality. We have many clinics in outlying areas and are looking at developing more. We should look very closely at our whole health care system and begin to place more emphasis on prevention and education.

With all of the progressive work we do in economic development, protection of tribal rights and in running a very complex organization, we must not forget who we are. We must pay attention to the protection and preservation of tribal culture. There are many definitions of tribal culture but we must sit down and define for ourselves those things we consider important to protect for future generations. In the past, promotion of tribal culture has been viewed as a function of the community and family, not of tribal government. But we've reached a point where we need to assume a leadership role.

We need to explore what we as a government can do to promote and protect our culture.

I don't think that anybody, anywhere can talk about the future of their people or of an organization without talking about education. Whoever controls the education of our children controls our future, the future of the Cherokee people and of the Cherokee Nation. There are many new programs I'm going to propose and I'm sure the council will propose regarding education. We're doing a lot of innovative things in education but there's more we can do. We have always placed a great deal of importance on education and that has helped us as a people. We must continue to do that.

In our education programs, I would like to incorporate education about tribal government and tribal history. If we know where we've been as a people, our history, our culture and our ancestry we have a better sense of where we are today, and certainly, a better sense of where we're going.

I've talked about some of the battles we face in terms of education, economic development. It is easy to talk about these problems but it takes the teamwork of many people to address them.

Finally, while there are a lot of external threats to the Cherokee Nation, the really great threat is one that is internal.

As any young organization and as officials elected to tribal government, we must develop an environment where dissent and disagreement can be handled in a respectful way. Dissent is natural and good. Out of respectful dissent and disagreement comes change that is usually positive. As tribal officials we can set an example how to disagree in a respectful and good way. We all have many goals for our tribe that will require myself, the deputy chief, the tribal council, the tribal citizens and tribal employees working together to reach.

We certainly can't do it if we focus on our disagreements. If we begin to focus on the things that we agree, we can forge ahead. We come from different backgrounds and certainly we're going to disagree. We must figure a way to balance that and the things we can work. The darkest pages in Cherokee history, the greatest tragedies that occurred to us as a people came when we were divided internally.

People say I'm a positive person, that I focus on positive things. I do. We've done a lot. I'm very proud of the Cherokee Nation, I'm very proud of the many people in our communities, I'm very proud of our history, I'm proud to be Cherokee. But that doesn't mean I don't know there are a lot of serious problems in our organization, that there are a lot of serious problems we still face in the communities and that I don't realize how much work remains to be done. As we continue to work on these problems, we need to be aware that the things we do will have a profound effect on the future of the Cherokee Nation, its government and the Cherokee people.

We take our responsibility extremely seriously. We work very hard and we welcome your input. As I said, we didn't acquire instant wisdom by being elected but we do take our jobs seriously and I think you'll see that over the next four years.

This is a very exciting time for me, for all these people. I hope that in the next four years we return in a very real sense to the golden era of the Cherokee Nation where we have economic prosperity, where we begin to do some really innovative things in education, where we do more in the health care field and continue the revitalization of our communities.

With that, I ask for your continued support throughout the next four years. You have certainly been supportive during this time, during the election and during the eighteen months I served as principal chief prior to the election. I thank all of those who helped me. I wouldn't want to start thanking everyone from my kindergarten teacher on up, but I would like to thank my husband. Without his support, I could not have run for office, nor could I continue in this position. I won't ask him to stand up but I would like to thank my husband, Charlie Soap, for all his help and all his work. I, too, would like to recognize the family of Clarence Sunday, because Clarence Sunday helped me an awful lot, not only in the campaign but by talking through a lot of issues.

So with that, again, I'd like to thank you for your attention, hope you'll stay very involved in the Cherokee Nation and continue to give us your ideas, your support and your prayers.

Thank you very much.

Source:

Text of speech delivered August 14, 1987 in Tahlequah (Cherokee Nation's capital). Reprinted in *Native American Reader: Stories, Speeches and Poems*, edited by Jerry D. Blanche. Juneau, Alaska: Denali Press, 1990.

CHINESE AMERICANS

The historical relationship between Chinese immigrants and their U.S. hosts has been somewhat tumultuous. In the early 1900s an influx of Asian Americans was referred to as the "yellow peril" and there were legislative efforts made to discourage Asians from coming to the United States. Most notably, western states such as Oregon, California, and Washington passed alien land acts which prevented certain immigrants, in particular those ineligible for citizenship, from owning land.

The Angel Island Immigration Station served as a waiting station for immigrants from China attempting to gain entry to the United States at the beginning of the twentieth century. Chinese immigrants were housed at Angel Island until state and federal authorities passed judgement on their eligibility. Approximately 175,000 Chinese immigrants that came to the United States between 1910 and 1940 had to pass through Angel Island. The waiting period was a painful and exhausting ordeal for the immigrants, in part, because restrictions were tightened while they awaited their fate. The immigrants had to go through a lengthy interrogation process during which they were asked minute details about their family history. The questioning was used as a means for restricting the number of Chinese immigrants allowed into the country. Many immigrants did not know whether they would be sent back home and severed from their families. Some immigrants documented their frustration by carving poetry on barrack walls. The message conveyed in the carvings was one of suffering, humiliation, and homesickness. The poetry on the barrack walls has been drawn into a larger opus of Asian American literature. It is considered by some to be one of the first literary expressions from the Asian American community.

Angel Island was a product of the 1882 Chinese Exclusion Act which was designed to discourage Chinese immigrants from coming to the United States. The 1882 Exclusion Act was followed by a 1924 law that prohibited Chinese immigrants that were ineligible for citizenship from entering the country. In addition, where the wives of other immigrant groups were automatically eligible for citizenship the wives of Chinese immigrants were excluded from this policy in accordance with the 1924 law. The law was challenged in Chang Chan et. al. v. John D. Nagle, however, the Supreme Court upheld the constitutionality of the policy. The law resulted in the separation of Chinese families which discouraged immigration from China. In large part because the Chinese fought on the side of the Allies during World War II, the exclusion laws were repealed in 1943.

United States officials closed the Angel Island Immigration Station in 1940; it was subsequently converted into a beautiful national park in the 1970s after the poetry on the barrack walls was discovered. The discriminatory policy toward the Chinese immigrants came to a formal end when President John F. Kennedy initiated a program that allowed over 18,000 Chinese immigrants to enter the United States over a three year period in 1962. President Johnson followed up with the initiative by allowing over 20,000 immigrants from each immigrant group to enter the country annually.

ANGEL ISLAND CARVINGS

Source:
Associated Press.

*T*ea drinking is an ancient tradition in China, dating back to the legendary Shen Nung. Shen is said to have personally sampled hundreds of different herbs and grasses to assess their toxicity and medicinal effects. By the Sung Dynasty (960-1280 A.D.) tea was a popular drink, and dim sum, as an accompaniment to the flavorful beverage, developed. After an exhausting day working in the fields in China's ancient agricultural society, people would often go to a tea house. Here, warm conversation was mixed with good tea and a sumptuous selection of dim sum, which translates to "a little bit of heart."

Today, dim sum is typically served as a luncheon meal, also known in Cantonese as yum cha, which literally means "drink tea." With the tea, shrimp dumplings wrapped in delicate dough bundles, steamed buns filled with seasoned meats, along with a variety of other small dishes, both sweet and salty, are served. The foods are served in bamboo steamers, and everything is rolled out on a trolley cart. Every several minutes, new dishes emerge from the kitchen, and diners simply point to select their choices. The quantity of each dish is relatively tiny, so that a many differnt items can be savored. Dim sum is popular everywhere, as evidenced by the number of restaurants serving this treat around the world.

DIM SUM
Potstickers

Dough
2 cups all-purpose flour
½ cup boiling water

Filling
½ lb ground pork
⅓ cup green onion, chopped
1 tbsp fresh ginger, minced
1 clove garlic, minced
1 tsp salt
½ tsp sugar
½ small Chinese cabbage (Napa), cored and shredded
1 small egg

To Cook
6 tbsp vegetable oil
1 cup water

Sauce
soy sauce
red rice vinegar
hot chile oil

Combine flour and water in a bowl, mixing to form a ball. Place on a floured board. After cooling, knead mixture with hands for 5 minutes. Shape dough into a ball, cover with a moist towel. Let stand for 10 minutes.

Filling is made by mixing all the filling ingredients thoroughly together, and refrigerate the mixture until ready to use.

To make the dumplings, knead the dough for 5 minutes. Roll it out into a cylinder approximately 1 inch in diameter. Cut off the ends, then divide the dough into pieces about ¾ inch wide. With your palm, press the dough down to flatten. Use a rolling pin to make the dough even thinner.

Spoon about 1 tablespoon of the mixture into the center of the wrapper. Fold the dough over to make a half-moon shape and pleat the edges of your dumpling firmly together.

Heat a heavy-bottom or cast-iron skillet over medium heat. Add 3 tablespoons of oil, coating the surface of the skillet evenly. When the oil is hot, place potstickers (seam side up) into skillet and gently shake for 1 minute. Pour in water, cover and simmer over moderate heat for 10 minutes. When

Dim sum is a Chinese luncheon meal, during which many tasty foods, including steamed buns and stuffed dumplings, are served with tea.

most of the water is gone, add the remaining oil, moving the skillet to ensure that all the potsticker bottoms become coated. Watch the dumplings carefully; bottoms should be browned, not burned or stuck to your skillet. Carefully remove from heat with a spatula when done.

Serve the potstickers with the sauce of your choice, either separately or mixed together to your taste.

Steamed Pork Buns

Dough
Makes 12

4 tablespoons sugar
½ cup warm milk
⅓ cup warm water
2 teaspoons active dry yeast
About 2½ cups flour
½ teaspoon salt

Filling

½ cup mushrooms
2 tablespoons cooking oil
½ cup minced green onions
2 teaspoons minced garlic
½ cup water
4 teaspoons hoisin sauce
4 teaspoons oyster sauce
1 tablespoon sugar

2 teaspoons cornstarch dissolved in 2 tablespoons water
1½ cups chopped Chinese Barbecued Pork

Dissolve 2 tablespoons of the sugar in milk and water. Sprinkle in yeast and allow about 10 minutes to activate. Mix in remaining sugar, 2 cups flour, and salt. If dough remains sticky, add small amounts of flour until you can work it with your hands without it sticking.

Place dough on a lightly floured board and knead until smooth and elastic. Pour oil over the top of the dough in a bowl, cover, and let rise in a warm place until doubled in size.

For filling, heat a wok and when hot add oil. Add onions, garlic, and mushrooms; stir-fry for 1 minute. Stir in water, hoisin sauce, oyster sauce, and sugar. Add cornstarch solution and stir until sauce boils and thickens. Stir in pork. Scoop into separate bowl, and allow to cool.

To begin assembly of the buns, punch the dough down and roll it out into a long cylinder. Cut the cylinder into 12 equal parts, rolling each part into a ball.

Flatten out each ball into a circle, with the thickness of the dough flattened to about 1/4 of an inch. Place a tablespoon of filling in the center of each circle. Pull the edges together over the filling, twisting and pinching the edges together (brushing a little beaten egg or water on the edges will help the seal stay put).

Cover the buns and let them rise again until they are puffy.

After rising, steam the buns over a high heat until the dough is smooth—about 12 minutes.

Source:
Anonymous.

Only two ways of making a living—restaurant and laundry work—were available to most Chinese immigrants in the early part of the twentieth century. Many were pushed into these service occupations when opportunities in manufacturing and agriculture were closed to them due to strong anti-Chinese bias.

The following account of life as a Chinese laundryman was woven into Paul C. P. Siu's important sociological study of the subject. In it a laundryman recounts the life he has chosen and the sacrifices he has made to ensure the welfare of his children. He stresses the benefits of education for the children, especially since he himself was denied a proper education in China, and he emphasizes the need to know English in order to advance in American society. Laundry work, he points out, takes a heavy toll on his health, and his only hope lies in his children's future.

THE CHINESE LAUNDRYMAN

Being a laundryman is no life at all. I work fourteen hours a day and I have to send home almost all my wages. You see, I have a big family at home. My mother is still living and I have an unmarried sister who is going to school. My own children, five of them, all are in school too. My brother here—he is no help; he has a family here and what he earns is just enough to support his family. I figure I send home about fifteen hundred dollars a year, at least, sometimes more.

I seldom go down to Chinatown—not every Sunday, anyway. Unless I have some business matter, I usually go to Chinatown only once a month. I sleep and read here Sunday. I don't go to movies often. You don't understand a lot of the things they say in the show. Sometimes I get tired and fall asleep in the movie theater.

I buy lottery tickets but do not patronize any other Chinatown gambling. I used to play ma-jong [majian] when I was in Canton. I do not have the energy to enjoy playing it any more.. . . I have never had any luck.

People think I am a happy person. I am not. I worry very much. First, I don't like this kind of life;

it is not human life. To be a laundryman is to be just a slave. I work because I have to. If I ever stop working, those at home must stop eating.

I am not healthy at all. I feel my backaches all the time. My health has improved however since my tonsils were removed. Then I have other troubles, like headaches. I am not an old man yet, but I feel old. How can a man feel good when he is forced into an occupation he doesn't like?

But I get used to it. After you are on it for so many years, you have no more feeling but stay on with it. After all, you can't get rich but you don't have to worry about money as long as you can work. If my father had let me stay in school, I could have graduated from middle school; then I might not have come. I could find something to do in China. It is better to be a poor teacher in China. You could have been happier.

In this country, one must know English enough to do something other than laundry work. I was not allowed to have a chance to study English when I first came here. My father and uncles had an idea that those who knew enough English were those who could become bad. He meant, to fool

Throughout a period of exclusion by the U.S. government (1882-1965), most Chinese Americans were confined to segregated ghettos, called Chinatowns, where they did work others did not want to do, such as laundry.

around with girls and so forth. I was foolish to listen to them though. Think of that sort of old ideas! How stupid!

I have a building in Canton. It cost my father about nine thousand dollars. My family is now living on one of the four floors; the other floors are rented. It is lucky we don't have to pay rent, otherwise my responsibility could be heavier. That was all my father left us.

Source:

"The Old-Timer," from *The Chinese Laundryman: A Study of Social Isolation*, by Paul C.P. Siu; edited by John Kuo Wei Tchen. New York: New York University Press, 1987. Originally presented as the author's thesis (Ph.D.)—University of Chicago, 1953.

The first Chinese in America arrived in the mid-nineteenth century, and their immigrant experiences were not as positive as Wong Chun Yau's in Greedy About Life Again. The Chinese were singled out for discrimination in America. Many states, led by California, passed discriminatory laws to exclude Chinese from owning land and gaining citizenship. The Chinese Americans were the first ethnic group to find itself the target of the U.S. Congress, who passed a law in 1882 to deny citizenship to Chinese immigrants. In the twentieth century, movies and television westerns depicting life in the West in the late 1800s cast Chinese immigrants in the stereotypical role of laundry men and social misfits who can not become an accepted part of the western community.

Chinese immigration occurred in three periods. The first, from 1849 to 1882, happened during the Gold Rush in California, and ended when Congress passed the Chinese Exclusion Act of 1882. Most of these early immigrants were young male peasants who landed in San Francisco and became contract laborers in mines and on railroads. Many returned to China, but at least 110,000 remained in the United States. During the second period, from 1882 until 1965, known as a time of exclusion, only diplomats, students and some refugees were able to immigrate. The new Immigration and Nationality Act of 1965 finally ended discrimination towards Chinese immigration, particularly by allowing relatives to join family members already in the United States. Thousands began to come yearly. In addition, around 250,000 students entered the United States to study for advanced degrees. Many of them stayed in the United States after completing school. Other Chinese have been granted refugee status as political instability and oppression compelled them to escape. By the time of the 1990 Census, 1.6 million Chinese Americans lived in the United States.

Wong Chun Yau's testimony about her life in China under the rule of Mao Tse-tung provides valuable details of ordinary life that were obscured for decades when access to China was closed to the West. It is particularly helpful to see the conditions under which she lived before coming to the United States in order to accurately understand her immigrant experience. Wong Chun Yau is exultant to be in the United States. Her memoir is also valuable because of her age. Her insights about Chinese and American cultures have been shaped by 70 years of living.

GREEDY ABOUT LIFE AGAIN
by Wong Chun Yau

Wong Chun Yau is seventy years old, heavy-set, with a deep infectious laugh. She is jovial and loud. She immigrated to the United States from China in 1979. She speaks no English. The interview was conducted in Cantonese (a dialect of Chinese).

"I look back at my life in China and I get scared. Now my life is worth something; it is precious again. In the past, I felt so what if I am shot, I just die. There wasn't anything to live for, anyway. But now, I am greedy about life again. I want to live.

"My daughter lived in San Francisco, so that's where I went when I arrived in this country in

1979. I was sixty years old. There was a social service agency there that provided orientation and training for new immigrants. So I enrolled in the eleven-week program. The first week, I was always sleepy because of the change in time differences. So I would rub my eyes and tears would come out. The teacher saw this and thought I had major problems in my life, and was troubled. By the fourth week she figured that maybe I needed some financial help, so after two hours of classes in the morning, she would send to a job, where I made three dollars and twenty-five cents an hour for three hours. I said, 'Wow, more than three dollars

A group of Chinese American women stretching before Tai Chi exercises in the morning.

an hour.' I had never made so much money in my life. I was ecstatic. My paycheck was over one hundred dollars a week. In China, I didn't even make one hundred dollars a month. And then they purged me there, too. In San Francisco I was sent to a hotel to clean bathrooms and pick up cigarette butts. It was work, and I couldn't believe I had such an opportunity to make money. People kept telling me how hard it would be in this country. But I say, this country is great. There is no comparison between China and the United States. One is striking the hot pot (a term for eating Mongolian hot pot), and the other, is striking the rear end. Not only did I make more money here, I could also buy whatever I wanted. How great it is. The U.S. government is excessively wonderful. Many of my friends tell me, 'Only you can get used to this country, many people can't.' I say it is true. I am very content. If I want something, I can buy it. So why not be satisfied? My sons have all prospered here, especially my youngest. He owns over six buildings. So, what is there to worry about? Noth-

ing. My eldest son has three buildings. He gave me five hundred dollars for Chinese New Year this year, and when my daughter-in-law returned from China recently, she gave me a gold necklace for taking care of her two children. So isn't that a fine life? I am absolutely satisfied. My daughter graduated from medical school in China, and knows acupuncture. But she studied Russian in school. When she was going to school, China was friendly with Russia, and she refused to learn English. So now she can't do very much in this country, so she sorts mail for some company. Her husband is a doctor too. But he can't get a job here either. He has a practice in Hong Kong, and visits her once a year.

"I came to New York because my two sons were here. They had opened up a Chinese restaurant. So I took the ten thousand dollars I made in San Francisco and gave it to them to open a takeout place. But the place lost money, and so we closed it. Now my youngest son is doing very well; he's in insurance. The oldest is in renovation work."

Escape from China

"In China, I owned two houses. And if you had money in China, it was a crime. If you were an intellectual, it was a crime. The really poor, who didn't have a thing, they were the average, so no harm came to them. But if you had a cent, they would purge you. If you owned land, they would purge you. I was purged by the Red Guards twice. This was in the 1960s. Every time they had some movement, they would drag me out, and make me the center of the event. They took everything-my money, my furniture. Even now the furniture hasn't been returned. They beat me—took off my jacket and beat me. I was sick for three months after that. They stuck me in a cow pen. And then they kept telling me to list my crimes. In the mornings, when I got up, I would have to write. But what could I say? I didn't kill anyone, or set any fires. So what was I supposed to write? So they told me to write down all the things I did against humanity. But I couldn't figure out what I did against the people. I was never a thief or anything. It was a very painful period.

"I worked as a nurse for over twenty years. From seven to five I would go to work. But then from seven to nine in the evening, I would have to go to class to learn about the Party and communism. I was envied by a lot of people where I worked, because I was making over eighty dollars a month. And those who were new were making maybe thirty dollars.

"My husband swam to Hong Kong in 1962, and then all my children swam out of China into Hong Kong in 1967. Then they came to this country as refugees in 1970. But I didn't leave China until 1979 when my son petitioned to have me join him in America.

"When I was in my forties I followed some local guys trying to make the break. I am a good swimmer so I swam for almost three hours to the outer territories of Hong Kong, and I saw this fishing boat, so I asked to get on board, thinking, I am so close, this must be a Hong Kong ship. But as it turned out, the fisherman was from China, and he took me back because he could get twenty for returning me to the government. So I was purged and beaten, and beaten and purged. They even took a knife and stabbed me in my face. I still have this scar where they split open my mouth.

"Things are fine now in this country. I want to live to be one hundred. In China, I always wanted to die. There was hardly anything to eat and you had to work all day. If you wanted one particular thing, you couldn't get that particular thing. You could get only one dollar's worth of meat a month. And a dime's worth of fish a month. And even

with the dime, you couldn't always find fish to buy. So I ate vegetables, lots of vegetables. I would salt them, and then dry them in the sun. Then I would steam them with some sugar. As for the salted fish—it was thirty cents a 'gun' (slightly over a pound), so I would buy the salted fish. For each meal I would just nibble at the fish for flavor, then eat a big mouthful of rice. A small nibble, then another mouthful of rice. If you had money, on pay day, you might go out to the farms and get the meat of some dead pigs or some real old pigs to eat. They rationed the rice—twenty 'guns' a month. Even if they allowed forty 'guns,' I would still be hungry. There was no oil, no meat. But here, I couldn't eat twenty pounds even if you gave it to me, because you have dishes such as chicken to go with the meal. In China, you ate chicken on New Year's Day and would have to wait until New Year's the next year to eat it again. Here, you could buy chicken by the pound. I love chicken so much, I eat it every meal now. Everything required ration tickets. Rice, bread, congee, everything required tickets. What's great about this country is I can buy a whole loaf of bread and even pastries and not need a ration ticket for them. Just the idea of being able to order a bowl of noodles, and not have to give a rice ticket—it's fabulous.

"They gave you just enough cloth to make one set of clothing. If you bought a pair of socks, it would be a few inches of material. All of it was rationed by the amount of material. The saying goes like this: 'A new set of clothes for three years, an old set for three years, and mending it again, you get another three years.' So it wasn't unusual to keep an outfit for nine years.

"My husband, at sixty, found himself another woman. She was thirty-two years old. He was in Hong Kong then and I was in China. He told everybody that I was missing and couldn't be found, so he divorced me and married her. He even had a huge banquet and invited all these friends. When I got to Hong Kong and applied to come to America, he was afraid I would go after him, so he sold everything and moved this woman and their two children to Canada. Now I can't even locate him there, because no one would give us their address. He's afraid I would come after him.

"At this senior citizen center I go to, I don't have to cook, and there is a meal for me. When I am finished, someone even wipes the table. I go there even though I have to pay thirty-five cents for lunch, because they give me a dollar back for car fare, so actually, I am ahead sixty-five cents. Another place I can eat free, but there is no reimbursement for car fare.

"I even got a picture from President Bush thanking me for voting for him. I don't know which party he belongs to, I just voted for the one who would be most helpful for old people."

Source:

Joann Faung Jean Lee. *Asian American Experiences in the United States: Oral Histories of First to Fourth Generation Americans from China, the Philippines, Japan, India, the Pacific Islands, Vietnam and Cambodia.* Jefferson, NC: McFarland & Co., 1991. pp. 78-81.

Sue Jean Lee Suettinger's life as told in a 1970s interview is representative of several aspects of the Chinese American experience in America, including the often prolonged process of assimilation into U.S. society. Sue Jean, born in Canton, China, came to New York City's Chinatown with her family at age four in 1952. Because of existing U.S. racial exclusion policies, her parents—though both college-educated—had to leave their professional fields and assume quite different careers. Many Chinese Americans, including her father, became involved in multiple small businesses, often involving import-export trading companies. In the 1950s, Sue Jean's father opened one of the first suburban Chinese restaurants in New Jersey. Sue Jean's mother, a non-English speaker, labored in a Chinatown sewing factory.

The traditional Chinese American life involved frugality and tolerance toward hardship and racial discrimination. Suettinger's family was no different. Though both parents worked, they were still poor. As Sue Jean relayed in her interview, "We were a poor family, and when I look back at it now I can see that. There were six of us living in a three-room flat. There were two small bedrooms and one room in the middle which had a sink and bathtub in it. We had to draw a curtain around us every time we washed. The bathroom was in the hall and we shared it with other families."

In a sort of second stage of immigration, Sue Jean became part of a later twentieth century emigration of Chinese Americans, particularly those better educated and affluent, out of Chinatowns. Upon leaving Chinatown to attend college in New England, Sue Jean reflected on how quickly she realized that Chinatown was a tight, closed community with limited interaction with mainstream America. Because of this isolation, she felt very unfamiliar with her new surroundings, and her socialization process took several months. However, her sheltered life of youth soon dissipated away as she became fully integrated with the people around her.

Graduating from Princeton University in 1970 Sue Jean joined the ranks of many other well-educated Chinese Americans. Indicative of racial intermarriage trends following the 1960s Civil Rights movement, she married a German Norwegian American and had to withstand the resulting strained relationship with her parents for not marrying someone of Chinese ancestry. Sue Jean's interview strongly reflected the persistent pride of her family heritage and how she would like to pass along knowledge of the Chinese American heritage to her children.

WEST SIDE STORY

Sue Jean Lee Suettinger

Sue Jean was born in Canton China and immigrated to the United States with her family in 1952, when she was four years old. She graduated Princeton University in 1970. She now works as a China consultant and is married to a fifth generation German Norwegian.

"I had a lot of fun growing up in New York's Chinatown. I remember the fun of having friends close by, or playing on the sidewalks—hopscotch, handball, tag, roller skating, and going around the block to the candy store. I remember the fun things. I was also aware, from a very young age, of the diversity in cultures that I encountered in school. I remember making very good friends with two Jewish girls. It was probably an odd sight to many, but the three of us did *Havah-Nagilah* on stage when I was in the fourth grade. I got to know their families pretty well, and remember tasting Jewish food. In that sense, it was very rich. It was a very Americanized environment.

"When I was thirteen or fourteen, I hung around with one group called the Continentals, and in keeping with the times, the boys wore black leather jackets, and hung around on street corners being cool, with ducktail type hairdos, and tight black pants. This was around 1963. There was almost a uniform of what the girls and guys who were a part of that social gang wore. Very often, girls would wear white shirts with black shorts. But I remember the white blouses with the initials on them. And we had our dances. The Continental group was a mixture of first, second and third generation Chinese teenagers, many of whom attended the Chinese school. And then there were other teenage groups, whose social life was centered around a church.

"Our idea of rebelliousness was hanging around street corners. Because we were the Continentals we would go around finding Lincoln Continentals and try to rip the little Continental symbols off the cars. That was the time of the movie, *West Side Story*, where teenage gang rivalry was depicted. These were gangs, but not as we know of them today—with access to guns, or extortion. These were social gangs much like the ones in *West Side Story*. They carried switchblades or chains—but that was as far as they would go in terms of weapons. And every now and then they would get into scuffles with Italian gangs, each maintaining dominion over their neighborhood block. And it was cool for us to be a part of that. And it was cool

for the girls to watch how the guys would get hurt in those things.

"I look back at my teenage years and think now that I was involved in some pretty off the wall stuff, being part of these gangs. And hearing the elders in Chinatown give us a bad name, and at the same time knowing we didn't do anything wrong—we just looked threatening because we hung around and shared that sense of rebelliousness—of wanting to be independent, grow up, and have an identity. My parents didn't know I was in a gang. They were very strict, and if we went to a party, often it was without the knowledge of my parents. We'd say we were going to the movies, and then we'd go to a party. At these parties, we'd do the twist, the cha-cha, the lindy, or jitterbug as it's called, and the Continental Walk. There were all-Chinese parties, and strictly limited to groups we hung out with. The extended group had forty to fifty people. Dating was certainly not the young man asking shyly whether I would go someplace like a movie or dinner, then having him show up at my door with a corsage or something, and being nervous about talking to my parents. The dating that we saw on 'Father Knows Best' was not the kind of dating experience I had. We didn't really date, one on one. We went out in groups to the bowling alley, ice skating, or to the movies. Then you paired off with someone. I don't remember being asked unless there was a dance or the movies.

"I remember being very insistent about going to Chinese school because my two older sisters went, and I wanted to go too. But I didn't start first grade Chinese school until I was two years ahead of that grade in American school. That was common. You often found older children in the lower grades because of ability. It was just the way the school was set up. We were all there, learning Chinese, memorizing the same lessons, and we were all competing for the same thing. But the social life was different. And the friends I eventually chose to develop a social life with were mostly second or third generation Chinese Americans. There was still that sense of competition, and the ones you competed with were the immigrants.

"School was from five to seven o'clock, five days a week. In my third year I started a Mandarin club because I was very interested in the dialect. I got our teacher to agree. Our Mandarin club would meet at four fifteen so that meant school started much earlier.

"Chinese school was comprehensive. We learned history, science, social studies (but from a Chinese perspective), geography about China, and in some cases, the world. Very seldom would I mix the lessons from Chinese school with American school. They were two distinct worlds. With only two hours a day, what we did was very selective. We learned composition; we learned how to write. The whole method of teaching was so different from American school. There was a lot of memorization. And penmanship, of course, was using the brush. It was learning how to write Chinese characters, with ink and brush. A very important part of that schooling was poetry.

"The Chinese school also had a tradition of drum and bugle corps. I was a baton twirler. And I was in it for four or five years. All this time that this was going on, it never dawned on me to think about how much out of the mainstream of society we were. It wasn't until I left Chinatown that I realized what a homogenous community Chinatown really was. What a tight, closed environment we lived in. We interacted with the rest of the city only as far as our activities took us. But in terms of sufficiencies, such as food and social activities, it was very contained.

"I can look back at my teenage years and see that is wasn't so different from other teenagers in other culture groups. It always amazes me how much of a New Yorker I was in terms of the environment. We had our dances, played our 45 records, had little transistor radios we played, and hung out in corners. Friends gathered after school at the local malt shop and had egg creams and french fries. These were all Chinese kids. Because the schools I went to were so close to the Chinese community, many of the students who went to the schools were Chinese, so invariably, I ended up hanging around with Chinese teenagers.

"In my early teens, my parents did not think it was appropriate for us to be seen with guys. So I just didn't tell them. The activities I would do with a guy would be done in a group setting. So there was no need for me to tell my parents I'm going with so and so, because I'd meet up with a group anyway. When my parents said to me, you're too young to be dating, I assumed they meant Chinese guys. There wasn't even a race issue in that, because it was understood that I would eventually end up with a Chinese. They certainly didn't have to warn me not to date Caucasians.

"At that point in my life, it never occurred to me to date anyone but Chinese because of the environment I grew up in. The school I went to had Italians, blacks, Jews, Puerto Ricans, whites—it was a pretty good mixture. But there was a sense of difference. I got along with people very well in school. I had some very good Italian friends—males and females—but it never occurred to me to date them. Or if I looked for cute guys, I'd be attracted to the Chinese ones and not the Caucasians. Although by the time I got to college, I could say my horizons broadened a bit, and I could say there were non-Chinese guys who were cute. You found them attractive, but not to the point where you'd say, 'Oh gosh, I wish he would call me up' or something. Again, I was looking for the Chinese or the Oriental guys. I grew up in a very sheltered environment in Chinatown, and there wasn't the need to look beyond. There were plenty of guys around to date, and enough to have crushes on. And there were some in the school environment as well."

Family:

"My father was in several businesses. He owned an import-export trading company, and for a while he worked in a Chinese butcher shop owned by some relatives. He also had his own business of producing monosodium glutamate which he sold to restaurants. And then he started one of the first suburban Chinese restaurants in New Jersey in the 1950s.

"My mother, because she did not speak any English, found work in Chinatown in a sewing factory. But both of them were pursuing ways of supporting a family that were not in line with their original interests. They were both college-educated people who had to essentially give up careers in their fields of interest to come to the States.

"We were a poor family, and when I look back at it now I can see that. There were six of us living in a three-room flat. There were two small bedrooms and one room in the middle which had a sink and bathtub in it. We had to draw a curtain around us every time we washed. The bathroom was in the hall and we shared it with other families. This living arrangement was supplemented by our father's store, which was where we had our kitchen and cooked our meals. In the back of the store was a hallway which we used as a kitchen. There was a living area in the back of this storefront and we spent most of our time there, so all we really did in the three-room apartment was sleep. My youngest sister and I slept in the same room as my parents and my two older sisters slept in a tiny bedroom of their own. As we grew up, there were times when the four of us would sleep in one bedroom. We were poor by middle class standards, but at the same time the families around us were living in the same situation. I never felt spiritually poor. I felt the difference when I visited beautiful homes and houses in suburban areas. When my sister and I went away for these summer programs sponsored by inner city churches that matched up city children with families in Connecticut, I remember visiting a family for two weeks, and living for the first time in my life, in a single family house with a big yard and a big kitchen. The little girl who was my age had a huge bedroom of her own, that was almost larger than the three room apartment that we lived in. I became aware of the difference in living standards in a situation like that. But I never really felt that I was poor.

"In looking back at the way my grandparents lived, I would say it was very poor. They lived in a garage that was in a city alley. It was a structure that was behind a building in Washington D.C.'s Chinatown that my grandfather was responsible for. And being a very humble man, my grandfather didn't see the need for a more comfortable environment. It was comfortable for him, so that was what he and his wife, my grandmother, would make do with. There was a bedroom in the upstairs portion of the garage with a little kerosene heater. And downstairs was a concrete floor of the garage. It was not covered with anything—just bare cement. He lived this way for over forty years. About a third of the downstairs was taken up with storage of very old things—like wood and glass. There was a junk pile stored in the garage and they lived in the other half of it. They set up a little living area of benches made out of wood and a wooden platform that my grandmother could lie down on. In the corner there was a two burner gas stove, that probably wouldn't meet anybody's fire codes these days. And they had a small old ice box. There was running water that came out of a pipe sticking out of the floor. There was a commode, but it was not one that you could flush. You had to pour water down there every time you used the bathroom. And that was it. If we took a bath, we had to use a tin bathtub. There wasn't any hot water, so we had to boil it. And there was no drain, so we would have to carry it and dump it down the toilet, or down a drain in the alley. And the running water from the pipe had to be caught by a tin bucket that rested on a cut off stool. So if you were going to wash your hand you had to wash it over the bucket, and then you dumped the water into the commode. My grandparents lived this way until my grandfather gave up his restaurant and retired in the mid-1960's. Then he moved to New York to be with us.

"We cared for family elders, respected them made them a part of our lives. I remember when my grandmother was still alive. There was a time when we had to face a decision of either putting my grandmother in a nursing home or keeping her at home. And it was pretty much unanimous, as diffi-

cult a woman as she was, she should stay at home, even in her handicapped state after her stroke."

Leaving Chinatown:

"I grew up in a very traditional family setting. I went to Chinese movies just about every week with my parents. As a first generation Chinese, I never even ventured a though of marrying anyone but a Chinese. So when my older sister married a non-Chinese, I was very, very upset. I was disappointed in her and felt betrayed.

"What changed my world completely was going away to a small college in Vermont to study Chinese in the end of my sophomore year. I had just been accepted to Princeton University for a special program and a summer of intensive Chinese at Middlebury College in Vermont was part of that.

"For the first eight weeks I knew nothing but the study hall, dorm, eating hall and language lab. That was my world in Middlebury. I kind of isolated myself from some of the students, and maybe in a way, I was reluctant to deal with it and rejected that kind of environment because it was so foreign to me. There were some Chinese Americans there—a few who were second or third generation. But the rest of the students studying Chinese were not Chinese. They were students from all over the country.

It wasn't until I left Chinatown that I realized what a homogenous community Chinatown really was. What a tight, closed environment we lived in.

"I was struck by the number of non-Chinese people who spoke the language very well and were studying the Chinese culture. They were studying history to an extent of being much more knowledgeable culturally of my heritage than my peers in Chinatown. I mean, to see a lecturer who acted more Chinese in terms of his mannerism and the way he spoke than some of my friends—when he was in fact Caucasian—was mind boggling. It was a shock. I was immensely impressed, and admired that. It was something that never occurred to me as being possible. I also met a Caucasian professor at Princeton, who had the grace, if you will, of a Chinese gentleman. He had more grace than many of the Chinese men that I have come across. The image of a Chinese scholar, of a Chinese gentleman that we grow up seeing in the movies—soft-spoken, very intellectual, who knew the social nuances of a Chinese setting, in terms of what to say, how to act, how to respond, patience—this man embodied much of that. He was married to a Chinese woman. I am sure the way he developed was very much affected by his marriage to this woman. If I closed my eyes, I would have seen someone who was Chinese.

"So it was like all different subcultures of this country converging on this little school. That was the first time for instance, I encountered a Californian—the free spirit of a Californian—who would take off on his Porche up the mountains of Vermont. You couldn't be in an environment like that without being affected by what was going on around you. And at the end of the eight weeks, I just broke down. I became more social. I was finally able to interact with them on their level, a level that was comfortable with me. It was like the layer of sheltered life I had led in Chinatown just slipped away. It took eight weeks, but I was finally comfortable. I don't know if it was purely a race issue, or if it was exposure to different social groups.

"I met my husband there that summer. He's the first of five generations not to carry on the family business. They had always lived in Wisconsin. He works for the government. He was one of the brighter students at Middlebury who really picked up on the language, and showed a real appreciation for the culture and history. I was very impressed.

"I couldn't have felt more loved from my first visit to meet his family. They were warm, loving, and they were not at all prejudiced against me. Or if they were, they certainly didn't show it. They had some concerns as to why their son was dating a Chinese girl before they met me. But they thought that was part of the weird things he was doing in terms of studying Chinese politics. But once I got there, I felt very much at home. And they were very much in favor of the wedding.

"My family was the complete opposite. My oldest sister married someone who was not Chinese and was the first in the family to do it. My father was very much against her marriage and tried to break them up anyway he could. And in the end, when he couldn't he did not speak to them for a long time. In my case, I was the second one to get married. He was so disappointed, hurt and maybe disgusted at the idea that this could repeat itself, that he didn't talk to me for a good six months before the wedding. So instead of doing everything he could to break us up, he just ignored me. It was

something I had expected. I had to consider that marriage very carefully because I knew all that I was giving up in terms of relationships with my family. So I was prepared for it, and in a way, respected his decision not to support me, and not to come to my wedding. In the end, about two days before I got married, my father and I had a long talk, perhaps worked out a mutual understanding, a respect for each other's decision, and things were fine after that. Now my relationship with my family is good. I often marvel at how well my husband and my father can communicate—even in Chinese.

"My children, unfortunately, do not speak Chinese. Language is very important to me. It would be very nice if they could. Unfortunately I don't offer them the environment where they can learn it and speak it on a regular basis to retain it. And when they were little I would teach them a couple of Chinese words, and it was confusing—more confusing than helpful. Even when we went to Hong Kong and lived for two years, it was still very difficult for them to learn, again because the kids they interacted with were not Chinese. But eventually I would like for them to make that decision on their own. I would encourage it. I don't go out of my way to force them or make them go to a Chinese school right now. But I hope that they will recognize the rich heritage that they come from and will eventually consider learning Chinese. But I want it to come from them. I don't want to force it.

"I've always seen myself as a Chinese—even today. Though there are time I recognize how Chinese American I really am. The music, the culture, the issues of the time, I can relate to them. So in looking back to the sixties to the things I enjoyed doing and the things that affected me, a lot of us in the States shared that. And I think that is very distinctly American, rather than Chinese."

Source:

Joann Faung Jean Lee. *Asian American Experiences in the United States: Oral Histories of First to Fourth Generation Americans from China, the Philippines, Japan, India, the Pacific Islands, Vietnam and Cambodia.* Jefferson, NC: McFarland & Co., 1991. pp. 38-44.

In the segregated South, Asians were caught in the middle, as Sam Sue's experience illustrates: "As a kid, I remember going to the theater and not really knowing where I was suppose to sit. Blacks were segregated then. Colored people had to sit upstairs, and white people sat downstairs. I didn't know where I was supposed to sit, so I sat in the white section, and nobody said anything."

The majority of the Chinese who settled in Mississippi formed a "middle class" of merchants who owned grocery stores that primarily catered to the black population, which was severely handicapped by dire poverty. Sue's family ran a "Mom and Pop" grocery store that sold "anything from shotgun shells to fresh meats to corn chop and hog shorts." Sue says his family and other Chinese occupied the same place in society as Jewish merchants—"marginal, economic roles." The white population shunned the Chinese, who had to live in the back of their stores or at the outskirts of town. With the expansion in recent years of large chain supermarkets, many of Mississippi's Chinese grocers have retired, gone out of business, or moved to urban areas.

GROWING UP IN MISSISSIPPI

Sam Sue is in his mid-thirties. He is a Chinese American and was born and raised in Mississippi. He speaks bitterly of his childhood. Today he is a lawyer in New York City.

"There is this shot in the opening scene of the movie, *Mississippi Burning*, where you see two water fountains. One is broken, and chipped, and water is dripping from it. The other is modern, and shining. A white guy goes up to the nice one, and the black kid goes up to the old one. I remember saying to myself, 'If I was in the scene, where would I drink?'

"As a kid, I remember going to the theatre and not really knowing where I was supposed to sit. Blacks were segregated then. Colored people had to sit upstairs, and white people sat downstairs. I didn't know where I was supposed to sit, so I sat in the white section, and nobody said anything. So I always had to confront those problems growing up. So these experiences were very painful.

"I guess I was always considered marginal with whites and blacks, though I think I got along better with blacks. I really didn't have any childhood friends. I just felt I had nothing in common with them. And I guess I felt there was this invisible barrier. I stayed mostly with my family—I have two older brothers and one older sister.

"I lived in a town called Clarksdale. At the time, there were twenty-five thousand to thirty thousand people there. In the sixties at the height, there were maybe forty to fifty Chinese families in town. Quite a number. They used to have Chinese

parties, and gatherings, and the funny thing about it was they all sort of came from the same village, or district.

"Chinese church was more of a social, rather than a religious event. I always hated the gatherings. I was basically ashamed of being Chinese. I think that's probably true for a lot of Chinese Americans—on the East and West Coasts. Whether they will acknowledge it is something else. But I think there is a lot of self-hatred, induced by society, culture, and circumstance. So I hated to go to these Chinese parties. Besides, it's not like you could date any Chinese girls, because they were all your cousins.

"I was lucky, in that the school I went to was mostly white, because our store was near the center of town, and the school was across the way. But most of the Chinese families lived in black areas so they went to black schools, and the kids got harassed a lot by the blacks. There was a lot of resentment against the Chinese by the blacks, because some of the Chinese families would rip off blacks, because it was part of giving store credit to the black farmers—they got surcharged excessively. Or they might be charged for things they didn't purchase.

"I didn't date at all—not in high school. It was totally unheard of. I remember very painful experiences of asking white girls to see if they were interested or anything, and them mumbling some excuse about being busy that night. But you knew what was going on. My cousin, for instance, had to take his cousin to the senior prom. I didn't think that kind of thing would be a good thing for me, so I didn't go to my senior prom. My reaction at the time to the dating scene was total alienation. I never considered dating a black girl. I don't know if it was racism, but I just felt there was no commonality. Because even though one wasn't accepted as a white at the time, dating a white was seen as going up—that was the thinking then. And I think Chinese women had it harder. I think it was okay for a Chinese man to date a non-Chinese, but not for a Chinese woman to go out with anything but a Chinese. Part of that was that Asian women are presumed to be exotic and submissive, and that's a common theme that runs through the stereotype images.

"Northerners see a Southern accent as a signal that you're a racist, you're stupid, or you're a hick. Regardless of what your real situation is. So I reacted to that by adapting the way I speak. If you talked to my brother, you would definitely know he was from the South. But as for myself, I remember customers telling my dad, "Your son sounds like a Yankee." I think I had a Southern drawl, but it wasn't pronounced. I also mimicked Northern accents because I was so alienated. Maybe I had this deep alienation, even as a kid. I used to read the Times. I'd see this stuff on the television. I grew up on the "Bowery Boys." The television and the radio were my links to civilization. I'd be waiting for eight P.M. to roll around, so that I could reach radio waves from Chicago or even New York. It was like Radio Free Europe for me."

Family: "My role model when I was growing up was my older brother because he was going to college when I was in elementary school. He was bilingual, so he was sort of the link for me between the old and the new country.

"My brother went to Ole Miss (University of Mississippi), and at one point, he was the first Chinese on campus invited to join an all-white fraternity. He was also in the ROTC. Actually it wasn't many years after that that they took away my father's and my oldest brother's citizenship. It was ironic—here he was teaching American government. He was about as American as you can get, and it sort of opened his eyes. Being denaturalized meant he was deportable, so he and my dad had to get waivers, and reapply for citizenship—doing the test again. So they had to be naturalized twice.

"There was a confession period for those who came into the country illegally. Many Chinese confessed, and things were okay. But what bugs me is my dad confessed, and he was nailed to the wall. He came into the U.S. illegally in the 1930s. Later on, he brought my mother and my oldest brother from China. The government took away his citizenship

by virtue of him coming here on false papers. He was denaturalized in 1965. That meant what the government gave, it could take away. I mean, Sue is not my real family name. I think it is Jiu."

The Family Store: "Dad said he went to Mississippi because that's where a good number of Chinese from his village had moved to. We, like other Chinese in Mississippi, ran a 'mom and Pop' grocery store. Anything from shotgun shells to fresh meats to corn chop and hog shorts. (Corn chop is feed for chicken, and hog shorts are grain for hogs.)

"My father would open his store about nine thirty in the morning, and close it about ten at night. We would eat after the store closed. We all ran the store, seven days a week. Only on Christmas would he close for half a day. He wouldn't even close the store when my brother got married. I had to run the store. I didn't want to go to Florida for my brother's wedding and let Dad stay home. So I let him go.

"It was a very rural area, and a number of Chinese had done well doing this. I guess economically they fit in to the area because their clientele were mostly black, rural farmers. I guess the black rural farmers couldn't get credit from white storekeepers. I guess that they presumed Chinese store keepers filled a need—providing credit to black farmers who couldn't otherwise get it. I remember for years on end, my father keeping records of people who owed him money. And that's what a lot of other Chinese did too. They filled that function.

"Our store was a social place, people would hang out on Friday, payday. So black customers would be hanging out, drinking beer, and eating sandwiches. It would be packed, with blacks and red necks. It was a place for them to meet.

"My dad didn't have much time to spend with me, so most of the time I would talk to the customers. We would kid around. I'd ask them, "How'd your skin go so black? And they would tell you stories to kid you. "Oh, I rolled down this river bank and got all this mud on me, and couldn't get it off." And I used to believe that stuff, and I thought blacks were really different. A lot of the blacks in our store chewed tobacco, so you'd think their spit was browner than white people's. But on a real gut level, you knew that people were treated different. And it's sort of weird on my parents' level, because on one hand they would make friends with a lot of black people, then on another, they would say racist things about them.

"Back then, the amount of poverty blacks suffered was profound. It doesn't come close to the experience of blacks in urban centers today. You're talking about people who didn't have running water, or who only got it recently. My father used to sell kerosene because people used it to light their lamps. I remember people using Clorox bleach to purify the water. It had chlorine in it, so they would let it sit in the water and kill the germs. Blacks were at the very low end of the scale, and the Chinese were sort of in between. We didn't really fit in. Very rich, aristocratic whites, were at the top end. Chinese really didn't have a place in society. Economically they were better than the blacks, but on a social scale, they didn't amount to very much. I think blacks saw us as Jews. We were in the same position as Jews were in the town. We all sort of played marginal, economic roles. There were quite a few Jews in town. They weren't accepted by blacks or whites either. I don't think whites knew what to make of us.

"Buying a store in California or some other urban center was expensive, whereas buying a store in Mississippi was cheap, so that's why a lot of Chinese families moved there. But you have to remember that there were still racial restrictions. A lot of the Chinese couldn't buy property, or had difficulty buying it. By the time my father paid off the mortgage, the owner said, 'I am not going to convey the title to you.' My understanding was that we had to threaten to sue him to get it."

Housing: "We had to live in the back of our store. It was tenement-like conditions, though we didn't know it at the time. I didn't know how poor we were until I left. Everyone slept in one big room. There was a kitchen in the back. We used to use the place to store goods too, so there would be boxes all around. If you went into the living room, you'd be sitting on a box of laundry detergent. We lived that way until 1970. It was only then that we could consider buying a house. We thought of buying a house in 1966, but it didn't work out. It was a white neighborhood, and the day before closing, we received a telephone call. Someone said, 'If you buy that house, we will burn it.' And we knew it was one of the neighbors calling. One of the Chinese families knew who had called—it was a Pepsi Cola distributor. Many of the Chinese families were so upset about what had happened that they boycotted Pepsi Cola for a long while. We didn't buy the house. The attitude was, if we're not wanted there, we just won't move there. Getting a house in a white neighborhood—it wasn't only impossible—there was no choice. You could either buy a house somewhere, if you could find an owner that would sell it to you, or you could buy property on the outskirts of town and build a house—which is what many Chinese families ended up doing. This way,

there were no problems from neighbors because there weren't any neighbors.

"Eventually, my family decided to buy a plot of land and build our home on the outskirts of town near some other Chinese families. We had to get a white man to buy the property and convey the title to us because certain property owners would not sell to Chinese families—and this was as recent as 1970."

Parents: "My father came to the United States in the 1930s from the Hoi Ping district of Canton. Like many Chinese of his generation, he went to California first. He didn't bring my mother. She came later. He worked in a restaurant with several other relatives around the San Francisco area. He said he borrowed money to come over, and the people working in the restaurant, including himself, were working to try to pay off his debt. They also wanted to save enough to go back to Hong Kong or China to get their wives. Eventually he did go back to China for my mother and my oldest brother.

Getting a house in a white neighborhood—it wasn't only impossible—there was no choice. . . you could buy property on the outskirts of town and build a house—which is what many Chinese families ended up doing.

"My dad was sixteen when he came to this country. He learned his English from customers, which would be blacks, or white rednecks. He did not finish school. He just finished the third or fourth grade in China. A friend of mine did a documentary on the Chinese in Mississippi, and she stayed with my dad in his home. She interviewed him, but never used the interview. She said his English was so strange that she would have had to use subtitles with it. He is a Chinese man who can speak English very poorly and does so with a black southern English dialect. It's quite difficult to understand. I can understand him, but it is difficult to communicate with him. And the gap gets even further when you want to get beyond the really simple language. Mom was less able to speak English than the others. One common thread that runs through many Asian lives is that parents spend so much time working for the future of their children, that they don't devote enough time to emotional needs. Either the parents are working and can't be there, or if they are at home, they are so tired they can't devote themselves to the children.

"The thing with Chinese parents is they make you feel like you owe them for the rest of your life—even when they're in the grave. My mother died when I graduated from college in 1977. My father made me feel terrible because he wanted me to work in the store even after I graduated. They had this idea that they were going to pass the store on to me, as stupid as it was. And they knew it was stupid. By the 1970s, the Chinese stores were declining due to mechanization. People used to be cotton pickers and we would sell these leather things for their knees so that when they crouched down they wouldn't have sore knee-caps. But with the advent of such things as cotton-picking machines and large supermarkets, it spelled doom for the Chinese store keepers. Also, kids my age didn't want to stay. Many chose to move to some urban area, such as Atlanta.

"My parents retired in 1978. But two months before the store officially closed, my mom died. It was a double shock for my dad. He not only lost his wife, but also his way of life. He had opened the store at nine AM and closed at ten PM, seven days a week. He did this for thirty years. He never went on trips. He just worked at the store. He felt there was nothing else.

"My dad is still in Mississippi. It's his life. He's been there since the Depression. It is all he knows. We actually tried to move him, but he is so attached to the area—not that he has affection for it, only that he's used to it—he feels it is home. There are still some Chinese there, though most have died, or moved away."

A Monolingual Chinese American: "I didn't learn how to use chopsticks until I left Mississippi. We never used chopsticks at home. I didn't even have any idea of what a Chinese restaurant was until I went to college. My first encounter with a Chinese restaurant was in Cleveland, Ohio. There just weren't any near where I was growing up.

"I can't speak the language, and you feel intimidated by it when you go into restaurants. Like you keep ordering the same dishes because those are the only dishes you can order. You feel that since you are Chinese, you should be able to speak to other people that look like you. Sometimes they have mistaken me for a *juk-kok* [foreign-born Chinese] and started talking to me; I can't understand a word.

"I don't feel Chinese, and I'm not. I identify myself as Asian American. I feel Chinese to some extent, but not necessarily to the extent of knowing much about Chinese culture or tradition. When I was in college, I met these Asian studies majors, and there was a certain amount of resentment in that they could speak the language and know the culture but they didn't know what it was like to be Chinese in a white society. They may have had a superficial understanding of the culture and language, but at the time I sort of felt they were expropriating our culture, and I felt very possessive about Asian women. It's like when I walk outside, I know I will be treated differently. It's not something I like saying. It's not even a political statement. It's just seeing reality. I'm not looking for, or am I supersensitive to, being treated as a Chinese person, or a nonwhite person, but it's there. It's even here in New York.

"One senses it in my profession as an attorney. You're arguing a case before a judge. And the other guy is white, and he's been around. The moment he walks in the office, it's like he says to the judge or the clerk, 'How's so and so?' But when I come in, it's like this stranger walks in—you don't belong here. But when he walks in, it's like family. I feel like I just walked into the wrong club—a place I don't belong.

"I never worked for a large firm. I never had the inclination to do that. It wasn't only a political choice, I really had nothing to talk to them about. There is this sort of Waspish mentality in the profession. I now work in a small Asian law firm. All the jobs I've had since college have been associated with Asian stuff.

"I don't have a burning desire to learn Chinese at this point, though it would be helpful in my work and in certain aspects of my life.

"If I went to China, I would be an American, and that is what I am in that context. So many of my views, as much as I may want to deny it, are American. If I were in a foreign country, I would be homesick. In terms of adopting American culture and values I'm an American. But in terms of feeling there is a difference, then I'm still Asian or Chinese. I feel different. Ask me what I feel different about, and I can't really say. It's not only that people may or may not treat you differently. It's that I am different.

"I left Mississippi in 1973. There was no future for me there. I was so alienated that even if I thought there was something concrete to be done there, I have such bad feelings for the place I wouldn't go back. Being Chinese in Mississippi was definitely a handicap.

Source:

Joann Faung Jean Lee. *Asian American Experiences in the United States: Oral Histories of First to Fourth Generation Americans from China, the Philippines, Japan, India, the Pacific Islands, Vietnam and Cambodia.* Jefferson, NC: McFarland & Co., 1991. pp. 3–9.

*T*he path Bette Bao Lord traveled to become a best-selling author and respected activist can best be described as circuitous, perhaps even a bit serendipitous. She was born in Shanghai, China, to Dora and Sandys Bao, an electrical engineer who worked for the Nationalist Chinese government. Shortly after the end of World War II, Sandys Bao left for an extended trip to the United States on behalf of his country, which was in the market for equipment to help rebuild China. As his assignment stretched from months into a year, he grew lonesome for his family. In 1946, he was finally given permission to send for his wife and two of his three daughters, including eight-year-old Bette. (An infant daughter, Sansan, stayed behind with relatives because her parents felt she was too young to make the long journey.) The Baos settled briefly in Brooklyn, New York, where Bette enrolled in public school. Later, they moved to Teaneck, New Jersey.

The family was still in the United States when civil war erupted in China between the Nationalist government and Communist rebels led by Mao Zedong. By the time the Communists claimed victory over the Nationalists in 1949, the Baos knew that they could not return home and that trying to spirit Sansan out of China would be dangerous if not impossible. So they remained in New Jersey, and it was there that Bette grew up.

An excellent student who was well-liked by her classmates, Bao graduated from high school in 1954 and went on to college at Tufts University in Boston. Although her intention was to major in chemistry because "every Chinese child is supposed to grow up to be an '-ist,' as in scientist," as she explained to a Chicago Tribune reporter, both she and her professors agreed that she would probably be happier in another field. So she switched to history and earned her bachelor's degree in 1959. The following year, she obtained her master's degree in international relations from the Fletcher School of Law and Diplomacy (also at Tufts).

Bao then headed to the University of Hawaii, where she began as an assistant to the director of the school's East-West Center and within a short time headed her own department. She left in 1961 for a job in Washington, D.C., as an advisor to the director of the Fulbright Exchange Program. There she became reacquainted with a former Tufts classmate, Winston Lord, who was then working in the U.S. Foreign Service. They married in 1963.

Meanwhile, Sansan Bao—separated from her family for more than fifteen years—was finally allowed to leave China, ostensibly to visit her ailing mother in Hong Kong. The "illness" was just a ruse, however, that enabled the Baos to help Sansan escape to America. Friends who were familiar with her lifetime of hardship under the Communist regime in China and eventual reunion with her family thought the story would make fascinating reading, and her sister agreed. When Bette could not find anyone else to take on the project (the fact that Sansan spoke no English was a major obstacle), she quit her job and tackled it herself. The result was Eighth Moon: The True Story of a Young Girl's Life in Communist China, published by Harper in 1964 to wide commercial and critical success.

From 1965 until 1967, Bette taught and performed modern dance in Geneva, Switzerland, where her husband had been sent as a member of the U.S. negotiating team involved in international tariff discussions. Not long after their return home,

Winston joined the administration of President Richard Nixon as a top aide to foreign policy advisor Henry Kissinger. In this capacity, Winston was very much involved in the events leading up to official U.S. recognition of Red China in 1972. The following year, Bette accompanied her husband on a journey to the land of her birth—her first visit since she had left there as a child. Her impressions of modern China eventually found their way into a historical novel she worked on during the late 1970s entitled Spring Moon. Like her first book, it was a hit with both readers and critics and was even nominated for a National Book Award.

In 1985, the Lords returned to China when Winston was named U.S. ambassador. There Bette once again devoted herself to cultural pursuits, becoming active in local theater and turning the American Embassy in Beijing into a meeting place for writers and artists. She also provided valuable assistance to her husband as an unofficial diplomat of sorts, guiding him through what proved to be an especially tumultuous time in Chinese history. Just as his term was coming to an end during the spring of 1989, student-led pro-democracy demonstrations erupted in at least twenty major cities, including Beijing. Although Winston had to return to Washington in April, Bette stayed behind and provided commentary on the unfolding events for CBS News and Newsweek magazine. She left China just days before exhilaration gave way to tragedy in Beijing's Tiananmen Square on June 6, when Army troops opened fire on the unarmed demonstrators, killing an estimated five thousand people and injuring thousands more. Hundreds of students and workers were subsequently arrested, and many were executed or imprisoned.

The horror of what occurred in Tiananmen Square to so many of those with whom she had talked and shared dreams of a brighter future compelled Lord to take action. Shortly after her return to the United States, she wrote the nonfiction book Legacies: A Chinese Mosaic, a selection of oral histories she had gathered while living in China that she hoped would "put faces and stories with what happened there [in Tiananmen Square]." Like her previous works, it was very well received

The events of Tiananmen Square also catapulted Lord into the human rights movement. In 1991, she joined the board of directors of Freedom House, a New York City-based organization (co-founded by Eleanor Roosevelt) that monitors and works for human rights around the world while promoting democracy as the key to preserving those rights. Two years later, she became its chairwoman.

It was in connection with her role at Freedom House that Lord appeared in Washington, D.C., before the foreign affairs committee of the U.S. House of Representatives on March 10, 1993, to offer her views on the role of U.S. foreign policy in strengthening human rights and democracy around the world. As she made clear in both her testimony and in the written statement that accompanied it, she regards American-style democracy as "the most successful model for nurturing a vibrant society, responsive government, a free press, effective unions, domestic harmony and global cooperation." At the same time, she condemns "neo-isolationism and disengagement from world affairs" now that Communism no longer appears to pose a threat as "precisely the wrong prescriptions at the wrong time.... In the end, the true power of America is its ideas."

BETTE BAO LORD'S SPEECH BEFORE THE HOUSE FOREIGN AFFAIRS COMMITTEE

As an immigrant, I have a singular honor to testify before this committee. As the chairman of Freedom House, I have the opportunity to speak on behalf of a bipartisan, nonprofit organization founded fifty years ago by Eleanor Roosevelt and Wendell Wilkie, on the subject that is our reason for being, promoting democracy and human rights.

While my written statement addresses your important questions in a more orthodox way, permit me to speak personally. I do so to provide a different perspective, one that native-born Americans cannot offer naturally. Taught to question every premise, they do not flinch from dissecting America's failings. It is a most admirable trait. But such clinical probes overlook the intangibles through which people living in distant lands discern America. I know. I am able to disappear among them and eavesdrop.

To the masses denied dignity by their rulers America is not just another country with material goods that they covet. It is the embodiment of intangibles—liberty, conscience, hope. The sun we enjoy blithely, they behold as a beacon from afar.

I recall how curious my Chinese friends were watching our presidential debates, but what they viewed as an earth-shaking phenomenon totally escaped even me. They were awestruck by the fact that a lowly TV journalist—apologies to Dan, Tom, and Peter—could politely, but in no uncertain terms, tell the paramount leader of the most powerful nation in the world that his time was up.

How confounding, just when technology and humanity's newest trials mock walls, borders, and oceans, some extol the efficacy of withdrawing to our shores or, worse, ethnically correct enclaves. Just when human rights, however mislabeled or mangled, must be given lip service by even the most repressive regimes, some Americans balk at invoking them at all. Just when there is but one superpower left, some question America's need to stay engaged.

How ironic, just when totalitarian states have imploded and democracy holds sway among more peoples than ever before, Americans are losing faith in the wisdom of promoting freedom and human rights abroad.

Some wonder if certain peoples will always be incapable or averse to ruling themselves. They fail to acknowledge that no man or woman has ever aspired to be a pawn. On the contrary, regardless of culture and history, everyone yearns to be the master of his or her own fate.

Some consider it culturally chauvinistic to project our own values elsewhere. They fail to understand that freedom is not a matter of "Westernization," it is the core of modernization. They also fail to recognize that human rights are not made in America, that they are universal, that every nation belonging to the United Nations has pledged to honor them, that international organizations from the CSCE to the OAS invoke them in their work.

"To the masses denied dignity by their rulers America is not just another country with material goods that they covet. It is the embodiment of intangibles—liberty, conscience, hope."

Some fret that promoting democracy and human rights is a luxury we can ill afford. They fail to understand that this pursuit not only serves our values but interests. Spreading democracy not only warms American hearts but cools foreign threats. What hundreds of billions worth of arms failed to do, rallies of converts did. Gone, the Berlin Wall, gone, the Warsaw Pact. Democracies do not war against one another, democracies make better partners. Democracies do not ignore the environment, shelter terrorists, or spawn refugees. Democracies honor human rights.

Now, for the third time in this century, destiny calls. America must step forth. We must earn the right to enjoy our myriad blessings. I speak about only two. First, the vitality of Americans. Where does it come from? From everywhere. Apologies to Michael Jackson; We are the world. Second, the stature of America. Believe me, despite all the venom the most arrogant dictators may spew they care profoundly where Uncle Sam points a finger, shakes hands, or pats them on the back. They hate losing face, but they crave respectability.

Thus, vitality and stature endow America with extraordinary gifts for making a difference in the

Bette Bao Lord

world. Like liberty, conscience hope, they are intangibles. To be true to our legacy, to enrich our future, America must invest in freedom.

Source:

The Future of U.S. Foreign Policy (Part II): Functional Issues—Hearings Before the Committee on Foreign Affairs, House of Representatives, 103rd Congress, 1st Session, U.S. Government Printing Office, 1993, pp. 260-261, 312-319.

*"**I** am not exactly sure when it happened, but somewhere during my childhood I decided I wasn't American." Thus observed Helen Zia in* Essence *magazine, recalling her sense of feeling like an "outsider" among her friends because she "didn't match the national color scheme." In a society that only recognized white and black during the 1950s and 1960s, Asian Americans were the "forgotten minority," and their concerns were of little import to the rest of the country. Zia has devoted her life to countering that trend, not just as an activist on behalf of Asian Americans, but for all people whose rights to justice and equality have often been ignored by mainstream society.*

Born in Newark, New Jersey, of parents who immigrated from China, Zia grew up amid the traditions of two very different cultures. "I liked hot dogs, Kool-Aid, apple pie and the two-tone Chevy wagon my dad drove," she has said. "But I ate my Spam with rice and could use chopsticks as well as an abacus." By the time she was eight, however, she and her family had endured so much racial prejudice on account of their perceived "foreignness" that Zia concluded "America didn't want me, and in that case I didn't want to be a part of it." During her teenage years, she very much identified with the black civil rights movement and its leaders. But she was also slowly becoming aware of other battles waiting to be fought.

After receiving her bachelor's degree from Princeton University in 1973, Zia worked briefly for the U.S. Department of State as a public affairs specialist before enrolling in the Tufts University School of Medicine, which she attended until 1975. She then headed to Detroit, where she pursued graduate studies in industrial relations at Wayne State University and was a factory worker for Chrysler Corpo-

ration from 1977 until 1979. During this same period, she began her career in journalism, contributing pieces to local and national publications.

It was also in Detroit that Zia became involved in a landmark civil rights case stemming from the racially-motivated beating death of Vincent Chin, a Chinese American. In June, 1982, the twenty-seven-year-old draftsman accompanied three friends to a bar to celebrate his upcoming marriage. Also in the bar that evening was an unemployed white auto worker named Ronald Ebens who blamed his joblessness on the shrinking market share of U.S. car manufacturers. Thinking Chin was Japanese, Ebens made some racial slurs that led to a fight, and all the participants were forced to leave. Later that night, Ebens and his stepson, Michael Nitz (who had also been involved in the bar incident), spotted Chin at a fast-food restaurant. They waited for him to come out and then, while Nitz held Chin, Ebens beat him with a baseball bat. Chin died several days later. Although initially charged with second-degree murder, Ebens and Nitz bargained their way into pleading guilty to manslaughter instead, for which they were fined about $3,000 each and put on probation for three years.

Asian Americans everywhere reacted with outrage at this clearly unjust outcome. Zia was one of the founders of American Citizens for Justice, the organization that sprang up to seek justice for Vincent Chin and to counter anti-Asian prejudice. Members of this group circulated and helped raise funds for legal expenses to challenge the Chin decision. Zia served as the campaign's national spokesperson and was elected president of the group for two terms. Nationwide protests eventually forced federal authorities to investigate, and Ebens was indicted for depriving Chin of his civil rights. While he was tried and found guilty, he saw his conviction reversed on appeal. A civil suit against Ebens proved more successful, however, and Chin's estate was awarded $1.5 million. Despite this less-than-satisfying resolution to the case, Zia and other Asian Americans counted it as a partial victory because it marked the first time they were able to demonstrate a direct link between anti-Asian prejudice and increasing rates of violence against Asian Americans.

Zia moved into the field of journalism on a full-time basis in 1983 when she joined the staff of Metropolitan Detroit *magazine as an associate editor; leaving in 1985 to become executive editor of* Meetings and Conventions *magazine, part of the Murdoch Magazines/NewsAmerica group located in Secaucus, New Jersey. She remained with the company for the next four years, serving as editorial director of* Travel Weekly *from 1986 to 1987 and then as editor-in-chief of* Meetings and Conventions *magazine from 1987 to 1989.*

In 1989, Zia moved to New York to become executive editor of Ms. *magazine, a post she held until 1992. She then headed to San Francisco, where she was vice-president and editor-in-chief of WorldView Systems (an electronic publishing company) through 1994. She now works primarily as a free-lance writer, lecturer, and media consultant. Zia is also a contributing editor to* Ms. *magazine and is at work on her own books of fiction and nonfiction. In 1995, she served as co-editor of the reference book* Notable Asian Americans.

In addition to her efforts on behalf of Asian Americans, Zia is also active in the feminist and gay/lesbian movements as well as other social justice causes. All of these interests figure prominently in her speeches, of which she may give up to two dozen or so in the course of a typical year. On August 27, 1992, for example, Zia was in Washington, D.C., to deliver the keynote address at the annual convention of the Asian American Journalists Association (AAJA), a group to which she belongs. The subject of her talk was media coverage of Asian Americans—particu-

larly by other Asian Americans. The following year, on March 6, 1993, Zia spoke at the "Equality and Harm Conference" at the University of Chicago Law School. Her focus that day was on hate crimes—specifically sexual assaults and murder—against women of color.

In the following speech, delivered at the Sixth Annual Gay Asian Pacific Alliance (GAPA) conference in San Francisco on January 29, 1994, Zia weaves together several of her interests as she reflects on the issue of achieving visibility and empowerment for gay and lesbian Asian Americans. Zia herself provided a copy of her remarks.

HELEN ZIA'S SPEECH BEFORE THE GAY ASIAN PACIFIC ALLIANCE

I'm truly honored and proud to be a part of GAPA's celebration of the diversity of Gay and Bisexual Asian Pacific Islander Men. Even before I moved to San Francisco a year and a half ago, I had heard of this magazine called *Lavender Godzilla* published by a really right-on group called GAPA that was doing incredible work to increase visibility of gay and bisexual men of Asian Pacific ancestry, to provide support around issues of coming out, community and family, HIV/AIDS, and to build powerful role models.

Building role models for visibility and empowerment is no small task. When you look in this wide world around us, where can you find us, the Asian Pacific Islander gay/lesbian/bisexual/transgender people?

Will you find us in media portrayals and popular images of the gay and lesbian community? No, you won't find us there. The quintessential standard for who is queer is white and male.

Will you find us in the leadership of the national gay and lesbian organizations and institutions? With a few exceptions that you can count on one hand, you won't find us there, either.

If you go home to the diverse Asian American communities across the United States where many of our parents and families are, you won't find us there. After all, our aunties and uncles and cousins watch TV, too, and have concluded that "homosexuality is white man's problem."

And this shouldn't come as a surprise either, because if we were each to trace our roots across the Pacific and visit one of our many sexually-repressive ancestral homelands in search of gays, lesbians and bisexuals, we'd again be very hard put to find our gay sisters and brothers—except perhaps in

mental wards, prisons, or living as outcasts who are infected with the dreaded Western "disease" of homosexuality.

Speaking of sexual repression, when we think about the popular concept of Asian sexuality, what do we find? Asian men in general are viewed as asexual, so being "gay" and "Asian" is an impossible construct. Meanwhile, Asian women are viewed as supersexual exotic creatures who are hot for white men, so it's similarly not possible to think of us as lesbians.

All this negation makes it incredibly tough to be a queer API [Asian Pacific Islander]. When there isn't a group like GAPA around, where in the world can we find validation of ourselves, let alone find positive images that build our sense of self-esteem and self-respect?

I know the damage this can do from my own personal experience, as I suspect most of you do. When I first became aware of my attraction to the same sex as a kid, I didn't have a place for it in my consciousness. And coming from an immigrant Chinese family, we never spoke of sex—ever. I got my sex education from reading the *Encyclopaedia Britannica*. Having read the entry on reproduction several times, I can assure you that there was no mention of homosexuality.

When I finally got the courage to go to lesbian bars, it was great to be around women-loving women, but I didn't exactly feel like I had found my home, either. All the dykes I met were white and I didn't know of any Asian lesbians. That situation made me feel like I couldn't be a real lesbian. And because I didn't think I could be a real lesbian, I also didn't feel I could be attractive to real lesbians.

But the worst part was how my fellow Asian American community activists reacted when they realized I was hanging out with a lot of white lesbians. This was back in the early 70s, before "gay" was an accepted word yet, and it was at the height of the Asian American movement and the radical Third World liberation movements, the days when the revolution was right around the corner.

I was one of those Asian American movement activists, and my strongest sense of myself at that time was as an Asian American. But my Asian American comrades—my Asian community/family—had determined that homosexuality was "counterrevolutionary" and a "petit bourgeois degenerate deviation." They called a special meeting to investigate my sexual proclivities. I remember sitting through that difficult meeting in rolled-up t-shirt sleeves and a leather bomber jacket that was too big for me, already confused and anxious about my sexuality. As you can imagine, this didn't help my coming-out process.

Luckily for me, I finally found my way to those Sapphic pleasures, and over time have struggled through many issues like being out in the straight Asian Pacific Islander community. Coming out to Asian community groups has its lighter moments. A few years ago, I was delivering a speech to the Asian American Journalists Association national convention in Washington, D.C., and the speech was going to be carried on C-SPAN. I tried hard to write something into the speech about being a lesbian, but it just wasn't going to fit the topic of my speech. So I asked the person who was going to introduce me to be sure to include the fact that I was a lesbian in the introduction—you know, just to blend it in with the other stuff and not to make it a big deal. She said "Fine, no problem." But when it came time for her to stand in front of AAJA and the C-SPAN cameras to introduce me, here's what she said: "Helen Zia is a longtime feminist and Asian community activist and she's a l-l-l-lesbian.. .." And then she sort of coughed, fiddled with the microphone, and said, "Is the microphone working? Did you all hear that, she's a l-l-l-lesbian.. .."

I just thought, "Well, so much for subtlety." But if the alternative was invisibility, I'm glad she went the other way. Because the price we end up paying for this invisibility is far too high. We have all experienced our own forms of personal hell as a result of being invisible. But there are other costs, too.

We all know how hate crimes bias-motivated crimes against gay men and lesbians have been increasing at frightening rates; in areas like Oregon and Colorado, where the anti-gay initiatives have

Helen Zia

been organized, it's open season against us. We also know that anti-Asian hate crimes have been increasing, especially as racist hysteria against Asian imports and Asian immigrants has heated up. Well, we—Asian Pacific queers—are directly in the fire for both hate trends.

Yet how can we effectively respond to and counter attacks when they happen? The unfortunate answer is that we can't when we're invisible to a community that is unable—or unwilling—to see us.

The quintessential standard for who is queer is white and male.

I'm sad to say that there have been several incidents of hate violence against Asian American gays and lesbians as well as an ambivalent response by our Asian communities. Only last year we witnessed the near fatal beating of Loc Minh Truong by a group of teenage boys near a local gay bar in Laguna Beach, California. Truong, a Vietnamese refugee who was fifty-five years old at the time of the attack, was so badly beaten that authorities could not initially determine his race. His left eye was out of his socket and a rock was impaled nearly an inch into his skull. Truong was in critical condition for several days; police described the attack as one blow short of murder.

Truong's attackers were apprehended and two pleaded guilty to attempted murder, felonious aggravated assault, and committing a hate crime against Loc Minh Truong. The attackers admitted to saying to Truong, "You fucking faggot. . .we're going to get you!" and "If a fag approached me, I'd beat him on the spot." They denied that Truong's race was a factor in the beating. Asian community anti-Asian violence activists monitored the case, but Truong's family and the local Vietnamese community denied that he is gay and did not want to associate him with being gay. Much Asian community energy went into speculating whether Truong was gay and to try to establish a race-biased motive instead. In point of fact, Truong's actual sexual orientation is irrelevant, since his attackers perceived him to be gay, and since sexual orientation and race are both protected under the California hate crimes law.

Does this mean that our Asian Pacific Islander community would be less likely to support a hate crime victim because of his or her sexual orientation? Well, as long as we remain invisible to our API communities, we make it easy for homophobia to rule their reactions.

Homophobia may have been the reason that there was little community response to the 1988 murder of Paul Him Chow, a gay Chinese American who was killed in New York City's Greenwich Village. Homophobia and racism may explain the subsequent lack of aggressive police investigation.

And both anti-gay prejudice in the API community and racism came into play in the 1991 murder of Konerak Sinthasimphone, a fourteen-year-old Laotian boy, by serial killer Jeffrey Dahmer. Then, the racist and homophobic police were all too willing to turn a naked, bleeding fourteen-year-old [over] to Dahmer, accepting the word of a white man that this Asian child was his adult lover. And after the atrocities were exposed, our Asian communities were again silent.

Actually, the only time I recall hearing of a grassroots community discussion of homosexuals was in the context of a community-wide alert against child sexual molesters of Asian boys—and the public posters suggesting that homosexuals were lying in wait to molest their sons. Not only was this homophobic, but also a complete heterosexual fantasy, since it's a well-established fact that the vast majority of child sexual abuse is committed by heterosexual men, and mostly toward girls.

As we all know, this silence, coupled with ignorance, can only mean death when it comes to a community-based response to HIV/AIDS. At a time when API men and women of all sexual orientations are at extremely high risk of HIV infection—largely because of community denial—we cannot afford to live with this invisibility.

That's why GAPA and the handful of other Asian gay, lesbian, bi, and transgender organizations are playing such a critical historic role today. Fighting for a spot in the Chinatown Lunar New Year parade, for example, is exactly the kind of VISIBILITY that we need to take on the challenges of today *and* tomorrow.

Looking forward to the future, what do we see? In six short years, we will be entering a new century, already dubbed the "Century of Asia and the Pacific." There will be a tremendous transfer of economic and political might to the nations of the Asia and the Pacific Rim, with incredible ramifications for APIs in the U.S.

To the extent that national visibility and power gets transferred to a sense of individual esteem, think of all the Asian gay men and lesbians who will potentially become more empowered. How many more will find the courage to be true to themselves and come out?

Let's do the math. In the U.S. today, there are 3.4 million Asian Pacific Islanders. Within a decade, that should more than double to 8-10 million, or 800,000 to 1 million gay, lesbian, bi, transgender Asian Americans. Next, I challenge you to think globally. Looking across the Pacific, there's 1-plus billion people in China, 1 billion in India, plus several hundreds of millions more in other Asian nations. At least 3 billion Asian people in the world, and if 10 percent are gay, lesbian, and bi, that's 300 million Asian Pacific Islander queers! It's more than the entire population of the United States—that's a lot of invisible queer power looking to come out!

And where will all these 300 million Asian gays, lesbians, and bisexuals be turning to for role models on what their lives can be and how they can be recognized for who they are?

I believe they'll be looking right here at GAPA and other courageous Asian queers, at all of you to learn who they are, to get reassurance that they have a right to live and love in dignity and respect and that as proud Asian queers they have an important contribution to make to their communities. That is the historic role and responsibility we have to play *today*.

So while you go about your daily lives and do all the important programs that you do for GAPA, think about how we must each strive to be good role models for each other and all those many other APIs who are desperately seeking some affirmation of who they are so they can be out and proud too. And get ready for the day that you'll have to crank out 100 million-plus membership cards. Now that's Lavender Godzilla power!

Source:

Helen Zia, transcript of speech delivered January
    29, 1994, before the Sixth Annual Gay Asian
    Pacific Alliance (GAPA) Conference held in
    San Francisco, CA.

CHOCTAWS

The Choctaw Indians were a North American Indian tribe that originally settled in the area now known as Mississippi. Although the Choctaws lived peacefully with the U.S. government for years, the Removal Act of 1830 forced them to migrate westward to what is now Oklahoma. The Choctaws, along with the other members of the "Five Civilized Tribes" were forced to sell their lands against their wishes. The federal government instituted a "detribalization" policy which left members of the Five Civilized Tribes with little authority over their own affairs. Today the Choctaw Indian reservation consists of ten and one-half counties in southeast Oklahoma. The Choctaw Nation is governed by twelve members of the Tribal Council each of whom represent a district within the Choctaw Nation. One of the central objectives of the Choctaw government is achieving economic self-sufficiency. The historical treatment of the Choctaws by the U.S. government explains why the nation places such a strong emphasis on independence.

In 1830, after peacefully co-existing with American colonists in Mississippi the U.S. government decided to force the Choctaws to move west to Oklahoma. The tribe was moved out in three phases in 1831, 1832, and 1833. The Choctaws were given two weeks to gather crops for the journey and were told that they had to leave all of their possessions behind including their livestock. The government promised them they would be compensated for these items when they were resettled. The poorly organized relocation project was a disaster for the Choctaws who trusted federal officials to bring them safely to a new land that was to replace their community. Thousands of Choctaws died during the journey from starvation, disease, and exposure to freezing temperatures. Before his departure to Oklahoma from Mississippi a Choctaw Indian wrote a farewell letter to the American people in which he wished prosperity to the state of Mississippi and made a plea to the government not to do further harm to Native Americans. "We hope, in the name of justice, that another outrage may never be committed against us, and that we may for the future be cared for as children, and not driven about as beasts, which are benefitted by a change of pasture."

It is fair to say that the government of United States did not honor the request of this Choctaw Indian. In fact shortly after the Choctaws were driven westward, in 1838 a similar "Trail of Tears and Death" was laid by the Cherokee Indians as they were driven off their lands in North Carolina, South Carolina, and Tennessee. Of the treatment of Native Americans by the U.S. government throughout history Moquin and Van Doren contend that "it can be asserted without qualification that no other ethnic group has been so consistently treated with such malevolence over so long a period of time."

FAREWELL LETTER TO THE AMERICAN PEOPLE

To the American People.

It is with considerable diffidence that I attempt to address the American people, knowing and feeling sensibly my incompetency; and believing that your highly and well improved minds could not be well entertained by the address of a Choctaw. But having determined to emigrate west of the Mississippi river this fall, I have thought proper in bidding you farewell, to make a few remarks of my views and the feelings that actuate me on the subject of our removal.

Believing that our all is at stake and knowing that you readily sympathize with the distressed of every country, I confidently throw myself on your indulgence and ask you to listen patiently. I do not arrogate to myself the prerogative of deciding upon the expediency of the late treaty, yet I feel bound as a Choctaw, to give a distinct expression of my feelings on that interesting, (and to the Choctaw) all important subject.

We were hedged in by two evils, and we chose that which we thought least. Yet we could not recognize the right that the state of Mississippi had assumed to legislate for us. Although the legislature of the state were qualified to make laws for their own citizens, that did not qualify them to become law makers to a people who were so dissimilar in manners and customs as the Choctaws are to the Mississippians. Admitting that they understood the people, could they remove that mountain of prejudice that has ever obstructed the streams of justice, and prevented their salutary influence from reaching my devoted countrymen? We as Choctaws rather chose to suffer and be free, than live under the degrading influence of laws, where our voice could not be heard in their information.

Much as the state of Mississippi has wronged us, I cannot find in my heart any other sentiment than an ardent wish for her prosperity and happiness.

I could cheerfully hope that those of another age and generation may not feel the effects of those oppressive measures that have been illiberally dealt out to us; and that peace and happiness may be their reward. Amid the gloom and honors of the present separation, we are cheered with a hope that ere long we shall reach our destined home, and that nothing short of the basest acts of treachery will ever be able to wrest it from us, and that we may live free. Although your ancestors won freedom on

the fields of danger and glory, our ancestors owned it as their birthright, and we have had to purchase it from you as the vilest slaves buy their freedom.

Yet it is said that our present movements are our own voluntary acts—such is not the case. We found ourselves like a benighted stranger, following false guides, until he was surrounded on every side, with fire or water. The fire was certain destruction, and feeble hope was left him of escaping by water. A distant view of the opposite shore encourages the hope; to remain would be utter annihilation. Who would hesitate, or would say that his plunging into the water was his own voluntary act? Painful in the extreme is the mandate of our expulsion. We regret that it should proceed from the mouth of our professed friend, and for whom our blood was commingled with that of his bravest warriors, on the field of danger and death.

But such is the instability of professions. The man who said that he would plant a stake and draw a line around us, that never should be passed, was the first to say he could not guard the lines, and drew up the stake and wiped out all traces of the line. I will not conceal from you my fears, that the present grounds may be removed—I have my foreboding—who of us can tell after witnessing what has already been done, what the next force may be.

I ask you in the name of justice, for repose for myself and my injured people. Let us alone—we will not harm you, we want rest. We hope, in the name of justice, that another outrage may never be committed against us, and that we may for the future be cared for as children, and not driven about as beasts, which are benefitted by a change of pasture.

Taking an example from the American government, and knowing the happiness which its citizens enjoy, under the influence of mild republican institutions, it is the intention of our countrymen to form a government assimilated to that of our white brethren in the United States, as nearly as their condition will permit.

We know that in order to protect the rights and secure the liberties of the people, no government approximates so nearly to perfection as the one to which we have alluded. As east of the Mississippi we have been friends, so west we will cherish the same feelings with additional fervor; and although we may be removed to the desert, still we shall look with fine regard, upon those who have promised us their protection. Let that feeling be reciprocated.

Friends, my attachments to my native land is strong—that cord is now broken; and we must go forth as wanderers in a strange land! I must go—let me entreat you to regard us with feelings of kindness, and when the hand of oppression is stretched against us, let me hope that every part of the United States, filling the mountains and valleys, will echo and say stop, you have no power, we are the sovereign people, and our friends shall no more be disturbed. We ask you for nothing that is incompatible with your other duties.

We go forth sorrowful, knowing that wrong has been done. Will you extend to us your sympathizing regards until all traces of disagreeable oppositions are obliterated, and we again shall confidence in the professions of our white brethren.

Here is the land of our progenitors, and here are their bones; they left them as a sacred deposit, and we have been compelled to venerate its trust; it is dear to us yet we cannot stay, my people are dear to me, with them I must go. Could I stay and forget them and leave them to struggle alone, unaided, unfriended, and forgotten by our great father? I should then be unworthy the name of a Choctaw, and be a disgrace to my blood. I must go with them; my destiny is cast among the Choctaw people. If they suffer, so will I; if they prosper, then I will rejoice. Let me again ask you to regard us with feelings of kindness.

Source:

Great Documents in American Indian History, edited by Wayne Moquin with Charles van Doren. New York: Praeger Publishers, 1973. pp. 151-153.

*T*he General Allotment Act of 1887, which separated Native American lands into smaller areas which the federal government could more easily control, is sometimes referred to as the Dawes Act. Its author was Henry Laurens Dawes (1816-1903), a Massachusetts representative and later senator who went on to chair the Dawes Commission, which oversaw implementation of the Act.

Dawes left the senate in 1893, the beginning of the second term for Grover Cleveland (1837-1908). Cleveland's his first term, when he signed the Dawes Act into law, had been a successful one; but his second term—following four years of Benjamin Harrison's presidency—saw numerous economic and labor problems. In an effort to ease the financial pressures in the East, Cleveland approved the Sherman Silver Purchase Act of 1890, which angered western farmers hoping for inflation to improve their own troubled circumstances.

No doubt, then, Cleveland was eager to show his western constituents measurable "progress" on the Indian question. At that time, the Secretary of the Interior, a position whose responsibilities include the development of natural resources and the preservation of public lands, was primarily concerned with issues involving Native American lands. Hence the occasion for Cleveland's May 4, 1895 letter to Secretary of the Interior Hoke Smith (1855-1931), a former Georgia newspaperman and future senator.

At that time the Dawes Commission, under the direction of Secretary Smith, was in negotiations with the "Five Civilized Tribes," which included the Choctaws, Cherokees, Chickasaws, Creeks, and Seminoles. All five tribes had originated in what is now the southeastern United States, and all had been forced to move westward—the Choctaws first among them—in the 1830s.

The Five Civilized Tribes had settled in what was then called Indian Territory, which later became the state of Oklahoma. Their adoption of a legislative form of government modeled on that of the United States had earned them the adjective "civilized," and no doubt many tribal leaders believed that thenceforth they would receive fair treatment at the hands of Washington. But the Choctaws' experience in the Civil War had already boded ill for future U.S.-Choctaw relations.

After Union troops all but deserted Indian Territory for the war back east, the Choctaws had sided with the Confederates, an allegiance that had virtually no effect on the war itself. But with the end of hostilities in 1865, Washington used the Choctaws' alliance with the Confederacy as justification for an 1866 treaty that took large tracts of land out of Choctaw hands.

Again, leaders of the Choctaws and other nations might have thought their people could then proceed peaceably with their lives; in fact they were seeing the beginning of the end of their control over Oklahoma. In 1890, with white settlers moving in, the western part of the area became the Oklahoma Territory. Settlers demanded the removal of Indians from the area, and the result was the formation of the Dawes Commission in 1893.

By 1895, the tide was clearly in favor of the United States—and so obviously against the Five Civilized Tribes—that President Cleveland and others could easily afford to take a gentle, conciliatory tone. Hence the wording of the president's letter to Secretary Smith, in which he related that "I am especially desirous that there shall be no reason, in all time to come, to charge the [Dawes C]ommission with any unfair dealing with the Indians . . . ."

Cleveland, undoubtedly with the utmost of sincerity, went on to outline what he considered fair treatment for the Choctaws and other tribes: U.S. citizenship, with all the rights and privileges such citizenship entailed. He then concluded with a wish that by arriving at an agreement with all due deliberation, the Dawes Commission and the Five Civilized Tribes could avoid the many "broken pledges and false promises" that might attend a more hastily penned agreement.

In fact there were few promises left to break, at least from the federal government's standpoint, and it is interesting to note the difference in tone between that of Cleveland, the man at the top, and Smith, who was closer to the actual dirty work. The latter, in the much more brief excerpt from his letter to Dawes, seemed to be saying that the Indians' best hope of an anything approaching a fair settlement would be under the present administration. Its tone was unmistakably threatening, and no doubt Dawes brought the same tone with him to the negotiating table.

The result of the 1895 negotiations for the Choctaws was an agreement, signed two years later, at Atoka in southern Oklahoma. The latter provided for allotment, or parceling off into lots, of tribal lands.

THE PRESIDENT TO THE INDIANS

A uniform letter has been sent by Chairman Dawes of the commission to the Chief of each of the five civilized tribes. In substance it states that the commission has been directed to present to the several nations, for their consideration, a letter from the Secretary of the Interior, in which he incloses one from the President, disclosing his interest in the success of the commission in coming to some agreement which will sanction all their just rights and promote their highest welfare. He asks the Chiefs to lay the matter before their people for favorable consideration. The letter from President Cleveland is as follows:

Executive Mansion,
Washington, D.C., May 4, 1895.

To Hoke Smith, Secretary of the Interior.

My Dear Sir: As the commission to negotiate and treat with the five civilized tribes of Indians are about to resume their labors, my interest in the subject they have in charge induces me to write you a few words concerning their work. As I said to the Commissioners when they were first appointed, I am especially desirous that there shall be no reason, in all time to come, to charge the commission with an unfair dealing with the Indians, and that whatever the results of their efforts may be the Indians will not be led into any action which they do not thoroughly understand or which is not clearly for their benefit.

At the same time, I still believe, as I have always believed, that the best interests of the Indians will be found in American citizenship, with all the rights and privileges which belong to that condition. The approach to this relation should be carefully made, and at every step the good and welfare of the Indian should constantly be kept in view, so that when the end is reached, citizenship may be to them a real advantage, instead of an empty name. I hope the commission will inspire such confidence in these Indians with whom they have to deal that they will be listened to, and that the Indians will see the wisdom and advantage of moving in the direction I have indicated. If they are seen willing to go immediately, so far as we may think desirable, whatever steps are taken should be such as to point out the way and the results of which will encourage these people in future progress. A slow movement of that kind, fully understood and approved by the Indians, is infinitely better then swifter results gained by broken pledges and false promises. Yours very truly, Grover Cleveland.

Secretary Smith says in his letter to Mr. Dawes: "The impossibility of permanently continuing their present form of government must be apparent to those who consider the great difficulty already experienced, even by an Administration favorable to the enforcement of treaties in preserving for them the rights guaranteed by the Government."

Source:

Ethnic Groups in American Life, edited by Gene Brown. New York: Arno Press and the *New York Times,* 1978. p. 34. Originally published by *The New York Times,* May 15, 1895.

Massachusetts Senator Henry Laurens Dawes (1816-1903) authored the General Allotment Act of 1887, sometimes called the Dawes Act. The latter provided for the allotment, or separation into smaller parcels, of Indian lands, with the intention of reducing Indian control over areas desired by white settlers.

Following their removal, in the 1830s, from homelands in what is now the southeastern United States, the so-called Five Civilized Tribes—Choctaws, Cherokees, Chickasaws, Creeks, and Seminoles—had been forced to settle in Indian Territory. The latter would become Oklahoma, and by 1890 the western half of the future state had been declared Oklahoma Territory. Clearly United States lands were encroaching on Native American areas, a fact signaled in 1893 when Dawes left the senate to head up the Dawes Commission, which oversaw implementation of the Act.

In 1895, the commission entered into negotiations with the Five Civilized Tribes, and on April 23, 1897, signed an agreement with the Choctaw and Chickasaw nations at Atoka, Indian Territory. (The New York Times mistakenly referred to the site of the agreement as Anoka, the name of a town and county in Minnesota.) The Chickasaws had refused to sign an agreement reached the previous year, but under threat of action from the federal government if they failed to comply, they joined the Choctaws in signing the Atoka Agreement.

The agreement provided for the Choctaw and Chickasaw government to remain in effect until 1906, when Oklahoma would be ready for statehood. In fact Oklahoma became a state in 1907, with the merger of Oklahoma Territory with Indian Territory. Allotment provisions allowed for each head of household to receive 160 acres, while orphans and single persons over 18 years of age received 80 acres, and all other single persons received 40 acres. What was left over would be sold to white settlers. The agreement provided for the disposition of Choctaw and Chickasaw "orphan lands"—that is, the areas from which they had been removed—in Mississippi, and set aside areas of one square mile (640 acres) for eleemosynary, or charitable, institutions.

The latter, along with provisions for churches and parsonages, and prohibitions against the liquor traffic, suggests the influence associations referred to as "Friends of the Indians." These were white Christian groups, the most notable of which was the Indian Rights Association of Philadelphia, whose stated aims included protection of the Indians from unbridled encroachment by white settlers. They also intended to "civilize" the Native Americans, and convert them to Christianity. The Friends of the Indians encouraged passage of the 1887 Dawes Act, and in the 1890s helped oversee the introduction of civil service rules to govern the Bureau of Indian Affairs.

Despite the efforts of the Friends of the Indians, the one-sidedness of the Atoka Agreement is quite apparent even in the language used by the New York Times to report it. The reference to Choctaw "freedmen," for instance, suggests that they were viewed as having a status akin to that of former slaves. More significant was the designation of the U.S. Senate as the tribunal for arbitrating disputes between the federal government and the tribes. This lends irony to the newspaper's statement that the two sides had "jointly executed an agreement"—an agreement which clearly favored one side.

Also notable are the provisions regarding valuable mines previously owned by the Choctaws and Chickasaws. These would fall under the control of two presidentially appointed trustees, figures whose loyalty to the federal government was unquestionable. Federal leases for coal and asphalt mines would run until 1928, by which time Oklahoma—and with it the Indian nations' lands—would have long been part of the Union.

Though the agreement allowed the Indian legislatures authority to raise the amount of payment received for mining privileges, in practice this was a moot point. The Choctaws did not receive money for the sale of their lands until 1920, nor for mines until 1949. By that time, the apportionment policy had had its disastrous effects on the Native American tribes.

By apportioning communally owned Indian areas into individual lots, the federal government pursued a "divide and conquer" strategy. This proved remarkably *effective: by 1934, when Washington discontinued the allotment policy, the Indians had given up 86 million of the 138 million acres of land they had owned in 1887.*

Much of the land transfer, as might be expected, had been clouded by fraud, but the Choctaws and others lacked the political power to put a stop to it. Only with the 1940 publication of And Still the Waters Run *by Angie Debo did much of the corruption in Oklahoma land dealings come to light—and then, because many of the principals still held prominent positions in Oklahoma government, Debo could not find a publisher in her home state.*

TREATY WITH THE INDIANS

The representatives of both the Dawes Indian Commission and the Choctaw and Chickasaw tribes, who five days ago at Anoka, Indian Territory, jointly executed an agreement, or treaty, for abolishing tribal organization and allotting lands in severalty, have reached here, and have announced formally the results of their conferences.

The agreement now has to be ratified by the Senate, and there is little likelihood of material delay in securing that approval. The substance of the agreement, brief announcement of which was wired to the Interior Department last week follows, a large part of the body of the text being similar to that executed with the Choctaws last year, but to which the Chickasaws then refused to agree:

The tribal governments are to continue for eight years from March 4, 1898, on the ground that no further change will be needed till the lands shall, in the opinion of Congress, be prepared for admission to Statehood. Provisions practically identical with those in the former unsanctioned agreements are made as to direct payment of per-capita funds; as to the Choctaw and Chickasaw trust funds and they payment to the Indians; as to Choctaw orphan lands in Mississippi; the assuming of citizenship on the expiration of tribal existence, and fixing the Senate as the arbitration tribunal for

claims between the United States and the two tribes; forty-acre shares are to be allotted Choctaw freedmen; 640 acres instead of ten each are given certain eleemosynary institutions designated; the Federal Government agrees to maintain strict laws in the territory of the two nations against the liquor traffic in any form; lots not exceeding 50 feet front and 100 feet deep for churches and parsonages in the towns are set apart and exempted from sale, with reversion to the tribes; all coal and asphalt mines are to be controlled by two Trustees appointed by the President and recommended by the heads of the tribes; past agreements for operating coal or asphalt mines are declared void, but all contracts hereafter made by the National agents thus authorized are ratified by the agreement. Coal and asphalt leases are to include 960 acres and to run 30 years. A royalty of 15 cents per ton on all coal mined and 60 cents on asphalt is provided for, subject to changes by the Indian Legislatures.

April 29, 1897

Source:

Ethnic Groups in American Life, Edited by Gene Brown, Arno Press, New York, 1978. Originally published by *The New York Times,* April 29, 1897.

COLOMBIAN AMERICANS

*E*lsa Chaney tracked the immigrant patterns of the Colombian Americans to answer basic questions like "Do they really take away jobs for Americans?" and "Do many return to Colombia?" Colombian Americans earned the dubious distinction of being second only to Mexico in the number of citizens in the United States without proper residence documents. In addition, for the closing 25 years of the twentieth century Colombia was first among South American countries in the number of legal immigrants. While U.S. Immigration and Naturalization Service officials work to ensure the legalities of entry, the scholars work to understand allure of entry. Documents such as Colombian Outpost in New York City present Chaney's findings, and are particularly valuable as baseline information against which later data can be compared. A close look at this first community provides insights into the problems Colombian Americans face, as well as the community dynamics that form when they live together in neighborhood enclaves.

The first Colombian immigrants were probably among the South Americans who arrived in the nineteenth century, but at that time the Federal Census did not specify the country of origin. The first Colombian American community formed in New York City after World War I. Most of these immigrants were professionals, and those who joined the community up until World War II were typically students working on advanced degrees.

When Colombia's civil war began in 1948, immigration numbers jumped from a few hundred to more than a thousand. Even after a measure of political stability was achieved, the immigrant flow steadily increased. The Immigration and Naturalization Service reported 116,444 Colombians came to the United States between 1960 and 1977. The Immigration Act of 1965 created strict controls, limiting the western hemisphere to 120,000 visas annually. Numerical limitations were only one aspect of the new rules. The law also sought to bar entry to all but the highly qualified workers, excluding many Colombians seeking to escape Colombia's political instability and drug trafficking conflicts. Illegal entry was the solution for many frustrated Colombians.

New York continued to be the most popular destination during the 1970s, though Colombian American communities in San Francisco, Los Angeles, Houston, Chicago and Washington D.C. also grew. Most immigrants found work in service industries, taking jobs the local population would not fill, thus in fact not taking jobs away from Americans. English language barriers proved less an obstacle for hotel housekeeping and similar service jobs. A continual problem for Colombian immigrants has been the lack of language training and few opportunities once they settle in America. The lack of English proficiency is a barrier against advancement for higher paying jobs. For immigrants in crowded urban settings, public schools were often sub-standard.

In the 1980s, Colombian Americans began to choose Miami as their most popular destination. Miami was not only home to a thriving Cuban community, but as *a bilingual city it presented a less difficult adjustment for Colombians. Many settled in Little Havana, the largest Cuban neighborhood, and found work in businesses involved in trade with South America. Others worked in factories or as domestic help. Prominent Colombians who fled for political reasons also settled in Miami. In the 1990s a new demographic trend began to emerge among Colombian Americans as they left metropolitan areas for the suburbs. This exodus was first seen in the New York area when a community began to form in Stamford, Connecticut, which had a population of 7,000 Colombian Americans by the mid-1990s. Communities in New Jersey also grew as the immigrants discovered more affordable housing in the suburbs.*

COLOMBIAN OUTPOST IN NEW YORK CITY

Afro-Caribbean and Latin American migration to the United States—today rapidly replacing the large-scale European migrations of earlier decades—poses urgent new policy issues for inter-American relations, a complex set of economic, political, and legal problems for the sending societies and the host country alike. Many similar issues have surfaced in other industrialized metropolitan centers which are receiving their former colonials and other third World nationals to undertake the menial tasks which persons born in the host societies no longer wish to do.

Tolerating Illegal Colombians

Colombians in the United States are a crucial population group to study, not only because they exhibit many of the same characteristics as other Latin American and Afro-Caribbean migrant groups, but also because Colombia recently was identified by the U.S. Immigration and Naturalization Service (INS) as the country second only to Mexico in the numbers of its citizens who are here without proper residence documents. Apparently, toleration of these new immigrant groups in the host societies has come about because these persons are necessary to the continued capitalist accumulation and economic growth in the industrialized centers. For the most part, these workers cluster in the low-paid, low-prestige jobs nobody else will do, but they nevertheless are often resented because they are viewed as "taking jobs away from Americans."

Thus the outcry against the new immigrants often has a spurious ring; for example, many people in the Colombian colony of Jackson Heights,

Queens, New York, believe that a great deal of the INS effort to round up persons without the requisite green card is *Paro teatro*, playacting by the service which is intensified in periods of economic contraction to satisfy U.S. labor unions. Getting caught is not much fun, but so far the statistical danger is slight. Indeed, some believe that U.S. officials must have informal agreements with several governments to permit the migrations to continue; Colombia, for example, is a "friendly democratic government" which the United States has no wish to offend.

Such toleration certainly does not lessen the problems that the migrants will experience on their arrival in the United States, nor the tensions not only between themselves and host society nationals, but among the different migrant groups. In the long run, however, the most important fact about the migration may be its distinct character and the implications this poses for both the host country and the sending societies.

Colombians on the Move

In order to understand the dimensions of the problem, it is important to note that not all Colombian migrant streams flow to the United States; possibly there is more concern about this migration because, while it is not the largest, it is believed to be by far the most selective. Representing far greater numbers is the over-the-border migration of Colombian agricultural workers in Venezuela, by now adding perhaps a million persons to—and accounting for about one-tenth of—the population of the neighboring republic.

This migration apparently follows the classic step or fill-in pattern; as Venezuelan *campesinos* depart for the booming centers of their country, Colombians move in to take over their jobs in the agricultural sector. While the sheer numbers who cross the long, permeable border pose delicate political problems for the two nations, certainly the economic advantage of this escape valve to Colombia is enormous. This migration functions in somewhat similar fashion to that over the American-Mexican border. Of course, many highly skilled persons go to Venezuela; most recently, large display ads in the Bogotá newspapers invite, among others, technicians from Colombia's highly developed textile industry to emigrate.

It is logical that steady, if not spectacular, numbers of Colombians have been going to their former territory of Panama since the end of the 1920s. More recently, perhaps 60,000 Colombians—with or without papers—have arrived in Ecuador because of the jobs created by the new petroleum enterprises. Although emmigration to the United States began in the 1940s, the massive numbers of Colombians (totaling perhaps 150,000-250,000 in the greater New York City metropolitan area and smaller colonies in Chicago, Miami, and Los Angeles) have come since 1960—with the total numbers reaching as many as 250,000-350,000 in the United States. These figures represent educated guesses, but are nevertheless—at the bottom—still speculation.

It is interesting to note that in all but two of the past twenty-five years, Colombia has been first among South American countries in numbers admitted legally to the United States, accounting for 34.7 percent of all the migrants from the continent. Many of these persons are highly qualified professionals; however, the migration since 1960, while continuing to include some top professionals, many middle-level white-collar and skilled blue-collar workers, also contains many more unskilled persons of the "lower classes" than came earlier—perhaps 60 percent of these are without proper residence documents. There is now evidence that at least the *indocumentados* among Western Hemisphere migrants, however, cluster in the secondary market regardless of their level of education and training.

Not only have massive numbers of Colombians been on the move beyond their country's borders, but this movement was preceded by a great deal of internal migration which has continued to the present day. In looking at both aspects, the distinctions often made between internal and international migration probably are artificial. Because of

the (relatively) short journey and cheap air fare—and the large numbers of Colombians clustered in Jackson Heights, Elmhurst, Corona, and Woodside (all in New York City)—there is little reason now for migrants to cross international borders. As Cruz and Castano neatly put it, the migratory flow to the United States is analytically discernible, but nevertheless fundamentally a p art of the entire migratory process involving Colombians.

I have likened the Colombian colony with its center at 82nd Street and Roosevelt Avenue in Jackson Heights—"Chapinerito," named after a middle-class suburb in Bogotá—to a distant province of Colombia, and believe the migratory processes probably are more similar than different, whether the destination is inside or outside Colombia's borders. From a structural perspective at least, the causes appear to be identical; like most of the new immigrants to North America from the Afro- and Latin American Caribbean, most Colombians view themselves as "economic exiles" whether they are heading for the nearest Colombian provincial city, Bogotá, or Queens.

The complex factors generating the rising indices of worldwide unemployment and underemployment have been analyzed by many scholars: capital-intensive productive techniques utilized not only in manufacturing but in agriculture and mining push people out of primary production with no possibility of more than a fraction being absorbed either by the new agricultural enterprises or, alternatively, by the manufacturing and service sectors. In Colombia the introduction of modern agricultural methods and machinery tended to exclude from the market all those who could not afford the new technology, contributing to an ever accelerating movement of people toward the cities. The agrarian reform program of the 1960s (much less radical than its public image) affected relatively few of Colombia's peasants; moreover, most analysts now agree that even if it had succeeded, the effort would have had little effect in stemming cityward migration because there simply was not enough land to give plots of viable size to sufficient numbers of peasants. An added ingredient was the high rate of population increase during the preceding two decades. As a consequence, some 25-30 percent of the work force in Colombia is unemployed or underemployed.

Many Colombians in the United States share the common conception that "La Violencia" was the principal cause of the arrival of Colombians in the 1950s and early 1960s. During a period of about ten to twelve years this phenomenon of La Violencia—widespread armed insurrection and guerilla activity in the rural areas stemming from complex political and social roots—precipitated large-scale movements of people within Colombia. Studies of internal migration in Colombia indicate that the rural population took refuge in the nearby towns (not only from La Violencia, but also from the poverty and misery of the countryside), while the residents of these smaller urban places headed for the cities and the capital. Thus, while it seems improbable that La Violencia had any direct effect on Colombian migration to the United States, there is strong evidence that the resultant uncertainty and malaise indirectly spurred migration during this period.

Colombians' Work

Colombian immigrants generally reflect the same phenomenon of downward mobility that is exhibited by other immigrant groups. Whatever their qualifications, the majority apparently go to work in factories or desire to do so. Not only are salaries better, but factory work is viewed as a bit more decent than washing dishes in a restaurant. Others work in a great variety of jobs—for example, there appear to be many mechanics, and the Colombian universally is considered to be highly skilled I this trade. Of course, some migrants prosper, and there are cases of successful entrepreneurs and professionals—some of them women—in the colony.

Interestingly, Colombian married women show higher indices of employment outside the home I the greater New York City metropolitan region than *either* married women in the general population or Puerto Rican women. This poses interesting questions on the changing role of Colombian women. The travel agent and real estate broker (mostly persons, again including women, who came in the years before the big influx of Colombians in the 1960s) are perhaps the best examples of business and leadership elite; the few Colombians of any prominence in cultural, community, and political (mostly related to Colombian politics) affairs come principally from their ranks.

Mainly, however, the Colombians—as do all the new immigrants—perform needed and useful services which, however, bring low rewards and little prestige or recognition. Despite the fact that they often are viewed as competitors, it appears that relatively few "take jobs away" from North American workers. Admittedly, at a time when the unemployment rate in the United States hovers around 8 percent, resident workers might gladly take on some of these tasks temporarily.

But it is the long-run trends, working themselves out since the mid-1950s if we take the Euro-

pean experience into consideration, that we are considering here. The evidence is somewhat contradictory: on the one hand, INS may well inflate the numbers of migrants (especially the persons without documents) and the dire implications of their presence—classic bureaucratic ploys to get a larger budget. On the other hand, a Labor Department study does appear to confirm that the largest majority of the illegals at least are not the drain on the welfare and tax systems that they so often are accused of being.

Observations and interviews among the Colombians confirm that they may fit the above profile—high in their contributions tot he system, low in their claims upon it. For every person who avoids the withholding tax (either through working "off the books" or through claiming an excess of dependents), there are probably two others who do not file for their tax refunds because of their irregular status; the national, as well as the state and local governments, are net gainers. As well, a large proportion of Social Security taxes never will be collected in the form of pensions by those who work in the United States for a few years and then return to their home countries. Finally, the influx of Colombians and other Hispanics into Jackson Heights has not changed the low indices of persons on welfare; in Jackson Heights welfare dependency increased by less than 1 percent between the 1960 and 1970 censuses.

An important sidelight on the question of work: many leading Colombian Americans are convinced that factory owners and other employers now are able to distinguish between Colombians and other Hispanics. It is their view—it is almost a mythology—that employers often *prefer* Colombians over Puerto Rican workers. This is so, they say, not only because they can be paid lower wages if they are without proper immigration documents, but also because Colombians are perceived as harder workers, more disciplined, more educated, and more refined than the uncultured, vulgar Puerto Ricans.

Part of this view of the docile Colombian as positive may stem from the fact that everyone realizes the necessity of shielding fellow workers without documents—many Colombians want to preserve a low profile and not make waves because of the large number of illegals in the colony. None of the leaders believe that the passivity and deference of the Colombian worker might be negative qualities, even though in the short run such docility apparently leads to great exploitation of the Colombian workers—factory salaries sometimes are as low as $70 a week—and to resentment on the part of the Puerto Rican workers who have no reason not to cause trouble over substandard working conditions and wages because they are citizens and cannot be deported. In the long run the growing reputation of Colombians as passive poses serious questions in the new *ambiente,* where conflict and hard bargaining are the normal tactics for extracting benefits from the political system.

Is there upward mobility for the Colombian through hard work, as has been the case for immigrants in the past? It is impossible to draw any firm conclusions from the very limited existing data. Yet several leaders believe that the more recent Colombian migrants lack aspirations. This is so, they say, not only because to rise from the dead-end jobs in which most work (which permit them little time for study, even for the essential mastering of English upon which moving ahead depends) is extremely difficult, but also because Colombians are inclined to view their stay in the United States as provisional. Therefore, they do not exert themselves sufficiently, even after some years of residence, to find better employment. Lack of achievement motivation is, of course, not the whole explanation; there are structural reasons for the lack of mobility from the lower echelons of the labor force—a growing literature attests to the widening gap between the highly skilled, creative positions at the top and the residual "drone" work at the bottom of the technological society.

Going Home: Myth or Reality?

Do Colombians in fact go back? The evidence on this question is inconclusive. Return for Puerto Ricans is now well established; return of European contract laborers is also well documented and, furthermore, tightly controlled. We can consider the relationship between Colombians and their homeland and speculate about the dimensions of the return.

There is one note of agreement among Colombian American leaders: no Colombian would make a permanent change in residence if he or she were not forced to do so by circumstances. Since Colombians come to the United States against their will, they will always be aliens. An official of the Colombian consulate has mentioned as other evidence the reluctance of Colombians to become American citizens, an attitude which the Colombian government does not oppose, he said, because it does not wish them to sever their last ties to their homeland.

Colombians in Jackson Heights are more interested in events in Colombia than in the local New York scene. They live glued to the happenings in the homeland; they are obsessive in their attachment to Colombia. This attachment is nurtured by the fact that the Colombian national newspapers—nine or ten of them from the capital and the principal provincial cities—can be bought in many places throughout the greater New York City area, with a lag of only a day or two. The most popular magazines from Colombia also are available, and there are at least two full-time correspondents based in New York City who report on the happenings in the colony to their newspapers in Bogotá.

It is routine for most Colombians to make a visit to the homeland at least every two or three years. The air fare offered by some of the non-IATA-affiliated airlines puts such trips within the reach of nearly everyone. The fact that Colombians also receive visits from political figures (and vote in their national elections), beauty queens, sports stars, folkloric ballet, groups, musical *conjuntos,* and singers keeps Colombians in constant touch with their own culture.

Yet this does not mean that Colombians are entirely dissatisfied with their situation and prospects. Many discover, upon arrival, that they must work harder than they ever did in Colombia to achieve their dreams; yet the dreams themselves suddenly become much more attainable. Relatively speaking, work of whatever type is better paid in the United States and enables families to join the society of consumers. Moreover, they routinely do things that many would only rarely if ever have been able to do in Colombia.

The easy American credit system, which enables consumers to use as they pay, contributes to the Colombian ambivalence about the work situation. With credit, it is possible to enjoy many amenities without waiting. Moreover, the fact that once a family has credit cards it often remains in debt, adding new items before the previous purchases are entirely paid, means that the breadwinner(s) must keep working. This situation may be the reason that the return to Colombia is postponed and postponed again, always advancing to a more distant future when the family has acquired all the consumer durables it wishes to take back to Colombia, paid off the installments, and has the requisite nest egg—the financial stake to invest in a small business enterprise and/or to purchase a new home that was the whole point in coming to the United States in the first place.

The crucial question of whether the "transient" situation of Colombian (and other) migrants continues may very well depend upon two variables: the continued influx of Colombians new to the colony, and the related question of whether a second generation develops socialized to the North

American environment and more receptive to its values and attitudes. New immigrants keep the links fresh and immediate, but a second generation pulls in the opposite direction.

The intention to return and the actual return may not make such a great difference to the older generation; lacking requisite skills and never completely secure in English, it may not ever really adapt to its surroundings, yet not outwardly rebel—the harshness of life tempered always by the rainbow at the end of the trail: the real or mythical return to Colombia. Most Colombians, particularly the mass of migrants who have come in the 1960s and early 1970s, view their lives as hard; find the New York *ambiente* (if not the Jackson Heights neighborhood) inhospitable and alien; suffer from the rigors of a climate which perversely produces both arctic winters and tropical summers; and come to view their situation as exploitative when they

realize that their wages—while high by Colombian standards—are low in relation to those prevailing in the United States.

Yet it is only a second generation that may simply refuse to accept the kinds of work its parents have had to do. To the extent that metropolitan countries succeed in preventing a second generation from growing up and being socialized to the host country's norms (as the second-generation Blacks and Puerto Ricans have been in the northern cities of the United States), they will avoid explosive class/racial clashes such as the United States experienced in the 1960s.

Source:

Elsa M. Chaney, *Awakening Minorities: Continuity and Change*, edited by John R. Howard. 2nd edition. New Brunswick, NJ: Transaction Books, 1977. pp. 67-76.

Rita Flores, born in Colombia, South America in 1940, grew up during a period of pronounced socio-political unrest. During the late 1940s and 1950s, many Colombians died and others, economically displaced, were forced from farms to crowded urban areas. A deep economic recession followed and immigration to the United States increased. An interview with Rita relayed the story of how she became one of over 116,000 Colombians who immigrated to the United States between 1960 and 1977.

During the early 1960s, Rita worked in Colombia as a nurse for an elderly American woman. Suddenly, in 1965, the woman suffered a heart-attack. Needing to return to the United States for care, she wished to also retain Rita's services. Though concerns in the United States over rising immigration led to restrictions on entry in the 1960s, domestic servants were largely exempted. Consequently, many Colombians, like Rita, were still able to immigrate to the United States.

Settling into the Miami area, Rita's arrival predated the large wave of Colombian immigration to the city beginning in the late 1970s and continuing into the 1990s. Consequently, much was unfamiliar. Rita described that upon her arrival she found the United States very different than what she had learned in school. As she described, "When I came over here—well, surprise for me! Everything, everybody was strange. The people were different. Hard to say how. But they were different. Everybody here live independent. In our country, the people help more. They more friendly." Seeking familiarity like many homesick immigrants, Rita married a friend who had also immigrated from Colombia. Though very poor and living in a single room apartment, the option of returning to Colombia was unattractive due to rising unemployment back home. However, not making enough money to properly care for her new son, Rita took the infant back home to be raised *by her brothers and sisters relying on the traditional Colombian family network. Many Colombian Americans faced such family separations.*

Rita's story tells of the hardships Colombian immigrants endured as they struggled to fashion a new life in America. She and her husband worked hard day and night seven days a week for their two incomes. Like many Colombian Americans, her husband began his own small business, cleaning floors. Later, he found employment as a supervisor for a large business. Able to afford a nice apartment after four years, they were reunited with their son and their daughter was born. Rita was proud and very happy with the new life they had built in America.

RITA FLORES

A long time ago, when I was seventeen or eighteen, I studied something about United States. I read that United States is beautiful country. The people make money and live well. The people nice, the people work, make a lot of money. That made these things interesting for me to come over here. When I came over here—well, surprise for me! Everything, everybody was strange. The people were different. Hard to say how. But they were different. Everybody here live independent. In our country, the people help more. They more friendly. Something happen at the neighbor's and somebody else can help you right away.. . .

In Colombia I be a nurse. It was pretty good. I worked and I got not much money, but I could buy my things and give money to father and mother. I worked for a lady—American lady. She had a heart attack in Colombia, and I came to the United States with her to nurse her. Was 1965, I be twenty-five years old. I was in Miami, Florida. She was seventy-five or eighty years old and she can't take me out. I had to learn myself.

I remember, one Sunday I went to church and then I walked all night [*laughs*], because I got lost. I was afraid to ask somebody where to take the bus. I no find my telephone. I had money in my pocket but I was afraid to take the taxi, because I didn't know how to tell the taxi where I live. I was so hungry, but I was afraid to go to cafeteria to eat, because I didn't know how to ask for meal or coffee or anything. I got home around six-thirty in the morning.

I lived in the lady's house about six months. And then I made one mistake one night. I broke a glass. [*Laughs.*] Was a delicate glass, and it's easy to break, and I so tired. And she got mad with me. I told her, "Well, if you no like my job and I not able to pay your for glass I broke, I sorry."

Then I found job in the newspaper with Dr. Solomon. They really nice, fine people, really good. I stayed there for a year and then I quit—getting married! I met my husband in Colombia; but we never saw each other again. I didn't know he was here. Well, one day I was walking to buy pizza one Saturday night. And he drove the car and said, "Hey, Rita!" He said he was looking for me. [*Laughs.*] He knew I was here. And later on we got married.

We had tiny little room and we worked in hospital, in the laundry. We were looking both in there. Later on we had my son, Eduardo. And we had little tiny room—only one room. We had a stove, refrigerator, bed. It was difficult for us. I stopped working. My husband, he made little money. He made a hundred dollars for fifteen days. We had to pay thirty dollars a week for the room, and we paid the hospital and food and crib and stuff for the new baby, and diapers. We no had nothing.

Later on we decided to send my little boy to Colombia. We couldn't raise him with no money at all. I couldn't work; we didn't know anybody to take care of Eduardo. So I brought him back to Colombia. I have two single brothers and two single sisters and my father, and they lived with Eduardo there. All my sisters and brothers, they really good. And they love Eduardo very much.

My sister wrote me one time and said, "You have to come over here, because Eduardo very, very sick." The doctor told my sister he had homesick. He had fever, high fever, he vomited, he had headache. He stayed in the hospital for one week. They said he was sick, because I came over here and left him there. But I couldn't go, because no money to go. He stayed for four years.

My husband and I worked day and night. My husband, he is young man but he is really good. He had little own business. He was doing floor wax. He had the places to go. He was working seven days in the week, day and night. I worked with him. We so busy, sometime we no had time to think of Eduardo. We tried to make some home and make and keep some money and have different life than we have before. Be able to nice apartment.

Well, my sisters were really good. They told Eduardo, "Your mother's away. Your mother love you. Your mother write you. Your mother say hello to you. Your mother kiss with you." "Your mother"—always. Always my sisters reminded me to Eduardo. Then two years ago I went there to get my son. When I got there, it was seven in the morning, and he was just waking up, and he said, "Hello, Mamma," and he just looked at me. Because my sisters told him, "Your mother come tomorrow. When your mother come, tell your mother, 'Hello, *como esta*'"

But he was scared. He cried a lot. I had hard time, very hard time. He cried a lot in the airport. He said, "You no my mother." And he cried a lot, and I cried a lot. And he was mean, but I know it's hard for him and for us. We bought a lot of toys, we took him out a lot, played outside a lot. I stopped working, because I expected the other baby. And

then Eduardo was so happy, because later on he had sister. And he picked out the name—Victoria.

We had very hard time finding the apartment, because all the people say, "You have children?" "Well, I have one," "Oh, well, we no like children. They destroy. We no like children." But we found little apartment. My friend was living here and she moved, and we moved in. Now my husband found a new job. He is supervisor at IBM. He take care of floors. I work sometime, baby-sitting.

Now we so happy, because we have nice apartment, and we can speak a little English. Well, I want many things. [*Laughs*.] I would like to speak perfect English and writing and reading. If I have time, I would like to go to the school and finish my high school. I would like to be a nurse. But at this time, I so happy. I have my children, my boy and my girl. We wanted a boy and girl, and we have it. And we so happy.

Source:

American Mosaic: The Immigrant Experience in the Words of Those Who Lived It, by Joan Morrison and Charlotte Fox Zabusky. New York: E. P. Dutton, 1980. pp. 358-360.

CREEKS

*F*or centuries, the Muscogee Indians controlled areas in the American southeast. In their language, the name referred to the flood-prone ground on which they lived, and a similar convention was applied when the European explorers found them living on the banks of creeks and streams: the Europeans called them the Creek Indians. By that time, in the 1600s, the Creek controlled most of the area that would later become Georgia and Alabama. As such they were described as the most powerful Indian nations of the age, but in fact, the organizational structure of the Creek was unlike other Indian nations. Less a nation than a confederacy, they continually accepted as members, and married into, new tribes.

In early Creek history, the basic social unit was the clan. Made up of families, the clan had a distinct identity, starting with its name, which was taken from an animal. Membership in a clan determined a person's social relationships, from matters as small as whom one could joke with to significant questions such as eligibility for marriage. While the social structure could impose strict rules, in another way it was extremely open and communal: the clans lived together, six clans usually forming a Creek town. They shared work as well as property, which belonged to everyone. In turn, as members of the Creek confederacy, the towns fulfilled designated political functions, ranging from diplomacy to law-making.

Muscogee myths reflected the people's spiritual beliefs. These illustrate the deep importance of the natural world to the Creek. Traditionally, they believed in a supreme being, Esakitaummesee, or the Master of Breath. In the myth of the origin of the clans, the Creek begin as a disunited people who were lost in a thick blanket of fog until the Master of Breath cleared it away. Once they can see, the people swear an oath of brotherhood, form clans, and become united. As in many other Creek legends, animals are a significant aspect of their spirituality. Close observers of nature, on which they long depended for survival, they believed that humans and animals could communicate.

The myth concerns another significant aspect of Creek life. Unlike other Native American nations which were closed societies, the Creek tradition of accepting outsiders and intermarrying with them is explained as an order from the Master of Breath. Marriage within the clan is forbidden; indeed, Creek society regarded it as incest. By decreeing that marriage must occur outside the clan, the myth reinforces the flexibility and adaptability which were traditional mainstays of Creek culture.

HOW THE CLANS CAME TO BE

In the beginning, the Muscogee people were born out of the earth itself. They crawled up out of the ground through a hole like ants. In those days, they lived in a far western land beside tan mountains that reached the sky. They called the mountains the backbone of the earth. Then a thick fog descended upon the earth, sent by the Master of Breath, Esakitaummesee. The Muscogee people could not see. They wandered around blindly, calling out to one another in fear. They drifted apart and became lost. The whole people were separated into small groups, and these groups stayed close to one another in fear of being entirely alone. Finally, the Master had mercy on them. From the eastern edge of the world, where the sun rises, he began to blow away the fog. He blew and blew until the fog was completely gone. The people were joyful and sang a hymn of thanksgiving to the Master of Breath. And in each of the groups, the people turned to one another and swore eternal brotherhood. They said that from then on these groups would be like large families. The members of each group would be as close to each other as brother and sister, father and son. The group that was farthest east and first to see the sun, praised the wind that had blown the fog away. They called themselves the Wind Family, or Wind Clan. As the fog moved away from the other groups, they, too, gave themselves names. Each group chose the name of the first animal it saw. So they became the Bear, Deer, Alligator, Raccoon, and Bird Clans. However, the Wind Clan was always considered the first clan and the aristocracy of all the clans. The Master-of-Breath spoke to them: "You are the beginning of each one of your families and clans. Live up to your name. Never eat of your own clan, for it is your brother. You must never marry into your own clan. This will destroy your clan if you do. When an Indian brave marries, he must always move with his wife to her clan. There he must live and raise his family. The children will become members of their mother's clan. Follow these ways and the Muskhogeans will always be a powerful face. When you forget, your clans will die as people."

Source:

Creek Lifestyles, Customs and Legends. September 18, 1996. Creek Home Page at http://www.edumaster.net/schools/ryal/creek.html (accessed December 31, 1996).

*I*n the two hundred years following the arrival of Europeans in sixteenth century America, the Creek Indians suffered a fate not unlike other Native Americans. Considered to be among the most powerful Indian nations, the Creek confederation governed a sizable part of the American southeast. Not only strong, they were especially adaptive, their interactions with the Europeans proving them capable linguists, traders, and diplomats. In return, the Europeans deemed them one of the so-called five "civilized" tribes, and gradually treated them to massacre, geographical dislocation, confiscation of their land, and religious indoctrination by Christian missionaries. It was popularly believed in the eighteenth century that Indians would prefer white culture, if only they had the chance to learn it. This destruction of their culture was called assimilation.

The memoir "Refuse to Kneel," by the then-recent college graduate Bill Bray, was published in 1997. In a style by turns sarcastic and shocking, Bray describes his personal and family life as Creeks from Oklahoma. The title relates to an incident in his grandmother's childhood. Because her parents were too poor to support her, the girl was raised by Catholic nuns. The nuns wanted to convert her, but she refused to kneel for prayer, and so was locked in a closet as punishment. A serious ear infection developed. Even after her eardrums exploded, she was allowed out only to clean off the blood.

For the author, his grandmother's refusal to kneel is symbolic of his own refusal to bend before the dominant culture. As a boy, Bray also learns early on that outsiders view him as different when a classmate tells him Indians "don't read". Indeed, his culture is neglected except in one grade school music class, "the only place that Creek culture was allowed to intrude into our school." The literate, inquisitive child becomes an adolescent who has constant fights with white classmates. Though he will not kneel, he discovers there is a price for speaking up. When he reacts to overhearing prejudices about Indian society, some white friends reply that they were not referring to him because, as a mixed breed, he has "some human blood, too."

As an undergraduate at Dartmouth, Bray finds that his struggles are far from over. The unofficial college mascot is a caricature of a drunken Indian. In describing how the image wounds him, Bray thinks of his grandfather, a gentle and wise man, and imagines him beset by a mob who shave his head, paint his face, and transform him into the hideous mascot. Despite having other, deeper confrontations that arise from differences between his and the college's values, Bray enters graduate school at Stanford. As an Indian academic, he finds the Western university system is too alien to him, so he leaves the Ph.D. program to work for a non-profit organization on behalf of Native American education in order "to protect our children from the type of Western education my family and I have endured." Like his grandmother, he will face the wishes of the majority on his own terms.

REFUSE TO KNEEL
by Bill Bray

I am supposed to acquaint you with the Indian experience. I will apologize right now. There is no Indian experience with which to acquaint you. This is my experience and I happen to be Creek Indian. The two things are not interchangeable and not equal. The best I can hope for is to give you an experience that is slightly off the beaten track.

I am from Oklahoma. It is not at all the part of the country that you probably think of when the "Sooner State" crosses your mind, if it ever does. You are, no doubt, thinking of west Texas. My Oklahoma is a land of softly rolling hills and rich farmland. In my backyard, I have grown tomatoes as big as your cantaloupes and sweetcorn that bursts in your mouth. I have eaten as many as twenty ears at a sitting. We have peach trees and apple trees, mulberries and persimmons. But most remarkable, perhaps, is that we have locust trees.

These trees are part of the odd family of temporarily glorious trees. For most of the year, they look like a pile of overgrown shrapnel: dark and thorny with small oblong leaves, the size of a dime, growing in clusters. But in the spring, they bloom. Millions of tiny white flowers with a fragrance that would kill a rose with envy. Locust trees surrounded our house, bringing shade and protecting us from the brutal northern wind and the searing Oklahoma sun. And Mama hated them.

My mother hated things for many reasons, but her hate of the locust trees was one of the most strange. She hated them for their beauty. She hated the blossoms and said that the flowers were cheap and small, but most of all, she hated the fragrance. "It makes me sick," she used to say. Mama had a problem with cheap things, my father included. Mama fought a war against the locust trees. It was a war that she was denied to lose for one very important reason: I was a subversive firmly in the camp of the locust trees.

Locust trees were a good ally for me to choose. They are vibrantly alive and reproduce in rapid secrecy. They send runners underground and can spring up in clusters in a week. Mama bought a heavy lawnmower and would send me out to mow them down. I would mow some of them, but I would always manage to leave three of four under the fence line or next to rocks. I could always claim that I couldn't get close enough. In a month, they would grow enough so that no mower would be able to chop them down.

I realize that I may have made my mother sound harsh and brutal, but that is only occasionally true. That is one-dimensional view of her, and if anything can be said about my mother, it is that she is multifaceted. Mama has been married three times to three different men. Now this is an important distinction to be made, because in my part of Oklahoma people like to get married and will often marry and divorce the same person over and over just to alleviate boredom. In a good year, I have known the same couple to get divorced and remarried three or four times. My stepmother once pondered the idea of giving everyone gift certificates for a free divorce for Christmas. But, I was talking about Mama—my stepmother, Billye, is to complex a person to be taken on in passing.

Mama's first marriage was to my father. It was not a wonderful thing, although it did have its moments. In its most rudimentary form, this marriage was created out of a bit of bad luck. The first time my father and mother slept together she got knocked up. Due to the barbaric society of the time, wedding bells of course began to ring. My mother says, "When I first found out I was pregnant, I seriously considered jumping off a building. But then I thought that with my luck I would be pregnant with two broken legs. And few things could possibly be worse than being pregnant, crippled, and living with your grandfather." So much for the "Gidget Gets Married" scenario.

In spite of this, my mother and father did not marry at an exceptionally young age. She was seventeen and he was nineteen. That is still about the average where I am from. There is an old saying that goes something like, "A bride is not a bride without a little bulge." I could mention that my wife was bulging a little, too, but that would be jumping ahead in the story and might make you overly anxious.

My father is generally a very self-contained man with a great sense of propriety. My mother used to say, "your father is the most civilized man I know." To her "civilized" was epithet. I must agree that he is civilized sometimes, but his exterior can fool you. When my mother divorced him, he drove his truck into the community center through the front door, executed a right-hand turn that people say must have been almost impossible, and then drove out through the side door. Now I think that we are fortunate that he did this at ten at night when there was no one in the center. All he had to do was pay for new doors for the center and get his truck repainted. He was a very passionate man, but he did not know how to express it properly. My father was (and still partially is) crippled; he does not really know how to express love. This was the reason that I hated him for many, many years; this and the fact that after her divorce, my mother's bit-

terness toward him grew exponentially for years until she had no concept of him as a person. Instead, he became for her a stereotype of cold brutality. One of the verbal clubs she used to beat me with was, "You're just like your father." I heard this constantly for five years. This was a club that I was finally to take away from her; no one can beat you with a club that you do not provide yourself. I wish I had known that earlier.

My father is a prejudiced man. He is prejudiced in an old-time southern way. He is also a counterexample to the idea that prejudiced people are not intelligent. My father's family has always had an axe to grind against Indians. It is little wonder, then, that all of his Indian ancestors over the years suffered a profound racial and historical transformation, until finally I was no longer even permitted to ask about the dark-skinned people in our family pictures.

When I was a child, my mother worked in a sewing factory. At the time, I had a variety of babysitters, all of whom I didn't like. However, fate finally threw me a bone, as it is wont to do, and I finally did get one that I liked. Her name was Levina, but I called her Mama Harjo. She was a Creek woman who lived in a small company house that had three rooms. It was an old house, as there had been no companies located in Wetumka to build houses in over forty years. And it was a house that I loved almost as much as I loved Mama Harjo. Mama Harjo and I had a wonderful life together in her house. She kept other children, but I was her favorite. She said so. She even began to teach me Creek. I remember that I loved the way the words tasted and would walk around saying them constantly. This was my undoing.

My speaking Creek brought about the end of my being kept by Mama Harjo, because one day, my father said to my mother, "You get someone else. She's turning him into a little Indian." So that was the end of Mama Harjo. But I have heard it said that if the Catholic Church has you 'til you're five, you're theirs for life. I think that the same thing must be true of being Creek. And if my father could keep me away from Mama Harjo, he could not keep me away from my family, half of which was Indian, and he could not dictate the people I associated with in school, most of whom turned out to be Indian.

He also could not change where I lived. Oklahoma is an Indian state, the state of Sequoyah, both rabidly multicultural and zealously monocultural. Oklahoma recently celebrated the year of the Indian, in 1992, and in 1989, it observed the one hundredth anniversary of the "land run." To celebrate, Indian children were asked to dress as pioneers and reenact the taking of their ancestral land. Paradoxically, white children in Oklahoma now wish to dress in Indian regalia and dance in Indian ceremonies, some of which celebrate Indian victories over white people. In scholarly terms, we are caught in what's called a narrative conflict. We move in the silent interstitial spaces left for a people displaced and finding a home in their displacement.

This is where my family and I are from, and as the Creek author Linda Hogan has said, we are in a process of "always coming home." It is probably appropriate to think of my story as a travel narrative—one of those strange little stories that explorers used to tell about exotic people and strange locations and how they survived only through wits and cunning. It is impossible for me to separate my own adventures from those of my family. We are all tightly connected, and what might be considered distant anecdotes by others are actual parts of me. When I talk about my family, I am always talking about myself as well.

As a very young girl, my grandmother was taken to Catholic schools and given to the nuns. Her family was too poor to support her. They could not buy her food and shoes. The Catholics took her, even though she was not Catholic, because at that time they were still in the business of converting Indians "by any means necessary." When my grandmother would not kneel to pray, the nuns locked her in a broom closet. Aside from the fright of leaving home and being locked in a closet, my grandmother—like many Indians—was prone to serious ear infections and developed one in the days she spent in the broom closet. Her infection became so serious, and the pressure so intense, that her eardrums exploded and ran blood. When the nuns finally came to let her out of the closet, it was only to force her to clean the blood out of her own ears. The nuns did not help. No one has ever said if grandma knelt to pray after that. She will not talk about it. Knowing her, I assume she didn't. This is where formal Western-style education begins in my family. Where it stands now is with myself, a graduate of Dartmouth College and one dissertation away from a Ph.D. from Stanford University. I have spent most of my education like my grandmother, refusing to kneel. Kneeling in Ivy League institutions is a different matter than kneeling was for my grandmother. So that is what this history of personal education is going to be about: it is going to be about how not to kneel. It is also about the price you pay when you refuse. My grandmother paid with her ears; I paid with something quite different.

My grandfather had an experience different from either my own or my grandmother's. He went to the country school near town and was judged gifted (though that wasn't the term they used back then). He was treated well throughout school, and by the time he graduated, he had a love of words, a love of language. New ideas were rare fruit to him. He lived for his ideas and not from them. He was a strong man and worked construction. He ran a bulldozer and a motor grader, and to take the sting out of the work, at night he would travel the world in his mind. When I was a child, he had a paper globe with the oceans in deep black and continents and states in color. He would have me spin the globe and place my finger on a country. I never hit on a country that he did not know something about. There were times when I would picture myself small enough to slip inside the globe. Sitting in the center, I would look out through all of the countries of the world. I would imagine the sun shining through the translucent pastel countries and playing across me until my skin was a map of the world. This was the sort of education I had from my grandfather; landscapes and languages were his domain. He spoke Muscogee, English, and Spanish, and he taught me about the country around Wetumka. My grandfather taught me geology and archaeology by showing me places to find fossilized tree roots and ocean shells. He took me out to the old cemetery outside of town and showed me where my relatives lived. He taught me about soil by taking me to dig potatoes with him. He also gifted me with a love of words, beginning, as he had done with my mother and aunt, with the word "metempsychosis."

Now literally, metempsychosis has to do with the transmigration of souls, but for me it had to do with something quite different. It was a ticket that my grandfather granted me into the world of language and its power. It all has to do with his reasoning. Papa Lloyd taught me to understand metempsychosis as a way to protect me from schooling. He said, "Your teachers don't know this word. Now you know something that your teachers don't. You know a lot of things that your teachers don't. They aren't any smarter'n you. Don't ever believe that your teachers are any smarter'n you are. They're older so they know some things that you don't, but you know some things that they don't." I suppose any long and obscure word would have done, but metempsychosis is the word that I remember starting me on my collection of words.

I came to love words the way my grandfather did. I loved the way they tasted, the way they felt. I learned to read at about age four and read insatiably. I was starved to read. I recall stealing books from the classroom in first grade and taking them home because you could not check books out of the school library in the first grade. I would put them under my coat and smuggle them out. I remember vividly the lump I would get in my throat, because I was raised in a family where stealing was not tolerated, but I also remember just having to have those books. In the second half of first grade, they granted my library privileges after I proved that I could read the books, and a library card brought an end to my criminal career.

It was only in the second grade that I learned that Indians don't read. The person who taught me this was Zelda Morris. Even with my vast storehouse of words, I can think of no words sufficiently venomous to describe her. Let it suffice to say that she was cold and brutal enough to beat a second grader for reading "too fast."

The rest of my grade-school career was hit or miss. Some teachers I bonded with immediately, some I did not. Mrs. Osborn was a teacher whom I loved as only a fourth grader can love a teacher. Mrs. Osborn was that rare Oklahoma teacher who prized and valued Indians even though she was not one herself. Her music class was the only place that Creek culture was allowed to intrude into our school. She and Mrs. Yahola taught the music class to sing Creek hymns, and they took us out to the Indian churches to sing them. I recall getting ready to get on the bus to go out to Thlopthlocco, edging up to Mrs. Osborn in a shy fourth-grade way, and giving her a necklace that my mother had beaded. She kissed my on the cheek in front of the whole class, a major embarrassment for a nine-year-old, but a memory I hold very dear.

As a small child, both in and out of school, mostly I tried to be unobtrusive and collect information. I would always listen, believing somehow that if I had enough information, I would be safe. I would listen around the corners of doors or sit quietly until the adults became too drunk to notice and would absorb everything and store it away. I don't know why I came to associate knowledge with safety. I only know this fused into and pervaded my education. Abetting this was a drive to understand the way things work and to collect knowledge. I have always loved things that were curious and new and beautiful.

This is how my grade-school education proceeded. It was good and bad, but by high school, it had become simply bad. I honestly don't know when my adolescence began. I understand that some people can provide you with the exact hour and day. I am not one of them. My life runs along a continuum. I hope it is one of constant development; at least I like to think it is. Not a smooth continuum, but more punctuated equilibrium. I

basically went along steadily on one tangent until a crisis or event caused me to change course. I don't know of a pivotal event that signaled adolescence. I can only paint you a picture of how I remember it.

Sitting in your room alone, you have covered the windows with aluminum foil in order to block out all of the light. You do not like light in your bedroom, because it creates a web of shadows in the middle of the night. You have already figured out that it was not the dark you were afraid of in your childhood; it was the shadows in the woods outside your bedroom window. You have carried this fear into your adolescence. Only total darkness can alleviate it, so that is what you have created. You are waiting for sleep to come and it does not. It often does not. You usually sleep during the day or afternoon. You feel exhausted all of the time but not in early night. Instead your thoughts race, but not in the usual way. They are in a slow race. They are weighted and plod through your mind unstoppable, unwilling to give you peace, yet uselessly slow. Spiraling and painful, they continue on.

To escape the isolation, your ears seek out noise. They hear fighting in the kitchen. Your father is pounding on the kitchen counter, slurring his words already. Your stepmother's voice is rising, until you finally hear her yell that you are not hers. Your pain peaks although you know that this is merely drunk-speak. You sneak into the hallway and turn on the air conditioner. Its hum almost drowns out the sound. Back in bed, you put the pillow over your head. You squeeze it tighter and tighter until you are unable to breathe. Only after you have no more breath to give up do you lay the pillow aside and hope that the screaming has stopped.

Now you have the tone for my adolescence. I don't feel that I need to go into it any further. My adolescence was pain. My escape from this was reading. I read everything that I could get my hands on, and every spare moment. I would read during lunchtime instead of eating. In every school, I searched until I found a hiding place where I could read undisturbed. This was not always easy, because after my parents' divorce, my mother got an itchy foot; I moved and changed schools six times between sixth grade and high school graduation. My life was in constant flux, and this was not a simple thing to deal with. As I changed schools, I began to attend less and less. I would cut school and go to the library or go to the movies.

My mother saw no value in attending school more than the minimum time necessary to make good grades. She said that grades were like money; they bought you things. Based on this philosophy, we struck a deal. I was required to attend school for no longer than it would take me to make A's. It was my mother's contention that all other time invested was wasted. I discovered that I could make A's by attending school two to three days per week. The remainder of my time I spent researching or watching television. On the research end of things, I would pick a topic and go to the library. I picked topics like cryogenics, black holes, the Cree Indians, riboflavin, and Australia, just things that caught my interest. I would then set about learning everything available on the subject. I had a craving for knowledge that was not being met in schools. My schools were more war zones than educational institutions. Like my grandmother in Catholic school, I would not kneel, and so I was left to fight.

My fights at school were very physical. It seemed as though I had to fight all the time. The other Indian kids were the only kids that I never fought with at school. They were my friends. I spent a lot of my time fighting with the whites; the black kids I only fought with once—then we established a mutual respect. The white kids I fought with perpetually, year after year. Strangely, I didn't notice that they were all white until later; I just noticed that they were brutal. I always won, but that is not surprising. That is what I was raised to do.

I also believe that I have a fighting nature because I am a mixed blood. I have read various authors who say that it is in the dynamic. Now being a mixed blood is not an unusual condition in Oklahoma, nor is it particularly interesting. It is only when you have it slapped into you that the peculiar nature of the arrangement comes to the forefront. For me, this came in class one afternoon in the fall of my junior year of high school.

I was sitting at my desk staring out the window as many of us often did (school being the challenging thing that it is in rural Oklahoma), when I began to pick up on a conversation between two of my friends. They were bitching about the benefits that Indians received. Their complaints ranged from "free health care" to the pencils and notebooks that were delivered to the Indian kids by the government. I had just received mine two weeks before. Finally, they centered their complaints on Indian houses. They complained endlessly about the fact that Indians got heir houses free and about the fact that it was their tax money that paid for the houses. I found this interesting, since I knew that neither of them had ever paid a tax in his life; you generally don't as a junior in high school.

After listening to their tirade for a while, I felt compelled to barge in. After all, I come form a long line of "fools who rush in." I reminded them that I was Indian and that my family lived in one of those houses. I had also intended to tell them that the houses were paid for out of tribal money and that nobody's taxes had anything to do with it, but I didn't get the chance. Instead I was told, "We weren't talking about you. After all, you have some human blood, too."

These were casual friends, and it was readily apparent in the way that they phrased their response that they were actually trying to show solidarity with me. Lift me up a bit as it were. My reaction was to give them what my brother terms my "go to hell look" and turn around in my desk. Their conversation drifted on to who they wanted to take out and who they thought would win the upcoming football game—leaving me to my own partially human thoughts.

The one place I did enjoy spending time when attending school was the library. The librarian and I became good friends. When walking past the library one day, I was asked if I was going to take the PSAT, a test for high school juniors to gauge their chances for getting into college. I told her probably not, because I didn't have the two dollars. She told me she would give me the two dollars if I would take the test. I agreed because I liked taking tests. They were games to me and I loved games. It is still amazing to me that two dollars properly spent can change the entire course of your life. I did very well on the test and started receiving information and scholarship offers from universities across the country. This was something that was outside of my experience. I come from a world that is very small and very old. To me, New York and Mars were approximately the same. They were places that you see on TV and places where no real people live—infinitely expansive but with no more depth and reality than the TV screen itself.

I always tell people that my admission to college was happenstance: I just happened to be in school the day they were administering the PSATs; a librarian just happened to remind me and loan me the money to take the test; I just happened to do well, which made me a National Merit Scholar, which brought me letters from expensive colleges. I then tossed my letters in the air and the one from Dartmouth just happened to come out on top. This is how I picked my college. I only applied to one. I had never heard of it. I was sure, though, that being a small college in the backwoods, it would be desperate for students, so I did not apply anywhere else. I only realized after I got to Dartmouth that other people had worked and planned for years to go there. Some had hired coaches for the standardized admissions tests and had had their parents fly them in to look at the place. I recall thinking what a pain that would be and wondering why they had bothered. Many of these questions were answered upon my arrival.

My first impression of Dartmouth was that it was beautiful and cold. I was picked up at the airport by a junior who was Ojibway. He was friendly and I was freezing. Coming from Oklahoma in September, I didn't expect the chill and had packed my coat in my suitcase. My suitcases were lost at the airport in St. Louis, leaving me in a new place, a thousand miles from home, with only the shirt on my back. After walking around some and getting to know the place, I went to my room. I remember lying on a military-style bed with no sheets in a freezing room wondering just what I was doing there.

Dartmouth College, since its founding, has alternately used, courted, tossed aside, enticed, mocked, ignored, and occasionally, educated Native Americans. In some ways, it is almost a mini-America.

That was my first impression of Dartmouth and I guess that is what Dartmouth is to me: a random assortment of impressions with no specific chronological order. In a sense it is personal event and spectacle. I suppose this is true for everyone. Pervasive among my impressions is a strong sense of alienation from Dartmouth. This began the day after I arrived, when I received a notice from the Dean's office that I was to meet with a dean at 12:00 the next day. I could not believe how rude that was; back home, you never simply told somebody to show up one day in advance, and seldom was a week enough warning. We just didn't do things that way. I felt my sense of correctness assaulted, as a city person might feel if all stoplights were to start changing colors at random. It was one of those things that was so unconscious that I could not have told you why it struck me as rude if asked; it's one of those subtle cultural/regional "differences" that are so deeply ingrained that you have to trip over them to bring them to light. This happened to me quite often at Dartmouth. On a regular basis, I felt as if I and the other students, as well as the professors, were existing on very different planes of reality.

I should say before I go on that writing about my time at Dartmouth is difficult for several reasons. The primary one is that after my graduation, I made a decision to remodel Dartmouth in my house of memory. It seems that many of us did that; when I meet with other Indian alumni, we remember the place fondly. Much like all alums, we have

sealed up certain rooms, shifted a few doorways, and recast our experiences in a more pleasant hue. We remember our friends, and even our memories of our competitors grow fonder. Contradictions that once loomed enormous may not have been resolved, but they have been lived through. I think that Indians have a gift for this. There is so much pain in our histories that even the worst a small college has to inflict pales in comparison.

The "Indian symbol" provides a good example of this process of not forgetting specific events, but rather refocusing attention only on certain aspects of them. I think of it little these days, but at one time it commanded much of my attention and energy. The Indian symbol—a degrading, stupid-looking caricature of an Indian that was usually found drunk near a rum barrel—was the unofficial college mascot for many years, looked upon with pride by many old alumni. When I looked at it, though, I saw too much of home to find anything funny or heroic about it. Let me give you an example of what it feels like, since so much of its effect is in what some elders call the unseen world.

Imagine your grandfather. He has raised you with love and respect and given a great part of himself to you. He stands very straight, and the dignity of his presence is almost palpable. Grandfather once lived very vitally, and it still shows in his humor and stories. He has a gentle wit and cares about his family and the world. His spiritual strength brings forth light. This is grandfather.

Now people have come to visit grandfather. He invites them in and offers them food. They do not accept, but instead, begin to jeer. They say taunting things that are aimed to hurt and destroy. But this is not enough; they grab grandfather and shave his head. They paint his face with stripes and draw a scowl from the corners of his mouth. Still not enough, they take him and push him into the mud outside. You look at grandfather and realize that they have not diminished him. They did not have the power, but the world itself is now a smaller, darker place. This is how the Indian symbol made some of us feel.

Now I realize that the symbol was not and is not the most pressing issue facing Indian society, but seeing it is like walking past a stinging nettle; you chop it out of your path only to have it return from the roots. Its persistence only serves to underscore a contradiction that every Indian who has ever attended Dartmouth has felt to some degree. Dartmouth College, since its founding, has alternately used, courted, tossed aside, enticed, mocked, ignored, and occasionally, educated Native Americans. In some ways, it is almost a mini-America.

The Indian symbol was a general challenge to the Native American community at Dartmouth, but there were many personal challenges as well. I recall being out dancing one night with a friend of mine, a beautiful Indian woman from Denver. My roommate (a student from New Jersey whose informal motto was "Yeah, I'm an asshole. So what?") was at the party as well. After a few minutes of dancing near my roommate, my friend Jo asked if we could move away from him. I asked her why. She said that he was pinching her and feeling her up. Well, where I'm from, you don't do things like that. But as a freshman, I didn't know clearly what to do. I thought about it a while and then looked him up and down and told him he should apologize to her. He said he didn't have to and that it was none of my business, so I hit him a couple of times to emphasize the point. Then I was really confused, because at Dartmouth, you just don't hit people. Mental cruelty of all kinds is protected and tolerated by established rules of conduct, but physical violence, no matter to what end, is deplored. At home, the reverse is true; decent treatment of people is encouraged and, if the situation requires, justifiably demanded through physical coercion. Unsure, I called home and spoke to my grandfather. He said that I had done "just right and if they were decent people they'd understand." How could I tell my grandfather that I was in a place where by many of the values I was raised with, people were not only not decent, but not even sane? Fortunately, it never came up.

But I also took to parts of Dartmouth like a duck to water. It was all about learning and things that were new and beautiful. The first class that I took was "Folklore," an anthropology course. Anthropologists delight in the unique, and the professor who taught this course was really the first non-Indian I had ever met who valued Indian culture. At the time I hadn't spent much time thinking about culture. It was just a given. I recall, though, being very excited at the age of eighteen to meet someone who was Jewish. I had seen some Jewish people on TV and was certain that here couldn't be very many of them, since I had never met one. At that time, for me, all the world was Indian; it was only later that I was to realize the rare and beautiful wealth that we hold onto.

One of my friends described Dartmouth as a fantasy land. In my freshman year, this was how it seemed to me. The work was stimulating but not especially burdensome. I have always loved the stars, and in my first term, I found a perfect combination of courses: "Folklore" and "Stars." But it should be clear by now that what I loved was not the physics and astronomy, but the poetry of the stars. Black holes are places where time itself stops

and things become infinitely smaller and no older, an eventual horizon past which there is no force in the universe that could allow one to escape. The romance of these astrological concepts was incredible and fit in so wonderfully with the folk stories of the people who came out of the earth and the ancient spiders hanging fire in the sky. But as far as the math went, I was in way over my head. My math education had stopped after Algebra I in the tenth grade. Sadly, they expected more at Dartmouth. Upon making a D on my first exam, I was determined to leave the college. Fortunately, the Native American Program director took me in hand and reassured me that "Stars" was neither the last nor the most important course I would take in college. I got an A in "Folklore" and a C in "Stars"; not terribly unique.

What was unique about my freshman year in college was Val. Years later, I find it hard to write about her, but Val was an important part of the lives of many of us who attended Dartmouth at that time and her story is very much a part of my own. When I first saw Val on my second day at the college, she was so beautiful she literally stole my breath away. She was wearing a green army surplus coat that she had decorated herself with streaks of spray paint and red handprints. When she asked me if I was going to the NAD House for a picnic to welcome new students, I, of course, said yes.

Val was Yup'ik from Alaska. When she entered Dartmouth, she was a poet, a singer, and a person with the most boundless raw energy I have ever known. By the time she left the college, a couple of years later, she was addicted to alcohol and cocaine and physically and emotionally battered. By the age of twenty-seven, she was dead from drinking antifreeze. Much is said about walking in two worlds, about being "bicultural." These discussions are little more than mouthings of academic platitudes. Val, like myself, thought about the world in a way that I can only superficially describe. I was not raised with talk of career paths and planning ahead. When I though of the future, it was only a matter of days or weeks. I did not plan to finish college or got to graduate school or get married or have a son. I was raised thinking that things happen, and people adapt if they can. No one exercises much control over the world, and it is only those who are gullible who delude themselves into thinking that they do. My main concern was and is what happens to my family and community. My education, more than anything else, helped me to redefine and expand whom I include in my circle of concern.

All in all, my education has been a rather selfish thing. It took me away from my family and tribe and I did it just to satisfy my curiosity. I was a poet inseparable from momentary tribal dreams when I left, and I am a better poet now. Being away led me to understand the incredible wealth I was raised with. I recently went to the wedding ceremony of a Native friend of mine from Dartmouth. He began the ceremony by saying, "My family and I would like to welcome you. We've lived in this neighborhood for about thirty-five thousand years." That statement alone causes you to think in ways that are difficult to reconcile with Western education. This, I think, is the paradox that killed Val because she could not reconcile it. I try with greater or lesser success.

I would like you to understand that my experience at the college was not universally bad. On the contrary, Dartmouth provided me with gifts too numerous to count. The foremost among these are my ex-wife and my son. My ex-wife is mixed blood like myself. She is Slovakian, Irish, English, Italian, and some nameless Massachusetts Indian tribe. What all these thing add up to is a strikingly beautiful woman. She has flowing brown hair with red highlights, eyes the color of polished amber, and a body that won't quit. In addition to all of the aforementioned things, she speaks four languages, graduated at the top of her class, was a state champion athlete, and upon giving birth, immediately got up and walked back to her hospital room.

Diane and I might have been considered star-crossed lovers. It was almost a storybook formulation. She was a near-white girl from a wealthy family who had all the money in the world to give her, but very little love; they insisted on the best from her and usually got it, one way or another. They had great plans for her: to follow in the finest tradition and become a powerful, self-concerned doctor whose only loves were money and control. And her family must always take a distant second place, so as not to interfere with her work. I was a poor Indian from Oklahoma whose family seldom had enough money, but always had enough love. My family aspired that I stay out of prison, but beyond that I was free to make my own way. Now as it happened, I loved Diane the near-white girl and she loved me and that was how things stood until one night I loved her too much and she became pregnant. When she told me this, it did not surprise me in the least, because that is how things work in the real world. Since her pregnancy was a fact, Diane had some decisions to make. I say "Diane" and not "we" because I believe that while a baby is inside a woman's body, all choices should be hers. I did tell her though, that if she wanted to have the baby, then I would have a say; the baby would not go up for adoption. If she wanted no part of it, I would

take it back to Oklahoma and raise it myself with the help of my family. I had the benefit of knowing that my family loves children and that a new baby would be greeted with joy. This gave me a security that many white people, including Diane, unfortunately lack. Well, to make a long story short, Diane decided to have the baby. I was happy and hesitant and unsure and proud and a million other things all stirred together in one big pot. I think Diane was the same way. I was also feeling very good in a way that only living up to a difficult conviction can make you feel. The upshot of it all was that we went ahead with our plans for her to have the baby. We also decided to get married. Our fraternity provided the scene.

Diane and I belonged to the same co-ed fraternity, and our wedding was the event of the season. Our nuptials were paid for out of the social budget, and it seemed like half of the campus turned up. It was a mighty fine time. Diane was beautiful in green velvet, and I have to say that I made quite a striking figure in my mismatched jacket and beaded bolo tie. My brother the preacher came all the way from Oklahoma to New Hampshire to perform the ceremony, and all of Diane's family showed up. We had decided to let her parents attend on the condition that my brother and I could cripple them if they acted ugly (they didn't). It was a grand affair and seven months later, my son Scot was born. He is the finest thing Diane and I have ever done together, and between us and my family he is one loved chebonni. Since then, Diane and I have divorced, but that seems like a happy place to stop.

A Kiowa elder once told me that the victories to be won today are educational. Most of the time now, we fight with words. Dartmouth College taught me to use words as arrows, a skill which led me to Stanford. But I was not comfortable or happy in this academic environment, and it took me a while to figure out why.

For myself as an Indian academic, the problem of locating "home" within the academic structure was serious. More than any people in North America, Indians can point to a piece of the world where home lies, and they can often even trace it back to specific rocks, trees, and bodies of water. The university is not where we point. We cannot adopt academia in the way Euro-Americans can. Having no concept of links that cannot be broken, Euro-Americans can pull themselves up by the bootstraps and plant themselves firmly in the academic community, a community historically conceived to take care of them. Aside from a few minor scrapes and disharmonies, they fit academia like a hand sliding into a glove. What, however, can an Indian do? What can Indians do when the glove is tailored to the white hand, and the white hand is already happily inside it?

One of the things that an Indian can do is leave, and we do so in droves. Indians have the highest university dropout rate of any group in the United States, on the undergraduate, graduate, and faculty levels. This is not surprising to either the academic world or the Indian world. I'll attempt to explain why this is so.

As a constant and enthusiastic user of computers, I have occasionally come across programs that have serious bugs. These are programs in which you attempt to do something that the program is purportedly capable of doing, yet actually is not. The commands are there, and the computer should be able to perform the task. In fact, the computer will insist that it is able. On the Macintosh, this results in a system error. The system error is the bane of the Mac user's existence, because it offers only one solution: turn off your computer, lose everything you have recently put into it, and start again from the beginning.

This is the situation of the Indian who stays within academia: the academic structure insists that it can accommodate you, and even gives explicit instructions on how this can be accomplished. You enter the system, begin to give input, and then out of the blue, you get a system error, incapable of correcting itself. As the user, you learn merely to avoid using that particular function. Unfortunately, the only way to discover a system error is to stumble across it and be sent back to the beginning.

Indians come from a place where the primary program is different and has been running for an incredibly long time. Most of the bugs are worked out. Indians enter academia expecting a fundamentally functional program. They press keys labeled "voice," "expression," "meaning," "creativity," and "use," and expect to find that something extraordinary happens. Instead, the machine stops. So Indians go home, a place that Euro-American academics have often forgotten exists, or they stay in a world they never made and don't fully understand.

After leaving Stanford partway through my Ph.D. program in education, I was hired as executive director of The Native American Preparatory School (NAPS). I took the job in order to protect our children from the type of Western education my family and I have endured. I refuse to believe that education must be painful and cruel.

The Native American Prep School took me many places, and my "education" continued. I flew across the country from New York to L.A., had meetings at private clubs and on yachts where no one looked like me, and asked people to donate money to Indian education, because Indians are the people of the future. And then I would go home and cleanse myself and vomit, because that is what you do if you are Creek and believe in our traditional ways and find yourself living in a world that is increasingly strange. Then I would return to work and laugh myself through another day, clinging to thirty-five thousand years of dances and stories and philosophy and thought and the comfort, joy, pain, and work that its survival implies.

The chairman of the NAPS board, like many wealthy older people in Santa Fe, lives in a security-controlled condo. As executive director of the school, I often went to visit him. In the beginning, I was consistently stopped at the gate by a series of white men, and each time I told them my business. When I told them that their tenant and I worked together, they would ask exactly what I did. They would ask where I lived. They would ask how long I expected to be there. I told the same people the same things for two months. I got to know them well by sight, and I would have thought that as I came and went twice a day, they would have gotten to know me, but such was not the case. Each time, they said, "We'll have to call and get confirmation."

One day, about two months into this process, I arrived late for my appointment, and as is so often the case, desperation became the mother of invention. I was stopped and they asked who I was. Out of irritation, I sarcastically responded, "I'm the gardener. Who do you think?" This changed our relationship in a way that I could not have anticipated. The guard at the gate thrust a pass at me. "Here," he said, "remember to bring this with you." He stepped back into the guardhouse before I could explain that I had been joking. But I now had a pass that would allow me to go anywhere in the complex. Sometimes, with all the education and degrees in the world, you're still just the gardener. A gardener is a respectable thing to be. My grandfather was a gardener. He raised potatoes, and I raise money. So maybe the guards had me pegged after all.

I once read a story in which one of the characters refused to let reality take shape. Through the sheer power of his denial, things would begin to realign themselves and reality would reshuffle itself. He was not an Indian, but he might have been. I should not be here. We should not be here. I read that we were all supposed to be gone by 1910 or 1940 or 1970. It seems that for people who have outlived the end of several worlds, it is only denial and laughter that keeps us going.

I have been told that there are ceremonies going on in Native America to call people home. There is an in-gathering and those who walked, crawled, or were carried away will be brought back. I had to go away to know that my education was my grandfather and grand mother and aunts and uncles and cousins, and that the land and the turtles who live on it were my education, too. I was schooled in the cold mountains of New Hampshire, and in California, but I was educated in a warm green forest in the rolling hills of Oklahoma. Simply put, I am a rare bird trying to combine a traditional Muscogee life with an Ivy League education. When I go to work, whether it is as a teacher, grant writer, bead-worker, or poet, I go to war. I seek to protect people and cultures that are beautiful and unique and timeless. But mostly, I seek to protect children who should not have to kneel; children who might be my grandmother, my son, my friend Val—or me.

According to legend, there is a little yellow deer who lives in the forest. If you are very still and very fortunate, he will come and whisper secrets in your ear. This is my son's name, Eco Lvne-ce—Little Yellow Deer. Scot often whispers secrets to me, and in exchange I have taught him to say "metempsychosis." If I do my job well, my son need never leave the forest.

Source:

First Person, First Peoples: Native American College Graduates Tell Their Life Stories, edited by Andrew Garrod and Colleen Larimore. Ithaca, NY: Cornell University Press, 1997. pp. 23-42.

CUBAN AMERICANS

E*rnesto Reina was born in Havana, Cuba, in 1970. He made four attempts to leave the island but was captured each time. Three times he served jailed sentences. In August 1994, responding to the growing exodus of Cubans who were leaving the island illegally, Premier Fidel Castro (1926-) said that all those who wanted to go could do so. Tens of thousands boarded homemade rafts and ventured across the Caribbean Sea to Florida. One of them was Reina, who was twenty-five years old at the time, with a wife and a six-month-old child.*

Reina kept a journal of his experiences, which was published in Spain in the magazine El Mundo. This translation was prepared by Beth Wellington. More than just a harrowing true-life adventure, Reina's diary offers a compelling, first-person glimpse into the psychology of refuge. From the outset, Reina asks himself pointed philosophical questions about his actions: Why did I have to come to this extreme of risking my life? Why can't I live free in the land I love and adore?

Reina survived his journey and arrived in Miami, Florida, where he took a job in a supermarket. The end of his diary finds him, like many Latinos, working very hard to raise money to bring his family to the United States.

Reina's vision of the United States as a land of opportunity, despite the hardships it heaps on newcomers, differs sharply from that of the writer Reinaldo Arenas (1944-1990), who came to the United States in the Mariel boatlift of 1980. Deeply distrustful of institutions no matter who is in charge, Arenas saw the United States as simply the lesser of two evils. Reina's story does, however, bear striking resemblance to other migration narratives from the Caribbean and elsewhere. The Haitian-American writer Edwidge Dantikat's poignant, terrifying stories of Haitian boat people come to mind, as do Chicano writer Ramon "Tianguis" Perez's Diary of an Undocumented Immigrant. In that work, Perez describes crossing the Mexican-U.S. border in the trunk of a car with a man named Juan and a preacher. Although a car rumbling across a desert is a world away from an innertube on an open sea, it is by no means any less treacherous a means of transport, as this extract makes clear:

> *After about half an hour, the trunk is uncomfortably hot. Because I'm so close to the tire, it's completely impossible for me to stay still. The sheet metal beneath me little by little grows hotter until I have to change positions. I feel like a roasting chicken and I don't want to imagine how much hotter it could become.. . . "Accidents happen all the time," the preacher says, "and we're neither the first nor the last to travel in a trunk." Such comments are nothing more than a manner of infusing ourselves with confidence, because anecdotes always come to mind. In the house of Juan Serna, a wet[back] told us he'd seen three others fried like bacon in a trunk.*

SEVEN DAYS: DIARY OF A "RAFTER"
by Ernesto Reina

I couldn't believe my ears, I just couldn't believe it. Fidel Castro had announced that he would let anyone who tried to leave the island go free. Everyone in Cuba was talking about the same thing. At first, I thought that it was another one of his evil lies, but no, people I knew had taken the trip to freedom and no one had stopped them. This was my opportunity; the fifth time would be the charm.

I had tried four times to go to the U.S. but besides being unsuccessful I was arrested on three occasions. I spent time in Fidel's jail cells: eighteen months, six months and 3 months, respectively. On the fourth try, I avoided imprisonment thanks to a bribe of 3,000 pesos. Now the fifth adventure was about to begin. . .

Sunday, August 14

11:30 a.m. I got together with a few friends at a house belonging to one of our fellow rafters. No one was older than 25. Nervous, but hopeful, we decided that the time had come to flee to the U.S. We planned everything quickly. We bought, on the black market, naturally, six innertubes from truck tires to help keep us afloat. Six innertubes would be enough. Manuel, one of our "compañeros", promised to bring the rafts and the rope which we would use to construct the deck of our "vessel". I would contribute the board, Fidel would provide a sheet—that could be used as a sail. Each one got whatever necessary items he could find for the difficult crossing.

In addition, I had three flares given to me by an American visiting Cuba; I also owned a compass that had, fortunately, never been confiscated during any of my earlier attempts to abandon the island. We made all of the preparations in a moment. Nothing and no one could stop us now.

Tuesday, August 16

6:00 p.m. The fight to attain freedom has a very high price and I was about to pay it. At my house, my wife and my five month old son were sleeping. With a broken heart, I gave a little kiss to "Ernestico"—that's what I like to call him—I didn't want to wake my wife so as not to upset her. Perhaps, many people wouldn't understand why I left them behind but I did it for them and for myself. If my dream of arriving safe and sound in Miami came true, I could struggle and work in order to have

them join me, and in this way, become the happiest man in the world.

7:30 p.m. I met the rest of my friends on the beach. We are all prepared for the adventure that could cost us our lives, but could also allow us to be born again. With ropes, cloth and innertubes, we managed to construct a raft. The only "motor" it had would be the oars and our own strength. One out of four. This was not a bet. These odds keep churning in my mind. For every four rafts launched into the sea, only one reaches its goal. The other three become food for the sharks or are swallowed up by the sea, overturned in a storm. At the moment of departure, I remember that my wife, who has a good memory for dates, told me that today would be the second anniversary of Hurricane Andrew, the storm that left Florida looking as limp as my sock.

The atmosphere at the beach was totally surreal. The first time I decided to leave Cuba, it was absolutely forbidden to escape by raft: at the time it was considered a furtive act that could cost you several years in jail and now it was a celebration. Just as we were about to launch into the sea there were hundreds of people preparing their crafts in order to do the same. The beach had turned into an enormous open-air shipyard.

Meanwhile, a crowd of onlookers had gathered together to observe this depressing spectacle, a crowd that had grown increasingly demanding. When a small raft began to move in circles in the waters close to shore instead of going forward, the multitude began to jeer. On the other hand, when a craft set to and made headway, they applauded.

8:00 a.m. Sitting atop our raft, we pushed off to sea to see what would happen. My seven "compañeros" on the trip were riding on the main raft while I placed myself into an innertube attached to the main rig.

No one wanted to go in the innertube for fear of the sharks. I didn't care because I thought that we were risking enough just by being in the water.

A few friends waved good-bye from the shore and wished us luck. The raft went out to sea slowly as the darkness of night fell upon us. All was silent for a few minutes. I felt an inexplicable frustration. "Why did I have to go to the extreme of risking my life? Why couldn't I live free in my beloved coun-

Cubans leave the harbor in Mariel, Cuba, during the "Mariel Boat Lift," which brought tens of thousands of Cubans to South Florida.

try?", I asked myself over and over again. I was sure that these same questions were running through the minds of my fellow rafters. The faces of some of them reflected an irrefutable sadness.

Little by little, the silence was broken and we began to talk about the possibility of reaching Miami, and being able to see our relatives after years of painful separation, and finally, and most important, being free and able to throw off the burden of Fidel. The majority of those on this adventure had suffered physical oppression at the hand of "State Security", the forces that Castro uses to humiliate and control anyone who doesn't follow his instructions.

Wednesday, August 17

1:00 a.m. The sea began to rise up in anger. All was dark and we could barely see each other's faces. The waves were stronger and stronger and some of the "compañeros" showed signs of sea-sickness and began to be nauseous. I started to talk in order to calm them down. I told them that it was a little storm that would soon pass. I tried to comfort them by saying that it would be much worse to feel the stinging sun on blistered skin, as I had read once in *Relato de un naufrago* by García Marquez. Fortunately, the storm disappeared and spirits were restored without any further problems.

6:00 a.m. After the storm, comes the calm as the saying goes and a beautiful dawn blossomed before our eyes. We couldn't see land anywhere but we already felt free although we were probably closer to death than to freedom at that moment.

1:00 p.m. At this fateful hour we received our second fright. Fourteen miles off Cuban shore, the raft turned over. It was a terrible experience. We lost the few provisions that we had and everyone fell into the water. We ended up without anything to drink. If necessary we were ready to refresh our throats with salt water. We thought that would be the end, but fortunately, after much painful effort, we managed to get onto the raft again.

I was finally free. We took a stroll around the city and had my picture taken with the American flag. My skin exuded happiness and joy from every pore.

At this terrible moment I recalled once again the hair-raising stories that were circulating among the people of Havana about the many who had made the crossing and lost their lives on the high seas, about the empty rafts found by the American Coast Guard, about the sharks who ate the rafters. This last fear is one that I can speak of from experience. A shark began to circle around the innertube where I was sitting. A shark's fin appears harmless. It is green, the color of hope, and black, like death. Everyone knows that sharks prefer to attack white objects. Sharks are near-sighted and can only see objects that are white and bright. This was Garcia Marquez' theory. He must be here in spirit.

In our hurry to leave we hadn't been able to rub the raft down with gasoline, which would have

warded off those dangerous fish. Fear was running through my veins at the same time that I was bursting with energy—from who knows where— to keep on struggling. In the end we didn't have any problem with that darn shark who miraculously disappeared from alongside our raft.

3:30 p.m. The only part of our bodies that we could move without fear of falling back into the sea was our heads. Anxious and impatient, we would look in all directions hoping to spy a boat that would rescue us from that endless wait. We didn't know how many of the 140 kilometers we had crossed. The worst think about these makeshift boats is that they don't have a prow nor a stern. The sea spins them around like tops and you no longer know if you are going north or east.

Suddenly I spotted a black point on the horizon that looked like a ship. Shouting, I alerted my companions. When we saw the black dot, we were exhilarated. Tears came to my eyes. Without worrying that it might be an optical illusion, I threw my first flare and then the second. A precarious and nervous happiness came over us.

4:00 p.m. Half an hour later, I had used the third and last flare. Thank God, as it approached, the black dot turned out to be a United States Coast Guard launch. We looked at each other with tears in our eyes, and our lips broke into smiles of joy, that until then had been lost.

4:15 p.m. The Coast Guard realized we were rafters and they signaled to us with lights in order to alert us to wait for them while they came to our rescue.

4:30 p.m. Finally, we were rescued. The eighteen hours of danger and agony had been rewarded with the marvelous prize. Our transfer from the raft to the enormous Coast Guard vessel was symbolic of the huge change that we were making in our lives. It was stepping from the past into the present. A present that, for us, was full of promise. Our future needed only to begin.

4:45 p.m. We arrived at Key West on the coast of Florida. As soon as we were docked, the first thing I did was kiss American soil. We were interned in an immigration center in Florida where we were given food and clothing. There we were able to rest and recover from the difficult crossing. The sensation of having already been in the United States was very strange; I had not yet assimilated the idea of leaving behind Fidel Castro's cruel system.

Thursday, August 18

5:00 p.m. After a long four-hour journey on the highway from Key West we reached Miami. We had to be detained in another center for a few hours while our papers were processed. Finally, my uncle, who lived in Miami, came to pick me up. I was finally free. We took a stroll around the city and had my picture taken with the American flag. My skin exuded happiness and joy from every pore. I found it difficult to control my euphoria. The difference between the two places was so spectacular and rapid that I had not yet had enough time to digest the experience.

Friday, August 19

President Bill Clinton announced a change in his Cuban immigration policy. All rafters would be detained and transferred to the U.S. Naval base at Guantanamo, paradoxically located on the island of Cuba.

Such is destiny. In only a matter of hours, my future was shining bright, while that of my fellow rafters, who continued to arrive day after day, was uncertain and frustrating. While thousands were detained in Miami in order to be taken to Guantanamo, I enjoyed absolute freedom and started a job that my uncle had found for me in a supermarket.

However, as I said before, my goal does not end with reaching freedom in the U.S.A. Now I am working hard in order to save enough money to send for my family. I want them to know what life is like in paradise."

Source:
Seven Days: Diary of a "Rafter," by Ernesto Reina. 1994.

*T*he story of Cuban American Rodolfo de León as told in a 1970s interview chronicles the economic turmoil of Cuba after the fall of dictator Fulgencio Batista and end of U.S. domination. De León was born in rural Camagüey, Cuba. His family, who owned storehouses in Camagüey, stayed in Cuba for several years after the revolution led by Fidel Castro, and continued to prosper economically. De León, however, remembered pro-Castro crowds celebrating political victory and rounding up many people believed to have been Batista supporters. A Catholic seminary near his home became a holding camp for some of those gathered. The failed 1961 Bay of Pigs invasion led to even more persecution of those considered not supportive of Castro and to further nationalization of private businesses, including his family's. His father refused an offer by the Cuban government to continue administering the business.

Almost a quarter of a million Cubans, including the de León family, immigrated between 1959 and 1962 to the United States for political and economic reasons. Miami became the American center for Cuban American relocation. Rodolfo recalls the distasteful experiences in dealing with opportunists taking advantage of the newly arrived Cuban immigrants in Miami. Later in the 1960s many middle and lower class families, including his grandparents, aunts, and an uncle, took advantage of U.S. and Cuban policies allowing Cubans to join relatives already in the United States.

Rodolfo tells of the increasing hostile racial environment in Miami as the population of Cuban Americans swelled. It was an unhappy time for the de Leóns in many ways, including a diet of canned government meat for the first year. As with other Cuban Americans, their lives were forever changed. As stated by Rodolfo, "Bang. A whole new picture. Everything was misplaced. Everything that I knew, everything that I felt good with, that I felt secure." His mother found work peeling shrimp in a shrimp-packing factory. His father lost great stature, going from a prosperous business owner to picking tomatoes for six dollars a day near Boca Raton outside of Miami.

Characteristic of the socio-economic success of Cuban Americans in pursuing professional careers, Rodolfo graduated from Boston College with an economics *degree in 1976. The end of the interview found Rodolfo longing for the life they once had in Cuba even though he had become a U.S. citizen and director of the Cambridge recycling program.*

RODOLFO DE LEÓN—LEAVING CUBA

Rodolfo de León is one of more than 700,000 refugees who have left Cuba since the revolution in 1959. Unlike many of these, who came from Havana, Rodolfo was born in the rural province of Camagüey. His family remained in Cuba through the first few years of the revolution. They owned some storehouses in Camagüey, which were nationalized by the revolutionary government. In 1962, at age eleven, Rodolfo, his brother, and his mother left for Miami. His father followed a year later, and his maternal grandparents, two aunts, and an uncle came in the late '60s.

The waves of Cuban immigration to the United States roughly follow a class pattern. Those who left with Batista or immediately after the Castro takeover were from the wealthiest classes and the military and were closely tied to the Batista regime. In the early '60s, as the government became more socialistic, some Cubans lost their livelihoods, and what they saw as the betrayal of the revolution forced them out. Many members of the middle and lower middle class left in the early and middle '60s. Inasmuch as one of the primary aims of the revolution was to improve the life of the *quajiro*, or peasant, fewer poor or rural Cubans found their way to this country.

Cuba, after the revolution, was the only nation in this hemisphere given no restrictions on immigration to the United States. A Cuban refugee program, which was set up and administered by the federal government, provided at least some aid for most of the Cubans leaving Cuba after 1959. Even so, Mr. De León, his brother, and his mother had to wait a year and a half before they could leave Cuba. His father left later, and only after much difficulty. His aunt and uncle tried to leave for five years before meeting with success.

In the 19960s, Cuban refugees were often pawns in Cold War games. Some were used by the U.S. government as secret invasion and espionage forces against the new Cuba. The American media hailed them as valiant fighters against communism while Castro called them "worms" and betrayers of their country. Castro also claimed that if American Immigration had been as generous in its invitation to Cubans during the Batista years there would have been a mass exodus then. The American press responded that if Castro's Cuba was heaven, why were so many people leaving?

At the time of the de Leóns' settlement in Miami, tensions were growing between the Cuban and "Anglo" communities; gangs often formed, usually along ethnic lines. Today, Dade County has a large Cuban population, and disputes over jobs and the use of Spanish in the schools are frequently reported in the national press.

I met Rodolfo de León in the fall of 1972. When I began taping some conversations with him I was not working on a book. Later he consented to the use of most of those early tapes. Mr. De León has attended the Museum School of Fine Arts in Boston and has exhibited his paintings in regional shows. He was graduated from Boston College in 1976 with a degree in economics, and he is presently the director of a Cambridge recycling program. Since our first tapings, many years have passed and some of the attitudes he then expressed have changed. He no longer wishes to return permanently to Cuba. In January of 1976 he became a United States citizen.

Fall 1973, January 7 and 8, 1974—Cambridge, Massachusetts

I remember the last two weeks of '58. In la Sierra they had a radio station. I remember hearing every night all this static. You would hear what's happening. Everybody was pro-Castro—not everybody, but a lot of people. I remember, so that nobody would catch us, we would close the windows and try to get the radio.

Those two weeks were really the most exciting weeks because Castro was moving. Che Guevara over here, Camilo over here. They were going to cut the island in half and establish a government on one side.

Cuban immigrants use mirrors to signal another boat in the exile flotilla. The close proximity between the United States and Cuba and the lack of restrictions on Cuban immigration have led many Cubans to emigrate to the United States.

The day that we knew Batista fell, I was woken up very early. Everybody was out on the streets. I remember my aunt made three or four 26th of July flags and we went around in cars, BEEP-BEEP, and people were drinking. Plus it's New Year's—perfect timing. [Laughs.] And there was a strike all over the island.

I remember I saw Castro once, and that's it. Never saw him again. On January first, Batista leaves, right? At four in the morning. And there was a strike all over the island. And so, Castro is in Santiago. And there was this looting in Havana and tearing down of parking meters. Somebody said that they were going to take a Viscount plane and take Castro from Santiago to Havana. Meanwhile, he had declared Santiago de Cuba the capital of Cuba, because he didn't think Batista was going to leave—the island was going to be divided for a while. So Batista leaves. Castro got into Havana the 6th, I believe. He said he wasn't going to take a plane, he was going to march to Havana. That's

how I got to see him. Our street, General Gomez, [led to] the center of Camagüey. He was coming in a tank. He came through Camagüey, the second or third day. He was as near me as fifty feet, and he was on top of a tank. And there were people on the sides of the tanks, and people marching. We were all standing there.

But his face seemed very white. That's the impression I had that day, and I didn't get his features very well, since he was so far. He seemed very angelic, like Jesus Christ. He just went by.

The first few days, they started collecting people, the Batistianos. Not because of Castro, just popular demand. It was kind of brutal. I witnessed the whole thing. They came in a truck. I remember running after it. They had already four or five people inside the truck, tied up. They searched for Pataganzo. Pataganzo was this *gusano* henchman. He lived about two blocks away. That's what they called hm because of his leg. He had a defect. They dragged him out of the house. I think they tied him by one leg and just dragged him across the street. They tied him to the truck by the leg and pulled him. They didn't kill him then.

Who did this, the army?

Not the army, just people. He was very well known. Everyone was afraid of him. You couldn't look at him the wrong way. He was an informer. Batista paid people all over the island. He paid them $33.33 a month. They were *chivatos.* You had to watch what you said around him. We used to close the windows whenever he came by. He was really ruthless. I remember hearing of people disappearing, being taken in the middle of the night because of him. They killed him later on, they shot him.

In the summer of '59 we moved to Doble Vía. We rented a house there. About a year later we moved to Calle Siete. My father bought this big house, really nice. It cost something like $19,000. He made better money after the revolution till the business got confiscated.

From where we lived, two or three blocks away, there was a small community, marginal type of people, very poor. They came with signs and all, against us, "Gusano." I don't know what these signs read. I forgot. They kept going around our house. They were chanting things. They did that for about a half an hour. My brother came out with a jar of cold water and glasses. It was hot, so he started giving them water. From then on they call my brother the diplomat. After that they left.

What do you remember about the Bay of Pigs invasion?

The Bay of Pigs—the only thing I remember was that they captured a lot of people; the militia, the government, the regime. They captured a lot of people who were believed to be conterrevolutionaries. Just for national safety they captured them, rounded them up, you know. I don't know if it was the night before, or the same time that the Bay of Pigs was on.

There was a seminary, a Catholic seminary, about two blocks from my house, and they turned that into sort of like a concentration camp. Not a concentration camp—not that connotation—just a place where they put them. A friend of ours was one of the people captured. I remember they let him go.

I went near there. There were people standing inside a wall. There was a wall there. Just men. They were standing around. Families brought them food. There was a sense of thrill, because there were these people captured there. Going over there and sneaking and looking through.

In the seminary they put up a megaphone and about three times a day they used to sing the "International" [sings]: *"Qué viva los pueblos del mundo."* It went on a lot, maybe three or four times a day. It was a middle-class neighborhood so they figured they'd bother us playing it early in the morning, walking us up with it, going to sleep with it.

I remember once they started the day-care centers thing—everywhere for mothers to bring their children to the centers. The *gusanos' bola*—means rumor, *bola* means ball, which gets bigger and bigger, and it was rumored around that they were going to take the kids away from you and teach them Marxism-Leninism, but in a very naive counter-revolutionary *gusano* way, "Here's an apple; God didn't give it to you, Castro did." Those were the examples they gave us, and that we should hide. And we did. We did hide. We didn't go anywhere; we were inside. Any time trucks or anything came by, the paranoia was so much, we hid under beds and things like that. So we didn't go to school for a while.

We left Maristas, the school we were going to. We went to this private school which was all *gusanos.*

Often there [was a troop of about twelve people marching] up and down the street, the militia, I guess, I don't know where the hell they came from, and we sort of heard or guessed that they especially sent them to that street.

Did you realize something profound was happening?

During the first years of the revolution I had good experiences. My father was doing well. We went to Havana for the first time. We went to Varadero.

After the revolution, the changes began to be noticeable. In Havana there was this Yuri Gagarin Restaurant. It was self-serving. This was a new thing for Cuba. The Ten Cent Building in Havana had an escalator; they served all types of sandwiches. I remember once going to a militia camp about two miles from our house. They built all these apartments near my house, near Puerto Principe. They took *campesinos* and put them in these houses, even in '61.

A special trip I remember was with my father. We went fishing. It was in the river, and it was really fun, you know, catching fish. They were men, and it was very nice under different shades of trees. Just cooking. I remember looking when my uncle opened up a fish and took out the insides and fried it and ate it, everybody drinking beer and rowdy and playing dominoes, in the middle of the country.

In Santa Lucia, when my father bought a house—those were really nice times. I enjoyed that. I remember going swimming there three times a day. In the afternoon the tide went very high, so it was dangerous. I remember we went to the beach swimming, getting hot, and my skin was getting dark, going back to the house, and there was a shower outside the house so you could clean yourself up, to get all the sand off. The water felt cool and so nice. The water felt good. I would stay in the hammock in the afternoon and just relax.

We were at the beach, and my father called us. We waited for him at the entrance of Santa Luccia. We waited a lot that day, and he didn't come. Finally, he came with the news that his business had been confiscated. They had offered him the job of administering it. He refused. Immediately he brought the lawyer with him to make up papers and passports for us to leave.

From then on everything was downhill. I felt there was something bad gong on, that we were gong to leave the country. I didn't know what the hell that meant! I didn't know. I didn't know what that meant that I was going to go somewhere else; I didn't have any ideas of sociological orders, economic ideas, whatever. I wasn't aware of a lot of things.

I remember crying when he told us that. I was really upset.

But then we did a lot of traveling. My father was trying to get passports. I think that's the first time we spent a lot of time with him. We went different places, to Varadero, Havano. My father was spending a lot of money to get a suite in the Lincoln Hotel. It was kind of nice. I was feeling like a type of millionaire.

In August or July we got a telegram in the middle of the night saying that we were authorized to go. I remember being excited at first, then I *really* felt bad. I remember crying. I remember looking back. I said to myself, "This is the last time you're going to look back." I remember I kept on looking back at my house and feeling very bad, very sad, and then going to Havana and going to the plane. I don't remember how many days we stayed in Havana. My father was in a nervous state.

They looked through our baggage. They took my brother's watch, a couple of things of value. We got on the plane and took off. I kept looking at the coastline as far as I could, as long as I could. It was just maybe five minutes when we landed. It didn't take that long. So we landed in Miami.

The people who were waiting for us—they were opportunistic, *stupid, low-down rats!* They were the worst kind of people you can imagine. My father had sent money over here for us. The dollar was going very high on the black market. So my father had to pay I don't know how many Cuban *pesos* for a dollar. [He had sent] about $400 in different installments many times. We only got $200. These people were *stealing* it. They didn't give us any money. This was the only reference we had here. They were friends of [a friend]. They had done that before. They had "taken care of " people, sons who came.

We stayed at their house, two weeks, three weeks. My mother couldn't stand it, we couldn't sand it. We went to bed hungry.

Why didn't your father come with your family?

Why couldn't he come? Well, I'm not quite sure why he couldn't come, but he felt he had some business to take care of. He felt that he wanted us to be secure in this country before he left Cuba.

The second or third week we were here we started receiving help from the government. We collected food, and we got $100 a month. We rented one place first. The rent was . . . way too high. The rent was $95. We had five dollars left for the month.

After a month or something like that we found this other place, which was $72. We were renting the apartment for $72, and so we had $28 for the month. That meant a dollar a day. We lived on that for I think about a year and a half. Aside from my mother baby-sitting for about two dollars for six hours, that was the only income we had. I remember in that place we had only one pillow. One day my brother and I started fighting for the pillow. We really got into a brawl about it. I started chasing him. My mother was chasing us. Then my mother broke down crying. We stopped. I really felt bad. We were fighting for this . . . pillow.

And we were eating really bad food. It was not only bad, but we were eating it constantly. Canned government meat. A whole year. Breakfast. Lunch. Dinner. And Beans. My mother would soak them overnight, and then she would spend the whole next day cooking. We sort of had this pot that we found. She spent time cooking all day, and I remember we sat down to eat and it was very solemn, we sat down and started eating. Somebody made a remark about the beans, and we started laughing and then crying. Between all that a bean got stuck. It got stuck right in my nostril, and I couldn't breathe through my nose for about two weeks. I remember one morning I went to school. Here I was, they put me in the fourth grade. In Cuba I was in the eighth. It was early in the morning. I went *ah ah choo!* [Laughs.] Thing was green, starting to get some moss. They were still hard, you know?

So it was a kind of bad time. I remember I wanted to drink a Coca Cola. My mother had probably thirty cents in her pocket and I felt really bad that I wanted one. Really bad.

There are a lot of experiences like that. You know, going to school and being kind of odd. I was much bigger and older. And I would bring my spam meat sandwiches, which smelled. Everybody around just dispersed every time I sat, every place I sat.

We used to have dancing classes. It was part of gym; it was compulsory. All the boys would line up this way, and all the girls would line up next to them. I was interested in girls, but not American. It was funny, but it really hurt me that they did this. The girls would count, the first one in line, to see who got me. She would count, and she was trying to move back or front or somewhere so she wouldn't dance with me. So usually, after all this rearrangement of all the girls moving from one place to another, there was this very fat girl, who was completely unaware of anything, what was going on, who landed in that place and with me. And it got to my turn and it got to her turn and we danced. I don't know what the hell else. I was embarrassed to death. *My soul felt stale* through those years, through many years afterwards.

The first [two months] we were here my brother heard of this place where you could pick up doughnuts and sell them—make a couple of dollars. The first day they left us the doughnuts and a metal case to carry them. We went out with this stuff and walked around. Finally we found this guy out mowing his lawn. He thought we were just kids selling stuff so he called us over. He said he wanted one. We gave him the bag. As he gave us the money, he must have realized we were Cubans, not American kids. He took the package he'd bought and threw it in the garbage. My brother was really upset. He was upset like hell. He wanted to go home. At that time I didn't understand what Ricardo was doing. I said I'd do it. He was upset and shy. He was hurt. He was very hurt. I wasn't so much hurt but I figured—what were we going to do with all those doughnuts. We didn't try to sell the rest. My mother had to pay six dollars for them. We ate stale doughnuts for weeks.

We went trick-or-treating. They told us you could get a lot of candy that way. So we did that. We ate candy for a long time.

We used to file down pennies and use them for cigarettes. Then we heard that the telephone people and different people were complaining about it—high rate of filed pennies being poured into machines. [Laughs.] At night we'd just file pennies. We'd file about a hundred pennies [Laughs.] We only had *one* dime so we filed it to that point. We bought a file that cost thirty-two cents. We got a lot out of that file! My brother used to go to the cigarette machines. He used three pennies. We'd get thirty packages and sell them for fifteen cents, so we were making twelve cents a pack. We used it for food, candy, telephones. After we did that for a while, we thought they were checking. We took it easy. We went to different areas. Can yo imagine a guy opening up a machine and all those pennies come out? Not even good pennies? Struck a copper mine.

Let me tell you, necessity is the mother of invention. When we moved to the $67 place, we didn't use it as much. It took us all night filing pennies. Our hands were shaking. We filed pennies in the dark. I think we used a candle.

What did you miss most?

I missed the whole thing. I can't say I missed this particular thing. Everything was misplaced at once. Bang. A whole new picture. Everything was misplaced. Everything that I knew, everything that I felt good with, that I felt secure. I felt aggressive. I now became insecure, passive. I was in front of this thing I just didn't know how to deal with. Especially where I hadn't been born here. Also the bigness of it.

Seeing my mother was depressing. She was trying to get work. I remember she finally found work. I remember she finally found work before my father came, for maybe four, five, or six months. She was working in a *camaronera*, shrimp-packing, to get the thing out of the shrimp to be packed. Her fingers, a piece of her hand is wasted, you can see it—take a look at her hand. It's from peeling shrimps. She probably came home with $30 after about forty, forty-five hours. She came home at five, maybe six o'clock.

When we were in Miami in '62—'63 we used to look for my father many times. After the Missile Crisis, there were no more planes coming in. We didn't know when he'd get here.

We were visiting some friends in Tampa when we got word that my father was coming from Cuba. We drove back the next day to Miami. I remember I was very anxious to see my father. I remember, before, we kept waiting for him. We kept going to meet all the incoming people. They used to bring them all to the stadium in northwest Miami. At that time they were trading medicine.

He came over the *Máximo*, on a boat, a big boat. I'll explain. You know the Bay of Pigs thing? People that were captured, somehow they struck a deal with Cuba, where they were sent ships of medicine in exchange for troops, these people: prisoners, mercenaries. So that on the way back a lot of other people came, too. Most of them were well off. So my father left the car there. And he didn't know he was coming. He couldn't send us a telegram or anything. He'd been trying to come. And we had heard that he was feeling bad. He was doing all these weird things. He was praying. At home he would fall down on his knees.

It was very hard, first time I saw him. He looked very different, and I just didn't react the way I used to. And ever since then I haven't reacted the same way. Before we left Cuba, it was more like Daddy, Daddy—you know, father. It was more he represented something else before, and now he didn't. Something had been taken away. He didn't have the power he had before, the image that I had of him.

Even when we were together, my father couldn't work, couldn't find work. When he did, he found it in Boca Raton, sixty miles away from Miami He picked tomatoes. And that was sixty miles away. They had a car pool, and some guy took him. So he had to pay, I don't know how much. He went about five o'clock in the morning and came back about ten o'clock at night. He got paid six dollars a day. Two dollars for the car, something like that.

My biggest impression came when we were driving from Tampa to Boston. We stayed in Miami, then we went to Tampa. Here I was, *guiding my father a guajiro* from Camagüey. My mother, you can imagine! We were driving up to Boston in a Chevrolet '54. And you know that time was in '64. And my father drives *slow*. You can imagine what hassle, to New York and all that. We got lost once and went the wrong way in the Lincoln Tunnel.

I remember something the second night, or the first night. I remember my lips were bitten, you know, blood was coming out of my mouth, from nerves. I was riding with my chin on the dashboard. We got lost because of the traffic. We couldn't take a left and the traffic just took us along with it.

Do you think you want to go back to your country?

I would like to go back to my country. But I've been here such a long time! I'd like to be able to drive around the place where I was born, once in a blue moon, you know. And I like to be with my own people and say, that's where my father used to own his business, and that's where I lived, and this is where I played when I was a kid, and these are my people. When I get in trouble I don't have to give excuses, where I'm from and when I came here. Maybe I will, maybe I'll spend the rest of my life in this country, but I hope I don't have to do that.

Do I think my parents are happy here? No. But they have to keep their myth up. They belong to another generation—old Cuba.

I'd like to go back. Coming to this country, it's just like my whole life turned on me. I can't express myself. The whole thing is just changed, my new life, a new person. Everything turned worse the day I got off the . . . plane. From that day on everything, everything went bad. I wish I could go back.

Source:

First Generation: In the Words of Twentieth-Century American Immigrants. Revised edition. Edited by June Namias. Chicago: University of Chicago Press, 1992. pp. 154-163.

*R*emembered as Cuba's greatest patriot, José Martí (1853-95) led an unsuccessful revolution against his country's Spanish colonial government in 1868. For this he was deported to Spain in 1871, and spent the next seven years traveling in Europe and Central America. Soon after his return to Cuba in 1878, he was again exiled, and moved to New York City, where in 1891 he wrote "Our America" (originally published in La revista illustrada, January 10, 1891).

The latter essay is pivotal for its definition of Latin America as distinct not only from the English-influenced nations of North America, but also from Europe. A key statement is his observation, midway through his manifesto, regarding wine made from plantains, a type of banana grown primarily in Central America: "even if it turns sour, it is our own wine!" Martí was concerned, not only with preserving a distinctly Latin American identity, but also with encouraging his fellow Latin Americans to embrace that identity and reject attempts to imitate North Americans or Europeans.

"Our America" is filled with vivid imagery, and in places Martí piles on metaphors and clauses—not to mention references to figures from the history of the Americas—so elaborately that his meaning sometimes becomes obscured. Thus a single sentence, near the end of the essay, contains some 150 words. Yet throughout, Martí shows himself a master of pithy statements that have the ring of an aphorism, or a memorable saying. A powerful example is the lead sentence: "The conceited villager believes the entire world to be his village."

From that starting-point, Martí goes on to attack those who view their existence purely in terms of what is best for them, rather than keeping in mind the best interests of their nation or their people. Along the way, he draws in numerous references which illustrate both his own obviously thorough education, but that of his audience. For instance, Juan de Castellanos, mentioned in the first paragraph, was a Spanish soldier who went to the New World in the 1540s, then gave up the military to become a priest and poet.

Martí's reference to "carpenter's sons" in the third paragraph, however, is probably not an allusion to Christ: by that point in his essay, he has reached the heart of his concern, a scathing attack on Latin Americans who scorn their own heritage—with its heavy Native American influence—in order to follow the fashions of Europe. He follows this with harsh words addressed to his other targets, the North Americans and Europeans, portraying George Washington as a veritable traitor and the makers of the French Revolution as the very sort of aristocrats that their revolution opposed. Again and again, however, Martí returns the focus to his fellow Latin Americans, a people whose society is a unique mixture of Spanish, Indian, and African elements.

Around the time of his writing and thereafter, intellectuals throughout the world were divided over the issue of civilization, which was non-racial, non-nationalistic, and universal; and culture, which was closely tied to nation and race. If anything symbolized civilization, it was ancient Greece, a realm whose legacies in areas such as democracy and philosophy are the joint inheritance of all humankind. Martí, on the other hand, places himself squarely on the side of culture: hence his statement that "The European university must bow to the American university," and that the history of the Americas should be taught, even if it means that students fail to learn about Greece.

Particularly notable is Martí's proclamation that "Our Greece must take priority over the Greece which is not ours." Since Greece is most often the standard by which other societies measure themselves, this is a bold claim indeed, and Martí goes on to celebrate the great figures of his own people's history. Among those are "the two heroes [who] clashed": South American patriot leaders Simon Bolívar (1783-1830) and José de San Martín (1778-1850). Martí refers to the latter as "not the lesser, [who] handed the reins to the other" when he resigned leadership of the independence struggle in 1822.

Martí himself would one day be remembered along with those heroes. A year after writing "Our America," he founded the Cuban Revolutionary Party, and in 1895 incited his countrymen in Cuba to revolt against the Spanish. Martí landed in Cuba, hoping to command a rebel army, but was killed in battle soon afterward. During the twentieth century his name became a powerful symbol both to the Communist government of Fidel Castro, and to anti-Castro Cuban groups operating from the United States.

OUR AMERICA
by José Martí

The conceited villager believes the entire world to be his village. Provided that he can be mayor, or humiliate the rival who stole his sweetheart, or add to the savings in his strong-box, he considers the universal order good, unaware of those giants with seven-league boots who can crush him underfoot, or of the strife in the heaven between comets that streak through the drowsy air-devouring worlds. What remains of the village in America must rouse itself. These are not the times for sleeping in a nightcap, but with weapons for a pillow, like the warriors of Juan de Castellanos weapons of the mind, which conquer all others. Barricades of ideas are worth more than barricades of stone.

There is no prow that can cut through a cloud-bank of ideas. A powerful idea, waved before the world at the proper time, can stop a squadron of iron-clad ships, like the mystical flag of the Last Judgment. Nations that do not know one another should quickly become acquainted, as men who are to fight a common enemy. Those who shake their fists, like jealous brothers coveting the same tract of land, or like the modest cottager who envies the squire his mansion, should clasp hands and become one. Those who use the authority of a criminal tradition to lop off the lands of their defeated brother with a sword stained with his own blood, ought to return the lands to the brother already punished sufficiently, if they do not want the people to call them robbers. The honest man does not absolve himself of debts of honor with money, at so much a slap. We can no longer be a people of leaves living in the air, our foliage heavy with blooms and crackling or humming at the whim of the sun's caress, or buffeted and tossed by the storms. The trees must form ranks to keep the giant with seven-league boots from passing! It is the time of mobilization, of marching together, and we must go forward in close order, like silver in the veins of the Andes.

Only those born prematurely are lacking in courage. Those without faith in their country are seven-month weaklings. Because they have no courage, they deny it to others. Their puny arms—arms with bracelets and hands with painted nails, arms of Paris or Madrid—can hardly reach the bottom limb, and they claim the tall tree to be unclimbable. The ships should be loaded with those harmful insects that gnaw at the bone of the country that nourishes them. If they are Parisians or from Madrid, let them go to the Prado under lamplight, or to Tortoni's for a sherbet. Those carpenters' sons who are ashamed that their fathers are carpenters! Those born in America who are ashamed of the mother who reared them, because she wears an Indian apron, and who disown their sick mother, the scoundrels, abandoning her on her sickbed! Then who is a real man? He who stays with his mother and nurses her in her illness, or he who puts her to work out of sight, and lives at her expense on decadent lands, sporting fancy neckties, cursing the womb that carried him, displaying the sign of the traitor on the back of his paper frockcoat? These sons of Our America, which will be saved by its Indians and is growing better; these deserters who take up arms in the armies of a North America that drowns its Indians in blood and is growing worse! These delicate creature who are men but are unwilling to do men's work! The Washington who made this land for them, did he not go to live with the English, to live with the English at a time when he saw them fighting against his own country? These "iconoclasts" of honor who drag that honor over foreign soil, like their counterparts in the French Revolution with their dancing, their affectations, their drawling speech!

For in what lands can men take more pride than in our long-suffering American republics, raised up from among the silent Indian masses by the bleeding arms of a hundred apostles, to the sounds of battle between the book and the processional candle? Never in history have such advanced and united nations been forged in so short a time from such disorganized elements.

The presumptuous man feels that the earth was made to serve as his pedestal because he happens to have a facile pen or colorful speech, and he accuses his native land of being worthless and beyond redemption because its virgin jungles fail to provide him with a constant means of traveling over the world, driving Persian ponies and lavishing champagne like a tycoon. The incapacity does not lie with the emerging country in quest of suitable forms and a utilitarian greatness; it lies rather with those who attempt to rule nations of a unique and violent character by means of laws inherited from four centuries of freedom in the United States and nineteen centuries of monarch in France. A decree by Hamilton does not halt the charge of the plainsman's horse. A phrase by Sieyes does nothing to quicken the stagnant blood of the Indian race.

José Martí

To govern well, one must see things as they are. And the able governor in America is not the one who knows how to govern the Germans or the French; he must know the elements that compose his own country, and how to bring them together, using methods and institutions originating within the country, to reach that desirable state where each man can attain self-realization and all may enjoy the abundance that Nature has bestowed on everyone in the nation to enrich with their toil and defend with their lives. The government must originate in the country. The spirit of the government must be that of the country. Its structure must conform to rules appropriate to the country. Good government is nothing more than the balance of the country's natural elements.

That is why the imported book has been conquered in America by the natural man. Natural men have conquered learned and artificial men. The native halfbreed has conquered the exotic Creole. The struggle is not between civilization and barbarity, but between false erudition and Nature. The natural man is good, and he respects and rewards superior intelligence as long as his humility is not turned against him, or he is not offended by being disregarded—a thing the natural man never forgives, prepared as he is to forcibly regain the respect of whoever has wounded his pride or threatened his interests. It is by conforming with these disdained native elements that the tyrants of America have climbed to power, and have fallen as soon as they betrayed them. Republics have paid with oppression for their inability to recognize the true elements of their countries, to derive from them the right kind of government, and to govern accordingly. In a new nation a governor means a creator.

In nations composed of both cultured and uncultured elements, the uncultured will govern because it is their habit to attack and resolve doubts with their fists in cases where the cultured have failed in the art of governing. The uncultured masses are lazy and timid in the realm of intelligence, and they want to be governed well. But if the government hurts them, they shake it off and govern themselves. How can the universities produce governors if not a single university in America teaches the rudiments of the art of government, the analysis of elements peculiar to the peoples of America? The young go out into the world wearing Yankee or French spectacles, hoping to govern a people they do not know. In the political race entrance should be denied to those who are ignorant of the rudiments of politics. The prize in literary contests should not go for the best ode, but for the best study of the political factors of one's country. Newspapers, universities, and schools should encourage the study of the country's pertinent components. To know them is sufficient, without mincing word; for whoever brushes aside even a part of the truth, whether through intention or oversight, is doomed to fall. The truth he lacks thrives on negligence, and brings down whatever is built without it. It is easier to resolve our problem knowing its components than to resolve it without knowing them. Along comes the natural man, strong and indignant, and he topples all the justice accumulated from books because he has not been governed in accordance with the obvious needs of the country. Knowing is what counts. To know one's country and govern it with that knowledge is the only way to free it from tyranny. The European university must bow to the American university. The history of America, from the Inca to the present, must be taught in clear detail and to the letter, even if the archons of Greece are overlooked. Our Greece must take priority over the Greece which is not ours. We need it more. Nationalist statesmen must replace foreign statesmen. Let the world be grafted onto our republics but the trunk must be our own. And let the vanquished pedant hold his tongue, for there are no lands in which a man may take greater pride than in our long-suffering American republics.

With the rosary as our guide, our heads white and our bodies mottled, both Indian and Creole, we fearlessly entered the world of nations. We set out to conquer freedom under the banner of the virgin. A priest, a few lieutenants, and a woman raised the Republic of Mexico onto the shoulders of the Indians. A few heroic students, instructed in French liberty by a Spanish cleric, made Central America rise in revolt against Spain under a Spanish general. In monarchic garb emblazoned with the sun, the Venezuelans to the north and the Argentineans to the south began building nations. When the two heroes clashed and the continent was about to rock, one of them, and not the lesser, handed the reins to the other. And since heroism in times of peace is rare because it is not as glorious as in times of war, it is easier for a man to die with honor than to think with logic. It is easier to govern when feelings are exalted and united than after a battle, when divisive arrogant, exotic, or ambitious thinking emerges. The forces routed in the epic struggle with the feline cunning of the species, and using the weight of realities were under-mining the new structure which comprised both the rough-and-ready, unique regions of our halfbreed America and the silk-stocking and frockcoated people of Paris beneath the flag of freedom and reason borrowed from nations skilled in the arts of government. The hierarchical constitution of the colonies resisted the democratic organization of the republics. The clavated capitals left their country boots in the vestibule. The bookworm redeemers failed to realize that the revolution succeeded because it came from the soul of the nation; they had to govern with that soul and not without it or against it. America began to suffers, from the tiresome task of reconciling the hostile and discordant elements it inherited from a despotic and perverse colonizer, and the imported methods and ideas which have been retarding logical government because they are lacking in local realities. Thrown out of gear for three centuries by a power which denied men the right to use their reason, the continent disregarded or closed its ears to the unlettered throngs that helped bring it to redemption, and embarked on a government based on reason—a reason belonging to all for the common good, not the university brand of reason over the pleasant brand. The problem of independence did not lie in a change of forms but in a change of spirit.

It was imperative to make common cause with the oppressed, in order to secure a new system opposed to the ambitions and governing habits of the oppressors. The tiger, frightened by gunfire, returns at night to his prey. He dies with his eyes shooting flames and his claws unsheathed. He cannot be heard coming because he approaches with velvet tread. When the prey awakens, the tiger is already upon it. The colony lives on in the republic, and Our America is saving itself from its enormous mistakes the pride of its capital cities, the blind triumph of a scorned peasantry, the excessive influx of foreign ideas and formulas, the wicked and un-politic disdain for the aboriginal race because of the higher virtue, enriched with necessary blood, or a republic struggling against a colony. The tiger lurks behind every tree, lying in wait at every turn. He will die with his claws unsheathed and his eyes shooting flames.

But "these countries will be saved," as was announced by the Argentinean Rivadavia, whose only sin was being a gentleman in these rough-and-ready times. A man does not sheathe a machete in a silken scabbard, nor can he lay aside the short lance in a country won with the short lance merely because he is angered and stands at the door of Iturbide's Congress, "demanding that the fairhaired one be named Emperor." These countries will be saved because a genius for moderation, found in the serene harmony of Nature, seems to prevail on the continent of light, where there emerges a new realistic man schooled for these realistic times in the critical philosophy which in Europe has replaced the philosophy of guess-work and phalanstery that saturated the previous generation.

We were a phenomenon with the chest of an athlete, the hands of a dandy, and the brain of a child. We were a masquerader in English breeches, Parisian vest, North American jacket, and Spanish cap. The Indian hovered near us in silence, and went off to the hills to baptize his children. The Negro was seen pouring out the songs of his heart at night, alone and unrecognized among the rivers and wild animals. The peasant, the creator, turned in blind indignation against the disdainful city, against his own child. As for us, we were nothing but epaulets and professors' gowns in countries that came into the world wearing hemp sandals and headbands. It would have been the mark of genius to couple the headband and the professors' gown with the founding fathers' generosity and courage, to rescue the Indian, to make a place for the competent Negro, to fit liberty to the body of those who rebelled and conquered for it. We were left with the judge, the general, the scholar, and the sinecure. The angelic young, as if caught in the tentacles of an octopus, lunged heavenward, only to fall back, crowned with clouds, in sterile glory. The native, driven by instinct, swept away the golden staffs of office in blind triumph. Neither the Europeans nor the Yankee could provide the key to the Spanish American riddle. Hate was attempted, and every year the countries amounted to less. Exhausted by the senseless struggle between the book and the lance, between reason and the processional candle, between the city and the country, weary of the impossible rule by rival urban cliques over the natural nation tempestuous or inert by turns, we begin almost unconsciously to try love. Nations stand up and greet one another.

"What are we?" is the mutual question, and little by little they furnish answers. When a problem arises in Cojimar, they do not seek it solution in Danzig. The frockcoats are still French, but thought begins to be American. The youth of America are rolling up their sleeves, digging their hands in the dough, and making it rise with the sweat of their brows. They realize that there is too much imitation, and that creation holds the key to salvation. "Create" is the password of this generation. The wine is made from plantain, but even if it turns sour, it is our own wine! That a country's form of government must be in keeping with its natural elements is a foregone conclusion. Absolute ideas must take relative forms if they are not to fail because of an error in form. Freedom, to be viable, has to be sincere and complete. If a republic refuses to open its arms to all, and move ahead with all, it dies. The tiger within sneaks in through the crack; so does the tiger from without. The general holds back his cavalry to a pace that suits his infantry, for if the infantry is left behind, the cavalry will be surrounded by the enemy. Politics and strategy are one. Nations should live in an atmosphere of self-criticism because criticism is healthy, but always with one heart and one mind. Stoop to the unhappy, and lift them up in your arms! Thaw out frozen America with the fire of your hearts! Make the natural blood of the nations course vigorously through their veins. The new Americans are on their feet, saluting each other from nation to nation, the eyes of the laborers shining with joy. The natural statesman arises, schooled in the direct study of Nature. He reads to apply his knowledge, not to imitate. Economists study the problems at their point of origin. Speakers begin a policy of moderation. Playwrights bring native characters to the stage. Academies discuss practical subjects. Poetry shears off its romantic locks and hangs its red vest on the glorious tree. Selective and sparkling prose is filled with ideas. In the Indian republics, the governors are learning Indian. America is escaping all its dangers. Some of the republics are still beneath the sleeping octopus, but others, under the law of averages, are draining their lands with a sublime and furious haste, as if to make up for centuries lost. Still others, forgetting that Juarez went about in a carriage drawn by mules, hitch their carriages to the wind, their coachmen soap bubbles. Poisonous luxury, the enemy of freedom, corrupts the frivolous and open the door to the foreigner. In others, where independence is threatened, an epic spirit heightens their manhood. Still others spawn an army capable of devouring them in voracious wars. But perhaps Our America is running another risk that does not come from itself but from the difference in origins, methods, and interests between the two halves of the continent, and the time is near at hand when an enterprising and vigorous people who scorn or ignore Our America will even so approach it an demand a close relationship. And since strong nations, self-made by law and shotgun, love strong nations, and them alone; since the time of madness and ambition from which North America may be freed by the predominance of the purest elements in its blood, or on which it may be launched by its vindictive and sordid masses, its tradition of expansion, or the ambitions of some powerful leader is not so near at hand, even to the most timorous eye, that there is no time for the test of discreet and unwavering pride that could confront and dissuade it; since its good name as a republic in the eyes of the world's perceptive nations puts upon North America a restraint that cannot be taken away by childish provocations or pompous arrogance or parricidal discords among Our America nations the pressing need of Our America is to show itself as it is, one in spirit and intent, swift conqueror of a suffocating past, stained only by the enriching blood drawn from hands that struggle to clear away the ruins, and from the scars left upon us by our masters. The scorn of our formidable neighbor who does not know us is Our America's greatest danger. And since the day of the visit is near, it is imperative that our neighbor know us, and soon, so that it will not scorn us. Through ignorance it might even come to lay hands on us. Once it does know us, it will remove its hands out of respect. One must have faith in the best in men and distrust the worst. One must allow the best to be shown so that it reveals and prevails over the worst. Nations should have a pillory for whoever stirs up useless hates, and another for whoever fails to tell them the truth in time.

There can be no racial animosity, because there are no races. The theorists and feeble thinkers string together and warm over the bookshelf races which the well-disposed observer and the fair-minded traveler vainly seek in the justice of Nature where man's universal identity springs forth from triumphant love and the turbulent hunger for life. The soul, equal and eternal, emanates from bodies of various shapes and colors. Whoever foments and spreads antagonism and hate between the races, sins against humanity. But as nations take shape among other different nations, there is a condensation of vital and individual characteristics of thought and habit, expansion and conquest, vanity and greed which could from the latent state of national concern, and in a period of internal disorder, or the rapidity with which the country's character has been accumulating be turned into a serious threat for the weak and isolated neighboring countries declared by the strong country to be inferior and perishable. The thought is father to the deed. And one must not attribute, through a provincial antipathy, a fatal and inborn wickedness to the continent's fairskinned nation simply because it does not speak our language, or see the world as we see it, or resemble us in its political defects, so different from ours, or favorably regard the excitable, dark-skinned people, or look charitably from its still uncertain eminence upon those less favored by history, who climb the road of republicanism by heroic stages. The self-evident facts of the problem should not be obscured, because the problem can be resolved, for the peace of centuries to come, by appropriate study, and by tacit and immediate unity in the continental spirit. With a single voice the hymn is already being sung. The present generation is carrying industrious America along the road enriched by their sublime fathers; from the Rio Grande to the Straits of Magellan, the Great Sem, astride his condor, is sowing the seed of the new America through-out the Latin nations of the continent and the sorrowful islands of the sea!

Source:

Our America: Writings on Latin America and the Struggle for Cuban Independence. New York: Monthly Review Press, 1977. pp. 84-94.

One of the most influential—and controversial—members of Miami's Cuban-exile community is Jorge Mas Canosa, longtime chairman of the Cuban American National Foundation (CANF). The son of a Cuban army veterinarian, Mas was born in the port city of Santiago de Cuba. As a student activist in his native country during the late 1950s, he ran afoul of authorities after denouncing the corrupt regime of military dictator Fulgencio Batista on the radio. Mas's parents then sent him to the United States to attend school in Maxton, North Carolina. Following the Castro-led coup that ousted Batista from power in 1959, there was some hope among Cubans that their new leader would temper his radicalism and follow a more moderate course. But it soon became clear that the country had merely traded one authoritarian leader for another. Mas, who had returned home a week after the revolution to enroll in law school at the University of Oriente, soon became active in the anti-Castro movement and once again found himself facing arrest. So, in 1960 he fled to Miami.

In the city's Little Havana neighborhood, Mas joined the famous 2506 Brigade, which participated in the disastrous Bay of Pigs invasion of Cuba in 1961. Like the rest of the veterans of that unsuccessful U.S.-backed attempt to overthrow Castro, he was then offered a commission as a lieutenant in the U.S. Army, but as soon as he realized that another invasion was unlikely, he resigned his commission and returned to Miami, where he worked various jobs to support his growing family.

Later in the 1960s, Mas secured financial assistance that enabled him to enter the business world as a partner in a local contracting firm, Iglesias y Torres. It was a time of tremendous growth in the Greater Miami area, and Mas's company prospered doing construction work for utilities and other public service corporations throughout South Florida. By the end of the decade, he had bought out his partners and anglicized the firm's name to Church & Tower. As a result of the tremendous success he continued to enjoy throughout the 1970s, Mas began to branch out into other businesses as well and before long, the once-impoverished immigrant was a multimillionaire.

At the same time he was making his fortune in business, Mas forged close relationships with local and state government officials who were sympathetic to the anti-Castro exiles and encouraged them to adopt a tough, uncompromising approach toward Cuba. Following the election of staunch anti-communist Ronald Reagan to the presidency of the United States in 1980, Mas felt the time was right for Cuban Americans "to stop the commando raids and concentrate on influencing public opinion and governments." So he and 14 other wealthy members of the Miami exile community who shared his views established the Cuban American National Foundation (CANF) to disseminate information to the public on conditions in Cuba and promote the idea of fostering political change there.

Throughout the 1980s, Mas built CANF into one of the most powerful lobbying organizations in Washington by successfully persuading important members of both political parties—including presidents Ronald Reagan and George Bush—that Fidel Castro represents a continuing threat to democracy in the Western Hemisphere. (This perception in turn helped shape U.S. foreign policy during the period, especially in Central America and the Caribbean.) He also made overtures to a couple of dozen world leaders as well, including Russian President Boris Yeltsin, urging them to isolate Castro and Cuba. One of Mas's greatest triumphs, in fact, came when Russia ended all economic and military aid to Cuba in 1993.

Domestically, CANF has supported legislation and other measures aimed at making life difficult for Cubans and therefore for Castro, such as limiting the amount of money Cuban exiles can send back home to help out their families, cutting off flight service from Miami to Cuba for family members, and detaining those who attempt to flee Cuba by boat at the U.S. military base at Cuba's Guantánamo Bay. Mas has also worked out a special arrangement with the U.S. Immigration and Naturalization Service allowing Cuban exiles living in other countries to enter the United States if they are sponsored by CANF.

In late 1991, Mas played a key role in drafting the Cuban Democracy Act (S. 2918), a bill that proposed strengthening the decades-old trade embargo against Cuba. While opponents of the measure argued that it was unduly harsh and punitive and would only result in more suffering among the Cuban people, CANF and its supporters viewed it as a way to intensify the internal pressures on Castro and thus hasten his downfall. When first introduced in February of 1992, the bill garnered little support. The State Department opposed it as a "self-destructive" move guaranteed to anger our allies because it banned trade with Cuba by U.S. subsidiaries located in third countries. As he had done several times in the past for other pending legislation regarding Cuba, Mas personally appeared before members of the House and Senate to present the case in favor of the Cuban Democracy Act on August 5, 1992. The Cuban Democracy Act sailed through both the House and the Senate in the fall of 1992 and was signed into law by President George Bush. As predicted by some, it led to a greatly reduced standard of living for the Cuban people and it also triggered periodic refugee crises as desperate Cubans take to makeshift boats to escape across the Straits of Florida and the promise of freedom in the United States.

Mas, as a member of the older generation, always dreamt of the day when he could once again live in the town where he was born and grew up. As he declared to a reporter for the Los Angeles Times, as quoted in an Esquire article: "I am a Cuban first. I have never assimilated. I love America, and I would die for it. I'd never have been so successful in Cuba. But people like me need to be fed with more than success. I have all the money I'll ever need. I don't do this for the money. I do *this because I feel like a tree without roots." He died from lung cancer on November 24, 1997, at his home in Miami, never having seen a democratic Cuba.*

JORGE MAS CANOSA'S SPEECH SUPPORTING THE CUBAN DEMOCRACY ACT

Thank you, Mr. Chairman. It is my honor to appear before you and the distinguished members of the Senate Foreign Relations Committee to talk about U.S. policy toward Cuba. I sincerely hope that our discussion today will lead to decisions that in some way can bring an end to the suffering of the Cuban people, including the tragedy taking place in the Straits of Florida where thousands of Cubans are dying while trying to escape Fidel Castro's tyranny in unseaworthy rafts and boats.

Mr. Chairman, Fidel Castro's trip to Spain two weeks ago for the Ibero-American summit served as a telling indicator of the current state of his regime. Everywhere he went, he was heckled and jeered, the Spanish press criticized him, and all Latin American heads of state in Madrid openly criticized him in public. It was such a setback for Castro that he cut his visit several days short, and even shorter still when mere rumors about troop movements on the island caused him to flee back to Cuba.

Mr. Chairman, this growing global intolerance of Fidel Castro, evident in numerous meetings I have had with heads of state around the world, demonstrates that a policy of isolating Fidel Castro is not simply a United States position, but it is one that is gaining the increasing support of the world community.

If Castro is a pariah, it is the Cuban people who continue to bear the very heavy burden of his arrogance and intransigence in the face of the global march toward freedom and democracy. Press reports out of Cuba and personal testimonies describe an ever more depressing situation on the island; an economy grinding to a halt, pervasive rationing, a skyrocketing underground economy, widespread discontent and alienation, and widespread repression of human rights.

Just in case any Cuban citizen gets the idea that they may want to publicly disagree with the regime, rapid action brigades—thugs reminiscent of Hitler's brown shirts—have been organized to tor-

ment and physically abuse anyone considering such action. These measures, Mr. Chairman, actually are desperate reactions to a growing phenomenon in Cuba today: increasing numbers of Cubans who will not accept socialism or death, who are moving decisively beyond dissident activity to outright open opposition to the regime.

This leads me into the topic of today's discussion—U.S.-Cuba relations and specifically, S. 2918, the Cuban Democracy Act of 1992, which forty-seven of your colleagues, Mr. Chairman, have signed on as co-sponsors. I am grateful that we have moved beyond the sterile debate over whether to engage in dialogue with Fidel Castro to a more promising discussion on options for accelerating Castro's departure from power and building a foundation for a new and democratic Cuba.

Mr. Chairman, we believe the current situation, both inside and outside Cuba, mandates a new approach to promoting a peaceful transition to democracy in Cuba. That is why we in the Cuban American Foundation support the Cuban Democracy Act, which applies the stick to Castro by tightening U.S. sanctions against his regime, and extends a carrot to the Cuban people by facilitating humanitarian assistance and expanding lines of communication.

I might add that a recent poll of Cuban Americans showed sixty-nine percent of the community also supports the bill. More importantly, so do numerous peaceful opposition groups on the island, including the Cuban Democratic Coalition, the largest opposition organization on the island, several groups of the Cuban Democratic Convergence, and twelve more independent opposition groups. In fact, one jailed dissident, Pablo Reyes, was told by Cuban security forces the reason he was arrested was because of his public support for the Cuban Democracy Act. He is now facing a sixteen-year sentence.

Jorge Mas Canosa

The Cuban Democracy Act is reminiscent of the U.S. approach toward South Africa, where a comprehensive policy of economic and political isolation made a very real contribution toward fostering change in that society. The political and economic isolation of Fidel Castro must remain the cornerstone of U.S. policy as long as Castro continues to reject any meaningful reform and refuses to surrender power. Why? Number one, it sends a message to those in leadership positions around Castro that he, Castro, is the obstacle to Cuba's reintegration into the family of nations.

Also, engagement with Castro does not work, Mr. Chairman. Just look at the former Soviets; they were engaged with Castro for thirty years and they have no influence over his behavior whatsoever. Two days ago, in the *Washington Post* a former United Nations Ambassador, Jeane Kirkpatrick, observed that in the current crises in Iraq, Yugoslavia, and Cambodia, Saddam Hussein and the others like him used peace negotiations and other agreements as tactics to buy short-range advantages. She writes it is standard practice for cutthroats to make agreements when the heat is on and to break them later. That could be used as a preview of coming attractions should we travel that road with Castro, Mr. Chairman. The Cuban American Foundation also supports the measures in the Cuban Democracy Act to tighten the U.S. embargo of Cuba, especially at this time when Fidel

Castro's functionaries are roaming the world in a desperate search for alternative sources of aid.

When you provide resources to Cuba, all of those resources go in the hands of Fidel Castro, and him alone. He has used the roughly $100 billion in aid received from the Soviet Union, not to help the Cuban people, who have been issued rationing books since 1960, but to buy the loyalty of those around him to sustain himself in power. The embargo deprives Fidel Castro of those resources and will continue to shrink his inner circle.

Indeed, to see who would benefit from trade relations with Cuba Mr. Chairman, follow the money. The Cuban American National Foundation has obtained from sources inside Cuba a financial audit of a Cuban front company in Panama called CIMEX, one of many he uses to circumvent the U.S. embargo to get U.S. products into Cuba and to get Cuban products into the United States.

CIMEX was cited, incidentally, in the recent letter made public from former General Patricio de la Guardia, who is serving thirty years in a Cuban jail for his part in the Ochoa affair, as one holding 500 kilos of cocaine for shipments to the United States. These financial records show, Mr. Chairman, that at a time of outrageous austerity measures being imposed on the Cuban people, Fidel Castro is hoarding $300 million in total assets in CIMEX, one of his personal piggy banks, including $100 million in cash, twice the amount of the total reported cash reserves held by the Castro regime.

These are the types of activities Fidel Castro continues to be engaged in, and it is why we want to make the U.S. embargo more effective. One measure in the Cuban Democracy Act that does so is what is known as the Mack Amendment, which you, Mr. Chairman, have supported in the past, a provision that would restore the embargo to its original language by closing the loophole opened in 1975 that allows foreign subsidiaries of U.S. companies to trade with Cuba.

It is truly distressing that at a time when Russia has radically reduced trade relations and eliminated subsidies to Castro, U.S. companies are extending a trade lifeline to Fidel Castro through their foreign subsidiaries. Even more so when subsidiary trade is not allowed with any other nation embargoed under the Trade With the Enemy Act.

Equally important to increasing economic pressure on the Castro regime is the idea of improving communications with the Cuban people. We support the elements of the Cuban Democracy Act that would institute careful and direct openings to the Cuban people quite apart from the regime, to

A Cuban flag is placed on the coffin carrying Cuban exile leader Jorge Mas Canosa (d.1997). He was laid to rest after a procession through Little Havana in Miami.

contribute to the opening up of Cuban society. What can we communicate to the Cuban people? That there is life after Castro and that the international community is in solidarity with them.

In every available forum, the U.S. must reiterate that the Cuban people face no threat from the United States, that they should not fear a change in government, and that the United States is eager to restore traditional ties of economic and diplomatic cooperation with a free Cuba. We should not let Castro get away with the fear and hysteria over an American invasion that never seems to come.

We can also go a long way in rebutting the ludicrous charges made regularly in certain media circles that sinister Cuban exiles are plotting to return to Cuba and seize property and resources once Castro is gone from power. Indeed, if one were to believe his reporting, you would think that people on the island are vehemently anti-American,

fearful of an invasion by Cuban exiles and foreign capitalists, and repulsed by the free-market system.

This cartoon caricature of the Cuban people could not be more inaccurate. Cubans on the island are painfully aware that communism does not work and that Cuban Americans enjoy tremendous opportunities that are denied [them]. Let us not delude ourselves by automatically equating Cuban nationalism with anti-Americanism. It is not that simple. Let me also state for the record that Cuban exiles have no intention of going back to Cuba to buy the island, to conquer the island, to hold people in Cuba accountable for the actions in Cuba during the last thirty-three years.

We must reassure the Cuban citizens on the island that we, the Cuban people, are one nation divided by one man, this outdated dictator, Fidel Castro. The only one who fears the reunification of the Cuban people is Castro. Finally, Mr. Chairman, the last dimension of the Cuban Democracy Act, stating what the U.S. is prepared to do to help Cuba, once Castro is out of power and free and fair elections are held. This includes, among other measures, removing the U.S. embargo.

I cannot overestimate the symbolic importance of this for the Cuban people. It says that this powerful nation is waiting to help and will do what it can to alleviate the inevitable and tremendous difficulties of transforming a country decimated economically and spiritually by thirty-three years of Marxist dictatorship. It will also make a positive contribution to ensuring that those positions of power in Cuba, around the Castro brothers, support a peaceful, nonviolent transition.

Fidel Castro has attempted to crush the Cuban people's hopes for the future and the future of their children. I believe the Cuban Democracy Act will restore that hope. We must not let the Cuban peo-

ple down. The Cuban people are going to decide for themselves their own destiny.

It is our responsibility to do what we can to hasten the demise of the Castro regime and the advent of a free democratic and prosperous Cuba. All that is needed is the vision and the will to seize this opportunity to help eliminate, once and for all, a bizarre political experiment that has plagued our era. Then, and only then, can the suffering of the Cuban people be replaced by a new golden age of national self-determination and economic revival. Thank you very much.

Source:

The Cuban Democracy Act of 1992, S. 2918: Hearing Before the Subcommittee on Western Hemisphere and Peace Corps Affairs of the Committee on Foreign Relations, United States Senate, 102nd Congress, 2nd Session, U.S. Government Printing Office, 1992.

*M*iami *is home to approximately 600,000 Cuban-Americans, and Cuban-Americans are the third largest Hispanic community in the United States. When Mireya Navarro wrote* Generations of Exiles, *Cubans had succeeded in integrating into the community in Miami. Cuban Americans held the positions of mayor of the city, mayor of the county, county police chief, county state attorney, president of the largest bank, owner of the largest real estate developer, and managing partner of the largest law firm. Yet Cuban immigrants came from radically different Cuban societies, and immigration over time has made Miami so distinctly Cuban that the cultural conflicts are no longer between Americans and Cubans as they are between various waves of Cuban immigrants. Navarro points out that Cubans who fled in the 1960s were largely products of a capitalistic society, whereas Cubans who came to the United States after that time had lived with Communism, where the state provided services. The capitalistic society of the United States was often a shock to the latter wave of Cuban-Americans.*

Cuban immigrants began arriving in the United States as early as 1868. Prior to the mid-1900s, New York City was one of the primary destinations for Cuban immigrants. When rail, highway links, and ferry service were created between Miami and Key West and Havana, the immigration pattern shifted, and Miami became the principle staging area for incoming immigrants. In 1959, Fidel Castro's Fidelistas took control of the government, and this initiated a tremendous influx of immigrants. As Communism became dominant, the United States initiated measures such as a trade embargo and an unsuccessful invasion at the Bay of Pigs in retaliation for the nationalization of hundreds of millions of dollars of United States Property and private business. In 1960, Castro established a full diplomatic relationship with the Soviet Union, which until 1991 was Cuba's major trading partner. Cuban immigrants fled because they feared persecution under the new regime. They were considered victims of Communism and were given special treatment by the

United States government, which had an open door policy towards Cuban immigrants. The Cuban Refugee Program, conducted between 1961 and 1978, dispersed incoming Cubans throughout the United States, focusing on New York, New Jersey, California and Illinois. During this time airlifts, conducted from 1965 until 1973, brought over 200,000 Cubans to the United States. In another influx, the Mariel boatlift took place in 1980 and lasted for six months, bringing in 125,000 Cubans. The open-door policy ended in 1987 when the United States and Cuba signed an agreement providing for 20,000 Cuban visas annually, chosen by lot. In 1994, however, a number of balseros (rafters) attempted to cross the Straits of Florida. Many of these would-be immigrants were intercepted and sent to refugee camps in Guantanamo naval base or Panama. A new agreement made in September of 1994 re-established the quota of 20,000 visas, but excluded cases where Cubans wanted to reunite with immediate relatives living in the United States.

The 1990 Census showed that nearly 60 percent of all Cuban Americans lived in Miami. This is likely due to the availability of employment, and a familiar cultural environment. Miami's Cuban community is a distinct economic grouping of immigrants who have organized their own services and ethnic market. Ethnic bonds provide a level of support and help the immigrant in the adjustment process, but does not necessarily help the immigrant adjust to the new culture. Most Cubans use only Spanish at home, and Miami has effectively become a bilingual city. The community serves to preserve the culture of the homeland, but the generational differences that Navarro portrays have the potential to diminish the influences of the traditional culture. What is more, Navarro also discusses the fact that Miami is becoming home to other ethnic groups such as Salvadorans and Colombians. This, too, will make Miami less of a Cuban cultural enclave and more of a multicultural city.

GENERATIONS OF EXILES
by Mireya Navarro

Miami, Feb. 10—In a classroom of newly arrived Cubans, Alex Alvarez, a Cuban transplant himself, wasted no time scaring his students straight. "Welcome to the capitalist system," he said.

"Each one of you is responsible for the amount of money you have in your pocket. The Government is not responsible for whether you eat, or whether you're poor or rich. The Government doesn't guarantee you a job or a house.

"You've come to a rich and powerful country, but it is up to you whether or not you continue living like you did in Cuba."

Such warnings were not necessary 40 years ago, when Cubans fleeing Fidel Castro settled down here to await, some to plot, his downfall. They came from a capitalist system, with enough education and ambition to fulfill the American dream. But Mr. Castro has lasted so long that Miami now reflects different Cubas.

The people from today's Cuba are the children of a revolution that provided social guarantees but limited opportunities.

They include those filling out job applications in Mr. Alvarez's class at the Training and Employment Council of South Florida, where he admonishes them, "Put down 'High School, Havana, Cuba.' Do not write 'secundaria Ho Chi Minh.'"

The people from an earlier Cuba, and their children, have grown into a Miami Who's Who. The mayors of the city and county of Miami, the county police chief and the county state attorney are all Cuban-born or of Cuban descent. So are the president of the largest bank, the owner of the largest real estate developer, the managing partner of the largest law firm, nearly half of the country's 27-member delegation in the Legislature and two of its six members of Congress.

About the only accomplishment Cuban-Americans cannot claim is regaining their country.

Cuban American children carry crosses that represent people who have died under the Castro regime.

"There's an irony and pathos about the situation," a University of Miami sociologist and expert on Cuban affairs, Max Castro, said. "They have succeeded as immigrants and failed as exiles."

That success and failure is etched on Miami, the main repository of Cuban dreams and dissent in the United States, where the news one day can be about a Cuban-American company's shares being traded on the New York Stock Exchange, and the next about the arrest of four aging exiles on a mission to assassinate Mr. Castro.

But the immigration over the decades has made Miami so distinctly Cuban that the cultural clash is no longer between Cubans and Americans as much as between different waves of Cuban immigrants.

With each batch of immigrants who win the annual visa lottery, each of the smuggled boatloads of Cubans that land almost daily in South Florida, Cuban Miami becomes less cohesive, encompassing a people who differ in social class, race, generation and politics, who increasingly come from different worlds.

The first and the latest waves of Cubans, particularly, said a sociologist at the University of Michigan, Silvia Pedraza, "live side by side but remain aloof from one another."

Until recently the Federal Government had an open-door policy for Cuban immigrants, welcoming

them as victims of Communism. They still get special treatment. Each year, 20,000 are granted visas by lot.

The New Wave

Despite Welcome, A Hard Transition

Immigrants from Cuba still count on welcoming relatives like Efrain Veiga, who left Cuba as a child in 1962 and now, at 47, is the successful owner of the Yuca restaurant in Miami Beach. Mr. Veiga has visited Cuba twice and regularly sends money to relatives there.

But even Mr. Veiga was startled by his latest experience with a cousin, whom he had helped leave the island, put up in his own home here and given a job in his restaurant.

Mr. Veiga said he was surprised when his cousin balked at working weekends. And the restaurant owner was outright shocked, he said, when one of his waiters showed up for work wearing a pair of expensive shoes he had given his cousin. "Where did you get those shoes?" Mr. Veiga asked. "Your cousin sold them to me," the waiter replied..

Mr. Veiga has hired other new-comers from Cuba and found many of them also stuck in the day-to-day survival mode of modern Cuba, where trading shoes for dollars could put food on the table.

"Their life style and way of thinking is different," Mr. Veiga said. "Deep down they feel we owe them something, that we've had it better."

The shock is mutual. Mr. Alvarez's students said one of their biggest surprises in the United States was how hard people work. Another is how "Americanized" their compatriots have become, they say.

"People are so materialistic," said Olga Rodriguez, 40, who came legally last year with a son, 22 and daughter, 15. "It's like they have the dollar sign on their forehead. It hasn't happened to me yet. I offer rides to classmates in language school even if I have to go out of my way."

Eduardo Marquez, 30, arrived in the United States after a year in American refugee camps Panama and Guantanamo Bay, Cuba. Only one of several distant relatives offered to put him up when he finally got here in 1995, and then only for two weeks. He said no thanks.

"They think we all steal," he said. "Mr. Marquez, a painter and sculptor who sold his art on the streets of Havana, said his relatives had also painted too rosy a picture of life here. "I thought that this was a wonderland, that you'd kick a rock and money would fall out," he said. Instead, he has bounced from job to job while struggling to start a pest control business.

Mr. Marquez does not regret leaving Cuba. The island, however, still has the pull of the 7-year-old daughter and a brother.

"I'm not political but from a human standpoint, they're killing of hunger the people, not Fidel," Mr. Marquez said, explaining why he opposed the American trade embargo of Cuba. "People here think that in Cuba a group could get organized to take Fidel out. That's really easy to say with a full stomach."

The First Wave

A Cuba Recalled, Then Recreated

It is true that many older exiles have lost touch, living off of memories that may or may not be accurate. But full stomachs have not tempered the craving for their homeland of those who settled her in the 1960s, fleeing the radicalization of the island and fearing political persecution and Communist indoctrination of their children. They have recreated pre-revolution Cuba here, renaming streets after Cuban martyrs, reactivating Cuban social clubs, trade organizations and businesses, filling supermarket shelves with "Cubano" versions of coffee, cheese and bread.

In this parallel Cuban universe, Jose Lopez-Silvero, 78, and Alfredo Blanco, 80, president and vice-president of the Sugar Producers of Cuba Inc., which represents those whose companies were nationalized by the Castro regime, can say exactly how much their former sugar mills are producing today and how much the workers earn. They have not seen Cuba since they left in 1960, but their information is all first-hand, gleaned from recent arrivals and letters from Cuba. Their ties, while no longer familial, remain emotional.

The former sugar producers want to recover their nationalized properties, which had been with some families for generations and which they regard as stolen. Their group also has a plan for restoring the sugar industry to its past glory in "post-Communist Cuba," one of many reconstruction plans hatched all over Miami for the moment Cuba gains its "freedom," as if Mr. Castro's four-decade rule has been just a temporary setback, a bad dream.

In their long exile, Mr. Blanco, a retired sugar trader and executive, and Mr. Lopez-Silvero, a retired corporate legal consultant, have supported the 37-year-old American embargo. They blame its failure to induce democratic change in Cuba on past Soviet subsidies and what they deem lax enforcement of its toughest provisions.

They have seen changes come close—before the Bay of Pigs invasion failed, after the Berlin wall fell—only to be let down. Now, they say, it is only a matter of time.

"Castro has to die some day," said Mr. Blanco, who is eight years older than the ruler.

Many of the early immigrants' children, however, are not waiting Mr. Castro out. Fed by their parents' nostalgia, aided by the contacts allowed with Cuba and driven more by curiosity than patriotism, they help fill clubs that feature bands from the island, and the charter flights to Havana that leave several times a week from Miami International Airport.

Richard Blanco, 30, a civil engineer born in Madrid to Cuban exiles and raised in Miami, visited Cuba in 1994 for the first time. He said the country did not deviate much from the descriptions he had heard growing, "except for the poverty," and he felt totally at ease. Last year he published a book of poems that laid out some of the feelings of his generation. One poem, "Mail for Mama," reads:

Monthly, you would peel eggshell pages,
The white onionskin paper telling details:
Kiki's first steps, your mother's death,
Dates approximated by the postmarks.

Sometimes with pictures: mute black and whites,
Poor photos of poor cousins I would handle
Looking for my resemblance in the foreign
Image of an ear, an eyebrow, or a nose.

The Next Wave

Other Ethnic Groups Dilute Cuban Flavor

While Miami's Cuban population evolves with American-born generations and newcomers, other demographic forces at work are changing the face of Hispanic Miami.

Cubans are still the single largest Latin American group, making up about 60 percent of the total Hispanic population, which accounts for more than half Miami-Dade County's population. But while the Cuban influx was accompanied by the flight of local whites, it coincided with the arrival of other Hispanic immigrants.

The Latin Americanization of Miami is slowly chipping away at the dominant Cuban identity. In Little Havana, storefronts advertise Salvadoran corn pancakes and waitresses hail from Honduras and Peru; on the radio, only one of three stations continue Cuba-oriented talk, and the area's highest-rated Spanish-language station is Colombian.

But if the voices are more diverse, and even politically moderate and liberal Cuban-Americans have come out in the open, Miami's political discourse and much of the media coverage is still largely defined by hard-edged conservatism. At times the city has the feel of a bubble suspended in time, where issues are debated as if Mr. Castro had just taken over, where "communist" is still the ultimate insult.

Polls have shown that a majority of Cubans here oppose even beginning a political dialogue with the Cuban government under Mr. Castro, a position zealously guarded by Cuban-Americans whose influence in Washington was personified by the founder of the Cuban American National Foundation, the late Jorge Mas Canosa, a man Presidents consulted on policy toward Cuba.

That unwavering stance, coupled with an image of political intolerance and violent episodes of right-wing extremism, has won the exiles little international sympathy. Mr. Castro, some political experts say, has proven far more shrewd at public relations than his opponents.

"We're seen as a narrow-minded," said Professor Castro, the University of Miami sociologist. "The one political success has been to turn U.S. policy in a hard-line direction, and that hasn't worked because it has the negative connotation that it hurts Cuban people."

Cuban-Americans like Bill Teck, editor of the magazine "Generation Ñ," a term applied to bicultural Hispanics members of Generation X, said his readers and staff differed on Cuba policy issues but shared a frustration that so many see Cuba through a romantic prism, blind to its political prisoners, its lack of democratic elections, its human rights violations.

"What we talk about is the failure of the cause of a free Cuba to permeate the pop culture," said Mr. Teck, who was born here of an American father and Cuban mother.

But among the younger generations, the conservative message has become less strident.

Alex Penelas, the Miami-born, 37-year-old mayor of Miami-Dade County and an ambitious politician many here expect to someday run for President, has inherited the conservatism of his parents. His father narrowly escaped a death sentence for plotting against Mr. Castro in 1960, said Mr. Penelas, who blames Mr. Castro for his never having met his paternal grandfather, who died in Cuba.

"I'm not convinced of this generational gap people talk about," said the Mayor, who is fluent in both English and Spanish.

Unlike many of his elders, however, Mr. Penelas has bicultural sensibilities. He said he would not have snubbed Nelson Mandela for his friendship with Mr. Castro, as Miami's Cuban leadership did when the South African leader visited here in 1990. The incident, which included the withdrawal of an official welcoming proclamation, prompted a three-year black tourism boycott of Miami-Dade County and worsened feelings of alienation among blacks here. "I would have met him, given the proclamation and use the opportunity" to give Mr. Mandela his opinion of Mr. Castro, he said.

And although he has lobbied for traditional Cuban-American causes like the embargo, he has also reached out to black constituents, championed gay rights and taken up the concerns of the numerous ethnic groups who now call Miami home.

Cuba still beckons, however. Mr. Penelas envisions "migration challenges" when the Communist Party loosens its grip on the island, as Cubans here expect after Mr. Castro's death. But he also sees an economic bonanza for Miami in trade and tourism if the embargo is lifted.

Mr. Penelas also expects to play some role in Cuba's transition to democracy, plans shared by many other Cuban-Americans, which some predict will create new conflict as a post-Castro Cuba is reshaped. But like most Cuban-Americans, naturalized or native born, he would stay put in Miami.

Less than 30 percent of the about 600,000 Cuban-Americans here would move to the island, polls show. This is where more than half of all Cubans in the United States have chosen to live, where the old have doctors, pensions and offspring, and where the young find opportunity and their own roots.

Miami, after all, is home.

Source:
New York Times, February 11, 1999.

CYPRIOT AMERICANS

An interview with Cypriot American Nikos Liadis profiled the will of a poor farming family's son in Cyprus to persevere and thrive despite major socio-economic hurdles. Nikos was born on the Greek island of Cyprus during a period of British rule early in the twentieth century. He remembered growing up in a large peasant family greatly susceptible to the effects of droughts resulting in periods when little food was available. Predating most moves to the United States by Greek Cypriots, Nikos' older brother immigrated to America in 1929 and established a restaurant. On Cyprus, Nikos was able to pursue his education beyond elementary school through sheer determination despite his family's poverty. After graduating from high school, Nikos became an interpreter for the British army during World War II.

Following the war the United States, representing the land of opportunity, beckoned young Nikos. In 1950, with increased political unrest and a weakening agricultural economy Nikos joined a growing Cypriot exodus that later peaked in the 1970s. Nikos first worked at his brother's restaurant. A typically hard working, family-oriented Cypriot American, Nikos eventually married and had three children. Greatly valuing education, Nikos was able to complete law school while working long hours at a family diner he started in 1955.

The Cypriot government was not a participatory form of democratic government while Nikos was growing up. No doubt like many other Cypriot Americans of his time, Nikos found political life in the United States new and exciting, particularly through his law school exposure. Also in his interview, Nikos observed that in order to survive in America, immigrants must be better than average in their daily lives in whatever they choose to do. Nikos asserted " you cannot expect to survive unless you are better than average. Everything else is not equal. We are a minority. And I've got to be better than the next person, if I'm going to survive. And besides, who wants to be a mediocrity?"

The process of immigrant children more fully assimilating into mainstream American society did not go unnoticed by Nikos. As he somewhat lamented, despite he and his wife's efforts to preserve a family awareness of their ancestry, his children considered themselves full-blooded Americans, not minorities.

NIKOS LIADIS: FROM CYPRUS, 1950

I come from a very poor farming family. We had eight brothers and sisters and two parents, was ten. And the farming and, generally speaking, the peasant's life wasn't such an enviable one, especially on the island of Cyprus, when you depend on rain; and we had very bad drought at the time. There was no rain and no crops, and the animals couldn't eat—there was no grass—and the peasant, the farmer, and the shepherd were really having quite a few difficult times. In fact, most of the people were lucky to get a piece of bread and olives and onion for breakfast, and then skip lunch and try and get a pot of beans for the evening.

Our village was at the time about five or six hundred people. When I finished the elementary school in the village I was the first one in the class, and that was out of curiosity, nothing more. I don't have any brilliant mind or any faculties better than the next person, but I was always first in my class, and when I graduated I remember the schoolmaster told my father, "If you don't take this kid to high school, you are going to do him an injustice." We needed two and a half shillings to go and pay for the fee to be examined if you qualify to go to high school. And as I said, in 1932 or '33, I think it was, my father didn't have it.

We didn't have the two and a half shillings, and he was delaying and postponing, and then, finally, one day I got angry and I said, "Dad, September is coming. I haven't gone for the examination yet. The year is gong to start and I'm not going to be in high school."

So he says, "Well, tomorrow."

"No! This is it!" I lay down in front of the cows and I said to my father, "If I can't go to high school, I don't want to live anymore. Go over me with the plow."

I remember I saw tears in his eyes, and he says, "Okay."

He tied up the cows and went to the village. He borrowed—I'll never forget this—he borrowed five shillings from the local grocer, who happened to be a second cousin of ours, and he took me right to Nicosia—it was about two or three miles—where I went for the examination. We went either on a donkey or in a cart, I don't remember.

When we got to the *gymnasium*—that's a high school, you know—a couple of the teachers saw me and asked, "What are you doing here?" I said, "I came here to take the examinations." They said the examinations were three months ago. I said, "Nobody told me." They said, "Too bad." And then I started crying. So a schoolmaster came I and he saw me. He says to me, "Why are you crying?" I said, "I came to take the examination. I want to go to high school." So—I'll never forget this man, he's still alive—he said, "Sit here. I'm going to arrange it." So he went out and he got to the mathematics teacher, who had pull, and he says, "This boy is crying and he wants to go to school. Why shouldn't we give him a chance?" So he called me over and he said, "Okay, we make an exception. We examine you." So that was the beginning of my high school, really. Even now when I think about it, I start crying.. . .

Then I began to wonder what is beyond the high-school education. Do the universities offer anything more, higher, finer, and better than what we were taught in high school? But that was more or less a dream. There is no university in Cyprus, and to go abroad and have to spend money for rent and books and tuition and what have you—it was out of the question at that time. But I had that inner desire, and I said, "If I don't go to university to learn something, I am being cheated."

But after high school the war broke out and we were limited to the island. Of course, it was a good thing to be there at that time. Because of security reasons we had the British navy. In fact, we never had any—other than a few sporadic attempts by the Italian air force to bomb the harbor of Famagusta—we didn't have anything else really. I was an interpreter in the army during the war—the English army. We had what we called the Cyprus regiment and the Cyprus volunteer force, and I was interpreting for the British instructors. It was quite an interesting experience. In fact, for a little while I was out in the field, which I enjoyed very much.

Then, after the war, I spent about a year in Cyprus doing odd jobs. Like I was helping on a farm. At one time I tried to raise chickens, but I wasn't too successful, thank God. So I decided that I have to try a little harder to get out of the island so I can go to the university, where I thought an education was necessary in order to satisfy my intellectual curiosity. I knew then that the United States was the country of opportunity, and since I was a child of a poor family, and I knew I had to more or less do it on my own, I felt this was the best place. And I had a brother here—he came in '29, I think. My brother became an American citizen, and after that he arranged for me to get my visa and come over to the United States.

My brother had a restaurant, and I started there, washing dishes. After a week or so I learned my way around; so I came out, I became a counterman for two or three weeks, and then I became a night assistant manager, and slowly, slowly, I became the manager and ran the place for two or three years. And that was my first trade, so to speak.

My brother and I found out there was a diner here for sale, so we bought the diner and we started in the diner business in 1955. At that time my one nephew came over from high school. I enrolled him at D—— University. And six months or a year after that, my next nephew came in, his brother. And I said to myself, "I'm going to help these two boys through college," because really I was resigned to the idea that I'm not going to do it myself. I might as well help somebody in the family. Also, this was an old debt that I was paying back, because these boys' father helped me go through high school in Cyprus. So I figured, to pay back the old debt I'd see to it that his two sons get a college education.

Now when they got here—especially when the second one got here—I was traveling back and forth, going by D—— University. And I said to myself, "Isn't this a shame? I go by every day; why don't I stop in to see what it looks like from the inside? And besides, while I spend the time to help these boys with their schooling, I might do something for myself." So I considered the idea that—uh—let me try it. By this time I had a family, three children. Although an old man, what have I got to lose?

So I started with D—— University for two courses in a semester, as a special student. I took Greek drama and political science, and I got very much interested in the work. I said, "Well, I'm going to finish." so I continued the next semester. I took either nine or twelve credits, and I kept working in the diner all the time. I went to summer school, and I think I took four courses a semester, which gave me perhaps a year's work. I completed three-quarters of the bachelor's degree. That was the minimum required for getting into law school. So I applied to law school and I was accepted. I was a poor candidate, because my law aptitude was so low, but somehow I impressed them with my grades, and I—you know—cried that I never took examinations of this kind before, and it was some

absolutely new thing to me, and that's why my record is so low. So I remember the dean of admissions says to me, "You impress me as a person and as a student, and I'm going to give you a chance. But you have to take the examination again." so I said, "Why not?" I took the examination the second time, but I was already admitted into the law school. At the time I got into law school I was thirty-eight or thirty-nine.

I worked through my college and through my law school. Well, in fact, when I was going to college I worked day and night; all night long, and I went to school half a day, that is, the morning. I started at eight and I finished at seven, and my brother used to put in the extra hour, God bless his soul. The diner was open twenty-four hours a day, and he was working thirteen hours a day and I was working eleven, to make the twenty-four hours. And when I finished at seven, I went home, washed, changed my clothes, and ran down to D—— University. I sat there from eight to eleven the first semester, and then until one in the following years.

My wife, during the time that I was going to college and law school, was really a saint. She was working at night as a waitress when I was sleeping to get ready for law school the following day. She used to come in from six at night to one in the morning and, you know we had a rough crowd there to feed. She was working there, and about one she woke me up to come to the diner and relieve her so she could go home, so she'd be ready in the morning to take care of our children to go to school.

Sometimes I couldn't keep awake in class. I told the fellow who was sitting next to me to give me the elbow once in a while. But I didn't have any problem really—I was so interested in what I was learning. But it was very difficult for me the first semester. I remember I just couldn't keep my eyes open—reading—and I remember I took American politics or American government. You know, where I come from there was no political life, as such, at the time. It was just that you're governed, and that's it. I didn't know what the structure of the American politics was. That was all new to me.. . .

We raised our children to know where they come from and what is their place in the American society. I believe to try to preserve the best we have in each nationality, and you don't preserve the best you have unless you are aware of your nationality, of your origin. For instance, I like to have my children know that Plato was a Greek, Aristotle was a Greek, *Oedipus Rex* was a Greek drama.

Of course, you cannot make the children understand that they are part of a minority. No, they feel they are full-blooded Americans, and there is no distinction, for instance, between an Irishman and a Greek, or a Jew and a German, or. . . . You know, it's very hard to make them understand that this is a country of different nationalities and perhaps discrimination in a subtle way. It's always around. They know that they've got to do better than the average child; otherwise I'm not satisfied. Because you cannot expect to survive unless you are better than average. Everything else is not equal. We are a minority. And I've got to be better than the next person, if I'm going to survive. And besides, who wants to be a mediocrity?

Source:

American Mosaic: The Immigrant Experience in the Words of Those Who Lived It, compiled by Joan Morrison and Charlotte Fox Zabusky. Pittsburgh: University of Pittsburgh Press, 1993. pp. 340-343.

CZECH AMERICANS

When Antonín Dvořák's Symphony No. 9 premiered on December 16, 1893, the Czech composer was 52-years old. His music was already celebrated throughout Europe and the United States. In some ways, he had reached the pinnacle of his career. From poor origins, the son of a butcher had overcome adversity early in life and gained an international reputation for his symphonies and string quartets. He traveled abroad frequently to conduct his own works in Germany and England and, in 1892, had begun a four-year residency in New York as director of the National Conservatory of Music. There he set about creating a new and ambitious piece of music.

In his native Czechoslovakia, Dvořák (1841-1904) had pursued a distinctive vision of his music. He was extremely proud of his heritage, and his art reflected this: he wanted his music to be at once Czech and European. Through his efforts, he succeeded in taking elements of his national folk music and incorporating them into contemporary European music. In 1893, while in New York, he attempted something similar. His study of Native American music and folk tales informed his latest work, which he subtitled "From the New World." The composition received its premiere at Carnegie Hall.

For a composer accustomed to honors, a positive response to a new composition was pleasant yet hardly a surprise. But the response to the Symphony No. 9 was hardly typical. As this review from the New York Herald newspaper explains, the audience was ecstatic "to the point of frenzy." A modest and humble man, Dvořák was personally overwhelmed. He later wrote to his publisher that he had been applauded through so many bows that he felt like a visiting member of royalty.

No less enthusiastic was the Herald's reviewer. Praising the symphony as "noble," "a great work," and "gorgeous," the review anticipated the larger critical reception that would follow in the years to come. Indeed, it ultimately became Dvořák's best known and perhaps best loved work. Its continuing popularity has made it one of the most performed symphonies in the twentieth century.

The review also speaks to another aspect of the audience's response. According to the reviewer, it was moved not only by the beauty of the music but by a sense of patriotism, too. This pride came from Dvořák having been inspired by his visit to America. The source of his particular inspiration was Native American music—ironically, a kind of music largely ignored in the nineteenth century United States. In fact, most of the melodies in the symphony are Czech in origin, artfully arranged to seem like Native American melodies. Yet for the writer of the Herald review, the United States—through the achievement of a visiting foreign genius—was on the map musically, at last. The New World could now claim to have spawned a music that would take its place among the masterpieces of the old.

AMERICA ADOPTS DVOŘÁK'S MUSIC

Dr. Antonín Dvořák, the famous Bohemian composer and director of the National Conservatory of Music, dowered American art with a great work yesterday, when his new symphony in E minor 'From the New World' was played at the second Philharmonic rehearsal in Carnegie Music Hall. The day was an important one in the musical history of America. It witnessed the first performance of a noble composition.

It saw a large audience of usually tranquil Americans enthusiastic to the point of frenzy over a musical work and applauding like the most excitable "Italianissimi" in the world.

The work was one of heroic proportions. And it was one cast in the art form which such poet-musicians as Beethoven, Schubert, Schumann, Mendelsohn, Brahms and many other 'glorious ones of the earth' have enriched with the most precious outwelling of his musical imagination.

And this new symphony by Antonín Dvořák is worthy to rank with the best creations of these musicians whom we have just mentioned. Small wonder that the listeners were enthusiastic. The work appealed to their sense of the aesthetically beautiful by its wealth of tender, pathetic, fiery melody; by its rich harmonic clothing; by its delicate, sonorous, gorgeous, ever varying instrumentation.

And it appealed to the patriotic side of them. For had not Dr. Dvořák been inspired by the impressions which this country had made upon him? Had he not translated these impressions into sounds, into music? Had they not been assured by the composer himself that the work was written under the direct influence of a serious study of the national music of the North American Indians? Therefore, were they not justified in regarding the composition, the first fruits of Dr. Dvořák's musical genius since his residence in this country, as a distinctive American work of art?

Source:

Czechs in America, 1633-1977: A Chronology & Fact Book, compiled and edited by Vera Laska. Dobbs Ferry, NY: Oceana Publications, 1978. p. 102.

The Bohemians who immigrated to the United States in the 1850s were farmers. Their country, Bohemia, which would later become part of Czechoslovakia, had grown too small and too violent for them. Settled by the Slavs in the sixth century, the central European kingdom enjoyed ten centuries of independence before its more powerful neighbor, Austria, swallowed it up. From the seventeenth century onward, Bohemia was a province of Austria-Hungary. By the 1850s, the Bohemians were weary of its aggressive rulers' ongoing wars, which cost them taxes and the blood of their young men, who were conscripted to fight. At the same time, thanks to improved agriculture, the population had exploded. There was not enough land in the agrarian society for everyone to work. Even housing was becoming scarce.

Following the advice of how-to books and rumors of cheap farmland, many Bohemians settled in the American Midwest. Midwestern states, which wished to grow, employed representatives who would meet emigrants at European ports and encourage them to choose the state as a destination. One such state was Wisconsin, which attracted many Bohemians from the district of Landskron, then about 115 miles north of Vienna. Drawn not only by economic potential, the Landskroner Bohemians were accustomed to living in a feudal society in which the ruling class dictated their limited rights. The promise of freedom in the new world was inspiring.

By the time the immigrant V. V. Vlach wrote "Our Bohemian Population" for the Wisconsin Historical Society, the Bohemian presence in the state was half a century old. From the financial panic at mid-century to the tumult of the American Civil War, it had been an eventful fifty years. The immigrants had found that farm land could be bought, but often only by working hard and saving for several years. Along with faring much better economically than they would have in the old world, they had developed a solid foothold upon the New World. With pride, they could point to their thriving communities; to the first Czech newspaper in America, Slowan Amerikansky ; to Czech-American members of the leading professions; and even to national heroes such as Charles Jonas, of the large Czech settlement in Racine, Wisconsin, who held American ambassadorships in Europe and was elected lieutenant-governor of the state.

Vlach's article is a kind of historical pulse-taking. He measures the progress, status, and political tendencies of his people. While there is much cause for pride in their accomplishments, Vlach's statement is notable for its exquisite humility. The Bohemians try "to be good American citizens," he wrote, and beg other Americans to forgive them for their failings. This quaint sentiment seems to spring from an authentic source—the earnestness with which immigrants in the nineteenth century sought to belong to, care for, and be respected as citizens of their adopted nation. Written nearly one hundred years ago, Vlach's prescient conclusion anticipated a future in which the old world's ethnic and cultural ties fade into historical memory, and yesterday's immigrant is today's American.

OUR BOHEMIAN POPULATION

Aside from an exceedingly personal interest which the Bohemians always take in every election, their duties to their homes and families have overshadowed any temptation to become political leaders or conspicuous public characters. Thus far in this state they have proven themselves content with gradual financial success as laborers, farmers, mechanics, and business men. They follow admirably the wise saying that "an unwise thirst for public employment is the worst of social maladies." Of course, if either of the two great political parties recognizes them with an appointive office, they take great pride in the fact; or, when one of them is elected to an office, he always, so far as I know, tries to perform its duties honestly. I am still looking for a Bohemian-American who, whether appointed or elected to an office, proved himself false or dishonest. It may be said of the Bohemians that, just as Hollanders are and always were unswerving Republicans, so the Bohemians were always loyal Democrats; but in recent years many of them are changing their polit-

ical views and are joining the ranks of the Republicans. Let scorn or wit exhaust their sneers and jibes, one fact must be admitted and cannot be truthfully denied of Bohemians—that as "Mugwumps" they have always exerted themselves for something higher and nobler than mere official patronage, and they cannot be accused of office-begging. This alone gives them a right to respect, and in it can be discerned a principle of political action, which should be an inspiring and elevating force in a government like our own.

Among the few men who have held positions of political prominence, and have been more or less influential in shaping the political choice of the Bohemians in America, was the lamented Charles Jonas of Racine, who, serving this country as consul to Germany, came to an untimely death. With deep affection for and trust in his own people, he made it his life-work to try to better their condition. He was recognized as the Bohemian authority of this country. His close application to literature and journalism, and his own ambitious efforts, undermined his health. He was editor of the *Slavie*, and author of various useful books; among these were translations of American laws and the constitution, and English-Bohemian and Bohemian-English dictionaries—books which may be found in almost every Bohemian home.

In conclusion, I will only add that the Bohemians do not pretend to be better than any other of the many nationalities that establish their homes in this state; but I do claim that they try their best to be good American citizens, and they only ask from their American fellow-citizens charitable indulgence for their imperfections and deficiencies. In a decade or two there will no longer be

Germans, Bohemians, Irish, Hollanders, Poles or other foreign elements, but one great, invincible, and liberty-loving American nation. The many nationalities that now occupy the United States will only live in history. And the Bohemians, like others, try to bequeath to their children and descendants an honest and untarnished name, so that in after years they need not be ashamed of their Bohemian ancestors; but may with pride own that they are Americans of Bohemian descent.

Source:

Czechs in America, 1633-1977: A Chronology & Fact Book, compiled and edited by Vera Laska. Dobbs Ferry, NY: Oceana Publications, 1978. pp 104-105.

*T*he earliest Czech immigrants, often called Bohemians because they were originally from Bohemia, Moravia, and Silesia, settled in farming communities in Wisconsin. The first major group of Czech immigrants arrived in the Unites States in 1848, fleeing the political persecution of the Hapsburgs. By the late 1850s, about 10,000 Czechs lived in the United States. The largest Czech settlement was in Chicago because rail transportation made it accessible to immigrants. Other Czech concentrations were located in St. Louis, Cleveland, New York, and Milwaukee.

Unlike other immigrants who arrived as individuals, most Czech immigrants came as families, with some large families requiring more than one trip by the head of the household to accompany everyone to the United States. In Wisconsin these immigrants settled alongside German, Irish, and Norwegian immigrants in rural communities. Second and third generation Czech Americans married into families with ethnic backgrounds different from their own. Assimilation into American culture was hastened by the willingness to live and work in communities with other ethnic groups. Most Czech families Americanized their names upon arrival. Some names were translated into English and other were simply changed to American-sounding equivalents. Czechs preferred to be called "Czech" but many Americans referred to them with the pejoratives "Bohunks" and "Hunkies," or by using the also unacceptable term "Bohemians."

The first major Czech farming town in Wisconsin was established at Caledonia, north of Racine. Racine was referred to as Czech Bethlehem. Wisconsin entered the Union on May 29, 1848, as the thirtieth state, with a population of less than 305,000, and only nine percent classified as urban. By 1870, the population exceeded one million. Wisconsin continues to be an important agricultural state today, typically ranking in the top ten states in annual farm income. Though Wisconsin eventually became known as "America's Dairyland" in the time that the first Czech immigrants arrived, the lumber industry was the backbone of the state's economy. By 1848 the United States had finished acquiring title to all the land of Wisconsin from Native Americans, including Winnebago, Menominee, and other

Mississippi Valley Native American cultures. All this land was opened to public sale beginning in the 1830s. Czech immigrants who purchased small tracts of land were able to produce their own necessities as well as a cash crop. Wisconsin's climate was similar to that of the Czech's homeland, so agricultural cycles were very similar. Beginning in the 1880s, farmers of cash grains such as wheat converted these farms for dairying.

The majority of Czech immigrants were literate, unlike most nineteenth-century immigrants. The Austrian regime had made education compulsory to age 14 throughout Moravia and Bohemia. Wisconsin opened its first public elementary school in 1845 and the first public high school in 1849. The first kindergarten in the United States was established in Wisconsin in 1856. Educated Czech immigrants contributed to the strong public school system established in Wisconsin. Czech Americans were hard workers who valued freedom and social equality. Many volunteered for military duty during the Civil War (1861-1865).

Originally published in Charities on December 3, 1904.

BOHEMIAN FARMERS IN WISCONSIN

The early settler bought from forty to sixty acres of land, making only a small cash payment, and giving a mortgage for the rest. The price ranged from five to ten dollars an acre. With the help of his neighbors, who blazed trails as they came lest they should not be felled a few trees to give space for a vegetable patch. Then came the serious work of cleaning the land, and at the same time earning enough outside money to live the ways. Sometimes the head of the family and the eldest son worked part of the year in the nearest sawmill or they went to the large farms to the south of Michigan to help during the harvest. Very often they made hand-shaved pine shingles of the trees on their land, and exchanged them at the nearest market for what they most needed.

These were, indeed, hard years for our pioneers, but better times came after 1861. The war broke out and the forest products of which they had such an abundance, increased in price. Tan-bark, cedar posts for fencing, cord-wood, railroad ties—all found a market so good that the village shippers bought they as fast as they could be made and brought to the shipping piers. Many of these merchant lumbermen advanced money to the farmers with which to buy oxen and sleighs. They also took timber products in exchange for flour, cloth and other necessities, and in other ways the struggle for existence became less

severe, the clearing of the lands went on more rapidly, and the farmers were able to meet more easily their living expenses and debts, notwithstanding war prices on food products and clothes, which put flour at $12 a barrel, coffee at 60 cents a pound and ordinary sheeting at 85 cents.

But the war, even with its attendant prosperity, was not an unmixed blessing. Enthusiasm and patriotism, everywhere rife, was further encouraged among the Bohemians by their newspaper *The Slavie*, then published in Racine, Wis. Many entered the volunteer army, and when later a draft was ordered, large numbers of farms were left without men. There remained usually a large family with only a mother, and perhaps a fourteen-year-old son, to overwhelm the most courageous of women. Yet our Bohemian wives were not disheartened and it is remarkable that in all that war-time not one mortgage was foreclosed in Kewaunee county, and not one of these brave women forfeited the homestead that was given into her care.

Source:

Source: from *Czechs in America, 1633-1977: A Chronology & Fact Book*, compiled and edited by Vera Laska. Dobbs Ferry, NY: Oceana Publications, 1978. pp. 78-79.

This Czech American couple started their own business selling traditional Czech dishes such as kolache.

DANISH AMERICANS

*T*he year of Erik Christian Jensen's birth, 1870, was a time of major economic change in Denmark. The economy, shifting from general agriculture to specialized dairy and pork production and industrialization, was unable to absorb the country's rapid population growth. Work opportunities were clearly limited. A 1939 interview with Jensen highlighted the difficulties and challenges facing Danish immigrants seeking employment in the United States.

Danish immigration to the United States began to escalate after 1860, peaking in the early 1880s. The Mormon Church recruited a large number of Danes to settle in Utah, while many others sought agricultural opportunities in the Midwest. By the 1890s ten percent of the Danish population had emigrated out of the country seeking employment, with most headed primarily to the United States. Danish immigrants increasingly were single, journeying outside the family context. Among those immigrants in 1893 was Erik, enticed by a friend who earlier immigrated. Erik found work in a wire mill in Worcester, Massachusetts.

After four years in the United States, Erik briefly returned to Denmark to marry and bring his new bride back to the States. When the U.S. economy worsened, Jensen still speaking little English, found work on a farm and began a bicycle repair service as a second job. Carrying newly gained skills with him, Erik returned to his wire mill job and began to work on specialized products such as fine strings for musical instruments.

Danish Americans, including Jensen, found life in America satisfying. He worked in the mill for 46 years and was well liked and respected by his peers. As Jensen described in the interview, ". . . mine missus and me belong to a Danish club; its the Danish-American Friendship Society. There's only about three or four hundred Danish people in Worcester, so we all stick together, but we do mix it up with the Swedes." Danes carry a reputation of loving to eat and enjoying social gatherings and Jensen was no exception. He reminisced about the traditional celebrations in Denmark with lots of food, drink, music, and friends, something he found not common in America. Further reflecting on the Danish family orientation, Jensen fondly remembered how Danish families kept Bibles filled with family names on a table visible to all visitors. Though favorably remembering Denmark, the Jensens liked their new country. Like most Danes, they easily assimilated into American society.

ERIK CHRISTIAN JENSEN—DANISH STEEL WORKER

Date of Interview: June 1, 1939
Title: Living Lore
Topic: Danish Steel Worker

"You think I'm Swede, (laughs) Jah! not only you thinks that—everybody does, if he don't know Erik. Denmark was where I was born, in 1870, and not 'til 1893 do I come to this country. Well, you see, in Denmark, all the country is flat, very low, and if there was anything to see, you could see it as far away as Boston. I think the best sight I ever see, it vos the rocks and stones I see coming to Worcester,—why they stick right out of the ground, and they build houses on rocks, and make buildings on rocks! Jah! When I want me to build mine house, all around I looks for a place on the rocks or the hills, and I find me one, and I says to my missus, 'On this rock hill, will we build, and here it is; we can see 'out' and down; we can look down and see water, and look out and see hills.' All my life in Denmark, never once did I see a hill.

"Not much work in Denmark for young men, and I have a friend who comes to America and works in wire mill. He writes me letter to come on, so I come. No, I don't work in mill in Denmark, I teach High School. Well, when I'm a very young boy, maybe 14 or 15, I work on a farm and in the fields, and one day we carry logs on our shoulder, for lumber. I carry the front end and he carries the back, and he trips and lets his end fall, and it goes on my back, and I breaks three joints. Well, I have one doctor, and he says I can get no better; then I have another doctor, and the same things says he. I think to myself, 'the Jensen family are well family and good family, and they should not suffer, but die in their sleep.' My father had two brothers, and they all go to sleep and die, and the some should I do. My father was well, eat good supper, and lay down on the bed, and my sister put shawl over him, and we play cards at the table. We go to bed, and in morning, my father just like we left him, only dead. He never suffer, just sleep away. Only three doctors we have there, and two tell me I should just die. I go see other doctor and he says, 'Why you come to me when other doctors tell you that you should die?' I said to him, 'I don't want to die; why should I die just because three of my bones is dead; that's not the best part of me! I am goin' to live!' Well, the doctor says, 'With your strong will to live, you

can live, and I'll help you!' Now, five years he doctors me, and all the time, I read and study, and when I can go about, I am a teacher. Oh, I teach Danish talk, arithmetic, and handicraft,—but I don't like that, so I come to America.

"Like this, it is; I get to Worcester on Sunday night, and on Monday morning, I go to work at the wire mill. (Washburn-Moen). I worked there two months, then the work went flat. I didn't know what to do, then, but the rich people here was all riding bicycles, the big high ones, so I went to all the people and see if I could fix their bicycles, and that's how I got started. I stayed on a farm and worked for my board, and fixed bicycles at night. No, I couldn't talk English, but I had a boy that could talk, go with me. Well, I could talk Swedish, and most of the men I talked to was Swedes. Well, I learnt it myself.

In Denmark we had a paper called 'the Youth's Companion' and I always read that, and when I come here the only paper I could ask for was 'Youth's Companion.' I knowed the kind of stories they had, and I'd learn one work, and then guess the next two. I didn't think it was so hard, for I didn't have anything much to do and I knowed how to study. In six months I could talk English, and after that it wasn't hard.

"I worked at odd jobs for a year, and then they called me back to the wire mill. Oh, I worked at first, with pick and shovel, and it was hard on my back. I used to get wire for the bicycle repairing, and the bosses got to know me, and I made some good advice about the wire, and sometimes the owners, mind you, would come by and stop and talk to me and ask me things. One day I was, 'tin plating' some wire for my bicycle 'spokes' and they come up and talked to me, and asked me if I could 'tin plate' all the wire, and I said 'yes', and they gave me all the wire to 'tin plate.' After that time, I did all the 'tin plate' and I have my own end of the mill. Now, I do all the fine wire for pianos, guitar strings and all music wires. Nobody knows about them but Erik Jensen , and they always come now and talk to me, and when the United States Steel took over the factory, they told me I would always have my shop, just like when Washburn had the wire mill.

"Accidents, Jah! Lots of accidents them days, but now they never happen. One time I saw a man get scattered all over the place. His legs went one way, and his arm another way, and his brain was throwed by me feet. He was painter and was up high on a ladder, and he had a white duck suit on, so we could see him. He got caught in the 'frame' and was pulled apart in every direction. Now, at the mill, we have a lot of safety, and we only have small accidents, like maybe a finger or sometimes, only a foot, but not big accidents. Every day a inspector comes around and write on a paper what he sees, and once a month we all have to go to a meeting and they tell us how to be careful. Then we have the relief, and if we get hurt, they take care of us. No, I don't mean the Social Security, that's something different. I think it's good, for they have that in Denmark for a long time. Over there they all pay into it and then when you get too old to work, you get money back. You don't get back just what you put in it, but if a man puts money into it, and dies, what he puts in, they divide, and everybody gets part of what he put in. Jah! the wire mill's a good place to work, and if I was starting in again, I'd work there, but there's trouble in young fellows stayin' one place too long. Maybe if I'd gone some other place, I might be a superintendent!—but I ain't got no kick comin', I'm just like my own boss; they never bother me none. Why,—when I built mine house here, they sent someone to tell me to come to the office; all the big owners was there, and they said to me, 'Erik , you're a good man, and we like you, and you're building a house. Now, if you need any money, all you got to do is tell us how much, and you can have any amount you need. Better to not go in debt, and we want to do all we can for good men like you.' I said, 'I thanks you all, but I have money for the land 10 years ago, and now I have money for the house, and I don't need anything, but mebbe to go out oncet or so to see if they do the work right.' Well, now, they said I could go, and I did go out lots of times. That was good for me, so, you see, I ain't got no kick comin'; they was good to me.

"One thing I don't like too much, and that's the pension. Generally, people looks forward to it, but I don't. When I was a young fellow, I looked old, and now that I'm old, I look young and I feel young and want to keep on working. My mudder said when I was 15 I looked old, maybe 25. Next year I'll be 70 and the new laws say I have to quit work. They's givin' me half pay, but I don't like that. I likes to work for what I get. I don't feel no older now than I was 30 years ago.

"Jah! I married my woman from Denmark. I worked for four years and then went back and got her. She's a good woman and always stands by. Mine girl is good girls. Well, a few years ago I thinks the young people were all wrong; that they was goin' too fast, but now I think they have straightened themselves out. The young American people drink too much, but the trouble about that is they don't start till about high school days. The Germans and the Danes always drink beer from the time they's little kids, and then when they grow up, it don't mean nothin' to them. A few years ago mine girls belonged to a Danish Club and we thought they all went crazy, but now, about 15 couples of them got married and got nice homes, and the rest of them are alright now. Oh, yes, mine missus and me belong to a Danish club; it's the Danish-American Friendship Society. There's only about three or four hundred Danish people in Worcester, so we all stick together, but we do mix it up a bit with the Swedes.

"There wasn't much for a young man to do here, when I come here; but work, but on Sundays we'd take bicycle rides. I had a bicycle, a high one, with a tandem, and I used to take my missus for long rides. We go with about 20 other couples, and take our lunch, or stop for a ice cream soda; that was something new for us, for we never had ice cream mixed with anything in Denmark. About all my good times was bicycle riding. We had a club of riders, and we used to have what they called 'Century Rides', and manys the time I rode 100 miles on Sundays. They didn't have good roads, and I don't know which was the worse, for as soon as the good roads got here, the traffic got too bad. If people only knowed what was good for them, they'd ride a bicycle. Just last summer a woman 65 years old come to me and told me she has something the matter with her 'innerts' and she was told to do some high-falutin' exercise with her legs, and it was like bicycle ridin', so she thought she'd get a bicycle and ride; and get the air at the same time. Well, she got a bicycle from me, and she come back in two months, and she looked like a different person. I think bicycle ridin' keeps me young, and my missus and me ride whenever we get a chance."

At this point the shop door banged and in marched a couple of towheaded youngsters with a disreputable piece of machinery they referred to as "the bike." Old Erik forgot me entirely as he began to work with battered wires and bolts, all the time keeping up a stream of conversation with his customers.

Paper #2

Erik Christian Jensen was born in Denmark in 1870 and came to Worcester when he was twenty-three years old. He is a tall, old man, stooped and misshapen, with a thatch of pale yellow hair, deep blue eyes, a booming voice and a kindly courteous manner. A boyhood accident injured his back so that his life was long despaired of, but Erik , as he will tell you with a twinkle, came from a family "who die old", and not even a bad back was going to deter this determined young man. Today, "Old Erik" is hale and healthy. He moves with the deftness of a man years younger, his hands are quick and sure. Only his bent body and extremely long arms are reminders of the long-ago injury.

The Jensens , father, mother and two daughters, have lived for many years in a comfortable little home set high on a hill on Grove Street near the outskirts of the city. It is a trim tidy little home, well-painted with bright flower gardens and a strip of green lawn, Mr. Jensen's pride and joy.

Mr. Jensen has worked in the wire mill ever since he came to Worcester, forty-six years ago. He appears to be a much valued worker. It has been suggested by those who profess to know, that at one time, Mr. Jensen worked out a method of tin plating which proved to be of such value to the company, that they were able to make great improvements in their products. If this is true, Mr. Jensen does not seem aware of it. He tells of his work simply, with pride in a job well done, but makes no reference to having materially aided the "company."

Very early in his life in Worcester, Erik found it necessary to turn to a "side line" when the wire mill was "low." Naturally deft with tools and machinery, he began repairing bicycles. Business boomed, for it was the age of the "League of American Wheelmen," of tandems and "bicycles built for two." In the past few decades, the bicycle industry was mainly confined to youngsters, but with the new vogue of recent years, "Old Erik" does a steady business.

The little bicycle shop, neat and scrupulously clean, is in the cellar of his house. It is really the first floor for on one side, the hill has been cut away to allow Mr. Jensen room enough for an entrance to his shop.

Mr. Jensen speaks English fairly well if he thinks about it. But when he becomes excited or strives to explain a point about which he is none too certain, his voice becomes blurred and thick and his words come out helter-skelter, crowding and pushing one another. It is with the children who came in with broken "bikes" of all makes and stages of repair, that Mr. Jensen appears most at ease. A broad smile, twinkling blue eyes and a quick hearty laugh form a language universally understood.

Paper #3

It was raining torrents but I had told Mr. Jensen I would be around for a visit, so at precisely 3 o'clock, I opened the door of the bicycle shop and said "hello."

Old Erik was very much troubled for fear I had "catched cold". With my rubbers and umbrella safely stowed away I sat down on the little stool and we began our chat.

"Bad day you should come, but I like to see you . Jah! Last time I tell you when you come again I take you upstairs to see my missus, but she say her talk not so good, and I better tell you. Much she remembers 'bout her days in Denmark and mine, too, and lots of things is done different here. We both laugh when we talk about the funerals in this country. You bury your dead too quick. One day they die and next day they get buried. In Denmark a funeral lasts sometimes a week, and rich people have them longer. Everybody comes and they eat. No, just eat and talk, and in the evening we had church music and prayers. On name days and christenings we have plenty to eat and drink and music to dance. We have everything out of the house, but in the bedrooms, then we dance or play cards or sing. The young people usually dance, maybe four or eight couples, but sometime in the evening, everybody dances.

"Like I tell you, in Denmark the houses are all on one floor, a big sitting room, and a dining room and kitchen, and bed rooms to the size of the families. If lots of children, there is one room for them, and lost of places the beds is made right in the wall, like you say—'bunks' and all around the room is 'bunks'. For the father and mother, they have beds, but they make them out of wood and the springs is made of rope, but the 'ticks' is made of feathers, you cover up with feather 'ticks', only not so thick, like you sleep on. If you have hired girl, you make for her, room back of kitchen. My missus says what she don't like when she first comes here is the stoves. In Denmark the stoves is in the corner and they are high and every room has his own stove. Sometimes they is high as the ceiling, and that is sometimes 10 or 12 feet. Sometimes theys about 3 feet high. When she comes to Worcester, they is little round stoves and in the middle of the room, or they is little holes in the wall and all open and they blaze up, and sometimes they is big fireplace and big logs is burned. It takes my missus long time to like American stoves. Now, by golly, she has electric stove and she likes.

"You know, in Denmark, when you go in somebody's house, right in the middle of floor is a table, and on top is a big Bible, and in it is all the names and ages of everybody in your family. Here, you never no more see a Bible on the table.

"Jah! Denmark is nice, but I like better here. You go into a house in Denmark of a evening, you see the children all sittin' round the tables studying their school books, and the missus, she sits by and does needlework, and the Pappa he sets by the stove and smokes and reads, too. No, never do you smoke cigars in your house—the men smoke big pipes, so big—you can put a big handful tobacco in them, and they last all night.

"Danish families are good families and the children always obey the father and mother, and never fights. Always on the name days (birthday) they give presents, even if it's wild flowers, but never forgets the name days of family. Christmas time in Denmark is good, too. A big tree is put up in the big hall and everybody comes and dances and sings and gives presents. The rich and the poor people mix up that one time in the year. Weeks and mebbe months the wimmin' make the *aebleskiver* and they give it to everybody that comes. Oh, that's make of apples, and sugar and flour, and like candy and cake, and its hard and you can keep it long time. There's always a big feast, like your banquets, and everybody eats gruel, made out of milk, and they roast duck, stuffed with prunes or chestnuts, and give you that with 'beer sauce'. Oh, Jah! dot iss goot! The beer sauce gives it taste—very good. Why, in Denmark, they use beer like in America they use water. The wimmin make soup out of beer and float slices of rye bread on top. Jah! that is goot, too. We use lots of soup in Denmark, and on Saturdays we have *Baenkavalling*, that's is made out of soup that's left over every day, and they call it soup made in a bench—well just like you say 'leavings' after each day. Oh, we have lots of different soup, and the favorite soup of the Danes is 'Prune Soup'. My missus makes it from prunes, milk, eggs rice and vegetables. Jah,—that's the best soup.

"Never do I eat breakfast in a lunch cart or outside mine house. First when I come here I must eat out, and they laugh at me, but now I have my house and my missus gives me kind of breakfast Danish people eat.—Well, here you eat bacon or ham with eggs and fried potatoes. My missus makes me my *smorrebrod*—why, that is a slice of rye bread, with butter and a slice of meat or fish, with beer or tea. That is a national dish of a Danish man. They laugh if you eat that in the outside here. My girls they don't eat that, but my missus and me do. When you come to Danish home for a meal you get some soup, then hot meat with horseradish, then some cake or sweet, and then you have cheese and bread. You must know how to slice the cheese thin, or you're not good cook.

"When you get up from Danish table you say 'thanks for meal'. You see, lots of things different here. You say 'excuse, please' and if you say excuse in Denmark, that means you're sorry, so—you see how it does? Danish people are good, quiet people, always very slow moving, and when you move slow, you think slow, and when you think slow, you never in trouble get. Why, it is true, in Denmark they have the clocks at the railroad station five minutes fast, so the people don't miss their train. The only thing that moves fast is the dogs, and they have lots of racing dogs, and that is funny, now, don't it? Never do you see a Dane walking fast.

"This will be nice time of year in Denmark, for they get ready for Easter; they start with Holy Thursday and everything is shut tight till Monday after Easter. Even the shops and business is closed up, and people are sad, but happy too. They go to church everyday, and then they walk all around the town. In Denmark the churches are on a hill."

Source:

Library of Congress. *American Life Histories: Manuscripts from the Federal Writers' Project, 1936-1940* from the American Memory website (http://memory.loc.gov/ammem/wpaintro/wpa-home.html).

Dominican Americans

T*he Dominican Republic is a country in the eastern part of the island called Hispanolia. The island is also occupied by Haiti. Hispanolia lies off the Southeast coast of Florida in the Carribean. The island was colonized by the French who occupied the west and the Spanish who settled in the east. The Dominican Republic has been governed by a series of dictatorships since its inception in 1844. The U.S. Marines occupied the country between 1916 and 1924 but the political system was eventually won over by Rafael Trujillo who held despotic rule over the Dominican Republic from 1930 until his assassination in 1961. Although Trujillo improved economic conditions for the country he ruthlessly suppressed any political opposition that challenged his power. The United States occupied the capital city of Santo Domingo in 1965 and assisted the country's long transition to democratic governance. The political relationship that developed between the United States and the Dominican Republic enabled segments of this Hispanic group to migrate to the United States.*

The Hispanic population in the United States to which immigrants from the Dominican Republic belong as well as descendants from other Central and South American countries such as Mexico, Cuba, Puerto Rico, Colombia, and Venezuela, has grown dramatically in recent years. In 1950 the population was estimated at four million and by the year 2000 it is expected to exceed 30 million. Strong Hispanic American communities have developed across the United States in New York, Florida, California, and Texas. The strength of these communities serves as a support group for incoming immigrants. The Hispanic American community is among the more "Americanized" group of immigrants that come to the United States because of their proximity and economic relationship with the United States. This makes their transition to American society easier, however, it also makes it difficult for parents to pass on to their children the values that are inherent to their own culture. One account from a Dominican Republic girl named Martha provides an indication of how difficult it is for immigrants to retain their cultural heritage.

Martha's mother came to New York after her husband left her while living in the Dominican Republic. She earned a living as a nanny and sent for her daughter after she secured working papers. In the Dominican Republic young girls are not allowed to be alone with boys without a chaperone. Martha, who is sixteen, would rather dispense with the tradition but her mother insists on accompanying her on dates. Martha's mother is struggling to pass on traditional values such as respect for authority, self-discipline, and love for family to her daughter. She wants a better life for Martha which is why she worked so hard to come to the United States and start a new beginning. Martha is resistant but her mother believes that setting strict curfews, limiting her daughter's use of the telephone, and chaperoning her on dates will lead her in the right direction.

MARTHA, AGE 16

The Dominican Republic shares the island of Hispaniola with the country of Haiti. A ridge of soaring mountains divides them. Located in the Caribbean, this Spanish-speaking nation is the size of Maryland and Massachusetts combined, but with half their population, six and a half million. Santo Domingo, the capital, founded in 1496, is the oldest European settlement in the Western Hemisphere. "Today," says Martha, "there are more Dominicans in New York City than in the town where I was born." One steamy June afternoon, we talk in the offices of a Bronx, New York, job placement center for high school students. With Martha is Brenda, her cousin, best friend, and occasional translator. Martha, who emigrated five years ago, begins with a brief history of her country and her family.

The Dominican Republic is a little country that everybody's taken advantage of. Columbus landed there in 1492 and that started it all. The Spanish, the French, the Americans, and then the people from Haiti were in there at some time, too, taking advantage of my people. February 27 is Dominican Independence Day, the day we liberated ourselves from the Haitians.

My great-grandmothers on both sides were from Spain. They were white. My grandfather on my mother's side was from the Indians, the Arawak. He had the brown skin and very fine hair. His wife, my mother's mother, practiced the religion "Brujeria," spiritism. She became an important witch. She was dead three years before I was born, but they say she was very good. In the Dominican Republic it's against the law to practice spiritism. The government just allows what they call the "real religions" like Catholic and Pentecostal.

Some people still practice witchcraft, but not openly. It's like voodoo and Santeria, except voodoo is more from Haiti and Santeria, with the animal sacrifices, is more from Cuba, Afro-Cuban. With spiritism, we don't have animal sacrifices. We sit down and the medium calls different spirits. Some people put fruit out for them, but more often it's tobacco or rum. The spirits like to party. They like alcohol. I was surprised when I came to the United States and saw people advertising themselves as practicing spiritism.

I don't know that much about the rest of my relatives. I guess we have a couple of negroes in there, too, maybe on my mother's side, because our hair is not so fine anymore. I don't know what moment they go into the family, though. Anyway,

I'm a mixture of black and white. The majority of people in my country are like that. We call them mulattoes.

We also have a lot of prejudice there. I'm going to tell you this. Once I went to a restaurant in the Dominican and this lady said if they served me, that "negra"—that's like saying that "nigger"—that she was leaving the restaurant. The people from there might tell you that we're not prejudiced, but that's a joke. And it's based on the color of our skin—the whiter the better. I have never felt the prejudice in the United States that I felt in my country. Sometimes people made me feel like s——.

Now don't get me wrong. The Dominican is a beautiful country, a great resort, and you can find anything you want, if you have money. You will find people from the jet set there, people enjoying vacations. If you have money, you will live like a king, even more than here. And the people who have money are the most prejudiced. They treat the poor people like garbage! They have made it part of the culture that when we introduce someone, we must use your title. If we leave out the title, we are insulting you. The military is very important, also. If someone says, "My father is a captain," we know you are threatening us. If we don't have a title, we are nobody.

My mother tells me that for many years in the Dominican, you are either rich-rich or you are poor. The people live under the rule of dictators. Now there is a democratic government. Life improves a little, but still the United States gives my country a lot of money. We grow up hearing and talking about "Nueva Yorque"—New York. That is where everybody is rich and wears gold chains.

Unemployment is really high in my country and those few who have money don't want to invest it there because the country hasn't been stabilized for the longest time. So poor people come to America for better jobs and rich people come here to make more money. At least, this is what my mother says.

Not so long after I was born, my father left. My mother tells me that he loved to dance the merengue more than he loved us. The merengue is LIFE in my country, but my mother says it shouldn't be more important than your family. He shouldn't have run out on her when she had no money and a little baby. I don't see him and his family very much.

The only thing she could think of to do was to move to New York. She came here illegal, and that's all I know. I was only a year old. She got a job taking care of other people's babies. I lived with my aunt, my uncle, and my five cousins. They took care of me.

Every Christmas my mother would come visit. I thought of her as a stranger. She called me sometimes but I didn't always want to talk to her. I didn't feel very warm toward her. I felt better toward my aunt. Then when I was ten my aunt told me that I was going to New York. She said it had been very hard for my mother to get papers for me, but after two years of trying, she did.

The next thing I knew I was on a bus to Santo Domingo and then to an airplane where I could drink all the Coca-Cola I wanted. I cried the minute the plane landed at JFK [Airport] and I was still crying when we got to my mother's apartment in the Bronx. I cried for fourteen straight days. Then my mother said, "I'm tired of your crying. Settle down or I'm going to send you back." That was the start of her "talks" with me.

I have talks and rules for everything. My mother's favorite is this: "Be careful when you go out. Open your eyes and close your legs. Study to get good grades. Have a career." And I have a curfew. If I break it, I'm in forever. My mother says, "I give you a curfew of nine and you want nine-thirty. I say ten and you want ten-thirty. The more I tell you something, the more you want."

I'm allowed a total of fifteen minutes, three calls, on the phone each day. Brenda calls me, five minutes. I time it. For six months I couldn't use the phone at all because a bill had come in for $150. My mother put a lock on it, kept the only key, and said, "You should be grateful for a phone."

I couldn't wear makeup until last year, when I turned fifteen. I couldn't date until after my six-teenth birthday, two months ago. I brought a guy home that I liked and my mother put him by the open window in the kitchen and asked him questions. "What do you hope to pursue?" "What are your intentions with my daughter?" She told me, "If I don't like his answers, there's a bat behind the curtain that's going to come out!" It made the guy nervous.

Then he had to ask my mother permission to ask me out. She said, "Okay," but we still had to have a chaperone—her. A good Dominican girl is never supposed to be alone with a guy. We couldn't go out on a real date. He could only come over and sit on the couch and watch TV with us. So what I did was told my mother I was going to the library, but instead I met him.

Another thing is that she won't let me be on the volleyball team. She says, "Volleyball isn't going to get you anywhere. It's better in school, not on the street." But I'm really good at it, one of the best. After school Brenda and I play handball at some courts near here. We're usually the only girls playing. Once the guys wanted to play with us and we beat them! They said, "It's embarrassing. Don't tell anyone that two girls beat us."

I suppose that someday I will become a U.S. citizen. My mother is. A couple years ago she paid $250 to some lawyer to start the paperwork, and now he tells her no one can find my records. I'm a lost person. My mother laughed when she told me that. I said, "I'm ready to be on my own now, get my own apartment. I feel American now." She laughed some more.

Source:
Janet Bode, *New Kids on the Block: Oral Histories of Immigrant Teens*. New York: Franklin Watts, 1989. pp. 29-37.

DUTCH AMERICANS

*E*dward Bok (1863-1930) was born with the name Den Helder in the Nether-lands. He immigrated to the United States when he was seven years old, and at the age of 23 formed the Bok Syndicate to publish the sermons of noted minister Henry Ward Beecher (1813-87). Eventually he developed a syndicated women's features column called the "Bok page," and served as editor-in-chief of Ladie's Home Jour-nal from 1889 to 1919. Bok became involved in a number of public causes, and in 1923 established the Bok Peace Prize. His autobiography, The Americanization of Edward Bok, won the Pulitzer Prize in 1920.

Bok devoted the last two chapters of his autobiography to summing up, first of all, "Where America Fell Short with Me," and finally, "What I Owe to America." Both in his complaints and in his words of praise, Bok reflects the spirit of a Dutch immigrant who has never forgotten the conditions of life in his homeland—and their contrast with life in America.

Bok's criticisms of America are as familiar, many years after he made them, as they were in the 1920s. His chief areas of concern include Americans' wasteful-ness; their lack of integrity in completing a job; the deficiencies of their educational system; their lack of respect for authority; and their ignorance of their rights and duties as citizens, particularly those related to suffrage.

With regard to wastefulness, it is clear that Bok was raised in a nation where thrift was a virtue. Whereas Holland is a tiny country where floodwaters threat-ened to overrun what little land the Dutch possessed, America was a realm of wide-open spaces, where people had little regard for precious resources. These wasteful habits, he found, were a part of the American mindset: hence, he noted, Ameri-cans viewed someone who saved their money as being "stingy."

Coupled with this attitude was a similarly casual regard toward work, and here again Bok found an ingrained mindset represented by everyday figures of speech: "That's good enough." Had he been writing at a later time, he might have thrown in the expression, "It's close enough for government work." Thus he found Ameri-cans incapable of activities which required tireless attention to detail.

The issue of wastefulness, tied as it is with concerns about the environment, is certainly a timely one; so to is the issue of short attention spans and the deficiences of the American educational system. Bok, who completed his grade-school educa-tion in about 1881, wrote that "I gained nothing from the much-vaunted [praised] public-school system . . . ."

One might think that problems between youth and the police are something new, but Bok makes it clear that they are not. Though he does not mention Ameri-cans' concern with rights and civil liberties, it is no doubt Americans' strong emphasis on those ideas that helped breed what Bok perceived as a lack of respect for authority. Hence police were seen not as friendly public servants, as the Dutch were brought up to perceive them, but as a threat to freedom. Particularly notewor-

thy is the distaste of Bok, himself a journalist, for attacks on public officials in print. He seems to suggest that the liberty of journalists to write what they want should be as closely supervised as threats to the public peace.

Addressing the issue of suffrage, Bok shows the foreign-born citizen's appreciation for his rights, an appreciation seldom shared by those who have never known anything else. Only after speaking with Seth Low (1850-1916), the reformist mayor of New York City, did he finally have his questions regarding the vote answered. Hence his suggestion that rather than trying to Americanize the foreigners in their midst—that is, to teach them what it means to be an American—Americans should seek to Americanize themselves.

Bok closes his memoirs with lavish praise for Americans, and in this he resembles another famous commentator on the subject, Alexis de Tocqueville (1805-59), whose Democracy in America (1835) is one of the one most important works on America by an outsider. Like Tocqueville, Bok points out Americans' belief in ideals such as fair play, comments that almost seem to contradict his earlier concern about their lack of integrity in doing their jobs.

Bok also notes Americans' lack of self-consciousness in being American. For his own part, he makes it clear that he has always been quite consciously American, and near the end of his observations, he states an idea that has run through many of his thoughts on Americanization: "I wonder whether, after all, the foreign-born does not make in some sense a better American.. . ."

THE AMERICANIZATION OF EDWARD BOK (EXCERPT)

Where America Fell Short With Me

When I came to the United States as a lad of six, the most needful lesson for me, as a boy, was the necessity for thrift. I had been taught in my home across the sea that thrift was one of the fundamentals in a successful life. My family had come from a land (the Netherlands) noted for its thrift; but we had been in the United States only a few days before the realization came home strongly to my father and mother that they had brought their children to a land of waste.

Where the Dutchman saved, the American wasted. There was waste, and the most prodigal waste, on every hand. In every street-car and on every ferry-boat the floors and seats were littered with newspapers that had been read and thrown away or left behind. If I went to a grocery store to buy a peck of potatoes, and a potato rolled off the heaping measure, the groceryman, instead of picking it up, kicked it into the gutter for the wheels of his wagon to run over. The butcher's waste filled my mother's soul with dismay. If I bought a scuttle

of coal at the corner grocery, the coal that missed the scuttle, instead of being shoveled up and put back into the bin, was swept into the street. My young eyes quickly saw this; in the evening I gathered up the coal thus swept away, and during the course of a week I collected a scuttleful. The first time my mother saw the garbage pail of a family almost as poor as our own, with the wife and husband constantly complaining that they could not get along, she could scarcely believe her eyes. A half pan of hominy of the preceding day's breakfast lay in the pail next to a third of a loaf of bread. In later years, when I saw, daily, a scow loaded with garbage of Brooklyn householders being towed through New York harbor out to sea, it was an easy calculation that what was thrown away in a week's time from Brooklyn homes would feed the poor of the Netherlands.

At school, I quickly learned that to "save money" was to be "stingy"; as a young man, I soon found that the American disliked the word "economy," and on every hand as plenty grew spending grew. There was literally nothing in American life to teach me thrift or economy; everything to teach me to spend and to waste.

I saw men who had earned good salaries in their prime, reach the years of incapacity as dependents. I saw families on every hand either living quite up to their means or beyond them; rarely within them. The more a man earned, the more he—or his wife—spent. I saw fathers and mothers and their children dressed beyond their incomes. The proportion of families who ran into debt was far greater than those who saved. When a panic came, the families "pulled in"; when the panic was over, they "let out." But the end of one year found them precisely where they were at the close of the previous year, unless they were deeper in debt.

It was in this atmosphere of prodigal expenditure and culpable waste that I was to practice thrift: a fundamental in life! And it is into this atmosphere that the foreign-born comes now, with every inducement to spend and no encouragement to save. For as it was in the days of my boyhood, so it is to-day—only worse. One need only go over the experiences of the past two years, to compare the receipts of merchants who cater to the working-classes and the statements of savings-banks throughout the country, to read the story of how the foreign-born are learning the habit of criminal wastefulness as taught them by the American.

Is it any wonder, then, that in this, one of the essentials in life and in all success, America fell short with me, as it is continuing to fall short with every foreign-born who comes to its shores?

As a Dutch boy, one of the cardinal truths taught me was that whatever was worth doing was worth doing well: that next to honesty came thoroughness as a factor in success. It was not enough that anything should be done: it was not done at all if it was not done well. I came to America to be taught exactly the opposite. The two infernal Americanisms "That's good enough" and "That will do" were early taught me, together with the maxim of quantity rather than quality.

It was not the boy at school who could write the words in his copy-book best who received the praise of the teacher; it was the boy who could write the largest number of words in a given time. The acid test in arithmetic was not the mastery of the method, but the number of minutes required to work out an example. If a boy abbreviated the month January to "Jan." and the word Company to "Co." he received a hundred percent mark, as did the boy who spelled out the words and who could not make the teacher see that "Co." did not spell "Company."

As I grew into young manhood, and went into business, I found on every hand that quantity counted for more than quality. The emphasis was almost always placed on how much work one could do in a day, rather than upon how well the work was done. Thoroughness was at a discount on every hand; production at a premium. It made no difference in what direction I went, the result was the same: the cry was always for quantity, quantity! And into this atmosphere of almost utter disregard for quality I brought my ideas of Dutch thoroughness and my conviction that doing well whatever I did was to count as a cardinal principle in life.

During my years of editorship, save in one or two conspicuous instances, I was never able to assign to an American writer, work which called for painstaking research. In every instance, the work came back to me wither incorrect in statement, or otherwise obviously lacking in careful preparation.

One of the most successful departments I ever conducted in The Ladies' Home Journal called for infinite reading and patient digging, with the actual results sometimes almost negligible. I made a study of my associates by turning the department over to one after another, and always with the same result: absolute lack of a capacity for patient research. As one of my editors, typically American, said to me: "It isn't worth all the trouble that you put into it." Yet no single department ever repaid the searcher more for his pains. Save for assistance derived from a single person, I had to do the work myself for all the years that the department continued. It was apparently impossible for the America to work with sufficient patience and care to achieve a result.

We all have our pet notions as to the particular evil which is "the curse of America," but I always think that Theodore Roosevelt came closest to the real curse when he classed it as a lack of thoroughness.

Here again, in one of the most important matters in life, did America fall short with me; and, what is more important, she is falling short with every foreigner that comes to her shores.

In the matter of education, America fell far short in what should be the strongest of all her institutions: the public school. A more inadequate, incompetent method of teaching, as I look back over my seven years of attendance at three different public schools, it is difficult to conceive. If there is one thing that I, as a foreign-born child, should have been carefully taught, it is the English language. The individual effort to teach this, if effort there was, and I remember none, was negligible. It was left for my father to teach me, or for me to dig it out for myself. There was absolutely no indication on the part of teacher or principal of responsibility for seeing that a foreign-born boy should acquire the English language correctly. I was taught as if I were American-born, and, of course, I was left dangling in the air, with no conception of what I was trying to do.

My father worked with me evening after evening; I plunged my young mind deep into the bewildering confusions of the language—and no one realizes the confusions of the English language as does the foreign-born—and got what I could through these joint efforts. But I gained nothing from the much-vaunted public-school system which the United States had borrowed from my own country, and then had rendered incompetent—either by a sheer disregard for the thoroughness that makes the Dutch public schools the admiration of the world, or by too close a regard for politics.

Thus, in her most important institution to the foreign-born, America fell short. And while I am ready to believe that the public school may have increased in efficiency since that day, it is, indeed, a question for the American to ponder, just how far the system is efficient for the education of the child who comes to its school without a knowledge of the child who comes to its school without a knowledge of the first word in the English language. Without a detailed knowledge of the subject, I know enough of conditions in the average public school to-day to warrant at least the suspicion that Americans would not be particularly proud of the system, and of what it gives for which annually they pay millions of dollars in taxes.

I am aware in making this statement that I shall be met with convincing instances of intelligent effort being made with the foreign-born children in special classes. No one has a higher respect for those efforts than I have—few, other than educators, know of them better than I do, since I did not make my five-year study of the American system for naught. But I am not referring to the exceptional instance here and there. I merely ask of the American, interested as he is or should be in the Americanization of the strangers within his gates, how far the public school system, as a whole, urban and rural, adapts itself, with any true efficiency, to the foreign-born child. I venture to color his opinion in no wise; I simply ask that he will inquire and ascertain for himself, as he should do if he is interested in the future welfare of his country and his institutions; for what happens in America in the years to come depends, in large measure, on what is happening to-day in the public schools of this country.

As a Dutch boy I was taught a wholesome respect for law and for authority. The fact was impressed upon me that laws of themselves were futile unless the people for whom they were made respected them, and obeyed them in spirit more even than in the letter. I came to America to feel, on every hand, that exactly the opposite was true. Laws were passed, but were not enforced; the spirit more even than in the letter. I came to America to feel, on every hand, that exactly the opposite was true. Laws were passed, but were not enforced; the spirit to enforce them was lacking in the people. There was little respect for the law; there was scarcely any for those appointed to enforce it.

The nearest that a boy gets to the law is through the policeman. In the Netherlands a boy is taught that a policeman is for the protection of life and property; that he is the natural friend of every boy and man who behave himself. The Dutch boy and the policeman are, naturally, friendly in their relations. I came to America to be told that a policeman is a boy's natural enemy; that he is eager to arrest him if he can find the slightest reason for doing so. A policeman, I was informed, was a being to hold in fear, not in respect. He was to be avoided, not to be made friends with. The result was that, as did all boys, I came to regard the policeman on our beat as a distinct enemy. His presence meant that we should "stiffen up"; his disappearance was the signal for us to "let loose."

So long as one was not caught, it did not matter. I heard mothers tell their little children that if they did not behave themselves, the policeman would put them into a bag and carry them off, or cut their ears off. Of course, the policeman became to them an object of terror; the law in my boyhood days. A law was something to be broken, to be evaded, to call down upon others as a source of punishment, but never to be regarded in the light of a safeguard.

And as I grew into manhood, the newspapers rang on every side with disrespect for those in authority. Under, the special dispensation of the liberty of the press, which was construed into the license of the press, no man was too high to escape editorial vituperation if his politics did not happen to suit the management, or if his action ran counter to what the proprietors believed it should be. It was not criticism of his acts, it was personal attack upon the official; whether supervisor, mayor, governor, or president, it mattered not.

It is a very unfortunate impression that this American lack of respect for those in authority makes upon the foreign-born mind. If is difficult for the foreigner to square up the arrest and deportation of a man who, through an incendiary address, seeks to overthrow governmental authority, with the ignoring of an expression of exactly the same sentiment by the editor of his next morning's newspaper. In other words, the man who writes is immune, but the man who reads, imbibes, and translates the editor's words into action is immediately marked as a culprit, and America will not harbor him. But why harbor the original cause? Is the man who speaks with type less dangerous than he who speaks with his mouth or with a bomb?

At the most vital part of my life, when I was to become an American citizen and exercise the right of suffrage, America fell entirely short. It reached out not even the suggestion of a hand.

When the Presidential Conventions had been held in the year I reached my legal majority, and I knew I could vote, I endeavored to find out whether, being foreign-born, I was entitled to the suffrage. No one could tell me; and not until I had visited six difference municipal departments, being referred from one to another, was it explained that, through my father's naturalization, I became, automatically, as his son, an American citizen. I decided to read up on the platforms of the Republican and Democratic parties, but I could not secure copies anywhere, although a week had passed since they had been adopted in convention.

I was told the newspapers had printed them. It occurred to me there must be many others besides myself who were anxious to secure the platforms of the two parties in some more convenient form. With the eye of necessity ever upon a chance to earn an honest penny, I went to a newspaper office, cut out from its files the two platforms, had them printed in a small pocket edition, sold one edition to the American News Company and another to the News Company controlling the Elevated Railroad bookstands in New York City, where they sold at ten cents each. So great was the demand which I had only partially guessed, that within three weeks I had sold such huge editions of the little books that I had sold such huge editions of the little books that I had cleared over a thousand dollars.

But it seemed to me strange that is should depend on a foreign-born American to supply an eager public with what should have been supplied through the agency of the political parties or through some educational source.

I now tried to find out what a vote actually meant. It must be recalled that I was only twenty-one years old, with scant education, and with no civic agency offering me the information I was seeking. I went to the headquarters of each of the political parties and put my query. I was regarded with puzzled looks.

"What does it mean to vote?" asked one chairman. "Why, on Election Day you go up to the ballot-box and put your ballot in, and that's all there is to it."

But I knew very well that that was not all there was to it, and was determined to find out the significance of the franchise. I met with dense ignorance on every hand. I went to the Brooklyn Library, and was frankly told by the librarian that he did not know of a book that would tell me what I wanted to know. This was in 1884.

As the campaign increased in intensity, I found myself a desired person in the eyes of the local campaign managers, but not one of them could tell me the significance and meaning of the privilege I was for the first time to exercise.

Finally, I spent an evening with Seth Low, and, of course, got the desired information.

But fancy the quest I had been compelled to make to acquire the simple information that should have been placed in my hands or made readily accessible to me. And how many foreign-born would take equal pains to ascertain what I was determined to find out?

Surely America fell short here at the moment most sacred to me: that of my first vote!

Is it any easier to-day for the foreign citizen to acquire this information when he approaches his first vote? I wonder! Not that I do not believe there are, and so do I. But how about the foreign-born? Does he know it? Is it not perhaps like the owner of the bulldog who assured the friend called on him that it never attacked friends of the family? "Yes," said the friend, "that's all right. You know and I know that I am a friend of the family; but does the dog know?"

Is it to-day made known to the foreign-born, about to exercise his privilege of suffrage for the first time, where he can be told what that privilege means: is the means to know made readily accessible to him: is it, in fact, as it should be, brought to him?

It was not to me; is it to him?

One fundamental trouble with the present desire for Americanization is that the American is anxious to Americanize two classes—if he is a reformer, the foreign-born; if he is an employer, his employees. It never occurs to him that he himself may be in need of Americanization. He seems to take it for granted that because he is American-born, he is an American in spirit and has a right understanding of American ideals. But that, by no means, always follows. There are thousands of the American-born who need Americanization just as much as do the foreign-born. There are hundreds of American employers who know far less of American ideals than do some of their employees. In fact, there are those actually engaged to-day in the work of Americanization, men at the top of the movement, who sadly need a better conception of true Americanism.

An excellent illustration of this came to my knowledge when I attended a large Americanization Conference in Washington. One of the principal speakers was an educator of high standing and considerable influence in one of the most important sections of the United States. In a speech setting forth his ideas of Americanization, he dwelt with much emphasis and at considerable length upon instilling into the mind of the foreign-born the highest respect for American institutions.

After the Conference he asked me whether he could see me that afternoon at my hotel; he wanted to talk about contributing to the magazine. When he came, before approaching the object of his talk, he launched out on a tirade against the President of the United States; the weakness of the Cabinet, the inefficiency of the Congress, and the stupidity of the Senate. If words could have killed, there would have not remained a single living member of the Administration at Washington.

After fifteen minutes of this, I reminded him of his speech and the emphasis which he had placed upon the necessity of inculcating in the foreign-born respect for American institutions.

Yet this man was a power in his community, a strong influence upon others; he believed he could Americanize others, when he himself, according to his own statements, lacked the fundamental principle of Americanization. What is true of this man is, in lesser or greater degree, true of hundreds of others. Their Americanization consists of lip-service; the real spirit, the only factor which counts in the successful teaching of any doctrine, is absolutely missing. We certainly cannot teach anything approaching a true Americanism until we ourselves feel and believe and practise in our own lives what we are teaching to others. No law, no lip-service, no effort, however well-intentioned, will amount to anything worth while in inculcating the true American spirit in our foreign-born citizens until we are sure that the American spirit is understood by ourselves and is warp and woof of our own being.

To the American, part and parcel of his country, these particulars in which his country falls short with the foreign-born are, perhaps, not so evident; they may even seem not so very important. But to the foreign-born they seem distinct lacks; they loom large; they form serious handicaps which, in many cases, are never surmounted; they are a menace to that Americanization which is, to-day, more than ever our fondest dream, and which we now realize more keenly than before is our most vital need.

It is for this reason that I have put them down here as a concrete instance of where and how America fell short in my own Americanization, and, what is far more serious to me, where she is fall short in her Americanization of thousands of other foreign-born.

"Yet you succeeded," it will be argued.

That may be; but you, on the other hand, must admit that I did not succeed by reason of these shortcomings: it was in spite of them, by overcoming them—a result that all might not achieve.

What I Owe to America

Whatever shortcomings I may have found during my fifty-year period of Americanization; however America may have failed to help my transition from a foreigner into an American, I owe to her the most priceless gift that any nation can offer, and that is opportunity.

As the world stands to-day, no nation offers opportunity in the degree that America does to the foreign-born. Russia may, in the future, as I like to believe she will, prove a second United States of America in this respect. She has the same limitless area; her people the same potentialities. But, as things are to-day, the United States offers, as does no other nation, a limitless opportunity: here a man can go as far as his abilities will carry him. It may be that the foreign-born, as in my own case, must hold on to some of the ideals and ideas of the land of his birth; it may be that he must develop and mould his character by overcoming the habits resulting from national shortcomings. But into the best that the foreign-born can retain, America can graft such a wealth of inspiration, so high a national idealism, so great an opportunity for the highest endeavor, as to make him the fortunate man of the earth to-day.

He can go where he will: no traditions hamper him; no limitations are set except those within himself. The larger the are he choose in which to work, the larger the vision he demonstrates, the more eager the people are to give support to his undertakings if they are convinced that he has their best welfare as his goal. There is no public confidence equal to that of the American public, once it is obtained. It is fickle, of course, as are all publics, but fickle only toward the man who cannot maintain an achieved success.

A man in America cannot complacently lean back upon victories won, as he can in the older European countries, and depend upon the glamour of the past to sustain him or the momentum of success to carry him. Probably the most alert public in the world, it requires of its leaders that they be alert. Its appetite for variety is insatiable, but its appreciation, when given, is full-handed and whole-hearted. The American public never holds back from the man to whom it give; it never bestows in a niggardly way; it gives all or nothing.

What is not generally understood of the American people is their wonderful idealism. Nothing so completely surprises the foreign-born as the discovery of this trait in the American character. The impression is current in European countries—perhaps less generally since the war—that America is given over solely to a worship of the American dollar. While between nations as between individuals, comparisons are valueless, it many not be amiss to say, from personal knowledge, that the Dutch worship the gulden infinitely more than do the Americans the dollar.

I do not claim that the American is always conscious of this idealism; often he is not. But let a great convulsion touching moral questions occur, and the result always shows how close to the surface is his idealism. And the fact that so frequently he puts over it a thick veneer of materialism does not affect its quality. The truest approach, the only approach in fact, to the American character is, as Viscount Bryce has so well said, through its idealism.

It is this quality which gives the truest inspiration to the foreign-born in his endeavor to serve the people of his adopted country. He is mentally sluggish, indeed, who does not discover that America will make good with him if he make good with her.

But he must play fair. It is essentially the straight game that the true American plays, and he insists that you shall play it too. Evidence there is, of course, to the contrary in American life, experiences that seem to give ground for the belief that the man succeeds who is not scrupulous in playing his cards. But never is this true in the long run. Sooner or later—sometimes, unfortunately, later than sooner—the public discovers the trickery. In no other country in the world is the moral conception so clear and true as in America, and no people will give a larger and more permanent reward to the man whose effort for that public has its roots in honor and truth.

"The sky is the limit" to the foreign-born who comes to America endowed with honest endeavor, ceaseless industry, and the ability to carry through. In any honest endeavor, the way is wide open to the will to succeed. Every path beckons, every vista invites, every talent is called forth, and every efficient effort finds its due reward. In no land is the way so clear and so free.

How good an American has the process of Americanization made me? That I cannot say. Who can say that of himself? But when I look around me at the American-born I have come to know as my close friends, I wonder whether, after all, the foreign-born does not make in some sense a better American—whether he is not able to get a truer perspective; whether his is not the deeper desire to see America greater; whether his is not less content to let its faulty institutions be as they are; whether in seeing faults more clearly he does not make a more decided effort to have America reach those ideals or those fundamentals of his own land which he feels are in his nature, and the best of which he is anxious to graft into the character of his adopted land?

It is naturally with a feeling of deep satisfaction that I remember two Presidents of the United States considered me a sufficiently typical American to wish to send me to my native land as the accredited minister of my adopted country. And yet when I analyze the reasons for my choice in both these instances, I derive a deeper satisfaction from the fact that my strong desire to work in America for America led me to ask to be permitted to remain here.

It is this strong impulse that my Americanization has made the driving power of my life. And I ask no greater privilege than to be allowed to live to see my potential America become actual: the America that I like to think of as the America of Abraham Lincoln and of Theodore Roosevelt—not faultless, but less faulty. It is a part in trying to shape that America, and an opportunity to work in that America when it comes, that I ask in return for what I owe to her. A greater privilege no man could have.

1922

Source:

Edward Bok. *The Americanization of Edward Bok.* New York: Charles Scribner's Sons, 1922. pp. 434-452.

EGYPTIAN AMERICANS

*T*he story of Karim and Aziza Mohammed is not of impoverished immigrants, but people of elevated status in their homeland. Many Egyptian professionals, like Karim, sought new careers in the United States during the decade from 1967 to 1977 for economic reasons. In an interview, Karim and Aziza described how and why they left Egypt for America, and some ramifications on their family.

Karim studied medicine in Egypt specializing in obstetrics. He established a practice and also joined the faculty at a university in Cairo. Despite his achievements, he still had to work long hours to support his family. Though competition in the Egyptian medical field was limited, so were the incomes in comparison to American incomes. While serving on an international vaccination team in the Gaza Strip, a U.S. physician, noting Karim's mounting frustrations, suggested he should relocate to America. In 1967 Karim decided to move. Many Egyptian immigrants sought the warmer southern climate of the United States, but Karim settled his family in Cleveland, Ohio.

Stress posed by disruption of traditionally close Egyptian family relations was evident as Aziza expressed reservations over their move. Aziza, detached from her family and experiencing a new climate and a new language, quickly became homesick. Like many Egyptians, Aziza was struck by fundamental differences between Egyptian and U.S. societies, such as dating, the selection of marriage partners, and the level of family support for new couples. She found life in the United States different in other ways as well. Aziza lamented, "Another difficult thing for me was housework. In Egypt I had a cook and I had a butler and I had a maid. I just supervised all that work at home. . .I didn't do the cooking, I didn't do the shopping, I didn't do the bathrooms. Oh, I was so tired the first three months here!"

On the other hand, Egyptian American professionals, such as Karim, found their careers rejuvenated. Karim was struck by the excellence in U.S. hospital facilities. But still, like many American minorities, Karim recognized how foreigners, always having to prove themselves, must work harder than others to be successful. Despite the hardships of change experienced by their children, they were convinced their children's futures were brighter in the United States than in Egypt. Concurrently with their desires to assimilate, the Mohammeds maintained a pride of their Egyptian heritage and customs shared with fellow Egyptian Americans.

KARIM AND AZIZA MOHAMMED

Karim: I did not come as an immigrant. I came as an exchange professor. I took a leave of absence to go to the university of Case Western Reserve. I had an open mind. I said, "I may stay, I may not."

I was a full professor in Cairo, and I had a private practice, too. I was very successful. In the university you have to work certain hours, from nine to two. Before that, before nine and after two, you are on your own, you have your own private patients. I used to start surgery at five in the morning. And I'd finish at eight or eight-thirty so that I'd be at the university on time. You leave the university, do your work, and by the time you reach home at six or seven, they call you for an emergency. And the system in Cairo is that you work six days a week. The weekend is only one day. You have only one day a week as holiday, and that is Friday. And even Friday morning we used to have surgery, because everyone is free. I was very busy and there was not much time for the family.

At first it was fun and a challenge, you know. You feel proud of it. And then it becomes a burden. And the only way out of it is to leave it all. When Dr. Edwards suggested to me that I come to the United States in 1967, I said, "This is not too hot, the life I've got. To make money, I don't have time for anything else." So I said to my wife, "Let's go. We have never been to the United States. Let's go there and take a chance of working there for some time." There was the challenge to grow. In Egypt, competition is limited. I had reached the top. I had nowhere else to go. I had achieved everything I wanted. I wanted to try to do something more.

My wife didn't like to leave Egypt because of her family. You know, our families are attached, and if one moves from Cleveland to Columbus, your family will think that's very bad and they cry and so on. She said, "Why should we leave? We have everything we wanted. What else do want?" She couldn't understand why should we move.

Aziza: I didn't want to come, because I didn't want to leave my family. Maybe if I was a working woman I would have been more occupied with my work. But it's the family that was the hardest thing, to leave the family.

I was very homesick—very, very homesick; because family life in Egypt is still very strong, you know. I wasn't working—I never worked in my life. But still, I wasn't one minute bored or lonely in Egypt. I'll tell you why. Besides regular visiting, we

have the sporting clubs, like the country clubs. It isn't a place to go just to play sports. You can sit in the sun, you know. Every day I passed by my mother—oh, definitely, every day—and my in-laws. We had the alumnae of my school, the American College for Girls, in Cairo. And we met once a month. All of our family went there—my mother and my sisters and now my niece. We do the social work-volunteer housewives, mostly from educated, high-middle-class families, are the ones that do this work. That was the outlet for women to go out and to do some work but not paid work. That was acceptable. In my time everybody went to have the education, even master's. But we didn't work. We stayed home. We did the social work. Egypt has illiteracy, so one of the work was to teach, educate the poor in the villages, teaching reading and writing. We do that with the servants, too, by the way. It's not like servants here.

Servants usually come from villages, not educated at all. So we get them, we dress them, we feed them, we educate them, we dress them we feed them, we educate them, and we pay them. All my own servants I taught.. . .

You know, in Egypt we have the arranged marriage. It's safe, because you look at the background of each other. The family of the bride will know that that man has a good future. It is a safer way of marriage, because, you know, when you marry here, young and just love, you don't look to other things. It's not only love, you know. There's economical, financial, social.. . . So usually, even if you didn't have time for dating, usually it works, because it's the same background. You don't know exactly the other person, but it's more predictable—his manners and his conduct and so on.

People approached my father many times, but he wouldn't ask me all the time, because if he always told me someone was interested, maybe then I'd spend all my time thinking about his man or that man. So he match. So one day he came to me and he said, "How about? Are you interested in getting married?" I said okay. Then they made an appointment, and the young man, Karim, came with his family to visit. We had a little party, especially so we can meet. He looks at me to see if he likes the way I look, if I'm pleasing to him. I look at him to see if I like his face, if he's not repulsive. In our case, we actually had seen each other before, because my cousin was a colleague of his, so it was not a new face. We talk, we try to know a little bit about each other. And the families talk. We were interested. Afterwards my father said to me, "Well, what do you think? Are you interested?" I said, "Yes, I like him. I think? Did you like the girl?" and he said to his father, "Yes, okay. Go ahead."

Once we both agreed, then we made an engagement party. An engagement party is different from what it is here. It's not a formal announcement. It's really a symbol that we can date, because in Egypt there's no dating. But now we can date. Oh, with chaperones! Who is the chaperone? Maybe my younger sister or his brother or my cousin. It can be anybody, but there has to be someone along.

Some engagements take three months, some take a year. It depends on how long it takes the father of the girl to get together the money for the household and to prepare all the furnishings. The system is that the bride always furnishes the house. The bridegroom pays a certain amount of money, and the bride supplies almost all the furniture. Not like here, not both start with nothing. In my case, we were engaged for three months, and when we married our house was all ready for us.. . .

When my husband decided to come here, we were married for ten years. He was one of the best doctors, and he was earning a lot. We just moved a few months before to a new house, and you get attached to certain things that you are used to. I think my husband was sure he was going to stay, but I was trying to tell myself that I wasn't staying. I kept my house and my furniture in Cairo. Everything was locked.

When we first got to Cleveland, somebody was meeting us—a doctor, Egyptian. He took us to a hotel and from there we looked for apartments, because in Egypt houses are very expensive. It's apartment living, like New York, or something like that. We found one near the good school district, in Shaker Heights. It was a two-bedroom apartment, two rooms and a living room. It was too small. We couldn't bear it. The other thing—the sound from the rooms and the next-door apartment—that was something different. You hear the sound from room to room, because you build with wood. In Egypt it's all concrete, even small homes.

We bought furniture and so on, but we didn't settle. And that was a big emotional problem for me, because I didn't work, I was at home. And we weren't starting our life. At the beginning, especially for a person like myself, I couldn't find friends. I'm not an outgoing person.

Another difficult thing for me was housework. In Egypt I had a cook and I had a butler and I had a maid. I just supervised all that work at home. I just show that this room was to be cleaned, I tell the cook what to go and buy and what to cook. I didn't do the cooking, I didn't do the shopping, I didn't do the bathrooms. Oh, I was so tired the first three months here! It was so hard for me. My muscles just ached, and I'm not joking.

And the treatment of the elderly! When I first came, it really made me sometimes cry to see an elder person going in the freezing temperature, carrying shopping bags, to get food. You know, I stand up for an older woman or man. If someone's coming out of a store, I get out of the way and I open the door. That made me upset, when I saw other people not doing that for an older person.

Karim: I was impressed by the hospitals—excellent! You know, the facilities, the equipment, everything you wanted to have to perform your job is available—not true in my part of the world. And then the facilities for teaching and education and development! The journals, we had in Egypt, but not every journal available here. And the audiovisual aids—this impressed me. If you want to do research, you have all the facilities—go ahead and do it.

Some engagements take three months, some take a year. It depends on how long it takes the father of the girl to get together the money for the household and to prepare all the furnishings.

As regards the climate, what impressed me is the green color—beautiful lawns and huge trees. This I liked so much. Egypt has green, but it doesn't rain, so the green is different. Here is as if you wash every leaf on the tree. And the maple trees are just gorgeous.

When the winter came, I realized how difficult it can be. The Cleveland is very rich in maple trees. The weather is very cold, very humid. My wife was not used to the ice, and she fell on the ice coming out of the house. She had a severe knee injury that required hospitalization. It was really a disruption of our life. I think it was an emotional trauma for the kids. They were young, they didn't know the language very well—because, you know, we came in July and she had the accident in January.

Aziza: My mother came then to keep me company, because I was so homesick, so depressed. But my mother doesn't know how to do tea, even, so I had to have somebody to serve her, too, while I was in the cast. Then my mother-in-law came after three or four months. Each one came, stayed three months. My mother came three times; my mother-in-law came twice. When we first came, we thought it was too far away, we'd be cut off; but once you go and they come, you find it becomes easier.

Karim: My father died while I was here. I didn't have a chance to see him. If my mother dies—I expect it to happen and I hope I will be there before she dies, but if she dies. . .I'll be sorry. I don't want to feel a sense of guilt all my life for this. As I said, I would feel sorry, but I don't want it to be a traumatic thing all my life—keeping myself guilty and trying to punish myself for not being there. Because I could be in Egypt and out on a trip and then she might die. My mother was here, visiting, and my father died when she was here, so it could happen. It could happen to anyone. I tell Aziza, too, the same thing. If her mother dies while she's here, it's bad, but this is God's will.

Aziza: It will happen to me. It is going to happen. . . I knew that my husband wanted to stay for good, but I was hoping for any reason he wouldn't like it, or the government wouldn't give us residency status in the United States, or something. That's why I insisted to have our house there closed, not rented. But after two years, once we had our residency, our green card, I said, "Okay, sell the house there."

My brothers take care of everything. When we became residents here, in order to go back to Egypt again we have to have the approval of our government—that they approve that we became immigrants to the United States. Bureaucracy—took six months, seven months, for my brother to run from one place to another. The papers, the papers, you know. That is something that you don't find in the United States. Nobody does for you anything except you yourself, but there—family.

So we moved to a house and we started to be settled. The first day, all the neighbors came and they said, "Welcome." A neighbor across the street—they were Jewish and they knew that we're Egyptians—they came, too, and they found people are people. It doesn't have anything to do with politics. Most of our friends now are Jewish. It seems that they are attracted to foreigners, or maybe it's because our customs are similar to theirs. Really, I think it's because of our feelings about the family. We notice that they, too—their families are very close, the children are still at home, and that's what we like about each other. But we don't talk about politics, because they are biased and we are biased. We found when we first started to talk about it, it's not good. So now we just have a rule: We don't talk about politics and we don't let it interfere with our friendship.

I am American in a way of simplicity. When I first came, I was too conscious of how I'm dressed. When I went out, even to the supermarket, I had to get dressed, with my shoes and my handbag dark blue if my dress is dark blue, and with my jewelry. Because I couldn't go out in Egypt without being completely dressed and perfectly matched, because I might see someone I know, and they'll say, "Oh, I saw so-and-so and she wasn't dressed quite right. Her shoes didn't match." But here I find that nobody knows me, nobody cares what I am—which is very good, the simplicity. That's something that I like here, because life is easier.

Karim: You know, since I came, there is a challenge all the time, and that kept my mind busy—work. It's very hard for a foreigner. You work harder than the others and you want to excel. I definitely feel that there has been discrimination because I'm foreign born. Not because I'm Egyptian, but because I'm not Anglo-Saxon, not American born and not American graduated. For example, in Egypt I was a full professor, and here I'm an associate professor. I think it's definitely because I'm not American. I think ultimately I will become a full professor, but, of course, I will have to publish 150 percent more than an American doctor, and I'll have to prove myself more. But eventually I will reach my aim. I like what I'm doing here. The hospital is great. I do clinical care, teaching, and research. I like that very much. It's hard to do the three, but I like the three—like having three children, you like each one. I think I would be bored if I left one go. I wouldn't be happy.

And then, only lately, after I finished writing my second book, I had some time to think. And I was a little bit depressed and homesick. I wouldn't say I would be sorry that I made the change. You know, the older you get, the more you realize that there is no perfect place or perfect person. Each place has its advantage and disadvantage. I don't think I would have grown as much as I did if I stayed in Cairo or been known nationally or internationally if I stayed in Cairo. But I regret something—for the kids—because of their religion and their language. There are no facilities here, no church—we call it a *mosque*. But at the same time, they know they are Moslems. I wouldn't mind if my children married an American, but I hope my grandchildren will keep the Moslem religion. The religion is very important, definitely, to us and to them, too. They know.

Aziza: Because I pray five times a day, and they see me praying. You don't have to go to a mosque to pray. You pray at home. There's a Moslem student association at the university. My children go to prayer and they take a religious class and Arabic class there. But when it's our holiday or our feast, they see we are the minority. It's not like being in the middle of everybody celebrating.

Karim: But, you know, they have advantages here. The education is better, their future is better. There are better opportunities when they graduate, more opportunity in the job market. I think the future here in the United States.. . .You know what will happen, you can plan for fifty years. You can plan for the children. We don't know what the conditions in Egypt will be in two years. You can't plan.

The children are Americans. There's nothing wrong with that But I say: "Until I die, I cannot and will not give up three things: my religion, my Arabic name, and my family." I hope they realize this, too. The important thing is that we should not

give up a culture for a culture. The equation would be zero. You have to take the good of both cultures, because every culture has something to offer. And this is what I expect my children to do. Egypt has had civilization for thousands of years, and I think one should be proud of this background and origin. If you can combine both cultures. . . .

Aziza: If you ask me if I'm sorry we came, I still wish I could have stayed in Egypt. I wish I could have been there all this time. Yes, I do. I wish I could have been there with my family.

Source:

American Mosaic: The Immigrant Experience in the Words of Those Who Lived It, compiled by Joan Morrison and Charlotte Fox Zabusky. Pittsburgh: University of Pittsburgh Press, 1993. pp. 378-384.

*N*awal El Saadawi is an Egyptian physician who practiced medicine in the area of thoracic medicine and psychiatry prior to becoming an internationally renown spokeswoman for women's issues. A novelist of international success, Nawal El Saadawi has been denounced by the Arab governments for her radical feminist writings. In this excerpt for her book Memoirs from the Women's Prison, El Saadawi describes the difficulties she endured and the impressions that she held during her prison experience in Egypt.

Nawal El Saadawi was born in 1931 in the village of Kafir Tahler in the Egyptian Delta, to a family of nine children. Her father was an official in the Egyptian Ministry of Education. All nine children received a university education, and Nawal El Saadawi became a physician in 1955. In 1958, she was appointed to the Ministry of Health, a position she held until she was dismissed in 1972 in response to her book on sexuality titled Women and Sex. From 1973 to 1976, she researched women and neurosis in the Ain Shams University's Faculty of Medicine. In 1979, she was appointed the United Nations Advisor for the Women's Program in Africa and the Middle East.

In 1981, during a round-up of Egyptian intellectuals, El Saadawi was imprisoned by Egyptian President Anwar Sadat. She was released after Sadat died in 1982. The experience inspired El Saadawi to write The Fall of the Imam, a novel that was denounced by Islamic groups. In 1982 she founded the Arab Women's Solidarity Association, an international organization seeking to help Arab women raise their awareness of women's issues. The organization was granted consultant status as an Arab non-governmental association in 1985 with the Economic and Social Council of the United Nations. The Egyptian government terminated the organization in 1991. Nawal El Saadawi took the Egyptian government to court but lost the case.

Nawal El Saadawi has published twenty-four books in Arabic. Her widely diverse writings have been studied, translated, and reviewed by Western advocates of *women's studies. She is greatly esteemed by feminists internationally, especially in the United States, where she is known as the Egyptian feminist. Nawal El Saadawi's writings are complicated. She wrote her first novel at age 13, and has written fiction and nonfiction, medical texts, short stories, plays, prison memoirs, critical essays, travel texts, and novels. She often examines the dynamics of the male-female relationship. For example, in* The Fall of the Imam, *there are first-person and third-person narrators of both genders. The story-line takes* The Thousand and One Nights *and redefines the relationship between major characters, redefining male theology in the process. The book is a highly complex literary work that evoked a strong, negative response from Arab males.*

El Saadawi's work is important because she is the voice of Arab women in the last decade of the twentieth century. Opposition to her work has taken the form of much published misinformation about her, including her medical specialty, her year of birth, and her publisher. Because of the seriousness of the death threats against her, Nawal El Saadawi lives in both Egypt and the United States, where she is a much-sought after lecturer.

MEMOIRS FROM THE WOMEN'S PRISON

Prison

If the most difficult moment in the life of one sentenced to execution comes just before the guillotine falls on his neck, then the hardest moment I'd ever known came just before I entered the cell.

My eyes follow the movement of the chain clutched in the cracked fingers of a blotchy brown hand, around which the massive keys swing. The one key resembles a huge mallet with the head of a hammer and a long steel arm indented by jagged teeth.

In the dark, the shadows of the steel-barred doors are reflected on the high walls like legendary phantoms. Steel clanging against steel, the sound colliding with the walls and the echo reverberating over the inner walls, as if hundreds of steel doors are being closed and locked. A whistle as sharp as utter silence, and voices resounding like a whistle, like a waft of trapped smoke escaping through a narrow aperture.

The plastic sandals on the two cracked brown feet strike the ground. Her back is stooped inside a greyish overcoat, its collar blackened with old sweat. On one shoulder, raised higher than the other, a black stripe perches like a black feather on the head of a mythical bird or legendary beast of ancient times. The keys in her hand, though, give her more the appearance of a gang leader whose band haunts the forests or deserted wilds.

The gloom is growing heavier, pressing on my eyelids with a new density. The air, becoming sluggish, takes on a piercing odour which burns through the mucous of my nose like suffocating gas.

Her back to me, the woman stopped before one of the enormous steel-barred doors and inserted the key. Her breathing is audible, as if she were panting.

Her voice rang out in the darkness, remote, as if it were coming to me from beneath the earth or from an era long past.

'Go on in.'

She pushed open the heavy steel door with difficulty, budging it just enough so that my body could pass through. Her cracked fingers stood out against my white dress as she helped me to enter.

I've witnessed this scene before, long ago: now I remember. The dark cracked fingers encircling my mother's body, encased in its white shroud, and pushing it slowly into the open hole in the ground. Around me, my father and family stand in mourning garb, their eyes glistening with tears. My eyes are open and tearless, as my head collides with the steel of the door.

'Careful.'

Her voice, too, is familiar. She is still standing at the threshold; her eyes dilate with a fleeting light before disappearing.

The key turned in the door three times and the silence, like a single continuous scream, invaded my ear just as the sharp whistling had done. I blocked my ears with my fingers and placed the white handkerchief over my nose. On the ceiling was an electric light staring like a strangled, bulging eye. Metal bunk beds. Bodies moving inside black cloaks. Heads wrapped in white or black; the *higaab*, which shields the head and neck, covering the wearer's hair completely. Faces concealed beneath *niqaabs*—all-enveloping face-veils with small holes through which I could perceive the steady gaze of human eyes.

Had I fallen to the bottom of a well? Or sprung on to another planet? Or returned to the age of slaves and harems? Or was this a dream? Was I asleep?

No, I'm not sleeping. I'm awake, standing up, totally conscious that I am inside prison. This is the cell. Four walls and the steel-barred door.

I closed and reopened my eyes. The ghostly shapes were still before me. I could make out one of the faces under the yellow light, and I called out in delight.

'Safinaz!'

We hugged each other. She was a journalist and writer whom I hadn't seen for many years, and she had greatly changed. She hadn't been wearing a *higaab* then.

A pair of eyes were gazing at me through two holes in a black *niqaab*. 'Who is our new colleague?'

'Dr. Nawal el Sa'adawi,' answered Safinaz. 'Author of dangerous books full of heresy.'

I saw a body moving on an upper bunk; she rose suddenly from her sleep and called out 'Greetings, Nawal.'

It was Dr Amina Rashid, a professor at Cairo University. Having met her a number of times in gatherings at my house and in the homes of friends, we had become friends. Happy to see Amina, I embraced her as Safinaz asked, 'Have you read the books Nawal has published?'

'Of course I've read them,' Amina replied, 'and my women students at the university have, too. They asked me to invite Nawal to the College so they could talk with her. These are important books which many people admire and like.'

'They're the books of an unbeliever and an atheist,' Safinaz responded.

Nawal El Saadawi

'Have you read them?' Amina wanted to know.

'I read only the Book of God.'

'How can you judge books which you haven't read?'

I don't know why I opened my eyes. I could have died with my eyes closed, but I discovered something I hadn't known before: a person dies with open eyes, as if wanting to see the process, or as if defending one's life with all senses.

A moment of silence passed. Some of the young women in *niqaabs* began probing me with questions about these books. Two eyeholes approached me and I heard a voice asking 'do you pray? Do you fast during Ramadan? Isn't a woman's face a blemish upon her, a shameful private part to be covered?'

'The shameful blemishes are oppression, falsehood, and the eradication of the human mind, whether a woman's or a man's,' I said. 'the blemish is our presence in this prison when we haven't committed any crimes, and no investigation has been undertaken.'

The eyes inside the holes widened and took on a shine. I turned towards Amina: 'When did you arrive?'

'Two days ago. An armed group came to my house. My son was with me, and I was busy with moving my furnishings to my new flat. I asked them to delay my arrest at least until my son's departure and completion of the removal, but they refused, and brought me to prison. We weren't in this cell at first, but in the hospital quarters, in the same room with Farida al-Naqqash and Shahinda Muqallid. I didn't feel like I was in gaol. We had newspapers, a radio, and our own food. The door was open all day long. But they transferred us to this place, and deprived us of everything. What happened to you, Nawal?'

'They knocked on the door, and I refused to open it for them, since they had no warrant from the Chief Prosecutor's office. They broke down the door and brought me here.'

Amina's eyes widened. 'Broke down the door?'

Suddenly we heard the key turning. The door to the cell opened and a woman entered. The door was locked behind her.

I could see her face in the yellowish light as she came towards us. 'Latifa!'

Dr Latifa al-Zayyat. I'd met her twenty years ago and our shared artistic and literary predilections had been the basis of a friendship. Delighted, we hugged each other.

'I read my name in the evening paper, among the list of those who had been taken into custody,' Latifa said. 'When I got home, I found the policemen waiting. They were convinced that my sister was me.' She laughed and looked at me. 'Nawal, what about you? What happened to you?'

'I refused to open the door for them without a warrant from the Chief Prosecutor, so they broke in.'

'Things really have reached the limit for them to arrest an independent writer like Nawal,' Latifa commented. 'God have mercy upon democracy and freedom of opinion.'

It was nearly dawn.

'We really must sleep a bit so we can resume the struggle tomorrow,' I said, and we laughed. But the laughter came from heavy hearts, exhausted faces and anxious eyes. Amina returned to her top bunk, next to a Christian girl with a very young face named Nur. Latifa tried to get to sleep on half of a bunk, next to Safinaz, but after a bit she got up and placed her mattress on the ground. Wrapping a white headband around her eyes, she fell asleep.

I remained open-eyed, contemplating my surroundings: the scabby black ceiling, cracked walls, steel bars, a small window high in the wall, next to the ceiling, blocked with a steel grille. Women's and girls' bodies lying on the ground or on the black metal bunk beds.

I stretched out my arm and looked at my fingers, moved one hand and grasped the other with it. Everything that had happened was real, not a dream. I was still wearing the white dress and the open-toed shoes which I had donned hurriedly as they were knocking at the door. My feet were slightly swollen—a sign of the long day's weariness. My throat was dry, and a ringing in my head accompanied a succession of filmstrip-like images. Events as old as childhood and new ones: the violent knocks, the noise of the door breaking, the yawning mouths of rifles, the shifting eyes of glass, the voice of the old man. The dark cramped vault, the horizontal pole rising and falling. The cleft in the great black door, the heavy, stifling atmosphere. I stretched out on the ground. Next to me was an iron bunk bed; on the bottom level lay a woman whose long hair covered her face entirely, and on the top bed was a woman wrapped in black from head to toe. Some of the other bodies extended full-length on the beds or the ground were half naked, while others were wholly swathed in black. I noticed an empty bed. Supporting myself with one hand on the ground, I raised myself, got to my feet, and walked towards the bed. No sooner did I sit down on it, however, than its fractured iron slats collapsed, so that I could see the ground below. I lifted the rubber mattress from the bed, placed it on the ground, and stretched out on top of it. Above my head was a black wall from which an unblinking electric light spilled red rays directly into my eyes, like a melting steel rapier, while ringing sounds, or perhaps a sharp whistling, poured into my ears like long strings of caustic liquid. Where were these sounds coming from?

I placed the white handkerchief over my face, blocked my ears with my fingers and closed my eyes. But the sounds continued to pierce my ears, and the light penetrated through my handkerchief and eyelids. Opening my eyes, I sensed a large space of burning pain between the eye and the lid which did not lessen, and a long stretch of time which would never come to an end.

Time is no longer time. Time and the wall have merged into one. The air is motionless. Nothing moves around me except the cockroaches and rats, as I lie on a thin rubber mattress which gives off the odour of old urine, my empty handbag placed under my head, still wearing the white dress and shoes in which I left the house.

I raised the handkerchief from my face and stuffed it into my ear. Continuous ringing and sharp screaming, whose source I could not place. Weird voices and a commotion I'd not heard before. From where does all of this come? Do these sounds pass through the four walls, the ceiling, the earth's depths, to arrive here? Human and non-human voices alike. A sharp scream like that of a newborn child; wailing and moaning akin to the howling of wolves, quarreling and cursing and a stifled sobbing. Raspy coughing, hands slapping and the sound of kicking. The whinnying murmur of water, what sounded like pleas of supplication, and chanting like the ritual of prayer. Frogs croaking, cats meowing and dogs barking, and over all a sharp whistling, the cockroaches' calls.

I was lying on my back in order to keep my head as far away as possible from the odour of the mattress beneath me. In the oppressive heat, I could feel the sticky sweat plastering my dress to my body. There was not a drop of breeze, and my chest seemed no longer able to move, either to rise or fall, to exhale or inhale. I imagined that I was dying, or that I had in fact died.

With the instinct of self-preservation, my eyes opened in alarm, as if of their own accord. I wasn't alarmed, or panicking in the true sense of the word, because I was sapped of all energy, in a state of fatigue and powerlessness near to death in which all reactions and feelings, including that of panic, were creeping away.

I don't know why I opened my eyes. I could have died with my eyes closed, but I discovered something I hadn't known before: a person dies with open eyes, as if wanting to see the process, or as if defending one's life with all senses.

In that instant it occurred to me that through my eyes I was sucking in the air which my chest had been unable to absorb. Perhaps this was the reason I didn't die. Although I could still feel and see, my chest failed to move.

And what did I see in that moment?

Above, I noticed a large yellow gecko clinging to the ceiling, creeping slowly along. A strange thought came to me: my gaze might draw him towards me, so that he would fall right on top of me. I closed my eyes, and then opened a single eye with extreme caution. I saw the gecko's legs moving before he fell suddenly.

If I had been in my normal state, I would have sprung up in fright before the gecko could fall on me. But I didn't budge. I felt the gecko running over my leg but I didn't move. Then I saw him jump off, startled, and disappear into a fissure in the wall.

My eyes widened in amazement, and suddenly incomprehensible feelings of happiness engulfed me. I closed my single eye in peace and slept until morning.

To this moment, I do not know how I slept, and I don't know the secret of that repose or the happiness which came over me all of a sudden—perhaps because it was the gecko which had taken fright of me rather than the other way around. Or perhaps it was the happiness of self-discovery, when there appears before one's eyes a new courage or self-confidence of which one was previously unaware, or when one disperses a fear or a phantom with which one has been living.

Source:

Nawal El Saadawi. *Memoirs from the Women's Prison*. Translated from the Arabic by Marilyn Booth. Berkeley: University of California Press, 1986. pp. 27-33.

ENGLISH AMERICANS

Jamestown, a former village in Virginia on the James River, was the site of the first English settlement in the New World. It was founded in 1607 by John Smith and named for King James I of England. Jamestown was home to the first representative government established by the colonists, the House of Burgesses (1619). Initially Jamestown was structured with a somewhat utopian ideal. The community shared the harvest and distributed food to families according to need. When the Communist-like system ultimately failed, the settlers turned to privatization.

Captain John Smith documented some his experiences in Jamestown during the settlement for the benefit of the London Company, which commissioned the venture. One of the subjects addressed by Smith in his reports was the weather in Virginia. Smith explained that, "Some times there are great droughts, other times much raine, yet great necessity of neither, by reason see not but that all the variety of needful fruits in Europe may be there in great plenty by the industry of men, as appeareth by those we there planted." At first glance Smith's words seem like a banal account of the climate and the promise of agricultural development in the fertile lands of southeast Virginia, but recent discoveries by scientists paint a more ominous picture.

The Jamestown settlers were nearly decimated by starvation because they came to the New World during one of the worst droughts of the millennium. Archeologists are now suggesting that the drought may have played a major factor in the famous disappearance of settlers of Roanoke in North Carolina. Researches have analyzed rainfall data from cypress trees and concluded that the years between 1606 and 1612 witnessed the worst drought in 770 years. Historians refer to the period as "the starving time." Of the roughly 8,000 settlers who came to Jamestown, only an estimated 1,218 survived. Nevertheless, the colony persevered and the site became the capital city of the colonists until 1699, when it was moved to Williamsburg, Virginia.

The Jamestown settlement is now home to Colonial National Park. Visitors from around the nation come to see artifacts and reconstructed domiciles and forts which enrich the experience. Tourists are also invited to wear costumes replicating the attire worn at the time of the settlement. Although the site stands as an historic relic celebrating the first English settlement in the New World, archeologists are still busy digging up the region in search of clues that will confirm historians' accounts of what appears to be both a triumph and a tragedy.

THE JAMESTOWN SETTLEMENT IN 1607

by Captain John Smith

Virginia is a Country in America, that lyeth betweene the degrees of 34 and 44 of the north latitude. The bounds thereof on the East side are the great Ocean. On the South lyeth Florida: on the North nova Francia. As for the West thereof, the limits are unknowne. Of all this country wee purpose not to speake, but only of that part which was planted by the English men in the yeare of our Lord, 1606. And this is under the degrees, 37, 38, and 39. The temperatures of this countrie doth agree well with English constitutions being once seasoned to the country. Which appeared by this, that though by many occasions our people fell sicke; yet did they recover by very small meanes and continued in health, though there were other great causes, not only to have made them sicke, but even to end their daies, etc.

The sommer is hot as in Spaine; the winter colde as in Fraunce or England. The heat of sommer is in June, Julie, and August, but commonly the coole Breeses asswage the vehemencie of the heat. The chiefe of winter is halfe December, January, February, and halfe March. The colde is extreame sharpe, but here the proverbe is true that no extreame long continueth.

In the yeare 1607, was an extraordinary frost in most of Europe, and this frost was founde as exteeame in Virginia. But the next yeare for 8 or 10 daies of ill weather, other 14 daies would be as Sommer.

The windes here are variable, but the like thunder and lightning to purifie the aire, I have seldome either seene or heard in Europe. From the Southwest came the greatest gustes with thunder and heat. The North-west winde is commonly coole, and bringeth faire weather with it. From the Northe is the greatest cold, and from the East and South-East as from the Barmadas, fogs and raines.

Some times there are great droughts, other times much raine, yet great necessity of neither, by reason we see not but that all the variety of needfull fruits in Europe may be there in great plenty by the industry of men, as appeareth by those we there planted.

There is but one entraunce by sea into this country, and that is at the mouth of a very goodly Bay, the widenesse whereof is neare 18 or 20 miles.

The cape on the South side is called Cape Henry in honour of our most noble Prince. The shew of the land there, is a white hilly sand like unto the Downes, and along the shores great plentie of Pines and Firres.

The north Cape is called Cape Charles in honour of the worthy Duke of Yorke. Within is a country that may have the prerogative over the most pleasant places of Europe, Asia, Africa, or America, for large and pleasant navigable rivers: heaven and earth never agreed better to frame a place for mans habitation being of our constitutions, were it fully manured and inhabited by industrious people. Here are mountaines, hils, plaines, valleyes, rivers and brookes all running most pleasantly into a faire Bay compassed but for the mouth with fruitfull and delightsome land. In the Bay and rivers are many Isles both great and small, some woody, some plaine, most of them low and not inhabited. This Bay lieth North and South in which the water floweth neare 200 miles and hath a channell for 140 miles, of depth betwixt 7 and 15 fadome, holding in breadth for the most part 10 or 14 miles. From the head of the Bay at the north, the land is mountanous, and so in a manner from thence by a Southwest line; So that the more Southward, the farther off from the Bay are those mounetaines. From which, fall certaine brookes, which after come to five principall navigable rivers. These run from the Northwest into the South east, and so into the west side of the Bay, where the fall of every River is within 20 or 15 miles one of an other.

The mountaines are of diverse natures, for at the head of the Bay the rockes are of a composition like miln-stones. Some of marble, &c. And many peeces of christall we found as throwne downe by water from the mountaines. For in winter these mountaines are covered with much snow, and when it dissolveth the waters fall with such violence, that it causeth great inundations in the narrow valleyes which yet is scarce perceived being once in the rivers. These waters wash from the rocks such glistering tincturess that the ground in some places seemeth as guilded, where both the rocks and the earth are so splendent to behold, the better judgements then ours might have beene perswaded, they contained more then probabilities. The vesture of the earth in most places doeth manifestly prove the nature of the soile to be lusty and very rich. The coulor of the earth we found in diverse places, resembleth bole Armoniac, terra sigillata ad lemnia, Fullers earth, marle, and divers other such appearances. But generally for the most part the earth is a black sandy mould, in some places a fat slimy clay, in other places a very barren gravell. But the best ground is knowne by the vesture it beareth, as by the greatnesse of trees or abundance of weedes, &c. The country is not mountanous nor yet low but such pleasant plaine hils and fertle valleyes, one prettily crossing an other, and watered so conveniently with their sweete brookes and christall springs, as if art itselfe had devised them. By the rivers are many plaine marishes containing some 20, some 100, some 200 Acres, some more, some lesse. Other plaines there are fewe, but only where the Savages inhabit: but all overgrowne with trees and weedes being a plaine wildernes.. . .

Source:

British in America, 1578-1970: A Chronology & Fact Book, compiled and edited by Howard B. Furer. Dobbs Ferry, NY: Oceana Publications, 1972. pp. 78-79.

As colonial America began to rise in the seventeenth century, laborers were greatly needed to work the fields of the mostly agricultural economy. In England, simultaneously, unemployment was high, and conditions for the poor were made even more harsh by English law. The so-called Poor Laws made unemployment a crime, even when no jobs existed for people. The combination of need abroad, a surplus of unemployed workers at home, and a harsh legal system helped to revive an old form of contractual labor called indenture. Workers who indentured themselves—called indentured servants—signed contracts to work for a number of years. In return, they received free passage to the colonies, where they would be given room, board, and work by their employer, known as their master.

Nearly a century later, advertisements around London tried to lure new recruits by describing life in the colonies as an adventure. Puncturing this lie is what the Englishman William Eddis has in mind in his letter from the colony of Maryland, where he was stationed as a royal officer in the 1770s. A rich source for historians, Eddis' letters home make detailed, critical, and often moving observations of colonial life, and his view of indenture is no exception. The "seducing encouragement of adventure" portrayed in the advertisements was, he argued, far from the truth that awaited servants. Eddis wrote that they discovered indenture was no better than being a convicted felon.

In fact, the lot of indentured servants was a little better than that of slaves—the other huge source of labor forced to build colonial America. The two practices differed significantly: slavery was a permanent condition into which slaves, who were mainly Africans, did not enter voluntarily, while voluntary contracts of indenture for white Europeans usually lasted only five years or so. However, in other respects, the conditions were similar. Food was scarce, housing barely adequate, hours of work long. And, like slaves, many indentured servants had not wished to be in the colonies. Convicted felons were sent en masse to the colonies; estimates range as high as one-fourth of all British immigrants during the colonial period. Destitute women and children were often pressed into indenture.

As the legal property of the master, the servant had almost no legal rights. Punishment for disobeying or trying to run away was typically whipping—plus additional years added onto the length of the indenture. The colonial courts upheld the con-

tracts of indenture, leaving the long-suffering employee to wait until the contract expired. The practice continued until being abandoned as outmoded and unjust in the nineteenth century.

The following letter was originally published in William Eddis's Letters From America, Historical and Descriptive; Comprising Occurrences from 1769 to 1777, Inclusive, *London, 1792.*

STIMULATING ENGLISH EMIGRATION—1769

In your frequent excursions about the great metropolis, you cannot but observe numerous advertisements, offering the most seducing encouragement to adventures under every possible description; to those who are disgusted with the frowns of fortune in their native land, and those who are an enterprising disposition who are tempted to court her smiles in a distant region. These persons are referred to agents, or crimps, who represent the advantages to be obtained in America, in colours so alluring that it is almost impossible to resist their artifices. Unwary persons are accordingly induced to enter into articles by which they engage to become servants, agreeable to their respective qualifications, for the term of five years, every necessary accommodation being found them during the voyage, and every method taken that they may be treated with tenderness and humanity during the period of servitude, at the expiration of which they are taught to expect that opportunities will assuredly offer to secure to the honest and industrious a competent provision for the remainder of their days.

The generality of the inhabitants in this province Maryland are very little acquainted with those fallacious pretences, by which numbers are continually induced to embark for this continent. On the contrary, they too generally conceive an opinion that the difference is merely nominal between the indented servant and the convicted felon; nor will they readily believe that people who had the least experience in life, and whose characters were unexceptionable, would abandon their friends and families, and their ancient connections, for a servile situation in a remote appendage to the British Empire. From this persuasion they rather consider the convict as the more profitable servant, his term being for seven, the latter only for five years: and I am sorry to observe that there are but few instances wherein they experience different treatment.. . .

Source:

British in America, 1578-1970: A Chronology & Fact Book, compiled and edited by Howard B. Furer. Dobbs Ferry, NY: Oceana Publications, 1972. p. 118.

T he Massachusetts report to the U.S. House of Representatives in April of 1836 (House Document 219) may be the first documented appeal to restrict immigration policy in the United States. It came in response to a number of British "paupers" that came to the United States in the early to mid-nineteenth century. The report claims that the British government was encouraging economically disadvantaged groups to migrate to the United States. In the absence of any alternative to stop the "evil" of incoming paupers, members of the Massachusetts legislature made an appeal to the federal government to employ some kind of measure to prevent impoverished immigrants from entering the United States. The report requests that

Congress *"use their endeavors to obtain the passage of a law by Congress to prevent the introduction of foreign paupers into this country."*

A number of subsequent efforts have been made to limit the number of immigrants admitted into the United States since the Massachusetts report. In 1882 Congress passed the Chinese Exclusion Act which prohibited Chinese immigrants who would be ineligible to become naturalized citizens. The law was revised in 1917 to include all Asians. In the 1920s Congress passed laws designed to limit the number of Italians, Jews, Catholics, and Greeks entering the United States. Although some past immigration policy such as the ban on Asians was racially motivated, other concerns such as employment during the 1930s and foreign policy during war times also influenced policy makers.

Historically, immigration policy in the United States has been based on a quota system. The quota system heavily favored immigrants from South and Central America and Canada as well as immigrants from Great Britain, Sweden, Ireland, and Germany. Although the ban on Asians was eventually repealed, the quota system did not allow for the admission of many Asians. President Truman called for an appraisal of immigration policy because of its discriminatory bias. Among the findings of the President's Commission on Immigration and Naturalization was that the quota system "discriminated on the basis of race, creed and color." In response, in 1965 U.S. immigration policy was revised to account for immigrants who wished to enter the United States in order to reunite with family members.

The shift in policy was designed to make for a more judicious immigration policy. However, the result was a dramatic increase in the amount of immigrants admitted into the United States. Since 1965 an estimated 18 million immigrants have entered the United States illegally. In 1995 the Jordan Commission recommended that the number of immigrants allowed into the United States should be reduced from 825,000 to 550,000 in an effort to mitigate education, urban congestion, and employment problems in the United States.

In spite of the many efforts made by various interest groups and state and federal legislators, the federal government has historically supported the notion that the United States has a history of being a "melting pot" of diverse peoples and is enriched by cultural and ethnic diversity. Belief in this concept has been reflected in immigration laws and policies which tend to support a relatively generous posture toward the admission of foreign peoples. According to journalist John Schidlovsky, "[n]o country in the history of the world, historians agree, has been as generous in accepting so many millions to its shores as has the United States."

BRITISH PAUPERISM IN MASSACHUSETTS—1836

Commonwealth of Massachusetts,
House of Representatives

April 9, 1836

The Committee appointed by this House, on the 25th ultimo, "to consider the expediency of instructing the Senators and requesting the Representatives of this Commonwealth in the Congress of the United States, to use their endeavors to obtain the passage of a law by Congress to prevent the introduction of foreign paupers into this country, or to favor any other measures which Congress may be disposed to adopt to effect the object," have attended to the duty assigned them, and respectfully ask leave to report:

That, at this late period in the session of this Legislature, they have not thought it advisable to go into the minute details of this most interesting, not to say alarming, subject, especially as it has occupied so much of the attention of this House for several of the last years, and so much valuable information relating to it has heretofore been communicated. They have preferred to come directly to the point referred to their consideration, adverting only so such circumstances as seemed to have a direct bearing upon it.

The immense, insupportable, and by us almost inconceivable, burden of pauperism in England, which originated at first in a well intended but ill judged and most disastrous provision of law, would most naturally occupy the attention of her statesmen and philanthropists, and induce them to look in every direction for some efficient mode of relief. And it is not at all surprising that the peculiar facilities and inducements for the emigration of paupers to this country, in our immediate contiguity to the British provinces, in our extended seacoast, and more than all perhaps, in the comfortable provision here made for the poor, and "our open philanthropy and freedom in giving strangers a hearty welcome to our shores," have decided them to fix upon emigration hither as the most available measure. Former Committees of this House have perceived and pointed out the gradual developments of a plan to this effect. They have also perceived the insufficiency of any State enactments "effectually" to prevent the rapid ingress of paupers to this country, under the operations of such a plan. An appeal to Congress has been considered the only adequate remedy of the evil. But, so far as your Committee

have been informed, no such appeal has yet been made. They are solemnly of the opinion, however, that it cannot safely be any longer delayed. They have ascertained that the plan of His Majesty's poor law commissioners, recommending the emigration of their poor, has not only reached its maturity in positive enactments of law, but has actually gone into operation.. . .

Your committee find that. . .320 paupers, from nineteen parishes, in eleven different counties, are reported to have emigrated during the last year. Of these 320, the cost of whose transportation was 2,473, or about £ 7,15s.6d. per head, 9 went to Prince Edward's Island, 261 to Upper Canada, and the remaining 50 to the United States, notwithstanding the regulation restricting them "to some British colony."

Now let it be considered that England contains 15,635 parishes and that if they should all conclude, this year to follow the example of the 19 reported, so "signally beneficial" in its results, our proportion of them would be about 41,145. But, alarming as this simple calculation may seem, it is but a trifle to what we have every reason to fear. When we consider that these paupers have no claim whatever upon the provinces to the United States; and the fact, so many times communicated to this Legislature, that nearly all of the host of foreign paupers, with which we are already infested, have come in by land through the provinces; is there not reason enough to fear that we shall soon be inundated with population of this kind, if it cannot, by some means, be speedily prevented? — No comment, surely, is necessary upon the fact that 261 of the 320 above-mentioned emigrants came to Upper Canada. Can it be for a moment supposed that England intends thus to burden her colonies, or that her colonies will quietly receive and provide for such accessions to their population?

As the result of their inquiries, therefore, your committee will only add the appended resolve. . . .

Resolved, That it is expedient to instruct the Senators and request the Representatives of this Commonwealth, in the Congress of the United States, to use their endeavors to obtain the passage of a law by Congress to prevent the introduction of foreign paupers into this country; or to favor any other measures which Congress may be disposed to adopt to effect the object.

Source:

*British in America, 1578-1970: A Chronology & Fact
    Book,* compiled and edited by Howard B.
    Furer. Dobbs Ferry, NY: Oceana Publications,
    1972. pp. 132-133.

*I*n the Victorian period, many Englishmen and women traveled abroad, and Englishwomen, especially, had never traveled so widely as they did in the early nineteenth century. Improvements in transportation, the decreasing cost of travel and increasing leisure and income made travel more feasible. As a result, people traveled for a multitude of reasons — to improve their physical health, for spiritual pilgrimages or to interact with new cultures. Women frequently traveled as lecturers for interest groups, as governesses for families, or simply in order to better understand world events. Many traveled alone. Though many English women travelers in this era believed that their British citizenship brought with it certain rights and privileges and therefore expected special treatment, they also felt a responsibility to record their experiences in journals and diaries, providing a record of what they saw. Indeed, the fact that women often wrote about their experiences often provided public recognition, authority and purpose. Victorian women's travel writing frequently appeared in the serial publications of the day, and gave women a measure of social authority that extended beyond the bounds of the household. Travel writing allowed Victorian Englishwomen to voice their opinions on other lives, histories and cultures.

As a destination, the United States represented the boundaries of personal and professional independence. Isabella Lucy Bird's The Englishwoman in America was the result of a trip that Bird took in 1854 when she was twenty three years old and suffered from a spinal disease. Bird sought both physical recovery as well as intellectual stimulation during her travels. Published in 1856, Bird's work is reflective of much of women's writing about America: it focuses on the details of everyday life, rather than on the dangers of travel or the landscape. Bird writes in detail about the inhabitants of Ohio, the prairie, and Chicago. In this chapter, she describes her train trip and the people traveling on the train with her, including people heading west. She gives a vivid picture of the changing scenery from the Ohio River Valley into the prairie, and describes the city of Chicago in crystalline terms. Her description of a rooming house and its meals, and the lamentable experience she has in this situation provide some flavor of the difficulties that a woman traveler in this era might encounter. Bird states, in spite of her troubles, that "Chicago is more worth a visit than any other of the western cities. Even one day at it was worth a voyage across the Atlantic, and a land-journey of eighteen hundred miles."

THE ENGLISHWOMAN IN AMERICA (EXCERPT)

CHAPTER VIII

A bright September sun glittered upon the spires of Cincinnati as I reluctantly bade it adieu, and set out in the early morning by the cars to join my travelling companions, meaning to make as long a detour as possible, or, as a "down-east" lady might say, to "make a pretty considerable circumlocution." Fortunately I had met with some friends, well acquainted with the country, who offered to take me round a much larger circle than I had contemplated; and with a feeling of excitement such as I had not before experienced, we started for the Mississippi and the western prairies en route to Detroit.

Bishop M'Ilvaine, anxious that a very valued friend of his in England should possess something from Ohio, had cut down a small sapling, which, when divested of its branches and otherwise trimmed, made a very formidable-looking bludgeon or cudgel, nearly four feet long. This being too lengthy for my trunks was tied to my umbrella, and on this day in the cars excited no little curiosity, several persons eyeing it, then me, as if wondering in what relation we stood to each other. Finally they took it up, minutely examining it, and tapping it as if to see whether anything were therein concealed. It caused me much amusement, and, from its size, some annoyance, till at length, wishing to leave it in my room at a Toronto hotel while I went for a visit of a few days, the waiter brought it down to the door, asking me "if I wished to take the cudgel?" After this I had it shortened, and it travelled in my trunk to New York, where it was given to a carver to be fashioned into a walking-stick; and, unless the tradesman played a Yankee trick, and substituted another, it is now, after surviving many dangers by sea and land, in the possession of the gentleman for whom it was intended.

Some amusing remarks were made upon England by some of the "Buckeyes," as the inhabitants of Ohio are called. On trying to persuade a lady to go with me to St. Louis, I observed that it was only five hundred miles. "Five hundred miles!" she replied; "why, you'd tumble off your paltry island into the sea before you got so far!" Another lady, who got into the cars at some distance from Cincinnati, could not understand the value which we set upon ruins. "We should chaw them up," she said, "make roads or bridges of them, unless Barnum transported them to his museum: we would never

keep them on our own hook as you do." "You value them yourselves," I answered; "any one would be 'lynched' who removed a stone of Ticonderoga." It was an unfortunate speech, for she archly replied, "Our only ruins are British fortifications, and we go to see them because they remind us that we whipped the nation which whips all the world." The Americans, however, though they may talk so, would give anything if they could appropriate a Kenilworth Castle, or a Melrose or a Tintern Abbey, with its covering of ivy, and make it sustain some episode of their history. But though they can make railways, ivy is beyond them, and the purple heather disdains the soil of the New World. A very amusing ticket was given me on the Mad River line. It bore the command, "Stick this check in your ———," the blank being filled up with a little engraving of a hat; consequently I saw all the gentlemen with small pink embellishments to the covering of their heads.

We passed through a large and very beautiful portion of the State of Ohio; the soil, wherever cultivated, teeming with crops, and elsewhere with a vegetation no less beautiful than luxuriant; a mixture of small weed prairies, and forests of splendid timber. Extensive districts of Ohio are still without inhabitants, yet its energetic people have constructed within a period of five years half as many miles of railroad as the whole of Great Britain contains; they are a "great people," they do "go a-head," these Yankees. The newly cleared soil is too rich for wheat for many years; it grows Indian corn for thirty in succession, without any manure. Its present population is under three millions, and it is estimated that it would support a population of ten millions, almost entirely in agricultural pursuits. We were going a-head, and in a few hours arrived at Forest, the junction of the Clyde, Mad River, and Indiana lines.

Away with all English ideas which may be conjured up by the work junction—the labyrinth of iron rails, the smart policeman at the points, the handsome station, and elegant refreshment-rooms. Here was a dense forest, with merely a clearing round the rails, a small shanty for the man who cuts wood for the engine, and two sidings for the trains coming in different directions. There was not even a platform for passengers, who, to the number of two or three hundred, were standing on the clearing, resting against the stumps of trees. And yet for a few minutes every day the bustle of life pervades this lonely spot, for here meet travellers from east, west, and south; the careworn merchant from the Atlantic cities, and the hardy trapper from the western prairies. We here changed cars for those of the Indianapolis line, and, nearly at the same time with three other trains, plunged into the depths of the forest.

"You're from down east, I guess?" said a sharp nasal voice behind me.—This was a supposition first made in the Portland cars, when I was at a loss to know what distinguishing and palpable peculiarity marked me as a "down-easter." Better informed now, I replied, "I am." "Going west?"—" Yes." "Travelling alone?"—" No." "Was you raised down east?"—" No, in the Old Country." "In the little old island? well, you are kinder glad to leave it, I guess? Are you a widow?"—"No." "Are you travelling on business?"—" No." " What business do you follow?"—" None." "Well, now, what are you travelling for?"—" Health and pleasure." "Well, now, I guess you're pretty considerable rich. Coming to settle out west, I suppose?"—" No, I'm going back at the end of the fall." "Well, now, if that's not a pretty tough hickory-nut! I guess you Britishers are the queerest critturs as ever was raised!" I considered myself quite fortunate to have fallen in with such a querist, for the Americans are usually too much taken up with their own business to trouble themselves about yours, beyond such questions as, "Are you bound west, stranger?" or, "You're from down east, I guess." "Why do you take me for a down-easter?" I asked once. "Because you speak like one," was the reply; the frequent supposition that I was a New Englander being nearly as bad as being told that I "had not the English accent at all." I was glad to be taken for an American, as it gave me a better opportunity of seeing things as they really are. An English person going about staring and questioning, with a note-book in his hand, is considered "fair game," and consequently is "crammed" on all subjects; stories of petticoated table legs, and fabulous horrors of the bowie knife, being among the smallest of the absurdities swallowed.

Our party consisted of five persons besides myself, two elderly gentlemen, the niece of one of them, and a young married couple. They knew the governor of Indiana, and a candidate for the proud position of Senator, also our fellow travellers; and the conversation assumed a political character; in fact, they held a long parliament, for I think the discussion lasted for three hours. Extra-ordinary, and to me unintelligible names, were bandied backwards and forwards; I heard of "Silver Grays," but my companions were not discussing a breed of

fowls; and of "Hard Shells," and "Soft Shells," but the merits of eggs were not the topic. "Whigs and Democrats" seemed to be analogous to our Radicals, and "Know-Nothings" to be a respectable and constitutional party. Whatever minor differences my companions had, they all seemed agreed in hating the "Nebraska men" (the advocates of an extension of slavery), who one would have thought, from the epithets applied to them, were a set of thieves and cut-throats. A gentleman whose whole life had been spent in opposition to the principles which they are bringing forward was very violent, and the pretty young lady, Mrs. Wood, equally so. After stopping for two hours at a wayside shed, we set out again at dark for La Fayette, which we reached at nine. These Western cars are crammed to overflowing, and, having to cross a wide stream in a ferryboat, the crush was so terrible, that I was nearly knocked down; but as American gentlemen freely use their canes where a lady is in the case, I fared better than some of my fellow-passengers, who had their coattails torn and their toes barbarously crushed in the crowd. The steam ferryboat had no parapet, and the weakest were pushed to the side; the centre was filled up with baggage, carts, and horses; and vessels were moored along the river, with the warps crossing each other, to which we had to bow continually to avoid decapitation. When we reached the wharf, quantities of people were waiting to go to the other side; and directly the gang-way-board was laid, there was a simultaneous rush of two opposing currents, and, the insecure board slipping, they were all precipitated into the water. Fortunately it was not deep, so they merely underwent its cooling influences, which they bore with admirable equanimity, only one making a better complaint, that he had spoiled his "go-to-meetins." The farther west we went, the more dangerous the neighbourhood became. At all the American stations there are placards warning people to beware of pickpockets; but from Indiana westward they bore the caution, "Beware of pickpockets, swindlers, and luggage-thieves." At many of the depots there is a general rush for the last car, for the same reason that there is a scramble for the stern cabins in a steamer,—viz, the explosive qualities of the boilers.

We travelled the whole of that night, our fellow-passengers becoming more extravagant in appearance at every station, and morning found us on the prairies. Cooper influences our youthful imaginations by telling us of the prairies—Mayne Reid makes us long to cross them; botanists tell us of their flowers, sportsmen of their buffaloes—but without seeing them few people can form a correct idea of what they are really like.

The sun rose over a monotonous plain covered with grass, rank, high, and silky-looking, blown before the breeze into long, shiny waves. The sky was blue above, and the grass a brownish green beneath; wild pigeons and turkeys flew over our heads; the horizontal line had not a single inequality; all was hot, unsuggestive, silent, and monotonous. This was the grass prairie.

A belt of low timber would bound the expanse, and on the other side of it a green sea would open before us, stretching as far as the eye could reach — stationary billows of earth, covered with short green grass, which, waving beneath the wind, completed the oceanic illusion. This was the rolling prairie.

Again a belt of timber, and a flat surface covered with flowers, brilliant even at this season of the year; though, of the most gorgeous, nothing remained but the withered stalks. The ground was enamelled with lilies, the helianthus and cineraria flourished, and the deep-green leaves and blue blossom of the lupin contrasted with the prickly stem and scarlet flower of the euphorbia. For what purpose was "the wilderness made so gay where for years no eye sees it," but to show forth his goodness who does what he will with his own? This was the weed prairie, more fitly termed "the Garden of God."

These three kinds of prairie were continually alternating with belts of timber and small lakes; but few signs of population were apparent during that long day's journey. We occasionally stopped for water at shanties on the prairies, and took in two or three men; but this vast expanse of fertile soil still must remain for many years a field for the enterprise of the European races.

Towards evening we changed cars again, and took in stores of refreshment for our night's journey, as little could be procured along the route. What strange people now crammed the cars! Traders, merchants, hunters, diggers, trappers, and adventurers from every land, most of them armed to the teeth, and not without good reason; for within the last few months, Indians, enraged at the aggressions of the white men, have taken a terrible revenge upon western travellers. Some of their rifles were of most costly workmanship, and were nursed with paternal care by their possessors. On the seat in front of me were two "prairie-men," such as are described in the 'scalp-Hunters,' though of an inferior grade to St. Vrain. Fine specimens of men they were; tall, handsome, broad-chested, and athletic, with aquiline noses, piercing grey eyes, and brown curling hair and beards. They wore leathern jackets, slashed and embroidered, leather small-clothes, large boots with embroidered tops, silver spurs, and caps of scarlet cloth, worked with somewhat tar-

nished gold thread, doubtless the gifts of some fair ones enamoured of the handsome physiognomies and reckless bearing of the hunters. Dulness fled from their presence; they could tell stories, whistle melodies, and sing comic songs without weariness or cessation: fortunate were those near enough to be enlivened by their drolleries during the tedium of a night detention. Each of them wore a leathern belt—with two pistols stuck into it—gold earrings, and costly rings. Blithe, cheerful souls they were, telling racy stories of Western life, chivalrous in their manners, and free as the winds.

There were Californians dressed for the diggings, with leather pouches for the gold-dust; Mormons on their way to Utah; and restless spirits seeking for that excitement and variety which they had sought for in vain in civilized life! And conveying this motley assortment of human beings, the cars dashed along, none of their inmates heeding each other, or perhaps Him

"—— who heeds and holds them all In his large love and boundless thought."

At eleven we came to an abrupt pause upon the prairie. After waiting quietly for some time without seeing any vestiges of a station, my friends got out to inquire the cause of the detention, when we found that a freight-train had broken down in front, and that we might be detenus for some time, a mark for Indian bullets! Refreshments were produced and clubbed together; the "prairie-men" told stories; the hunters looked to their rifles, and polished their already resplendent chasing; some Mexicans sang Spanish songs, a New Englander Yankee Doodle;' some guessed, others calculated, till at last all grew sleepy: the trappers exhausted their stories, the singers their songs, and a Mormon, who had been setting forth the peculiar advantages of his creed, the patience of his auditors—till at length sonorous sounds, emitted by numerous nasal organs, proving infectious, I fell asleep to dream confusedly of 'Yankee Doodle,' pistols, and pickpockets.

In due time I awoke; we were stopping still, and there was a light on our right. "We're at Rock Island, I suppose?" I asked sleepily. A laugh from my friends and the hunters followed the question; after which they informed me in the most polite tones that we were where we had been for the last five hours, namely stationary on the prairie. The intense cold and heavy dew which accompany an American dawn made me yet more amazed at the characteristic patience with which the Americans submit to an unavoidable necessity, however disagreeable. It is true that there were complaints of cold, and heavy sighs, but no blame was imputed to any one, and the quiescence of my companions made me quite ashamed of my English impatience. In England we should have had a perfect chorus of complaints, varied by "rowing" the conductor, abuse of the company, and resolutions to write to the Times, or bring up the subject of railway mismanagement in the House of Commons. These people sat quietly, ate, slept, and smoked, and were thankful when the cars at last moved off to their destination.

On we flew to the West, the land of Wild Indians and buffaloes, on the narrow rims of metal with which this "great people" is girdling the earth. Evening succeeded noon, and twilight to the blaze of a summer day; the yellow sun sank cloudless behind the waves of the rolling prairie, yet still we hurried on, only stopping our headlong course to take in wood and water at some nameless stations. When the sun set, it set behind the prairie waves. I was oblivious of any changes during the night, and at rosy dawn an ocean of long green grass encircled us round. Still on—belts of timber diversify the prospect—we rush into a thick wood, and, emerging from it, arrive at Rock Island, an unfinished-looking settlement, which might bear the name of the Desert City, situated at the confluence of the Rock River and Mississippi. We stop at a little wharf, where waits a little steamer of uncouth construction; we step in, a steam-whistle breaks the silence of that dewy dawn, and at a very rapid rate we run between high wooded bluffs, down a turbid stream, whirling in rapid eddies. We steam for three miles, and land at a clearing containing the small settlement of Davenport. We had come down the Mississippi, mightiest of rivers! half a mile wide seventeen hundred miles from its mouth, and were in the far West. Waggons with white tilts, thick-hided oxen with heavy yokes, mettlesome steeds with high peaked saddles, picketed to stumps of trees, lashing away the flies with their tails; emigrants on blue boxes, wondering if this were the El Dorado of their dreams; arms, accoutrements, and baggage surrounded the house or shed where we were to breakfast. Most of our companions were bound for Nebraska, Oregon, and Utah, the most distant districts of which they would scarcely reach with their slow-paced animals for four months; exposed in the mean time to the attacks of the Sioux, Comanches, and Blackfeet.

There, in a long wooden shed with blackened rafters and an earthen floor, we breakfasted, at seven o'clock, on johnny-cake, squirrels, buffalo-hump, dampers, and buckwheat, tea and corn spirit, with a crowd of emigrants, hunters, and adventurers; and soon after re-embarked for Rock Island, our little steamer with difficulty stemming the mighty tide of the Father of Rivers. The machinery, such as it was, was very visible, the boiler patched in several places, and steam escaped in different directions. I asked the captain if he were not in the habit of "sitting upon the safety-valve," but he stoutly denied the charge. The vernacular of this neighbourhood was rather startling to an English ear. "Who's the alligator to hum?" asked a broad-shouldered Kentuckian of his neighbour, pointing to a frame shanty on the shore, which did not look to me like the abode of that amphibious and carnivorous creature. "Well, old alligator, what's the time o' day?" asked another man, bringing down a brawny paw, with a resounding thump, upon the Herculean shoulders of the first querist, thereby giving me the information that in the West alligator is a designation of the genus homo; in fact, that it is customary for a man to address his fellow-man as "old alligator," instead of "old fellow." At eight we left Rock Island, and, turning my unwilling steps eastward from the land of adventure and romance, we entered the cars for Chicago.

They were extremely crowded, and my friends, securing me the only comfortable seat in one of them, were obliged to go into the next, much to their indignation; but protestations were of no use. The engine-bell rang, a fearful rush followed, which resulted in the passage down the centre being filled with standing men; the conductor shouted "Go a-head," and we were off for Lake Michigan in the "Lightning Express," warranted to go sixty-seven miles an hour! I had found it necessary, to study physiognomy since leaving England, and was horrified by the appearance of my next neighbour. His forehead was low, his deep-set and restless eyes significant of cunning, and I at once set him down as a swindler or pickpocket. My convictions of the truth of my inferences were so strong, that I removed my purse, in which, however, acting by advice, I never carried more than five dollars, from my pocket, leaving in it only my handkerchief and the checks for my baggage, knowing that I could not possibly keep awake the whole morning. In spite of my endeavours to the contrary, I soon sank into an oblivious state, from which I awoke to the consciousness that my companion was withdrawing his hand from my pocket. My first impulse was to make an exclamation, my second, which I carried into execution, to ascertain my loss; which I found to be the very alarming one of my baggage-checks; my whole property being thereby placed at this vagabond's disposal, for I knew perfectly well, that if I claimed my trunks without my checks, the acute baggage-master would have set me down as a bold swindler. The keen-eyed conductor was not in the car, and, had he been there, the necessity for habitual suspicion, incidental to his position, would so far have removed his original sentiments of generosity as to make him turn a deaf ear to my request, and there was not one of my fellow-travellers whose physiognomy would have warranted me in appealing to him. So, recollecting that my checks were marked Chicago, and seeing that the thief's ticket bore the same name, I resolved to wait the chapter of accidents, or the re-appearance of my friends. I was scarcely able to decide whether this proof of the reliance to be placed upon physiognomy was not an adequate compensation for the annoyance I was experiencing, at the probability of my hoarded treasures falling into the hands of an adventurer.

During the morning we crossed some prairie-country, and stopped at several stations, patches of successful cultivation showing that there must be cultivators, though I rarely saw their habitations. The cars still continued so full that my friends could not join me, and I began to be seriously anxious about the fate of my luggage. At mid-day, spires and trees, and lofty blocks of building, rising from a grass-prairie on one side, and from the blue waters of Lake Michigan on the other, showed that we were approaching Chicago. Along beaten tracks through the grass, waggons with white tilts drawn by oxen were proceeding west, sometimes accompanied by armed horse-men.

With a whoop like an Indian war-whoop the cars ran into a shed—they stopped—the pickpocket got up—I got up too—the baggage-master came to the door: "This gentleman has the checks for my baggage," said I, pointing to the thief. Bewildered, he took them from his waistcoat-pocket, gave them to the baggage-master, and went hastily away. I had no inclination to cry "Stop thief!" and had barely time to congratulate myself on the fortunate impulse which had led me to say what I did, when my friends appeared from the next car. They were too highly amused with my recital to sympathise at all with my feelings of annoyance, and one of them, a gentleman filling a high situation in the East, laughed heartily, saying, in a thoroughly American tone, "The English ladies must be 'cute customers, if they can outwit Yankee pickpockets."

Meaning to stay all night at Chicago, we drove to the two best hotels, but, finding them full, were induced to betake ourselves to an advertising house, the name of which it is unnecessary to give, though it will never be effaced from my memory. The charge advertised was a dollar a day, and for this every comfort and advantage were promised.

The inn was a large brick building at the corner of a street, with nothing very unprepossessing in its external appearance. The wooden stairs were dirty enough, and, on ascending them to the so-called "ladies' parlour," I found a large, meanly-furnished apartment, garnished with six spittoons, which, however, to my disgust, did not prevent the floor from receiving a large quantity of tobacco-juice.

There were two rifles, a pistol, and a powder-flask on the table; two Irish emigrant women were seated on the floor (which swarmed with black beetles and ants), undressing a screaming child; a woman evidently in a fever was tossing restlessly on the sofa; two females in tarnished Bloomer habiliments were looking out of the window; and other extraordinary-looking human beings filled the room. I asked for accommodation for the night, hoping that I should find a room where I could sit quietly. A dirty chambermaid took me to a room or dormitory containing four beds. In one part of it three women were affectionately and assiduously nursing a sick child; in another, two were combing tangled black hair; upon which I declared that I must have a room to myself.

The chambermaid then took me down a long, darkish passage, and showed me a small room without a fireplace, and only lighted by a pane of glass in the door; consequently, it was nearly dark. There was a small bed with a dirty buffalo-skin upon it; I took it up, and swarms of living creatures fell out of it, and the floor was literally alive with them. The sight of such a room made me feel quite ill, and it was with the greatest reluctance that I deposited my bonnet and shawl in it.

Outside the door were some medicine-bottles and other suspicious signs of illness, and, after making some cautious inquiries, we found that there was a case of typhus fever in the house, also one of Asiatic cholera, and three of ague! My friends were extremely shocked with the aspect of affairs. I believe that they were annoyed that I should see such a specimen of an hotel in their country, and they decided, that, as I could not possibly remain there for the night, I should go on to Detroit alone, as they were detained at Chicago on business. Though I certainly felt rather out of my element in this place, I was not at all sorry for the opportunity, thus accidentally given me, of seeing something of American society in its lowest grade.

We went down to dinner, and only the fact of not having tasted food for many hours could have made me touch it in such a room. We were in a long apartment, with one table down the middle, with plates laid for one hundred people. Every seat was occupied, these seats being benches of somewhat uncouth workmanship. The floor had recently been washed, and emitted a damp fetid odour. At one side was a large fireplace, where, in spite of the heat of the day, sundry manipulations were going on, coming under the general name of cookery. At the end of the room was a long leaden trough or sink, where three greasy scullery-boys without shoes, were perpetually engaged in washing plates, which they wiped upon their aprons. The plates, however, were not washed, only superficially rinsed. There were four brigand-looking waiters with prodigious beards and moustachios.

There was no great variety at table. There were eight boiled legs of mutton, nearly raw; six antiquated fowls, whose legs were of the consistence of guitar-strings; baked pork with "onion fixings," the meat swimming in grease; and for vegetables, yams, corn-cobs, and squash. A cup of stewed tea, sweetened with molasses, stood by each plate, and no fermented liquor of any description was consumed by the company. There were no carving-knives, so each person hacked the joints with his own, and some of those present carved them dexterously with bowie-knives taken out of their belts. Neither were there salt-spoons, so everybody dipped his greasy knife into the little pewter pot containing salt. Dinner began, and after satisfying my own hunger with the least objectionable dish, namely "pork with onion fixings," I had leisure to look round me.

Every quarter of the globe had contributed to swell that motley array, even China. Motives of interest or adventure had drawn them all together to this extraordinary outpost of civilisation, and soon would disperse them among lands where civilisation is unknown.

As far as I could judge, we were the only representatives of England. There were Scots, for Scots are always to be found where there is any hope of honest gain—there were Irish emigrants, speaking with a rich brogue—French traders from St. Louis—Mexicans from Santa Fe—Californians fitting out, and Californians coming home with fortunes made—keen-eyed speculators from New England—packmen from Canada—"Prairie-men," trappers, hunters, and adventurers of all descriptions. Many of these wore bowie-knives or pistols in their belts. The costumes were very varied and picturesque. Two Bloomers in very poor green habiliments sat opposite to me, and did not appear to attract any attention, though Bloomerism is happily defunct in the States.

There had been three duels at Chicago in the morning, and one of the duellists, a swarthy, dark-browed villain, sat next but one to me. The quarrel originated in a gambling-house, and this Mexican's opponent was mortally wounded, and there he sat, with the guilt of human blood upon his hands, describing to his vis-a-vis the way in which he had

taken aim at his adversary, and no one seemed to think anything about it. From what I heard, I fear duelling must have become very common in the West, and no wonder, from the number of lawless spirits who congregate where they can be comparatively unfettered.

The second course consisted exclusively of pumpkin pies; but when the waiters changed the plates, their way of cleaning the knives and forks was so peculiarly disgusting, that I did not attempt to eat anything. But I must remark that in this motley assembly there was nothing of coarseness, and not a word of bad language—indeed, nothing which could offend the most fastidious ears. I must in this respect bear very favourable testimony to the Americans; for, in the course of my somewhat extensive travels in the United States, and mixing as I did very frequently with the lower classes, I never heard any of that language which so frequently offends the ear in England.

I suppose that there is no country in the world where the presence of a lady is such a restraint upon manners and conversation. A female, whatever her age or rank may be, is invariably treated with deferential respect; and if this deference may occasionally trespass upon the limits of absurdity, or if the extinct chivalry of the past ages of Europe meets with a partial revival upon the shores of America, this extreme is vastly preferable to the brusquerie, if not incivility, which ladies, as I have heard, too often meet in England.

The apparently temperate habits in the United States form another very pleasing feature to dwell upon. It is to be feared that there is a considerable amount of drunkenness among the English, Irish, and Germans, who form a large portion of the American population; but the temperate, tea-drinking, water-drinking habits of the native Americans are most remarkable. In fact, I only saw one intoxicated person in the States, and he was a Scotch fiddler. At the hotels, even when sitting down to dinner in a room with four hundred persons, I never on any occasion saw more than two bottles of wine on the table, and I know from experience that in many private dwelling-houses there is no fermented liquor at all. In the West, more especially at the rude hotels where I stopped, I never saw wine, beer, or spirits upon the table; and the spectacle gratified me exceedingly, of seeing fierce-looking, armed, and bearded men, drinking frequently in the day of that cup "which cheers, but not inebriates." Water is a beverage which I never enjoyed in purity and perfection before I visited America. It is provided in abundance in the cars, the hotels, the waiting-rooms, the steamers, and even the stores, in crystal jugs or stone filters, and it is always iced. This may be either the result or the cause of the temperance of the people.

Ancient history tells us of a people who used to intoxicate their slaves, and, while they were in that condition, display them to their sons, to disgust them early with the degrading vice of drunkenness.

The emigrants who have left our shores, more particularly the Irish, have voluntarily enacted the part formerly assigned to the slaves of the Spartans. Certain it is that their intemperance, with the evils of which the Americans are only too well acquainted, has produced a beneficial result, by causing a strong re-action in favour of temperance principles.

The national oath of the English, which has earned for them abroad a horrible sobriquet, and the execrations which belong to the French, Italian, and Spanish nations, are unfortunately but too well known, because they are too often heard. Indeed, I have scarcely ever travelled in England by coach or railway—I have seldom driven through a crowded street, or ridden on horseback through quiet agricultural villages—without hearing language in direct defiance of the third commandment. Profanity and drunkenness are among the crying sins of the English lower orders. Much has been said upon the subject of swearing in the United States. I can only say that, travelling in them as I have travelled in England, and mixing with people of a much lower class than I ever was thrown among in England—mixing with these people too on terms of perfect equality—I never heard an oath till after I crossed the Canadian frontier. With regard to both these things, of course I only speak of what fell under my own observation.

After dinner, being only too glad to escape from a house where pestilence was rife, we went out into Chicago. It is a wonderful place, and tells more forcibly of the astonishing energy and progress of the Americans than anything I saw. Forty years ago the whole ground on which the town stands could have been bought for six hundred dollars; now, a person would give ten thousand for the site of a single store. It is built on a level prairie, only slightly elevated above the lake surface. It lies on both sides of the Chicago river, about a mile above its entrance into Lake Michigan. By the construction of piers, a large artificial harbour has been made at the mouth of this river.

The city has sprung up rapidly, and is supplied with all the accessories of a high state of civilisation. Chicago, in everything that contributes to real use and comfort, will compare favourably with any city in the world. In 1830 it was a mere trading-post, situated in the theatre of the Black Hawk

war. In 1850 its population was only 28,000 people; it has now not less than 60,000. It had not a mile of railway in 1850; now fourteen lines radiate from it, bringing to it the trade of an area of country equalling 150,000 square miles. One hundred heavy trains arrive and depart from it daily. It has a commerce commensurate with its magnitude. It employs about 70,000 tons of shipping, nearly one-half being steamers and propellers. The lumber-trade, which is chiefly carried on with Buffalo, is becoming very profitable. The exports of Chicago, to the East, of bread-stuffs for the past year, exceeded 13,000,000 bushels; and a city which, in 1840, numbered only 4000 inhabitants, is now one of the largest exporting grain-markets in the world.

Chicago is connected with the western rivers by a sloop canal—one of the most magnificent works ever undertaken. It is also connected with the Mississippi at several points by railroad. It is regularly laid out with wide airy streets, much more cleanly than those of Cincinnati. The wooden houses are fast giving place to lofty substantial structures of brick, or a stone similar in appearance to white marble, and are often six stories high. These houses, as in all business streets in the American cities, are disfigured, up to the third story, by large glaring sign-boards containing the names and occupations of their residents. The side walks are of wood, and, wherever they are made of this unsubstantial material, one frequently finds oneself stepping into a hole, or upon the end of a board which tilts up under one's feet. The houses are always let in flats, so that there are generally three stores one above another. These stores are very handsome, those of the outfitters particularly so, though the quantity of goods displayed in the streets gives them rather a barbaric appearance. The side walks are literally encumbered with bales of scarlet flannel, and every other article of an emigrant's outfit. At the outfitters' stores you can buy anything, from a cart-nail to a revolver; from a suit of oilskin to a paper of needles. The streets present an extraordinary spectacle. Everything reminds that one is standing on the very verge of western civilisation.

The roads are crowded to an inconvenient extent with carriages of curious construction, waggons, carts, and men on horseback, and the sidewalks with eager foot-passengers. By the side of a carriage drawn by two or three handsome horses, a creaking waggon with a white tilt, drawn by four heavy oxen, may be seen—Mexicans and hunters dash down the crowded streets at full gallop on mettlesome steeds, with bits so powerful as to throw their horses on their haunches when they meet with any obstacle. They ride animals that look too proud to touch the earth, on high-peaked saddles, with pistols in the holsters, short stirrups, and long, cruel-looking Spanish spurs. They wear scarlet caps or palmetto hats, and high jack-boots. Knives are struck into their belts, and light rifles are slung behind them. These picturesque beings—the bullock-waggons setting out for the Far West—the medley of different nations and costumes in the streets—make the city a spectacle of great interest.

The deep hollow roar of the locomotive, and the shrill scream from the steamboat, are heard here all day; a continuous stream of life ever bustles through the city, and, standing as it does on the very verge of western civilisation, Chicago is a vast emporium of the trade of the districts east and west of the Mississippi.

At an office in one of the streets Mr. C——took my ticket for Toronto by railway, steamer, railway, and steamer, only paying eight dollars and a half, or about thirty-four shillings, for a journey of seven hundred miles!

We returned to tea at the hotel, and found our viands and companions just the same as at dinner. It is impossible to give an idea of the "western men" to any one who has not seen one at least as a specimen. They are the men before whom the Indians melt away as grass before the scythe. They shoot them down on the smallest provocation, and speak of "head of Indian," as we do in England of head of game. Their bearing is bold, reckless, and independent in the extreme; they are as ready to fight a foe as to wait upon women and children with tender assiduity; their very appearance says to you, "Stranger, I belong to the greatest, most enlightened, and most progressive nation on earth; I may be the President or a millionaire next year; I don't care a straw for you or any one else."

Illinois is a State which has sprung up, as if by magic, to be one of the most fruitful in the West. It was settled by men from the New England States—men who carried with them those characteristics which have made the New Englander's career one of active enterprise, and successful progress, wherever he has been. Not many years ago the name of Illinois was nearly unknown, and on her soil the hardy settler battled with the forest-trees for space in which to sow his first crops. Her roads were merely rude and often impassable tracks through forest or prairie; now she has in operation and course of construction two thousand and seventy miles of those iron sinews of commercial progress—railroads, running like a network over the State.

At seven o'clock, with a feeling of great relief, mingled with thankfulness at having escaped untouched by the terrible pestilence which had ravaged Chicago, I left the hotel, more appropriately termed a "caravanserai," and my friends placed me in the "Lightning Express," warranted to go sixty-seven miles an hour.

Unless it may be St. Louis, I fancy that Chicago is more worth a visit than any other of the western cities. Even one day at it was worth a voyage across the Atlantic, and a land-journey of eighteen hundred miles.

Source:
Isabella Lucy Bird. *The Englishwoman in America.* Madison: University of Wisconsin Press, 1966.

ERITREAN AMERICANS

*B*etween 1962 and 1993, Eritrea faced relentless war, famine and poverty. The northeast African region was engaged in a bitter struggle for independence from Ethiopia, which had claimed it as part of the Ethiopian Empire in 1962. A historic region which for centuries determined its own destiny, Eritrea, whose name is derived from the Latin for the Red Sea, which it borders, refused to be ruled by its larger neighbor. Guerrilla soldiers of the Eritrean People's Liberation Front (EPLF) carried the war into Ethiopia until the Ethiopian army collapsed from famine and bankruptcy in 1991. Two years later, Eritreans voted overwhelmingly for independence.

As fighting intensified during the 1980s, thousands of refugees fled southwest into Sudan, where camps swelled as they waited hopefully for international relief agencies to help them. Many Eritreans wished to become U.S. citizens, but this was far from easy. Not only did U.S. immigration policy tightly cap the numbers of Eritreans who could immigrate, but some Eritreans who had fought for the EPLF were seen as unfit for immigration. Their offense was having opposed foreign rule at a time when the United States backed the Ethiopian regime.

Luckily for Tesfai and Lem Lem Gebremariam, the Eritrean husband and wife were granted immigrant visas in 1984. As he explains in this oral history published in 1988, Tesfai had been in the EPLF, but this did not hinder his immigration. Others were less fortunate: he knew some who, having failed their immigration hearing and lost the chance to escape war and famine, committed suicide in despair.

Like immigrants throughout history, the family tried to preserve cultural traditions upon becoming citizens of a new country. In some ways for the Gebremariams, this was possible. Eritreans have traditionally helped their neighbors in times of need, and the Gebremariam family received the help of friends in Washington, who contributed furniture and household items for them. Similarly, in a traditional showing of support for those in grief, they gathered in the homes of other Eritreans to cook for and comfort those who had suffered the death of a family member. The strong communal ties of their people were preserved.

But some essential traditions could not be practiced in the United States. Unlike women in Eritrea whose traditional role was to raise children or help their husbands farm, Lem Lem worked outside the house in a job cleaning hotels. This was a necessity for economic reasons, but one which she acknowledged her peers in Eritrea—perhaps one percent of whom hold regular jobs—would not understand. Similarly, the family found that their demanding work schedules meant making profound adjustments in their life. They shared responsibility for the children, primarily a woman's role in Eritrea. Moreover, the children now played outside without their parents watching, something common in the United States but uncommon to them.

Despite these adjustments grand and small, Tesfai noted that they had gradually become more comfortable with their radically different lives by "shift[ing] our expectations." Echoing a theme sounded by generations of other immigrants, the family saw advantages even amid ongoing change and hard work. For their children, there was the promise of a good education, and of a better life.

TRADITION

Tesfai and Lem Lem Gebremariam
Refugees from Eritrea Province, Ethiopia
Medical Technician and Hotel Chambermaid
Hyattsville, Maryland

TESFAI: We arrived in Washington, D.C., from the refugee camps in Sudan in August 1984. My wife was five months pregnant with our youngest child. Right away, we asked friends how to find work. We said, "If there is a job available, we will do it."

LEM LEM: The second week we were here, the Convention Center hired us. For six days, Tesfai and I worked together, busing tables. After that, I found a full-time job at the Ramada Inn. But, three months later, I had to stop working when the baby was born. The children were too young for me to be away from them.

TESFAI: At that time, we had to take public assistance for the family, because we couldn't afford to pay the $4,000 or $5,000 hospital bill. We didn't have insurance, and I was attending a medical-assistant training program without bringing home a paycheck. This caused great conflict. I told myself, "We need to take the money to pay the rent. But if we take it, I feel completely worthless."

Immediately after finishing my training, I found a job at Saint Elizabeth Psychiatric Hospital. My job has been to take care of the more than one hundred Cubans who came during the Mariel boatlift. They are kept in a separate part of the hospital, because they need a lot of help. Some are very tough guys, some are crazy. Many were criminals—some were thieves, others were into drugs. Some killed people.

It's ironic that in Eritrea, for many years, my wife and I were fighting for our freedom against Cuban soldiers. Now that we have freedom in this country, I am taking care of Cubans. And even though I didn't have time to take advanced English classes, I was sent to Spanish classes by the hospital.

Now, most days I attend medical-laboratory-technician classes in Washington from 8:00 A.M. until 2:20 in the afternoon. Then I get into my car and drive for a half-hour to Saint Elizabeth Hospital. I work until 11:30 P.M. By midnight I am home.

It's very difficult to live this way. But my wife and I don't have any second thoughts about our jobs. We have rent to pay and two young children. Our baby, Jerome, is fourteen months. And our daughter, Adiam, started kindergarten this year.

She is very American. When we arrived here, she was only three years old, so she doesn't know much about Ethiopia. She plays with American children and speaks perfect English. When we go to the shopping center, we don't know some foods. Adiam tells us everything, because she sees them advertised on TV.

LEM LEM: Now that the baby is a little older, I'm back at the Ramada Inn doing housekeeping. And some evenings I work part-time at the Westin Hotel. Two jobs, twelve hours a day. It's very hard being on my feet all that time.

TESFAI: She is also trying to attend English classes and to complete her high-school equivalency. Lem Lem was just a young teen-ager when she had to flee her parents' home in Asmara to escape the Derge's soldiers. Even before she escaped, schools were closed, because the Derge were killing and arresting students.

Since the Derge took power, thousands of refugees have fled Ertrea. The United States accepts relatively few people from Ethiopia each year. But there are ten times that many Eritreans in Sudan who need to be resettled.

I know some people who were rejected by American Immigration officers and killed themselves on the same day. They made up their minds that they had to live in America. They failed the immigration hearing because the [Eritrean resistance] Fronts had also fought against the previous Ethiopian regime, which the U.S. supported. So these rejected refugees went off and committed suicide. They didn't have any alternatives.

LEM LEM: Most Ethiopians accepted to the United States are from the cities and have some schooling. Many poor farmers from Eritrea can't flee to Sudan, because the Derge army blocks their escape. Even when some of these people do manage to reach Sudan, they refuse to leave Africa. They still feel very connected to their land and families they left behind. They say, "If we go to America, we are lost.". . .

TESFAI: My wife and I registered as refugees through the United Nations. UN officials introduced us to the American Joint Voluntary Agency office, where we were interviewed to see if we qualified for acceptance to America. After we passed the JVA interview, we were sent to the American immigration officers.

We knew that they looked unfavorably on former members of the Front. [Because some members had embraced Marxism and had been trained by the Soviet bloc during Haile Selassie's rule.] But I told them the truth, that I had been a fighter. I had done nothing to be ashamed of. Fortunately, we were accepted and began a four-month orientation program.

We had three hours of classes every day about life in America and the English language. For those of us who already knew English, we had classes on culture: how to ride subway, how to use a shopping center, and many other necessary activities in this country. Those classes were very helpful, because in our country there are no large supermarkets and we don't have refrigerators to keep food fresh or frozen for long periods of time. We go to small shops and bargain over prices with the merchants. And in the countryside, we grow most of our food. We only need to buy little things, like coffee, sugar, or oil, which are not very expensive. A nickel's worth of salt can last you three or four months.

Besides attending classes, I continued working in the clinic until we departed for the States in August 1984. We were informed in Khartoum that we were going to Washington, D.C., and given the address of our sponsor, the International Rescue Committee.

As we flew into New York at night, we saw the harbor lights from the plane's window. The city lights reminded us of Asmara. The most difficult part of our arrival was that we didn't have relatives to greet us. It was after midnight when our connecting flight arrived in Washington. We were so exhausted from the long trip and the time change that we rested the entire first day.

On the second day, we went to the IRC office. We were so happy to meet some Eritrean friends there who we had known in Sudan. They were waiting to apply for jobs. Afterwards, they invited us to their apartments. We had lunch at one place and dinner at another friend's home. They told us how to get around the city, how to use the bus. I told them, "Our main concern is finding any kind of work."

LEM LEM: Even though we had the orientation about American life in Sudan, we still felt a little awkward in Washington. We spoke enough English to understand what people said, but it was difficult for Americans to understand what people said, but it was difficult for Americans to understand us because of our accent. [Laughs]

We moved into this apartment complex in Hyattsville. We are just a short bus ride from Wash-ington, and many of our friends were already living in this apartment complex. When we first moved in, they helped us to find furniture. They brought us a dining-room set, a king-size bed and a small bed for our daughter, a sofa for the living room, and enough cooking and kitchen materials. Since then, little by little, we've been buying what we need to decorate the apartment.

In the beginning, one friend or another would drive us to the store to buy whatever food we needed. In our culture, we like to have a lot of relatives or friends eating together. The way Eritreans eat, we cook a bowl of spiced beans or chicken or lamb stew. We then cover a large round tray with a kind of soft, thin pancake called *enjira*. On the *enjira* we serve the main courses of food, with smaller pieces of *enjira* on the side. Everyone shares the meal, eating with their hands by using pieces of *enjira* to pick up the food, like a small sandwich.

TESFAI: I have come to like American food, but it took time, because the spices and texture of Ethiopian food are very different. After living here for two years, we have shifted our expectations and feel more comfortable being a part of this society. It's true that we went through many changes, trying to forget about life in our country before the war and adjusting to this life style. Living in a large apartment complex, my wife and I working different shifts, sharing responsibility for the children—this is a big change from how we lived before.

In Ethiopia, we don't feel good when little children, like my daughter, play outside without parents' being with them. But it is common for children in the apartment complex to play in the large parking lot by themselves. We have good communication with the neighbors, and we keep an eye on each other's kids.

LEM LEM: In our country, families usually have between five and ten children. In the cities, the wife stays home to take care of the children most of the time; maybe one percent of the women hold regular jobs. But in the countryside, wives cannot stay home, they have to work on the farms. When the husband cultivates the land with the oxen, the wife follows behind, planting the seeds, and women have to do all the housework and cleaning. Men never cook, only do the outdoor jobs. Inside the home, women have equal rights, but in public, men have the dominant role in our culture.

TESFAI: I came from a big family, nine brothers and sisters. My mother always helped my father grow food during the planting season and she helped cut the crops at harvest. They worked side by side.

LEM LEM: But in the city, my mother didn't have an outside job. The only women who work are nurses, teachers, and bankers. People in Asmara wouldn't understand if I told them that I was working in the hotels here doing housekeeping.

TESFAI: We have both worked hard for the two years we have lived here. The rent hasn't been too high, so we've been able to save a little money for each of the children's college education, little by little. Our son, Jerome, was born here, so he is automatically an American citizen. The rest of us must wait five years from the date we arrived to apply for American citizenship. For now we are mostly concerned with working and trying to save.

My wife and I leave for work or school at the same time in the morning. But with the shifts we work, we see each other for only a short time in the evening and early morning. When I get home from the hospital and Lem Lem gets home from her second job at night, we go right to sleep. We are so tired. The only time we get to talk is in the morning, when we are driving in the car.. . .

TESFAI: Tonight a friend called on the telephone to tell us that her mother died in Ethiopia. We are going to her apartment this evening with three or four other families so she will not have to be alone. We will stay until late, then come home for a little rest before we go to work in the morning.

In Eritrea when somebody dies, a member of the family will notify all the people in the surrounding area. Everybody takes time from what they are doing to come to the home. For two weeks, day and night, some friends help to cook and do the housework to make it easier on the family. In the evenings, other friends and relatives bring food from their homes for everyone to eat together. They make jokes and everybody laughs, even though they are very sad. Guests stay until around 1:00 A.M. so the family won't have to cry alone.

Now, in America, we try to do the same thing, but only for three or four days. In American culture, people are too busy.

No matter how long we live in America, we remain very concerned about our families back in Ethiopia. Our parents are always on our minds. If any friend's father or mother dies, we are all deeply touched. We cry and shout just like a baby, because it is like death twice over. First is the actual death. Second is the fact that we cannot be with them, even for the funeral. We are far away from home, but we always hope to be reunited with our families.

We would like our children to grow up in America. That is our decision. They have a chance to get a good education. And to live in any other country as a refugee we would have problems being accepted. Everybody says, "You are foreigners."

In America, we have the same rights as everyone. It's true that my wife and I have to work very hard, to be an American, you have to work hard. But nobody asks us, "Where are you from?" They can tell when they hear me speak that I was not born here. My accent is still very noticeable. But nobody makes a big deal out of it. This is our chance to live.

Source:

New Americans: An Oral History: Immigrants and Refugees in the U.S. Today, by Al Santoli. New York: Viking, 1988. pp. 85-102.

ESTONIAN AMERICANS

Herbert Henry Lehman (1878-1963) came from the highly influential New York family that founded Lehman Brothers bankers, and became a partner in the family firm in 1908. His first major political office was as lieutenant governor of New York state in 1928. After four years he became governor, and served in that position for a decade. Lehman was known for his philanthropic activities, and with the outbreak of World War II became director of the Office of Foreign Relief and Rehabilitation. After leaving the relief office in 1946, he ran for the U.S. Senate, where he served from 1949 to 1957.

The occasion for Lehman's speech on September 11, 1951 was a report concerning some 84 persons who had fled from Estonia, by way of Sweden, to the United States. These were part of a larger exodus from that nation which occurred in the years from 1945 to 1951. The numbers of fleeing Estonians, however, were never large for two reasons: first of all, Estonia is a small country, and more important, the odds of survival—with the escapees pitted both against the forces of nature and those of the Soviet police state—were not high.

Precisely because these 84 brave people were not likely to attract a great deal of world attention, Lehman spoke up on their behalf before the Senate. As it stood, the U.S. immigration bureaucracy was prepared to turn the Estonian refugees back, which would have meant certain death.

At that time, Estonia and the whole of the Soviet Union were under the control of Josef Stalin (1879-1953), perhaps the most brutal and bloodthirsty dictator the world has ever known. Though Stalin's sometime ally Adolf Hitler attracted considerably more attention—partly because his killings were racially motivated, and partly because the United States fought Nazi Germany in a war—Stalin killed far more people than Hitler.

By eliminating his enemies, Stalin had gradually assumed control of the Soviet Communist state after the death of its founder, V. I. Lenin, in 1924. He greatly enhanced the police-state apparatus set up by Lenin, and developed a vast network of concentration camps in which millions upon millions of people lost their lives. Many millions more, who managed to survive years of grinding slave labor, were destroyed emotionally and mentally, if not physically, by Stalin.

It is not surprising that Stalin found much in common with Hitler, and this led to a pact between the two in August 1939. Hitler ultimately broke the pact by invading the Soviet Union in June 1941, thus leading to an alliance of Stalin with the leaders of the free world against Nazi Germany in World War II. During the almost two years of Nazi-Soviet cooperation, however, both sides benefited greatly from the pact. Hitler's main interest was Poland, but he also gave Stalin a large portion of that country; more important from the Soviet perspective, Stalin was able to take over Estonia, Latvia, and Lithuania.

He did this by forcing the leaders of the three countries to sign "security treaties" with the Soviet Union. It would be more than 50 years before any of the *three republics saw the light of freedom again: as Stalin told the foreign minister of Latvia, "So far as Germany is concerned, we can occupy you."*

Upon assuming control of the three nations, Stalin liquidated all possible opposition with rounds of arrests, "trials," imprisonments, and executions. The situation was so bad in eastern Europe that many nations welcomed the German invaders as liberators—until the Nazis began their own wave of murders. After World War II ended, Stalin launched a new campaign of killings.

It was against this backdrop that the 84 Estonians had escaped. From Sweden, as Lehman noted, they had made a dangerous Atlantic crossing, proving that they were more afraid of Stalin than of the ocean's perils. One might wonder why they did not stay in Sweden, itself a free country; however, Sweden, which had also done business with Hitler in order to save itself from Nazi invasion, had chosen to recognize the Soviet occupation of Estonia. Therefore, Stockholm would have simply extradited, or returned, the Estonians to the terrors that awaited them back home.

Apparently the United States was willing to do the same, despite attempts by President Harry S Truman to secure asylum for the refugees. Because Congress, as Lehman indicated, had failed to make arrangements for such situations, it became necessary to request special legislation to allow the refugees to remain in the United States.

As a result of Lehman's speech, Congress passed the new legislation. Partly as a result of his efforts, it became American policy to give special preference to immigrants fleeing tyranny, whether it be Soviet-style Communism, South African Apartheid, or other forms of repression.

SENATOR LEHMAN'S SPEECH

September 11, 1951

I am today introducing a bill to provide asylum in this country for 84 individuals now in the United States who, in 1948 and 1949, fled from tyranny in Estonia, their native land.

These individuals came to this country by way of Sweden. They came in three groups, in small open boats, across the North Atlantic, preferring the rigors of the open sea to Soviet rule and oppression. At the time of their arrival, there were many newspaper accounts of the dangers and hardships which these individuals had faced and overcome to get to our shores. Storm and sea were only the first of the hazards of this flight to freedom.

Shortly after the arrival of these groups in the United States, President Truman, exercising his emergency authority, granted them temporary asylum pending disposition of their cases in the Congress. Last year Congress considered a measure to grant permanent residence to these people. That bill was not acted upon. Now these Estonians are

faced with deportation—deportation to certain death—or what might be worse than death—the concentration and slave-labor camps of Siberia.

These individuals came to this country directly from Sweden. They can of course be deported to that country. Sweden has, unfortunately, accepted as a legal fact the violent incorporation of Estonia into the Soviet Union. Hence, under the laws of Sweden, these people are Soviet subjects and would be deported from Sweden, back to their native land and, as I have said, to death, persecution or imprisonment.

Our Immigration and Naturalization Service has now issued deportation orders for these people. I hope that the Senate will speedily consider and approve my bill which will permit these men, women and children, after proper screening, to remain in this country. After escaping from behind the Iron Curtain and after heroically overcoming the hazards of the North Atlantic in their small motor and sail ships, these refugees from tyranny should certainly be given harbor and haven in this country. That gesture on our part would be well understood the world over, especially behind the Iron Curtain. We would thus provide a happy ending to this flight from terror, to this break from the Soviet prison-house.

I do not know these individuals personally or individually, nor do I know their exact political or intellectual orientation. The have, indeed, been vouched for by reputable American organizations. I know one thing, that these people were seeking freedom and were trying to escape from oppression. America meant to these individuals—as it has always meant to all the peoples of the world—the land of freedom. Let it ever remain so. Let us show the great heart of America, and the hospitality of America, and the meaning of America as the homeland of freedom, by giving prompt and sympathetic consideration to this bill.

Herbert H. Lehman

Source:

Estonians in America, 1627-1975: A Chronology & Fact Book, compiled and edited by Jaan Pennar. Dobbs Ferry, NY: Oceana Publications, 1975. pp. 107-108.

FILIPINO AMERICANS

The Tydings-McDuffie Act, signed into law on March 23, 1934, provided for the creation of the Commonwealth of the Philippines, and promised independence for that nation after ten years. The term "commonwealth," also applied to Puerto Rico and other U.S. possessions, indicated that the Philippines would maintain a local system of government, but would become part of the United States. In spite of this fact, the Tydings-McDuffie Act provided that Filipinos would be treated as aliens thenceforth, and Filipino immigration numbers would be severely limited.

Named for King Philip II of Spain, the Philippines had been controlled by Madrid for more than three hundred years when the United States won possession of the islands following the Spanish-American war of 1898. In the latter years of Spanish rule, hopes for Philippine self-determination had been raised by nationalist leaders José Rizal (1861-96) and Emilio Aguinaldo (1869-1964)—and, according to Aguinaldo, by U.S. officials. Rizal was executed by the Spanish, and Aguinaldo, who felt he had been misled by American representatives with whom he had met in 1898, led a failed resvolt against the victorious American forces.

By 1901, the U.S. military had suppressed Aguinaldo's insurrection and established control over most of the nation's seven thousand islands. Despite what many Filipino intellectuals perceived as heavy-handedness in its dealings with the Philippines, the United States did introduce valuable educational and land reforms. The American government established schools, among them the University of the Philippines in Manila; and sold some four hundred thousand acres, purchased from the Catholic church, at low prices to the poor.

Still, a rising generation of Filipino leaders clamored for independence. In place of the idealists Rizal and Aguinaldo had come two much more pragmatic men, Manuel Quezon (1878-1944) and Sergio Osmeña (1878-1961). Uneasy allies in the cause of the nation, both built power bases on the strength of promises made by President Woodrow Wilson. The latter supported passage, in 1916, of the Jones Act, which promised independence as soon as the Philippines developed a stable government.

Philippine hopes for self-determination were dashed in 1921 when Wilson—by then an invalid—left the White House, and Warren G. Harding inaugurated 12 years of Republican leadership. Because Republican foreign policy went against Philippine independence, the issue was shelved; meanwhile, however, Filipino nationalists gained some unlikely allies.

In the 1920s, farmers, labor groups, and isolationists on the West Coast—an array of entities whose concerns ranged from nationalism or racism to fear of cheap imports and labor—began petitioning Washington to set the Philippines free. Once the latter became an independent nation, these unexpected advocates of Philippine independence reasoned, a lid could be placed on both immigration and imports.

These forces helped pushed through the Hare-Hawes-Cutting Bill in December 1931. The new legislation, passed over the veto of President Herbert Hoover, *established an unequal import—export arrangement whereby U.S. goods would enter Philippine markets without any import taxes, or tariffs, whereas Philippine goods would carry increasingly higher tariffs over a ten-year period. It also limited Filipino immigration to just 50 persons annually.*

Quezon, incensed by this proposal—which Osmeña had accepted—went to Washington in 1933 to meet with the new Democratic president, Franklin D. Roosevelt. He got few concessions, but the following year, Congress attempted to settle the Philippine question with the Tydings-McDuffie Act.

The latter, of course, favored the United States over the Philippines. It contained no specific trade provisions, but with regard to immigration, it placed the Philippines under restrictions already applied to Japan and other nations with laws passed in 1917 and 1924. Thus the 50-person limit stood. On the other hand, the Tydings-McDuffie Act did provide for the creation of a Philippine government as a step toward independence.

Over the years that followed, the numbers of Filipinos in the United States continued to increase. This was partly through births to the already sizeable number of Philippine immigrants already in the country. More Filipinos came as a result of a program set up much earlier, whereby promising students from the Philippines could come to America to gain an education. By the 1970s, the Philippines would become, after Mexico, the nation with the second-largest number of immigrants annually entering the United States.

Meanwhile Quezon won the first Philippine presidential elections in 1935, and Osmeña, the second-most powerful man in the Philippines, became his vice president. When Japan invaded the islands early in 1942, the two would evacuate to Australia with General Douglas MacArthur. Quezon oversaw the government-in-exile from Washington until his death in 1944, when Osmeña took over. On July 4, 1946, the United States granted the Philippines its independence, but maintained military bases in the Philippines—and a substantial interest in local politics—until the 1990s.

TYDINGS-McDUFFIE ACT

To provide for the complete independence of the Philippine Islands, to provide for the adoption of a constitution and a form of government for the Philippine Islands, and for other purposes.

Be it enacted by the Senate and House of Representatives of the United States of America in Congress assembled.

Convention to Frame Constitution

Philippine Islands

Section 1. The Philippine Legislature is hereby authorized to provide for the election of delegates to a constitutional convention, which shall meet in the hall of the House of Representatives in the cap-ital of the Philippine Islands, at such time as the Philippine Legislature may fix, but not later than October 1, 1934, to formulate and draft a constitution for the government of the Commonwealth of the Philippine Islands, subject to the conditions and qualifications prescribed in this Act, which shall exercise jurisdiction over all the territory ceded to the United States by the treaty of peace concluded between the United States and Spain on the 10th day of December, 1898, the boundaries of which are set forth in Article III of said treaty, together with those islands embraced in the treaty between Spain and the United States concluded at Washington on the 7th day of December, 1900. The Philippine Legislature shall provide for the necessary expenses of such conventions.. . .

Section 8. (a) Effective upon the acceptance of this Act by concurrent resolution of the Philippine Legislature or by a convention called for that purpose, as provided in Section 17.

(1) For the purpose of the Immigration Act of 1917, the Immigration Act of 1924 (except Section 13 (c)), this section and all other laws of the United States relating to the immigration, exclusion, or expulsion of aliens, citizens of the Philippine Islands who are not citizens of the United States shall be considered as if they were aliens. For such purposes the Philippine Islands shall be considered as a separate country and shall have for each year a quota of fifty. This paragraph shall not apply to a person coming or seeking to come to the Territory of Hawaii who does not apply for and secure an immigration or passport visa, but such immigration shall be determined by the Department of the Interior on the basis of the needs of industries in the Territory of Hawaii.. . .

Section 14. Upon the final and complete withdrawal of American sovereignty over the Philippine Islands the immigration laws of the United States (including all the provisions thereof relating to persons ineligible to citizenship) shall apply to persons who were born in the Philippine Islands to the same extent as in the case of other foreign countries.

Certain Statutes Continued in Force

Section 15. Except as in this Act otherwise provided, the laws now or hereafter in force in the Philippine Islands shall continue in force in the Commonwealth of the Philippine Islands until altered, amended, or replaced by the Legislature of the Commonwealth of the Philippine Islands or by the Congress of the United States, and all references in such laws to the government or officials of the Philippines of Philippine Islands shall be constructed, insofar as applicable, to refer to the government and corresponding officials respectively of the Philippine Islands. The foremost of the Commonwealth of the Philippine Islands shall be deemed successor to the present government of the Philippine Islands and of all the rights and obligations thereof. Except as otherwise provided in this Act, all laws or parts of laws relating to the present government of the Philippine Islands and its administration are hereby repealed as of the date of the inauguration of the government of the Commonwealth of the Philippine Islands.

Section 16. If any provision of this Act is declared unconstitutional or the applicability thereof to any person or circumstance is held invalid, the validity of the remainder of the Act and the applicability of such provisions to other persons and circumstances shall not be affected thereby.

Effective Date

Section 17. The foregoing provisions of this act shall not take effect until accepted by concurrent resolution of the Philippine Legislature or by a convention called for the purpose of passing upon that question as may be provided by the Philippine Legislature.

Source:
The Filipinos in America, 1898-1974: A Chronology & Fact Book, compiled and edited by Hyung-Chan Kim and Cynthia C. Mejia. Dobbs Ferry, NY: Oceana Publications, 1976. pp. 77-78.

Willie Barientos was born in April of 1908, in Caoayan I Sur, the Philippines. He immigrated to Hawaii in 1924 to work on the pineapple plantations, but as he said in this interview, conducted in 1976, he was soon cutting sugarcane. He points out here that immigration was used by planters as a tool against labor unionizing in Hawaii. "We had to have a salary of one dollar a day, " he said. "Until you had twenty-three days working in land you cannot have no bonus, ten cents bonus."

In 1929, Barientos made the journey to California, where he cut asparagus in the fields. After attending a school for adults, he worked as a janitor in San Francisco. In 1946, just after World War II (1939-1945), Barientos went to Delano, California, and there he learned how to cultivate grapes. "We take care of the grapes like a baby," he remarked. "Like a baby!"

After working almost twenty years in the Delano grape fields, Barientos took part in the famous Delano grape strike of September 1965. A few months earlier, Filipino grape pickers had formed the Agricultural Workers Organizing Committee of the AFL-CIO. The Filipinos refused to work for less money than imported Mexican laborers, against whom the landowning companies had pitted them in an effort to keep wages low. The Mexican American labor leader Cesar Chavez, seeing an opportunity to work with the Filipinos, brought them into the newly formed United Farm Workers and thus created a multiethnic farm workers' collective that won improvements in agricultural labor conditions.

SOME ARE BOUGHT, SOME FIGHT

Willie Barientos—Filipino Farmworker

March 6, 1976, Agbayani Village
Delano, California

When I was young, I was a fighter. I was born that way. My mother raised me that way. I left them when I was young. Then my old grandpa said, "Well, young man, I don't have no money in the world, but you're still young. You know how to work." "Sure I can work. How you live if you don't work?" I said. My grandpa told me, "Young grandpa fight for the freedom of the people, for the freedom of the Philippine. Put that in your head." My own grandpa, he said, "He fight for the freedom of the people in your nation. I raised you more than anybody else. Don't let nobody kid you, because I raise you good. And don't be afraid to nobody so long as you are right. Nobody!" That's what he told me. And I fight. I fight until today.

I was about eighteen. They opened immigration just to break the strike in Hawaii, just like they are doing in Mexico now. When they opened immigration in the Philippines, all young kids they came in this country. In 1850, they do that to the Chinese, until 1890. They immigrate the Chinese first. They work and drive them to Chinatown down there in San Francisco. Then came the Japanese, 1924 is Japanese exclusion also, until 1934. Then the Filipinos also came in 1924. Thirty thousand Filipinos came to the United States, 1924. And then in 1952 we got only a chance of quota, fifty to one that means that the quota is only one hundred Filipinos can come in this country, see? That is the historical background I have in my head. I know history! See? Immigrate all these people. Also in the South, the Negro, they are farm workers. They work in the cotton. They know that history. They have sold them for another. They don't take me, I know.

In Hawaii I was stationed in the plantation. We cut sugarcane. We had to have a salary of one dollar a day. Until you had twenty-three days working in land you cannot have no bonus, ten cents bonus. This is terrible.

The big giant corporation opened the plantations. They were the Del Monte, they were Dole.

I was stationed very close to Honolulu, and close to Waikiki in the east part of the Hawaiian Islands. I don't know how to work in the field before. My mother was worried because I was too young and I never do work before. When I went to Hawaii I cut sugarcane, and that is hard work. I confronted the plantation that I could not do this cutting sugarcane. "I don't wanna do this job." They gave me a hoe and let me cut the grass. I said to my brother, "Like hell. I didn't do this all my life."

One time, I went to the main house where we sleep down there in Hawaii. I didn't go inside because I almost cried. I was still young. I don't like to hold that hoe. Hell, I didn't hold no hoe in my life, and I told my brother, "Hey, Magnon, is this here work in Hawaii, huh?" I complain. They give me a better job. Guys, they load the cane and put it in the boxcar until it's full. I got to record all those cars.

I went to Hawaii. I saw Hawaii. I saw the people working in the pineapple; I saw the people working in the sugarcane. That's a hard job, a dollar a day. S---. More than highway robbery. I am poor people. I came from a poor family. I had that in my heart and my mind, to fight for the poor people. I want to see my brother. I want to send him back home [from Hawaii]. I don't want to come to America unless I put my brother to work in the family. I have only one brother, two sisters. We are poor. I stay in Hawaii till 1929, after he left maybe two weeks. I came in this country December 20, 1929. I landed in San Pedro, then I got a job in Stockton.

They wanted me to work in the asparagus. I worked for one week, I guess. They teach me. They

For years, the only way for Filipinos to emigrate to the United States was through Hawaii, when it was still a territory.

got some knife and they cut the asparagus this way. And you bend with your back, you know. I said, "I cannot do this job." I told to my cousins and the workers I don't want this kind of work. Then I went to San Francisco.

In San Francisco, I had a friend there. He's working with a family. I go there so someone would hire me and I would go to school. Maybe they got small pay, but they send me to school. I want to learn. I want to see my way better. That's what I got in my head.

So I went up there. I work as a schoolboy. I go to school a little bit, then I change. I got another job. A janitor job. At night time I learn a little bit English.

I got $30 a month as a janitor. That's depression, that's very hard. Well, I heard from some guys that there is work in the field, so I took a bus from San Francisco. Then I met some Filipinos here. I came to Delano in 1946.

They teach me how to plant the grape, how to pick the grape, how to prune, how to thin, how to thick, all the whole operation of the grape. Mostly Filipinos then. Eighty or seventy-five in the camps.

What were the conditions like?

Conditions is not good. That's why I was there. I see them and I watch them very close, what they are doing to the workers. And then I put them in a plan in my head until the union came along.

We started this union September eight, nineteen hundred and sixty-five. I have been waiting for this time, because I want to join the union. And I was one who can stand again to fight the growers.

My boss told me, "Willie," he said, "you've been working for me ten years. But now you are the leaders against me? What's wrong?"

I said, "You don't know? But I'm going to tell you. Me, I build you up from your head to your feet, with all my pals, with all my brothers here. Where are you today without my brothers here? Now, I

Many Filipino immigrants in the early twentieth century arrived to work on plantations in Hawaii.

want my share. We want our share to live as a human being, so we can also send our children to school and be educated like your children. That's what I've been wanting," I told him. And I look him in the eye also. And he think I am scared. "No, I am no scared at you. I build you up, and you think I don't know it, huh? My brothers are here. That's why we had the strike this day, September eight, nineteen hundred and sixty-five, because we want a higher wage, and better conditions. Because we have been exploited for centuries. Here is the time. I have been waiting for this time."

We, the Filipino people, are the one who started this strike, four weeks before Cesar Chavez came out. Don't ever nobody tell you lie, because that is the truth, that we the Filipinos wanted this strike before Cesar Chavez came along. We have identical purposes. He realizes that when the Filipinos and Mexican, Arabian — all the farm workers working the field—should unite, they may be stronger to fight them back.

This is not the first time we strike here. No, they tried before but they fail. Why? Because of the divisions, that's the weapon, that's their weapon: divide and control. I know it, even they don't tell me. I saw it with my two eyes.

How did they do that?

Just like this. When you got the Filipino foreman here, Chicano foreman here, they bribe these people and they sell their own people down the river. They do it in Hawaii, and they do it here, and they do it everywhere. It is the historical problem of the union, and it is heartache. Among the workers, they know it. Some are sold, some fight.

Later we march to Sacramento. We started from Delano, and from every city we pick up. And when we reach Sacramento, that was Easter Sunday. You know how many people are there? Maybe around ten thousand there in Sacramento that day. Then it came the investigation when Robert

Kennedy came around. We had a meeting down at that auditorium in the high school.

When we started this strike, wages is only $1.10 an hour and now when we have this September 8, 1965, we ask for $1.40. Here in Delano we had $1.20; when we had the strike we ask for $1.40. And gradually we move. Today we come to $2.60. Teamsters, they got $2.54. That's the difference, they are lower all the time. Today we got a contract for $3.35. We have ten minutes' rest in the morning, ten minutes' rest in the afternoon. We don't have that before in the whole history of the labor movement until we have this United Farm Workers of America, today.

Are you married?

No, because when we came here 1924, the Filipino cannot marry a white. That's the law. This hurt me. We cannot marry. We cannot buy land, until we fight the war. That's all hurt me. That's why I get old in my head and in my heart and in my hand. When I was young, I was strong.

I have seen all those experiences in my life, I saw it. They pass in my hands. I see it with my eyes, that's how I know. I did not go to college and learn this. I know it. I have seen the war in Vietnam. I saw what they are doing in the Philippines right now.

What they are doing in the Philippines? This big giant that they are in Hawaii before, they are moving in the Philippines now. They had the pineapple, all kinds. They want to get all the big pieces in there.

Do you live in Agbayani Village?

I don't live here at Agbayani Village yet, but I am gonna live here because I'm the one who is campaigning all over the state to get this village here. We fight very hard for this village. You see, there is discrimination. These associations in Delano, they came to the court and fight that we cannot build this building.

At the court people talk, then they said, "Anymore who want talk?" "Yes, I want to talk. Your Honor, I want to talk. You tell me you are going to build a building for the old men when they retire? Or would you rather we build a building for them so that they would not sleep on the sidewalk when they cannot walk anymore?" I point them one by one in the court. I point them, all these big shot in here.

"You have a big house, but what about the other side of the road? On the other side of the road, we couldn't get a house there. You mean to tell me we cannot irrigate over here? Why? What reason? You are talking about not supporting Delano. We are the one who build Delano. We buy our shoes, we wear our clothes, come back to the town, put in everything. We are not supporting Delano? The hell," I said, "The hell. You are lying." We build them up.

"Who plant the grapes? We plant the grapes. We take care of the grapes like a baby. Like a baby!" I said. "From roots to the top. We made them rich. Where is our share? We want to a small one. Small share, so that we could also live like human beings, like anybody else. So that we could also send our children to school, like anybody else. The hell [tears in his eyes]. Who bring all those fruits on your table? But I want my share, that's all I ask."

They've got money; I don't have it. But there are other things: your cause, your rights, your dignity as an individual, that's what I'm talking about. That's in me, that's inside, and the only way they are going to stop me is when I die, because I am going to fight until I die.

They make the laws, but they are the one who break the laws. They have the big businessman, they have the banker, the politician. Two hundred and fifty people are running this country. What about us? We elect them. They broke my two legs in the picket line. They tried to kill me. August 23, 1972. They hit me in the picket line, three of us. The sixth rib was broken. Beat my arms. One guy was thrown in the side road, I thought he was dead already. We are lucky. He was still alive.

They tried to get me in Salinas; they tried to get me in Phoenix, Arizona; they tried to get me in Coachella Valley. I'm still alive. They want to break my morale? The hell.

The future of the world is in the younger generation. I might not be here to witness all these things, but I know they will come. We are going to live in a better world.

Source:

First Generation: In the Words of Twentieth-Century American Immigrants. Revised edition. Edited by June Namias. Chicago: University of Chicago Press, 1992. pp. 71-79.

"*T*he one constant in my life is that. . .I could get people together to fight a cause." Thus observed Filipino American activist, feminist, and educator Irene Natividad (1948-) about herself in an International Examiner *article discussing her activism on behalf of women and minorities, particularly Asian Americans. It is a path she has followed for over twenty-five years and one that has seen her rise to top posts in several major organizations, including the National Women's Political Caucus, the National Commission on Working Women, and the Philippine American Foundation. The common goal that links these endeavors is Natividad's commitment to making sure those who are often overlooked or ignored gain power and influence through political action. "The price of citizenship is political involvement," she asserts. "To be silent is to not be counted, and we can't afford not to be counted."*

A native of Manila, the capital and largest city of the Philippines, Natividad is the oldest of four children born to a chemical engineer whose job took him around the world. She thus spent her childhood in a number of different countries, including Japan, Iran, Greece, and India, and is fluent in a half-dozen languages. To this day, Natividad credits her family's frequent moves with making it easier for her to work with people from other cultures. It also made her especially sensitive to the limited opportunities afforded to women in many nations where they were not allowed to hold jobs outside the home.

Natividad completed her high school education in Greece, and from there she went on to attend New York's Long Island University, from which she graduated in 1971 at the top of her class. She then enrolled at Columbia University, earning her master's in American literature in 1973 and her master's in philosophy in 1976. She has since completed the course work toward her doctorate but increasing demands on her time have made it impossible for her to finish her dissertation.

During the early 1970s, Natividad taught at Lehman College of the City University of New York and Columbia University. The late 1970s and early 1980s saw her move into the administrative ranks as director of continuing education at Long Island University and then at New Jersey's William Paterson College.

Her first brush with activism was while she was working as a waitress. Exercising her natural talent for organizing, she rallied her fellow waiters and waitresses to demand higher wages. Although she lost her job as a result, Natividad was not discouraged. She subsequently became active politically, distributing campaign leaflets for 1968 presidential candidate Eugene McCarthy. Later, as her interest in women's issues grew, she became involved in a number of organizations devoted to their concerns. For example, in 1980, she founded and headed a group known as Asian American Professional Women and was a founding director of both the National Network of Asian-Pacific American Women and the Child Care Action Campaign.

Natividad became active on the national political scene in the early to mid-1980s. After a two-year stint as chair of the New York State Asian Pacific Caucus early in the decade, she went on to serve as deputy vice-chair of the Asian Pacific Caucus of the Democratic National Committee. During the 1984 presidential campaign of Walter Mondale, she was chosen by Democratic party officials to act as liaison between the Asian American community and Mondale's choice for vice-president, Geraldine Ferraro—the first woman ever selected for the post by a major U.S. political party. Even Mondale and Ferraro's loss in the election to Republicans Ronald Reagan and George Bush could not completely dampen Natividad's spirits, however, for as she later declared to a reporter for the Honolulu Star-Bulletin, *Ferraro "broke the credibility gap for all women candidates.. . . I don't consider '84 a loss. I consider it a win."*

In 1985, Natividad made history herself when she became the first minority woman to head a mainstream political organization—the National Women's Political Caucus, based in Washington, D.C. Founded in 1971 by a small group of prominent feminists, including congresswomen Shirley Chisholm, Patsy Mink, and Bella Abzug, the National Women's Political Caucus is a bipartisan group that concentrates its efforts on electing more women to public office.

During her four-year tenure, Natividad took steps to ensure the flow of potential women candidates for national office would continue by emphasizing the need for them to gain political experience at the local level first. To that end, the Caucus conducted training sessions throughout the country for women candidates and their staffs (including the first-ever program for minority women) on the ins and outs of running a successful campaign. Members of the Caucus also collected and analyzed data to help them understand the influential factors in congressional races involving women. In addition, the Caucus monitored political appointments of women at the state and national level and promoted women candidates for such posts.

Since stepping down as head of the National Women's Political Caucus, Natividad has remained busy with a number of other endeavors on both the national and international level. In 1991, for example, she became chair of the National Commission on Working Women, which is devoted to improving the economic status of working women in the United States. The following year, she served as co-chair of the Women of Color Committee for Clinton/Gore. She maintains affiliations with many Asian American organizations as well, among them the Philippine American Foundation; its efforts to reduce poverty in her native Philippines include fostering grassroots rural development. In addition, Natividad heads her own consulting firm, Natividad & Associates, which provides services to groups that are trying to reach specific segments of the voting population.

In a keynote address delivered in 1991 at a symposium held in Washington, D.C., at the National Museum of American History (part of the Smithsonian Institution), Natividad reflected on the many achievements of women in American political life over the past few decades. The speaker herself provided a transcript of her remarks.

Irene Natividad's Address on Women's Achievements

When the scribes of history sit down to write a chapter on the past three decades, they ought to call it "The Wonder Years.". . . From the first shaky steps out of our kitchens in the late fifties, to the fortifying sessions of consciousness-raising groups formed in our own parlors during the sixties, and the growing pains of entering the work world in the seventies and eighties, women in the nineties have indeed come of age. Unquestionably, we are now enjoying the largest measure of personal and political freedom in this country's history. There are those among you in this audience who will agree that the path to progress has been a bumpy one, but no one doubts that indeed we have moved forward.

As we have come of age, from the very basic and revolutionary struggles of our early foremothers who are celebrated by this exhibit, through the seasoning experience of our more recent fights for equality, we have all learned that the personal is indeed the political. You might say we have gone public over the years, and the world has not been the same. The result today is that we are in the fortunate position of having power, serious power, within our reach—power to win our rights, to fulfill our dreams, and to assume full partnership in the public business of this nation.

Today we are fortunate to have Ann Richards serving as the governor of the third-largest state in this country, Texas. The nation's capital is governed by a woman, Sharon Pratt Dixon. And she is joined by many other women mayors: in Houston, for instance, with Kathy Whitmire; in Dallas with Annette Strauss; in Charlotte, North Carolina, with Sue Myrick. Kansas distinguishes itself by being the only state that has a woman governor, Joan Finney, a woman senator, Nancy Kassebaum, and a woman congressional representative, Jan Meyers, all serving at the same time. Equally important, women of color have broken through the dual barriers of race and gender, so that for the first time, there are four African American women serving in Congress—Cardiss Collins, Eleanor Holmes Norton, Barbara Rose Collins, and Maxine Waters—as well as one Asian American, Patsy Mink, who was there long before, and one Hispanic American, Ileana Ros-Lehtinen.

The leadership breakthroughs in business and the professions are legion. Mickey Siebert's history-making feat in the early seventies—being the first woman to buy a seat in the New York Stock Exchange—no longer confounds us, as a series of firsts have happened in rapid succession: the first woman on the Supreme Court, Sandra Day O'Connor; the first woman astronaut, Sally Ride; most recently, the first woman surgeon general, Antonia Novello, and so on.

We have come to accept that certain notoriety that comes with being the first woman to enter the rooms of power, be they economic, political or social. Men have entered those rooms in the past, assuming their rightful place as if they had been expected. Well, we are not yet expected in large numbers, for the time being, but as more women enter the room the spotlight will dim and not focus exclusively on the newest member of the club. Instead, the focus will shift to our numbers. Women are now the majority of students in colleges and graduate schools all across this nation. Large numbers of women are studying in medical schools, law schools, and business schools. Women are projected to be the majority of workers in the next century, and the majority of new small businesses are now started by women.

But the most important numerical fact, which underscores our power to shape the forces of twenty-first century America, is that women are the majority of voters in every state of the United States. That means that no one can get elected without our votes, not to the House, not to the

Irene Natividad

Senate, not to the presidency, let alone to school boards. The gender gap—or the women's vote, as I prefer to call it—provided the margin of victory for Ann Richards in the last election, for Governor Doug Wilder in Virginia, and for Mayor David Dinkins in New York City in the 1989 elections.

Equally important, the threat of the women's vote propelled the issue of child care into the 1988 presidential campaign. And we saw candidates for the first time tripping over themselves at child care centers. It's not that they had discovered children lately. It's just that the mediagenic politics of the last decade dictates that you go to a child care center because it resonates among women voters.

"[W]omen] are now enjoying the largest measure of personal and political freedom in this country's history."

Lastly, the large female electorate has encouraged officeholders interested in re-election to make record numbers of women's appointments at both the state and the federal levels. Right now, President Bush's record stands at twenty-two percent of all senior-level positions held by women, beating all prior presidents' records. I don't think it's an accident that President Bush suffered a gender gap against him prior to being elected.

The successes of the past three decades that I've been recounting to you were the result of efforts from the early suffrage movement to the modern women's movement. These extraordinary gains challenge us to reach yet another plateau in history—to top our gains, so to speak. But I didn't come here tonight merely to sing the praises of women's achievements of these past thirty years. I came to provide, if I can, a frank assessment.

The organized women's movement is far from being a small band of feminists doing consciousness-raising, or "hell-raising," as some would have said a few decades ago. Over the years the movement has acquired sophisticated, grass-roots organizing, coalition-building, political skills that have helped to win many a victory. The quest for equality in employment, education, in all areas of public life, has been embraced by this nation. The pioneers of women's freedom of the late sixties have been transformed into the largest mainstream movement of the late eighties.

Yet the test that confronts this movement is one of durability. It is, in effect, a dare—a dare to continue to thrive when powerful vehicles, such as the presidency and the courts, are no longer available to support basic rights won earlier in the struggle for social reform along gender lines. All successful movements must face the fact that with successes come failures. To live beyond the moment of ascendancy, to live to get the whole job done, great movements must reinvest themselves. To sustain themselves, movements must not only grow, they must change. That great feminist theorist, Simone de Beauvoir, phrased it well when she titled one of her last essays "Feminism: Alive, Well, and in Constant Danger." The fact of the matter is that, ironically, women have created enough change to be significant, but too little change to be sufficient. This uncomfortable dichotomy makes it difficult to chart a future course as definitive as that pursued during the seventies, when equal rights, embodied in the fight for the Equal Rights Amendment [ERA], made the mission so clear and seemingly so simple.

The contradictions to women's successes have proved most frustrating. The public consensus we had for women's equality has had little effect on the wage gap. Today women still earn only two-thirds of what men earn, no matter what area or level of employment. As Jesse Jackson said so well, the loaf of bread does not cost the woman any less, so why pay her less? It seems so clear, but no one is listening. The consensus for women's equality has not produced a coherent and caring system of child care for families and for the women that society has encouraged to work. The equal rights majority has not been able to gain recognition and protection for the rights of women in the nation's most basic legal document, the Constitution of the United States. Reproductive choice has been won and now is threatened state by state.

These mixed results confuse and confound. So while women are buoyed by their successes, they are simultaneously bedeviled by the inability to sustain the fast pace they had set for themselves in the sixties and seventies. The result is frustration. Frustration is inevitable for a country in which we still must reargue the basics of reproductive choice, affirmative action, and civil rights as a whole. Frustration is justified when a group that is fifty-three percent of the population numbers as its representatives only two percent of the Senate, only six percent of the House, only sixteen percent of the state legislatures, and only nine percent of the federal district court judges. Frustration is justified when there seems to be an inverse relationship between the number of women in public life and the degree of power that they exercise. The higher you go, the less accessible it seems. Frustration is justified when a majority of the poor are still women and children and women workers are still clustered, for the most part, in low-paying clerical, sales, and service jobs. Frustration is justified when the largest industrialized nation in the world is unable to pass a family and medical leave bill at a time when two-earner families are the norm in this country.

These frustrations make the organized women's movements' efforts seem sisyphean at times. For every step up the hill, we roll back a few times. But women are resilient and persistent, and so are our organizations. Women's groups didn't fold up their tents and go home when the ERA failed or when the Supreme Court handed down the Webster decision almost two years ago. Instead, they learned to coalesce, not just among themselves, but with civil rights groups, labor groups, and, in some instances, even business groups to fight for issues demanding their attention. The results are palpable: the passage of a child care bill (many of us do not deem it to be sufficient but, at least, a significant first step); the passage of the Civil Rights Restoration Act, which restored institution-wide coverage of civil rights bills for minorities, women, the aging, and the handicapped; the defeat of judicial nominations deemed to be contrary to the interests of the disadvantaged in this society. In addition, women have become experts in using the media to reach the majority of Americans, so that more than any one piece of legislation, the women's movement's best achievement of late is the creation of a growing constituency for a family support system in a society where women's disproportionate responsibilities for work at home and work at work often make time more valuable than money.

The thread to women's reproductive rights actually proved to be a boon to a movement that had not been able to attract young adherents in large numbers prior to the Supreme Court's Webster decision. For the first time, women leaders were able to make a direct connection for young women—as they had never been able to do before—between politics and their daily lives, between the act of voting and preserving a right. Young women understood, all of a sudden, that indeed the personal is the political. The challenge, of course, is how to maintain the commitment of these young women, energized and politicized by an issue that is no longer on the front pages of the nation's newspapers, and, equally important, how to extend that commitment to choice to the other issues affecting women.

The women's vote remains the most powerful tool for social change in the coming decades. Not always voting as a bloc, except recently on the issue of choice, women have increasingly come to view their vote as the expression of their hopes and dreams for a better world. The candidate who makes direct appeals to this vote wins, as Governor Doug Wilder discovered. Women are also much more likely to cross party lines to vote their interests.

The enlightened, self-interest dimension of the women's vote is, to a large extent, a product that we might call an economic gender gap. Focus groups of infrequent women voters were asked in 1988 what the issues were that propelled them to vote. The results were not surprising. "Not earning as much as a man" was the number-one answer—not pay equity, not comparable worth, but "not earning as much as a man." Crime, or personal vulnerability as a whole, was the second most important issue. Employment. Environment. And the prism through which women saw all of these issues—children.

It is important to note that there is a strong correlation between the increasing number of women in the workplace and the increasing number of women voters. The more women become charged with their economic destiny, the more likely they are to vote. Shirley Chisholm phrased it well when she said that women vote according to their pocketbooks. The truly liberating issue for women is economic security.

The task that remains, however, is how to mobilize that vote. Like most Americans, women are still voting only half their strength—a fact which I find personally frustrating. I have told women all across this country that if they do not

vote, then they have not earned the right to complain about crime, about education, about discrimination, about the environment. I remind them that in other countries—in Latin America, for instance—people get shot for exercising their right to vote. But in this country, we take that right for granted. On election day, many of us go shopping, which is all right as long as we shop as well for a candidate who represents our interests. I tell them the story of my friend who lost a state legislative race in South Dakota by one vote, even after a recount. And most recently, in that same state, an anti-choice bill was defeated in the senate, again by one vote.

There is no substitute, however, for promoting social reform through our own leaders, our own representatives. The impact of one Pat Schroeder, who pushes for a child care bill, the impact of one Claudine Schneider, who sponsors an environmental bill, one Connie Morella, who pushes for legislation for the aging, one Marge Roukema, who fights for family and medical leave, would be even more dramatic if there were 290 of them in Congress out of 435 instead of 29 out of 435. Clearly, token numbers of us on the inside cannot speak for the millions of us who are out here. And it remains the most challenging task of the women's movement to make those numbers grow bigger. It is not an easy task. It is an effort that's a little bit like carving a woman's face on Mount Rushmore. It will take years to chip away at stubborn rock before a woman's face begins to emerge. But trust me, emerge it will.

"The women's vote remains the most powerful tool for social change in the coming decades."

A 1987 survey of voters' attitudes towards women candidates, commissioned by the National Women's Political Caucus, revealed that the future of women candidates is positive. From school board to Congress to the presidency, the poll showed that the bias against women candidates is eroding. In part, this is due to the public's becoming more accustomed to the notion of women holding office. Madeleine Kunin so eloquently articulated this when she said, "I couldn't have been elected governor of the State of Vermont. . .without Dixie Lee Ray, without Martha Layne Collins. In a very real way we create public confidence through one another."

Given the changing demographics of the United States, which project a next century when minorities will be the majority, the Madeleine Kunins of the future will come from various ethnic groups. The next plateau for the women's movement, which so far has been largely white and middle class, is how to embrace pluralism in its maturity. How to arrive at consensus in the future—given the possibility of emerging political tensions between the ethnic groups that will come into ascendance—will pose a difficult challenge for many of us.

Where the women's movement will be in the new political mosaic of the coming decades will be interesting to see, as Hispanics conflict with Asian or African Americans, or vice versa, in carving out new districts. How do you coalesce the interests of the young with the interests of the old? Will it be child care versus Medicare at a time when twenty-five percent of the American population will be older Americans, the majority of whom will vote, when children can't?

Clearly the task before us is enormous. But we women are more than up to it. Like Wonder Woman, we are smart, we are patient, we are persevering. There are more of us and we live longer. The hurdles that we face are real. But we cannot move forward if we spend our time bemoaning our fate and the foibles and arrogance of the other gender.

Nancy Astor, the first woman to sit in the British House of Commons, said it best when she said, "Mercifully, women have no political past. We have all the mistakes of one-sex legislation with its appalling failures to guide us. We should know what to avoid. It is no use blaming the men. We made them and now it's up to us, the makers of men, to be a little more responsible."

Thank you very much.

Source:

Irene Natividad. Transcript of speech delivered at the National Museum of American History, 1991.

FRENCH AMERICANS

As waves of Europeans immigrated to the United States in the late nineteenth and early twentieth centuries, most could barely speak English. Some knew only fragments, others none at all. One of the biggest tasks of assimilation was simply learning to speak. Because children always find languages easier to learn than adults, immigrants' children swiftly became more adept than their parents, and second generation immigrants' English was indistinguishable from that of the third and fourth generations. Even well beyond the mid-twentieth century, one still heard the thick accents of first-generation immigrants, especially in eastern cities like New York.

Language skills had significance in society as well, where they were often marked as a means of dating an immigrant's arrival and establishing a social pecking order. Eager to be seen as Americans, immigrants commonly tried to hide their linguistic origins. Many households insisted upon speaking in English to their children, and in this process some descendants lost the ability to speak their parents' and grandparents' language.

The French, however, were not among this group. Historically proud of its culture, and especially of its linguistic and literary traditions, France had a long tradition of preserving "proper" French from decry and encroachment by other languages. From its inception in the seventh century, L'Acadamie Francaise—the French national Academy—set forth to purify the French language. It sought to accomplish this goal through the publication of official dictionaries and the granting of awards to authors who upheld the nation's cultural traditions.

"Bad Advice in Good French" is the title of a New York Times staff writer's essay published in 1910. The humorous title indicates the writer's bemusement with those who would resist linguistic assimilation. In New York, the essay noted, there were newspapers in as many languages as there were immigrants. As the author correctly observes, the city was far from homogenous, but instead broken into a number of enclaves that reflected the ethnic identities of its occupants. This phenomenon seemed natural, given the city's importance as a port of destination for most immigrants.

But the author is less sanguine about an argument advanced in L'Opinion, a French newspaper published in Worcester, Massachusetts. By the turn of the century, the manufacturing town of Worcester had drawn a number of French-Canadian immigrants. The Times writer objected to their linguistic separateness, and ridiculed their newspaper's claim to be written in "pure and uncorrupted" French. Not only is the French spoken by the immigrants a patois—or hybrid—but literary writing in the dialect is increasingly respected, the writer argued. In one sense, the essay is trying to tweak the nose of L'Opinion's editors. Yet in another, mocking the idea that French American children devote themselves to improving their French, it is a reminder that the pressures of assimilation were once great and made exceptions for no one.

Janine Caubit Williams wears her French Resistance armband and holds a little stack of French coins, sitting outside her Kentucky home. Both items are reminders of a time nearly 60 years ago when she was a frightened young refugee fleeing her home near Paris.

BAD ADVICE GIVEN IN GOOD FRENCH

That New York, the gateway of a Nation, or, rather, of a continent, should have a newspaper for each group of strangers arriving, and only too often setting, here, is natural enough. Indeed, this has come to be, or at least to seem, rather a congeries of colonies, each with its own language, than a city in the older sense of a homogeneous community. Much more remarkable is it that Winnipeg, so new and so remote, should already have, according to a report of origin to make it credible, periodical publications in forty-two languages and dialects, including the Canadian variant of English.

To be really startled, however, one must have his attention called to the fact that even in the heart of New England foreigners not yet even lingually assimilated are come to be so numerous that they prefer, demand, and get the news printed for them in words that the waning representatives of the "old stock," so recently almost unalloyed by an alien admixture, cannot understand. Such a shock, with a lancinating little pain, is the result of receiving from Worcester, Mass., a chance copy of *L'Opinion Publique,* a French paper, well edited and better printed than most of those that come from Paris, and "carrying" enough advertising to indicate prosperity.

Of course we all know that Worcester is a big manufacturing town, containing many artisans of French Canadian origin, but why do they thus stand apart from their neighbors? And as if to emphasize their separateness, *L'Opinion Publique*, gives prominent editorial space to a vehement, almost passionate, defense of the language spoken by its readers as being, not as certain base detractors have said, a "*français déformé*," but the real thing, pure and uncorrupted. That contention is just a bit amusing, since the Canadian patois not only exists with its innumerable and interesting reminders of the old French provinces whence came, to be thereafter isolated from later changes, the original settlers of New France, but that patois has in recent years won for itself a respectable, though small, place in dialectic literature, both prose an verse.

Of course *L'Opinion Publique* does not claim that all the Frenchmen in Canada and the United States speak "good" French, but it says that many of them do, and, under the impulse of a strange and lamentable misguiding, it urges its readers to see to it that their children devote more of their schooltime hours to the learning of correct speech—in French: A deadly enemy could not give worse advice.

October 22, 1910

Source:

Ethnic Groups in American Life, edited by Gene Brown. New York: Arno Press and the *New York Times*, 1978. p. 87.

In July of 1621, French and Belgian Protestants, under the leadership of Jesse de Forest, presented a petition to Sir Dudley Carleton, British ambassador to the Hague, to settle in Virginia. These immigrants, called Huguenots, were routinely persecuted for their religious beliefs in sixteenth and seventeenth century France. The Wars of Religion, which began in the mid-1500s and concluded at the end of that century, left thousands of Protestants dead. In 1598, King Henry IV signed the Edict of Nantes. King Henry IV was a Protestant who, upon being made King, accepted Catholicism. The edict provided religious and political freedom for the Protestants, but in spite of these provisions, civil wars occurred again in the 1620s under King Louis XIII. Once more, Protestant Huguenots were persecuted and forced to convert to Catholicism. Louis XIV formally revoked the Edict of Nantes in 1685 and by the early 1700s, Louis XIV claimed to have removed Protestantism in France. As a result of this continued persecution, more than 400,000 Huguenots emigrated from France in the seventeenth century. Many of them migrated to England, Prussia, the Netherlands and America.

At the time, it was customary for citizens of other nations wishing to settle in America to request permission, and sometimes a grant of land, from the English monarch. "A Huguenot Petition to the British Ambassador, 1621" (originally published in The French Blood in America, by Lucian J. Fosdick. New York: Baker and Taylor, 1911) made such a request, and was presented by the Huguenots in seven articles. The petition made requests for land, for freedom of religion, and for protection under the British Crown. In the document, the Huguenots proposed to build a city, establish industry, designate land for nobles and use the natural resources for hunting, fishing and timber. In short, they asked "whether they might make use of everything above and below ground according to their will and pleasure" while preserving the royal rights to the land.

HUGUENOT PETITION TO THE BRITISH AMBASSADOR, 1621

His lordship the ambassador of the most serene king of Great Britain is humbly entreated to advise and answer us in regard to the articles which follow.

I. Whether it would please his Majesty to permit fifty to sixty families, as well Walloons as French, all of the Reformed religion, to go and settle in Virginia, a country under his rule, and whether it would please him to undertake their protection and defense from and against all, and to maintain them in their religion.

II. And whereas the said families might find themselves near upon three hundred persons; and whereas they would wish to carry with them a quantity of cattle, as well for the cultivation of the earth as for their sustenance, and for these reasons would need more than one ship; whether his Majesty would not accommodate them with one, well equipped and furnished with cannon and other arms, on board of which, together with the one they would provide, they could accomplish their voyage; the same returning to obtain merchandise for the regions granted by his said Majesty, as well as that of the country.

III. Whether he would permit them, on their arrival in said country, to choose a convenient spot for their abode among the places not yet cultivated by those whom it has pleased his Majesty to send thither already.

IV. Whether, having secured the said spot, they might build a city for their protection and furnish it with the necessary fortifications, wherein they might elect a governor and magistrates for the maintenance of order as well as justice, under those fundamental laws which it has pleased his Majesty to establish in said regions.

V. Whether his said Majesty would furnish them cannons and munitions for the defense of said place, and grant them right in case of necessity to make powder, fabricate balls and found cannons under the flag and arms of his said Majesty.

VI. Whether he would grant them a circuit or territory of eight English miles radius, that is sixteen in diameter, wherein they might cultivate fields, meadows, vineyards, and the like, which territory they would hold, whether conjointly or severally, from his Majesty in such fealty and homage as his Majesty should find reasonable, without allowing any other to dwell there unless by taking out papers of residence within said territory, wherein they would reserve rights of inferior lordship; and whether those of them who could live as nobles would be permitted to style themselves such.

VII. Whether they would be permitted in the said lands to hunt all game, whether furred or feathered, to fish in the sea and rivers, and to cut heavy and small timber, as well as for navigation as other purposes, according to desire; in a word, whether they might make use of everything above and below ground according to their will and pleasure, saving the royal rights; and trade in everything with such persons as should be thereto privileged.

Source:

The French in America, 1488-1974: A Chronology & Factbook, compiled and edited by James S. Pula. Dobbs Ferry, NY: Oceana Publications, 1975. pp. 127-128.

The history of French Protestantism is bloody. Over three centuries, from the 1500s through the late 1700s, they suffered constant persecution under the ruling French Catholic majority. In one successive monarchy after another, Catholic leaders harassed, imprisoned and killed members of the religious minority. Known by the name of the Huguenots, the French Protestants fought back. They launched a political movement which agitated for religious freedom. Yet their calls for reform only led to greater repressions and, repeatedly, war. During the sixteenth century, French dukes fought eight bloody religious wars against the Huguenots. And in 1572, this bloodshed produced the infamous Massacre of St. Bartholomew when, between the months of August and September, French Catholics slaughtered 20,000 Huguenot citizens.

Ending the wars, King Henry IV ushered in a period of relative peace for the Huguenots. The King, who had Huguenot blood through his mother, had been educated as a Protestant and sympathized with them, despite having claimed to renounce his faith at one point to escape death in the Massacre of St. Bartholomew. In 1598, the King issued a royal decree called the Edict of Nantes. It established political and religious freedom for Protestants, granting them rights equivalent to those enjoyed by the Catholic majority. Now they could live and worship where they chose. The edict even gave them fortified towns in which to live. Although the Edict of Nantes did not entirely end persecution of the Huguenots, the rights with which it armed them were a vast improvement as the seventeenth century began.

Ironically, France pursued two very different courses in the next century. First, between 1618 and 1648, it sided with Protestants in their war with Catholics during the so-called Thirty Years War, lending military aid to German Protestants. Despite its religious origins, the war took on political dimensions as nations vied for control of Europe, and France sought power through its alliance with the Protestants against the nations of Spain and Bavaria. After the war, in fact, France emerged as the dominant power on the continent. Once this cynical end was served, however, it soon turned upon its own Protestants again. In 1685, King Louis XIV revoked the Treaty of Nantes.

Eight decades after the royal edict had guaranteed their rights, French Protestants faced terrible repression again. They had no protection under the law, which even forbid them to leave the country. But to hundreds of thousands of Huguenots, staying in France as second class citizens was not a choice. A mass exodus began, as the Huguenots spread out across Europe and to colonial America. Not until the French Revolution nearly a century later was religious freedom restored in France.

This letter from a Huguenot to friends in America described the terror that was experienced in France in 1685. The Protestant church has been outlawed, its ministers given hefty fines, Protestant citizens barred from working in the trades, and worse injustices—soldiers at the door—are "expect(ed) every day." With one of the nation's greatest waves of immigration about to commence, the letter writer looks hopefully to America and its promise of freedom. If a ship could be sent, the writer suggests, there would be money in it for someone.

FRENCH PROTESTANT'S LETTER TO AMERICA

[If] I and my family were with you, we should not have been exposed to the vengeance of our enemies, who rob us of the goods which God hath given us to the sustinence of soule and body. I shall not assume to write all the miseries that we suffer, which cannot be comprehended in a letter, but in many books. I shall tell you briefly, that our temple is condemned, and razed, our ministers banished forever, all their goods confiscated, and moreover they are condemned to the fine of a thousand crowns. All the other temples are also razed, except the temple of Re, and two or three others. By act of Parliament we are hindered to be masters in any trade or skill. We expect every day the lord governour or Guiene, whom shall put soldiers in our houses, and take away our children to be offered to the Idol, as they have done in the other countrys.

The country where you live [New England] is in great estime; I and a grat many others, Protestants, intend to go there. Tell us, if you please, what advantage we can have there, and particularly the boors who are accustomed to plow the ground. If somebody of your country would hazard to come here with a ship to fetch in our French Protestants, he would make great gain.

Source:

The French in America, 1488-1974: A Chronology & Factbook, compiled and edited by James S. Pula. Dobbs Ferry, NY: Oceana Publications, 1975.

FRENCH-CANADIAN AMERICANS

*F*rench explorers discovered the Canadian mainland in the sixteenth century. The subsequent settlement established French speaking communities in Canada, particularly in the eastern province of Québec. When economic conditions deteriorated in the nineteenth century, French Canadians immigrated to newly established New England mill towns, many around Boston. U.S. businessmen expanded their textile mills in the region to take advantage of the increasing influx of French Canadians. Typical of these French Canadian immigrants was Philippe Lemay whose family settled in Manchester, New Hampshire. By the late 1830s almost half of the population of Manchester was French-Canadian and was the largest single nationality group in the area.

Lemay's commentary, as relayed in a lengthy 1930s interview, reflected the experiences of many French Canadians whose lives centered around extended families and French-speaking communities bound by strong religious ties. A general lack of social acceptance by mainstream American society further compelled this ethnic closeness.

Lemay was born in 1856 in the rural community of St. Ephrem d'Upton, not far from Montreal, Québec. French Canadian families were commonly large and Lemay's was no different having 14 children. Reflecting predominate migration patterns, the Lemays immigrated as an extended family with aunts and uncles and parents, first to Lowell, Massachusetts in 1864, then to Manchester in 1872. Lemay began work in the mills at the age of eight. By the 1870s, New England was home to so many French Canadian immigrants, they warranted their own priests and schools. As Lemay described:

> After 1870, there were enough of our children to make schools necessary for them, with lay teachers for the first ten years or so. In Manchester, Father Chevalier, who came here in May, 1871, having been the first resident parish priest from Québec in New Hampshire, started to build St. Augustine's church in 1872 and it was opened for worship in 1873.

The French-Canadians arrived without much money wearing homespun clothing and appearing quite distinct from the American population. The close-knit ethnic communities expanded through the 1880s, becoming a prominent aspect of the New England cultural landscape. Lemay recalled various persons important to the early settlements, including physicians, merchants, bakers, and photographers. Lemay also recounted that workers labored long and hard for low pay and their home was often in a crowded tenement. Lemay expressed pride that many fought for the new country in the Civil War, Spanish-American War, and World War I. Lemay worked in the textile mills for over 50 years witnessing many changes in technology, working conditions, and communities.

THE FRENCH-CANADIAN TEXTILE WORKER

By Philippe Lemay
Reported by Louis Pare

"French Canadians from the province of Québec have worked in the mills of Manchester for a long, long time. There was one as far back as 1833, and for more than 50 years they kept on coming until now we are 35,000 strong, 40% of the entire population of the city. Ours is said to be the largest single nationality group.

I am going to tell you as well as I can the story of the French Canadian textile worker; what brought him here; how he came, lived, worked, played and suffered until he was recognized as a patriotic, useful and respected citizen, no longer a 'frog' and 'pea soup eater,' a despised Canuck. And it's the story of all the French Canadians who settled in New England mill towns. The picture of one French Canadian textile worker and the picture of another are just as much alike as *deux gouttes d'eau,* or, as we have learned to say in English, like two peas in a pod.

Let me say, first of all, Monsieur, that the current of immigration was strongest between 1850 and the early 70's. Some came before, as you will see, others after, as long as there was no limit by law on immigration, no head-tax nor passport required. In 1871, French Canadians here were strong enough to have a resident priest of their nationality and a parish of their own. A second parish was founded in 1880 on the west side of the Merrimack. At the time, New Hampshire was a part of the Portland diocese. In 1884, thanks to French Canadian immigration, the Manchester diocese was created.

Why did our people leave Canada and come to the States? Because they had to make sure of a living for their family and themselves for a number of years, and because they greatly needed money. The wages paid by textile mills was the attraction.

Here and wherever else they went, they didn't forget their duty to God: the churches, schools and other institutions they built testify to that. But their duty to the country that was feeding them, that was another thing. They didn't like to become citizens and feared it for more than one reason. They couldn't speak English, and that, let me tell you, was a big handicap. They were afraid of war and might be drafted. Most of them were still tax-payers in the province of Québec and the different

places from which they came, and they felt that they couldn't pay taxes here too. Most of them hadn't come here to stay. What they wanted most was to go back to their Canadian farms with the money earned in the textile mills. So they kept putting off taking out naturalization papers.

But we already had able leaders, among them Ferdinand Gagnon, and they preached Americanization to all those who intended to stay in this country. They pointed it out as a duty to ourselves as well as to the country. They told us that naturalization was something that gave to a foreigner all the rights belonging to the citizen in the country to which the foreigner swears allegiance. Our people began to realize that their ideas against being naturalized were wrong. They saw the privileges as well as the duties, and so, as early as 1871, we had fifty voters in Manchester, fifty men who, supporting good Father Chevalier, were able to obtain from the city authorities, without cost to the French-speaking Catholics, a French language school; building, heating, lighting, books and lay teachers. This success was encouraging. Naturalization increased, and that, if you take account of the many births, tells you why so many of us are voters and tax-payers today, why so many of our folks settled here for all time.

Before we had the railroads, immigrants from the province of Québec came to Manchester in wagons or other horse-drawn vehicles. If they brought their household goods with them, and that was rare enough, they travelled in hay-racks. Did some travel on foot from Canada? No, I don't think so. Perhaps from places near the border to northern Vermont, but if any immigrant had walked as far as Manchester, we certainly would have heard about it from old settlers, and there were quite a few left in 1872. Anyway, travelling in wagons was bad enough. Even the trip by train in 1864 was terribly slow. There wasn't much comfort for the voyageurs and it was expensive, because we had to stop over more than once and even children were obliged to pay full fare.

Here is the case of my own family, for example. It took us four days and as many nights to go from our home town, St. Ephrem d'Upton, to Lowell. Train engines weren't big and powerful in those days. Besides, they were wood-burners, and you couldn't put enough wood in the tender to make

Work in the logging industry or in textile mills drew many French Canadians to the United States in the late nineteenth century. Here, an old French Canadian, who worked in a paper mill, is sawing wood in front of his house in Connecticut

long trips. So trains didn't run far and never during the night. We started from St. Ephrem in the afternoon and went as far as Sherbrooke and slept there. The next days we reached Island Pond, in Vermont, and spent the night in that customs town. It was a very small place, too. The following morning, the old Grant Trunk took us to Portland, Maine and again we passed the night there, because the train went no further. After another night's rest, on a different railroad, we were on our way to Boston where we had to find lodgings once more. At last, the fifth day, we landed in Lowell where we were to live for eight years.

Many things can happen on such long trips, and something did while we were coming to the States, *aux Etats,* as French Canadians say it even today. At Island Pond, my mother was taken sick and couldn't go on with us when we left for Portland on the third stage of our journey. Father remained with her. We were told to continue towards Lowell and to mind our uncle and aunt who

were making the trip with us from St. Ephrem. We promised to be good and followed our good aunt and uncle, but we worried on account of our parents. We weren't separated for long, though, for mother was a strong, healthy woman, of good Canadian stock. Father and mother arrived in Lowell only three days after we did, and what do you think they brought with them? A new little Lemay whom we all welcomed to our already rather large family.

Train engines weren't big and powerful in those days. Besides, they were wood-burners, and you couldn't put enough wood in the tender to make long trips. So trains didn't run far and never during the night.

The majority of French Canadian immigrants came to Manchester at their own expense. In fact, all of them did, so far as I know, and they didn't have to be coaxed, either. It is true that some companies, seeing in the type Québecois an honest, able workman, asking little for himself and rather unwilling to lot himself be fooled by strike agitators, brought here a certain number through recruiting agents sent to Canada for the purpose. The companies built homes to house these new hands. However, if their fares and other expenses were paid by the textile corporations, it was never mentioned and I don't believe it was done.

Our people didn't come to the States with money they had saved up, though, since they emigrated because they were really obliged to go where they could earn their daily bread and butter. To raise enough money to buy railroad tickets for the family and pay for food, rooms and other expenses on route, they had to faire encan , sell all their household goods at auction. That money was practically all gone when they arrived here, and all they possessed was the clothes they had on their backs, you might say. Parents and children alike were dressed in homespun and homemade clothes and they were recognized as coming from Québec province the very moment they left the train. Most of them, you see, were from small towns and farming districts, very few coming from large cities like Montreal and Québec. As they were poor, all those who were old enough went to work without waiting to take a much needed rest.

They boarded at first with relatives, if they were lucky enough to have any here, or in some French Canadian family until they could rent a tenement for themselves, mostly in corporation houses, and buy the furniture that was strictly needed.

Money was very precious to us in those days and we spent it carefully, getting along with only the things we couldn't do without, but we were able to make a living and save something besides. You understand that food, clothing, lodging, fuel, everything was much cheaper then than now. For lighting, we used kerosene lamps and the streets were lighted the same way. It was some time later that we had gas.

Our kitchen had to serve also as dining-room and living-room. There was no such thing as a parlor and no place for one, because all the other rooms, including the front one, were bedrooms and there weren't too many, you can bet on that. We had no draperies or sash-curtains in the windows, just paper shades without roller-springs such as we saw later. A narrow strip of wood, of the same width, was sold with this paper shade and we nailed it across the top to the window frame. In the morning, the shade was rolled by hand and held up by a string fastened to a nail. The floors, not always of hard wood, were bare and had to be scrubbed on hands and knees with lye or some other strong stuff, once a week at least, on

Saturdays. The only floor coverings we knew were round braided carpets and catalognes , seven or eight feet long and three wide, all homemade with rags carefully put away for that purpose.

Once a week, sometimes twice, our women folks broke their backs over the washboard and wrung the family washing by hand, washing machines and wringers being unknown at the time. There was no hot water in large, convenient tanks, only the one you heated on the kitchen stove in the washboiler, pans and pots, or if you came to afford it, a tea-kettle. This hot water served for cooking, washing the dishes, clothes and floors and to take the weekly bath in the wash tub.

But we had big appetites and ate well and slept well, going to bed and getting up early every day in the week, except Sunday. Sunday nights, we had our veillees du bon vieux temps , as we had them in Canada. The younger folks enjoyed birthday parties, but early French Canadian textile workers, even in the 'seventies, never thought of celebrating their golden or silver wedding anniversaries. In 1871, our first parish was established and our new church was opened in 1873. In the meantime, we worshipped in Smyth Hall and in the church located on the corner of Chestnut and Merrimack Streets. A few years later, we had two parishes, so we really could practice our religion as easily as we did in old Québec. We said our morning prayer separately, but after supper, before the dishes were washed, we recited the beads and evening prayer en famille , father or mother alternating with the children and the boarders.

After a while, the children became young men and women. They had been earning money for a few years and, being prouder, thought of changing from homespuns, worn even on Sunday, to more fashionable store clothes. We saved pennies until they became dollars and when there was enough, we dressed up, you bet, paying in full for what we bought, not a little down and so much a week, as so many do today with the creation and the spread of the installment plan.

"You must have heard about the earliest French Canadian settlers in Manchester, M. Lemay," M. Pare inquired.

"Yes, I learned much about then when I was a very young man, and I can tell you they all started In the textile mills where most of them stayed. The first one to come here was Louis Bonin, in 1833. I understand that a Madame Jutras kept a boarding house in Amoskeag village (the northwest corner of Manchester) in 1830. Hyacinthe Jutras was another old timer. In 1848, he was the best man at the marriage of Louis Bonin and Miss Henriette

Bonenfant, the other witness being Miss Catherine Bonenfant. M. Jutras, who died in 1893, had a remarkable memory and was able to tell us much concerning the beginnings of the local French Canadian colony.

The records of births, marriages and deaths at City Hall were far from being complete. When the names of our people weren't changed so that no one could recognize them, they were left out altogether. It is true that the law wasn't strict so long ago, but certain doctors seemed to find it useless to register the names of children born of French Canadian parents. In some cases, they would simply report that on a certain day a boy or a girl had been born in a Frenchman's home.

The old records show that Louis Marchand married Sarah Robert in 1839. The first birth recorded is that of a child born of M. et Mme. Cyrille Lebran in 1852. Mme. Jean Jacques died in 1853. Others among the earliest settlers were J.P. Lariviere, John Montplaisir, Julie and Amelie Prevencher, Pierre Bonenfant, Michel Hevey, Jean Biron, Telesphore Lemire who died at Stoke Centre, P.Q., in 1891, Nazaire Laflotte, Joseph Janelle, Joseph Berard and Michel Cote, one of the men who, in 1849, chopped down the trees on the site of Saint Anne's church located on the corner of Merrimack and Union Streets where it still stands. The pastor was Father William McDonald who had come here in 1844. There was also a Thibodeau family and another by the name of Rocheleau.

In those early days, there was a City directory, but it was published only every two years. Those who came and left between the times names were taken didn't figure at all in the book. Here is, as far as we are concerned, a remarkable markable thing about this Directory: after almost every French Canadian name, you found this occupation mill-worker and the addresses were always something like these Amoskeag Corporation, Stark Corporation, Machine Shop, Print Works, with the number, just as you'd say today John So-and-So, 40 Main Street.

Some doctors came to Manchester from Canada more than eighty years ago to minister to their sick fellow-countrymen, but none of them stayed very long because business wasn't very good or for some other reason. The first was Dr. Joseph A. Parent who came here in 1852, had his office at 20 Amherst St. and went away in 1854. That year, a Doctor Belisle became the resident French Canadian physician. He was still here in 1856 and had his office at No. 3 Granite Block, his residence at 12 Manchester St.

The first photographer of our nationality group was Benjamin Milette with a studio at No. 79 Elm St., his home at 20 Pine St., corner of Manchester St. He came in 1858 and was gone in 1860. Dr. Elzear Provencher arrived in 1858 but remained only a short time, not so long as those who came before. Olivier Desmarais, who also took pictures, lived here about 1882. In 1862, Nazaire Laflotte entered the employ of the Barton Company, owners of a dry goods and notions store, and was probably the first French Canadian store clerk in Manchester. Our first merchant was Joseph Duval who opened a grocery and liquor store in 1863. In 1870, Nestor Goudreault rents half of Marchand Beausoleil's grocery store on Elm St. and starts the first French Canadian bakery. Godefroi Messier is doing so well with his oyster and refreshment shop opened in 1869, that he takes his sons Pierre and Luther as partners and moves to a larger place at 285 Elm St. In 1870, H. Girard owned a shoe store at No. 5 Well's Block; the same year, L. Lacroix was a wheelwright and carriage-maker on Elm St., opposite the Tremont building. In 1869, Dr. A.L. Tremblay, who came to Manchester in 1867, formed a company and started the first French language newspaper, *La Voix du Peuple,* with Ferdinand Gagnon, noted leader and pioneer of our newspaper man, as editor. In 1871, Father Joseph Augustin Chevalier became the first resident priest and founded St. Augustine's parish. In 1872, he resided on the north side of Laurel St., No. 62, between Pine and Union Streets.

There are now eight Franco-American parishes, each with its cure and most of these with vicaires or curates. By Father Chevalier and those priests who followed him to Manchester from Québec province, parish records were very carefully kept. Every birth, marriage and death is written down with all the names spelled as they should be, and if you want any information, you have it complete and right. A census is taken each year in all the parishes; that tells us the number of Franco-Americans at any time. That may be a difference of two or three hundred between that number and the real total because some French Catholics married into Irish families and belong to Irish parishes, and others lost their faith and joined Protestant denominations.

In 1871, there were about two thousand French Canadians in the city. After Father Chevalier's coming and the opening of the first church in 1873, immigration was speeded up for a while, as many as five or six families arriving on the Canadian train, the train du Canada , every day.

What was the pay of these earliest settlers? Well, in 1845, Michel Cote mixed mortar for five shillings a day, but in the mills where every other

French Canadian was employed, the pay was fifty cents a day and the board cost two dollars a week. The workday began at five o'clock in the morning and finished at eight o'clock at night. The workers had a half hour off for breakfast, dinner and supper. Later, every day of the week, in summer as in winter, the working hours of millhands were from six in the morning till 6 at night and that schedule was continued for many years. Nobody complained because everybody was happy and contented. It was good to have a steady job and a steady pay with the assurance that you didn't have to loaf unless you wanted to.

Today, we live in other times and fit ourselves to new conditions. The workweek has been considerably shortened and there is talk of making it even shorter. Machinery has been perfected, everything is modern. Between yesterday and today, what a difference. During my fifty-three years in the local mills, I have seen a seventy-five percent improvement. New looms in which the machine stopped if a thread broke were introduced about 1885 and saved much time and cloth. Ring spinning succeeded fly spinning with fine results for everybody. In 1872, the mills made fancy shirting, fleeced and plain cotton cloth, as well as blue and brown drilling for frocks and over-alls; then came gingham and ticking and finally woolens, worsteds, every kind of textile product.

People work as hard now as they did years ago, but life is better, easier, more satisfactory for the mill-worker of the present time and we old timers are glad that it is so. We are glad that we have brought it about to a certain extent. We were proud and insisted on working for our living, instead of depending on charity. We wanted to better our condition; own our home; set aside something against a rainy day; give our children a better education than we had ourselves. So we did our work honestly and well in order to keep our jobs and got better ones. Out of our wages, we built churches, then schools, while supporting public schools and the government of our country, state and city. Our children, better educated, are already in higher positions or prepared to fill them with honor. Some of us have retired to the homes we worked so hard to buy, while others have bought farms and gone back to the occupation which was that of their fathers and ancestors in the country where we were born.

Some French Canadians were not afraid and fought for the Union during the Civil War; there were many more in the war against Spain, but the greatest number served in the World War, hundreds having enrolled as volunteers in 1917. Our men would be ready and willing to answer another such call tomorrow. They'd rather have peace, just as the rest of the nation does, but if the fight is brought to them, they'll want to be in it, just as sure as you're there. I guess those early settlers I told you about won't have to be ashamed of us, because we've done our best.

You would like to have me introduce myself? Because it will lead me up to my first job in the mills, I will try to satisfy you, but we'll make it short, because there are so many things much more interesting to tell.

I was born in St. Ephrem d'Upton, P.Q., not far from St. Hyacinthe and Montreal, June 29, 1856. I was the fourth in a family of fourteen children, five of whom are still living. I told you that my mother was of good old Canadian stock. She was 97 years old when she died. My father was killed in an accident while at work; he was 80 and in perfect health, so he might have lived for quite a few more years, don't you think so?

When we came here in 1872, we lived in 'squog, on the west side of the river. After I was married, I occupied the same tenement for 44 1/2 years in an Amoskeag corporation house, on the north side of Stark Street, between Elm and Canal Streets. For the last ten years, we have lived in this cottage I own on Candia Road, near Lake Massabesic. I have with as my granddaughter, the housekeeper, and her son, 17 years old and a Freshman at St. Anselm's College.

I have always loved to travel, especially since I have been out of the mills. I have a son living in Florida and I have spent seven or eight winters with him. I drove my car both ways every time. This year, again by automobile, I went to Canada three times. No, I haven't forgotten my birthplace where father, mother and others of my family are buried.

I use glasses to read, but when it comes to see from a distance, my eyes are just as good as they were fifty years ago. Do I eat well? Mon cher ami , I can eat baked beans for supper and not feel the worse for it. I do quite a bit of work around the house. From spring until fall, I take care of my garden. My granddaughter thinks I work too much and often scolds me in a nice way; you hear her scold even now, but look at her smile. When I'm not working, I read and that brings me to a little nap in my rocking-chair. When you are going on 83, you too will like your petit somme in the afternoon. I am still considered the head of the family, loved and respected. With all that, who wouldn't be happy in his old days? As you see, we are able to speak English without a trace of accent, and that is natural; I have been in this country so long and the children were all born here.

After working for over sixty years, stomach ulcers began to bother me. I thought I wouldn't be able to go on any longer and spoke of leaving the mills, but they didn't want to let me go. The company in May and June, 1924, gave me a vacation with pay and told me that would put me on my feet. I did come back in July but things went from bad to worse with my stomach. In December, I was forced to retire and the Amoskeag, giving me a month's extra pay, had to let me quit my job as overseer of the Coolidge spinning mill. I went to the hospital where I spent quite a while and recovered my health.

I liked the people who were with me in the mills and I sympathized with them. I helped them as anybody else would have done in my place. Did I, when I was a boss, hide some who weren't quite sixteen, when inspectors visited he mills? I wouldn't have mentioned that if you hadn't put the question, but there is some truth in it, though I wonder who could have told you. You see, I started working in the Lowell mills when I was only eight years old and I could understand. If boys and girls were big and strong enough to work, even if they were a little under the legal age, I gave them a chance to keep their jobs. Their parents were poor and needed every cent they could get. So I'd tell these younger workers to keep out of sight until the inspector had gone away. There was no harm to anybody in that and it did a lot of good. And besides, the law wasn't so strict in those days. Looking back over the years, when I think of those who worked with me and for me, I feel in my heart that I miss a lot of friends and I'd be lonesome at times if I didn't have something to keep me busy around here. But let me talk about something else, about my first job, for instance, and then we'll go along.

When we landed at Lowell in 1864, there were very few French Canadians, only five families at one end of the city, fifteen at the other. Many more came after the Civil War was over. I was only eight years old, but that didn't stop me from going to work. My first job as a textile worker was in the Lawrence mill, No. 5, where I worked as a bagboy and doffer for about three years. Then I wanted to do outside work and one of my jobs was driving a one-horse wagon. In 1872, when I was sixteen, our family moved to Manchester. In 1875, father and mother returned to St. Ephrem.

Here, in the beginning, I started in a card room as roping and bobbin boy, but I wanted to be a spinner, not a mule-spinner. I had seen mule-spinning in Lowell and didn't like it at all; fly-spinning that makes cotton into thread, ready for the weave-room, that's what I wanted to do. But it wasn't until 1875,

the year my folks went back to Canada for good, that I got my chance. How I landed in No. 1 spinning mill of the Amoskeag, where no French Canadian could be hired before, is a little story in itself.

Each spring and fall, it seems, the older immigrants had a touch of homesickness. Most of them still had farms in old Québec. "I want to see if it is still where I left it," they'd smilingly tell the boss when they asked permission to be away for five or six weeks. So they went back to Canada twice a year. While there, they visited friends and relatives, that's sure, but their principal reason was a serious one, and they had to make many sacrifices in order to save up enough money to pay railroadffares and other necessary expenses.

At heart, Monsieur, they were still farmers like their ancestors had been, and they wanted to get something out of those farms, some of which had been in the family for many generations. In the spring, they attended to ploughing, harrowing and sowing; in the fall, to the harvesting of the crops. During the summer, some relative or neighbor kindly gave a look once in a while to see that all was well.

I went back to No. 1 with a job that paid me $1.30 a day, 20 cents more than I was getting at No. 4.

While they were absent from the mills—others having to loaf on account of sickness or for some other reason, spare-hands had their chance to work. That's how I got into spinning. The overseer was kept at home by sickness and the second hand hired me. When the boss came back, I was giving all my attention to my work and not losing a minute. We all did that. But the overseer didn't look pleased and he was mad when his assistant told him my name. He wanted to know why I had been hired when he didn't want any Frenchman working there in his mill. The second hand said he'd discharge me right away and I felt that my dream of becoming a fly-spinner was coming to an end quickly. I kept on working. The boss looked at me, seemed to think twice before he spoke and then said: "Don't do it now; wait until Smith comes back to work."

Smith did come back and I was out of a job, but not for long. The boss was sorry to let me go, that was plain. He took my address and said he'd let me know as soon as he needed me. He had changed his mind about hiring French Canadians after he had seen one of them at work. The very next day, at noon, he sent for me and after that I had a regular job in the Amoskeag. And that same boss hired many of my people, and that is the point I want to bring out in my story.

Later, I was transferred to No. 4 mill where there were, besides the overseer, three second hands in a department of 18,000 spindles. You can imagine how little work those assistant overseers had to do. They ought to have been running some of the frames to keep themselves busy. I went back to No. 1 with a job that paid me $1.30 a day, 20 cents more than I was getting at No. 4. 1 was roping-boy, oiled the shafts and pulleys and did other jobs.

The boss of No. 4 mill wanted me back and offered me $1.45 a day. I went, of course. One day, another overseer tried to got me, and when I spoke of leaving, Hamilton, boss of No. 4, wouldn't hear of it. To keep me, he offered me extra pay if I would do the work of a sickly operative who had to loaf at times, and more extra pay if I wanted to take the place of a third hand once in a while. I accepted, did my own work besides and, as long as the arrangement lasted, I got $2 a day and a little more. I was finally given a regular job as third hand, quite a promotion for a French Canadian at the time. In 1881, I was made second hand and, in 1901, overseer in No. 1 spinning mill. It included No. 2, where I had such a hard time getting a small job twenty-six years before.

It was a big event when I was appointed overseer of the 1 and 8 spinning mills. There was to be a vacancy very shortly. I knew about it and, being convinced that no one would say a good word for me, I decided to speak for myself. I wasn't bashful any more. So, one day, I asked the super if he wouldn't give me the chance. He was so surprised that he couldn't speak for a long time, or so it seemed to me. He was looking at me as if he had been struck by thunder and lightning. What! A Frenchman had the crust to think he could be an overseer! That was something unheard of, absolutely shocking. And the super was shocked, I'm telling you. When he recovered enough to speak, he told me he'd think it over, turned his back on me and walked off. He was certainly upset.

The next day, he came to me and, still with a doubting expression spread all over his face, said he'd try me for six months. But I didn't want six months, I answered back. I wasn't going to clog up that spinning department. Either I was the man for the job, I said, or I wasn't. If I was, it wouldn't take six months to find it out. If I wasn't, I'd get out in a hurry. No six months for me. One month, that's all I wanted to show what I could do. The super seemed to be wondering again but answered it was all right with him just as I said. So I became the over-seer of No. 1 Spinning where I had made my shaky debut in 1875.

That was another step ahead for the French Canadians, wasn't it? But this time, it was an awful scandal. The sad news didn't take long to spread. Americans and Irish were mad clean through. They looked at me and spoke to me only when they were strictly obliged to, but as far as friendship was concerned, there was no more, you bet. I, a Frenchman, had jumped over the heads of others who thought themselves the only ones entitled to the job of overseer; here was a sin that could not be forgiven, and what was the world coming to, anyway?

My disappointed former friends had another shook of the same kind two years later when Theophile Marchand—we called him Tofil—was named overseer of weaving, and he was included with me in their hate. Tofil, who had been a first class weaver, was then a first class loomfixer, a big job in those days. His promotion, like mine, became the talk of "Milltown" and was a terrible scandal.

Later, those who were afraid of us got used to these things and took them in a better spirit, for several other French Canadian textile workers got well deserved promotions. Theophile Marchand, better known as John, was one of my own second hands, and I recommended him. He was a boss just three days, then he came back to his old job with me, after telling the superintendent that he'd be happier and healthier that way. 'An overseer's job has too many worries,' he said. 'the first thing you know, I'd be loafing because I was sick, and I can't afford to do that, because I have quite a family to support.' And so, my friend Tofil had the distinction of being the first French Canadian , perhaps the first one of any nationality group, to refuse an overseer's job.

Others who didn't worry were a Mr. Lalime who was made a superintendent of weaving; Frank Houde who came with me to the Coolidge mill as a second hand and went later to No. 1 spinning mill as an overseer; Wilfred Lemay, one of my sons, who was second hand for the one who took my place as boss of old No. 1 when I was transferred to the Coolidge in May, 1910. Then there was Domicile Nolet, superintendent of carding at the Stark Mills, and a M. Blais, overseer of spinning for the same company, when Amoskeag bought Stark in 1922. They stayed as bosses for the Amoskeag until it shut down for good. M. Nolet became overseer for the Pacific Mills who opened a plant here a few years ago in a part of old Amoskeag. Pacific moved to Dover this year, Domicile followed and is still there.

An overseer has a good chance to got even with those who hate him and have been mean to him and his people, but such a thought didn't come to my mind. As soon as I had been appointed, the super came over and said to me: 'Lemay, now is the time to get rid of your first second hand. He never liked you and he's no good anyway. You are now able to discharge him and pay him back what he did to you.' 'I'm giving this man a chance to make good with me if he wants to. Besides, he's just as good as I am. I won't punish him nor anybody else that way because I have been treated meanly. Don't expect me to got rid of John until I have good reason to, and that goes for all those who work under me.' So I kept my first second hand. I recommended him to take my place in No. 1 when I was transferred to the new Coolidge mill. Again the super couldn't understand me. 'But can he do the job?' he asked. 'sure,' I answered, even better than I can.' 'there you are again,' replied the big boss. 'Whether it's to keep a second hand I don't want or to get him the job of overseer, you insist he's a better man than you, and the man isn't a French Canadian either.' 'He doesn't have to be one of my people, Mr. Super. If he's all right, I say so, and that's justice. Go ahead and try him out and find out what a fine man he is.' The super did, the man made good and I had my revenge twice against John, a Christian's revenge. I got no credit for what I had done but wasn't disappointed. My own good luck had brought me the congratulations and good wishes of only one American official, the superintendent of the Machine shops. The others kept their grudge until the time to congratulate had passed and then made the best of a thing that couldn't be avoided."

"What schooling did you have, M. Lemay?" M. Pare asked.

"None at all when I was a boy, " he replied, "and none until I had been made a second hand, and that was in 1881. I had three terms at evening school, each term beginning in October and ending sometime in March. Afterward, I took one term in a business college, again attending evening classes, of course. When I started to go to school, I already could speak English pretty well, and that was a great help to me.

When I was a young boy in Lowell, my father wanted me to attend day school, but I didn't care much for reading, writing, spelling and arithmetic. Father left home early in the morning to go to work in the sawmill, as he had to walk about a mile and a half, coming back only for supper. As soon as he was gone, I went in my turn, but not to school; I went to the mills. At night, I got a good spanking, this happening every day, but I couldn't change my ways. I wanted to work, that's all, to do something for my parents who needed all the help they could get, with the family they had to feed and take care of. Father had to let me have my way, but he didn't like to and showed it more than once.

In general, French Canadian children living here could have had some schooling in the grammar school grades if their parents had been able to get along without the earnings of these boys and girls, but most of them couldn't afford that. The only ones who had a chance to get an education were the youngest of the children, because older brothers and sisters were in the mills, helping their parents at the time. There were even boys who went to college and became priests, doctors, lawyers, newspapermen, and girls who studied to be religious teachers thanks to the hard-earned money of textile workers in their families.

After 1870, there were enough of our children to make schools necessary for them, with lay teachers for the first ten years or so. In Manchester, Father Chevalier, who came here in May, 1871, having been the first resident parish priest from Québec in New Hampshire, started to build St. Augustine's church in 1872 and it was opened for worship in 1873. Young women helped the pastor by teaching catechism to the children in church each Sunday. It was as late as January, 1881, that the Sisters of Jesus-Marie were brought to Manchester from Sillery, near Québec, by the cure of St. Augustine, to teach both French and English, besides religion, which ranked first, as it does now, in the school program, to young Franco-Americans."

Immigrants from the province of Québec settled not only in Manchester but in other Now Hampshire mill centers, Great Falls (now Somersworth), Salmon Falls and Newmarket, to name only a few. In each community, they built church first of all, then a presbytere or residence for the pastor, as soon as possible a school for their children (which the children had to attend), and they finally bought a tract of land on the outskirts of the city for a cemetery. To protect their homes and families, they later organized mutual benefit or fraternal societies, the first of which was the *Saint-Jean-Baptists Society*, *Union Saint-Pierre*, *Societe Saint-Augustin* and *Union Saint-Georges*. The first of these groups and *Union Saint-Pierre* have ceased to exist but they lived remarkably long; *Union Saint-Georges* and *Societe St. Augustin* have joined the *Association Canada-Americaine* founded in 1896, I know of some *St. Jean-Baptiste Societies*, some started as early as 1867, that are today strong and active as independent fraternal groups.

Finally, to link themselves more closely, they had their newspapers. Some didn't live long like *Voix du Peuple*, the first one, and *Echo des Canadians*, but *L'Avenir-National*, started as a weekly fifty years ago, is one of the important French dailies in New England. We have also two monthlies, *Echo de*

Notre-Dame and *Republique* and *Canadao-Americain*, the monthly organ of *Association Canado-Americaine*. The church, the school, the societies and the press are what have kept Franco-Americans alive as a group. Let them all disappear, and we go into the famous American melting pot.

"From what I have already told you," M. Lemay continued, "it can be guessed that the children of Québec immigrants, like most of their parents, had no school education when they arrived here. They had been well and religiously brought up by devout parents in their Canadian homes; their mother had taught them to pray, but they could neither read nor write. One of the exceptions was Joseph E. "Joe" Pellerin. Joe was 17 when he came to Manchester with his folks in 1881. He had been to grammar school under religious teachers at Yamachiche where the family then lived and which was the birthplace of Joe's Canadian ancestors. He then had four years of classical studies at the seminary of Trois-Rivieres. He followed this up with two terms of business college in Manchester, attending night classes and learning bookkeeping, English and penmanship. He was a first class weaver and what did his education do to him? It took him off the looms in the early 90's and placed him in the weave room office. There he kept books, including the workers' time, for overseer Adam Graf, and marked the new cotton until 1922, at which time he was made a cloth inspector in another room. He remained there until he retired from the mills in 1930.

Joe was born in *Baie-du-Fevre*, near Nicolet, and is now 75 years old. He came here from Yamachiche with his father, step-mother, two brothers and sister. In the order of birth, he was the second of this family of four. His parents and sister returned to Yamachiche in 1884; one brother married and settled in Lowell, while the other, also married here, moving to Canada with his family some time later. My friend was an investigator for a local bank until 1933. He then retired and lives with his wife and unmarried daughter, Miss Germaine, in a corporation house he has occupied for the last forty years and is located at 59 West Bridge St. M. Pellerin has four children, two daughters and two sons. A son, Alfred, is an attendant in a State hospital, and the unmarried daughter is a fine pianist and the able organist of St. George's church.

Joe is a nice talker, has a wonderful memory and, with his distinguished appearance, could pass just as easily for a doctor, a lawyer or a professor as for a retired textile worker . But Joe was one of the best weavers known in his time, and that's what he's proud of. He tried his hand at polities twice. The first time, running for the City Council in

1889, he was defeated at the Ward 1 caucus by 25 votes. He tried again the following year and was elected as he had told his political enemies he would be.

Like myself, Joe says we owe our success in the mills to the fact that we were faithful, honest workers, giving our attention to what we had to do instead of losing time talking to our fellow-workers. Joe is a man of fine character, a loyal citizen who'd rather go without eating or postpone a trip to Canada than to miss a chance of voting on election days. He loves his adopted city and country in a practical way, being ever ready to serve them, yet he remains at 75 loyal to the land of his birth and to his nationality group here. He speaks English fluently while preserving his faith, his mother tongue and customs of our people. He is a very active member of St. George's parish, of parish and fraternal groups, a worker for every good cause. Yes, Joe sets a fine example for us to follow, he is a real leader among Franco-Americans in Manchester and he's a jolly good fellow."

"You wish to know about a French Canadian textile worker who was neither a boss nor an office clerk in the mills? Then let me tell you about Stanislas Gagnon. M. Gagnon is 63 years old and lives at 100 Orange St., near St. George's Church. Stanislas served the Amoskeag Manufacturing Company for 47 years, always ways in the card rooms where has done every kind of work that department offers to a textile operative. He was just twelve and a half years of age when he started to work as a mill hand, and he's still at it, a carder. He came to our city in 1888 with his mother, his grandmother on his father's side and his brothers and sisters. They lived first on Pearl Avenue, near their present residence, and Stanislaus has never moved out of that district, though he has belonged to two parishes. Our friend now occupies a very neat tenement and lives in comfort with his wife and their unmarried daughter. A married daughter is a resident of Boston.

M. Gagnon, when he was a young mans wanted his share of gold and adventure, so he left the mills to go to the Klondike where he spent three years.

He returned to Manchester and worked for a while in the card room of the Amory mill. During the strike of 1922 and after the final shutdown of Amoskeag, he worked for several months at Exeter, this State, Lewiston, Me., Lawrence and Fall River, Mass., and Brattleboro, Vt., but he passed the greater part of his 47 years as a textile worker in the service of Amoskeag. He is a good hand and enjoys his work which he does faithfully and well. Everybody likes Stanislas who is a fine, good natured and good looking man, a six-footer and just a little shy, with a fair complexion, blue eyes, square shoulders and large, capable hands, all of which gives the impression that he is not a day over fifty.

For three whole days, M. Gagnon was an employee of the Stark mills. He was a boy of 13, full of fun and innocent mischief. He enjoyed himself until the third day when he got a good scolding from his boss. Stanislas liked it so little that he quit his job without giving notice and went back to Amoskeag. Like many youngsters of his day, Stanislas got his job in the textile mills by pretending to be 16. He was tall enough, but not built to look like a strong and able workman, and the bosses, though guessing that the truth was being stretched, gave him and other boys a chance.

As Stanislas was telling me one day, there were difficult moments in the lives of these young mill workers. If they happened to be loafing, they were generally out on the streets. Sometimes, a truant officer would come along and ask questions. Why weren't the boys in school? How old were they? Where did they live? Stanislas says he and his friends were in hot water all the time this third degree business lasted. They had to think up some reasonable answers in not too much time and apparently satisfied the officer, since they kept their jobs in the mills. If they had been forced to go to school, the loss of their small earnings, added together, would have made quite a difference in the family budget.

Ask any French Canadian textile worker and he will tell you how well he got along with his overseer. Stanislas Gagnon, who never was a boss, says that he never had any trouble with his, nor with his fellow-workers, and thousands of other French-Canadians say the same thing. We got along well because we never killed time, gave our attention to our jobs and turned out work that the company could sell. That is why we got the reputation of being skillful operatives who could be trusted to remain on their jobs even if the bosses weren't always around to watch them. It is for that same reason the local textile corporations sent agents to Canada and to American textile centers to bring more of those French Canadians.

Our American overseers were always fair and just to us and it is fair and just to admit it. They were fine men and knew their business. They never bothered those who did their duty. We can certainly be thankful to them for their decent treatment of us. Stanislas Gagnon tells this story to prove it.

'my second hand,' says Gagnon, 'was an Irish-American who took away some work from an Irish operative. It was extra work for me without any extra pay. At first, being a little timid, I told the

second boss I'd do the work, but the more I thought it over afterward, the more convinced I was the second hand was favoring his countryman at my own expenses and I refused to be anybody's goat. I went to my overseer and told him all about it. He thought I was right and told me so. He then went to the Irish assistant boss and asked him if what I had said was true. The second hand admitted it was and went on to say that I lost a lot of time talking with women operatives and killed time otherwise. Speaking louder, he continued: 'He has plenty of time to do this extra work I gave him and he's going to do it or somebody's going to get out.' To which the boss answered: 'Yes, somebody's going to get out and it won't be Gagnon. I'm keeping him, so you'd better change your mind pretty soon about that extra work you gave him, because he isn't going to do it. Think it over if you care anything for you job.' The second hand changed his mind in a hurry and the Irish operative got his work back again.

The overseer trusted Gagnon, that is why he stood by him. The company itself had much confidence in us and gave us big and important tasks to do. Not the least of these was the job of setting up the machinery and putting in operation the spinning department in the new Coolidge Mill, in 1910. We started in May. In December, the executives were told the job had been completed. They couldn't believe that it had taken only seven months, and only a personal investigation could convince them. If all those who worked with me hadn't given their full cooperation, it couldn't have been done, so the greater part of the credit belongs to them. We had set up in record time what was said to be the largest single spinning department in the world, 105,000 spindles and 150[?] hand on one floor, and there were also the picker-room men in the basement. Many French Canadians worked for me and my first assistant was Theophile Marchand.

It lasted nearly ten months and was the worse thing that ever happened. It was bad for the city, its merchants, tenement owners, business in general. It destroyed Amoskeag's trade and the Company, never recovering from the blow, kept going down until it had to close its doors. My sympathy, however, goes first to all the workers for they are the ones who suffered the most. They lost all their savings, went deep in debt and lived on canned beans while the hope of winning the fight was kept dangling before their eyes. They were told almost every day by the strike leaders to be patient and tighten up their belts because victory was in sight. But there was no victory, only defeat for all concerned.

As an overseer, I couldn't join their ranks in the labor union nor help them in any way, but neither could I be against them. As a boy, a young man and a middle-aged man with a family, I had worked long hours for anything but high wages. I knew what it meant to be poor, what sacrifices must be made if you want to lay something aside for a rainy day. The workers wanted more pay; I would have given them a living wage if it had been in my power to do so, every worker having a right to that. They wanted shorter hours; I would have given them a reasonable work-week if I had anything to say about it. Even as a second hand and an overseer, I never forgot my humble beginning and always considered myself a textile worker . Those strikers were textile workers too, and I was sorry for them. Yes, that strike of 1922 was really a terrible thing.

Where did we meet the girls we married? Why right here in Manchester. No, we weren't in love before we left Canada.

We were too young to think of such things when we came to the States. Very few had known in childhood the girls they were going to marry; so many of us, you see, came from different parishes and villages.

This is the day of my wedding, the happiest day of my life; beloved, I am yours and forever.

The young lady who became my wife in 1878 was Miss Selima Laliberte. She lived in a private home, that of her friend Miss Laurence who kept house with her two brothers and worked in the mills besides. Now Damase and Georges Laurence, Moise Verrette, and Joseph Baril and myself were intimate friends. Joe Baril's mother wasn't in good health, I had only one small room, so we spent our evenings together with the Laurences or at the home of Moise Verrette, never dreaming then that he would later be the owner of a large grocery store and meat market and twice mayor of Manchester. While visiting Georges and Damase, I became acquainted with Miss Laliberte. She was a fine, attractive girl and interested me. Soon I was going to the Laurence home mostly to see Selima, then for herself alone, We had fallen in love, we became engaged and were married by Father Chevalier in St. Augustine's church.

Joe Pellerin, once more the exception to the rule, found his wife in Canada, she was a stranger to him. He went to Yamachiche in the late summer of 1891 while on vacation after an illness. He was coaxed to take a job in a general store at Maski-nonge, only a few miles away. He got the job and stayed thirteen months. His pay was five dollars a month with room and board, but it was a lucky day

for him, he says, when he went to Maskinonge, for it was there he met the girl he was to make his wife.

He came back here in the spring of 1892, leaving his heart in the little Canadian village, and went to work for Adam Graf. In the fall of 1892, having decided not to wait any longer, he took the train for Maskinonge, married the girl he loved and brought her to Manchester where they have lived happily ever since.

We had family reunions, mostly on Sunday, to amuse ourselves. They were real veillees canadiennes and we certainly enjoyed ourselves. We sang without piano accompaniment songs of old Québec, danced square and round dances and jigs, played games like l'assiette tournante (Spin the Platter) for forfeits, and played cards for the fun of it, mostly euchre, a game we learned here.

Sometimes, one sang alone; at other times, we sang in chorus. There were also *chansons a repondre* a sole with certain lines repeated in chorus by *la compagnie*, the gathering. Everybody who was asked to sing cleared his throat—that was the usual ceremony—, saying he or she had a cold, and called on the others to help him: *Vous allez m' aider bien?* What did we sing? Well, Monsieur, we sang *Vive la Canadienne* and other popular songs of the Canadian folklore; sentimental songs, and one of them—I don't remember all the words because I didn't sing much myself—began like this:

C'est aujourd'hui la jour de mes noces,
C'est aujourd'hui la plus beau de mes jours.
Ah! oui, cher amant que j'aime,
Je suis a toi aujourd'hui pour toujours.

I couldn't translate that in verse, but here is what it means: This is the day of my wedding, the happiest day of my life; beloved, I am yours and forever.

Some were very good at singing comic songs, like Zozo in which the words are so misplaced that sense becomes nonsense, the kind that makes you laugh. I believe I remember the first verse. Here it is, and it's crazy:

Je suis Zozo, par mes actions comiques,
J'ai fait parler de moi pendant-z-onze ans.
Je suis le fils de mon seul pere unique
It pour le sur aussi bien de Mouman
Un jour, la nuit, cette pauvre Valere
Tomba malade, mon pere me dit: Zozo,
Va chercher du bouillon pour ta mere
Qu'est bien malade la-bas dans un petit pot,
Va chercher du bouillon pour ta mere,
Qu'est bien malade la-bas dans un petit pot.

This part of another verse is even worse:

Mais v'la t'y pas que ma maladresse
Je chavirai les assiettes at les plats;
Je fis une tache sur ma veste de graisse
Et les culottea de ma jambe de drap. . . .

In the first, Zozo, the son of his only fathers is told to fetch some broth for his mother who is sick over there in a little pitcher. In what there is of the second, Zozo knocks down the dishes and spills the broth over his fat vest and the trousers of his woolen cloth leg.

Another song, this one a *chanson a repondre*, a sort of catechism and mentioned one God, two Testaments, etc. up to the ten Commandments. As he went along the singer, as we do in *Alevette*, repeated backwards what he had sung and finished as he had begun, with the words: *Il n'y a qu'un seul Dieu, Il n'y a qu'un seul Dieu*, which the others repeated after him in chorus.

For our round and square dances as well for jigs, the music was furnished by a fiddler who always played the same tune as long as you wanted him to—he knew no other—and by a fellow who played the accordion but they never played together because their tune was different. We didn't care about that and we danced and had great fun. In St. Ephrem, even these home dances weren't allowed because our people believed that the devil himself was present as a cavalier wherever people danced. Stories of tragic happenings were told and made you shiver. Here, we never went to public dance halls but weren't afraid of the devil being in our homes if we conducted ourselves as decent people should.

In 1874, Father Chevalier, wishing to encourage the study of music among his parishioners and to give more prestige to the French Canadians of Manchester, called a group of young men to his home and proposed that they should start a band. The idea was quickly accepted and in a short time and after much work, we had the Fanfare Canadienne de Manchester . Instruments and uniforms were bought. At Father Chevalier's invitation, Joseph Lafricain came from Marlboro, Mass., to help in the organization of the musical group and to be its leader.

The men practiced in a small hall and were seated. There came a time when they had to learn to play while marching. So, one day, they went in carriages to the vicinity of Alsace and Amory streets where there was a park in those days but no homes. There they marched and played to their hearts' content. The Fanfare Canadienne became an institution. It paraded many times in our city and gave concerts which were well attended. It was engaged by fraternal groups and travelled an far as Québec. There were twenty-seven members in the Fanfare called the French Military Band by the English newspapers. It was reorganized in 1882 as the City Band which ceased to exist only a few years ago. Father Chevalier's band was composed of textile workers and I played the slide trombone. I have hare a list of the charter members. I'll read it off to you:

J. R. Lafricain, leader, clarinet; Solyme Daigneault, bass; Charles Blanchard, cornet; Edouard Harrington, bass; John Harrington, alto; Jean-Baptiste Blanchette, cornet; Joseph Gagaon, bass; Charles-Borromee Boulanger, slide trombone; Napoleon Monette, cornet; Hormidas Manseau, baritone; Jules Provencher, cornet; Fred Sansouci, alto; Edouard Geoffroy, cornet; Joseph Marcotte, bass; Victor Hébert, clarinet; Victor Sansouci, cornet; Edouard Brown, fife; Cyrille Lebrun, cornet; Damase Laurence; cornet; Philippe Archambault, alto; Joseph Letendre, cornet; Philippe Lemay, slide trombone; James Manseau, snare drum; Joseph Desjardins, bass drum and cymbals; J. Champagne, bass drum. Five of them died and the band escorted them to the church and cemetery.

"It has often been said, Mr. Lemay, that the French Canadian immigrants here and in all industrial centers had much to suffer from a certain nationality group for a number of years. Please tell us something of those troublous times," said Mr. Pare'.

"Those days of petty persecution, beating, rock-throwing swill-slinging and tragedy are not nice to remember," M. Lemay answered sadly, "Besides, Monsieur, a big book couldn't tell all the story. Our troubles came mostly, not to say entirely, from Irish people who, it seems, were afraid that we had come here to take their jobs away from them in the mills and who tried hard to send us back to Canada by making life impossible for us in America. They wanted us to speak the English among ourselves when we only knew French and it made them mad because we didn't. They had forgotten—or didn't know—that French Canadians had taken into their homes many orphaned children of Irish immigrants to Canada and brought them up as their own. Yes, Irish-Americans should have been our best friends over here, not our worst enemies.

It was bad enough here in 1872 and later, but it was worse in Lowell about 1864. It was impossible to get drinking water from public pumps in the daytime. Irish boys threw dirt in our pails, so we had to go at night, in the darkness and by roundabout ways.

Sundays, we went to mass at the Irish church. There was no other. Irish lads sat behind us and, with needles or pins stuck in the ends of their boots, they'd dig into us. We jumped and yelled, and other people in the church were disturbed.

We had our ears boxed by the man in charge of children. When we couldn't stand it any longer, we stopped going to church. The priest visited our homes to inquire about our absence. We told him why we stayed at home, the guilty boys got a licking and then we could attend Sunday services in peace.

My father worked in a saw-mill located almost in the center of the city. For a time, the men mere obliged to work at night and the owners had to build a shack where the workers could eat their lunch without fear of being injured or killed by rocks thrown at them. The job was lit up by flaming rosin placed in large irons pans, but all around the place, it was very dark, so it was easy to hide and throw rocks or bricks and you'd never know where they came from.

Irishmen were fond of clay pipes, 'T. D. s", they were called, but they must have thought nobody else had the right to use the some kind. When they met a French Canadian smoking a clay pipe, they'd break it off between his teeth. If he'd smoke a briar pipe, they'd push it down his throat. Not liking this sort of sport, our fathers and big brothers smoked nothing but short "T. D. s" that couldn't be shortened any more nor pushed in.

In Manchester, it was in those parts of the city where only Irish people lived, especially what was called l'Irlande, all around Park common which was called la commune d'Irlande, that we found plenty of trouble. Our family was then living in the 'squog section of West Manchester, and the shortest way to St. Augustine's church, the only French church at that time, was over Granite St. bridge, across Elm St., up Lake Avenues through the Commune d'Irlande and up Spruce St. to the corner of Beech where the church was located. Well, sir, we couldn't pass there without having our Sunday clothes ruined by filthy swill thrown at us from yards and alleys. Rocks flew also, and many of us youngsters received painful beatings from young Irish-Americans who were nearly always armed with sticks. The only way for us to save our clothes and our skins was to go to church by making a long detour and approaching St. Augustine's from the east instead of from the west as we would have naturally done if there had been no enemies on the way.

No, we didn't fight back because we were afraid of having trouble with the law. Being strangers, we didn't know how it would turn out for us. The first Greeks who came to Manchester weren't so timid. Welcomed as we had been by the Irish, they thought they hadn't come from far-off Greece to be chased away without some resistance.

They paid back with interest everything they received from the residents of the district. Often they were arrested but just as soon acquitted after they had proved that they had acted in self-defense. The Irish hated Chief of police Healy for that, though he was an Irishman himself, but he was a just man and a fine chief who made Manchester the orderly city it is. Anyway, the Greeks did so well that the commune d'Irlande is now called the commune des Grecs where people may pass without being insulted or beaten up.

Some years later, French Canadian grown-ups were treated more decently. There were too many of us then and we weren't so bashful about defending ourselves. Irish boys alone remained mischievous. Armed with sticks and stones, they often chased French Canadian boys through streets and back yards, even into homes where the attacking "army" didn't always dare to follow.

But the worst blow struck at us was the killing of Jean-Baptiste Blanchette, a member of the French Band of which he was then the leader and a fine fellow if there ever was one.

On the night of September 309 1880, Blanchette and four friends, who also belonged to the band, were talking quietly about the Fanfare and its leadership, in French , of course, on Amherst St., near the corner of Vine. The friends were Georges Laurence, Edouard Harrington, Joseph Desjardins and Frank Manseau. Blanchette, called John Blanchard by the English-speaking people, had met them at the Excelsior House, Concord St., where he owned a lager beer parlor, his other place being at 34 Amherst St. All five walked to Amherst St. where they continued their conversation. It was a little after 11 o'clock.

Three Irish young men—no need of mentioning their names—came out of another beer parlor located nearby, on the same street. They, like many others, hated to hear French spoken and called on the five "frogs" to "talk United States". They rushed the French Canadians as they passed them. The three attackers were drunk. Blanchette pushed them away, One of the three came back at Jean-Baptiste who met him once more, and the assailant, either struck or pushed, fell on the sidewalk. A large, round beer bottle, containing a small quantity of hard liquor, was broken in the fall. The man was now furious. He got back to his feet, seized the upper part of the broken bottle and holding it by the neck, he threw it and it struck Blanchette on the left side of the throat. Blanchette had run into the street and there he fell. The jagged edge of the broken bottle had made a wound one inch deep and two inches long and cut the jugular vein.

Blanchette was soon bathing in his blood which was coming out so fast nobody could stop the flow.

Quickly, Harrington and Laurence picked up their friend and carried him to his room over the saloon. They laid him down on the floor where another pool of blood was soon formed. There was now a wide, sticky red trail leading from the street, onto the sidewalk and the stairs and into the room. A piece of glass, the pointed end sticking out, was still in the wound. It was removed and one of Blanchette's companions held his hand over the gaping hole, trying to stop the constant flow of blood. Officer John Cassidy, later deputy chief, was patrolling his beat when a woman shouted to him from an open window that a man was dying upstairs. Officer Cassidy went to the bloody room then called his captain and he soon arrived on the scene with four doctors who did all they could but couldn't save the terribly wounded man. He died twenty minutes after being hit, having lost all his blood.

The news spread like wild fire around the usually quiet city. The next morning, at 7 o'clock, hundreds of French Canadians stood near the corner of Vine and Amherst Streets.

The bloody spot was still there and staring at it, they said: 'this is where three Irishmen killed Jean Blanchette last night.' The crowd was excited and you could hear a low grumbling, but there was no other demonstration. They held themselves as they had done whenever they had been made to suffer. Only this was worse and could hardly be believed. A man had been killed by a "frog" hater. Those hundreds of men could have cried as if Blanchette had been the near relative of all of them while they kept looking at that awful red spot which nobody had thought of cleaning up.

The Irish lads were arrested and locked up in cells at the police station. Two were charged with being drunk and fined, being held afterward as witnesses. The bottle-thrower who admitted throwing the top half of the beer bottle but insisted he didn't know where it landed, was accused of murder. At the January term of Superior Court, he was sentenced to five years in prison. He served his sentence and died a few months after coming out. He was only 18 years old at the time of the tragedy; his father and mother were dead and he lived here with an uncle. He had worked in the mills but had been idle for some time.

Jean-Baptiste Blanchette was 23 years of age and had come to Manchester thirteen years before. He had worked for the Amoskeag in a weave room, then in the Langdon mill. Later, though still a young man, he had saved up enough money to run two small lager beer parlors where French Canadi-

ans liked to gather and talk of the things that interested them. They had no social clubs at the time.

Blanchette wasn't married. He roomed with the family of Alexandre Boucher and boarded at 22 Concord St. His body was laid out at the home of his good friend, M. Harrington, 51 Pearl St. The funeral took place at St. Augustine's church on Sunday morning, October 2nd, at 9 o'clock. As early as 7 o'clock, there was a large crowd of French Canadians in front of the Harrington home. At half past eight the long funeral procession started its march to the church.

In front was the Fanfare Canadienne led by Joseph Lafricain its first conductor, who had come back to honor his friend John, one of the founders of the band. Then came the Societe St. Jean-Baptiste, 104 members wearing their insignia and carrying their banners, the president, Charles Robitaille, leading the imposing group. Blanchette had been voted in as a member but had not yet signed the society's constitution and by-laws, so he wasn't an active member, but the Societe turned out just the same. From 200 to 300 young men, all intimate friends of Blanchette, marched in ranks behind the hearse. There was also the French Republican Club of which John was a member. Then followed carriages in which were Blanchette's relatives. His father lived somewhere in New Hampshire but no one knew his address. Following the carriages, in the procession, were about 1,000 persons of all ages. Crowds lined the streets on the way to the church and all seemed to sympathize with the relatives who escorted the body. In a few minutes, the church was filled. Father Chevalier officiated at the high mass for the dead and gave absolution. On the casket, we could see the uniform our friend wore and the cornet he played in the band, with a crown of natural flowers made by Miss Emelie Harrington.

After the church service, the procession was formed just as it had been before and marched to St. Augustine's cemetery, in the southern end of the city, where the body was buried.

The French weekly, Echo des Canadiens, wrote nice things about Jean Blanchette, and that was quite natural. But the Daily Union calling him John Blanchard, praised him even more. In the story of the murder, it described John as a 'genial and pleasant fellow' and, in its edition of Mondays Oct. 3rd,—here is the clipping—after relating the details of the funeral, it says: 'the large number of friends of the deceased who turned out to show their respect shows plainly the esteem in which he was generally regarded. Blanchard was popular, well liked by all who knew him. It is the general opinion that he had no enemies and that he was upright in all his dealings.' The Union called the killing a 'terrible and bloody tragedy.'

Only a few hours before Blanchette met his death, I had visited him at his room. I was terribly shocked when I heard what had happened. He was a very dear friend of mine, always cheerful, quiet, minding his own business, kind to everybody. I asked myself how anyone could have struck him down in this awful manner just because he was talking to fellow-countrymen in the language that was most natural to him, his mother tongue. I can't understand now, after almost sixty years.

That tragic episode of 1880 brought much grief to the French Canadian colony and, compared to it, the mean things that had been done to us seemed very small indeed. Feeling ran high among us, but not one of us thought of a avenging our murdered friend. As always, we suffered in silence with the hope that some day, our right to live peacefully in America would be recognized. We had so much confidence in God and in this adopted country of ours. Well, the day did come. Now, the surviving French Canadian textile workers of long ago, their children, grandchildren and great-grandchildren have won the respect and esteem of their fellow-citizens. Yes, a we surely have found our place in the sun of American liberty. Franco-Americans are prominent in all lines of business and namy are quite successful in politics. Since 1918, Manchester has had four mayors and they were all Franco-Americans. We have distinguished doctors, lawyers, educators, judges, artists, architects, bankers and clergyman, one of these having been the third bishop of Manchester for 25 years.

To what do we owe our success? I believe we owe it to the self-sacrificing French Canadian immigrants from old Québec, to the courage that made them refuse to accept defeat and quit when that would have seemed the natural thing to do; to the cheerfulness that carried us through our trials and tribulation and helps us old-timers to wait happily for the final bell calling us home to rest after our long, hard life in the textile mills. And perhaps the bloody death of Jean-Baptiste Blanchette, a martyr in the true sense of the word, had its share in bringing about the conditions we are enjoying today.

Source:

Library of Congress. *American Life Histories: Manuscripts from the Federal Writers' Project, 1936-1940* from the American Memory website (http://memory.loc.gov/ammem/wpaintro/wpahome.html).

GERMAN
AMERICANS

*T*he events of a brutal century drove the Palatine Germans to America. When their emigration began in 1709, the region in which they lived, the Palatinate, was an area of Germany west of the Rhine and north of the French border. Its recent history was woeful. Half a century earlier, it had been devastated by the Thirty Years War (1618-1648), the religious conflict between Catholics and Protestants which became a war between nations to dominate Europe. As subjects of one of Europe's most powerful Protestant rulers, the Palatine Germans paid dearly during the crisis, with most of the population being killed and the country in ruins. New persecutions of Protestants at the start of the eighteenth century led the Palatines to flee, usually penniless and starving.

Leaving hardship in the old world, the Palatines encountered different hardships before they even reached the new one. This legal document, a pleading written nearly a decade after their arrival in the American colonies, still has the horrors of the passage fresh in mind. Flight from Germany had been accomplished by way of underground railroad, smuggling families along the Rhine to Netherlands, and then to England. In London, refugee camps swelled as unsanitary conditions bred disease, and conditions did not improve once the refugees were packed into vermin-ridden boats for transport to the colonies. Hundreds died from disease during the three to six week trip.

Passage was not free. A fee was collected upon arrival in the colonies, and for the destitute travelers, the alternative to paying was grim: bond servitude for a period of four years to an owner, known as a master, who paid off the refugee's fee. A variation of the practice of indentured servitude—and not far from the practice of slavery—this was a cozy arrangement for the wealthy land owners, who paid a pittance to own a worker. For the Palatine, it meant that families were split up. Orphaned children fell into the hands of owners until the age of 21.

As the document indicates, appearances were deceptive, too. The Palatines who embarked for New York in 1709 and survived the passage did not receive what they were led to expect—land, money, and tools to help them get started. Instead, they ended up shuttling from one inhospitable tract of land to another, being ordered to work for a landowner, and having to buy land. The worst indignity came when the Palatines were informed that their newly-purchased acreage was owned by someone else. This led to a bitter legal conflict in which the authorities of Albany lined up against the Palatines, making arrests and threatening to deport them.

By 1717, the situation had deteriorated to the point that the Palatines begged the English authorities to intercede. The document is in the form of a pleading to the Lords Commissioners of Trade and Plantations, who, more than a half century before the American Revolution, exercised authority over land disputes. The pleading asks for the right to continue living upon and cultivating the land "that they might not be starved for want of Corn & food." It recounts the miseries of exile, *takes pride in survival against all odds, and expresses hope that all the colonists' difficult work will not be undone.*

*This document was originally published by Edmund Bailey O'Callaghan (ed.)
in* Documents Relative to the Colonial History of New York *(Albany, 1855).*

PALATINE GERMANS IN NEW YORK—1720

That, In the year 1709. The Palatines, & other Germans, being invited to come into England about Four Thousand of them were sent into New York in America, of whom about 1700 Died on Board, or at their landing in that Province, by unavoidable sickness.

That before they went on Board, they were promised, those remaining alive should have forty acres of Land, & Five pounds sterling per Head, besides Cloths, Tools, Utensils & other necessaries, to Husbandry to be given at their arrival in America.

That on their landing their were quartered in Tents, & divided into six companies, having each a captain of their own Nation, with a promise of an allowance of fifteen Pounds per annum to each commander.

That afterwards they were removed on Lands belonging to Mr. Livingstone, where they erected small Houses for shelter during the winter season.

That in the Spring following they were ordered into the woods, to make Pitch & Tar, where they lived about two years; But the country not being fit to raise any considerable quantity of Naval Stores, They were commanded to Build, to clear & improve the ground, belonging to a private person.

That the Indians having yielded to Her late Majesty of pious memory a small Tract of Land called Schorie for the use of the Palatines, they in fifteen days cleared a way of fifteen miles through the woods & settled fifty Families therein.

That in the following Spring the remainder of the said Palatines joined the said fifty families so settled therein Schorie.

But that country being to small for their encreasing families, they were constrained to purchase some Neighbouring Land of the Indians for which they were to give Three hundred pieces of Eight.

And having built small Houses, & Hutts there about one year after the said purchase some gentlemen of Albani, declared to the Palatines, that themselves having purchased the said countrie of Schorie of the Governor of New York they would not permit them to live there, unless an agreement were also made with those of Albanys; But that the Palantines having refused to enter into such an agreement, A Sheriff & some officers were sent from Albany to seize one of their Captains, who being upon his Guard; The Indians were animated against the Palatines; but these found means to appease the Savages by giving them what they would of their own substance.

That in the year 1717 the Governour of New York having summoned the Palatines to appear at Albani, some of them being deputed went thither accordingly, where they were told, that unless they did agree with the Gentlemen of Albany, the Governor expected an order from England to transport them to another place, And that he would send twelve men to view their works & improvements to appraise the same & then to give them the value thereof in money.

But this is not being down the Palatines to the number of about three Thousand, have continued to manure & to sew the Land that they might not be starved for want of Corn & food.

For which manuring the Gentlemen of Albani have put in prison one man and one woman, & will not release them, unless they have sufficient security of One Hundred Crowns for the former.

Now in order that the Palatines may be preserved in the said Land of Schorie, which they have purchased of the Indians, or that they may be so settle in an adjoining Tract of Land, as to raise a necessary subsistance for themselves & their families, they have sent into England Three Persons one of whom is since dead humbly to lay their Case before His Majesty, not doubting but that in consideration of the Hardships they have suffered for want of a secure settlement, His Majestys Ministers and Council will compassionate those His faithful Subjects;

Who, in the first year their arrival willingly and cheerfully sent Three Hundred men to the expedition against Canada, & afterwards to the Assistance of Albani which was threatened by the French and Indians, for which service they have never received One Penny tho' they were upon the Establishment of New York or New Jersey nor had they received on Penny of the five pounds per head promised at their going on board from England. Neither have their commanders received anything of the allowance of fifteen pounds per Annum, and tho' the arms they had given them at the Canada expedition which were by special order from Her late Majesty, to be left in their possession, have been taken from them, yet they are still ready to fight against all the enemies of His Majesty & those countrys whenever there shall be occasion to shew their hearty endeavors for the prosperity of their generous Benefactors in England as well as in America.

Therefore they hope from the Justice of the Right Honble the Lords Commissioners of Trade and Plantations, to whom their Petition to their Excellencies the Lords Justices has been referred That they shall be so supported by their Lordships Report, as to be represented fit objects to be secured in the Land they now do inhabit or in some near adjoining lands remaining in the right of the Crown in the said Province of New York.

Source:

The Germans in America, 1607-1970: A Chronology & Fact Book, compiled and edited by Howard B. Furer. Dobbs Ferry, NY: Oceana Publications, 1973. pp. 87-88.

*T*he German Society of New York served thousands of German immigrants coming to the United States. The goal of the organization was to provide for immigrants who came to the country without family or friends, who may have been in need of medical attention, or initial financial assistance. The 1840s were difficult times in Germany: there was revolution within the German Confederation, a depression had seriously impeded industrial expansion, and crop failures had resulted in a major famine throughout Europe. The Zollverein, or Customs Union, came into existence in 1834 and not only served to achieve commercial unification within the German Confederation, but also made it much easier for movement in and out of the German harbors of Bremen and Hamburg. This made emigration more feasible for the poor Germans as well as the rich. Between 1834 and 1900, some five million German immigrants came to America. In 1847 alone, the German Society of New York recorded over 70,000 immigrants in its books.

As the following document points out, many Germans arrived in America with resources. They often saved money and had agricultural skills, mechanical skills, or education. Many Germans were not driven to emigrate by poverty, but came to America to preserve their family and economic traditions, such as farming and the management of small shops, which were more difficult to maintain in an industrialized Germany. Chain migration was common, whereby a family who had come to America wrote letters of encouragement to family and friends in Germany. This group would bring others to the country and they would create a community. The German Society of New York took credit for helping reduce the cost to the State of New York's Commissioners of Emigration for immigrants by providing several types of services to the immigrants. These services included the provision of free medical care for the German poor, provided by the German physicians in New York and Brooklyn. The Society pointed out that German immigrants came to the Society first because they spoke their language. If they did not find the help necessary, they turned to the German community.

The sheer numbers of German immigrants and their needs strained the resources of the community and of the society itself. Therefore, in this proposal before the New York Legislature, the German Society of the City of New York asked that an act be passed requiring the Commissioners of Emigration to pay the German Society a certain amount each year, equal to half the sum of voluntary contributions, to help support their efforts.

The following was originally published in "Memorial of the Officers of the German Society of the City of New York to the New York State Legislature, Demanding a Share of the Head Tax Receipts," New York Assembly Document, No. 165, 1848.

THE GERMAN SOCIETY OF NEW YORK—1848

The memorial of the undersigned officers of the German Society of the city of New York respectfully showeth:

That the immigration from Germany at this port during the last year, was greater then that from any other country, while the expenditures arising therefrom, which had to be borne by the Commissioners of Emigration, were trifling in comparison with the great burden thrown upon said Commissioners by the immigration from other countries.

According to the report of said Commissioners, submitted to the Honorable the Legislature of the State of New York, there arrived at this port from the 5th of May to the 31st of December, 1847, 129,069 immigrant passengers, of whom 53,180 were natives of Germany, 52,946 were native of Ireland and 22,943 were natives of other countries.

The number of those who became chargeable to the Commissioners was 10,422 and the amount expended for their support was, from the commutation fund, $65,317.44; from the hospital fund, $82,829.87; in all, $148,147.31. Which sum, divided by the above number of those for whose sake it was expended, say 10,422, shows the average cost of each to have been $14.21 1/2.

The report of the Commissioners does not state distinctly how many of said 10,422 persons whom they had to support were Germans, inasmuch as it includes 3,416 persons admitted into the marine hospital from ship board, without mentioning places of nativity; but your memorialists believe the Germans among said 3,416 persons were proportionately not more numerous than among those sent to the hospital from the city. The number thus sent was 2,802, of whom 196 were Germans; hence,

of the 3,416 admitted from ship board, 238 were Germans. Adding these 238 to the number enumerated as natives of Germany, in Table B, appended to the Report of the Commissioners of Emigration, it appears that the total number of Germans, who became chargeable to the Commissioners, out of an immigration of 53,180, was 872.

Your memorialists feel confident that this estimate is quite large enough and that they may safely refer to the Commissioners of Emigration themselves for the correctness of this view. In fact the latter will readily admit that the patients sent to the marine hospital from ship board were almost exclusively natives of Ireland, and assuming 238 to have been Germans, is a larger number than should fairly be allowed. But your memorialists desire to be on the safe side, and prefer, if err they must to do so to their own disadvantage.

Your Honorable Body is aware that the tax collected from emigrant passengers is one dollar from each, commutation money, and fifty cents from each, hospital money. Hence the money collected from 53,180 Germans, at $1.50 each, is $79,770.00. The expenditures for the support of 872 Germans, who became chargeable, at $14.21 1/2 each, is $12,395.48. And thus the surplus of receipts over expenditures of the German immigration at this port, is $67,374.52.

The number of immigrants, other than Germans was 75,889, and the hospital and commutation money collected from them, at $1.50 each, was $113,833.50. Of these 75,889 immigrants, 9,550 became chargeable to the Commissioners, at a cost of $14.21 1/2 each, amounting in the aggregate to

$135,753.25, showing an excess of expenditures over receipts of $21,919.75.

Thus then it is shown by the Report of the Commissioners of Emigration that the receipts from immigrant passengers, natives of Germany, overran the expenditure caused by the same, $67,374.52, while on the other hand the receipts from the immigrants from other countries a loss of $21,919.75.

This result is no doubt principally owing to the fact that the immigrants from Germany arrived in better condition than the great mass of those from other countries, but it would be incorrect to take this fact as a full and satisfactory explanation of the remarkable disparity. Your memorialists feel convinced, and beg leave to show, that in a great degree it is brought about by the working of the German Society.

The German immigrant, on his arrival here, if he requires assistance, does not call on the Commissioners of Emigration, but at the place where his native language is spoken, he calls on the German Society; and the German Society does not send him to the office of the Commissioners (except in extraordinary cases) because the Commissioners have made it a rule to grant relief only in their own institutions. But ample proof is daily furnished by the visitors of our Society, that it is next to impossible to induce the German immigrant voluntarily to become an inmate of those institutions; he will rather submit to actual suffering, and thus, ignorance of the language of the country, and the dread of the alms-house, which the German looks upon as a sort of penitentiary, throw the chief burden of the indigent German immigration on the German Society, and the latter, by the force of a portion of the expenses, which, by the act of May 5, 1847, "concerning passengers in vessels coming to the city of New York," are intended to fall on the Commissioners of Emigration. For the truth of this, your memorialists may confidently refer to the Commissioners themselves.

The enormous immigration at this port from Germany, which, during the year of 1847, according to the books kept at the office of the German Society, amounted to 70,735 persons, proves a serious burden to the citizens of German origin. It will be readily admitted that among such a mass of people there must be many having neither friends nor relatives among the resident Germans, but requiring medical as well as pecuniary assistance.

As already stated, the suffering and needy will in the first place apply to the German Society, but failing to receive all the aid they require, they will throw themselves, not on the Commissioners of Emigration, but on the sympathy of their countrymen, and these cannot possibly resist the appeal. Hence it is that the indigent and suffering German immigration proves a constant and daily increasing tax upon all the resident Germans, and this explains the circumstance, that out of 10,000 German voters, only about 500 are members of the German Society. It is not an unfriendly feeling towards the society which prevents so many from joining the same, but the consciousness of doing enough without contributing towards its funds. On the other hand, the society feels keenly the absence of that general co-operation which it would enjoy, but for the reasonable objection urged by so many of its well wishers.

There are now 58 persons actively engaged in carrying on the business of the society, viz: 15 members of the executive council, 17 physicians, 24 district visitors and 2 employees in the agency office. The services of all are gratuitous, with the exception of the agent and his clerk, who receive salaries. The total expenditures during the last twelve months was $7,823.10, which sufficed to afford substantial and adequate relief to 3,721 deserving applicants, while the agency procured employment to 4,743 persons. Your memorialists would say that it would be impossible to accomplish a greater amount of good with equally limited means.

There is one channel through which the German Society is constantly endeavoring to extend the sphere of its benevolent action, which your memorialists take leave to notice more particularly. This is an arrangement with the regular German physicians of New York and Brooklyn, now numbering about twenty, by which the latter are represented in the board of officers of the society, and take charge of all the sick German poor, attending them gratuitously, the society paying for medicines, nurses, etc. According to the last annual report of the society, its physicians, during the last twelve months, prescribed medicines in 2,808 cases, and had under treatment, for account of the society, 714 patients. Considering that the inmates of the hospitals under the control of the Commissioners of Emigration cost $14.21 1/2 each, it will not be deemed extravagant on the part of your memorialists to say that the medical department of the German Society has saved the city and the Commissioners of Emigration many thousand dollars.

But the extraordinary exertions made by the society during the last twelve months have exhausted its means and it is now threatened with the prospect of having to suspend its usefulness. Your memorialists, therefore, compelled by the embarrassing condition of the society, and in consideration of its being so efficient an auxilliary to the Commissioners of Emigration, venture to ask your honorable body for aid, and they also venture to hope their prayer will be satisfactorily responded to on the ground that the German immigrant, as shown in the beginning of this "Memorial," has not derived the same amount of benefit from the operation of the act of May 5, 1847, as the emigrant from other countries, having in fact furnished the means by which not his own wants but those of others have been relieved.

It is not the intention of your memorialists, nor the object of their prayer, to relieve the members of the German Society from the claims on them to keep alive, and if possible, to enlarge the springs of private charity; and the prayer of your memorialists is this:

That an act be passed requiring the Commissioners of Emigration to pay to the treasurer of the German Society for its use, the sum of ——— dollars, and further authorizing aid commissioners to pay annually to said treasurer on or before the 1st of March of every year an amount equal to one-half the sum of voluntary contributions, collected during the preceding twelve months from the members of said society, so long as said commissioners can satisfy themselves that the German Society has a fair claim to such support, and provided, also, the such annual payment shall not exceed the sum of $3,000; these payments to be made out of the Commutation Fund.

Source:

The Germans in America, 1607-1970: A Chronology & Fact Book, compiled and edited by Howard B. Furer. Dobbs Ferry, NY: Oceana Publications, 1973. pp. 113-116.

Celebrating the arrival of a new year has been a popular festival for people from all over the world since nearly the beginning of civilization. Long before Americans developed the custom of donning tuxedos and black dresses, gathering in Times Square, and un-corking a chilled bottle of champagne there were less formal customs. Some earlier civilizations celebrated the new year's festival by symbolically or actually killing off the old king and anointing the new. Others customs involved sacrificing animals.

There are, in fact, a multitude of ways in which people inaugurate a new year. Jewish Americans, who celebrate the new year on September 16th, share an apple dipped in honey with some round challah bread. The Chinese, who celebrate the new year on February 10th, hold elaborate feasts, ignite fireworks, and have parades. Other customs include eating a piece of herring or some black-eyed peas which is supposed to bring wealth. In Greece and among Greek Americans there is a tradition of baking bread with a coin in it and cutting it up like a pie. The person who gets the coin will have good luck in the coming year. In Africa, where music plays a big roll in cultural life, drummers play in the streets the entire day in honor of the coming year. In Switzerland large cow bells are used to ring in the year. The ominous tone resonates throughout the villages and is supposed to purge the previous year's evil spirits.

The Romans celebrated the coming of the new year before the birth of Christ. According to Janine Roberts, co-author of Rituals For Our Times, the Romans named the month of January after the God Janus who had both a forward-looking and a backward-looking face. The tradition of drinking alcohol dates back to old European times which represented casting off the chaos of the previous year, according to Tad Tuleja, author of Curious Customs.

Early German-Americans celebrated the flipping of the Gregorian calendar by chanting a hymn after which a group of men would fire guns in the air. The tradi-

tions of setting off pyrotechnics as well as the expression "bringing in the new year with a bang," undoubtedly owe their origin to this German-American ritual. A group of twelve men, presumably one for each month of the year, would approach a random home and, after chanting a brief but eloquent verse, would discharge their rifles in the air. The proprietors would subsequently invite the "Christmas Shooters" into their home for "sausage as big as a stove pipe," "cake as big as a barn door," and hard cider.

The content of the hymn can be loosely described as an appeal to God to end the misery of war and other forms of suffering on earth. The hymn ends with a request for permission from God to "shoot in the new year for him" after which the soldiers say, "Since we hear no complain, You shall hear our shot."

GREETING THE NEW YEAR

New Year's festivals once included rites which were supposed to ward off the barrenness of winter and insure the return of spring with its fertility. In pre-Christian times among certain peoples, these midwinter rites included the actual or symbolic killing of the king of the old year and the welcoming of a new king. Sometimes a sacred animal was sacrificed, to be replaced by a new one; sometimes a scapegoat, upon whom the sins of the tribe were visited, was driven out to wander or die. New Year's in America, which occurs at the midpoint of the Twelve Days of Christmas and aside from Christmas itself is the most festive celebration of this joyous season, brings to the Christ-Mass many pagan vestiges: the veneration of evergreens, the burning of the yule log and kindling of new fires, indulgence in sexual license and intoxicating drink, processions of mummers and maskers, ritualistic combat between opposing parties, and the pledging of good resolves in order to redeem the bad behavior of the past.

Our German forefathers had a custom of saluting the incoming New Year. They exchanged visits of greeting on the night wherein the Old Year ended, and the New Year began. Parties would be formed, to deliver these greetings to the families in the neighborhood. An hour before midnight their calls began, and were continued till towards morning. Usually a few guns were taken along to fire the salutes. Musicians, if any such were in the neighborhood, took their flutes and violins along, to accompany the New Year's hymn, sung before the door. One of the party committed and delivered the address (*Spruch*). This usually consisted of a New Year's hymn, to which a few original sentences were added, to suit the occasion. Sometimes the custom led to scenes of rioting and drunkenness, disgrace-

ful to the neighborhood, and through an imprudent use of firearms, disastrous to the guilty parties.

A venerable friend informs us, that fifty years ago he occasionally helped to salute his neighbors with a New Year's greeting. In the dead of night they quietly approached a home. After each had gently taken his place before the chamber window, where the parents slept, the spokesman, with a solemn voice, recited the beautiful New Year's hymn:

Nun lasst uns gehn and treten
Mit Singen und mit Beten
Zum Herrn, der unserm Leben
Bis hieher Kraft gegeben.
Wir gehn dahin und wandern
Von einem Jahr zum ander;
Wir leben und godeihen,
Vom alten zu dem neuen.
Durch so viel Angst und Plagen,
Durch Zittern und durch Zagen,
Durch Krieg and grosse Schrecken,
Die alle Welt bedecken.

Now let us go
Singing and praying
To the Lord, who up to now
Has given power to our lives.
We walk along and wander
From one year to the other,
We live and grow
From the old (year) to the new,
Through so much anguish and torment,
In fear and trembling,
Through war and great terrors
Which cover the entire world.

At the close of the hymn the speaker continued:

Damit will ich mein Wunsch beschliessen
Und euch das Neue Jahr anschiessen.
Wann es euch aber sollt verdriesen,
So müsst ihr's sagen, ehe wir schiessen,—
Indem wir hören kein Verdruss,
So sollt ihr hören unsern Schuss.

With this I want to close my wish
And shoot in the New Year for you.
But if it should annoy you
Just say so before we shoot—
Since we hear no complaint,
You shall hear our shot.

And then a dozen guns were pointed skyward. The leader's command, "ready," "aim," "fire," was followed by an ill-concerted discharge of arms. For in those peaceful days, the country had no well-drilled warriors yet. Noise enough the firing made, which brought all the children out of bed in one leap. The horses and cattle in the stables sprang to their feet, and the frightened poultry on their roost set up a great cackling.

By this time the door was opened, and the greeters invited to enter. Hard cider, cakes, pies and all manner of delicacies were set before them. After singing a few more hymns, they proceeded on their mirthful tour.. . .

A few lines we remember of the *Spruch* [speech] in the neighborhood of our boyhood home:

Ein glück-seliges Neues Jahr,
Eine Brathwurst wie ein Ofen-rohr,
Ein Kuchen wie ein Scheuer Thor

A happy New Year,
A Sausage as (big as) a stovepipe,
A cake as (big as) a barn door.

Source:

Pennsylvania Dutchman, V (January 1, 1954), 3. Reprinted from "New Year's Eve" by B. Bausman, which first appeared in *The Guardian*, Philadelphia, January 1868.

When World War I (1914-1918) broke out—but before the United States entered the war in 1917—a number of German Americans not only continued to celebrate their heritage but made no secret of their devotion to the German cause in the war against France and Great Britain. In the 1910s, Germans were by far the largest group with strong foreign ties in the United States (those who were within only one or two generations of having immigrated). Of some 32 million people falling into this category, Germans and German-speaking Austrians accounted for about 10 million. They often faced intense hostility from other Americans—especially Americans of English descent—who questioned the German Americans' loyalty to the United States. They were frequently attacked in newspapers and popular magazines such as Life, which printed this nativist cartoon and song in 1918.

President Woodrow Wilson (1856-1924) and former president Theodore Roosevelt (1858-1919), who disagreed on many fundamental national policy issues, both condemned the perpetuation of German culture in America. In fact, it was Roosevelt who coined the expression "hyphenated Americans" to express his displeasure of groups that, in his opinion, held on to their cultural traditions and refused to assimilate into American society. For his part, Wilson, despite urging Americans to be "impartial in thought as well as in action," was suspicious both of the Allies and of Germany. But Wilson turned decidedly against Germany after that nation's U-boats began sinking U.S. ships (which, in the opinion of Germany, should not have ventured into a war zone) and especially after the infamous Zimmermann telegram (named for the German ambassador to Mexico) was intercepted and published in a U.S. newspaper. The Zimmermann telegram called for a military alliance between Mexico and Germany, for which Mexico would be rewarded with the acquisition of Texas, New Mexico, and Arizona in the event of war with the United States.

After Wilson won a declaration of war from Congress in April of 1917, he proved adept at organizing public opinion against Germany and Germans generally. His Committee of Public Information (CPI) produced such films as The Kaiser: The Beast of Berlin, an attack on the emperor of Germany, and distributed 75 million copies of pamphlets in several languages explaining American motives in the war and decrying Germany's.

The deep-seated hatreds that the war aroused compelled many German Americans to change their names. Common German words were changed (albeit only for a short time); thus, for example, sauerkraut became "liberty cabbage." German businesses were crippled, and their social organizations were threatened. The very existence of the German-language press was put in doubt. In one notorious episode, a mob of 500 people stripped a German American man near St. Louis, Missouri, bound him in an American flag, and lynched him.

MY COUNTRY, 'TIS OF THEE

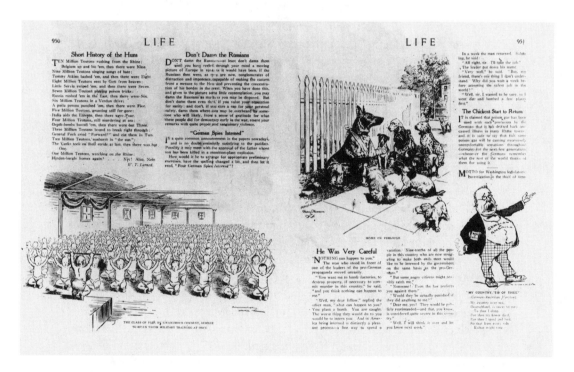

Source:

Originally published in *Life*, 1918. Courtesy of
Library of Congress.

World War I (1914-1918) was a devastating global conflict that threatened the balance of power in Europe and drew in Asia, Africa, and the Americas before its tenuous resolution at Versailles. At the center of the conflict were two groups of alliances in Europe: the "Central Powers," which included Germany and Austria-Hungary; and the "Allies," which included Britain, France, and Russia. During the early stages of "The Great War," to which it was referred at the time, Germany invaded France, which resulted in brutal trench warfare at the Marne River. The trench warfare would continue for three years and result in the loss of millions of lives.

The Germans, who fought aggressively during the trench warfare, were the subject of propaganda campaigns issued by the French and British. The propaganda campaigns were designed, in part, to draw the United States and other countries into the war on the side of the Allies. The two nations dropped thousands of flyers from airplanes to neutral nations describing alleged atrocities committed by German soldiers. One particularly graphic flyer suggested that the Germans were tossing up babies and catching them atop their bayonets. In reality both sides engaged in drastic measures in an effort to gain leverage during the stalemate. The propaganda campaigns, although exaggerated, misleading, and sometimes altogether false, were successful in depicting the Germans as ruthless killers. The propaganda campaigns as well as Germany's use of U-boats (submarines) to sink three U.S. merchant ships, not only drew the United States into the war but also helped foster anti-German sentiments in the United States which would prove difficult to reverse.

In an effort to encourage patriotism on behalf of the war effort the federal and state governments began to proliferate their own propaganda campaign against the Germans. The propaganda efforts included attempts to ban the sale of German newspapers, prevent advertisers from using the German language, and revoke the charters in German American communities. In addition, studying the German language was banned from study in many public schools. Some schools even burned German textbooks. So thoroughly was the propaganda rhetoric absorbed into the American psyche that people began questioning the sanity of Germanic peoples.

World War II exacerbated the American public's view of Germans as the world witnessed the worst war time travesty in history—the Holocaust. The systematic extermination of six million Jews in Europe confirmed many Americans' suspicions about the nature of Germans even though most German Americans denounced the atrocities committed by the Nazis. Hollywood has done little to ameliorate the German stereotype. Some Germans feel that the motion picture industry only portrays Germans in two ways: as mad scientists or Nazis. Michael Medved, an author and critic for PBS, explains that "the German has emerged as a convenient symbol for evil or mad brilliance. When a film calls for somebody sinister, or a crazed genius, the producers will create a German character every time." Steven Spielberg, arguably, tempered the German stereotype with his 1993 adaptation of Thomas Kenealy's Schindler's List. The film depicts the poignant struggle of German millionaire Oskar Schindler, an otherwise callous opportunist, to save 1000 Polish Jews during the Holocaust. However, the image of Germans as ruthless killers contrived during World War I has altered Americans' perception of Germans and is indicative of the detrimental side-effects of war time propaganda campaigns.

This piece was originally published in Julius Drachsler's Democracy and Assimilation: The Blending of Immigrant Heritage in America (New York, 1920).

ANTI-GERMAN FEELING IN AMERICA—1917

The declaration of war by Congress seemed to have silenced all dissenting voices. Henceforth there was only one goal for all loyal Americans, a complete and crushing victory over the arrogant German war-machine. Among the immigrants, the psychological characteristics of the pre-war period were brought into still stronger relief. Organization of "loyalty leagues" grew apace. Passage of resolutions of "unflinching loyalty to our country, the United States of America" became part of the regular order of business of every immigrant social organization. Spontaneous requests were made by Czecho-Slovaks, Poles, Jews, Armenians, to the government to organize foreign legions as distinct fighting units in the American army, while the international composition of the American expeditionary forces was pointed out as proof of the unanimity of spirit among the native and the foreign born. Relief campaigns for sufferers in the war zones were inaugurated on a scale unimaginable before the War.

Nor were patriotic societies, and the government slow to take advantage of the rising tide of feeling among the foreign-born and to harness this dynamic sentiment to urgent national tasks that had to be carried through as pre-conditions of final victory.

Simultaneously with these positive efforts to awaken and stiffen the will to fight to the bitter end, there developed a definite anti-German propaganda throughout the country. The slow, but relentless coercion of a changing public opinion manifested itself in all degrees of suppression. Sensitive citizens, bearing unmistakable "American" names. Local communities rechristened streets and avenues, business concerns and social welfare agencies appealed to their clients and patrons in the name of the "new management." But these self-imposed metamorphoses were, after all, only superficial and mild in their effects. Much more stringent were the attempts to have Federal and State authorities revoke the charters of incorporated German-American societies; to have municipalities prohibit the sale of German papers by barring them from news-stands; to persuade advertisers not to use the German language press; to prevail upon news-dealers not to sell these publications; to hold mass-meetings to stir up sentiment in favor of a press in the English language only. This hostile attitude towards the German language and German culture was clearly reflected in the action of the State and local school authorities of almost forty States of the Union. German was either banished from the curricula of many public schools and high schools by direct order of the educational authorities, or by the refusal of students to elect it as a language study where they had the option to do so. The effort was made to stimulate interest in other languages as substitutes, such as Spanish and French. Text books, magazines or newspaper publications were sedulously censored or excluded from the schools, lest they might serve as channels of insidious German propaganda. In one city the German texts were not only taken from the students but "tons of the volumes were burned as though they were under the ban." Another community "not only put the German text books out of the schools but provided cans in the principals streets, where pupils and the public might throw all the volumes they wished to have destroyed."

As the war-fever rose, serious doubts began to be expressed by many earnest citizens as to the sanity of the German people in permitting the awful carnage to go on at such a fearful cost to themselves. An enterprising student of national psychology even suggested in a letter to the editor of a metropolitan daily, the appointment of a scientific commission to study the "German type of mind."

Source:

The Germans in America, 1607-1970: A Chronology & Fact Book, compiled and edited by Howard B. Furer. Dobbs Ferry, NY: Oceana Publications, 1973. pp. 133-134.

In a 1930s interview, German American Judge Faudie describes a life frequently on the move, from one region of his new country, America, to another searching for a better life. Faudie was born in Legelhurst of Baden Germany in December of 1851 during a period of national political instability. His father, a German farmer who raised wheat, barley, hemp, fruit and clover, died in Faudie's youth. Subsequently, young Faudie traveled to France and worked as a linen weaver until joining the German army at age 20. German leader Kaiser Wilhelm I at the time was busily suppressing the rapidly rising socialist working class. Many Germans were leaving their country simply to avoid serving in the army during this period of social unrest. Following an early release from service, young Faudie similarly chose to seek greater freedom by immigrating to America.

New Orleans had remained a common entry point for Germans since the French had attempted to colonize Louisiana in the early eighteenth century using German immigrants. The latter nineteenth century saw an expanded German immigration to the United States in which over 750,000 migrated in the 1870s. Faudie, immigrating with many others from Baden, arrived in New Orleans on board a steamer ship in early 1873.

Much was new to young Faudie as he moved about in the South, Midwest, and West Coast. Faust marveled over the American Southern black culture in Louisiana and Arkansas and the Chinese workers he encountered in California. In 1890 he and his wife moved to Texas settling in a German settlement near the town of Perry. After his first wife died, he married another German American. Faudie had 14 children.

Faudie proudly recalled the early history of Texas Germans, the role they played in the Texas Revolution against Mexico and subsequent service of German Americans in various U.S. wars. Faudie proclaimed,

> *I have become an American citizen long ago, and was glad that my boys could serve this country of my adoption . . . to help pay the debt that the Americans owed to France (for being its support in the American Revolution), even if we were not here in those early days (of the nation). In my wanderings in America have not found any place that has been equal to this central part of (Texas) where I have lived ever since I came here in 1890.*

GERMAN JUDGE FAUDIE

"I was born in Legelhurst, in Baden, Germany on the first day of December 1851. My father's name was George Faudie, he was a farmer and raised wheat, barley, hemp, fruit and clover and had some cattle and horses. He worked oxen to the plow. He died when I was two years old and my mother married again, she had four boys and one girl.

"When I was in my 'teens I went to France and worked as a linen weaver until I was twenty years old. Then I had to serve in the army in Germany.

We were supposed to serve three years. I served one year and received four cents a day and my board. This did not buy my clothes so after a year of service I got a furlough and went on a visit to my mother. When I reached home there was a couple going to America, and I told my mother that if I had the money I would go too.

"She made some arguments and gave me enough to pay my fare to the new country of America where we were told that we could have freedom to live our lives as we wished. My ship fare was about twenty dollars in money (American). We took an old merchant ship from France and changed to a steamer in Liverpool bound for America. It took us six weeks to arrive at New Orleans, we arrived there the 9th, day of April 1873. When I reached New Orleans I found many strange sights.

"The strangest sight that greeted me was the Negroes unloading the ships at the wharves. They seemed to be very happy as they worked, they would sing songs in a low tone, so different to the songs of my native land that I was thrilled by them. I remember one song that they sang which was something like this,

"Happy darkies workin' on de levee,
Happy darkies workin' on de levee,
Happy darkies workin' on de levee,
Waitin' for de steamboats to come down.
What is dat I hear a whistlin' loud an' clear?
O O—O— O— O— O ah—a!
I think hit is de Natchett or de Robert Lee.
Come along an' jine our ban'
An' how happy we will be.

"Well I did not join their ban' but instead I got a job as ice man. My boss's name was Rothschild, he taught me the city and the ice route. When I took the ice into the stores and the saloons I had to take a drink with him, first he, and then myself would treat to the drinks. After I learned the route it was turned over to me and so I kept this job until one of my friends from the old country came, on his way to Illinois to live with an uncle, so I went with him and worked for his uncle who owned a brick yard. I worked in his brick yard until I finally left and went down into Arkansas.

"When we went to Illinois we took a steamboat and went up the Mississippi River to Grandtower. It took us four days to make the trip and cost us three dollars each. We stayed on the deck and did not take a berth. This was in the summer of 1834 and I married my boss daughter, her name was Elizabeth Erhardt. When we went to get the license we had to take my boss partner to prove that she was old enough to marry and that her parents gave their consent. She was only fifteen years old.

"We were married by the County Judge in Murfreesboro, Ill. We went home and her parents gave us a big wedding supper with all kinds of good things to eat and wine and beer to drink. This was in 1875 and we lived there two years. I had been working in a rock quarry and it went out of business and some friend moved to Arkansas and we decided to go with him. So we hitched up our teams to our

wagon and drove down to Oceola Arkansas. It took me six weeks to make the trip, for the roads were rough and rocky and when we would have to go up a hill we would have to unload and carry our things in our arms some of the time. When we crossed the Arkansas River we had to ford it.

"There were so many hills that one of my horses got loose from us and could not be found. That left me with just two horses. When we reached Mississippi County, Arkansas we rented some land from an Irishman. The next spring it rained so hard that the whole country was under water and when I went anywhere I had to go in boats for some time after the rains, had to haul our fuel, wood and coal in boats and had bad times all that spring. So finally it was getting to be summer time.

"When the summer came I took the malarial fever and so had to have Negroes to finish my crop. You will remember that I had never seen any Negroes to amount to anything except when I reached New Orleans, and I was amused to hear them sing of their work as they did. I was told that before the war between the states that the burden of their song was freedom, but now after the war was over they would sing of their work and to me it was a source of amusement. I lay on my bed of illness and from my window I could hear their voices as they sang,

"I'se goin' from de cotton field,
I'se goin' from de cane,
I'se goin' from de little log hut
Dat sets up in de lane.
Dey tell me up in Kansas,
So many miles away,
Dey tell me up dere, honey,
Dey're gettin' bettah pay.

"Much as I loved the South I had to go back to Illinois to get well so in the year I farmed in Arkansas I had to go to the hospital in St Louis to get treated for the malaria and when the doctors told me to leave the malarial country I took my wife and two children and went to Jacksonville and lived there until 1888. About this time there was a boom on in California and I joined a company of emigrants and went to this state and worked in a rock and stone quarry.

"Where the people use the Negro labor in the south, in California they use the Chinese. There were four white men who were foreman and each white man had from twenty to thirty Chinamen working under him. The white men were paid $1.75 a day and the Chinese were paid a dollar a day. They were good workers but it was hard to make them understand what we wanted them to do.

"After the boom was over in California the people commenced to talk about Texas, there were men there boosting Texas so we decided, my family and myself, to come and see if Texas was what it was advertise to be, rich land, and plenty of it and cheap as well. So we came to Waco Texas on the train and I met a man by the name of Torrance on the square and rented a place from him near Axtell Texas, made a crop, but there was pasture land joining my place and the stock got into it and destroyed my crop, so I left this lace place and found one in the German settlement near Perry Texas.

"It seemed that my bad luck had at last left me and I bought land in this community in 1895 and paid $20.00 an acre for it. We were in the Alexander school settlement, two miles from Perry, had two churches, the Lutheran and the Methodist, Rev. Schuler was the Methodist preacher I believe at one time, and later lived in Waco. There was fine hunting and fishing up and down the Brazos bottom and plenty of wild game out on the prairie.

"My wife died in 1904 and in 1905 I married Mrs Ernestine Hamburg. I had fourteen children, eight lived to be grown. Two sons, Charlie and August went to the World War. Charlie died soon after he returned. August was in France, and was in the army of occupation after the war closed. They paid my debt for me to the old country, I never went back to serve my time in the army, for had I gone I might have been punished as well as had to serve it out.

"I have become an American citizen long ago, and was glad that my boys could serve this country of my adoption when they crossed, to help pay the debt that the Americans owed to France, even if we were not here in those early days. In my wanderings in America have not found any place that has been equal to this central part of the state where I have lived ever since I came here in 1890.

"As I understand it the German settlers assumed the duties and the responsibilities of American citizenship. They took part in the Texas Revolution, the war against Mexico, the War Between the States, the Spanish-American War, and the World War, thus proving their loyalty to their adopted country."

Source:

Library of Congress. *American Life Histories: Manuscripts from the Federal Writers' Project, 1936-1940* from the American Memory website (http://memory.loc.gov/ammem/wpaintro/wpa-home.html).

W*hen the Nazi regime came to power in Germany in 1933, it launched racial policies that ultimately climaxed in genocide. The immediate targets were opponents of the regime and the German Jews. The Nuremburg laws passed in 1934 consigned Jews to a pariah caste. As the severity of the repression grew, so did the number of refugees. A formidable obstacle to their coming to America was the quota restrictions imposed in 1924. An eloquent spokesman for modification of these obstacles was the German-born Senator Robert Wagner (1877-1953) of New York. The architect of New Deal welfare legislation, he was a liberal voice. He was joined by George Cardinal Mundelein (1872-1939) of Chicago, the son of German immigrants who vigorously denounced Hitler. The appeal to admit children carefully aimed to avoid arguments against admitting refugees such as their "becoming public charges, or dislocating American industry or displacing American labor." As it turned out, Congress refused to admit the children. It convinced Wagner that Congress would not act to reduce the catastrophe overtaking the European Jews.*

WAGNER/NOURSE ROGERS BILL

ADMISSION OF GERMAN REFUGEE CHILDREN

Mr. WAGNER. I introduce a joint resolution and ask that it may be properly referred and printed in the Record, together with an explanatory statement and a statement by a number of distinguished clergymen.

The VICE PRESIDENT. Without objection, the joint resolution introduced by the Senator from New York will be received, properly referred, and, together with the statements referred to, printed in the Record.

The joint resolution (S. J. Res. 64) to authorize the admission into the United States of a limited number of German refugee children was read twice by its title, referred to the Committee on Immigration, and ordered to be printed in the Record, as follows:

Whereas there is now in progress a world-wide effort to facilitate the emigration from Germany of men, women, and children of every race and creed suffering from conditions which compel them to seek refuge in other lands; and

Whereas the most pitiful and helpless sufferers are children of tender years; and

Whereas the admission into the United States of a limited number of these children can be accomplished without any danger of their becoming public charges, or dislocating American industry or displacing American labor; and

Whereas such action by the United States would constitute the most immediate and practical contribution by our liberty-loving people to the cause of human freedom, to which we are inseverably bound by our institutions, our history, and our profoundest sentiments: Now, therefore, be it

Resolved, etc., That not more than 10,000 immigration visas may be issued during each of the calendar years 1939 and 1940, in addition to those authorized by existing law and notwithstanding any provisions of law regarding priorities or preferences, for the admission into the United States of children 14 years of age or under, who reside, or at any time since January 1, 1933, have resided, in any territory now incorporated in Germany, and who are otherwise eligible: Provided, That satisfactory assurances are given that such children will be supported and properly cared for through the voluntary action of responsible citizens of responsible private organizations of the United States, and consequently will not become public charges.

The statements presented by Mr. Wagner are as follows:

The joint resolution I have just introduced authorizes the admission into the United States of 10,000 German refugee children of every race and creed, during each of the calendar years 1939 and 1940.

Millions of innocent and defenseless men, women, and children in Germany today, of every race and creed, are suffering from conditions which compel them to seek refuge in other lands. Our hearts go out especially to the children of tender years, who are the most pitiful and helpless sufferers. The admission of a limited number of these children into the United States would release them from the prospect of a life without hope and without recourse, and enable them to grow up in an environment where the human spirit may survive and prosper.

This resolution does not suspend existing quota restrictions on the immigration of adults. It merely authorizes the admission during a limited period of a limited number of refugee children, 14 years of age or under. This could readily be accomplished without their becoming public charges and without any danger of dislocating American industry or displacing American labor. Their admission would be predicated on satisfactory and voluntary undertakings by responsible American citizens or private organizations that adequate provision would be made for their maintenance and care in homes of their own faiths.

Thousands of American families have already expressed their willingness to take refugee children into their homes. Recently 49 of the outstanding Catholic and Protestant prelates of the United States, including His Eminence Cardinal Mundelein, joined in a statement urging our people to join together without regard to race, religion or creed in offering refuge to children as a token of our sympathy and as a symbol of our faith in the ideas of human brotherhood. Both branches of the labor movement have now joined in expressing sympathy for this objective.

Such action by the United States would follow the precedent of England and Holland, which have given sanctuary to many of these unfortunate victims of persecution. It would constitute our most immediate and practical contribution to the cause of human freedom, to which we are inseverably bound by our institutions, our history, and our profoundest sentiments. I have every confidence that there will be prompt and wholehearted response throughout the country to this noble cause, whereby the American people will give expression to their innermost cravings for liberty, justice, and international peace.

A Statement by Protestant And Catholic Clergymen of America

January 10, 1939.

The American people have made clear their reaction to the oppression of all minority groups, religious and racial, throughout Germany. They have been especially moved by the plight of the children. Every heart has been touched, and the nation has spoken out its sorrow and dismay through the voices of its statesmen, teachers, and religious leaders. Americans have felt that protest, however vigorous, and sympathy, however deep, are not enough, and that these must translate themselves into such action as shall justify faith.

We have been stirred by the knowledge that Holland and England have opened their doors and homes to many of these children. We conceive it to be our duty, in the name of the American tradition and the religious spirit common to our Nation, to urge the people, by its Congress and Executive, to express sympathy through special treatment of the young robbed of country, homes, and parents. A heartening token of the mood of America is to be found in the fact that thousands of Americans of all faiths have made known their eagerness to take these young children into their homes without burden or obligation to the State.

Working within and under the laws of Congress, through special enactment if necessary, the Nation can offer sanctuary to a part of these children by united expression of its will to help.

To us it seems that the duty of Americans in dealing with the youthful victims of a regime which punishes innocent and tender children as if they were offenders is to remember the monition of Him who said, "Suffer little children to come unto me." And in that spirit we call on all Americans to join together, without regard to race, religion, or creed, in offering refuge to children as a token of our sympathy and as a symbol of our faith in the ideals of human brotherhood.

Dr. Martin Anderson, Central Presbyterian Church, Denver, Colo.

Dr. Albert William Beaven, president of Colgate Rochester Divinity School, Rochester, N.Y.

Dr. Oscar F. Blackwelder, Lutheran Church of the Reformation, Washington, D.C.

Dr. Walter Russell Bowie, Grace Church, New York City.

Most Reverend John T. Cantwell, Archbishop of Los Angeles.

Dr. Samuel Cavert, executive secretary, Federal Council of Churches of Christ in America, New York City.

Dr. Allen Knight Chalmers, Broadway Tabernacle, 211 West Fifty-sixth Street, New York City.

Dr. Henry Sloane Coffin, Union Theological Seminary, New York City.

Dr. Henry Crane, Central Methodist Church, Detroit, Mich.

Bishop Ralph Cushman, Methodist Church, Denver, Colo.

Dr. Harry Emerson Fosdick, Riverside Church, New York City.

Rev. Graham Frank, First Christian Church, Dallas, Tex.

Rt. Rev. James Edward Freeman, Bishop of Washington, Washington, D.C.

Dr. Robert Freeman, Presbyterian Church, Pasadena, Calif.

Dr. Lewis W. Gobel, president, General Synod of Evangelical and Reformed Church, Chicago, Ill.

Dr. Louis Hartman, editor, Zion's Herald, Boston, Mass.

Dr. Ivan Lee Holt, St. Louis, Mo.

Rt. Rev. Edwin H. Hughes, Bishop of Washington area, Methodist Episcol Church, Washington, D.C.

Dr. Robert Scott Inglis, pastor emeritus of Third Presbyterian Church, Newark, N.J.

Dr. Edgar DeWitt Jones, Central Woodward Church, Detroit, Mich.

Dr. Meredith Ashby Jones, Atlanta, Ga.

Bishop Paul Bentley Kern, Methodist Episcopal Church South, Durham, N.C.

Rev. McIlyar H. Lichliter, First Congregational Church, Columbus, Ohio.

Dr. Mark Allison Matthews, First Presbyterian Church, Seattle, Wash.

Most Rev. Charles Hubert Le Blond, Bishop of St. Joseph, St. Joseph, Mo.

Rev. Oscar E. Maurer, moderator, National Council of Congregational-Christian Churches, New Haven, Conn.

Bishop Charles Mead, Methodist Episcopal Church, Kansas City, Mo.

Dr. Julius Valdemar Moldenhawer, First Presbyterian Church, New York City.

His Eminence George Cardinal Mundelein, Archbishop of Chicago, Chicago, Ill.

Rev. Roger T. Nooe, president, International Conventino of Disciples of Christ, Nashville, Tenn.

Rt. Rev. John O'Grady, secretary, National Conference of Catholic Charities.

Very Rev. Arthur A. O'leary, S. J., president, Georgetown University, Washington, D.C.

Rev. Joseph D. Ostermann, executive director, Committee for the Catholic Refugees from Germany.

Bishop G. Bromley Oxnam, Methodist Church, Omaha, Nebr.

Dr. Albert Wentworth Palmer, Chicago Theological Seminary, president, Chicago, Ill.

Rev. Daniel Alfred Poling, editor, Christian Herald and Christian Endeavor World, Baptist Temple, Philadelphia, Pa.

Dr. George W. Richards, president, Theological Seminary of the Reformed Church, Lancaster, Pa.

Most Rev. Joseph Francis Rummell, S. T. D., Archbishop of New Orleans, New Orleans, La.

Most Rev. James H. Ryan, S. T. D., Bishop of Omaha, Omaha, Nebr.

Rt. Rev. John Augustine Ryan, director, social action department, National Catholic Welfare Conference, Washington, D.C.

Rt. Rev. William Scarlett, Bishop of Missouri, Protestant Episcopal Church, St. Louis, Mo.

Dr. Avery A. Shaw, president, Denison University, Granville, Ohio.

Rev. Maurice S. Sheehy, head, department of religious education, Catholic University of America, Washington, D.C.

Most Rev. Bernard James Sheil, Auxiliary Bishop of Chicago, Ill.

Rt. Rev. Henry K. Sherrill, Bishop of Massachusetts, Protestant Episcopal Church, Boston, Mass.

Dr. Joseph Richard Sizoo, St. Nicholas Church, New York City.

Dr. Ralph W. Stockman, Christ's Methodist Episcopal Church, New York City.

Dr. Robert Elliott Speer, president of the board of trustees, Princeton Seminary, Princeton, N. J.

Dr. Anson Phelps Stokes, canon of Washington Cathedral, Washington, D.C.

Dr. John Timothy Stone, president, Presbyterian Theological Seminary, Chicago, Ill.

Dr. Howard Thurman, dean of chapel, Howard University, Washington, D.C.

Dr. Ezra Allen Van Nuys, Calvary Presbyterian Church, San Francisco, Calif.

Dr. John Anderson Vance, First Presbyterian Church, Detroit, Mich.

Source:
Wagner/Nourse Rogers Bill. February 9, 1939.

*C*hain migration, *by which people would decide to emigrate based on reports from friends and family already settled in a new land, was commonly used by Germans, including Fritz and Frieda Schmidt, seeking new homes in America. A 1930s interview chronicles the Schmidts' experiences. Fritz was born in the 1880s to a prosperous German merchant and Frieda was born nine years later. They married and Frieda gave birth to their only child in her native rural village located at the edge of the Black Forest during World War I. Following the war, many German soldiers, including Fritz, returned home to find the local economy in disarray as the Weimar Republic attempted to deal with war debt, inflation, and loss of territory. Receiving news from friends in the United States that the North Carolina region was well adapted to growing grapes, the Schmidts arranged for their move through a German*

emigration agency. Seen as a means to relieve population pressures and quell political unrest, emigration agencies had risen in popularity in the nineteenth century.

Though they spoke no English, the Schmidts arrived in America in the 1920s and settled. North Carolina was a region less commonly selected by German Americans than the Midwest or Texas. In recounting the difficulties in adjusting to their new home, Frieda spoke of initially missing the old country's cobbled community squares, community baking ovens, and living in centuries' old houses and villages. But through hard work and savings, they eventually purchased their own farm, planting cuttings brought from Germany. Their story was a one of fortitude, rebuilding a neat new cottage reflecting traditional German customs after a devastating fire.

Through the 1930s German Americans' interest in returning to Germany, even for a brief visit, waned as political upheaval wrought by Adolph Hitler became increasingly prevalent. Though the Schmidts sought to perpetuate traditional customs, their children more quickly adopted their new country's ways. To Fritz's dismay, their son chose not to carry on the family farm in the German tradition. As Frieda related, "Since his first success Fritz has planned that Friedrich should become his partner and successor. But his son now has the American idea of planning his own life. He has gone to work as an operator in a hosiery mill, meaning to learn the business by starting at the bottom. It is a blow to Fritz. Relations are strained between the father and son." Such were the stresses common to immigrant families.

THE SCHMIDTS

January 13, 1939

A winding road leads upward from the highway at Valkyria to the Schmidts' little house on the slope of Chieftain Mountain. A vineyard of 21 acres surrounds it, and in early autumn the air is sweet from the winepress and the vines. Fritz's winery had become famous, and sometimes he sells small lots of grapes to insistent visitors. He doesn't like to do that, as he nurses his treasured Black Hamburgs jealously for the wine because of their fine flavor and rich red color, but he is an amiable man not given to argument.

The vineyard crowds almost to the door of his neat cottage and only a very small space is saved for Frieda's little garden in the dooryard, where she has laid out patterns in field stone and flowers to make the cottage a picture from an old fairy tale. Down the mountain, rows of vines descend in tidy ranks.

The Schmidts have received final papers for American citizenship. They came from Germany in 1924.

Fritz was born in Wurzburg in 1884. His father, for whom he was named, was a prosperous merchant. Frieda is nine years younger than her husband and

was 21 when Friedrich, their only-child, was born during the first year of the World War in Frieda's native village on the edge of the Black Forest.

When Fritz returned from the War he found his family broken up and their money gone. He could not find work and his wife and child were hungry. Friends in the United States wrote of fine vinelands in the Thermal Belt of North Carolina and urged him to join them there. He made arrangements through a German emigration agency to finance the trip and left the Black Forest, as he thinks now, forever. Neither he nor Frieda knew a word of English.

Arriving in North Carolina, the little homesick, bewildered family were sponsored by Dr. Johannes von Hoff, an established vineyardist who was also an instructor in Romance Languages in the high school of a nearby town.

Friedrich was sent to school there and made the trip daily with Dr. von Hoff. The first few weeks were weeks of terror. The children flocked around him shouting, "Talk, Dutchie, talk! Say something in German!" Backed against the schoolhouse wall at recess, ringed in by grinning faces, he babbled in German—anything that came into his head—to please the children. His answers in class were slow and stumbling as he fumbled with unfamiliar words, and he cringed when the class shouted with laughter. But his sweet nature and engaging smile won him many friends. He quickly learned English and was intelligent in all his schoolwork.

Frieda studied too, but Fritz found the new tongue hard to master and even now lapses into German in moments of excitement or emotion. The two of them, unlike Friedrich, were miserably homesick for the fatherland. Their dream was to save enough for a long visit to their old home. Unlike most German girls of the prewar period, Frieda had inherited land instead of receiving a dowry, and the settlement of that property was the supposed reason, or excuse, for the visit.

Frieda was oppressed by all the newness about her. She missed the cobbled square where housewives baked in the community oven and gossiped and chattered in her own familiar tongue. She longed for the comforting stability and sense of permanence about the 15th century houses of her own village.

After a few years working for Dr. von Hoff, Fritz had saved enough for the journey, but, to their great surprise, they no longer wanted to go. The money would buy five acres of land on the mountainside, five fertile acres well suited to grape-growing. Fritz had been looking at that land and thinking. It would be a start for himself in the work he loved. He worried about approaching Frieda with the plan to buy, when for years she had been longing to return to Germany. But Frieda was delighted with the thought of starting out for themselves.

"Buy land now, Fritz," she said, "and go back later."

He cleared the land and put it into a vineyard. He rooted cuttings sent him from Germany, where the originals had come from Capri. He thinks these were the first Black Hamburg vines planted in the United States. From the beginning the vines flourished, and now he uses nothing else for his wine.

Frieda says they chose that strip along the mountainside for their home not only because the land was fertile and had the right exposure for growing grapes, but because it was a "dreamy-looking place," and the little stream falling down the hillside made them think of the old country. They built a cottage in the shelter of the mountain. It was small and pretty and they loved it. They were doing well.

Then came the fire. They do not know how it started. In the falling dusk Frieda stood stricken, holding the sobbing Friedrich, weeping and watching the little house go up in flames. She thought of

the family treasures and prized new possessions burning before her eyes, and it seemed as if the last ties with the old life were being destroyed as well as hope for the new. Fritz too was weeping. The loss of his violin seemed to hurt him most.

Neighbors saw the glow and hurried over to save what they could, but it was very little. The fire had spread too quickly.

Fritz moved the salvage into the packing shed and the garage. He agreed to let Frieda and the boy go to a neighbor's for temporary shelter, but he refused to move from the smoking foundation throughout the night. There were many offers of assistance. Fritz was moved and grateful but he refused them all.

"Ve done it vunst. Ve do it again," he said.

Next day he started making a new home of the well-built shed and garage, while they lived in a rented house. Fritz's industry and thrift had won him a good reputation and it was not hard to get a loan to start over.

When Fritz returned from the War he found his family broken up and their money gone. He could not find work and his wife and child were hungry. Friends in the United States wrote of fine vinelands in the Thermal Belt of North Carolina and urged him to join them there.

The new cottage is set on a rise overlooking their land. The long flight of stone steps that make the walkway lead through Frieda's rock garden to the hooded door opening into a large L-shaped room. There are casement windows and a great fireplace. On the ledge of stone forming the mantel rests a concave black candelabrum holding nine yellow candles, flanked by two yellow-and-black bowls filled with sweet potatoes now hidden by the leafy, hanging vines they have sprouted.

The furniture is good. Easy chairs and a sofa are covered in harmonizing colors. There is a beautiful old desk and a highly polished table or two. The other end of the L is the dining alcove, with built-in wall cabinets, drop-leaf table, and chairs. A handsome old chest of drawers with a mirror above it stands near the arch of the entrance. The dining table is decorated with a bowl of foliage, and casement windows are gay with plants in brightly colored pottery. A swing-door opens into a kitchen with spotless, shining modern equipment. Frieda no longer regrets the community oven in her German village.

Upstairs are two bedrooms and a bath. Old-fashioned dormer windows are set in the mansard roof. That was admittedly a sentimental touch, to remind them of the houses in their German village. There is an inset deep in the roof and the side of the house to accommodate a great tree they could not bear to cut down only because it stood a few feet in their way.

Behind the house are the new packing shed and garage. Running along the lane to the winery is a stone wall made beautiful with flowers, vines, and shrubs. On the hill to one side, the winery is built over the mountain stream for natural refrigeration. Here the grapes are put into the winepress and the juice stored for fermentation.

Fritz is nurseryman and landscape architect as well as vineyardist. The edges of his land are bordered with a variety of plants and shrubs for sale, his specialty being those used in rock gardens. When the town near which he lives voted land and funds for a municipal park, Fritz donated his services both as architect and planter. The result shows his natural skill, for he had no specialized training.

Since his first success Fritz has planned that Friedrich should become his partner and successor. But his son now has the American idea of planning his own life. He has gone to work as an operator in a hosiery mill, meaning to learn the business by starting at the bottom. It is a blow to Fritz. Relations are strained between the father and son. But Frieda only smiles and says, "Vait andt see, time makes things smooth!"

She is immensely proud of the land, the vineyard, the house, and the winery, and of the man who earned and built them. Her most visionary dreams have been realized. She and Fritz no longer have any desire to return to Germany for even a visit. Their families are scattered and Frieda's property long ago was sold to strangers. The country is in a condition they do not want to see. Frieda still cooks German dishes, and Fritz still lapses into German when excited. Though Friedrich speaks with only a trace of accent, Fritz's and Frieda's speech marks them unmistakably as German born. But their sympathies and allegiance are American. They are proud that it is so.

Source:

Library of Congress. *American Life Histories: Manuscripts from the Federal Writers' Project, 1936-1940* from the American Memory website (http://memory.loc.gov/ammem/wpaintro/wpahome.html).

GREEK AMERICANS

This New York Times *article dated August 4, 1873, preceded a wave of Greek immigration that began in the 1880s. It describes the Greek American community of a few hundred just before that community grew to 2,308 in 1890, and then to 15,979 in 1900, according to U.S. Census records. The Immigration Acts of 1921 and 1924 established quotas that greatly reduced the number of Greeks admitted to the United States. In spite of those restrictions, the 1990 census reported that 1,110,373 Americans claim Greek ancestry.*

"Greeks in America" provides a valuable portrait of the lives of the single Greek men who immigrated to the United States with the hope of making enough money to provide for their families back in Greece. During the 1880s, Greek economic conditions were extremely poor, and many Greeks immigrated in search of work to support their families. Most of these immigrants were from Laconia, in southern Greece. Some settled for a while in New Orleans where they could continue in the shipping occupations. As mentioned in the New York Times, many also settled in Chicago for the same occupational opportunity, and few ventured West as ranch owners. Many of these early immigrants returned to Greece after working a few years in the United States.

Early Greek immigrants were mostly sailors and laborers who found work in the mill towns of New England. Greeks in San Francisco worked in mines and on the railroads. Many immigrants were exploited by the padrone system, an indentured servitude system that kept the Greek worker from profiting from his work, usually with large mining corporations in the West. After the 1890s, immigrants came from all over Greece and entered a wide variety of professions. Many became grocery store owners, some were butchers and bakers, others operated coffee houses and barber shops. By the 1920s, Greeks owned thousands of candy stores and candy-manufacturing businesses and restaurants. Their willingness to work hard paid led to greater success as they became business professionals in communities such as the New England towns of Boston and Manchester.

The humble occupations of early Greek Americans contrast with those of Greek immigrants of the second half of the twentieth century, when most Greeks were professionals such as doctors, lawyers, pharmacists, dentists, and chemists. By the 1990s, Greek Americans were found in every occupation, and were one of the wealthiest ethnic groups in the United States. This document reveals that such high standing was the result of the hard work by several generations of Greek immigrants, who began at the bottom of the employment ladder.

THE GREEKS IN AMERICA

Greek Sailors—The Principal Greek Colonies—Their Love For Their Native Land

Comparatively little is known about the Greeks in America. Reference is made occasionally in the daily Press to the Greek merchants of the City, whose enormous transactions in cotton and grain form an important item in the exports of the country, but beyond that we seldom see a Greek name coming before the public in the daily incidents of this cosmopolitan city.

Greece is so thinly populated that she can hardly spare any hands to emigrate to foreign countries, and we seldom see any Greeks among the nationalities mentioned in the regular reports of our Commissioners of Immigration. Yet a great many Greeks arrive daily on our shores, but they come under the quality of sailors, working their passage on board sailing ships of various nationalities.

As soon as they land here they apply to their Consul in this City, Mr. D. N. Botassi, for work, when with few variations, the following dialogue takes place:

"When did you arrive?"

"This day."

"Any particular profession?"

"None."

"What did you expect to do?"

"Anything, your Excellency."

"Have you got any money?"

"Not a cent, your Excellency."

"Where are your lodgings?"

"Our traps are at the door; we shall go anywhere your Excellency will send us."

"Can you speak English?"

"Nothing but Greek, your Excellency."

There are two sailors' boarding houses in this City doing a thriving business. The Consul invariably sends them there, and it seldom occurs that they do not find work in a short time. They begin by doing rough work in loading and unloading merchandise at our piers, and being generally very temperate, they soon accumulate some savings.

Their first care is to send the little which they can spare to their families in Greece. The family ties are so strong among all her classes, particular the lower ones, that even years of absence in for-

eign lands cannot diminish their love for their native land and the dear ones they have left behind. The love of their country is one of the strong characteristics of the Greeks; they emigrate under compulsion to better their condition, but the hope to return one day to their country under more comfortable circumstances is always strong and paramount.

Few of the Greeks who arrive at this port go West to become agriculturists. This means to become in time owners of land whereon to build their new home. But, as we said before, the Greek has always the hope to return to his country. They mostly go to Chicago, where they easily find work in loading vessels and navigating the lakes. On the water they find themselves happy, being in their element. As soon as the lakes are frozen in the Winter time they go down the Mississippi River, and many of them are working on the steamboats plying between St. Louis, Cincinnati, Louisville, Cairo, and New-Orleans. Over 200 of them are to be found in the Crescent City, where they seem to be thriving under the more genial climate, not dissimilar to that of their own country. They have all sorts of professions; many are fruit dealers, keep little restaurants and coffee houses, where the American bar is combined with little tables a L'orientales, round which are seated Greeks talking all at the same time generally, all the idioms of the Grecian Archipelago, drinking coffee, and smoking paper cigarettes. Many of them are oyster dealers and oyster fishers, owning generally their little craft, which they navigate themselves, and trade all among the coast from New Orleans to Indianola and Matamoras, or on the other side through the lakes to Mobile and Pensacola. The writer tasted, some years ago, an excellent glass of sherry cobbler made by a Greek bar keeper on one of the steamboats on the Alabama River. In New Orleans the Greek colony is important enough to maintain a church of their own religion built some five years ago by subscription, and divine service is celebrated every Sunday in the Greek language by a priest educated in the National University of Athens.

The Greek colony in San Francisco numbers about 300 members, and is the best organized of all the Greek colonies in the States of the Union. They maintain a little chapel of their own, and have established a benevolent society. This latter was rendered necessary from the quantity of newcomers of their countrymen to the Golden State,

A group of Greek women arrive in the United States as brides for Greek men. Frequently in the past, men immigrated first, and then sent for their wives.

with the hopes of finding gold in abundance. It is strange with what great expectations these children of Hellas go to California, and their disappointment in not finding gold in the streets of San Francisco can be better imagined than described. They seem utterly astonished when they are told that they must work in San Francisco, as everywhere else, to gain their living, and the idea of gold is so deeply rooted in them, that many go to the mines of California and Oregon with the hope of enriching themselves one day by some sudden smile of fortune. Even in those distant localities they do not forget their native land. They write to their families in Greece from time to time, and are subscribers to Greek newspapers, to learn the news. To the positive knowledge of the writer eight copies of a Greek newspaper are sent to Greek miners in Piscer County, California, and a Greek roaster of pea-nuts in Galveston, Texas, is a subscriber to one of the best Greek newspapers. The only subscribers in America to an Ecclesiastical Review, published in

Athens, are an American Episcopalian clergyman in New-York and a Greek boarding-house keeper in Chicago, Ill.

There are not students from Greece in this country, with the exception of one, who is studying agriculture at the expense of the Greek Government, in the Illinois Industrial University, in Champaign, Ill., on the scanty allowance of $40 per month.

The average salary of sailors, on board Greek vessels, is about $10 per month; it is no wonder, therefore, that those who come to this country are hesitant to go back, getting as they do, from $30 to $40 per month. But they get even more on land. Last year a Greek vessel arrived at this port from Sicily with a cargo of brimstone. The crew, consisting of twelve men, refused to go to Havana, where the vessel was bound, and remained in New-York. They soon found their way to Athens, below Albany, where they engaged to work at the railroad

A group representing traditional Greek soldiers marches in Boston.

depot. They have worked there for one year, saved $300 each, which they sent to Greece through their Consul, and worked their passage home recently on an American vessel. Their abstinence from drinking and their hard work were much remarked by the employees of the railroad.

But the most remarkable incident of the strength of family ties among the Greeks which came to our knowledge is that of a Greek boy who came to this country thirty years ago. He was educated for the ministry and pursued his avocation. A year ago he made inquiries about his relatives in Greece, and finding that a sister of his, a widow, was still living, but very poor, he opened a correspondence with her. They have never seen each other, but the expatriated Greek felt an inherent duty to assist her. He sends her now very regularly a

yearly pension, with which she lives at present comfortably in Athens.

There are twelve commercial Greek houses in this city, dealing largely in cotton, grain, and East India produce; four more are in New Orleans, similarly engaged; one in Mobile, one in Memphis, Tenn., and two in Boston, Mass. These latter deal principally in Mediterranean produce, mostly dried fruit from Constantinople and Smyrna, exporting thither New England rum, machinery, and Yankee notions.

Source:

The Greeks in America, 1528-1977: A Chronology & Fact Book, compiled and edited by Melvin Hecker and Heike Fenton. Dobbs Ferry, NY: Oceana Publications, 1978. pp. 61-64.

By the late nineteenth century, social conditions were markedly improving in Greece, but the economy still languished. Seeking brighter economic opportunity, the first substantial wave of Greek immigrants to the United States began in the 1880s and continued through the 1890s. Among them were George Mehales, the subject of a 1939 interview, and his older brother.

George was the sixth son of an Athens family. Born in 1892 shortly after his father's death, George's destiny was soon determined as his mother decided her sons would have much better lives in America. Selling her property and borrowing money, she sent George, three years old, and a sixteen year old brother to live with an uncle who owned a restaurant in Brooklyn, New York. Not long after George's arrival, New York became a key destination of Greeks in America. Part of a growing Greek American community, George attended an American school in the mornings and a Greek school in the afternoons. He also began helping at the restaurant.

After temporarily returning to Greece upon the death of his mother to assist his ailing brothers, George came back to open his own restaurant in New York. With his business failing due to poor management, he turned to teaching the Greek language to Americans. With the onset of World War I, George joined the U.S. Army as an interpreter and cook.

Greek Americans frequently found life in America very satisfying, making many friends and facing little discrimination unlike other immigrant groups. George was no different being markedly outgoing, largely conforming to the American stereotype of a Greek with a zest for life. George's spirit saw him through several restaurant failures, the death of his wife, and losses in the Great Stock Market crash of 1929. Relishing life, George bemoaned the fast paced business-like American life he observed in his restaurants, "Seems like most Americans eat just because they have to. . .Eating should be a pleasure and not just something you have to do. Men rush in, order something, and gobble down their food. It takes them about five minutes to eat. . .They always say they are in a hurry. Well, they may be in a hurry but they are just hurrying to the grave when they gobble down their food." George's persistence in economically tapping into the ever increasing popularity of Greek American food eventually led to part ownership of a Greek restaurant in Spartanburg, South Carolina.

GEORGE MEHALES

Date of First Writing: December 1938
Name of Person Interviewed: George Mehales
Fictitious Name: None
Street Address: The Dixie Lunch E. Main Street
Place: Spartanburg, S.C.
Occupation: Part Owner of a Greek Restaurant
Name of Writer: R. V. Williams

On January 14, 1892, Penelope Mehales gave birth to her sixth son in the ancient town of Athens, Greece. Because she had once been to America, and because she believed her sons would find a much brighter future in the United States than in her native country, she gave her new-born child the popular English name of "George," not at all realizing that this name, like her baby, was of Greek origin and meant "farmer." The family was poor, and George's father had died two months before he was born, but the mother was determined that her boys should come to America. She sold what little property she had; borrowed money from her kin-folks, and sent George, when he was but three years old, along with his brother, who was sixteen, to New York.

The two Greek boys were taken in charge by an uncle who had come to America several years before and who operated a small restaurant in Brooklyn. Louis, the older of the two boys, immediately went to work for his uncle. George was sent to school when he was six years old, attending the public school during the morning and the Greek school during the afternoon. In spare moments, he helped his brother and his uncle in the restaurant.

George finished high school in 1909 and went to work for Stove Bekettas, who had purchased his uncle's restaurant. The death of his mother in Greece, and the fact that four of his brothers were ill with tuberculosis and unable to work, caused him to return to his native country. There, for a while, he engaged in farming, thus literally justifying his name. Later, he became a teacher.

"We had only a few schools in Greece where English was taught." George said. "At that time there were many Greeks who planned to come to this country. The immigration laws were not so strict in those days. Most everybody who had enough money for their boat passage could get into the United States. Some of these people wanted to learn to speak English. I earned enough by teaching English to some of these people to take care of myself and my sick brothers. My uncle and brother in Brooklyn sent me money to help out. At last, I

had enough money to care for my brothers for a while, and I came back to America.

"In New York, an old friend and I put our money together and opened up a restaurant. We bit off more than we could chew. (George's English shows a mastery of colloquialisms but has many indications of his foreign origin in its inflections and phrases). We couldn't pay for the expensive fixtures we bought. In three months we were broke and had to close our place. I found myself with no money and no job. Some friends get me a job in a Greek school. I had only twenty pupils. I taught Greek to Greek children who had been born in this country. I didn't make much money, but I managed to save a little and to send a little to my brothers.

"Nothing much else happened to me till the War. I enlisted in New York and came to Spartanburg with the 27th Division. When I enlisted, the officer told me I would be used as an interpreter. He said there were a lot of Greeks in the division who didn't understand English. When we got to Camp Wadsworth, they put me to cooking in Company "C", 100th Infantry, and there wasn't a Greek in the whole company. I was never used as an interpreter.

"Do you remember that big snow we had when the camp was here? I don't remember the exact date, but anyhow, I slipped on the snow and fell from the back of the mess shack. I broke my ankle. It was a bad break. They took me to the hospital and operated. They took tow bones out of my foot. Then they told me I could never walk again without limping. Six long weeks I stayed in the hospital."

Apparently, George's experience with his broken ankle is one of the outstanding experiences of his life. When he discusses it, he seems to a slough off his acquired shell of correct English, and begin to speak in the broken English so common with the majority of Greeks today.

"The officers came around see me," George continued. "They say I can get honorable discharge. I don't want to go. I beg them let me stay when I get well. Cornelius Vanderbilt, Jr., comes to the hospital. I tell my troubles, and he goes to see his father, Colonel Vanderbilt. Two or three days, officers tell me I can stay after doctors let me out of hospital.

"I went back mess shack on crutches. They told me I didn't have to go back yet. I wanted to. I sit in the kitchen and supervised all cooking. Meats, pies, everything. Soon word starts around that we move out any day for Frances. I was still crippled. I want to go with the boys, but Captain Cline tells me I can't go. The boys in the company hear I can't go. They sign paper asking officers let me go with them and do the cooking. I go back to hospital for another examination, but they say no use. It almost breaks my heart to see the boys go. I cried lots."

When the 27th Division left for France, George remained behind. He does not like to discuss the period of his war record. He had formed friendships with many men in the company, many of whom lost their lives when the 27th and 30th Divisions crashed through the Hindenburg Line.

"After the boys left," George said, "I went back to the mess shack on crutches. I got rid of them as soon as possible. I went to this officer and that officer and asked them what company I was to work with. They said they would take it up with headquarters, but I guess they were too busy with other things because nothing happened. For about two months, I was just loafing around. I slept on a cot in my old mess shack. I folded it up every morning and packed it away. I ate with the new men that came in. They were from Indiana and belonged to the 91st Division. They were swell fellows.

"By this time, I could walk almost without a limp. My pay stopped coming. The captain told me to go to headquarters to see about it. I hung around there about three days before I could get any attention. Then an officer heard my story. He told me to go back to my mess shack and stay there until something was done. I went back and began to work in the kitchen. The boys liked to have me there because it made less work for them. Inspection day came along, and the officers wanted to know what I was doing there. They said my name was not on the company list. For about the hundredth time, I told my story. About a week later, some officer came in the mess shack and told me to go with him to headquarters. When I got there, some officers told me that a mistake had been made in the records. They said that the records showed I had been discharged about two months before. They told me that the papers had got lost somehow. They had the doctors at the hospital look me over again. Then they shoved a lot of papers at me to sign. I don't know much what was in them but I didn't care. I was glad that somebody was paying some attention to me. They told me to go back to the mess shack and start to work. A few days after that, Captain Johnson came in and told me that I had been assigned to the company. On top of that, I got paid for the two months, and did that money look good. I guess for these two months, I was just lost to the United States Army.

"Armistice Day was a great day at the camp. Our company had not used up its allotment of food for the period. The quartermaster decided to put on a spread. He went to Spartanburg and bough turkeys. It took us all day, even with an extra detail, to get ready. But we had a small dinner that night."

After his discharge from the army, George found himself, like many other soldiers, without a job. For a while he worked in a restaurant owned by his brother, who had not gone to war, and who had profited during the period when some men amassed fortunes.

"My brother and I decided that it would be necessary for one of us to go to Greece to look after the property that Uncle Louis had left us. My brother said I was freer to go than he was. The trip was my second trip home. I was lucky to get it because the immigration officials told me I would have a hard time getting back. When they found out I was an American citizen and that I served during the war, I didn't have any trouble at all. I stayed in Greece about three months, and then came back here.

The immigration laws were not so strict in those days. Most everybody who had enough money for their boat passage could get into the United States.

"I stayed in New York for a while, and then came back to Spartanburg. I had always wanted to come back here. I lived here with some Greek friends for a while. I took up school teaching again while I was looking around for something better. Two of my brothers in Greece died within ten days of each other. They left me about three hundred dollars in American money.

"What did you do with the money," I asked him.

"Tell you, Bob, it was like this. I found an owner of a small restaurant here—not mentioning any names—that needed some capital. With what I had and what I borrowed from my brother, I went into business with him. Our business jumped up fast, and we had to hire extra people to take care of the trade. We were open day and night. Then his wife became sick—or should I say ill? She had the same disease that killed my brothers. He decided to take her to Arizona for her health, and he wanted to sell out to me. I bought it and was broke in less than six months. I couldn't get it out of my head that I wanted the best restaurant fixtures that money could buy. I was making good money but it wasn't enough to meet the expense of my new fixtures. And I was also playing the stock market. One day, one of my customers showed me how much money he was making in the market. I had never even thought about the stock market before. For a few days, I looked at the market page in the newspaper. It looked good to me, and I bit with what you folks call 'hook, line and sinker.' All the money I took in, I put into stocks. The first day of October in 1929 made me feel like I was rich. The stocks I bought had gone up and up. I sold some of them and bought others. I often thought about what my mother had said and that was "You'll get rich in America someday!' I should have paid for my fixtures, but I figured I could pay them any time. You might think I would have known better, but I didn't. I figured I could pay my debts any time, and I just let them ride.

"Trouble hit me hard during the last day of October of that year. I had become so interested with the market that I let my own business go down. I wasn't there half the time. I need my own place of business as a place to hang around in. Business dropped off, but I didn't care "cause I was making plenty money in the market.

"During the last days of October, my stocks began to drop. I was gambling on the margin. My brother called me and told me I would have to put up more cash. I went to the bank and put up all the cash I had in the bank with my brother. It seemed to me that things would soon get better. I sent a telegram to my brother and he sent me one thousand dollars. I had about five thousand dollars invested. On that day of October 29, they told me I needed more cash to cover up. I couldn't get it. I was wiped out that day.

"I guess disappointment comes mighty hard to some people, but that almost killed me. My brother lost in the market like me, and he couldn't help me out. I considered killing myself, 'cause I had nothing left. I found out what a fool I had been. I did manage to pay my debts by selling my cafe at rock bottom prices. I learned a lesson then. It almost killed me to see my cafe go at such a cheap price. It taught me that you've got to pay your debts to get along.

"Not long after my cafe was sold, I met a nice Greek girl named Penelope. Same as that of my mother. We kinda seemed what you call matched for each other. She lived in Charlotte and came here to see her brother when I met her. We started to going together. We decided to get married but I didn't have much to get married on. We got married anyhow and struggled along on almost nothing. The 'flu' took her after we had been together about six months. The doctor said it was 'flu' but I think it was pneumonia. Talk about committing suicide, I felt like it then sure enough. Just before

she died, she asked me to look out for her brother. He was always getting into some kind of trouble. His name was Nick. He lived with us. I got Nick a job in Greenville. He stole some money from Gus Trakas when he was working there. I told Gus I would pay everything back if he wouldn't have him arrested. Gus turned Nick over to me. I sent him to Greenville and he made good there. Owns a small interest in one of the best restaurants in that town. He paid me back every cent I ever spent on him.

"The rest of my life—there's nothing much to it. I have been working and saving my money. I own an interest in this cafe. I'm pretty well fixed and I seem to have a lot of friends and I happy here."

George is spending most of his spare time is reading such magazines as Time, Readers' Digest, etc., but his favorite magazine is *Asia*, because he says he often finds in it articles concerning his native country.

He has many interesting stories to tell of his experiences in the restaurant business, but his favorite one is what he calls the "Tramp Mark."

"One day a few years ago," George said, "a tramp came into my place and wanted something to eat. He said he had not anything to eat for three days. He said he would wash the dishes or do anything I wanted him to do if I would give him something to eat. I gave him a meal and some small change I had in my pocket. The next day, about six men came in with hard luck stories. Every day after that, a bunch of men would come in and ask for something to eat. I told a friend one day that I couldn't figure out where all the hoboes were coming from. He said I must have a "Tramp Mark" on my building. I had never heard of a "Tramp Mark" before. He said that when hoboes found a place where they could get a meal for nothing, they would put a mark on the building so that other tramps would know that the place was a place to get a free meal. I went back to my place and looked around. On the back door, I found the mark. It was a circle that somebody had put there in chalk. It was about as big around as a saucer, and it had something in it like a cross. I rubbed it out. From then on, I looked over the building every day to see if there was any marks. Those hoboes had about eat me out of a place of business. There was a lot of hoboes then. Don't find so many now."

"Which do you find the hardest to please, George, men or women?"

"What you call the average man," George replied, "isn't so particular. He'll pick up the menu, glance at it a second or so, and then say, 'Give me a roast beef dinner,' or something like that. He never tells you what vegetables he wants to go along with his dinner. That's the average man, but there are some like old maids that want everything just so and so.

"Take the average woman, now. She studied the menu a long time before she orders anything. Then she will say just what vegetables she wants. Women eat less than men, and a lot of them still order some kind of a sandwich instead of a regular meal."

George believes that Americans would greatly improve their health if they would be more careful about their diet and would eat more slowly.

"Seems like most Americans eat just because they have to," George said. "Eating should be a pleasure and not just something you have to do. Men rush in, order something, and gobble down their food. It takes them about five minutes to eat. Everybody should take at least a half hour to eat. They always say they are in a hurry. Well, they may be in a hurry but they are just hurrying to the grave when they gobble down their food."

George is pessimistic about the future of his native country, although he says Greece is in far better financial condition today than any other country.

"There is no unemployment in Greece," George said, "and everybody would be happy over there if the rest of the world would leave them alone. But they are all scared of Hitler. He's heading that way, and the Greeks think it won't be long before he takes over the Balkan states, and then he will want Greece. Nobody has stopped him yet in anything he wants, and the Greeks believe he wants Greece. Then they thin he will take Egypt and move on to India. They think he's trying to form a world empire.

"That may sound what you call 'far-fetched' to people over here," George continued," but they believe it will happen unless somebody stops Hitler. The Germans and Greek hat each other. Greece can't stop Germany by herself. Italy don't like

Greece. Roumania don't like Greece. And you know from history what the Turks think about Greece. The Greek's best friends are the English and the Americans. They might help out if the Greeks get in danger, but there is no promise of help. That's why they worry so much."

If a stranger went into George's restaurant today, he would probably find him in the kitchen, supervising the cooking. During the morning he busies himself in the kitchen and making the necessary purchases of food. At noon, he comes out of the kitchen in a clean white uniform and a round white cap to talk with his customers. At two o'clock in the afternoon, he leaves his restaurant to take his "siesta."

"In Greece," George said, "everybody stops work from twelve till two. It is why you folks say is an old Spanish custom. I have to take mine from two till four. I spend that time in resting and reading. The hours I like most are at night. I go back to work at seven and work till nine. People are through with their work and in no big hurry. They like to sit around and talk, and that suits me fine. I talk too much, I know, because I learn more from listening than from talking."

About nine o'clock, George turns over in restaurant to the night shift. The he invariably goes to his room and reads, retiring, he says, about eleven o'clock each night with his alarm clock set at seven the next morning.

"George," I asked him, "I have always heard the expression that 'The Greeks had a word for it.' Do you know the origin of that saying?"

"I don't, Bob," George laughingly replied, "but I can tell you this. As for me, and for thousands of other Greeks who are happy here, I'd say that that word is 'the United States.'"

Source:

Library of Congress. *American Life Histories: Manuscripts from the Federal Writers' Project, 1936-1940* from the American Memory website (http://memory.loc.gov/ammem/wpaintro/wpa-home.html).

*T*ensions *between Greece and Turkey go back, in a sense, to the Trojan War (c.1200 B.C.), when—as every student of Homer's Iliad and other myths of the war knows—the Greeks defeated the Trojans of Asia Minor after a ten-year battle of attrition. However, it would be more accurate to assign the origins of Greek-Turkish conflicts to the 1000s A.D., when Asia Minor was conquered by the Turks from central Asia. Up to then, the people of Asia Minor had been closely related to the Greeks; thereafter, the two regions were divided both by ethnicity and by religion, with the Turks bringing the new religion of Islam to the whole of Asia Minor. Greece, meanwhile, remained the center of Orthodox Christianity.*

A focal point of tension between Greece and Turkey has been the island of Cyprus in the Mediterranean. Historically linked with Greece, Cyprus fell to the Ottoman Empire of the Turks in 1571, and remained in Turkish hands for three centuries. During that time, particularly on the north end of the island, a significant Turkish Muslim minority began to develop.

Britain, which had taken an interest in Cyprus since 1878, when the Ottoman Empire was on the decline, assumed control of the island after Turkey entered World War I on the side of Germany. Cyprus began a British crown colony after the war, but in 1931, the Greek Cypriot majority began to agitate for enosis, or union, with Greece. This campaign began in earnest after World War II, as the National Organization of Cypriot Fighters—led by a retired Greek army officer—waged a campaign of terrorism against British authorities.

In the tense postwar environment, Cyprus became a strategic hotspot. On the one hand, the Soviet Union had a strong presence in eastern Europe, heightening American concerns over the region; on the other hand, both Greece and Turkey belonged to NATO (North Atlantic Treaty Organization), the principal military alliance of free nations in the region. Differences between Greece and Turkey over Cyprus thus threatened to undermine the power of NATO.

After a 1959 meeting in Zürich, Switzerland, however, Greek and Turkish Cypriot leaders showed their willingness to agree on sharing of power, and Cyprus became independent in the following year. Yet by the end of 1963, fighting had broken out, and in 1964 the United Nations (UN) Security Council sent in troops. This brought an end to the conflict—for a time.

The takeover of Greece by military officers in 1967 signaled a return to heated disagreements over Cyprus, and in July 1974, Greece forces overthrew the Cypriot government of Archbishop Makarios III. Turkish troops invaded later that month, and by the end of the summer, Turkey controlled the northern third of the island. In February 1975, the Turkish area declared its independence from Cyprus, though Turkey was the only nation in the world to recognize the breakaway state.

It was against this backdrop that the United Hellenic American Congress (UHAC) called on the government of the United States to take a stand on Cyprus. The UHAC, as the public affairs committee of the American Hellenic Institute, had long been influential in American politics, and it chose a highly visible place and time to make its position known: Philadelphia, Pennsylvania, on July 6, 1976. Just two days before, all of America had celebrated the 200th anniversary of the signing of the Declaration of Independence in Philadelphia's Liberty Hall.

The use of this setting by the UHAC was more than just idle grandstanding. At a time when the United States was celebrating its status as the world's oldest democratic government, the UHAC was able to draw on the great symbolic power of Greece, the nation where democracy was born some 2,500 years before. Though the UHAC resolution does not mention the Greek origins of democracy; however, that fact is implied. Certainly the statement calls on the highest American ideals: ". . . America has, from its inception, stood not only for freedom, justice, and liberty for its people, but as a beacon of freedom, justice, and liberty for all the peoples of the world . . . ."

Largely as a result of lobbying by Greek American groups, the United States imposed an arms embargo against Turkey on February 5, 1975. Despite U.S. refusal to sell weapons to its NATO ally, however, and despite lack of recognition by other nations, the Turkish sector declared itself a fully independent state, the Turkish Republic of Northern Cyprus (TRNC), in 1983. Beginning in 1988, the presidents of Cyprus and the TRNC engaged in talks, but success was limited.

The United States again made its voice heard over Cyprus in 1995, when it encouraged its allies in the European Union, an economic alliance of European states, to admit Cyprus as a member. Tensions and occasional violence continued in Cyprus throughout the 1990s.

The following document originally appears in the United States Congressional Record, *Extensions of Remarks, August 10, 1976, p. E 4491.*

UNITED HELLENIC AMERICAN CONGRESS RESOLUTION

HON. EDWARD J. DERWINSKI
of Illinois
In the House of Representatives
Tuesday, August 10, 1976

Mr. Derwinski. Mr. Speaker, I insert in the *Record* a resolution adopted by the executive committee of the United Hellenic American Congress, which met last month in Philadelphia.

The United Hellenic American Congress is a nationwide organization of Americans of Hellenic origin interested in developments in this country as well as developments affecting Greece and Cyprus. This group is a complete cross-section and has a truly representative membership of the American-Greek community.

The resolution follows:

Resolution

Whereas, the United Hellenic American Congress has conducted its National Meeting in the City of Philadelphia this 6th day of July, 1976, in conjunction with the observance of our country's Bicentennial celebration; and

Whereas, America has, from its inception, stood not only for freedom, justice, and liberty for its people, but as a beacon of freedom, justice, and liberty for all of the peoples of the world;

Now, therefore, be it resolved, that the Officers and Members of the Executive Committee of the United Hellenic American Congress assembled this 6th day of July, 1976, in the City of Philadelphia, do hereby proclaim liberty and reaffirm our dedication to the principles of the founding fathers of our Nation, and we hereby urge the Government of the United States to exert its full efforts and moral support for freedom and liberty and justice throughout the world; and

Be it further resolved, that the Congress of the United States is hereby memorialized to continue to support democracy, self-determination, and majority rule throughout the world, and to condemn and oppose aggression throughout the world; and

Be it further resolved, that the Congress of the United States is hereby memorialized to continue support to the democracy in Greece and to support the Rule of Law in prohibiting all arms transfers to until Turkey withdraws all her troops and civilians from Cyprus and allows all refugees to return to their homes.

Source:

The Greeks in America, 1528-1977: A Chronology & Fact Book, compiled and edited by Melvin Hecker and Heike Fenton. Dobbs Ferry, NY: Oceana Publications, 1978. pp. 117-118.

GUATEMALAN AMERICANS

During the 1980s, thousands of Guatemalans abandoned communities ravaged by civil war and found refuge in different countries in the Americas. Among these refugees were 12,000 Q'anjob'al Mayans who escaped the political violence that had destroyed some 440 villages. The Q'anjob'al settled in southern Florida, in a small farming community called Indiantown. There they joined other Central American and Mexican immigrants.

The American writer Allan F. Burns based his book Maya in Exile: Guatemalans in Florida on interviews with the Mayan residents of Indiantown. Through their conversations, several trends emerge. Most Mayan refugees in Florida lived for a number of years in refugee camps—mostly in Mexico—before undertaking the journey to the United States. Despite the problems of discrimination and persecution they face in Florida, they say they prefer to be in the United States for reasons of safety. Almost all give graphic descriptions of politically motivated violence. (Note: If you are sensitive to such material, you may not want to read this selection.)

Migration is a matter of compromise, however. Many of these indigenous people came from small, isolated villages in western Guatemala. Some admit that the new ways of life and the language they have encountered frighten them. For some, adapting to American culture means having to abandon some of their cultural traditions. In other cases, American culture has absorbed their Mayan ways.

Nearly every ethnic group that has migrated to the United States has had its Indiantown, its first home in the new country in which elders attempt to preserve tradition and the young and members of the first generation find tradition often at odds with their experience. One can see this pattern in such diverse narratives as Anzia Yezierska's The Bread Givers and Piri Thomas's Down These Mean Streets, among scores of others. It might be called an archetypal development in the literature of newcomers to a pluralistic society.

ESCAPE AND ARRIVAL

The number of Maya people who have to come to the United States as refugees is difficult to assess. Since 1981 the number of Guatemalan refugees inside and outside Guatemala has been estimated as being as high as 600,000, with up to 200,000 in the United States (Zolberg, Suhrke, and Aguayo 1989:212). Of these, only a very few have been given political asylum. Between 1983 and 1986, when the first wave of close to 100,000 Guatemalans fled to the United States, only 14 petitions for political asylum were granted while 1,461 were denied (United States President's Advisory Committee for Refugees 1986:9). The numbers of people applying for either temporary or permanent worker status, those receiving legal papers through one of the provisions of the Immigration and Reform Control Act of 1986, and those here illegally have not been assessed.

Nor are there accurate figures for the number of Mayas in Florida. According to one newspaper account in late 1988, there were probably between fifteen and twenty thousand Maya in the state at that time (Palm Beach Post, Dec. 12, 1988). Of this number, probably close to five thousand live in Indiantown during the harvest season. Other communities with significant Maya populations include West Palm Beach, Homestead, Boynton Beach, Immokalee, and Okeechobee. These communities each have between five hundred and several thousand Maya immigrants. Small groups composed of individuals and families are found in most other agricultural communities in the state. But Indiantown is the historic, cultural, and numeric center of the Maya in the state. Indiantown and Los Angeles are considered the two major centers of Maya immigration in the United States.

As we saw in Chapter One, the violence in Guatemala in the 1980s was overwhelming for many Maya groups. Hundreds of villages were destroyed, lands were appropriated, and people were tortured and murdered with a ferocity that traumatized much of the indigenous population. The Maya of northwestern Guatemala were caught between the military forces of the government and the guerilla movement. The guerilla movement sought food, recruits, and ideological legitimacy from the Maya. The military sought to destroy the subsistence base of the guerrilla movement by a scorched-earth policy of rural destruction.

Not all Maya were caught by the military violence, nor were all communities in Guatemala affected. Some groups were able simply to stay isolated and outside of the zones of conflict. Others sided with the government in order to save their villages. Still others stood up to both the government forces and the guerrillas and were left alone. But many were not so fortunate. The area of the Cuchumatan Mountains was especially susceptible to both guerilla and military campaigns through the 1980s. This chapter focuses on the stories of some of the people from this region who have now come to the United States.

The Maya who fled this modern devastation of their culture their homes, and their families did not know where they were going or what they would find. Once in Mexico they set up temporary camps, which were soon raided by the Guatemalan military (Carmack 1988). Forty-two thousand of them were given refugee status by the Mexican government and put in camps near the Guatemalan border. When the Guatemalan army made several attacks on the camps in 1982 and 1983, several thousand were taken to isolated lands in the states of Campeche and Quintana Roo, Mexico.

One community leader, Joaquim Can, recounted the forced journey between the camps in Chiapas and Campeche:

Allan Burns: What was it like to travel from the camps in Chiapas to Campeche?

Joaquim Can: They brought us in big school buses from Chiapas. It took several weeks to bring us all here. I remember that at night they would put us in big warehouses and we had to all sleep on the floor next to each other. It was crowded and many people died, especially children and those who had infections. There was no sanitation and no way to care for those of us who were sick. Many people died.

In Campeche, the refugees constructed stick shacks with corrugated cardboard roofs. In 1989, when I interviewed residents of the camps, the same cardboard was there, only now the rains and storms had opened many houses to the elements. Despite the pathetic conditions, however, people preferred to live her than to live near the border or return to Guatemala.

Those who could fled farther north, through Mexico and into the United States. They crossed deserts at night, where they saw the bodies of people who had gotten lost in the wilderness of the border, and eventually they arrived in Phoenix and other cities. Once in the United States many

The tradition of Guatemalan weaving has been brought to United States through recent immigration from Central America.

applied for political asylum, while the majority entered the illegal alien world.

Receiving political asylum has been an important hope for many of the Maya. During the early years of the Maya immigration to the United States and especially to Florida, American Friends Service Committee and Florida Rural Legal Services worked to secure documentation for political asylum cases. As more and more Maya arrived in the United States, however, asylum hearings turned hopeless; only a small handful of applicants achieved legal status through these means. Application for political asylum was still a viable strategy in the short term, however, since it enabled those Maya who applied for the status to receive temporary work permits. This temporary status allowed people to work legally and have access to hospitals and other facilities.

One of the problems with applying for political asylum status for the Maya was the fear that had been engendered in Guatemala and in the United States concerning government institutions. Refugees feared that providing their names or any information about their families to a lawyer or an immigration judge would lead to their immediate deportation to Guatemala. For this reason, individuals were loath to step into the limelight of a court hearing, especially when it became well known that asylum application hearings seemed always to lead to denial.

The case of one woman, Maria Gonzalez, is illustrative of the summary nature of the hearings. Paralegals wrote up their experience with the case in a letter to the public after her immigration hearing:

From the first defendant, Juan Francisco, the judge heard of the brutal massacre of eleven men, including his father and two brothers, in his village of Ixcanac. Juan was away working on a coffee plantation during the massacre and received a warning from his mother never to return. Another defendant, Carlos Juan, spoke of the killings in the town of San Rafael by guerrillas of the people who did not support their movement. Maria Ana, the last defendant to be heard described in detail how she witnessed the army massacre of El Mul in which eleven men were killed, and on the stand Maria described to the court how many soldiers stormed into her home and brutally beat and hacked her father and two brothers to death with machetes. The soldiers also beat women and children, stole and villagers' animals, possessions, and burned homes to the ground.

The contention of the authorities all along has been that the Kaniobal people have come here for economic reasons rather than fleeing political violence. Another position of the government is that the refugees should have gone to UN-sponsored refugee camps in Mexico rather than continue on to the United States. Judge Foster told the defense attorneys that it was not enough that one's family had been killed for one to prove persecution and qualify for asylum.

In many ways the trials showed the cultural conflicts between a Maya people . . . and the court. An example was Maria. Confident in the telling of the brutality she experienced, she nonetheless is not even sure of the months of the year, is unschooled in numbers and mathematics, and during her long flight she was often sick and unable to document how long she remained in each place. So afraid was she by what she had witnessed that she assumed a false name in Guatemala to protect herself, and continued using it when caught by the immigration authorities and put in detention in the United States. (Camposeco, Silvestre, and Davey 1986)

It is difficult to convince the U.S. immigration authorities of the reality of the violence and fear that are at the heart of the Maya immigration to the United States, and attitudes about work and being a productive member of society contribute to misunderstanding as well. Maya people take great pride in their dedication and commitment to work. Their abilities to work well in diverse places such as the mountains of Guatemala, coastal coffee plantations, and now the migrant streams of the United States are a source of pride. To work hard and long is a value assumed to be appreciated in any country. When Maya women or men are asked why they are here in the United States, it is much more common for them to say that they came to work than to say that they came to escape repression. The violence, the betrayal of families and communities by neighbors, and the brutality of the Guatemalan government during the 1980s are issues that are simultaneously overwhelming and difficult to express. It is much easier to tell someone that you came to the United States because you are a good worker, in the hope that this virtue

will be better received than will a sad story of your homeland. A newspaper article titled "Strangers in a Strange Land" (Palm Beach Post, Aug. 19, 1990) quoted a Maya who was learning English. The first phrase he proudly spoke was, "I need a good work."

The irony of this is that identifying oneself as a good worker or in immigration terms, an "economic refugee," is the one sure way not to have a chance at gaining legal status through political asylum. Economic refugees are popularly seen as workers who take jobs from U.S. citizens, even though this is not so and as unskilled laborers, even though many of the Maya once held positions as shopkeepers, cooperative officials, and school teachers. Economic refugees are seen as a drain on the U.S. economy because of the remittances they send back home. As George Waldroup, the assistant district director of the INS in Miami, said in a newspaper interview, "Most of these claims are based on economic need, but there is no such thing as economic asylum" (Palm Beach Post, Aug. 22, 1990).

A final problem with political asylum as a strategy for achieving legal status in the United States is the time that it takes for Maya people to travel from Guatemala to the United States. The United States is not a country of "first asylum" for most of the Maya. A very few have managed to fly directly to the United States, but the vast majority who come by land often spend months or even years moving surreptitiously through Mexico. Sometimes individuals spend a year or more in Mexico earning enough money to move slowly toward the U.S. border. Once here, they continue with the same strategies of being unobtrusive migrant workers.

Jose Xunche, a recent arrival to Florida, had spent several years in Mexico, working in the oil fields of Tabasco and in a restaurant in Mexico City, before coming to the United States:

Allan Burns: When was the last time you were in Guatemala?

Jose Xunche: I left on January 10, 1982, and went to Mexico for two years. I heard that the military was going to come into our hamlet. I came back in 1984. I lived near Rio Azul and every day the army would come there with a truck of guerrilla captives. They would stand at the bridge, cut them up with machetes, and throw them into the river. Half of them weren't dead but they just threw them in with the dead ones. I couldn't stay, so I left and made my way up here.

Rodrigo Antonio, another immigrant, talked with Julian Arturo, a University of Florida anthropology student from Colombia, about his journey from Guatemala through Mexico:

Well, it was for the war. There in Guatemala. In my town, I am from San Miguel. But I am from Guatemala. Well, then, when there was war there it was hard for us to leave. Also we didn't have any money. Then finally I left there, fleeing. I left without hardly saying goodbye to my family because of the fear I had of the army, the ones that were killing people. It was of the government, as we say. The guerilla was also active, killing people once in a while. But it was the army that I feared more; I feared that they would come and kill me. For example, if you went out to work there and the army came upon you, it was really easy for them to kill you, because the army could do it there. The guerilla was up in the mountains, but the army could come upon you on the road or in the milpas or wherever. This is what happened to my best friend. He was in his milpa and the army came upon him and killed him there. This is what happened to him. That's why it frightens you to live there. And that's how I came here. I hardly said goodbye to my family because I left so quickly. I came here.

Since recording this interview, Rodrigo has returned to Guatemala to bring his wife and children to the United States.

Rodrigo's matter-of-fact telling of the personal terror in Guatemala is common in refugee accounts of terrorism. For him and others, the conditions in Guatemala can be described, but the killings and destruction of villages need no stress when told to others. Victor Montejo's Testimony: Death of a Guatemalan Village (1987) has a similar style of unexaggerated description: "Before going down to rescue the captives I had learned of the death of one patrol member: the boy of fourteen.. . . It was now two thirty, and the day had begun to cloud over. The bullet-riddled bodies of the dead civil defenders remained where they had fallen. No one, not even the widows, dared to leave the group to weep over the bodies of their husbands" (Montejo 1987:29).

In Rodrigo Antonio's case, the journey through Mexico to California and subsequently to Florida was in itself traumatic. After staving in Mexico City for several months, Rodrigo and a group of four companions (three men and a woman) made their way by train to the U.S. border:

Rodrigo Antonio: Well, we got there to Mexicali and we got a ticket for Tijuana. We got to Tijuana and we arrived—how do you say it?—real nervous. There were two women with us as well.

Julian Arturo: Two women with you?

Rodrigo Antonio: Yes, two women with their husbands. They were almost dead. When we were on the train, we couldn't even get up. People just

walked over us, because we felt so weak for lack of food. When we got to Tijuana, we still had a few pesos. The brother of the coyote [a person who brings people across the border for money] found us and we went to his house. There we bathed, ate some eggs, then we went to buy a few beers, so that was the end of that money. That was the last dollar I had; we spent it on beer with that coyote. We were in the hands of one of those coyotes, in his house.

I went with the coyote myself. The migra [Immigration and Naturalization Service agents] was there in front of a church. I was really tired and hungry. But when I saw the migra, I didn't worry about being tired or hungry, nothing! Thanks to God the church had something, a little park with flowers and everything. That's where I hid.

Julian Arturo: The Mexican migra or the United States?

Rodrigo Antonio: The United States migra! We were in the United States, in Chula Vista, in California. We had already passed on to California. And the migra chased me, but thanks to the little park that was in front of the church, I was able to get away. I hid in the flowers and then escaped out the fence to a road that was in front with a lot of cars. I was running behind the coyote. We got to another house where they had—how do you call them, those things to carry horses?

Julian Arturo: Horse trailers.

Rodrigo Antonio: Horse trailers. An old one was parked there by the side of the house. The migra was still after us, but I was hidden in there, in the trailer. I waited while the migra stopped looking. After a while they came back, but I was still hidden in there. Luckily there was a little hill there. That's where I hid myself. I lost the coyote; I was all alone; everyone else, including the coyote, was gone.

Rodrigo Antonio's story is similar to that of many of the Maya who have come to the United States. California is often the first place that they try to find work, as it is the place where most Mexican coyotes, the people who are paid for bringing people across the border, know well. Connover's book Coyote (1987) presents a powerful story of what it is like to come across the United States—Mexican border with the help of the coyotes.

Rodrigo describes his life in both California and Florida almost as if they were neighboring villages:

Rodrigo Antonio: Yes, one of my cousins left when I was in California, the other later. I was by myself. I went up north by myself. The other one stayed in Fort Myers. There a lot of people in Alabama. Too many people. We didn't get anything for our work. It was really hot. Everyone was sweating a lot, even the women who were working there in the sun. We were all sweaty. It was like it was raining; you couldn't even go to the bathroom. And we didn't get anything for it. So after this I went to Michigan.

Julian Arturo: And did you do well there?

Rodrigo Antonio: Yes. I went with a woman friend up there to Michigan. We got up there and began picking cherries. We went in June. In one week we made three hundred dollars. "Ay, here there is money," I said. We stayed there for the entire cherry harvest, three weeks. Then we picked apricots, cucumbers. It was really good there. I had work there usually every day. After the apricots, then we picked apples. Then after the apple harvest, when it gets cold in November, we came back here again.

Julian Arturo: Where did you go?

Rodrigo Antonio: First I spent a few days in Fort Myers; then I came here to Indiantown.

Julian Arturo: How did you know about Indiantown?

Rodrigo Antonio: I had a friend there who had a car, and he brought me here once to visit some friends who live here. I knew about Indiantown because when I was living in Fort Myers I came here to visit now and again. I knew how it was here. I had friends who gave me a ride here.

One of the first places the Guatemalan Maya can find to live in Indiantown is in the apartment complexes built to house migrant workers. These apartment buildings are privately owned but are called "camps" like the farmworker housing found in the citrus and vegetable farms of the area.

Julian Arturo: Did you come to one of the camps, like Blue Camp when you came?

Rodrigo Antonio: No, I always came here to Seminole Street. Near the house of Luis. That's where my friend lives. I picked oranges.

When Rodrigo Antonio returned to Guatemala to find his family, he found himself conscripted into the "civil patrol," one of the more burdensome organizations now instituted in many of the villages such as San Miguel, where Rodrigo was born. These patrols are made up of local men who are expected to give up their time to defend the villages from guerrilla soldiers. A list of every adult man is made in each village, and the men take turns doing "guard service." Suspicious strangers are reported to military authorities by these patrols, and often jealousies or old conflicts between families are settled by a patrol member's telling the military government that the other party is "subver-

sive." In this way the current system installed by the Guatemalan government to lessen the threat of guerrilla insurgency has been transformed into a means for indulging feuds and personal conflicts. Some men pay others to take their turn at patrol. Many who now work in the United States send back money for years to pay a neighbor or relative to do their patrol duty.

Rodrigo Antonio: When I went back, it had changed a lot. It wasn't at all like it was when the war was going on. Now there is the patrol. You have to be a part of the patrol and not miss a day. When I went back, I had to patrol three times a week. You can't work at all. You have to be on patrol so much that you can't get any work done.

Julian Arturo: They don't let you work?

Rodrigo Antonio: No. There is no time to work. You have to patrol when it's your turn.

Julian Arturo: In the camps?

Rodrigo Antonio: No, in our town. We are, as we say, guarding our town. The army is there making sure we do.

Julian Arturo: So you can't work more than four days a week?

Rodrigo Antonio: Yes, you can't work five days, just four days a week. Most of the time you can only work two or three days a week. You see, that is why the people are so . . . in poverty now. It's because of the patrols, the war. Lots of things have been destroyed.

As we have seen, because political asylum was the most viable strategy for staying in the United States, the Maya like Rodrigo who came here were encouraged to apply for it, even though it was seldom granted. The year or more that it took for cases to go through the appeals process at least gave applicants a period of relative safety when they could legally find jobs and live without fear of deportation. With support from the Indian Law Resource Center in Washington, Jeronimo Camposeco began working with lawyers and other advocates to advance as many political asylum cases as possible through the court systems. The strategy taken by Jeronimo and other advocates was to be forthright about the presence of the Maya in the United States. The filing of political asylum applications provided people with legal status as long as the process of deciding on the individual cases continued. The Maya did not want to remain "undocumented aliens," illegal people. They wanted a chance to maintain their families until it was safe for them to return to Guatemala.

The case of Jeronimo Camposeco is indicative of this process.

Allan Burns: Were you working there in the seventies on a school project or what?

Jeronimo Camposeco: Yes, I was a teacher there in the parochial school teaching little kids. I was teaching them how to write and literacy. And many of these refugees here were my students.

Allan Burns: Were you teaching them to write in Maya as well as in Spanish?

Jeronimo Camposeco: Yes I was, because they don't speak Spanish. I was teaching Maya, in Kaniobal language. It's a Maya language, one of the many Maya languages in Guatemala.

Allan Burns: So you devised an alphabet that could be used.

Jeronimo Camposeco: Yes, we have an alphabet. We are using the modern alphabet of the modern script, but we have to have some changes in the alphabet. We need to learn and then to teach the children. In other words, we teach the children in the modern alphabet, because when they are going to school, they can read in Spanish also. So this is a good help for them. Not only [because to] learn from their own language . . . is more easy, but because if you impose the Spanish since the beginning then.. . . There is a program of the government that is called "Castellanizacion" that is for the little Indians to learn Spanish before starting school. What I did was teach directly in the Indian language.

Allan Burns: Did the people accept that; did you have a lot of students?

Jeronimo Camposeco: Yes, it was very . . . they accepted that, because they didn't have to do big . . . they didn't have problems to understand the teacher; because they trusted the teacher because the teacher speaks the language. Of course the teacher was another Indian like them.

Allan Burns: You grew up in Jacaltenango, speaking Jacaltec.

Jeronimo Camposeco: Yes, Jacaltenango is a village not too far from San Miguel. We are only divided by two rivers and a mountain. So the Kaniobals go to the market place in Jacaltenango every Sunday carrying their . . . they make, from the maguey fiber, crafts like bags and ropes and all those good things. And also pottery, and also wood for construction. They are very good for those kinds of things like carpentry.. . . So I learned Kaniobal because my father was some kind of instructor also and he had many deals with the Kaniobal.

In the 1970s, Native Americans from New York and Pennsylvania contacted the Maya of Guatemala as part of a pan-Indian movement that crossed national boundaries. Jeronimo and several others from the northwestern highlands were invited to speak and perform marimba music in reservations across the United States and Canada.

Allan Burns: But how did you end up here in Indiantown; why did you leave Guatemala?

Jeronimo Camposeco: Because I could learn Spanish. I am an Indian like everybody else. Since I was a kid I helped my father in the fields, working in the lands and working to grow milpa and bringing wood to myself. And so I had the opportunity to go to the school. Later I worked at the National Indian Institute. We were a team of people there, and we were connected with the North American Indians. And some of them were working with us in the villages, because in 1976 was an earthquake, and so some just came to work. And some of them stayed there after the earthquake until 1980. And this work, for the government, for the paramilitary groups and the death squads, and even the army was looking for all the people who were working to try to have a better life in the countryside. Because we are the people in Guatemala, we are very poor. You know that since colonial times the people in power took our lands—we only have tiny lands in the mountains, and the good lands are in the lowlands in the hands of the companies. Exporting all the products like sugar cane, coffee, bananas, but there is nothing for our consumption, so I teach the Indians how to develop their own lands.

Allan Burns: Did the army come for you?

Jeronimo Camposeco: Yes. First of all the army came and killed some of my friends and my co-workers. Even a North American Indian was killed by the army; his name was Kayuta Clouds. He was tortured. And because we worked together, the death squads found my name in a letter I sent to him inviting him to come to Guatemala. And so the American Embassy called to my office saying that I need to be careful because some people are looking for me because they found the body of Kay. After that they were looking for me. So I went to my house and told my wife and my children that I am leaving because the death squads are looking for me. So I escaped to Mexico. My family went to another house. There was a store next to my house. The people there saw three men in a car looking for me, but fortunately my family and I were not there. So I could escape to the United States. And I came to Pennsylvania because there is a place where my friends there, American Indians, farm. And so they gave me refuge there for six months. My family came later, and they joined me in Pennsylvania.

When the Maya of Florida immigrated to the United States in the early 1980s, like many groups of people before them they found the new language, customs, and communities both fascinating and frightening. On the one hand, they found a haven from the disarray of Guatemala, a community that was hospitable to their plight and their work ethic. One woman, Maria Andres, put it quite succinctly:

Maria Andres: Well, we left Guatemala for the problem that was there, for the war. We wanted to save ourselves in Guatemala, so we came to this land. We looked for each other here in this land. We like living here in this land. Now we don't want to go back to Guatemala.

Allan Burns: What year did you come here?

Maria Andres: In '80 or '81.

Allan Burns: Did you come directly to Indiantown?

Maria Andres: No. We first came to Los Angeles. We came to Los Angeles first. We can't live in our own country, because they are killing a lot of people there. It's because of that. We don't want to die; we want to live in peace, and so we came here. That is the problem that we have.

Allan Burns: And are these your two daughters?

Maria Andres: Yes, one is a niece, but her mother was killed, so she's here with me.

Allan Burns: Did they come with you?

Maria Andres: One of them, yes; the other arrived earlier.

Allan Burns: When did your mother die?

Eugenia Francisco (the niece): In '79.

Allan Burns: Did she die here or where?

Eugenia Francisco: In Guatemala. There was an accident.

Allan Burns: And here in the United States, how is life for women?

Maria Andres: No, we don't have problems here. We just want to work here. We just want to live and work here.

Allan Burns: What did you do in Guatemala?

Maria Andres: There in Guatemala, we didn't work. We were in the house, taking care of it and raising our children. That's what we did in our houses.

Allan Burns: Were you making things of clay?

Maria Andres: No, it was others who did that. Where we lived we didn't. We made food for those who worked, the campesinos. That is what we were doing. Now, we have to go and look for work elsewhere, well, because here there isn't any work. We won't be able to work anymore here. We'll leave and then we'll return here again after the work.

Allan Burns: Where will you go?

Maria Andres: To New York.

Allan Burns: To New York? Maria Andres: All of us, the whole family will go. We are taking the number of the center here with us in case our application comes up and they have to call us for an appointment. If they do, we'll come by plane for the appointment for political asylum. That's what we're going to do.

Allan Burns: What do you need here in Indiantown?

Maria Andres: If the president would let us, we would buy a little land here so we could live better.

Maria Andres and others from Guatemala came to Florida and found jobs, first in the citrus groves, later in construction and the service industries. They found their friends who had fled several years earlier, and some went back to bring wives and children. With the passing of years, their children learned English and some went to college. Others moved away from Indiantown to see other parts of the United States and to see what it means to be a Maya American.

The narratives of the violence of Guatemala, the flight to the United States, and the difficulties of staying in the United States legally now make up a new oral history among the Maya of the United States. The narratives are not just stories of a journey, but are at the intersection of personal history and political adaptation. People like Maria Andres who are not practiced in public speaking have had to talk about events that are personally tragic and that run counter to the prevailing beliefs of U.S. citizens and immigration authorities. Their stories are met with incredulity, an incredulity often fueled by the legal expectation of precision with regard to dates and locations. The narratives have been honed through interactions with lawyers working for political asylum, but even when dates and places are precisely given, new challenges are brought forward. Sometimes it is the challenge of time itself: after a few years threats and persecution are thought to disappear, and dangers experienced a few years ago are not seen as real today. Sometimes the challenge is to the veracity of the asylum seekers, as when an immigration hearing judge doubts that a gentle Maya person could recall such tragic events in a voice without emotion.

Source:
Maya in Exile: Guatemalans in Florida, by Allan F.
    Burns. Philadelphia: Temple University Press,
    1993.

GYPSY AMERICANS

Separated by six countries, three continents, and a thousand years of cultural development, the separate bands of musicians who make up Gypsy Caravan find they all speak a similar musical language. When they jam together, they recognize traces of their own music—of melody and of rhythm—in each other. Yet their music belongs to no single country or famous composer, let alone any recognized classical tradition. The performers seldom meet, and their music rarely if ever fills the world's concert halls. As the article on this unique meeting of diverse musicians explains, they recognize similarities because of a distant, common heritage: they are ethnic Gypsies—or, more properly, Roma.

Diversity marked the Roma from the beginning. This diverse people originated in northern India where, prior to the eleventh century, they were organized into armies by the Indian rulers as a means to resist the eastward expansion of Islam. At some point in the 1200s, the Roma began to migrate across Europe, and from there to points as northern as Russia and as southern as Australia. They reached the United States as well, where anywhere between 100,000 and one million Roma are believed to live today.

If the Roma have long been a nomadic people, it was not necessarily by their choice. Historically, nations have shunned them. Prejudice, founded upon stereotypes of them as thieves and vagabonds, has given them centuries of status as outsiders. As such, Romani identity has long had adaptability at its center. The Roma have long had to live with constant change on the periphery of societies that were, and still are, hostile to them. During the 1980s, for example, Bulgaria sought to extinguish the Romani presence that had been a part of it for centuries. And even when societies are less openly antagonistic, they tend to trivialize Romani culture by viewing its members as an exotic, romantic, and hence irrational people—the so-called "noble savage." Historically, one exception was Russia, where aristocrats, rulers, and writers celebrated the Russian Roma.

But while neither the Western nor Eastern world has exactly opened its arms, more people in the 1980s and 1990s began to take Romani culture seriously. Along with academic scholarship, helping to popularize this new evaluation were movies such as the drama "Time of the Gypsies" (1989), a European hit filmed in a Romani dialect, and the documentary "Latcho Drom" (1993), which focused on Romani music.

By 1999, the Gypsy Caravan was on tour. Organized by the World Music Institute, a U.S.-based promoter of traditional and contemporary world music, the tour brought together six Roma bands with members from India, Bulgaria, Romania, Hungary, Russia, Spain and the United States. There was striking diversity in their music. The Indian group Musafir, which contains no Roma members, performed folk songs and dances that may have formed the basis of Roma tradition before their twelfth century exodus began. From Romania, Taraf de Haidouks spe-

cialized in dizzyingly fast accordion, fiddle, and vocal performances. And the Russian Kolpakov Trio offered seven-string guitar songs.

Notably, as the article suggests, the Gypsy Caravan tour afforded a glimpse into a traditionally secret side of Romani culture. Over the centuries during which they learned the language and customs of the countries through which they traveled, the Roma found that music was a commodity they could often sell. This was a means of subsisting, and also of meeting foreign expectations: outsiders primarily wanted a certain stereotypical gypsy sound at weddings and public performances. And yet just as the Romani preserved their own language, so too have they kept a more personal music for themselves. In this personal music was a tradition hoarded and kept safe from a hostile world—a music by, and for, a people with no home.

ON THE ROAD WITH GYPSY SONG AND DANCE

In a rehearsal room above City Center, three Russian guitarists, the Kolpakov Trio, struck up a bouncy, slightly mournful gypsy tune. Kalyi Jag, a Hungarian group, joined in, strumming guitars and tapping on a milk can, playing a variant of the tune that came through their own tradition. Taraf de Haidouks, from Romania, chimed in with the hammered strings of a cimbalom and stuttering, breakneck lines from its accordionist.

Grins began to flash between the musicians. Yuri Yunakov, a Bulgarian saxophonist, took up the melody, zigzagging all around it, while the percussionists in Musafir, a group from Rajasthan, India, started to double time the beat with wooden clappers and a hand drum. A flamenco dancer, Antonio El Pipa, stepped forward, his back arched like a drawn bow as his heels clattered cross-rhythms. Next to him, Masafir's dancer, Sayari Sapera, tried the swaying, sensual hip movements of a dance originally used to charm snakes. Her hands traced arabesques akin to flamenco gestures; she was barefooted, twirling, with bells around her ankles jingling at every step.

It was, in its way, a family reunion. The musicians and dancers were about to start touring together as the Gypsy Caravan, a sextuple bill, produced by the World Music Institute, that comes to City Center on Friday and Saturday. They were rehearsing a potential grand finale, bending history and musicology a little bit to make a point: that the Gypsy heritage stretches all the way from India to Australia. It's a musical diaspora that has survived poverty and persecution while transforming, and being transformed by, every culture it has touched.

"We can all speak together," said Gusztav Varga, the leader of the Hungarian band Kalyi Jag (which means Black Fire). "We have one language."

The story of Gypsy music is one of flexibility backed by hidden tenacity. Lately, the itinerary has been documented in films like "Latcho Drom" and on albums like "The Gypsy Road" (Alula), which has selections from five of the six bands on the Gypsy Caravan tour.

The Roma, as gypsies call themselves, began to spread across Europe from northwestern India in the 11th century. (The word Gypsy comes from the mistaken idea that the Roma originated in Egypt.) They were not welcomed. The Roma were distrusted, exploited, scapegoated, sometimes enslaved, as the familiar Gypsy stereotypes grew. They were shunned and marginalized; they were also pressured to assimilate. In the Austro-Hungarian Empire and more recently in Eastern Europe, Rom language and traditional dress were outlawed. In Spain, where it was banned from 1499 to 1800, the Rom language is virtually lost, even as Spain has come to prize the flamenco tradition that merges Rom, Andalusian and Moorish roots.

As nationalism has surged in Eastern Europe, the Roma still face discrimination. Bulgaria outlawed Rom language, music and dress in the 1980's in a stated effort to cleanse Bulgaria of outside influences, despite the fact that Roma people had been in Bulgaria for centuries. Mr. Yunakov, a Rom of Turkish descent who was a member of Ivo Papasov's renowned wedding band in Bulgaria, said band members often had to flee the police if they chose to perform a Gypsy song. He and two other members of his current band were imprisoned for playing the wrong songs, and threats were made against Mr. Yunakov's children. At that point, Mr. Yunakov emigrated to the United States. For the last five years, he has been performing on Tuesday nights at the Turkish Kitchen restaurant in Murray Hill. There, he plays not Rom or Bulgarian music but Turkish songs.

Like other minorities, the Roma learned to live between cultures: to present different faces to the outside world and their own communities. They picked up the language and musical styles where they settled yet held on to their own traditions. Across Europe, the Rom language still uses words and structures that can be traced back to Sanskrit and Punjabi. And behind closed doors families passed down the old tunes and dances.

Most of the musicians in the Gypsy Caravan play at least two repertories. One is for listeners who expect to hear so-called Gypsy music and simply adds Rom touches to a local folk and pop repertory. The other, rarely revealed to the wider public, is the music and dance they perform for one another, and the Gypsy Caravan tour is intended to present the purer Rom styles. "It is a completely different sound," said Mr. Varga, who started Kalyi Jag in 1978 to hold on to the old Hungarian Rom music. (Contrary to stereotype, there's no violinist in the group.) More recently, he founded a school to teach children the Rom language along with English and computer literacy.

Mr. Varga said he could hear common characteristics in much of the music on the Gypsy Caravan program, like a certain clipped, 2/4 rhythm that appears in flamenco, in his own repertory and in the Indian songs of Musafir. Rom songs often use a raw, incantatory vocal style that clearly has non-Western roots, although scales and structures change with every regional style. Three-part harmonies, for voices or instruments, are widespread, and much of the dancing shares a percussive approach, from the heel taps of flamenco to the thigh-and boot-slapping dances of Hungary. Improvisation is an essential part of the music, as it is in many local folk styles along the Rom route.

And in many parts of Eastern Europe, rom musicians have long been especially prized for wedding celebrations, at which the dancing can go on nonstop for hours or days. But as Manole Ionel, who plays accordion in the Romanian band Taraf de Haidouks, said: "You arrive as a musician, and you are welcomed. But you leave as Rom, and nobody wants to pay you."

Still, there is more variety than similarity in the styles of the Gypsy Caravan. Despite their cultural kinship, the groups on the bill represent styles that have long been separated from one another, geographically and historically.

Musafir, the Rajasthani group, is not made up of Rom musicians; as Hameed Khan, the group's founder and tabla player explained, the Roma were the ones who migrated, not the people who stayed in India. "What is a memory of people who left nearly 1,000 years ago?" he asked. " The migration never came back." Musafir (which means traveler in Farsi) was organized to include as many of Rajasthan's performing traditions as possible, including North Indian classical music and devotional music. Its musicians come from three groups that live in the Thar desert: Langas, Manghiyars and the nomadic Saperas. For the Gypsy Caravan concerts it will concentrate on the vigorous folk songs and dances that are a likely part of the Rom heritage.

The Kolpakov Trio reflects the history of Russia's reaction to the Rom presence. Writers like Pushkin celebrated Rom music; aristocrats became patrons. After the revolution, Stalin was also a fan, and in 1931 the Government built the Moscow Romen Theater, institutionalizing Rom performance styles but also homogenizing them and adding Western influences. (Only later, under Khrushchev, did the Soviet Union start to restrict the Roma severely.) Alexandre Kolpakov, the group's leader, was trained at the Romen Theater.

But he began to play the seven-string guitar, a traditional Russian Rom instrument, as a boy in his hometown among the Servo, the oldest Rom group in Russia. The trio reflects an intimate older style of Rom music, with rich vocal harmonies and songs that start out moody and introspective then accelerate dramatically. His 18-year-old nephew, Vadim Kolpakov, studied with him and joined the trio in 1997. "The most important thing is to further the culture, to transmit it to the next generation." Alexandre Kolpakov said. "To give what you have and to see people taking it—that makes you rich."

Antonio El Pipa's flamenco group focuses on the dancers, whose imperious postures and explosive foot-stamping depict vignettes of pride and desire. But the group also includes his aunt Juana Fernández Reyes, who sings with an indomitable, gravelly voice that conjures age-old melancholy and resolve. She learned the tradition through her family, which had generations of musicians. The feeling, she said, "comes from inside; it is always there."

Taraf de Haidouks, which means "Band of Brigands," also brings together musicians from two generations, playing Romanian songs that work their way up to dizzying speeds, with raw, quavering voices and endless variations spun out on accordion and fiddles. The elder musicians have spent their lives playing at local weddings, baptisms and parties; the younger ones have turned their ears to the outside world, adding influences from around the Balkans and playing newer tunes on the old instruments. "We play the old songs as they are and as they have ben," Mr. Ionel said. "Each musician puts something into the piece, but the traditional part cannot be changed." (Along with the Gypsy Caravan tour, Taraf de Haidouks will perform a New York club show at the Bottom Line on April 14.)

The Romanians and the Bulgarians are the speed demons on the bill; their versions of the old tunes ought to leave jet trails behind them. Mr. Yunakov's Bulgarian—which began replacing the trumpet in Bulgarian bands in the 1970's—and an electric keyboard alongside the more traditional accordion. Carrying on the age-old tradition of Rom musicians, who have kept their ears open all the way along their 1,000-year itinerary, Mr. Yunakov continues to extend his music; along with his Rom, Turkish and Bulgarian songs, he has taken up Albanian music since arriving in New York.

"On every road," Mr.. Yunakov said, "you find something new to learn."

Source:
Jon Pareles, "On the Road with Gypsy Song and
    Dance." In *New York Times*, April 4, 1999. p. 7.

HAITIAN AMERICANS

T his Haitian woman's memoir of coming to America in 1983 gives voice to her experience as a non-English speaking, uneducated, and unskilled female refugee, who left her Caribbean island country in a boat seeking to reach Miami. U.S. Immigration records for 1983 show that 8,424 Haitians came to the United States. In 1992, Haiti's population reached about 6.5 million, with about 600 persons per square mile, one of the highest population densities of the world. Immigration waves typically corresponded with political turmoil in Haiti, but poverty has also been a motivating factor to leave.

Many Haitian refugees and immigrants settled in Little Haiti, which was once known as Lemon City. When 60,000 Haitian boat people arrived in South Florida between 1977 and 1981, the area became a spirited community with a unique Caribbean marketplace with shops offering Caribbean arts and crafts, foods and music. By the 1990s, the population was about 33,900. Businesses along North Miami Avenue and Northeast Second Avenue showcase ethnic pride and entrepreneurial energy. Tourists seeking world famous colorful Haitian primitive art shop the mom-and-pop businesses that offer Haitian goods. The historic Buena Vista district in Little Haiti is a residential enclave of Mediterranean style stucco cottages. The urban renewal of the Little River commercial district has happened as a result of the aggressive business efforts of the immigrant community, a renewal taking place in other U.S. cities with growing immigrant communities. Little Haiti's renewal began during the early 1980s when Haitian professionals and entrepreneurs migrated from New York to Miami and established businesses and restaurants along Fifty-fourth Street and Northeast Second Avenue.

Paulette Francius left Haiti to seek a better life for herself. While conditions for her hardly improve in Little Haiti, as the Haitian community in Miami has come to be known, conditions for her children born in the United States are good. With public assistance and public schooling, the outlook for Francius and her children seem worth her struggles. She mentions her fear of violence, particularly robbery, and contrasts conditions in Haiti as more favorable in this regard. However, Francius is not nostalgic about Haiti: she mentions the Tonton Macoute, a patronage system that assumed political control through strong-arm techniques that Francius calls "bullying people all the time." The Tonton Macoute functioned within the army and gave peasants no voice in the political process. As late as 1989, they were the main obstacle to free, fair, and popular elections in Haiti.

LITTLE HAITI

Paulette Francius
Born near Saint Marc, Haiti
Unemployed Single Parent
Miami, Florida

It was April 6, 1983, when we finally reached the Florida coast. The night was so dark that we couldn't tell we were just outside of Miami. Some people said, "We are in Nassau, Bahamas." But other people on the boat, who knew Miami, said, "No, this is Florida." When an American coast-guard boat approached, we knew that we were in Miami. I didn't know whether to be happy or afraid.

The coast guard came with other police. They took our names and gave us something sweet to eat. People who were very sick were taken to a hospital. A woman who worked for Immigration told the rest of us that we were being taken someplace comfortable, where our families would come to pick us up. That was a lie. The next morning, we were taken in a big bus to Krome prison. They gave us uniforms to wear.

The Krome Center is built like a regular prison for illegal immigrants.

All the detainees live in big white cement buildings. There is barbed wire surrounding the compound. Men and women are separated by a large steel chain-link fence, but we were allowed to socialize certain times of the day. The women's quarters was one huge room lined with bunk beds. There were around a hundred women from different countries. Most were Haitians. I cried all the time.

Every day, we would just sit there. Women who knew how to sew kept busy on machines. I met a Haitian man in Krome who I came to love. It seems unbelievable, but I became pregnant in Krome. I became very ill and asked the authorities for permission to go to a hospital. They told me that I was insane and refused to accept my pregnancy, even though my stomach and breasts were obviously swelling with all the clear symptoms.

The authorities said that they always had guards watching us, so it was impossible for me to be pregnant. But my boyfriend and I found ways to have private time together, such as when everyone went to the cafeteria for meals. He and I planned to get married when we were released from Krome.

In September, five months after we had been imprisoned, my stomach was so swollen that the authorities had to send me to the hospital for a

checkup. I had dizziness and was vomiting, as well as swelling breasts—all the signs of pregnancy. But they kept saying that I wasn't pregnant. I got into a big argument with them in the hospital, because they said my condition was just an infection.

My boyfriend was desperate, so he sent a tape-recorded plea to Father Jean-Juste at the Haitian Refugee Center in Miami. I spoke in Creole, and he did an English translation. We explained that we were afraid that the Krome officials were concealing my pregnancy in order to give me an abortion and then deport us. My boyfriend said, "I am the father of the baby. Paulette will be my wife when we get out of this jail. That is something we planned before she became pregnant."

Father Jean-Juste came to visit me at the hospital. He photographed my large stomach and gave the picture to a newspaper. I was shocked when the immigration officers released me from Krome. I stood outside the huge steel fence and said, "Thank God, I'm free."

Because I have no relatives here, I was put under the responsibility of the Haitian Refugee Center, pending an asylum hearing. I moved in with relatives of my boyfriend and waited for him to be released. I looked forward to getting married and began looking for work right away.

I applied for jobs at many hotels and restaurants in the Miami Beach area, but every place only wanted to hire women who spoke some English. During that time, I had a miscarriage and lost the baby. Then I got the news that my boyfriend had been sent back to Haiti. My dreams were shattered.

I realized that there was no work for me in Miami. I met people who were going to work on farms in another part of Florida, but I didn't have close friends or relatives there, so I was afraid to go on my own. I met another man, who I began to spend time with. We moved into an apartment on 58th Street in Little Haiti in January 1984, when I was again pregnant. My son Paul was born one year after I arrived in Florida.

I didn't have a good relationship with Paul's father. So, although I was kind of afraid, I began to look for a place of my own. I felt very insecure and took up with a man who was working. Paul was not even a year old when the twins, Gerard and Gerald, were born.

While I was in the hospital giving birth, the twins' father took care of Paul. It was a very difficult time for me. In Haiti, when a woman has a baby, her mother or sister helps take care of the other children. Even a friend might help. Here I felt so isolated and alone. I cried so much because of that. I had a Cesarean operation, and when I came home from the hospital, there was nobody to help. Right away I had to take care of the children, do the housework, everything by myself, even though the doctors at the hospital had warned me to take it easy. The father worked during the day. I was home by myself with the children. We lived in an upstairs apartment.

Occasionally one neighbor, an American woman married to a Haitian, came by to help with the children. Sometimes other neighbors would stop by. But they thought my husband was there, so they didn't come very often.

For two and a half years, ever since I moved back out on my own, I have just stayed home with the kids. I can't socialize, because I don't have anyone to leave the kids with. In Haiti, especially in the countryside, women work hard. Here, because of the lack of jobs, women don't work as much as men. This gives the man more power in the household. He tells the woman, "You're not working. You take what I give you."

In Haiti, if wives don't hold a job, they find other ways of making money by doing small home-style business. They sell food that they cook or bake at the marketplace or outside of their homes. Some women buy and resell small quantities of rice or canned food, others sew or make clothes. This is a way of life for Haitian women.

In Miami, some women have been able to find similar ways to make a little money from their homes. Some cook and open their home like a small restaurant for a few hours each day. If I had a sewing machine, I would try to do some work for friends. First I need to learn how to sew well. And with the kids, I have no time to make money. I just stay home. . . .

After the birth of the twins, when I regained my strength, I decided that it would be better if I had my own place. I found this apartment even though I don't speak English, because the landlord is Haitian. I've learned how to get around, because people I've met give me advice. And there is a Haitian radio station, newspapers in Creole, and a pretty active grapevine.

When Americans talk to me, I can understand some words, but I cannot comprehend exactly what they are saying. If I had someone to watch the kids, I would take English class. At home, I can't even learn English from watching television, because the kids are usually running around. I know how to count in English, and the days of the week. That's about all.

In the four years I've been in Miami, I've had limited contact with Americans. I only see Haitian people. I am afraid of Americans. Robbers come into people's houses with guns and say, "Give us everything you have, or we will kill you." It's happened many times on this street. A thief came into my next-door neighbor's apartment just this week, but the lady was home and heard the noise. She ran outside, yelling for help.

Many times, thieves come when everyone is asleep and steal even decorations on window ledges. That is why we all have iron bars on our windows. And I make sure to lock my door every night. The robbers are both Haitians and black Americans. The Liberty City neighborhood is seven blocks away. That's a pretty rough area. What can we do? The white police can beat us up, and the blacks come in and rob us.

In Haiti, there wasn't this kind of problem with robbery. The problem was the Tontons Macoute bullying people all the time. They controlled everything. And after Duvalier, social chaos. . . .

I don't know what will happen to me. My immigration case is still on appeal before the judge. Periodically I am called into the INS building for the judge to ask if what I have already told them is true. But they still haven't scheduled my final hearing. If my plea fails, they can send me back to Haiti. My children are American citizens, because they were born in Miami. They would leave with American passports and could come back any time. But I wouldn't be able to come with them. My hope is for the children to go to school, so they can become *someone*.

I am very worried about my status, but I don't like to complain while I am in this country, because the American government has given me food to eat. They provide medical care and enough money to pay the rent. In Haiti, there is no welfare program or American-style clinic for the children.

I worry. Not about these children's future: I believe that nothing bad will happen to them. But I worry about my son in Haiti. He is eleven years old now. I would like to send money to my mother to take care of him or to send for him, but I cannot afford to. And my mother is very poor. She sent me a letter recently and asked me to take him. The government took some of her land and left her without anything. In Haiti, there is no justice.

I have no regrets about coming to Miami. Even though my life is uncertain, I have food. I can say anything I want to say. There are no Macoutes or police who bother me. Still, I miss my relatives and wish that I could do more for them.

If I could find work now, I would be happy. Any type—on a farm, in town—it doesn't matter. But I can't look for work, because in this neighborhood there is only one day-care center, on 22nd Avenue. You have to sign a waiting list. It takes two years, sometimes they forget about you. And a requirement for day care is that you must already be working. They won't take children if the parent is trying to find a job. Where does that leave me?

Source:

New Americans: An Oral History, by Al Santoli. New York: Viking Penguin Inc., 1988. pp. 360-365.

*T*here have been four significant waves of Haitian immigration to the United States. Each of these periods was precipitated by political upheaval, along with economic turmoil. There was the stage of French colonization; the Haitian revolution (1791-1803); the United States occupation of Haiti (1915-1934); and the period of the Duvaliers (1957-1986). During the last period, political persecution that resulted from the rule of François "Papa Doc" and Jean-Claude "Baby Doc" Duvalier led to an exodus of students, the middle class, and Haitian professionals to several different countries, including the United States. Many Haitians attempted to enter the United States by boat, but they were not always welcome, as the American government at the time supported the Duvalier government.

Moreover, by the 1990s there was an increase in xenophobia and racism throughout the United States. Many advances made on the behalf of minorities became threatened, as affirmative action plans and equal opportunity programs were discontinued, as they were now considered policies of reverse discrimination. There were also demands to halt or restrict immigration. In 1995, voters in California passed Proposition 187, which denied illegal aliens and their children government funding for education, health care and other state benefits. The measure never took effect, however, as it became mired in lawsuits. In 1997, most of the proposition was declared unconstitutional by a federal court. This was the climate that prompted the political cartoon depicted here.

No Haitians Need Apply

Source:
Copyright Neil R. King.

HAWAIIANS

The Kumulipo is the great Hawaiian creation chant containing the most ancient traditions of the Hawaiians about their gods, the origin of the sky, seas, and the world, the sea's islands and all the creatures, and the myths of their human and Polynesian ancestors. Chants were passed from one generation to the next by special bards, called haku mele, who spent their lives composing, reciting and teaching Hawaiians to perform the ancient chants. The Birth Chant for Kau-i-ke-ao-uli is an offshoot of that great creation chant that was composed in the nineteenth century to celebrate the birth of the Kamehameha I's second son, Prince Kau-i-ke-ao-uli, who ruled Hawaii from 1825 to 1854 as Kamehameha III. This chant was composed in 1813, seven years before the arrival of the first New England missionaries, who would deeply affect Hawaiian culture. In pre-Christian Hawaii, hula troupes, or chanters, performed ritual chants, dances, and songs to celebrate the festival of first fruits and to summon magic and power to the ceremonial and sexual union of high chiefs. The birth of a royal child needed this magic to ensure that he become a great leader.

Birth chants eulogized the ancestry of the newest heir to the chiefdom in order to add distinction to him. At the first signs of pregnancy for a royal couple, bards composed name songs to celebrate the coming child. The bards taught the name chant to hula dancers, who memorized the words and particular attitudes and gestures to accompany the chant. The chant was joyfully performed until the birth of the child.

Alternating refrains throughout the Birth Chant for Kau-i-ke-ao-uli chant ask the questions: "Who shall be above? Who shall be here below?" These questions are thought to refer to the Hawaiian premonition that the ruling chiefs would be transformed into mere human beings instead of sacred heads of government. The name of this child, who was stillborn but "prayed into life" by the priest, meant "placed in the dark sky," a reference to regaining consciousness and achieving mental enlightenment. In the chant, the birth of the prince is linked to cosmic events that are personified in the mating of the sky father, named Wākea, and the earth mother, named Papa. Four major gods are invoked during the chant, the source god of sun, water and light, the god of healing, the god of canoe-making and war, and the god of fertility, agriculture, and fishing.

The Kumulipo was a genealogical prayer chant containing the earliest beliefs about Hawaiian origins. German anthropologist Adolf Bastian borrowed a copy of the chant from the king, and called European attention to the document when he compared it with origin myths from Polynesia and ancient Asiatic civilizations in a work published in 1881. Other Polynesian cultures, notably the Marquesas and the Tuamotus, also celebrated with recitations.

King Kalakaua published his document in the native language in 1889 in a 66 page pamphlet printed in Honolulu. Historian Mary Kawena Pukui noted in The Echo of Our Song, that the printed versions of chants were reasonable facsimiles

*but could never take the place of the living poem in its primary language. But print-
ed records became extremely valuable by the twentieth century. Two pages attached
to Kalakaua's pamphlet described the circumstances under which the chant was
composed and recited in the old days. The printed version of the Kumulipo was
translated into English in 1897 by the dethroned Queen Liliu'okalani, sister of King
Kalakaua, who had died. The manuscript copy of the Kumulipo that belonged to
King Kalakaua is the property of the Bishop Museum in Honolulu, given to the
museum in 1922 by the nephew of the former rulers.*

*Hawaiian chants generally fell into two categories: mele oli chants unaccom-
panied by any instrument and performed by an individual; and mele hula chants
performed by a group and accompanied by dancing and musical instruments. Within these categories there were dozens of different kinds of chants both formal and
informal for such occasions as surfing, expressions of affection, chants to make a
request, chants to complain or praise, and prayer chants, to name a few. Chants
were the poetic expression of the native Hawaiian, fulfilling a need that was satisfied by songs and written poetry in other cultures. Chants were composed according
to rules that governed styles of performance. For example, the kepakepa style was
a rapid-speech, rhythmic recitation that was used for game chants and prayer.
Modern American rap music has similarities to some types of Hawaiian chanting.*

*Kamehameha III, the honoree of the Birth Chant for Kau-i-ke-ao-uli, ruled
Hawaii during a time of significant change. He approved Hawaii's first constitution.
Thirty-six years after his death the monarchy was destroyed, as hinted in the birth
chant's questions, "Who shall be above? Who shall be here below?" Kamehameha
III died 105 years before Hawaii became the fiftieth state of the United States.*

MELE HĀNAU NŌ KAU-I-KE-AO-ULI

Birth Chant for Kau-i-ke-ao-uli

I

The chiefess gave birth,
she bore in labor above,
she lay as in a faint, a weakness at the navel.
The afterbirth stirred at the roots, crept in darkness,
in waves of pain came the bitter bile of the child.
This was a month of travail,
of gasping labor,
a writhing to deliver the chief.
He is this chief, born of a chiefess.

Now a chief shall be here above.
Who shall be below?

Born was the earth, rooted the earth.
The root crept forth, rootlets of the earth.
Royal rootlets spread their way through the earth to hold firm.
Down too went the taproot, creaking
like the mainpost of a house, and the earth moved.
Cliffs rose upon the earth, the earth lay widespread:
a standing earth, a sitting earth was the earth,
a swaying earth, a solid earth was the earth.

II

O hānau a hua Kalani,
O ho'onā kū i luna,
O momoe o ma'ule ka piko,
O kolokolo ia pō ke ēwe,
O mulea, o malahia ka nalu, ke a'a.
O ho'onā kū o ka malama,
O ka'ahē a ka 'īloli,
O ho'owiliwili e hānau Kalani.
'O ia ho'i, 'o Kalani, hānau Kalani.

'O Kalani ia ho'i auane'i kō luna nei la.
'O wai la ho'i auane'i kō lalo la?

O hānau ka honua, a mole ka honua.
O kolokolo ka a'a, ka weli o ka honua.
O lani weli ka honua, o lani'i'ī.
O holo pu ka mole, o 'u'ina ke a'a,
O hale ka pou lewa ka honua.
O pali nu'u ka honua, ākea ka honua,
O honua kū, o honua noho ka honua,
O honua lewa, o honua pa'a, ka honua,

Four year old Lei Ku'u I'ini performs a Hawaiian dance in front of a lion's mask in Chinatown Plaza, Las Vegas.

The earth lay below, from below the earth rose.
The earth was Kea's, to Kea belonged the earth.
The earth was Papa's, to Papa belonged the earth,
the earthly firstborn borne by Papa.
He is this earth, the earth that was born.

The earth shall be here below.
Who shall be above?

II

Born was the night above,
born was the night up here.
The heavens slid away into the night, swift came the afterbirth.
The nights came closer together, stretching along
until came a separation, making distinct the night of Mahina-le'a.
The night turned, closeness became separated.
This is the royal offspring of night borne by Kea,
first child of the night, second child of the night,
third child of the night.
The night lay in travail
to give birth to the night.
He is this night, the night newly born.

Who shall be below?
Who shall be upon the island?

III

Born was the island, it grew, it sprouted,
it flourished, lengthened, rooted deeply, budded, formed tender leaves.
That was the island over Hawai'i.
Hawai'i itself was an island.

Ka honua ilalo, ilalo nu'u ka honua.
O honua a Kea, nā Kea da honua.
O honua a Papa, nā Papa ka honua,
'O ka hiapo honua a Papa i hānau.
'O ia ho'i, 'o ka honua, hānau ka honua.

'O ka honua la ho'i kō lalo nei.
'O wai la ho'i auane'i kō luna la?

II

O hānau ka pō iluna,
Hānau ka pō i luna nei.
O lani hāne'e ka pō, o pīna'i ke ēwe.
O pipili ka pō, o moe anana le'a,
O kōhi ana, le'a ka pō o Mahina-le'a,
O huli ka pō, o ka'awale ka pili.
'O ke keiki pō lani keia a Kea i hānau,
Keiki 'akāhi a ka pō, keiki 'alua a ka pō,
Keiki 'akolu a ka pō.
'O ke kuakoko a ka pō,
E hānau mai auane'i ka pō,
'O ia ho'i o ka pō, hānau ka pō,
'O ka pō la ho'i auane'i kō luna nei la.

'O wai la ho'i auane'i kō lalo?
'O wai la ho'i o ka moku?

III

O hānau ka moku a kupu,
A lau, a loa, a a'a, a mu'o, a liko.
Ka moku ia luna o Hawai'i.
'O Hawa'i nei nō ka moku.

The land was unstable, Hawai'i quivered,
moved freely about in space,
Wākea recognized the island, Hawai'i recognized remained.
Visible were island and earth,
held in heavenly space by the right hand of Wākea,
Hawai'i was held, Hawai'i was seen, an island.

Down here shall be an island.
Who shall be above—Who?
The cloud, that is who it shall be.

IV

The cloud was born, it rose and appeared.
The cloud thrived, it rose and appeared.
The cloud came at dawn, it rose and appeared.
The cloud flushed with a reddish tinge, it rose and appeared.
The cloud rose and appeared in clearest configuration,
        turned yellow and menacing.
The horizon cloud hung yellow over a calm sea.
A swelling cloud, a dark cloud,
a cloud whose deepening darkness turned to black
in a sky already black with feathery clouds of dusk,
a sky heavy with blackness, rough, lowering,
a sky speaking in threat:
a vast cloud foretelling the approach of rain.
The sky writhed in labor to give birth.
He is this cloud: thus it was born.

A cloud shall be up here.
Who shall be below?
The mountain, that is who it shall be.

V

Born of Kea was the mountain,
the mountain of Kea budded forth.
Wākea was the husband, Papa Walinu'u was the wife.

Born was Ho'ohoku, a daughter,
born was Hāloa, a chief,
born was the mountain, a mountain-son of Kea.
Jealous was Wākea, he revealed his fault,
told of his smiting Kāne with a club
in battle, fought in Kahiki-kū.
Wākea was routed, fled in confusion with his family.
None spoke to Wākea save in whispers, but Kāne shouted.
Wākea returned to the sky seeking a wife.
He mated, sleeping beside Papa as mate.
The sun was born to Wākea,
a sacred offshoot of Wākea,
the growth of Wākea was Wākea's own.
He was this mountain's growing, this chief: so was the
        mountain born.

The mountain shall be down here.
Who shall be above?
The sun, that is who shall be above.

He pūlewa ka 'āina, he naka Hawai'i,
E lewa wale ana nō i ka lani lewa,
Hanou mai e Wākea, pā hano ia.
Mālie 'ikea ka moku me ka honua,
Pa'a 'ia lewa lani i ka lima 'ākau o Wākea,
Pa'a Hawai'i, la'a Hawai'i, 'ikea he moku.

O ka moku la ho'i kō lalo nei.
'O wai la ho'i kō luna, 'owai la?
O ke ao, 'oia ho'i hā.

IV

O hānau ke ao, o hiki a'e.
O 'ohi a'e ke ao, o hiki a'e.
O mokupawa ke ao, o hiki a'e.
O aka 'ula ke ao, o hiki a'e.
O moakaka ke ao maāla'e.

'Ōpukupuku ke ao melemele.
O memele ka 'ōpua he la'i.
O 'ōpua nui, uli ka 'ōpua hiwahiwa,
O hiwahiwa ka 'ōpua lani'ele,
'Ele'ele ka lani huhulu weo,
Lani'eka'ekahā'ele'ele,
Hākona, hākuma, hākumakuma,
'O ke ao nui mai he'e ua kaia.
E ho'owiliwili ana e hānau,
'O ia ho'i, 'o ke ao, hānau ke ao.

'O ke ao ho'i hā kō luna nei.
'O wai la auane'i kō lalo la?
'O ka mauna, 'oia ho'i.

V

O hānau ka mauna a Kea,
'Ōpu'u a'e ka mauna a Kea.
'O Wākea ke kāne, 'o Papa, 'o Walinu'u ka
        wahine.
Hānau Ho'ohoku he wahine,
Hānau Hāloa he ali'i,
Hānau ka mauna, he keiki mauna nā Kea.
O ka lili o Wākea, o ka ha'i i ka hala,
O ke kū kukū lā'au 'ana me Kāne,
I ho'oūka ai iloko o Kahiki-kū.
He'e Wākea, kālewa kona 'ōhua.
Kuamū 'ia e Kāne, kuawā 'ia e Kāne.
Ho'i mai Wākea a loko o lani momoe.
Moe Wākea, moe iā Papa.
Hānau ka lā nā Wākea,
He keiki kapu nā Wākea,
'O ka uluna a Wākea nā Kea nō.
'Oia ho'i hā, o ka mauna, hānau ka mauna.

'O ka mauna auane'i kō lalo nei.
'O wai auane'i kō luna la?
'O ka lā, 'oia ho'i hā.

VI

The sun was born to be mine,
mine the sun of Kupanole.
At Kupanole the sun held back,
the sun held back for Hina's sake.
Rays of the sun made secure
the boundaries of Hilinamā, of Hilinehu,
joined the branch of a *kamani* tree
to the linked branches of the red *kamani*.
The wings of Halulu were broken, broken.
They were severed by the sun,
by the sky-voyaging sun of Kea.
Wākea was below, above was the sun,
the sun-child born to Kea.
He it was, the sun-child: the sun brought to birth.

The sun shall be above.
Who shall be below?
The ocean, that is who shall be below.

VII

The ocean was born of Kea,
the surf for Kea, the sea for Kea,
the wild sea, the gentle sea for Kea,
the coral beds, coral caverns that grow for Kea,
the fish who twist and turn in the surge.
Deep black were the headlands pointing seaward,
broad lay the ocean spread out below.
Who shall be above?
Kū, Lono, Kāne, Kanaloa,
Ka'eka'e and Mauli,
composers of prayers, givers of prayers,
high priests who uttered solemn prayers in sacred places,
voiced them in places free: free of kapu was the place
    of the chief!

Born was Kū, let him remain above.
Who shall be below? Who indeed?

From Hāloa men came forth, chiefs multiplied.
Chief Ka-mehameha was conceived above,
the first chief, the first up here.
The Chiefess Kau-i-ka-'aleneo was the second up here.
They joined, clung together. Was it not so?
Ka-lani-nui-kua-liholiho was the first
to inherit the kapus, the first up here.
Chief Kau-i-ke-ao-uli was the second up here.
Brothers are they, close joined: they hold firm to one another.
So it is. 'Oia e.

VI

O hānau ka lā a nā'ū,
O nā'ū ka lā o Kupanole.
'O Kupanole ka lā kōhia,
Kōhia ka lā iā Hina.
'O ke kukuna o ka lā pa'a,
'O ka pe'a o Hilinamā, o Hilinehu,
'O ka lālā o ke kamani,
'O ka hui o ke kamani 'ula.
'O ka 'ēheu o Halulu,
Ke ha'ina mai lā, ha'i,
Ke hakia mai la e ka lā,
E ke keiki hele lani ā Kea.
'O Wākea ka i lalo, o ka lā ka i luna,
'O ke keiki ia ā Kea i ho'okauhua ai.
'O ia ho'i o ka lā, hānau ka lā.

'O ka lā auane'i kō luna.
'O wai auane' kō lalo nei?
'O ka moana, 'oia ho'i hā.

VII

Hānau ka moana ā Kea,
O nā nalu nā Kea, o ke kai nā Kea,
O kai kāne, o kai wahine nā Kea,
O ko'a kū, o ko'a hālelo ulu nā Kea,
O ho'owiliwili a ka i'a iloko o ka moana.
Uliuli, 'ele'ele nei lae o ka moana.
O ka moana auane'i kō lalo nei.
'O wai auane'i kō luna e?
'O Kū, 'o Lono, 'o Kāne, 'o Kanaloa,
'O Ka'eka'e, 'o Mauli,
O haku o ka pule, o nu'u pule,
O nu'u kahuna, o 'eli'eli holo i mua kapu,
O 'eli'eli holo imua noa, noa ka hānau
    'ana o ke ali'i.

Hānau Kū, 'o Kū la auane'i ho'i kō luna.
'O wai la ho'i kō lalo nei, 'o wai la?

'O Hāloa, puka kānaka, laha nā ali'i.
Loa'a i luna nei 'o Ka-lani Mehameha,
'Ekāhi ka lani la, 'ekāhi o luna nei.
'O Ka-lani Kau-i-ka-'alaneo 'elua o luna nei.
Pili lāua, ua mau paha, 'oia paha?
'O Ka-lani-nui-kua-liholiho 'akāhi,
I ke kapu la, 'akāhi o luna nei.
'O Ka-lani 'o Kau-i-ke-ao-uli, 'alua o luna nei,
Pili lāua, ua mau paha.

Source:
The Echo of Our Song: Chants & Poems of the Hawaiians, translated and edited by Mary Kawena Pukui &
    Alfons L. Korn. Honolulu: University Press of Hawaii, 1973. pp. 14-25.

*I*n 1881, the Hawaiian King Ka-lã-kaua became the first Hawaiian Island monarch to leave his kingdom to meet with heads of state around the world. Feted by royal parties and even granted an audience with the pope at the Vatican in Rome, the king's diplomatic journey helped combat the belief by Europeans that Hawaiians were an uncivilized people with little cultural complexity. King Ka-lã-kaua's ten-month adventure included two weeks in Japan as the guest of Emperor Mutsuhito, visits to the Chinese port cities of Shanghai, Tientsin, and Hong Kong, as well as visits to Indonesia, India, Africa, Europe, and the United States. In Europe he met with German Prince William (who later became Kaiser William II) and the Austrian Archduke Albrecht.

After his arrival back in the Hawaiian Islands, he composed a chant that he used to address his people about his trip. It concludes with his assessment that in his own kingdom, the island of Hawaii, he finds the most cherished treasure of all, and that is that he can be among his people without fearing bodily harm. Though the king was impressed with the power of the heads of state in Europe and the United States, because of the number of people they ruled, he did not miss the reality that heads of states were threatened by their own citizens. The Pearl reveals the personal impact of the King's journey as he assures his people through his chant that their loyalty to him has become his greatest treasure. It is interesting to note that the concept of a "pearl of great price" is a Biblical concept espoused by Jesus in the Gospel according to Matthew, chapter thirteen. In that context, the pearl is symbolic of the kingdom of heaven.

It was typical in Hawaiian culture to compose a chant to commemorate significant events, offer explanations for philosophical topics, and to pass knowledge along as oral tradition. Chants were complex and lyrical, with imagery, hidden meanings (called kaona) and poetic themes. The power of the chant lay in its kaona. Kaona often held double meanings. Listeners might believe a chant told a general story of love and passion when the chant actually recounted a specific event. The use of metaphor, such as rain symbolizing love, allowed for this complexity. These sophisticated literary devices in the chants demonstrated the intelligence of the early Hawaiians.

The oldest chants in Hawaii before contact with Europeans were of two broad categories, mele oli and mele hula. Mele means "poetic language" and these earliest chants were spoken, not sung. Mele came to mean song, but the earliest Hawaii chants were not sung. Chanters, called haku mele, were trained as children and spent a lifetime composing, reciting and teaching others to chant. Mele oli chants were performed by one person and were not accompanied by any instrument. Mele hula chants were performed by more than one person and sometimes accompanied by dance and/or musical instruments.

Hawaiians dismantled their legal system in 1819, which had been based on sacred taboos. The restructure brought about cultural changes but did not end the use of chants. The introduction of the first printing press and area newspapers in the nineteenth century encouraged interest in the written versions of ancient chants. By the time of Ka-lã-kaua's trip in 1881, chants were still a part of cultural life for Hawaiians. King Ka-lã-kaua's political goals for Hawaiians were to revive the political and racial pride and a deep sense of the Polynesian and southeast Asian origins. But the monarchy was destroyed in the 1890s, and in 1896, the use of Hawaiian language was forbidden in public schools. The art of chanting was threatened by the ensuing language barrier for subsequent generations.

In the late 1980s, a rebirth of Hawaiian language through immersion classes for school children brought the ancient art of chanting to public attention. Unfortunately, many chants were not written down during the years when the Hawaiian language was neglected, and thus many chants were lost.

KA MOMI
The Pearl

I have traveled over many lands and distant seas,
to India afar and China renowned.
I have touched the shores of Africa and the
    boundaries of Europe,
and I have met the great ones of all the lands.

As I stood at the side of heads of governments,
next to leaders proud of their rule, their authority
    over their own,
I realized how small and weak is the power I hold.

For mine is a throne established upon a heap
    of lava.

They rule where millions obey their commands.
Only a few thousands can I count under my care.

Yet one thought came to me of which I may boast,
that of all beauties locked within the embrace of
    these shores,
one is a jewel more precious than any owned
    by my fellow monarchs.
I have nothing in my Kingdom to dread.

I mingle with my people without fear.
My safety is no concern, I require no bodyguards.

Mine is the boast that a pearl of great price
    has fallen to me from above.
Mine is the loyalty of my people.

Ua ka 'ahele au maluna o ka 'ili honua me nā moana,
A 'Inia mamao me Kina kaulana,
Hō'ea i nā'ae kai o Aferika a me nā' palena o Europa,

A hālāwai me ka ikaika o nā'āina a pau.

A ia 'u i kū ai ma nā 'ao'ao o nā po'o aupuni,
Ka po'e mana maluna o lākou me ka hiehie,

Ho'omaopopo iho la au i ka 'uka iki a nāwaliwali o ko'u,

Me ko'u noho ali'i i ho'okahua 'ia maluna o kāhi
    pu'u pele,

A ma kāhi he miliona i ho'okō i ka keia mau mō'ī,
    He mau tausani wale nō mlalo o ko'u malu.

Akā, ke 'upu nei loko, na'u ke kaena hiki,
Aia he mau nani maloko o nā pō'ai o
    ko'u mau 'ae kai,
I 'oi aku ka makamae i ka o'u mau
    hoa ali'i.
'A 'ohe o'u kumu hopo maloko o ko'u aupuni.

He hiki ke hui me ko'u lāhui me ka weli'ole.
'A 'ohe maka'u no'u iho, me ke kia'i pa'a ole ia.

A na'u ke kaena, he momi i ho'oūna
    'ia mai luna mai na'u,
Eia me a'u ke aloha pili pa'a o ko'u lāhui kānaka.

Source:
The Echo of Our Song: Chants & Poems of the Hawaiians, translated and edited by Mary Kawena Pukui & Alfons L. Korn. Honolulu: University Press of Hawaii, 1973. pp. 153-155.

After the defeat of Spain in the Spanish-American War (1898), the United States took control of Spanish island colonies in the Western Hemisphere and the Pacific Ocean, including Puerto Rico and the Philippines. At the height of the war, flush with victory against the Spanish fleet in Manila Bay, in the Philippines, and preparing to attack the Spanish colony of Cuba, the United States annexed Hawaii, where sugar plantation owners, all of them American citizens, had overthrown the independent government of Queen Liliuokalani (1838-1917) in 1893.

The move was indirectly related to the war. Spain had no interests in Hawaii, and the United States already had a small military base there, for which the Hawaiian government received rent. But the utility of having bona fide possessions in the Pacific Ocean had been suggested before the war, and the fighting in the Philippines had focused attention on that need.

The question of annexing the Hawaiian Islands had been debated and rejected in 1893, but five years later, in the midst of war, the U.S. Congress and the administration of President William McKinley (1843-1901) decided to take the opportunity to expand in the Pacific in 1898.

Two years later, with the war over, Congress passed the Organic Act, which made Hawaii a U.S. territory and established a self-governing territorial administration for a period of sixty years. The act extended U.S. voting rights to native Hawaiians, though not to Asians residing in the Hawaiian Islands.

The Organic Act also banned contract labor in Hawaii, the indentured servitude that had made the sugar industry profitable. Congress had already banned the practice of contracting laborers abroad for short- or long-term work in the United States. The earlier ban, adopted in 1885, was intended to keep the number of southern and eastern European immigrants down following a public reaction against them after 1880. The provisions of the Organic Act—including the ban on contract labor—were widely known during congressional debate of the bill, and the Hawaiian Sugar Planters' Association, aware that it would lose an important source of labor, imported thousands of workers, many of them from Japan, just before the bill was passed. This massive, last-ditch effort to increase the pool of labor contributed to making Hawaii the ethnically diverse society it is today.

THE ORGANIC ACT

Section 1

That the phrase "the laws of Hawaii," as used in this Act without qualifying words, shall mean the constitution and laws of the Republic of Hawaii, in force on the twelfth day of August, eighteen hundred and ninety-eight, at the time of the transfer of the sovereignty of the Hawaiian Islands to the United States of America.

The constitution and statute laws of the Republic of Hawaii then in force, set forth in a compilation made by Sidney M. Ballou under the authority of the legislature, and published in two volumes entitled "Civil Laws" and "Penal Laws,"

respectively, and in the Session Laws of the Legislature for the session of eighteen hundred and ninety-eight, are referred to in this Act as "Civil Laws," "Penal Laws," and "Session Laws."

Section 2

Territory of Hawaii

That the islands acquired by the United States of America under an Act of Congress entitled "Joint resolution to provide for annexing the Hawaiian Islands to the United States," approved July seventh, eighteen hundred and ninety-eight, shall be known as the Territory of Hawaii.

Kathy Uluwehi Knowles and other members of Mahina's Halau perform outside the U.S. Capitol in Washington. The event was part of a two-day demonstration marking the 100th anniversary of the annexation of the Hawaiian Islands and calling attention to the plight of some native Hawaiians in re-securing the lands.

Section 3

Government of the Territory of Hawaii

That a Territorial government is hereby established over the said Territory, with its capital at Honolulu, on the island of Oahu.

Section 4

Citizenship

That all persons who were citizens of the Republic of Hawaii on August twelfth, eighteen hundred and ninety-eight, are hereby declared to be citizens of the United States and citizens of the Territory of Hawaii.

And all citizens of the United States resident in the Hawaiian Islands who were resident there on or since August twelfth, eighteen hundred and ninety-eight, and all the citizens of the United States who shall hereafter reside in the Territory of Hawaii for one year shall be citizens of the Territory of Hawaii.

Section 5

Application of the Laws of the United States

That the Constitution, and, except as herein otherwise provided, all the laws of the United States which are not locally inapplicable, shall have the same force and effect within the said Territory as elsewhere in the United States:

Provided, That sections eighteen hundred and fifty and eighteen hundred and ninety of the Revised Statutes of the United States shall not apply to the Territory of Hawaii.

Section 6

Government of the Territory of Hawaii

That the laws of Hawaii not inconsistent with the Constitution or laws of the United States or the provisions of this Act shall continue in force, sub-

Native Hawaiians fly the state flag upside down to signal their distress over the higher poverty rates and health problems suffered by Native Hawaiians. They seek compensation for state use of former kingdom lands. A Hawaiian language motto says, "The life of the land is perpetuated in righteousness."

ject to repeal or amendment by the legislature of Hawaii or the Congress of the United States.

Section 7

That the constitution of the Republic of Hawaii and the laws of Hawaii, as set forth in the following acts, chapters, and sections of the civil laws, penal laws, and session laws, and relating to the following subjects, are hereby repealed. . .

Section 8

Certain Offices Abolished

That the offices of President, minister of foreign affairs, minister of the interior, minister of finance, minister of public instruction, auditor-general, deputy auditor-general, surveyor-general, marshal, and deputy marshal of the Republic of Hawaii are hereby abolished.

Section 9

Amendment of Official Titles

That wherever the words "President of the Republic of Hawaii," or "Republic of Hawaii," or "Government of the Republic of Hawaii," or their equivalents, occur in the laws of Hawaii not repealed by this Act, they are hereby amended to read "Governor of the Territory of Hawaii," or "Territory of Hawaii," or "Government of the Territory of Hawaii," or their equivalents, as the context requires.

Section 10

Construction of Existing Statutes

That all rights of action, suits at law and in equity, prosecutions, and judgments existing prior to the taking effect of this Act shall continue to be as effectual as if this Act had not been passed; and those in favor of or against the Republic of Hawaii, and not assumed by or transferred to the United States, shall be equally valid in favor of or against the government of the Territory of Hawaii. All offenses which by statute then in force were punishable as offenses against the Republic of Hawaii shall be punishable as offenses against the government of the Territory of Hawaii, unless such statute is inconsistent with this Act, or shall be repealed or changed by law. No person shall be subject to imprisonment for nonpayment of taxes nor for debt. All criminal and penal proceedings then pending in the courts of the Republic of Hawaii shall be prosecuted to final judgment and execution in the name of the Territory of Hawaii; all such proceedings, all actions at law, suits in equity, and other proceedings then pending in the courts of the Republic of Hawaii shall be carried on to final judgment and execution in the corresponding courts of the Territory of Hawaii; and all process issued and sentences imposed before this Act takes effect shall be as valid as if issued or imposed in the name of the Territory of Hawaii:

Provided, That no suit or proceedings shall be maintained for the specific performance of any contract heretofore or hereafter entered into for personal labor or service, nor shall any remedy exist or be enforced for breach of any such contract, except in a civil suit or proceeding instituted solely to recover damages for such breach:

Provided further, That the provisions of this section shall not modify or change the laws of the United States applicable to merchant seaman.

That all contracts made since August twelfth, eighteen hundred and ninety-eight, by which persons are held for service for a definite term, are hereby declared null and void and terminated, and no law shall be passed to enforce said contracts in any way; and it shall be the duty of the United States marshal to at once notify such persons so held of the termination of their contracts.

That the Act approved February twenty-sixth, eighteen hundred and eighty-five, "To prohibit the importation and migration of foreigners and aliens under contract or agreement to perform labor in the United States, its Territories, and the District of Columbia," and the Acts amendatory thereof and supplemental thereto, be, and the same are hereby extended to and made applicable to the Territory of Hawaii.

Section 11

Style of Process

That the style of all process in the Territorial courts shall hereafter run in the name of "The Territory of Hawaii," and all prosecutions shall be carried on in the name and by the authority of the Territory of Hawaii.

Chapter 2—The Legislature

Section 12

The Legislative Power

That the legislature of the Territory of Hawaii shall consist of two houses, styled, respectively, the senate and house of representatives, which shall organize and sit separately, except as otherwise herein provided.

The two houses shall be styled "The legislature of the Territory of Hawaii."

Section 13

That no person shall sit as a senator or representative in the legislature unless elected under and in conformity with this Act.

Section 14

General Elections

That a general election shall be held on the Tuesday next after the first Monday in November, nineteen hundred, and every second year thereafter:

Provided, however, That the governor may, in his discretion, on thirty days' notice, order a special election before the first general election, if, in his opinion, the public interests shall require a special session of the legislature.

Section 15

Each House Judge of Qualifications of Members

That each house shall be the judge of the elections, returns, and qualifications of its own members.

Section 16

Disqualifications of Legislators

That no member of the legislature shall, during the term for which he is elected, be appointed or elected to any office of the Territory of Hawaii.

Section 17

Disqualifications of Government Officers and Employees

That no person holding office in or under or by authority of the Government of the United States or of the Territory of Hawaii shall be eligible to election to the legislature, or to hold the position of a member of the same while holding said office.

Section 18

No idiot or insane person, and no person who shall be expelled from the legislature for giving or receiving bribes or being accessory thereto, and no person who, in due course of law, shall have been convicted of any criminal offense punishable by imprisonment, whether with or without hard labor, for a term exceeding one year, whether with or without fine, shall register to vote or shall vote or hold any office in, or under, or by authority of, the government, unless the person so convicted shall have been pardoned and restored to his civil rights.

Section 19

Oath of Office

That every member of the legislature, and all officers of the government of the Territory of Hawaii, shall take the following oath or affirmation:

I solemnly swear (or affirm), in the presence of Almighty God, that I will faithfully support the Constitution and laws of the United States, and conscientiously and impartially discharge my duties as a member of the legislature, or as an officer of the government of the Territory of Hawaii (as the case may be).

Section 20

Officers and Rules

That the senate and house of representatives shall each choose its own officers, determine the rules of its own proceedings, not inconsistent with this Act, and keep a journal.

Section 21

Ayes and Noes

That the ayes and noes of the members of any question shall, at the desire of one-fifth of the members present, be entered on the journal.

Section 22

Quorum

That a majority of the number of members to which each house is entitled shall constitute a quorum of such house for the conduct of ordinary business, of which quorum a majority vote shall suffice: but the final passage of a law in each house shall require the vote of a majority of all the members to which such house is entitled.

Section 23

That a smaller number than a quorum may adjourn from day to day, and compel the attendance of absent members, in such manner and under such penalties as each house may provide.

Section 24

That, for the purpose of ascertaining whether there is a quorum present, the chairman shall count the number of members present.

Section 25

That each house may punish by fine, or by imprisonment not exceeding thirty days, any person not a member of either house who shall be guilty of disrespect of such house by any disorderly or contemptuous behavior in its presence or that of any committee thereof; or who shall, on account of the exercise of any legislative function, threaten harm to the body or estate of any of the members of such house; or who shall assault, arrest, or detain any witness or other person ordered to attend such house, on his way going to or returning therefrom; or who shall rescue any person arrested by order of such house.

But the person charged with the offense shall be informed, in writing, of the charge made against him, and have an opportunity to present evidence and be heard in his own defense.

Section 26

Compensation of Members

That the members of the legislature shall receive for their services, in addition to mileage at the rate of ten cents a mile each way, the sum of four hundred dollars for each regular session of the legislature, payable in three equal installments on and after the first, thirtieth, and fiftieth days of the session, and the sum of two hundred dollars for each extra session of the legislature.

Section 27

Punishment of Members

That each house may punish its own members for disorderly behavior or neglect of duty, by censure, or by a two-thirds vote suspend or expel a member.

Section 28

Exemption from Liability

That no member of the legislature shall be held to answer before any other tribunal for any words uttered in the exercise of his legislative functions in either house.

Section 29

Exemption from Arrest

That the members of the legislature shall, in all cases except treason, felony, or breach of the peace, be privileged from arrest during their attendance at the sessions of the respective houses, and in going to and returning from the same:

Provided, That such privilege as going to and returning shall not cover a period of over ten days each way. . .

Section 55

Legislative Power

That the legislative power of the Territory shall extend to all rightful subjects of legislation not inconsistent with the Constitution and laws of the United States locally applicable. The legislature, at its first regular session after the census enumeration shall be ascertained, and from time to time thereafter, shall reapportion the membership in the senate and house of representatives among the senatorial and representative districts on the basis of the population in each of said districts who are citizens of the Territory; but the legislature shall not grant to any corporation, association, or individual any special or exclusive privilege, immunity, or franchise without the approval of Congress; nor shall it grant private charters, but it may by general act permit persons to associate themselves together as bodies corporate for manufacturing, agricultural, and other industrial pursuits, and for conducting the business of insurance, savings banks, banks of discount and deposit (but not of issue), loan, trust, and guaranty associations, for the establishment and conduct of cemeteries, and for the construction and operation of railroads, wagon roads, vessels, and irrigating ditches, and the colonization and improvement of lands in connection therewith, or for colleges, seminaries, churches, libraries, or any other benevolent, charitable or scientific association:

Provided, That no corporation, domestic or foreign, shall acquire and hold real estate in Hawaii in excess of one thousand acres; and all real estate acquired or held by such corporation or association contrary hereto shall be forfeited and escheat to the United States, but existing vested rights in real estate shall not be impaired. No divorce shall be granted by the legislature, nor shall any divorce be granted by the courts of the Territory unless the applicant therefor shall have resided in the Territory for two years next preceding the application, but this provision shall not affect any action pending when this Act takes effect; nor shall any lottery or sale of lottery tickets be allowed; nor shall spirituous or intoxicating liquors be sold except under such regulations and restrictions as the Territorial legislature shall provide; nor shall any public money be appropriated for the support or benefit of any sectarian, denominational, or private school, or any school not under the exclusive control of the government; nor shall the government of the Territory of Hawaii, or any political or municipal corporation or subdivision of the Territory, make any subscription to the capital stock of any incorporated company, or in any manner lend its credit for the use thereof; nor shall any debt be authorized to be contracted by or on behalf of the Territory, or any political or municipal corporation or subdivision thereof, except to pay the interest upon the existing indebtedness, to suppress insurrection, or to provide for the common defense, except that in addition to any indebtedness created for such purposes the legislature may authorize loans by the Territory, or any such subdivision thereof, for the erection of penal, charitable, and educational institutions, and for public buildings, wharves, roads, and harbor and other public improvements, but the total of such indebtedness incurred in any one year by the Territory or any subdivision shall not exceed one per centum upon the assessed value of taxable property of the Territory or subdivision thereof, as the case may be, as shown by the last general assessment for taxation, and the total indebtedness for the Territory shall not at any time be extended beyond seven per centum of such assessed value, and the total indebtedness for the Territory shall not at any time be extended beyond seven per centum of such assessed value, and the total indebtedness of any subdivision shall not at any time be extended beyond three per centum of such assessed value, but nothing in this provision shall prevent the refunding of any existing indebtedness at any time; nor shall any such loan be made upon the credit of the public domain or any part thereof, nor

shall any bond or other instrument of any such indebtedness be issued unless made redeemable in not more than five years and payable in not more than fifteen years from the date of the issue thereof; nor shall any such bond or indebtedness be incurred until approved by the President of the United States.

Section 56

Town, City, and County Government

That the legislature may create counties and town and city municipalities within the Territory of Hawaii and provide for the government thereof. . .

Chapter 3—The Executive

Section 66

The Executive Power

That the executive power of the government of the Territory of Hawaii shall be vested in a governor, who shall be appointed by the President, by and with the advice and consent of the Senate of the United States, and shall hold office for four years and until his successor shall be appointed and qualified, unless sooner removed by the President. He shall be not less than thirty-five years of age; shall be a citizen of the Territory of Hawaii; shall be commander in chief of the militia thereof; may grant pardons or reprieves for offenses against the laws of the said Territory and reprieves for offenses against the laws of the United States until the decision of the President is made known thereon.

Section 67

Enforcement of Law

That the governor shall be responsible for the faithful execution of the laws of the United States and of the Territory of Hawaii within the said Territory, and whenever it becomes necessary he may call upon the commanders of the military and naval forces of the United States in the Territory of Hawaii, or summon the posse comitatus, or call out the militia of the Territory to prevent or suppress lawless violence, invasion, insurrection, or rebellion in said Territory, and he may, in case of rebellion or invasion, or imminent danger thereof, when the public safety requires it, suspend the privilege of the writ of habeas corpus, or place the Territory, or any part thereof, under martial law until communication can be had with the President and his decision thereon made known.

Section 68

General Powers of the Governor

That all the powers and duties which, by the laws of Hawaii, are conferred upon or required of the President or any minister of the Republic of Hawaii (acting alone or in connection with any other officer or person or body) or the cabinet or executive council, and not inconsistent with the Constitution or laws of the United States, are conferred upon and required of the governor of the Territory of Hawaii, unless otherwise provided. . .

Chapter 5—United States Officers

Section 85

Delegate to Congress

That a Delegate to the House of Representatives of the United States, to serve during each Congress, shall be elected by the voters qualified to vote for members of the house of representatives of the legislature; such Delegate shall possess the qualifications necessary for membership of the senate of the legislature of Hawaii. The times, places, and manner of holding elections shall be as fixed by law. The person having the greatest number of votes shall be declared by the governor duly elected, and a certificate shall be given accordingly. Every such Delegate shall have a seat in the House of Representatives, with the right of debate, but not of voting.

Section 86

Federal Court

That there shall be established in said Territory a district court to consist of one judge, who shall reside therein and be called the district judge. The President of the United States, by and with the advice and consent of the Senate of the United States, shall appoint a district judge, a district attorney, and a marshall of the United States for the said district, and said judge, attorney, and marshall shall hold office for six years unless sooner removed by the President. Said court shall have, in addition to the ordinary jurisdiction of district courts of the United States, jurisdiction of all cases cognizable in a circuit court of the United States, and shall proceed therein in the same manner as a circuit court; and said judge, district attorney, and marshall shall have and exercise in the Territory of Hawaii all the powers conferred by the laws of the United States upon the judges, district attorneys, and marshals of district and circuit courts of the United States.. . .

Section 87

Internal-Revenue District

That the Territory of Hawaii shall constitute a district for the collection of the internal revenue of the United States, with a collector, whose office shall be at Honolulu, and deputy collectors at such other places in the several islands as the Secretary of the Treasury shall direct.

Section 88

Customs District

That the Territory of Hawaii shall comprise a customs district of the United States, with ports of entry and delivery at Honolulu, Hilo, Mahukona, and Kahului.

Chapter 6—Miscellaneous

Section 89

Revenues from Wharves

That until further provision is made by Congress the wharves and landings constructed or controlled by the Republic of Hawaii on any seacoast, bay, roadstead, or harbor shall remain under the control of the government of the Territory of Hawaii, which shall receive and enjoy all revenues derived therefrom, on condition that said property shall be kept in good condition for the use and convenience of commerce, but no tolls or charges shall be made by the government of the Territory of Hawaii for the use of any such property by the United States, or by any vessel of war, tug, revenue cutter, or other boat or transport in the service of the United States.

Section 90

That Hawaiian postage stamps, postal cards, and stamped envelopes at the post-offices of the Hawaiian Islands when this Act takes effect shall not be sold, but, together with those that shall thereafter be received at such offices as herein provided, shall be canceled under the direction of the Postmaster-General of the United States; those previously sold and uncanceled shall, if presented at such offices within six months after this Act takes effect, be received at their face value in exchange for postage stamps, postal cards, and stamped envelopes of the United States of the same aggregate face value and, so far as may be, of such denominations as desired.

Section 91

That the public property ceded and transferred to the United States by the Republic of Hawaii under the joint resolution of annexation, approved July seventh, eighteen hundred and ninety-eight, shall be and remain in the possession, use, and control of the government of the Territory of Hawaii, and shall be maintained, managed, and cared for by it, at its own expense, until otherwise provided for by Congress, or taken for the uses and purposes of the United States by direction of the President or of the governor of Hawaii. And all moneys in the Hawaiian treasury, and all the revenues and other property acquired by the Republic of Hawaii since said cession shall be and remain the property of the Territory of Hawaii.

Section 92

That the following officers shall receive the following annual salaries, to be paid by the United States: The governor, five thousand dollars; the secretary of the Territory, three thousand dollars; the chief justice of the supreme court of the Territory, five thousand five hundred dollars, and the associate justices of the supreme court, five thousand dollars each. The salaries of the said chief justice and the associate justices of the supreme court, and the judges of the circuit courts as above provided shall be paid by the United States; the United States district judge, five thousand dollars; the United States marshal, two thousand five hundred dollars; the United States district attorney, three thousand dollars. And the governor shall receive annually, in addition to his salary, the sum of five hundred dollars for stationery, postage, and incidentals; also his traveling expenses while absent from the capital on official business, and the sum of two thousand dollars annually for his private secretary.

Section 93

Imports from Hawaii into the United States

That imports from any of the Hawaiian Islands, into any State or any other Territory of the United States, of any dutiable articles not the growth, production, or manufacture of said islands, and imported into them from any foreign country after July seventh, eighteen hundred and ninety-eight, and before this Act takes effect, shall pay the same duties that are imposed on the same articles when imported into the United States from any foreign country.

Section 94

Investigation of Fisheries

That the Commissioner of Fish and Fisheries of the United States is empowered and required to examine into the entire subject of fisheries and the laws relating to the fishing rights in the Territory of Hawaii, and report to the President touching the same, and to recommend such changes in said laws as he shall see fit.

Section 95

Repeal of Laws Conferring Exclusive Fishing Rights

That all laws of the Republic of Hawaii which confer exclusive fishing rights upon any person or persons are hereby repealed, and all fisheries in the sea waters of the Territory of Hawaii not included in any fish pond or artificial inclosure shall be free to all citizens of the United States, subject, however, to vested rights; but no such vested right shall be valid after three years from the taking effect of this Act unless established as hereinafter provided.

Section 96

Proceedings for Opening Fisheries to Citizens

That any person who claims a private right to any such fishery shall, within two years after the taking effect of this Act, file his petition in a circuit court of the Territory of Hawaii, setting forth his claim to such fishing right, service of which petition shall be made upon the attorney-general, who shall conduct the case for the Territory, and such case shall be conducted as an ordinary action at law.

That if such fishing right be established, the attorney-general of the Territory of Hawaii may proceed, in such manner as may be provided by law for the condemnation of property for public use, to condemn such private right of fishing to the use of the citizens of the United States upon making just compensation, which compensation, when lawfully ascertained, shall be paid out of any money in the treasury of the Territory of Hawaii not otherwise appropriated.

Section 97

Quarantine

That quarantine stations shall be established at such places in the Territory of Hawaii as the Supervising Surgeon-General of the Marine-Hospital Service of the United States shall direct, and the quarantine regulations for said islands relating to the importation of diseases from other countries shall be under the control of the Government of the United States.. . .

The health laws of the government of Hawaii relating to the harbor of Honolulu and other harbors and inlets from the sea and to the internal control of the health of the islands shall remain in the jurisdiction of the government of the Territory of Hawaii, subject to the quarantine laws and regulations of the United States.

Section 98

That all vessels carrying Hawaiian registers on the twelfth day of August, eighteen hundred and ninety-eight, and which were owned bona fide by citizens of the United States, or the citizens of Hawaii, together with the following-named vessels claiming Hawaii register, Star of France, Euterpe, Star of Russia, Falls of Clyde, and Wilscott, shall be entitled to be registered as American vessels, with the benefits and privileges appertaining thereto, and the coasting trade between the islands aforesaid and any other portion of the United States, shall be regulated in accordance with the provisions of law applicable to such trade between any two great coasting districts.

Section 99

That the portion of the public domain heretofore known as Crown land is hereby declared to have been, on the twelfth day of August, eighteen hundred and ninety-eight, and prior thereto, the property of the Hawaiian government, and to be free and clear from any trust of or concerning the same, and from all claim of any nature whatsoever, upon the rents, issues, and profits thereof. It shall be subject to alienation and other uses as may be provided by law.

Section 100

That for the purposes of naturalization under the laws of the United States residence in the Hawaiian Islands prior to the taking effect of this Act shall be deemed equivalent to residence in the United States and in the Territory of Hawaii, and the requirement of a previous declaration of intention to become a citizen of the United States and to renounce former allegiance shall not apply to persons who have resided in said islands at least five years prior to the taking effect of this Act; but all other provisions of the laws of the United States relating to naturalization shall, so far as applicable, apply to persons in the said islands.

Section 101

That Chinese in the Hawaiian Islands when this Act takes effect may within one year thereafter obtain certificates of residence as required by "An Act to prohibit the coming of Chinese persons into the United States," approved May fifth, eighteen hundred and ninety-two, as amended by an Act approved November third, eighteen hundred and ninety-three, entitled "An Act to amend an Act entitled 'An Act to prohibit the coming of Chinese persons into the United States,' approved May

fifth, eighteen hundred and ninety-two," and until the expiration of said year shall not be deemed to be unlawfully in the United States if found therein without such certificates:

Provided, however, That no Chinese laborer, whether he shall hold such certificate or not, shall be allowed to enter any Sate, Territory, or District of the United States from the Hawaiian Islands.

Section 102

That the laws of Hawaii relating to the establishment and conduct of any postal savings bank or institution are hereby abolished.. . .

Section 103

That any money of the Hawaiian Postal Savings Bank that shall remain unpaid to the persons entitled thereto on the first day of July, nineteen hundred and one, and any assets of said bank shall be turned over by the government of Hawaii to the Treasurer of the United States, and the Secretary of the Treasury shall cause an account to be stated, as of said date, between such government of Hawaii and the United States in respect to said Hawaiian Postal Savings Bank.

Section 104

This Act shall take effect forty-five days from and after the date of the approval thereof, excepting only as to section fifty-two, relating to appropriations, which shall take effect upon such approval.

Source:

Act of April 30, 1900. C 339, 31 Stat 141. Full text available from the *Hawai'i: Independent and Sovereign* website at http://www.hawaii-nation.org/ (accessed September 27, 1999).

Storytelling is a great Hawaiian tradition. Before the Hawaiian language was written, the literature was spoken. The Hawaiian legend King of Ku-ai-he-lani *is similar to the western tale of* Cinderella; *and* Au-ke-le *recalls* Rip Van Winkle, *or perhaps* Odysseus. *Religious stories describe the many Hawaiian deities and their complex relationships with humans. The following creation story incorporates both Native tradition and the biblical stories introduced by Christian settlers on the islands.*

LEGEND OF CREATION

The three gods Kane, Ku, Lono come out of the night (*po*) and create three heavens to dwell in, the uppermost for Kane, the next below for Ku, and the lowest for Lono, "a heaven for the parent (*makua*), a heaven for Ku, a heaven for Lono." Next they make the earth to rest their feet upon and call it "The great earth of Kane" (*Ka-honua-nui-a-Kane*). Kane then makes sun, moon, and stars, and places them in the empty space between heaven and earth. He makes the ocean salt, in imitation of which the priests purify with salt water. Next an image of man is formed out of earth, the head out of white clay brought from the seas of the north, south, east, and west, the body out of red earth (*apo ula*) mixed with spittle (*wai nao*). The right side of the head is made of clay brought from the north and east, the left side is made of clay from the south and west. Man is formed after the image of Kane with Ku as the workman, Lono as general assistant. Kane and Ku spit (or breathe) into the nostrils,

Lono into the mouth, and the image becomes a living being. "I have shaped this dirt (*lepo*); I am going to make it live," says Kane. "Live! Live!" respond Ku and Lono. The man rises and kneels. They name him *Ke-li'i-ku-honua* (The chief *Ku(mu)honua*) or *Honua-ula* because made out of "red earth." They give him a delightful garden to live in called *Kalana-i-hauola*, but later *Paliuli*, situated in the land of *Kahiki-honua-kele* (The land that moved off), and fashion a wife for him out of his right side and call her *Ke-ola-Ku-honua* (or *Lalohana*). "Great Hawaii of the green back and mottled seas" this land is called. A law is given him but he breaks the law and is then known as *Kane-la'a-(kah)uli*, "a god who fell because of the law."

Source:

Martha Warren Beckwith. *Hawaiian Mythology.* New Haven: Yale University Press, 1940.

HMONG
AMERICANS

Living in the mountains of China, Vietnam, Laos, and Thailand, the Hmong are a distributed population. They are also called the Miao, Hmung or Hmu, and there are 70 to 80 different groups, each with distinct traditions, dialects, and customs. As the story "Why Farmers Have to Work So Hard" suggests, agriculture is the primary activity for all of these groups. In their homeland, they grow corn, rice and opium. This Hmong folk tale tells the story of why "Hmong farmers have to walk long distances to the fields and carry their harvests on their backs." It is an instructive tale, in the tradition of a people without a written form of language.

The Hmong first came to the United States after the American withdrawal of troops from South Vietnam. During the Vietnam war, the Hmong served for the United States Central Intelligence Agency as a "secret army" in Laos, fighting against Vietnamese and Laotian forces. When the American military effort in Vietnam stopped, the Hmong fled into Thailand and lived in United Nations refugee camps until they could be relocated. Nine thousand Hmong came to the United States in 1975 and 43,000 arrived between 1979 and 1981. An additional 66,000 arrived by 1990. Refugee families were widely dispersed, so as not to burden the social services and local budgets in cities accepting refugees. However, many Hmong migrated within the United States, relocating to cities in central California and in the Midwest, near St. Paul, Minnesota and in central Wisconsin.

When the Hmong refugees came to the United States, many were farmers, but others were also small entrepreneurs. Some Hmong immigrants started grocery stores, butcher shops, or sold crafts; but the largest portion of the immigrant population were employed in low paying service, clerical and manufacturing positions, such as janitors, parts assemblers or sewing machine operators. Though many Hmong immigrants wanted to return to the farming life that they knew, it was only a remote possibility, and only a few families were able to become established farmers. Some Hmong in the Midwest were able to farm on a smaller scale and produce vegetables for sale at farmers' markets, or worked as migrant farm laborers.

As this document indicates, the Hmong world view is based on a complex spirit world. Spirits of all types were believed to have power in the daily lives of Hmong people. Shamans intercede with the spirit world to protect and negotiate for the living. Some Hmong embraced Christianity, but often they continued to make use of traditional shamans to protect and guide them in their approach to the spirit world. Stories help bridge the gap between these worlds, and allow the Hmong to preserve the traditions of their homeland. In addition to practicing their oral traditions, the Hmong create paj ntaub, or story cloths, which show scenes from daily life in the homeland. Community groups perform traditional dances and tell folk tales on a communal level, at once maintaining traditions and promoting the Hmong culture.

WHY FARMERS HAVE TO WORK SO HARD

Long, long ago, plants and animals of all kinds were able to talk. They used words just like we do today. Here is what happened.

Lou Tou and his wife Ntsee Tyee were the first people of the Hmong. When they came to the surface of the earth from a crack in the rocks on a mountainside, Lou Tou carried a flower with him.

Each day Lou Tou and Ntsee Tyee ate a few seeds from the flower, until one day they saw that the seeds would soon be all gone. So they decided to plant the few remaining seeds.

After some time, a single stalk of corn grew where they had planted the seeds. But this was a special corn stalk, because on it grew several different kinds of grain. There were an ear of corn with seven leaves, an ear of yellow sticky corn, an ear of early white corn, a larger ear of late white corn, and three ears with three different kinds of millet. The last ear of corn on the stalk was white sticky corn, and the tassel at the very tip of the stalk was covered with rice.

All the grains on the special corn stalk grew and ripened. The first to ripen was the seven-leaf corn, and it returned to Lou Tou and Ntsee Tyee's house. "Mama and Papa, if you please, open the door," it said.

Lou Tou and Ntsee Tyee looked at each other. They did not recognize the voice, so they replied, "We would be willing to open the door, but you must tell us who you are."

"I am the seven-leaf ear of corn. I am part of the flower you brought with you from inside the earth."

"Where are you going to stay if we let you come in?" asked Lou Tou.

"Since I am small and don't want to be cold, I would like to be hung from the ceiling joists under the attic platform."

Shortly after that the yellow sticky corn ripened and came to the couple's door. "Mama and Papa, please open the door," it said.

"Yes, we will open the door, but who are you?" they asked.

The answer was, "We are part of the flower you brought from inside the earth."

"Where are you going to find room if we let you come in?" they asked again.

"We would like to hang under the attic floor, from the ceiling joists," answered the ears of yellow sticky corn. When the door was opened, they came in and were hung beside the ear of seven-leaf corn.

A few years later the early maturing corn asked to come into Lou Tou and Ntsee Tyee's house. "Who are you?" they asked the corn.

"We are part of the flower. We are the early corn," was the answer.

"Where do you want to be put?" the couple asked.

"Hang us under the attic floor," said the early corn. And so they were hung alongside the other corn.

Several days later, the late maturing corn came and said, "Mama and Papa, open the door for us."

"Who are you?" Lou Tou and his wife asked.

"We are part of the flower. We are the ears of late corn," came the reply.

"Where do you want to stay?" the couple asked.

"There are a lot of us. We want to stay in a special small room." So Lou Tou and Ntsee Tyee built a granary on tall poles, to keep the small room off the ground. That way the rats could not get to the room. There they stored the late maturing corn.

Shortly after they finished building the granary, the couple heard again, "Mama and Papa, please open the door."

"We will open the door, but who are you?"

"We are part of the flower. We are grains of millet. We have had a lot of trouble living and growing. Most of our grains died, but we have managed to come home," the millet said.

"Where do you want to stay?" asked the couple.

"We would like to stay in a basket up in the attic, right over the fireplace."

Lou Tou had to weave a basket to hold the millet. When he was finished, he put the millet in the basket in the attic.

A few days later, the grains of another kind of millet asked to come in. "Who are you?" asked Ntsee Tyee and Lou Tou.

"We are part of the flower. We are millet grains. Many of us had trouble growing and each cluster of us is only half filled out. We are ripe though. Please let us come back home."

"Where do you want to stay?" the couple asked the millet.

"We would like to stay in a large storage basket." And so a large bamboo storage bin was made ready to hold the grain.

Several days later, the grains of rice arrived and asked, "If you please, Mama and Papa, open the door."

"Who are you?" demanded Lou Tou and his wife.

"We are part of the flower. We are ripe and want to come back home," the rice said.

"Where do you want to stay?" the couple asked the rice.

"We would like to stay in a large, strong basket."

So Lou Tou had to weave another basket like the large storage bin for the grains of rice.

Lou Tou and Ntsee Tyee now had all kinds of grain. They had all they needed to plant and grow crops to eat. That was the way it was on earth for a long time: The grains always came to the home of the farmer when they were ripe and ready to use.

Many, many years later, a Hmong farmer went out one day to clear land to make a new field to plant grain. First he cut down the bamboo and trees. They cried and cried without stopping.

Then he cut away all of the plants already growing on the ground and set fire to them. The fire spread to the whole field and all the plants, trees, and bamboo sobbed and wailed. They cried without stopping.

The Hmong farmer planted the field in rice and corn. A short time after he planted the grains, they sprouted all together and began to grow. But oh! When the little plants were as big as the curved feathers in a rooster's tail, all the wild plants began to grow back, too. The wild plants began hitting the rice and corn and breaking them down.

"This will never do," said the corn and rice. So they went and told the farmer what was happening. "Mr. Hmong Farmer, you went out and planted us in the heart of the forest. Now the bamboo groves and trees that are growing there are banging into us and hitting us. They are breaking off our hands and

our feet. Why did you plant us there? If you don't help us we won't survive."

The farmer told them, "Dear corn and rice, go and wait for seven days and I will come. In seven days I will come to where you live. I will make sure those wild plants won't hurt you anymore."

When the rice and corn got back to the forest field, they said to the wild plants and trees, "You better quit hitting and hurting us. We have a strong farmer who is going to come and see you. When he comes he will make trouble for you. There is no telling what he might do to you! We have told him all about you."

The bamboo, trees, and plants answered the grain, "If that is so, tell us what your farmer looks like."

"Our farmer is a man who wears a broad-brimmed, wool felt hat. His clothes are black and he carries a big knife. He will be puffing on a pipe. Just keep watching and when you see a man like that, he is the one," replied the grain.

The next day a tiger passed through the field. The bamboo, trees, vines, bushes, weeds, and grass started hitting the rice and corn and sneered, "Is this your owner?"

"No, it is not, no, it is not, no, it is not," chanted the rice and corn. "Not this one."

The very next day a bobcat sauntered by. While the bobcat passed, the wild plants began hitting the rice and corn again. "Is he the one?"

"No, he is not, he is not, no, he is not," came the reply. "Please, don't hit us like that! It hurts so much."

The third day a rat came scurrying through the field, pushing his way through the leaves and grass. The wild plants laughed and taunted, "Ha! Is this little creature with the long tail your chief? Your leader? Your owner?"

"No, he is not, no, he is not, no, he is not," whispered the rice and the corn.

"You are lucky, corn and rice, because if he is, we could just fall on him and crush him. He is so little we could easily take care of him!"

During the fourth day, a snorting bull came through the field. He was going to eat the grass plants, but the plants were rough and had stickers on them that hurt his mouth, so he went on. The wild plants asked, "Is this one your chief?"

"No, he is not, no, he is not, no, he is not," came the answer.

The fifth day a wolf went by. The wild plants asked, "Is this the one or not?"

"No, he is not the one either," groaned the rice and corn.

The sixth day a chicken flew over the field. "Ha, ha, ha! Is that your brave owner?" the wild plants taunted.

"No, he is not, no, he is not, no, he is not," was the reply.

At last the seventh day arrived. The Hmong farmer walked and walked and walked on his way to the field. He walked for half a day to get there. When he arrived the weeds and other harmful plants asked the corn and rice, "Is this your chief, your owner and protector?"

The rice and corn sighed with relief. "Yes, he is. He is the very one. Take a good look at him!"

The Hmong farmer began to chop the weeds and wild plants with his big knife. The wild plants all started crying at once, wailing and lamenting without end. The farmer sliced their necks so their heads fell off, PLOP! He cut them all off, all of the weeds in the whole field.

And so, at last the rice and corn grew and got big. The rice told the farmer, "Ah, Mr. Hmong Farmer, you have helped us very much, in many, many ways. Now you can go home and rest. You planted us and took care of us, and now you can stay home. We will come to you when we are ripe. But you have one more thing to do. Make a granary for us to live in at your home. We will come to you on our own when we are fully grown."

So the farmers went home. He did nothing, however, but went straight to bed. He lazed around in bed for a long time. In fact, he stayed in bed so long that his ear became flat and stuck to his head.

When the rice and corn were fully grown they all came at once, like a stream of flowing water, to the farmer's home. But there was no place ready for them to stay. There was no storage house, no bins, no granary, nothing! That meant they would have to stay outside, and they would get wet and rot when it rained. The rats would be able to get at them and eat them. So the rice and corn told the farmer, "We have come to you as we promised. You do not have a place ready for us to stay. Since this is true, we will go back to the field and whenever you get hungry for something to eat, you will have to come and get us. Hereafter, you will have to work to bring us in."

And so the rice and corn plants went back out to the field in the middle of the forest and stayed there until the farmer came to get them. That is why, even today, Hmong farmers have to walk long distances to the fields and carry their harvests on their backs.

Source:

Folk Stories of the Hmong: Peoples of Laos, Thailand, and Vietnam, compiled by Norma J. Livo and Dia Cha. Englewood, Colorado: Libraries Unlimited, 1991. pp. 47-53.

*H*mong story cloths, sometimes called quilts, are a recent tradition among the Hmong (roughly pronounced "mung") people of China and Southeast Asia. Story cloths are needlework creations depicting stories of Hmong experiences. These cloths have became decorative works of art treasured by collectors. Hmong story cloths have scenes that artists wish to commemorate and remember. Through delicate appliqués and needlework, figures and settings are crafted: children fleeing soldiers, the homeland in the mountains of China, and even the journey by ship to America are represented.

Story cloths were first created in Thai refugee camps. In these camps, Christian missionaries taught the Hmong, using elaborate illustrations to help in language comprehension. Missionaries collected Hmong folk tales in Laos in the 1960s to use in school primers. The Hmong did not have any previous written language, and the missionaries in Thailand standardized the language from the many different dialects that existed among the Hmong. Ancient Hmong communication was oral or pictorial.

Story cloths developed as a result of boredom in the refugee camps. Hmong women transferred language textbook illustrations to cloth. Scenes captured in fabric told of everyday life, of major events, of a family fleeing disaster, or simply a wedding or courtship ceremony. Hmong story cloths evolved into valuable artifacts that preserve the record of thousands of years of Hmong history, also providing a way for the Hmong to retain their cultural identity. Many story cloths focus on the traumatic exodus of the Hmong people from their tribal homelands in southeast Asia during the 1970s and 1980s.

Creating a story cloth requires the same skills used to create Paj ntab (roughly pronounced "pandoa"), a phrase meaning flower cloths, that date back 2,000 years. Paj ntab is a complex form of textile art using cross-stitch, batik, embroidery and appliqué techniques that usually featured animals and geometric designs. Three or four layers of cloth are used in each design. Many are created on silk fabric. Women in North Laos found that Paj ntab silk belts and clothing could be sold to earn income for the family. Women and men learned the skills, but women produce the vast majority of story cloths. Story cloths retell history, beliefs, culture and family stories in much the same way that Giberti's bronze doors at the Baptistery in Florence, Italy tell Old Testament stories by a visual representation in sculptured relief. A cloth may involve several scenes from one event. While most story cloths commemorate historical events and cultural tradition, some have scenes telling about Hmong American life, with turn of the twentieth century cloths depicting students sitting in front of computers, for example.

The word Hmong means "human being" or "free man." The Hmong people have lived in mountainous regions of China since 2000 B.C., and anthropologists say the heritage can be traced to Siberia and Central Asia. The Hmong maintained ethnic distinction from other Chinese until the 1700s, when Chinese officials falsely assured them that surrender to China would result in a peaceful coexistence. Between 1850 and 1880 the Hmong unsuccessfully revolted against China. Many Hmong fled to Burma, Laos, Vietnam, and Thailand. In Vietnam they were oppressed by the French, who eventually establish an autonomous Hmong district. By the time of U.S. involvement in the Viet Nam War in the late 1960s, 40,000 Hmong soldiers fought to support U.S. interests on the condition that they would be allowed to resettle in the United States if defeated. When defeat occurred, the U.S. government resettled only about 1,000 Hmongs after withdrawing troops in 1973. Many Hmong crossed the border into Thailand where in 1999, 55,000 are estimated to live in refugee camps. It was in these camps that story cloths first developed.

In December of 1975 the United States agreed to resettle the Hmong people in America, and Congress admitted 1,466 people. A steady yearly increase lead to a U.S. Hmong population of 50,000 by 1980. By the time of the 1990 Census, over 100,000 Hmong people had resettled in America. Of these, more than 43,000 settled in California, with 17,000 selecting Minnesota and 16,000 choosing Wisconsin. While immigration officials actually targeted and sent Hmong immigrants to 53 different cities in 25 states, the Hmong immigrants moved in a secondary migration to California, settling in Fresno, Merced, Sacramento, Stockton, Modesto, and Visalia. In 1999, most street fairs in San Francisco have booths that sell traditional story cloths.

HMONG STORY CLOTH

Source:
Associated Press.

HOPIS

The Hopi Indians are a Pueblo Indian tribe from Northeast Arizona. They developed a complex matrilineal society with various clans which relied on agriculture for sustenance. At the center of the Hopis' society was the benevolent spirit god called kachina. When the Hopis were placed on a reservation life changed dramatically for the tribe.

In the nineteenth century many Native American tribes were forced to attend Americanized educational institutes after they were placed on reservations. The children's clothes were burned, their hair was cut, and many were given new "American" names. Many of the children resisted, hiding from whites who forced them to attend classes. The Indians were segregated into two classes: "hostiles" and "friendlies." Hostiles were those who resisted the white man's way and friendlies were submissive. The children of hostiles were rounded up by the police and forced to attend school. It was a frightening ordeal for the children, however, once they learned that they would not be harmed they began to adapt. The children learned to speak English, eat the white man's food and learned Christianity. Although some Native Americans benefitted from the assimilation process, many were left torn between cultures. The boarding schools set up by the white man caused families to fall apart and undermined the Hopis' relationship to traditional values, including their religion.

A new generation of Native American scholars is emerging, however, offering promise for the future. Some of the difficulties educators on reservation face is apathy, alcohol and substance abuse, and a lack of family support. Part of the solution involves having role models for students to look up. Evidence of success will encourage more students such as Jobey Williams, who proudly graduated from Marysville-Pilchuck High School, to excel. Graduation rates among Native Americans range between 70 and 80 percent but recent success stories are providing new hope. Laura Tohe earned a Ph.D. in English from the University of New Mexico after graduating from the Albuquerque Indian School in New Mexico. Tohe is now a professor at Arizona State University and hopes to clear a path for future Native American children to follow. Although Tohe feels more at home with American culture because of her academic exposure, she still feels torn between her Navajo roots and American society.

Inspired by the notion of preserving their rich cultural heritage the Native American community has developed a university system. The Native American Educational Service (NAES) based in Chicago, is an accredited University system founded in 1974. According to its co-founder, Faith Smith, NAES College is designed to help Native Americans bridge the gap between tribe and community. Many Native Americans have grown detached from their cultural roots and feel alienated from American culture. The university system helps Native Americans reacquaint themselves with their roots and, at the same time, nurture a sense of belonging to the larger community in which they reside. The NAES system primarily offers Bachelor of Arts degrees in community studies.

THE RESERVATION SCHOOL

I grew up believing that Whites are wicked, deceitful people. It seemed that most of them were soldiers, government agents, or missionaries, and that quite a few were Two-Hearts. The old people said that the Whites were tough, possessed dangerous weapons, and were better protected than we were from evil spirits and poison arrows. They were known to be big liars too. They sent Negro soldiers against us with cannons, tricked our war chiefs to surrender without fighting, and then broke their promises. Like Navahoes, they were proud and domineering—and needed to be reminded daily to tell the truth. I was taught to mistrust them and to give warning whenever I saw one coming.

Our chief had to show respect to them and pretend to obey their orders, but we knew that he did it halfheartedly and that he put his trust in our Hopi gods. Our ancestors had predicted the coming of these Whites and said that they would cause us much trouble. But it was understood that we had to put up with them until our gods saw fit to recall our Great White brother from the East to deliver us. Most people in Oraibi argued that we should have nothing to do with them, accept none of their gifts, and make no use of their building materials, medicine, food, tools, or clothing—but we did want their guns. Those who would have nothing to do with Whites were called "Hostiles" and those who would cooperate a little were called "Friendlies." These two groups were quarreling over the subject from my earliest memories and sometimes their arguments spoiled the ceremonies and offended the Six-Point-Cloud-People, our ancestral spirits, who held back the rain and sent droughts and disease. Finally the old chief, with my grandfather and a few others, became friendly with the Whites and accepted gifts, but warned that we would never give up our ceremonies or foresake our gods. But it seemed that fear of Whites, especially of what the United States Government could do, was one of the strongest powers that controlled us, and one of our greatest worries.

A few years before my birth the United States Government had built a boarding school at the Keams Canyon Agency. At first our chief, Lolulomai, had not wanted to send Oraibi children, but chiefs from other villages came and persuaded him to accept clothes, tools, and other supplies, and to let them go. Most of the people disliked this and refused to cooperate. Troops came to Oraibi several times to take the children by force and carry them off in wagons. The people said that it was a terrible sight to see Negro soldiers come and tear children from their parents. Some boys later escaped from Keams Canyon and returned home on foot, a distance of forty miles.

Some years later a day school was opened at the foot of the mesa in New Oraibi, where there were a trading post, a post office, and a few government buildings. Some parents were permitted to send their children to this school. When my sister started, the teacher cut her hair, burned all her clothes, and gave her a new outfit and a new name, Nellie. She did not like school, stopped going after a few weeks, and tried to keep out of sight of the Whites who might force her to return. About a year later she was sent to the New Oraibi spring to fetch water in a ceremonial gourd for the Ooqol society and was captured by the school principal who permitted her to take the water up to the village, but compelled her to return to school after the ceremony was over. The teachers had then forgotten her old name, Nellie, and called her Gladys. Although my brother was two years older than I, he had managed to keep out of school until about a year after I started, but he had to be careful not to be seen by Whites. When finally he did enter the day school at New Oraibi, they cut his hair, burned his clothes, and named him Ira.

In 1899 it was decided that I should go to school. I was willing to try it but I did not want a policeman to come for me and I did not want my shirt taken from my back and burned. So one morning in September I left it off, wrapped myself in my Navaho blanket, the one my grandfather had given me, and went down the mesa barefoot and bareheaded.

I reached the school late and entered a room where boys had bathed in tubs of dirty water. Laying aside my blanket, I stepped into a tub and began scrubbing myself. Suddenly a white woman entered the room, threw up her hands, and exclaimed, "On my life!" I jumped out of the tub, grabbed my blanket, darted through the door, and started back up the mesa at full speed. But I was never a swift runner. Boys were sent to catch me and take me back. They told me that the woman was not angry and that "On my life!" meant that she was surprised. They returned with me to the building, where the same woman met me with kind words which I could not understand. Sam Poweka, the Hopi cook, came and explained that the woman was praising me for coming to school without a policeman. She scrubbed my back with soap and water, patted me on the shoulder, and said, "Bright boy." She dried me and dressed me in a shirt, underwear, and very baggy overalls. Then she cut my hair, measured me for a better-fitting suit, called me Max, and told me through an interpreter to leave my blanket and go out to play with the other boys.

The first thing I learned in school was "nail," a hard word to remember. Every day when we entered the classroom a nail lay on the desk. The teacher would take it up and say, "What is this?" Finally I answered "nail" ahead of the other boys and was called "bright."

At first I went to school every day, not knowing that Saturday and Sunday were rest days. I often cut wood in order to get candy and to be called a "smart boy." I was also praised again and again for coming to school without a policeman.

At Christmas we had two celebrations, one in the school and another in the Mission Church. Ralph of the Masau'u Clan and I each received a little painted wagon as a reward for good attendance. Mine was about fifteen inches long with two shafts and a beautiful little gray horse.

I learned little at school the first year, except "bright boy," "smart boy," "yes" and "no," "nail," and "candy." Just before Christmas we heard that a disease, smallpox, was coming west from First Mesa. Within a few weeks news came to us that on Second Mesa the people were dying so fast that Hopi did not have time to bury them, but just pitched their bodies over the cliff. The government employees and some of the schoolteachers fled from Oraibi, leaving only the principal and missionaries, who said that they would stay. About this time my mother had a new baby, named Perry much later.

During the month of January I danced for the first time as a real Katcina. One evening I entered the Howeove kiva, to which both my father and grandfather belonged, and found the men painting for a dance. Even though I had not practiced I decided to paint myself and dance with them. When my father and grandfather arrived, they discouraged me, but the kind old man who had promised to protect me from the Giant Katcinas in the same kiva about a year before was an important man and insisted that I could dance. When I finished painting, my grandfather gave me a small black blanket to use as a sash, and, since there were not enough gourd rattles, someone gave me an inflated and dried bull scrotum which contained a few small stones and made a good rattle. We left the kiva for the women to enter and then one of

the Katcinas carried me down the ladder on his back which made the people laugh. I was at the end of the line and danced well enough for an old woman to pull me over by the stove so that all could see me. Then I went with the Katcinas to the other kivas. The people praised me and said that my reward might be a nice girl for a wife.

One day when I was playing with the boys in the plaza in Oraibi, the school principal and the missionary came to vaccinate us. My mother brought me in to the principal who was holding a knife in his hand. Trembling, I took hold of his arm which caused him to laugh. They had a small bottle of soaplike liquid which they opened, and placed a little on my arm. After it dried, they rubbed my arm with a cloth and the missionary took a sharp instrument and stuck it and set a good example for the rest of the family who were vaccinated in their turn. It was spring when the disease disappeared. We were lucky. The old people said that the vaccinations were all nonsense but probably harmless, and that by our prayers we had persuaded the spirits to banish the disease—that it was Masau'u, who guards the village with his firebrand, who had protected us.. . .

That autumn some of the people took their children to Keams Canyon to attend the boarding school. Partly because I was tired of working and herding sheep and partly because my father was poor and I could not dress like some of the other boys, I was persuaded to go to the Agency school to learn to read and cipher—and to get clothes. My mother and father took three burros and accompanied me to Keams Canyon. When we arrived at the end of two days, the matron, Mrs. Weans, took me into the building and gave me a bath, clipped my hair, and dressed me in clean clothes.

I ate my supper in the dining room with the other children. My father and mother ate outside in a camp. That night I slept in the dormitory on a bed. This was something new for me and felt pretty good. I was eleven, and the biggest boy in that dormitory; I did not cry. The next morning I had breakfast with the other children. My father and mother went tot he kitchen, where the cook fed them. For breakfast we had coffee, oatmeal, fried bacon, fried potatoes, and syrup. The bacon was too salty and the oatmeal too sloppy.

After breakfast we were all told to go to the office and see the superintendent of the Reservation, Mr. Burton, for whom my parents would have to sign their names, or make their marks, before going home. There were a great many of us and we had to stand in line. The agent shook hands with us and patted us on the head, telling us through an interpreter that we had come to be educated. Then he told us to pass into another room where we would receive some gifts. They gave my mother fifteen yards of dress cloth and presented an axe, a claw hammer, and a small brass lamp to my father. Then they asked him to choose between a shovel and a grubbing hoe. He took the hoe.

We did not go to school that day. We returned to the kitchen, where the cook gave my parents two loaves of bread and some bacon, syrup, and meat. Then we went to the camp, where my father saddled a burro and told my mother to mount. "Well, son," they advised me, "don't ever try to run away from here. You are not a good runner, and you might get lost and starve to death. We would not know where to find you, and the coyotes would eat you." I promised. My father climbed on a burro and they started off. I kept my eyes upon them until finally they disappeared in the direction of Oraibi. I moaned and began to cry, fearing that I should never see them again. A Hopi boy named Nash, whom I did not know, spoke to me and told me to stop crying. My parents would come back again, he reassured me, and they might bring me some good Hopi food. He took me through the Canyon to the other end, where the school building stood. There we gathered some wild roseberries and began eating them until I discovered that they were full of worms.

At noon we all lined up, with the smallest boys in the lead. I was the tallest and the last boy for our dining room. At the table somebody spoke a few words to God, but failed to offer him any of the food. It was very good.

After lunch we smaller boys were given a job cleaning up trash in the yard. When we had finished, Nash and I took a walk up the southeast mesa to the highest point. As we reached the top, Nash turned and said, "Look over tot he west." I looked and saw the top of Mount Beautiful, just beyond Oraibi. It seemed far away and I cried a little, wondering whether I would ever get home again. Nash told me not to worry, because I was put there to learn the white people's way of life. He said that when he first came he was homesick, to, but that now he was in the third grade and satisfied. He promised me that when his relatives brought some good Hopi food he would share it with me. His talk encouraged me. As we climbed down the mesa, we heard the supper bell ringing and ran but arrived late. The disciplinarian stepped up to us and struck Nash twice on the buttocks saying, "You are late." Since I was a new boy, he did not put his hands on me—was lucky.

We went to the dining room and ate bread and a thing called hash, which I did not like. It contained different kinds of food mixed together; some were good and some were bad, but the bad outdid

the good. We also had prunes, rice, and tea. I had never tasted tea. The smell of it made me feel so sick that I thought I would vomit. We ate our supper but it did not satisfy me. I thought I would never like hash.

I had trouble defecating, too. A person had to be very careful where he sat. Little houses called privies were provided—one for boys and another for girls. I went into one of them but was afraid to sit down. I thought something might seize me or push me from below and was uneasy about this several days.

After supper we played a little. Some of the older boys, who had been in school before, wrested with me. I had been a big, brave lad at home, but now I was timid and afraid. It seemed that I was a little nobody and that any boy could beat me. When it came time for bed the matron took us to the small boys' dormitory, where she made us undress except for our underwear, kneel, and put our elbows on the bed. She taught us to ask Jesus to watch over us while we slept. I had tried praying to Jesus for oranges and candy without success, but I tried it again anyway.

The next day we had to go to school. The little boys went both morning and afternoon. I had to commence at the very bottom in the kindergarten class. When we had entered the classroom and taken our seats, the teacher asked me my name. I did not like my name, Max, so I kept quiet. "Well," said the teacher, "your name shall be Don," and wrote it down in a little book.

The teacher used to pick up a stick, turn the leaves of a chart, and tell us to read. Some of the little boys from First Mesa, who had been there before, could read right along. Although I was the biggest boy in the class, I could not read at all. I felt uncomfortable, especially since they had dressed me in little brown knee "A cat," "A horse," "A cow," "An eagle," etc. Then came such things as "A cow has four feet," and "The man had two feet." Another step was, "Put a ball on the box," "Count up to ten." After several days I finally began to understand the words. Soon we were reading long sentences like "'A rat, a rat,' cried Mae."

I grew tired of school and thought of running away. But one of my father's nephews, Harry Kopi, was watching me and noticed that my face was growing sorrowful. One afternoon, as I was sitting still and sad in the building, he came to me and said, "Come out with me to the place where the pigs live." As we walked along he asked me if I were lonesome, and I almost cried. "I have brought you out here to see the pigs," he said. "When I used to get homesick I would come here and look at them;

they made me laugh and feel better." There were about twenty pigs in the pen, all of different sizes. They were funny animals—like dogs with hooves. They looked horrible with their little eyes, sharp mouths, and dirty faces. "Let's go into the pen and ride a pig," said Harry. He caught one by the tail and I clambered on its back and rode it about the pen. It was great fun. I felt better when I got off, and thought to myself that if my homesickness returned I would ride a pig again.. . . .

On June the fourteenth my father came for me and we returned home, riding burros and bringing presents of calico, lamps, shovels, axes, and other tools. It was a joy to get home again, to see all my folks, and to tell about my experiences at school. I had learned many English words and could recite part of the Ten Commandments. I knew how to sleep on a bed, pray to Jesus, comb my hair, eat with a knife and fork, and use a toilet. I had learned that the world is round instead of flat, that it is indecent to go naked in the presence of girls, and to eat the testes of sheep or goats. I had also learned that a person thinks with his head instead of his heart. . .

By the end of summer I had enough of hoeing weeds and tending sheep. Helping my father was hard work and I thought it was better to be educated. My grandfather agreed that it was useful to know something of the white man's ways, but said that he feared I might neglect the Hopi rules which were more important. He cautioned me that if I had bad dreams while at school, I should spit four times in order to drive them from my mind and counteract their evil influences.

Before sunrise on the tenth of September the police came to Oraibi and surrounded the village, with the intention of capturing the children of the Hostile families and taking them to school by force. They herded us all together at the east edge of the mesa. Although I had planned to go later, they put me with the others. The people were excited, the children and the mothers were crying, and the men wanted to fight. I was not much afraid because I had learned a little about education and knew that the police had not come without orders. One of the captured boys was Dick, the son of "Uncle Joe" who had stirred up most of the trouble among the Hostiles. I was glad. Clara, the granddaughter of Chief Lolulomai, was also taken. The Chief went up to Mr. Burton, who was writing our names on a piece of paper, and said, "This girl must be left until she is older." She was allowed to return to her mother. They also captured my clan brother Archie, the son of my mother's sister, Nuvanhunka.

When Mr. Burton saw me in the group, he said, "Well, well, what are you doing here? I thought you were back in school at the Agency." I told him that I was glad to go with him. This seemed to please him, and he let me go to my house to get my things. When I returned with a bag of fresh peaches, I discovered that they had marched the children to New Oraibi to be placed in the wagons. I followed and found my grandfather in a group near the wagons. When I noticed with a bag of fresh peaches, I discovered that they had marched the children to New Oraibi to be placed in the wagons. I followed and found my grandfather in a group near the wagons. When I noticed how crowded the wagons were, I asked Mr. Burton if I might ride a horse. He sent me with Archie, Dick, and my grandfather to ask the police. Two of them were my clan uncles, Adam from First Mesa and Secavaima from Shipaulovi. I walked up to Adam, smiling, shook hands with him, and introduced my clan brother Archie. "You don't need to fear us," said my uncle, "we are policeman." I asked him whether Archie and I might ride double on horseback to the Agency. They laughed and said that I had a brave heart. They warned me that the Hostiles might follow us on the road and give battle, but they were only teasing.

When we were ready to leave the police took us three boys behind their saddles. Near the foothill of First Mesa we made a short cut through the gap to the mission house, where we stopped and waited for the wagons to bring our lunch. After eating, Adam told me that his week's term as policeman was up and that this was as far as he was going. He took me to Mr. Burton, who told me that I might ride with him in his buckboard. When we were ready to start, I climbed on the buckboard. When we were ready to start, I climbed on the buckboard back of the seat. Rex Moona, an educated Hopi who worked in the office at Keams Canyon, was riding in the seat with the superintendent. We drove on ahead of the procession and reached Keams Canyon about sunset.

The children already at the school were eating their supper when we arrived. Rex and I went to the kitchen and asked for food. We each got a loaf of bread and ate it with some syrup. The cook asked me if I would like some hash. I said, "No." We ate our food at the door and told the people in the kitchen that the children were coming in wagons. Then we went to the dormitory and rested. The next morning we took a bath, had our hair clipped, put on new clothes, and were schoolboys again.

Source:

Great Documents in American Indian History, edited by Wayne Moquin with Charles van Doren. New York: Praeger Publishers, 1973. pp. 278-285.

Polingaysi Qoyawayma, or Elizabeth Q. White (c.1892-1990), was born in the village of Oraibi or Old Oraibi, later renamed Kykotsmovi, in what is now north-eastern Arizona. One of the oldest and largest centers of Hopi culture, it was estab-lished in about 1150 A.D., and became the site of a Franciscan Catholic mission established by the Spanish in the 1600s.

Around the time of Qoyawayma's birth, however, a new missionary movement had entered the area: the Mennonites, whose chief representative was Henry R. Voth (1855-1931). A denomination that arose in Switzerland during the 1500s, the Mennonite sect was distinguished by its adherents' belief in nonviolence. Thus although the arrival of missionaries in Oraibi inevitably constituted a form of cul-ture shock for Qoyawayma and other Hopi, the situation could have been much worse with a more strident group of Christians.

The Voths and their colleagues attempted to round up Hopi children and bring them to their school—and of course to convert them to Christianity—but their methods were not particularly coercive. Qoyawayma herself recalled being more intrigued than frightened, once she became used to the presence of the Bahana (whites) in the area.

The Hopi had their own highly developed and entrenched religious and cultural system, as described by Qoyawayma. They worshipped a sun god, one of the oldest and most prevalent types of deities, which can be found in cultures throughout the world, as well as a deity represented by a lion and her cubs. Presumably the latter was a mountain lion, since the Hopi would have had no contact with lions. Associ-ated with Father Sun was a figure referred to as the "Good Spirit."

These deities, in the belief of the Hopi, brought rain, a particularly crucial issue in the parched homeland of the Hopi; hence the importance of the kachina, spirits who interceded with the gods, on behalf of the people, for rainfall. During the grow-ing season, people dressed up as kachinas and performed sacred dances; later the kachina were represented as dolls, artifacts which became everyday playthings for Hopi children—and attractive crafts for tourists.

Central to the worship of the Hopi gods was the kiva, a shrine in an under-ground chamber. Little light entered the sunken room, accessed by a hole in the floor of a dwelling, and the darkness of the kiva only added to the aura of mystery sur-rounding it. Its subterranean location was a symbol of the Hopis' belief that they had come from the earth—a creation myth common to many Native American peoples.

A comment by Qoyawayma is telling: "The kiva was no longer used, but the older children told of strange noises down there, as though ghosts of the old rain priests haunted it." Clearly the old belief systems of the Hopi were under challenge, as they had been since the arrival of the first Spanish missionaries in 1629. The centuries that followed had seen continuing conflict between traditionalists and progressives.

Certainly the elder Lololoma, a prominent leader in Qoyawayma's childhood, was a traditionalist; yet he allowed the Mennonites and government officials to establish their school. No doubt his accession came from a desire for peace, but this led to disagreement with other traditionalists. Yet as Qoyawayma noted, the oppos-

ing forces had to come into agreement—and thus accept the school—because open conflict would have brought about more interference from government authorities.

Heightening that interference was the presence of policemen from the Navajo tribe. As Qoyawayma described, the lines between Bahana and Hopi were not the only ethnic boundaries in her childhood: almost as severe was the division between Hopi and Navajo. The Hopi regarded the latter as invaders, but in fact the Navajos' frequent trespassing on Hopi lands probably resulted from the fact that their own homelands had been greatly reduced by the federal government.

In the end, it was neither police nor religious dogma that persuaded Qoyawayma to attend the school, but simple curiosity and a desire not to be left out. Her mother's disapproving pronouncement, that for Qoyawayma there was "no turning back," proved prophetic. Qoyawayma went on to graduate from Bethel College in Newton, Kansas, and returned to the Hopi Reservation as a Mennonite missionary. A noted educator, she published several books; earned the Distinguished Service Award from the U.S. Department of the Interior; and established the Hopi Scholarship Fund at Northern Arizona University.

NO TURNING BACK (EXCERPT)

DURING HER EARLY childhood, Polingaysi had enjoyed the feeling of security that was the heritage of the Hopis. Her navel cord had been tied to a stirring stick and firmly thrust into the wattled ceiling to serve forever as the marker of her birthplace. While she was still an infant, her ears had been pierced as evidence that she was a Hopi. She had been accepted by her grandparents, named Polingaysi, Butterfly Sitting Among the Flowers in the Breeze, and presented to Father Sun on the twentieth day of her life, then honored by the community.

She was a member of her mother's Coyote Clan, and a child of her father's Kachina Clan. She belonged. She as a Hopi.

Like other children of the old village, Polingaysi spent her little girlhood playing. She dug holes in the moist sand, built tiny rock houses, hunted for broken bits of pottery to use for play dishes. Each spring she went with the mothers and children to gather greens. Gradually her back grew strong enough to carry a little *wigoro* from the deep funnel of the spring where the water serpent lived. Eventually she began helping to care for the smaller children in her family.

The white man came, but she did not remember the first one she had ever seen. She was shy, but she was not afraid of them, for her father did not fear them. He worked for the Mennonite missionary, H.R. Voth, and whenever possible Polingaysi

tagged along after her father, often carrying with her one or more of her flat Kachina dolls made of cottonwood root and adorned with bright paint and feathers.

She enjoyed attending religious services, for she loved to sing, and the missionaries were teaching the Hopi children many songs. Knowing not a word of English, they mouthed the strange syllables.

"Deso lasmi, desi no," Polingaysi sang. The words were, "Jesus loves me, this I know," but she had never heard of the Great Teacher.

Hopi equivalents of the strange syllables added up to, "the San Juan people are bringing burros," and this sent the children into gales of giggles. They agreed the white man was very silly to sing about San Juan people bringing burros, but the *Bahanas* gave them candy after the singing lessons, and the candy tasted good. Besides, whatever the words, Polingaysi loved to sing and to be where things were happening.

One morning she was to have her breakfast of corn cakes, *piki* bread, and water in her grandmother's house before going to the missionaries' services. She knew it was the duty of the youngest member of a Hopi family to feed the family gods and she was the youngest present, but she was in a hurry to be off and would have neglected the duty had not her grandmother reminded her.

The family gods, a crudely carved large stone that was supposed to represent a mountain lion, and two smaller carved stones that represented her cubs, were in a dark room above the mysterious kiva of the rainmakers. The kiva was no longer used, but the older children told of strange noises down there, as though ghosts of the old rain priest haunted it.

Never had Polingaysi been able to perform her simple duty without feeling goos pimples rising on her skin, but the thought of the singing, the kind missionaries, and the possible treats helped her to pick up a pinch of sacred corn meal for Father Sun and a pinch of *piki* flakes for the lion and her cubs, and to sidle into the dark room.

"Please don't hurt me," she whispered to the lion, hastily dropping the *piki* flakes before it. "Father Sun and Good Spirit, protect me," she added, tossing the corn meal into the aid before backing out of the room and hurrying back to the family.

They sat on the floor. The food was before them, the *piki* on a plaque, corn cakes in an earthen pot, and there was water into which they could dip the *piki*. They bowed their heads, remembering to be grateful for food made possible by the rain that had fallen and the sunshine that had warmed the Hopi fields,

Polingaysi bowed her head, then ate. A few minutes later, she was with the other small children of the village, lustily singing, "Deso lasmi, desi no."

She did not know the missionaries were on the mesa to teach the Hopis the sinfulness of their ways, to lead them from their ancient beliefs into the white man's way of worship. She was too young to have understood, had she known.

From earliest childhood she had been taught to pray. Getting up a dawn and going to the mesa's edge to voice one's thankfulness for life and all good was part of the established Hopi pattern.

Children who stayed in bed were reprimanded. "Would you have Father Sun carry you on his back?" They were scolded. Sometimes cold water was doused on them. Sometimes a maternal uncle would be sent to rouse them from their warm beds.

"Come now! I am your uncle, and have the right to punish you. Get up at once," he would say, and sleepy-eyed and ashamed, they would obey.

Those were the days of the hereditary Bear Clan chieftain, Lololoma. Often he would be sitting on the mesa's edge, wrapped in his blanket, praying with his face turned eastward long before the others came straggling out to join him.

"Why does he always sit there?" Polingaysi asked her mother. Sevenka tried to explain.

"He is responsible for the well-being of our village, and must make a daily pathway for us, his people, through prayer. He calls us his children. We call him our father. He prays for long life, purity, abundant crops, for all of us who live in Oraibi. He prays for rain. He prays for the essence of good in the plants we use, and in the clay we dig and crush for our pottery making, and in the rocks we pile one on top of the other in house building.

"Your father and I are responsible for the well-being of our own home and our children. It is our duty to see to it that our children have a place to live and food to nourish their bodies. It is why he prays in the mornings, and again in the evenings. He is the father of our spiritual home."

Polingaysi could not remember a time when she had not made her morning prayer, going with her mother, cousins, and aunts to the mesa's edge. First, to rid themselves of evils accumulated during the past twenty-fours hours, they turned and spat over their shoulders; then cleansed and ready to face the new day, they breathed on the corn meal in their hands their supplications for long life and good health before releasing the meal into the spirit world by tossing it outward, toward the rising sun.

As the first warming rays of the sun slid over the horizon, touching them with golden fingers, they reached out, symbolically drawing the beams to them and pressing them to their bodies, meanwhile inhaling deeply and praying that they might be made beautiful in body, face, and heart. Clothed in the armor of all good and all beauty, and protected from evil, they were strengthened to meet the day and its problems.

It would have shocked Polingaysi, as it shocked her parents and other Hopis, had she been old enough to understand that the missionaries considered them wicked and unsaved. Their religion was not a Sunday affair; it was a daily, hourly, constant communion with the Source, the Creator from whom came all things that were, large or small, animate or inanimate, the power behind Cloud People, Rain People, the Kachinas, and all the other forces recognized and respected by the Hopi people. But at that time the little girl mixed religions as confidently as she mixed Hopi parched corn and the *Bahana's* hard candy.

H.R. Voth, the Mennonite missionary, had built a home for his family on the fat side of Oraibi Wash, in the valley below Oraibi, and ancient city said to have been constantly occupied since about 1120. Polingaysi's father, called Freddie by Mr.

Voth, because his name, Qoyawayma, was too difficult for English-speaking tongues, made the trip to
and from the Voth home daily. He trotted down the
steep mesa trail each morning and back each
evening, and for his labors made a salary of fifty
cents per day.

It seemed to excite him when other white
men, bringing wagon loads of building materials,
began the erection of a building on the slope at the
foot of the mesa. They were building a schoolhouse,
but the word meant nothing to the children of the
mesa and their parents. They knew nothing of
white man's ways and had never been inside a
schoolhouse.

Since nothing had been said to excite her fear,
Polingaysi went about her play unalarmed until a
morning when her mother, whose voice was cus-
tomarily low and calm, called out to her in ago-
nized syllables.

"Polingaysi! Come! Come quickly!"

Frightened, Polingaysi gathered up the
younger brother she had been pulling on her shoulder blanket and ran home with him. He gurgled
with glee at the bouncing ride she gave him and
cried when their mother ran to meet them and
snatched him from Polingaysi roughly, saying, "Lie
down behind that roll of bedding, Polingaysi. I will
hide you with a sheep pelt. Hurry."

"Why?" Polingaysi asked in childish bewilder-
ment.

"Do as you're told!: her mother snapped.
Bahana is catching children this morning, for the
school. Sister is hiding at grandmother's house."

"Catching children!" What a fearful-sounding
phrase. It made Polingaysi think of the older boys
catching rabbits in snares. Without argument she
darted across the room and flattened herself behind
the rolled-up sheep pelts and blankets. Her mother
covered her and returned to the doorway.

Polingaysi could hear her sick brother whim-
pering on his pallet beside the fireplace, then she
heard a strange voice, speaking a language she did
not understand. When the mother made no answer,
another man began talking, this time in not very
good Hopi.

"He says, tell you we are going to take your
children to school. Where are they?"

"That sick boy is all I have, except for the
babies," Polingaysi's mother lied. "He is too sick to
go away form home."

There was more talk in the foreign language,
then the interpreter said, in Hopi: Bahana says the
boy doesn't look sick. We'll take him. Come!"

Polingaysi's sick brother wept aloud, but he
struggled to his feet and went with the men.

Almost smothered by the time her mother
removed the heavy pelt, Polingaysi began at once
to beg her mother not to let the men catch her.

"If they take you, they take you," her mother
said, her usually gentle voice harsh in her angry
helplessness. "What can we do? The Bahana does
not care how we feel toward our children. They
think they know everything and we know nothing.
They think only of themselves and what they want.
I don't know what they are going to do to our children, down there in that big house. It is not the
Hopi way of caring for children, this tearing them
from their home and their mothers."

All that day the village hummed with resentment and fear.

The children who had escaped the school
authorities sidled out of their hiding places only to
huddle together and run at the first hint of danger.

The Bahana, unable to speak Hopi, had
brought with him Navajo policemen, carrying guns
and clubs, and the Navajos terrified the Hopi children.

The "Foreheads," as the Navajos were called
by the Hopi children because they brushed their
hair straight back and apparently scorned bangs
such as the Hopi wore, were traditional enemies of
the Hopi people. Hopi farmers had suffered man a
Navajo raid, and had lost their ripe peaches, their
new corn and melons, to the raiders. Occasionally a
pretty girl was carried off. Small wonder they entertained no affection for the tall, thin-faced Navajos,
so different from the peaceful, farming Hopis.

In their play, Hopi children of that day often
acted out Navajo raids. Usually this play-acting
took place in late summer, after a heavy rain, when
all the potholes in the red rock of the mesa were
pools of rain water. The potholes made excellent
swimming pools.

This was the time of ripening peaches, which
the Navajo raiders liked, so the Hopi youngsters
would toss a few peaches into a pool, those who
were to play the part of Navajos would daub themselves with mud and slick their bangs back from
their foreheads, then hide behind the nearest rock
or bush, while the "Hopis" got into the pool with
the peaches.

At the first sight of a "Forehead" sneaking
toward their pool and their peaches, the "Hopis"
would set up a shrill warning.

"Foreheads! Foreheads!" they would shriek.
"They've come to steal our peaches."

This was the signal. The "Foreheads" would rush the "Hopis," snatching peaches if possible. When a "Forehead" was caught, he had only to duck under water and sweep his bangs back into place to become a "Hopi," whereupon he could change sides in the game.

Because of their long enmity, the Hopi people felt both hurt and insulted that the white man should enlist the aid of Navajos in forcing attendance at the new school.

Polingaysi's father had known what the *Bahanas* were planning, but since he had no answers for the many questions he knew his people would ask, he had kept silent. Actually, he did now know what "school" meant, and he had no inkling of what it would do for his people.

In spite of his pleasant association with the white missionary, Voth, and the red-faced, white-bristled Government man at the school, Polingaysi's's small Hopi father was a member of the conservative branch of the Hopi village and as eager as they to retain the ancient culture of his people. It was the so-called progressive group that had consented to adoption of white man's ways.

"When a Hopi becomes a white man," the conservatives said, meaning, of course, when the Indian is willing to take on an overlay of white culture, "he no longer has a face. We want to be Hopis, not white men. We want our children to learn Hopi ways and live by them."

But the white authorities had persuaded Lololoma, chief of the Bear Clan, to sanction their plans for his people. He had, as his people said, "taken the pencil." By making his mark with it, he committed the children of Oraibi to attendance at the new Government school. He had given his promise that they would attend.

The conservatives flatly refused to follow his lead. In the old days there would have been open war, a clash that would have resolved the issue, but times had changed. Warfare would have brought white soldiers. So only stubborn resistance ensued, with anger smoldering in the hearts of both factions-anger which would eventually lead to a wound from which Oraibi would never recover.

The conservatives were angry, and they were afraid. No one took the trouble to talk with them calmly, explaining what was planned for their children and that they were not being jailed. Or, if someone tried, perhaps the language barrier proved insurmountable.

Unfortunate incidents made those first days of recruiting students much worse than they should have been. A maiden was forcibly taken from the home of her husband's mother before her wedding rites had been completed. She had refused to remove her wedding garments for the garment of ticking, called a Mother Hubbard, which was the school uniform, and had wept steadily until Mr. Voth convinced the school authorities she should be exempted.

Polingaysi's older sister had escaped by hiding in her grandmother's house, and she and Polingaysi had orders to run to the grandmother if the police came again.

For the first time Polingaysi turned her thoughts toward the invading school authorities. A quick-moving, intelligent little girl, she could not accept the situation with a shrug, as some of her playmates did. She was stirred. She didn't understand what was going on, but she was intensely interested in it.

Why, she pondered, her smooth brow perplexed, should the children be confined all day to that big house below the mesa? They weren't hurt. They came back up the mesa trail in the evening, talking and laughing, even singing, after being locked up all day. Even her sick brother seemed none the worse for spending a few days there, though he no longer had to attend school, but was back on his pallet, feverish and coughing.

The Navajo police still patrolled the mesa, but she had been clever in hiding. She wondered if perhaps it might be better to allow herself to be caught and have the worry over. It was an irritating thing to have to be on guard every minute, peering around corners before walking down the streets of one's own village, afraid to be oneself, the old self that had been as free and unhampered as the wandering wind.

The conservative faction had devised a scheme whereby the still uncaught children were warned to run for cover at the sound of a certain high-pitched, prolonged call. Polingaysi heard it one day when she was playing on the hill near her grandmother's house. Forgetting her thoughts of capitulation, she fled from the approaching danger.

"Hide me! Hide me!" she screamed, dashing into her grandmother's house only a few steps ahead of her sister and two other village girls who had thus far evaded the authorities. "The *Bahana* comes."

"Sh-h!" her grandmother scolded, taking her by the hand and leading her toward the hiding room. "Are you forgetting how to behave like a Hopi? Be quiet. You are safe here."

The mountain lion and her cubs crouched beside the big *piki* plaque which the grandmother quickly removed from the loose floor stone it covered. Polingaysi shuddered and hung back as the old woman took her arm. She had never before been in the old kiva of the rainmakers. It was black down there, and musty smells smote her nostrils. Then she felt the dirt floor beneath her feet and her grandmother released her arm. A spider web brushed her nose, making her want to sneeze.

She heard, rather than saw, the other girls let themselves down into the darkness, but said nothing to them. The grandmother replaced the stone. Gradually her eyes adjusted to the darkness. A tiny ray of light from the air shaft revealed the other girls, huddled in silence. Momentarily Polingaysi expected to hear scuffle overhead, the sound of gruff voices, and removal of the floor stone. Trembling violently, she imagined how horrible it would be to be pulled screaming out of this blackness and carried off to imprisonment in the school. But no scuffle took place. No sound of voices reached them. Eventually the grandmother removed the stone and helped them out.

The grandmother was angry. Her black eyes were hot with hatred and her thin lips were compressed.

"They dared come into my house," she muttered. "Those Navajos! They pushed me aside when I tried to keep them out. And that fat *Bahana*. The one with white hairs sprouting from his red face. He watched them and said nothing. I think he hoped they would hit me." She breathed hard for a moment, while the girls brushed dirt from their blanket dresses. "They are gone, but they will come back. In time they will catch you."

The very next day Polingaysi's sister and her friends were trapped on the talus slope south of the village and taken to school.

Polingaysi pretended she felt no interest in the striped cotton dress her sister wore home that afternoon, but she was alive with curiosity. It looked clean and pretty. How did it feel? Was it warm, like their blanket dresses?

Pretending unconcern at home, she went to the home of one of her playmates and asked about the new garment.

"Will you let me try it on?"

The other girl was willing. They ran behind the house. Off came Polingaysi's one garment. Off came the ticking dress. On over Polingaysi's black head it went. The other girl was taller. Her dress came to Polingaysi's ankles. She felt grown up in it. She ran her hands over the smooth material approvingly. It was not harsh, like her home-woven wool blanket dress.

"I like it," she said, taking it off and returning it. "Tell me, do the *Bahanas* hurt you, down there in that big house."

"No," her friend said, with a shake of her head. "They don't do anything to us. We sit on a seat and make marks. We play in the schoolyard. When Father Sun is overhead, they give us food."

"Food? What kind?" Polingaysi asked, for this was one of her favorite subjects. *Nu-qui-vi? Piki? Som-ev-I-ki?*

The other girl shook her head.

"*Bahana* food" she said. "I don't know it's name."

The next day it seemed to Polingaysi that all the children except herself had gone to school. She was lonely. None of her games held her interest. The simple, ordinary pursuits had lost their tang. Her thoughts were down below, at the school.

"I am not happy," she admitted. "I am lonely."

Casually, she worked her way slowly across the mesa from her own home and sat down on a rock, letting her short legs dangle. She could hear the children calling to each other as they played in the schoolyard. They sounded happy.

She did not have her mother's permission to go down the trail, but down the trail she went, dodging behind rocks and bushes when she met villagers coming up the trail, then sauntering on, nearer and nearer the schoolhouse.

At noon, when the children came out of the schoolhouse again, she was playing beside a nearby boulder. Two of her friends saw her and came running to her. Shy as a little desert animal, she hid from them at first. Though she could no longer endure being left in the backwash of all this excitement, she knew the enormity of her action. No one had forced her to do this thing. She had come down the trail of her own free will. If she went into that schoolhouse, it would be because she desired to do so. Her mother would be very angry with her.

When she yielded to her desire to be with her friends and to savor the new experience at the cost of losing her freedom, the other girls took her hands, and between them, pulling back only slightly, she went to the schoolhouse.

A bell rang. The children lined up and marched past the kitchen where each was given a saucer of syrup, a piece of hardtack, and a tin cup of water. After they had eaten, the bell rang again and they lined up to march into the schoolhouse. The white man with the red face and the white whiskers stood beside the door, hairy hands on his hips. Polingaysi tried to sidle past him, but he stopped her. Her heart pounded like a Hopi drum as he said something to a Hopi girl, several years older.

"He says to take you and clean you up," the older girl said, taking Polingaysi's hand and leading her away. There was a big tub in the room to which Polingaysi was taken. The older girl poured water into it, instructing Polingaysi to undress. She helped her into the tub, soaped her generously, scrubbed her from head to toes, then rinsed and dried her body. As Polingaysi had hoped, the girl then gave her one of the ticking dresses and rolled her blanket dress, tying it with woven sash.

"Now, go to school," she said when Polingaysi had struggled into the strange garment. "They'll tell you what to do."

The teacher must have been waiting for her. As she hesitated at the door, he came over, took her by the arm, and walked her rapidly to a desk where two other little girls were sitting. He shoved her in beside them and pushed a pencil and a piece of paper in front of her. He was a thin, sour-faced young man with cold, unsympathetic eyes. She could not understand what he said to her before he turned away.

One of the other girls whispered to her, "Make marks like the ones he makes."

The marks the teacher made on the black-board spelled "cat," but Polingaysi did knot know it. She copied them as best she could, filling her paper on both sides.

Climbing the trail with the other children after school, she began to have misgivings. What would her mother say? She had no doubt wondered where Polingaysi had gone and worried about her. On the mesa once more, Polingaysi took a round-about way home, dragging her bare feet to prolong

the painful moment of confession. Her older sister reached home long before she did.

When Polingaysi stepped into the doorway, four pairs of eyes met her: her sick brothers', sad and reproachful; her sister's wide with excitement; her mother's sorrowful; and the baby brother's, warm and loving.

Her mother spoke.

"Who took you to school? I looked everywhere for you. The *Bahana* has not been in the village all day long."

Polingaysi hung her head, the rolled blanket dress clutched to her bosom.

"I took myself."

"So! You self-willed, naughty girl! You have taken a step in the wrong direction. A step away from you Hopi people. You have brought grief t us. To me, to your father, and to your grandparents. Now you must continue to go to school each day. You have brought this thing upon yourself, and there is no turning back."

She turned her gaze away from Polingaysi, emphasizing the finality of her words. A great sadness seized the little girl in the doorway. She had been condemned for committing herself to a new way of life. Tears rushed into her black eyes and spilled over. She dropped her rolled-up bundle and ran to the mesa's edge to shed her repentant tears in solitude.

Source:
Polingaysi Qoyawayma (Elizabeth Q. White) as told to Vada F. Carlson. *No Turning Back: A True Account of a Hopi Indian Girl's Struggle to Bridge the Gap Between the World of Her People and the World of the White Man.* Albuquerque: University of New Mexico Press, 1964. pp. 13-26.

HUNGARIAN AMERICANS

Written on July 3, 1853, the document The Koszta Affair *details the actions of Commander of the United States ship St. Louis, D. N. Ingraham, regarding the kidnaping of a Hungarian refugee, Martin Koszta. Koszta claimed the intent of becoming a United States Citizen, but was taken by an Austrian consul on Turkish soil and brought aboard an Austrian ship on June 23, 1853. Ingraham, wishing to protect Koszta from being sent to Trieste if he indeed was a citizen, prepared his ship for military action against the Austrian brig. After contact with the legation at Constantinople, Koszta was declared a citizen of the United States, and Ingraham decided to use his negotiating tactics to protect him. The prisoner was given up without the need to use military force and received the protection of the United States. Ingraham, aware that he took extreme measures on his own responsibility, wrote to request approval for his actions.*

The fact that Koszta was a Hungarian on Turkish soil, at the hands of Austrian officials, and claiming American allegiance should not be surprising. Hungarians were dispersed throughout the countries neighboring their homeland, and in the twentieth century they were considered exiles in European history. Hungarians were one of the largest groups of Europeans that lived outside of its homeland and were commonly located in Romania, Slovakia, the former Yugoslavia, Ukraine and Austria. Because of this, it was often difficult to determine a Hungarian person's national identity. And because immigrants to America were registered according to their country of origin and citizenship, and not according to their ethnic group or national identity, it was difficult to determine the actual numbers of Hungarian immigrants coming to American Soil. Hungarians did not actually begin to emigrate to the United States in large numbers until the late 1800s, though legend has placed Hungarians on the crew of Lief Erikson and among the first people who greeted Christopher Columbus when he landed in America. Hungarians who arrived in America in the 1800s were primarily farmers or unskilled factory and mine workers. They were generally poor, and left their villages for economic reasons. Many of the immigrants at this time worked specifically to save money and return to their home, and thus remained transient while they were in America, not becoming a part of the communities in which they lived.

THE KOSZTA AFFAIR

UNITED STATES SHIP *ST. LOUIS,*
Smyrna, July 3, 1853

SIR: It becomes my duty to report to you an affair at this place, in which I have taken upon myself to compromise the American flag.

I arrived here upon the 23d of June, and, soon after anchoring, was informed that an American had been kidnaped by the Austrian consul upon the Turkish soil, and sent on board an Austrian brig-of-war.

I sent for the American consul, and informed him of what I had heard. He told me the man was a Hungarian refugee, (named Martin Koszta,) who had a certificate of intention to become a citizen of the United States, and came here in an American vessel, but that he did not consider him under his protection, having, to his knowledge, no passport.

The consul and myself then went on board the brig and requested to see the commander, but were told he was not on board. We then went to the Austrian consul and demanded to see Koszta, which, after some demur, was granted. After a conversation with Koszta, I was afraid I had no right to demand him as a citizen of the United States, but determined neither to make a claim, nor acquiesce in his seizure, until I could hear from the legation at Constantinople. I was guided in this opinion by the consul, who seemed to think we could not use force without more evidence than the paper in his possession gave. I then requested the consul to write immediately to the legation, which he did. Before an answer could arrive, I received information that Koszta was to be sent to Trieste. I immediately wrote to the commander of the brig, protesting against this step, and received a verbal reply that he was ignorant of any such intention. Next morning, at daylight, I got under way and anchored within half-cable's length of the brig, and loaded my guns; the steamer, in which it was said Koszta was to be sent, being very near. At 11 A.M. an answer came from Mr. Brown, stating that Koszta was an American citizen, and advising the consul to give him all aid and sympathy, but in an unofficial way. I then told the consul he must insist upon Koszta remaining until I again heard from the charge. He did so, when the Austrian consul told him he had intended to send the man that day, but would wait until the next mail. On Saturday, the 2d of July, the capon ogland of the legation arrived with letters from the charge to the consul and myself to use stringent measures.

I immediately had an interview with Koszta, in which he claimed the protection of the American flag. I then addressed note "B" to the commander of the brig, demanding Koszta's release. I also directed the American consul to furnish the Austrian consul with a copy of the demand, which was done.

At this time the Austrian brig and a 10-gun schooner, that arrived the day before, prepared for action; having three mail steamers to assist. I did the same, and awaited the hour of 4 P.M. At 12 our consul came off with a proposition that Koszta should be delivered into the hands of the consul general of France, to be held at the joint order of the American and Austrian consuls until his nationality should be determined. After some consideration, and the advice of the English and French consuls to ours, I agreed to the terms. The prisoner was then landed, amid the cheers of the inhabitants and every demonstration of joy. I know, sir, I have taken a fearful responsibility upon myself by this act; but after Mr. Brown had informed me Koszta had taken the oath of allegiance to the United States, and forsworn all allegiance to Austria; that he was an American citizen, and had been under the protection of the legation at Constantinople, I could not hesitate to believe he was fully entitled to protection. It was a case of life and death, for if Koszta had been taken to Trieste his fate was sealed; and could I have looked the American people in the face again if I had allowed a citizen to be executed, and not used the power in my hands to protect him for fear of doing too much? The easy manner, also, in which he was given up, and the convention that he should be held by a third party until his nationality could be established, is evidence that they were not sure of their ground.

Should my conduct be approved by you, sir, it will be one of the proudest moments of my life, that I have saved this gallant man from a cruel and ignominious death. On the other hand, should the course I have pursued be disavowed, I must bow to the decision; but whatever may be the consequences to myself, I shall feel I have done my best to support the honor of the flag, and not allow a citizen to be oppressed who claimed at my hands the protection of the flag.

I enclose copies of all the papers (A to E) relating to this affair.

I have the honor to be, very respectfully, your obedient servant,

D.N. INGRAHAM,
Commander.
Hon. J.C. Dobbin,
Secretary of the Navy, Washington, D.C.

Source:

The Hungarians in America, 1583-1974: A Chronology & Fact Book. Compiled and edited by Joseph Széplaki. Dobbs Ferry, NY: Oceana Publications, 1975. pp. 64-65. [Originally published: United States. Congress. House of Representatives. Executive Documents No. 91. (33rd Congress, 1st Session).]

From 1892 to 1954, Ellis Island in New York harbor served as the chief processing station for persons entering the United States. As such it became a part of immigrant lore, charged with images of hope and apprehension. Much less well-known, however, is Castle Garden, site of the welcoming center prior to the designation of Ellis Island for that purpose.

At one time there was a piece of land at the tip of Manhattan, which was later joined to the larger island by means of a landfill. In 1808, New York state began building a fort on the spot in preparation for a war with England, and though that war came in 1812, it passed New York by. The fort came to be known as the Southwest Battery, and later Castle Clinton in honor a New York governor, DeWitt Clinton.

In 1824, the place took the name Castle Garden, and for several decades was the site of a concert hall. Then in the mid-1800s it was transformed yet again, this time to serve as a reception center for immigrants. At Castle Garden, people arriving from Europe were given medical care, changed their national currencies for dollars, and learned about available housing in New York City.

By 1879, the arrival of ships carrying immigrants from Europe to the New World was a common enough event, yet precisely because this was the heyday of European immigration, the New York Times saw fit to regularly report the numbers of new arrivals according to ship and port of origin. Thus on December 16, for instance, 354 immigrants arrived at Castle Garden on the City of Berlin, originating in Liverpool, England, and so on.

The fact that many of the ships themselves bore the names of cities and countries made the lists somewhat difficult to read. What truly stood out, however, was the arrival of "a large number of Hungarians . . . in a destitute [penniless] condition." Because of their apparent skill in the lumbering trade, they were quickly given jobs in the forests of Pennsylvania, but only with great difficulty did the superintendent at Castle Garden learn of these skills, since none of the Hungarians spoke any of the languages known by the staff there.

As the New York Times reported, after bringing in a Hungarian interpreter, officials learned that flooding in their homeland had ruined the Hungarians' crops, forcing them to scrape together what they could to get out of the country. Passage from Hungary to America was a costly affair at a time when transatlantic travel could only be accomplished by ship, since Hungary is located deep in the heart of the European continent.

The Hungarians' situation richly illustrates the vast distance between the lives of ordinary Europeans—farmers and workers such as these immigrants—and those of the privileged few who ruled their lands. Hungary had long been controlled by Austria, but with the weakening of the latter, Hungarian leaders' aspirations for national self-determination had grown. Following an uprising in 1848, Hungarians had attempted to set up an independent republic, an uprising crushed by combined Austrian and Russian armies.

Then in 1867, Austria's leaders—European rulers of long standing called the Hapsburgs—had conceded to Hungarian demands for autonomy by declaring dual rule over the newly renamed Austro-Hungarian Empire. The latter had a magnificent flag, complete with the royal arms of both countries, and indeed the empire was a splendid collection of more than a dozen nationalities. Simmering differences between those national groups would eventually bring about World War I, which ended the Austro-Hungarian Empire forever.

In such a troubled environment, it is not surprising that the immigrants mentioned in the New York Times *article would have fled their native land. The newspaper writer speculated that the steerage fare aboard the* Spain*—that is, the meals they received with their third-class tickets during the transatlantic crossing—was the best food they had eaten in their lives.*

A few decades after these Hungarians arrived in New York City, a new word entered the English language: luftmensch. Drawn from Yiddish, a blend of German and Hebrew spoken by many Jews in eastern Europe, luftmensch (whose plural is luftmenschen) meant literally "air man"—someone who spends their time on inconsequential matters. The hardworking Hungarians were the very opposite of luftmenschen, yet the term seems oddly applicable because, to the astounded American officials, they seemed capable of living on nothing but air. The superintendent of Castle Garden expressed tongue-in-cheek reservations regarding the apparent overconfidence of these people; but the resolve and steadfastness of the Hungarians, in laying claim to their new home, was quite clear.

DESTITUTE IMMIGRANTS

The arrivals of immigrants at Castle Garden since Saturday, are as follows: Per City of Berlin, Liverpool, 354; Elysin, London, 53; Spain, Liverpool, 255; Mass, Rotterdam, 135; Anchoria, Glasgow, 177; total, 974. Among this number of Hungarians, who arrived in a destitute condition. Thirty of these people came last week, and had immediately to be taken charge of, by the Castle Garden officers. Superintendent Jackson finally found employment for them at Lenhardtsville, Bucks County, in the lumber region of Pennsylvania. They were all woodchoppers and hardy forest laborers, hence the reason for sending them there. Yesterday, the Spain discharged 90 more of these people, equally destitute, on the Emigration Department. The astonished officers became alarmed, and instituted inquiries. It was not easy to communicate with the men, as they could not speak English, French, or German; but an interpreter was found with some trouble. It was learned that they had come from the flooded districts of Hungary, where the crops have failed and long continued rains have caused the inundation of the country, sweeping away the subsistence of the people. The immigrants sold everything they had to get money enough to pay their passage to this country, which was necessarily expensive as they had to come from the interior of Hungary, through Germany, to Liverpool. The section they come from rejoices in the unpronounceable name of Sarosmegye. They are all lumbermen and farmers. It is exceedingly likely that the steerage fare on the Spain was the best feeding they ever had in their lives. They were landed looking strong and hearty, but without so much as a rent among the whole lot, and they had to get their breakfast from the department people in whose charge they for the present will remain. Superintendent Jackson says they are honest, hard-working fellows, and he thinks there will not be much difficulty to find work for them; but he says what he rather dreads is, that when they have got $15 or $20 together, each man will be sending for his family, and a long string of equally destitute Hungarian wives and children will trail through the department for a year or more.

Source:

Ethnic Groups in American Life. New York: Arno Press and the *New York Times*, 1978.

After participating as a spectator in an unsuccessful revolt against the communist government of Hungary in 1956, Thomas Blatt risked his life to leave his country. This memoir gives voice to the emotional and physical hardships faced by 38,000 Hungarian refugees who entered the United States after the Revolution of 1956 failed to end communist rule in Hungary. Fear of retribution from the communist leadership, a retribution that occurred during the early years of the rule of János Kádár (1956 through 1988), led 200,000 citizens to flee the country, willing to take the risk of being shot. Hundreds were executed and thousands more were deported to the former Soviet Union. The U.S. Navy organized rescue efforts to assist fleeing Hungarians.

Thomas Blatt's memoir is valuable both for his exit report—the illegal border crossing to flee a communist country—and for his entry experiences as he encountered American culture in Boston in the late 1950s. Blatt left Hungary with only a swimsuit, a deck of cards, and his college records in his possession. He followed in the footsteps of 2,000 to 3,000 refugee intellectuals who had left Hungary in the 1930s. Those immigrants made impressive achievements that influenced American society. Lauri Ferni, author of the highly acclaimed study Illustrious Immigrants, published in 1968, popularized the stereotype of the Hungarian as a talented achiever. Indeed, Blatt easily gained admission to the Massachusetts Institute of Technology even though he confesses to "no background, nothing."

Blatt's testimony about the revolt of 1956, the internal conditions and the attitudes of citizens living during the communist rule is important as an eyewitness record. He captures the fear and desperation of life under a repressive government. He mentions the recurring nightmare that he and other escaped Hungarians often dreamed. Those fears lingered through the years until he returned to Hungary after the fall of communism. But it is important to preserve the record of his experiences as one of thousands with a similar story. His assessment that the immigration of 1956 removed the "cream of the crop" is an accurate description of the loss of the talented and educated members of his generation. Other writings show that many of these Hungarians intended to return, like Blatt, who told the Soviet guard, "We really want to come back, but we just really want to go out to study." Blatt's return twenty years later was only for a visit.

THOMAS BLATT—REMEMBERING HUNGARY

January 28, 1976
Weston, Massachusetts

I was twenty-three when I left; I had just finished college. I was reasonably adult so I remember everything in detail; in fact, the whole thing started at our university. The uprising was a completely spontaneous matter. If it hadn't been, it would have never happened at all because they would have stopped it.

It was very interesting the way it started. Even the day it started there was no indication. What happened was that Hungary became a Communist country more or less in 1949. Until 1954 [1953], when Stalin died, it was total repression. And then when Stalin died it became a little bit lighter. The intellectuals, the writers, and what have you became more and more open, and by 1956 it became pretty open with criticism of certain aspects of the system.

In 1848 there was a big revolution everywhere in Europe—the longest one was in Hungary, which lasted into 1849. There was a very famous Polish general who fought on the side of the Hungarians. In 1956 there was an uprising in Poland that was beaten down. The university students, as a gesture, marched on October 23rd, 22nd, to the statue of this General Bem. They put some flowers there to protest into the beating down of the youth movement in Poland.

The entire Hungarian government was outside the country—they visited Tito in Yugoslavia as a peace gesture. Suddenly about 100,000 people collected in front of the Parliament. That's the way the whole thing started. I wasn't there at the statue, but I was at the Parliament—it was a few blocks from where I lived.

Nobody got organized. We just saw a lot of people walking, and we started walking with them. The architects, in fact, started to put together some demands to the government. In 1848 the greatest poet in Hungary's history put together a list of fourteen points, what the people wanted, and the architecture students put a letter of fourteen points. I wasn't there, but then the fourteen points were read into the radio because the crowd occupied the radio station. But again, it was just a crowd, no leaders, nothing. And in fact the leader whom the crowd wanted was a Communist, who was a previous prime minister of Hungary, a moderate—Imre Nagy.

Then on October 23rd they started the shooting. It was very disorganized. The real fighting was outside the city, mostly by the armies. There were some individual groups who took it upon themselves to occupy a church or something. Anyway, it was pretty serious because the Russians had to regroup November 4th, which was ten days or two weeks later. On that day the tanks and everybody came in with two hundred thousand soldiers. It was just ridiculous at that point. On November 9th, we realized it's all over, and on November 13th we left.

I didn't have to get out of there. I always wanted to get out of there, but it was hopeless. There was no serious possibility because the border was mined. Hungary was completely surrounded by Communist countries: Czechoslovakia in the north, Yugoslavia in the south, and of course Russia in the east and Romania in the southeast. There is a very small border with Austria and that was completely mined, so there was no way to go through. They picked up the mines in the summer of '56 and that made it possible to go out. The Hungarian army did it because the tension relaxed.

The decision [to leave] was a spontaneous one. We were thinking about it before, but we never really materialized it in our mind. For a few days, after October 23rd, we thought the uprising might succeed, but even that was mixed euphoria, not quite complete euphoria. In Hungary there is a famous joke: "If you meet one Hungarian, that's a Hungarian; two Hungarians mean sex, three Hungarians mean four political parties." We had about twenty-five political parties there and nobody knew who wanted what. It was difficult to establish whether what is coming would be worse, better, or even different. There was no leadership. In fact, the new leaders were also members of the Communist party, so it was not quite sure at that point what was going to happen.

Saying good-bye wasn't so easy. I was an only child, and I lived with my mother and my grandmother. Two of my friends and I decided one evening to leave the next morning. I spoke to my mother. She was a very enlightened person, sort of an ideal woman, in many ways. My friends used to come to talk to her because they felt that my mother was a better mother to them than their mothers. The relationship between us was a very interesting one, a very intellectual relationship between us was a very interesting one, a very intellectual relationship, in a way. She was very wise.

I used my sarcastic sense of humor before leaving. When she said, "What are you taking with you?" I said, "I am taking with me my school papers, a bathing suit, and a deck of cards." I still have those cards, I was a great cardplayer in my life. When I was fourteen years old I was playing cards till three in the morning, making more money than my mother did at her job.

If you want to hear how I got captured and came out of Hungary, that is a long story. I have to drink when I talk about that one.

One of the three friends left earlier and he went through. I had a girl friend of whom I wanted to marry at the point, but she didn't want to come. It was difficult to leave her. It had a long-lasting effect on my life—but anyway, the remaining two of us left. He lives here now.

There was a general strike, there was no transportation. We carried our suitcases. Each of us had four bottles of apricot brandy and our bathing suits. You have to carry all this, because Hungarian apricot brandy is something with which you can bribe anybody any time.

So we waved down a military truck which was going in the correct direction. They stopped and we waved a bottle of brandy and they took us on the truck halfway to the Austrian border. We got blank permits and forged our name on them because there was a limit beyond which you couldn't go west. So we left. We hired a car. There is a city called Györ, which is halfway between Budapest and Vienna. We slept there at night. The next morning we rented this car and were taken to a canal. We had to go across that which was rather difficult and we started to build a raft. We went to a farmer and bought nails and what have you. We knew that to the right is Czechoslovakia and to the left is Austria. There is a bridge and Russians were there so we had to be careful. At night they were shooting right away, so we had to go during the day, at which point the worst that can happen is that they capture us, but they won't shoot us, so it was complicated.

Suddenly a third guy showed up, an older guy. He said he would like to join us. Well, fine. The problem was that this raft that we build would take only one man. So we decided that we would make a rope out of scarves. One guy goes over and pulls the scarves. Then we can pull the raft back with the scarf, and the next guy goes over and whoever is left can pull it back, and the third guy goes over. This third guy fell off the raft and into the water and started to yell; it was very cold water. At this point, for the first time in my life I got drunk.

Finally they captured us; they put us in a camp. We were there for six hours at the border. Then they put us on a truck, and they started to take us east. We didn't know whether they would stop in Hungary or take us to Siberia. By that time it was around midnight and we were back in the city of Györ. We came in this truck which was full of all the people they had captured. There was this guy who was driving the truck in front and there was a guy with a gun who was beside him, but he could not see us. The truck was going about thirty-five or forty kilometers per hours, not too fast. So we decided we are going to escape.

I was the one who jumped off first and my friend threw down the two small suitcases. Then he jumped down and then the third guy jumped down, who broke his leg. We picked him up, we took him to a house, and we left him there.

Next day we tried to escape again, which was a much more difficult situation because it started to snow. Then my friend said, "Let's go home, because there is the snow; they will capture us right away."

I said, "All right, let's try one more time and let's start walking." Then we walked down to the city. It's a city of about eighty thousand or one hundred thousand people. Suddenly we saw a big truck with all kids of people on it. "Where are you gong?"

They said, "Well, we are all truck drivers. We are gong to the border because a lot of truck drivers escaped from Hungary to Austria and there are all the empty trucks we have to pick up there."

So they took us and they drove us much further west than the previous time. There is a city called Sorpon, which is right on the border. They dropped us maybe five miles from the border. It was all covered with snow. We didn't know what to do. We didn't know where we were and we asked somebody.

Imagine this. Suddenly you see railroad tracks. It is like a groove in the land which is dug out for the train, and there are the tracks. This guy says, "Well, the best thing is to go down there, because they won't see you, because the Russians are all over at the top." So I started to go and suddenly there is a guy with a machine gun, a border guard.

He says, "Where are you going?" and we told him, "We want to go out." What can you tell him? We tell the guy the truth, "We want to get the hell out of here."

The guy started to go into a philosophical discussion. "You know that this is a nice country. Why do you wan to leave?

We said, "We really want to come back, but we just really want to go out to study. We are students." Finally I said, "Look, I give you all the money we have. We don't need it, anyway. Take it."

So the guy said, "All right. It is five miles to the border. It is five miles to go and you have forty-five-minutes. You have forty-five minutes because in about forty-five minutes the train will come," which is the Orient Express. "When the train comes you have two things to do, you either climb up there, in which case you would be captured, or you let the train run over you."

So we started to run. We passed about one hundred and fifty people. Apparently he let everybody through. We passed these people and we ran like crazy. I was in tremendous physical condition. So we were going like crazy and we were totally dead, and finally fell own onto the Austrian side of the border. Three more people came, then came the train. Then nobody came. We barely made it. That's the way I got out.

What happened after that? I didn't have a clue what I wanted to do. Twenty-three years, highly educated, highly intelligent, totally immature, and totally lost.

We were in Austria for a while and then we went to Paris, where my friend had relatives. I was in Paris for a while, which I loved. I thought, "I don't want to stay in Europe, I want to go to America for a while." so I decided to go to Canada.

I flew from Vienna in one of those really old airplanes which had to stop at every big tree, so it stopped in Belgium and Scotland and Iceland and had to stop in Gander and finally Montreal. My first experience you should write a book about. I arrived in Gander, Newfoundland. Yes, forty-three below zero, six feet of snow and the Salvation Army playing music for the refugees who arrived. Then you go into the inside of the airport and you see on the television wrestling—four guys are killing each other. I said, "Jesus, what a place we came to!"

There were agencies. There was the whole International, God knows what. They processed everybody—where you wanted to go—and got visas.

I decided I'd got o a place where I don't know anybody because I have relatives everywhere: Australia, South America, Sweden. I went to Montreal for awhile. I hated it, but looking back it's not such a bad place.

As to English I didn't know a damn thing. I started to learn it in Paris already—I didn't speak very well, but anyway, I got a job. Not so bad, actu-

ally. I didn't even have such a bad salary, in fact. And I rented a room in the best part of the city. That's the Hungarian philosophy, live in the cheapest room in the best hotel.

In Montreal there were seventy thousand Hungarians. Montreal is a fantastic Hungarian center. [But] I was too lonely. I was missing my girl friend and everything else, but anyway. I couldn't stand the cold winter, the hot summer. After three months I decided that I wanted to go back to school.

I choose M.I.T. very happily later, because that was on the East Coast and I didn't want to go far west. I thought, "The East is still closer to Europe" —there is still this attraction. So in September I came down. I saved $1,100 in six months, which was a lot of money since my salary was only $360 a month. I worked a lot of overtime. I also played cards. [Laughs.]

What were your first impressions of the United States?

What is the impression of a civilized people going into a jungle? This is not a different country, this is a different world. The difference between even western Europe and the United States is great. It's much, much bigger than even a Communist country and a non-Communist country, in my opinion. Number one, the whole place seemed like a nonpermanent residence.

It was a big shock walking in Central Square, Cambridge. You expected that you have to go to Africa to find a place like Central Square in Cambridge. Central Square in Cambridge is so primitive even today. You don't believe that people live permanently in tiny little wooden houses one beside the other, and then combined with the great ethnic and racial mixture: blacks, whites, Arabs! It was a big shock walking in Central Square in Cambridge and the downtown area of Boston, Washington Street. Compared with the Champs Elysees in Paris, it was a very depressing feeling.

My first impressions were negative. First, I remember there was the total lack of quality in municipal government. Second was the way they treat the old. Third was the lack of health care, and fourth was that I thought the people were so uptight sexually. At the time I felt that people had a wall; they were closed. My impressions were not all bad. These were cultural shocks, which were very difficult.

Of course there was much that was positive. You can go anywhere you want, any time you want. I was a student at M.I.T., had no background, nothing. And credit. They sold me a $1,500 car in 1958 and I didn't put down a penny. Nobody asked me questions. That was incomprehensible. That is fantastic!

I found people extremely generous here, much more involved, sometimes too much involved, in other people's affairs. People were friendly to me. I found that it might have been because I was an Hungarian.

You said you were in Hungary last year?

Last year I went to Europe. I went to Germany and Austria and Italy. So for the first time I decided to go back to Hungary.

All the people who had left Hungary had dreams—like you went back and they don't let you out again, all these things. I had that dream for a long time. But I was always feeling funny going back there. Finally I flew in. As soon as I got there, I didn't have any fears anymore. I had lots of relatives there, cousins and uncles and aunts. Several of them visited me here. My mother's family is extremely close.

The first major surprise was that I had no feelings about that place. I felt like a tourist except that I knew the streets and I knew the houses.

I met people. I met everybody in the family: cousins who were two years old when I left. I met my old girl friend, whose marriage I screwed up once, and interestingly enough I showed up from nowhere and it turned up once, and interestingly enough I showed up from nowhere and it turned

out that I arrived five days before she was to get married again. I had a wonderful time. I think if you like to eat and have fun, nowhere in the world can you eat like that.

The Hungarian immigration was different because it was the top of the society. It was the cream of the crop of the college population. Do you know that I went there, that layer is missing, the people who are forty to forty-five years now, of top executives, scientists, writers. Two hundred thousand people left; two percent of the population. It's a fantastic number.

I felt nostalgic about the reasonable easygoing life that those people have there. People see each other much more. They are much more socially outgoing than we are. People are poor, I'm sure, even in western European standards, certainly by American standards. The major value of my visit, I felt, was that what I remember was reality. That was the best thing I found out over there. You know, after twenty years you glorify certain things or make it look worse, and I think that my memory about Hungary and the life there and the people there was extremely realistic.

Source:

First Generation: In the Words of Twentieth Century American Immigrants, compiled by June Namias. Revised edition. Urbana: University of Illinois Press, 1992. pp. 146-153.

ICELANDIC AMERICANS

The document "A Party of Colonists from Iceland," about Icelanders who came to settle in Minnesota, dates from the July 29, 1879, New York Times. This was during the mass emigration from Iceland to the United States between the 1870s and 1880s. The first Icelanders to come to America, however, were Mormons. They arrived in Utah in the 1850s and, by the turn of the century, were 2,970 in number. Between 1870 and 1914, approximately 15,000 Icelanders emigrated to North America. The causes for emigration were numerous. In the late 1800s, Iceland was involved in a struggle with the Danish government for executive governmental autonomy. In addition, Iceland's growing population strained already eroded rural areas. The eruption of a volcano in the east of Iceland in 1875 and a smallpox epidemic gave many Icelanders reason to leave. Letters arriving from Norwegians who had gone to America and the willingness of Norwegian farmers to give new immigrants work as hired hands encouraged the belief among Icelanders that they could make a living in America.

In this article, the group of 76 people who arrived directly from Iceland in 1879 were described as the first large party of Icelanders to come to America. They were preceded by a group of their leaders who selected a colony in Minnesota. Minnesota was the location of the first sizable permanent settlement of Icelanders. Immigrants usually became farmers and raised sheep, and most were successful. Immigrants valued education, and nearly all were literate. Those who were not farmers, beginning with the first and second generation Icelanders, gained education and entered professional fields.

A PARTY OF COLONISTS FROM ICELAND

Among the steerage passengers of the steamship Anchoria who landed at Castle Garden yesterday, were 76 natives of Iceland, who are on their way to form a colony in Minnesota. There are 14 families represented in the group, with a plentiful sprinkling of children and babies. The grown persons are mostly middle-aged, there being only three really old women in the party. The men are all vigorous and healthy-looking, and they appeared perfectly able to take care of themselves in any country. The most noticeable thing about the women was the national head-dress, which nearly every one wore. It is made of black cloth, and resembles nothing so much as the old-fashioned long net purses with a sliding ring in the center. One end of the head-dress is pinned close to the head like a skull-cap. The rest hangs gracefully on one side, reaching the shoulder, and is ornamented with a shining metal ring from one to two inches wide. None of the party spoke English, and the Castle Garden officers talked a little with some of them in the language of Norway. This is the first large party of Icelanders that has come to America. It is said that this company of 76 has been preceded by leaders, who have selected a place for them in Minnesota. During the voyage one of the Icelandic women named Kier-

Icelandic American women harvesting crops.

stoum Rvanson died. Her body was brought here to be buried on Ward's Island.

July 29, 1879

Source:

Ethnic Groups in American Life. New York: Arno Press and the *New York Times*, 1978, p. 48.

Representative of Icelandic families, Gunnar Johanson's family lived in a small village depending on the fishing industry for their livelihood. Tragically, his father and brothers were all lost in accidents at sea. Consequently, Gunnar's mother encouraged her young son to pursue a different career. So with little else available in Iceland, eager to see the world, and unable to speak English, seventeen year old Gunnar immigrated to the United States in 1905. A 1930s interview with Gunnar is illustrative of a common migration route taken by many Icelanders.

Since immigration from Iceland to North America had escalated in the 1850s, many well established Icelandic contacts were available to Gunnar to assist in his adventure. Gunnar thus followed the path of many immigrant Icelanders before *him. Traveling alone, Gunnar described journeying to the port of Québec by way of Liverpool, England. Having contracted scarlet fever, Gunnar continued his travels under considerable difficulty. His journey took him through Winnipeg, Manitoba, settled by many Icelanders in the late nineteenth century. Using contacts there, he pushed on south to North Dakota arriving in Grand Forks by train.*

By the late nineteenth century, many Icelandic Canadians had moved further south to North Dakota where they had established the largest American Icelandic community. Gunnar found a new home there on a farm homesteaded by earlier Icelandic immigrants. Nursed back to health by an Icelander doctor, he worked as a hired hand for three years on the farm.

Although the farming community was home to many Norwegians and Icelanders, they still faced discrimination from the English-speaking Americans. As Gunnar later reflected,

> *It's kind of tough when you're young and you don't know the language. But it's lucky they were all Norwegians and Icelanders around here. There was hardly anything else in Grand Forks. There were Yankees. There were quite a few of them and they thought they were something, believe me, because they could talk English and we couldn't. They kind of ran the town, you know.*

Gunnar for a while tried his hand at logging, but at 36 he married an Icelandic American, settled back on a farm, and raised five children. Carrying on an Icelandic American tradition of intra-family support, one son eventually operated the farm next to his and they helped each other tend to their daily tasks.

GUNNAR JOHANSON: FROM ICELAND, 1905

I was almost eighteen when I came here on June 14, 1905. I came from a little fishing village in Iceland, and there was nothing to do there but work on the sea and unload the ships. Most of the boys there wanted to go out on the ocean and fish, but my mother said no. She was afraid for me, you see, because my father and two brothers had been lost on the sea, and, well, she didn't think that was the kind of life she wanted me to go into. She was absolutely against me going to sea. Well, one thing added to another and she finally consented that I should go to this country. I didn't want to stay home. I wanted to go out and see the world.

I came alone, but there was another boy from Iceland that left when I did. We went to Liverpool first and had to wait for a few days for the ship to Québec. That was how people came from Iceland in those days. I was all right when I got on the boat in Liverpool, but the trip over was rough and by the time we got to Québec I was very sick. I had a fever

of 102 degrees. Later I found out it was scarlet fever, but I didn't know that then. I must have caught it while I was in Liverpool, because it takes about ten days for the sickness to show. I didn't want to let them know at the port in Québec that I was sick, because I was afraid they wouldn't let me land, so I walked past the Immigration man and tried to stop myself from shaking. We had to go to a hotel there overnight until the train was ready to leave, and when we went out to catch the train we found it had gone two hours before. So we had to wait in the station and it was cold there and wet. We had to wait all afternoon for the train. When we got on I hardly knew what I was doing. I went and laid down on the berth, and for two days, three days, I couldn't eat and hardly drink. The boy who came from Iceland with me gave me a little water. That was all I wanted.

We got to Winnipeg and went to stay one night with a woman my mother had known, a woman from the old country. And the next day we had to get the train to go to the United States. It had been raining for days and we had to walk knee-high through the water. I was shivering and shaking, so I hardly knew what I was doing. We got on the train and came down here and got off in Grand Forks, North Dakota.

My mother had written to a family we knew from the old country, and I was to go to be a hired man on their farm. It was a homestead they had taken out years before. The farmer met me at the station and took me to his house, but I was so sick by then I went right to sleep. His family and his children nursed me. They were good people. The daughter of the house, who was twelve then, took special care of me. I didn't notice her much then because I was sick and so young, but that's the girl I married when we both were older. They got a doctor out, Dr. Lax. He wasn't a real doctor; he was an Icelander who knew about medicines and things like that, and he gave me some pills and by and by I got better. All the children of the family came down with the sickness about ten days after I arrived there. Only the mother and father were well. They all got better in a few weeks.

I really was too weak to work on the farm that summer, but I helped a little, and in the fall I began to do a man's work—taking care of the horses, getting the hay. I helped build a barn there, too. I worked as a hired man for that farm for three years. He had three other men—boys, really—working on the place, and we all had to sleep in one bed. We slept crosswise with our feet sticking out. I was tall, so I used to put a chair by the bed to rest my feet on. When you worked as a hired man, the farmer furnished the room and board and washed clothes and everything. You lived there. I didn't need to worry about living or anything. The wages wasn't high, but I thought it was okay.

They treated the hired men like one of the family then. Nowadays they won't even feed the hired man! Now a hired man got to go into town and eat. Pretty near everyplace that's true. They just give them the money and tell them to go into town. And they don't even want them to sleep at night. Now they got to go down to the hotel. That's why you got to pay such an awful price for a man these days—three or four dollars an hour, you know.. . . Well, it was different then.

I had to get used to things on the farm, like working with a plow. Of course, I hadn't worked on a farm in Iceland, and there we had just had little patches anyhow and you just used a hoe, you didn't have a plow. And I didn't know how to milk cows, but I learned. The farmer showed me. It was a lot of

work. We'd be walking, probably walk behind the plow all day. Twenty or twenty-two miles a day walking behind a plow. And we had to cut wood, of course.

It's kind of tough when you're young and you don't know the language. But it's lucky they were all Norwegians and Icelanders around here. There was hardly anything else in Grand Forks. There were Yankees. There were quite a few of them and they thought they were something, believe me, because they could talk English and we couldn't. They kind of ran the town, you know. But around here we're all Icelanders or Norwegians. It's like a little Scandinavian town. I didn't even have to talk English the first few years I was here. Not till I started working in the lumber camps.

After a while I thought I'd like more money, more cash to spend. I wanted to save up to get a farm of my own. So I decided to go lumbering. I worked in the woods for thirteen winters, cutting down trees and logging and chipping and all that. There's some hundred men working in the camps. You work all day, hard work. It's a rough life, you know, in the camps. You work all day and play cards every night until nine. Then the lights went out. First it was hot around the stove, then the stove would go out. Before morning you were pretty near frozen stiff, because there was nobody firing the stove. We had just a couple of boards to sleep on with some hay on them.

We didn't get to see women in those logging camps, not for four months; and they sure looked good when you got out of there. [Chuckles.] Yeah, we'd go to Minneapolis and the wages didn't last long there. Two or three days and you were broke and you had to go out again. You'd throw your money away. That's what you'd do, just throw it away. Have a drink, free drinks; you'd treat another guy, he'd treat you; pretty soon your money would be gone. Yeah, it's lots of fun, but you suffer afterwards, too.

I didn't save the money I thought I'd save. Year after year I'd spend it. I'd make it and spend it. But when I was thirty-six years old I'd had my fun and came back here and married this girl that had nursed me when I was a boy. We rented a farm then—two quarters of good land, good flat land. There was an old log house there; I fixed it up and right after we moved in we got a snowstorm for three days. The snow blew right in the room. We had one of them small wood stoves, you know, and we built a fire and we were warm. It was nothing because we were young, you know.

After we rented a few years, the family we rented from wanted the farm back, and we had a little money so we bought this place and I'm still farming it.

I work about five hours a day in the summer and spring, and I help with the harvesting, too. My son has the next farm and he helps me. He does the harrowing and the plowing and I work the cultivator. It's not much. You get up on the cultivator. You turn a lever, turn the wheel. The only problem is getting up on it, it's so high [*indicates with his hands about five feet high*] to the first step. But once I'm up on it, I'm all right. I have a mirror so I can see behind me. It's a little hard to turn around now for me. And I keep going. I do two hundred acres and do each one five times, so that's a thousand acres I cultivate. You see that pile of stones out there? I'm still getting stones out of the field. I put those on top this summer. It's easier to grow stones than it is to grow potatoes out here. [*Laughs.*]

We had five children out here and had some good times and some bad times. Lots of fun, lots of hard work. One year it snowed so high there were ten-foot drifts in the yard. You could walk straight into the loft over the snow. You couldn't see the barn door at all. And our last baby was born on Christmas Eve. The doctor came out and he said, "Well, you got a nice Christmas present," and that's my youngest boy, Fred. He's the one that lives on the next farm.

My wife died two years ago. She was in a rest home, a nursing home, for five years before that. I went on the bus to see her every day. Yeah [*sighs*], after all them years. Yes, she's dead now. I keep house for myself, make my coffee, keep the cookstove going. They say the first hundred years is the hardest. I've only got a little bit to go.

Source:

American Mosaic: The Immigrant Experience in the Words of Those Who Lived It, compiled by Joan Morrison and Charlotte Fox Zabusky. Pittsburgh: University of Pittsburgh Press, 1993. pp. 36-39.

INDONESIAN AMERICANS

The first batik cloths that traveled from Southeast Asia to Europe did so as a byproduct of the eastern spice trade that was underway in 1613. In that year Englishman John Saris reported, according to Woven Cargoes, that "twenty-one varieties of Cambay and Coromandel cotton cloths could be profitably bartered for cloves." European traders used silver and gold to purchase cloth in India that was traded for spices in Southeast Asia. Indian trade with the east had been established as early as the first century A.D., a time when textiles indicated wealth and position. In Southeast Asia societies, textiles were used in gift exchange and to seal political alliances. In Thailand and Malaysia, cloths were part of diplomatic and court protocol as well as important in marriage contracts of ordinary people.

There is historical evidence that suggests that batik, or resist-dying processes that developed in Southeast Asia, resulted from the stimulus of imported Indian textiles. The earliest form of Javanese batik is blue-and-white. Southeast Asian textiles from trading times prior to the mid-1550s are different from Middle-East textiles of the same time, though batik was practiced in both areas. Southeast Asian batik cloths survive as complete cloths because they were used in ritual and symbolic functions so they were carefully preserved, while Middle-East cloths are fragments because they served a utilitarian function.

The word batik is believed to mean "a cloth with little dots." Batik was practiced in Turkey, China, India, Japan, and West Africa, all countries involved in trading in the middle ages. However, the most intricate and highly-developed forms of batik are found on the island of Java in Indonesia. While the art form can be very intricate, the tools used to produce batik are simple. The cotton or silk cloths used must have a very high thread count, meaning a tight weave, to hold the tiny details in designs. Fabric is prepared for batiking by washing and boiling it to remove all starch, lime or chalk that are added to the fiber during the weaving process. These sizing substances will interfere with the dyes and must be removed. Next, a design is drawn on the fabric using melted wax. The area that is waxed will not be dyed.

The Javanese invented a handy wax dispenser, called a canting, that allows a great variety of styles and sizes of designs to be laid in wax. There are different kinds of wax, and the best are from the Indonesian islands of Timor, Sumbawa and Sumatra. Wax formulas are trade secrets because the wax affects the quality of the design. After the design is waxed into the fabric, the dye is applied. This process is repeated for as many colors as are needed. The wax is removed after the final dying. Because creating batik takes so much time, someone in the nineteenth century invented the cap (pronounced chop). This block of copper contained a unit of design that could be filled with wax and stamped on fabric. Modern batik is machine-made to produce large amounts economically, but beautiful handmade batik is still produced in Indonesia.

By changing the waxing and dying procedures, an endless number of designs are possible. However, batik designs can be described by two categories: geometric motif and free form designs that are stylized patterns or imitations of woven texture. The imitation of woven texture is thought to be the main reason that batik was originally developed. The most famous design with this effect is Nitik.

Particular designs were produced in certain areas and for certain functions. For example, certain batik designs were reserved for brides and bridegrooms. The Kawung design using intersecting circles was reserved for the royal court of the Sultan of Jogjakarta. The Parang pattern of slanting rows of thick knife-like segments running in parallel diagonal bands was used only by the royal court of Central Java. Batik from the north coast of Java show Chinese cultural influences and use brighter colors and more intricate flower and cloud designs.

Dyes, like wax, are essential ingredients and carefully guarded trade secrets. The traditional dyes used in Javanese batik were made from natural ingredients that produced beige, blue, brown and black. Blue, made from the indigo plant, is the oldest color used. Traditional dying was done in clay pots, but today dying is done in concrete vats. Special batik cloths called Prada were produced by adding gold leaf or gold dust that was glued to the fabric using a homemade glue of egg white or linseed oil. These cloths had ceremonial uses.

Additional historical information illustrated with color plates of private collections can be found in John Guy's Woven Cargoes, which traces the fabrics used by the spice traders. Guy is a respected authority who serves as Deputy Curator of the Indian and Southeast Asian Collection at the Victoria and Albert Museum.

BATIK CLOTH

Source:
Corbis.

Li-Young Lee was born in Jakarta, Indonesia, in 1957. He is of Chinese descent. His ancestors having migrated to Indonesia, and he, in turn, came to the United States at the age of six. Lee, a poet, has been the recipient of a grant from the National Endowment for the Arts, an award from the Mrs. Giles Whiting Foundation, and a fellowship from the Guggenheim Foundation. His books of poetry include Rose (1986) and The City in Which I Love You (1990).

In "The Cleaving," Lee likens immigrating to the butcher's act of cleaving a duck: the violent act—"two fast hacks of the cleaver"—is akin to the experience of immigrants uprooted from their homeland, from family, friends, and familiar surroundings, and thrown into a new country. The change is a violent one, but for Lee it is also a movement toward rebirth: "I did not know the soul / is cleaved so that the soul might be restored."

THE CLEAVING

He gossips like my grandmother, this man
with my face, and I could stand
amused all afternoon
in the Hon Kee Grocery,
amid hanging meats he
chops: roast pork cut
from a hog hung
by nose and shoulders,
her entire skin burnt
crisp, flesh I know
to be sweet,
her shining
face grinning
up at ducks
dangling single file,
each pierced by black
hooks through breast, bill,
and steaming from a hole
stitched shut at the a—.
I step to the counter, recite,
and he, without even slightly
varying the rhythm of this current confession or
     harangue,
scribbles my order on a greasy receipt,
and chops it up quick.

Such a sorrowful Chinese face,
nomad, Gobi, Northern
in its boniness
clear from the high

warlike forehead
to the sheer edge of the jaw.
He could be my brother, but finer,
and, except for his left forearm, which is engorged,
sinewy from his daily grip and
wield of a two-pound tool,
he's delicate, narrow-
waisted, his frame
so slight a lover, some
rough other
might break it down
its smooth, oily length.
In his light-handed calligraphy
on receipts and in his
moodiness, he is
a Southerner from a river-province;
suited for scholarship, his face poised
above an open book, he'd mumble
his favorite passages.
He could be my grandfather;
come to America to get a Western education
in 1917, but too homesick to study,
he sits in the park all day, reading poems
and writing letters to his mother.

He lops the head off, chops
the neck of the duck
into six, slits
the body
open, groin

to breast, and drains
the scalding juices,
then quarters the carcass
with two fast hacks of the cleaver,
old blade that has worn
into the surface of the round
foot-thick chop-block
a scoop that cradles precisely the curved steel.

The head, flung from the body, opens
down the middle where the butcher
cleanly halved it between
the eyes, and I
see, foetal-crouched
inside the skull, the homunculus,
gray brain grainy
to eat.
Did this animal, after all, at the moment
its neck broke,
image the way his executioner
shrinks from his own death?
Is this how
I, too, recoil from my day?
See how this shape
hordes itself, see how
little it is.
See its grease on the blade.
Is this how I'll be found
when judgement is passed, when names
are called, when crimes are tallied?
This is also how I looked before I tore my mother
    open.
Is this how I presided over my century, is this how
I regarded the murders?
This is also how I prayed.
Was it me in the Other
I prayed to when I prayed?
This too was how I slept, clutching my wife.
Was it me in the other I loved
when I loved another?
The butcher sees me eye this delicacy.
With a finger, he picks it
out of the skull-cradle
and offers it to me.
I take it gingerly between my fingers
and suck it down.
I eat my man.

The noise the body makes
when the body meets
the soul over the soul's ocean and penumbra
is the old sound of up-and-down, in-and-out,
a lump of muscle chug-chugging blood
into the ear; a lover's
heart-shaped tongue;
flesh rocking flesh until flesh comes;
the butcher working
at his block and blade to marry their shapes

by violence and time;
an engine crossing,
re-crossing salt water, hauling
immigrants and the junk
of the poor. These
are the faces I love, the bodies
and scents of bodies
for which I long
in various ways, at various times,
thirteen gathered around the redwood,
happy, talkative, voracious
at day's end,
eager to eat
four kinds of meat
prepared four different ways,
numerous plates and bowls of rice and vegetables,
each made by distinct affections
and brought to table by many hands.

Brothers and sisters by blood and design,
who sit in separate bodies of varied shapes,
we constitute a many-membered
body of love.
In a world of shapes
of my desires, each one here
is a shape of one of my desires, and each
is known to me and dear by virtue
of each one's unique corruption
of those texts, the face, the body:
that jut jaw
to gnash tendon;
that wide nose to meet the blows
a face like that invites;
those long eyes closing on the seen;
those thick lips
to suck the meat of animals
or recite 300 poems of the T'ang;
these teeth to bite my monosyllables;
these cheekbones to make
those syllables sing the soul.
Puffed or sunken
according to the life,
dark or light according
to the birth, straight
or humped, whole, manque, quasi, each pleases,
    verging
on utter grotesquery.
All are beautiful by variety.
The soul too
is a debasement
of a text, but, thus, it
acquires salience, although a
human salience, but
inimitable, and, hence, memorable.
God is the text.
The soul is a corruption
and a mnemonic.

A bright moment,
I hold up an old head
from the sea and admire the haughty
down-curved mouth
that seems to disdain
all the eyes are blind to,
including me, the eater.
Whole unto itself, complete
without me, yet its
shape complements the shape of my mind.
I take it as text and evidence
of the world's love for me,
and I feel urged to utterance,
urged to read the body of the world, urged
to say it
in human terms,
my reading a kind of eating, my eating
a kind of reading,
my saying a diminishment, my noise
a love-in-answer.
What is it in me would
devour the world to utter it?
What is it in me will not let
the world be, would eat
not just this fish,
but the one who killed it,
the butcher who cleaned it.
I would eat the way he
squats, the way he
reaches into the plastic tubs
and pulls out a fish, clubs it, takes it
to the sink, guts it, drops it on the weighing pan.

I would eat that thrash
and plunge of the watery body
in the water, that liquid violence
between the man's hands,
I would eat
the gutless twitching on the scales,
three pounds of dumb
nerve and pulse, I would eat it all
to utter it.
The deaths at the sinks, those bodies prepared
for eating, I would eat,
and the standing deaths
at the counters, in the aisles,
the walking deaths in the streets,
the death-far-from-home, the death-
in-a-strange-land, these Chinatown
deaths, these American deaths.
I would devour this race to sing it,
this race that according to Emerson
managed to preserve to a hair
for three or four thousand years
the ugliest features in the world.
I would eat these features, eat
the last three or four thousand years, every hair.

And I would eat Emerson, his transparent soul, his
soporific transcendence.
I would eat this head,
glazed in pepper-speckled sauce,
the cooked eyes opaque in their sockets.
I bring it to my mouth and—
the way I was taught, the way I've watched
others before me do—
with a stiff tongue lick out
the cheek-meat and the meat
over the armored jaw, my eating,
its sensual, salient nowness,
punctuating the void
from which such hunger springs and to which it
    proceeds.

And what
is this
I excavate
with my mouth?
What is this
plated, ribbed, hinged
architecture, this *carp head,*
but one more
articulation of a single nothing
severally manifested?
What is my eating,
rapt as it is,
but another
shape of going,
my immaculate expiration?

O, nothing is so
steadfast it won't go
the way the body goes.
The body goes.
The body's grave,
so serious
in its dying,
arduous as martyrs
in that task and as
glorious. It goes
empty always
and announces its going
by spasms and groans, farts and sweats.

What I thought were the arms
aching *cleave*, were the knees trembling *leave*.
What I thought were the muscles
insisting *resist, persist, exist,*
were the pores
hissing *mist* and *waste*.
What I thought was the body humming *reside*,
    reside,
was the body sighing *revise, revise*.
O, the murderous deletions, the keening
down to nothing, the cleaving.
All of the body's revisions end

in death.
All of the body's revisions end.

Bodies eating bodies, heads eating heads,
we are nothing eating nothing,
and though we feast,
are filled, overfilled,
we go famished.
We gang the doors of death.
That is, our deaths are fed
that we may continue our daily dying,
our bodies going
down, while the plates-soon-empty
are passed around, that true
direction of our true prayers,
while the butcher spells
his message, manifold,
in the mortal air.
He coaxes, cleaves, brings change
before our very eyes, and at every
moment of our being.
As we eat we're eaten.
Else what is this
violence, this salt, this
passion, this heaven?

I thought the soul an airy thing.
I did not know the soul
is cleaved so that the soul might be restored.
Live wood hewn,
its sap springs from a sticky wound.
No seed, no egg has he
whose business calls for an axe.
In the trade of my soul's shaping,

he traffics in hews and hacks.

No easy thing, violence.
One of its names? Change. Change
resides in the embrace
of the effaced and the effacer,
in the covenant of the opened and the opener;
the axe accomplishes it on the soul's axis.
What then may I do
but cleave to what cleaves me.
I kiss the blade and eat my meat.
I thank the wielder and receive,
while terror spirits
my change, sorrow also.
The terror the butcher
scripts in the unhealed
air, the sorrow of his Shang
dynasty face,
African face with slit eyes. He is
my sister, this
beautiful Bedouin, this Shulamite,
keeper of sabbaths, diviner
of holy texts, this dark
dancer, this Jew, this Asian, this one
with the Cambodian face, Vietnamese face, this
    Chinese
I daily face,
this immigrant,
this man with my own face.

Source:
Li-Young Lee. *The City in Which I Love You*. Brock-
    port, NY: BOA Editions, 1990. pp. 77-87.

IRANIAN AMERICANS

*I*ran is a populous country, located on the Asian continent. It is bounded by territories of the former Soviet Union, as well as Afghanistan, Pakistan, Iraq, and Turkey. The vast majority of Iranians are Muslim. Most Iranian immigrants in the United States arrived in the late 1970s and early 1980s and they were generally well-off economically.

Iran was formerly known as Persia, and Persian cuisine is quite flavorful and elaborate. Dishes are seasoned with herbs and spices such as scallions, parsley, coriander and saffron. A special butter known as ghee is a basic necessity in Iranian kitchens. Though rice is a staple, only basmati rice is used. It is cooked in a variety of ways. One way is to steam it with ghee, allowing a lightly browned crust to form at the bottom of the pot. Lamb is also frequently eaten in dishes such as stews, while chicken is considered a delicacy.

KHORESH-E-GEYMEH

2 large onions, peeled and thinly sliced
1 pound stew meat, cut into ½ inch pieces
5 tablespoons oil
4 whole dried limes, pierced with fork
1 teaspoon salt
½ teaspoon tumeric
1 large tomato, peeled and chopped
1 tablespoon tomato paste
1 tablespoon slivered orange or tangerine zest
½ teaspoon ground saffron, powdered, dissolved in
     2 tablespoons of hot water
⅓ cup yellow split peas

In a pot, brown onions and meat in 3 tablespoons of oil. Add the dried limes (or about two table-spoons of lime juice, or to taste), salt, pepper, and turmeric. Saute for 2 minutes.

Pour 1½ cups water and bring to boil. Cover and simmer over low heat 55 minutes.

Add fresh tomato, tomato paste, orange peel, and saffron water. Cover and cook another 45 minutes.

Cook yellow peas in 2½ cups of water and ¼ teaspoon salt for 30 minutes. Drain and add to the pot.

Enjoy over steamed white rice.

Source:
Anonymous.

360

IRISH AMERICANS

*T*homas Nast (1840-1902) was a political cartoonist for Frank Leslie's Illustrated Newspaper (1855-1859) and staff artist of Harper's Weekly (1862-1886). A biting satirist, he popularized many stereotypes and images of the Gilded Age, such as the Republican elephant, the Democratic donkey, and Santa Claus. From 1869 to 1872 he used the power of his published cartoons to attack the corrupt administration of New York City boss William Marcy Tweed (1823-1878) and was largely responsible for Boss Tweed's downfall.

Nast was also suspicious of Irish Catholics and helped perpetuate the notion that they were the bane of American society. In this cartoon for Harper's, he depicted an intractable and uncooperative Irish boy whose schoolteacher has confiscated his rum and weapons, items often associated with Ireland during this period. Note that Nast filled the schoolhouse with popular images of American virtue, such as the U.S. Constitution and the Bible, which he believed were threatened by the foreign culture of Irish Catholic immigrants.

But Nast was unaware of something. In 1931 the American Historical Association reinterpreted the findings of the U.S. census of 1790 and came up with some startling results. Whereas the Scotch-Irish population had long been thought to represent only 8.9 percent of the population in 1790, the analysis of 1931 showed that it really made up some 17.6 percent. Even though the majority of the Scotch-Irish of 1790 were Protestant, there was still a sizable population of Irish Catholics among them—6.5 percent of the total population of Maryland, 5.5 percent in Virginia, and 5.4 percent in Delaware and North Carolina (and a total of 3.6 percent of the entire country's population at that time). Figures like these are comparable to the Asian American population at the end of the twentieth century.

THE GOOD-FOR-NOTHING, IN MISS COLUMBIA'S SCHOOL

Source:
Harper's Weekly, 1871.

In the 1870s, anthracite ore miners in Pennsylvania went on strike to demand the right to organize a union and to protest low wages and poor working conditions. Since the Civil War (1861-1865), violence had permeated relations between miners and mine owners. Taking advantage of their control of the local government, owners used vicious intimidation tactics to stop the miners' unionization efforts. In response, several mine bosses were murdered and buildings destroyed, allegedly by members of a secret society of Irish workers—the Molly Maguires. The Mollies were members of the Ancient Order of Hibernians, an Irish American fraternal society that adopted the name and extralegal tactics of an association in Ireland that fought oppressive landowners.

In 1875, railroad owner Franklin B. Gowen (an Irish-Protestant immigrant) hired Allan Pinkerton's (1819-1884) anti-union detective agency to infiltrate the Molly Maguires. Pinkerton detective James McParlan (1844-1919) lived among the miners for two years and learned the Mollies' secrets. In 1876 John Kehoe and several other Hibernian members were brought to trial (Commonwealth vs. John Kehoe, et al). Based on McParlan's testimony, the men were convicted and hanged, and the organization was destroyed.

Issues of class and ethnicity had combined to form stereotyped images of Irish immigrants. To Americans who feared the increasing labor unrest throughout the United States, the Molly Maguires represented the threat posed by "outside" or "un-American" influences brought to the nation by immigrant agitators.

THE TRIAL OF THE MOLLY MAGUIRES

Tuesday, August 8, 1876.

At the opening of the Court this morning District Attorney Kaercher called for trial the case of the Commonwealth against John Kehoe, Michael O'Brien, Christopher Donnelly, John Donohue, alias Yellow Jack, James Roarity, Dennis F. Canning, Frank McHugh, John Gibbons, John Morris, Thomas Hurley, and Michael Doyle, charged with assault and battery with intent to kill William M. Thomas. All of the defendants but Hurley and Doyle were produced in custody. Judge Walker sat alone, the other judges being otherwise engaged.

George R. Kaercher, Esq., Hon. F. B. Gowen, Frank W. Hughes, Esq., Guy E. Farquhar, Esq., and Hon. Charles Albright appeared for the Commonwealth, and James Ryon, Esq., Martin M. L'velle, Esq., and S. A. Garrett, Esq., for the defendants.

Upon the opening of the case Mr. Ryon asked for a continuance, on the ground that Hon. John W. Ryon, of counsel for the defendants, was unable to be present on account of ill-health, and because Henry McAnally, Philip Nash, David Kelley, and Daniel Dougherty, material witnesses, were absent.

The morning session was consumed in the examination of witnesses and the argument of counsel on the question of continuing, when the Court finally refused the motion, and the usual recess for dinner was taken. After recess the case was proceeded with, the following jury being empanelled: Lewis Miller, Frailey; Henry Berger, North Manheim; John J. Thomas, St. Clair; Jacob Faust, Branch; Michael Kerkeslager, Schuylkill Haven; A. B. Herb, Hegins; Joseph Stetler, Pottsville; William Wilcox, St. Clair; Samuel Stoudt, Pottsville; Reuben Kieffer, Ashland; Uriah Good, Pottsville; Charles Rice, South Butler.

The Case for the Commonwealth

Opening of Guy Farquhar, Esq.

Mr. Farquhar opened the case for the Commonwealth, as follows:

With submission to the Court—Gentlemen of the Jury: John Kehoe, Michael O'Brien, Christopher Donnelly, John Donohue, alias Yellow Jack, James Roarity, Dennis F. Canning, Frank McHugh, John Gibbons, John Morris, Thomas Hurley, and

Michael Doyle are charged in this indictment with assault and battery with intent to kill William M. Thomas. Of these parties, Thomas Hurley, and Michael Doyle are fugitives from justice. The Commonwealth has not been able to arrest them, and you have only been sworn to try the other prisoners whom I have mentioned.

Before going into the details of this case, it will be necessary for me to explain another matter so that you may more fully understand the attack which was made upon Mr. Thomas. For a number of years there has existed in this county an organization known as the Ancient Order of Hibernians, also known as the Mollie Maguires. It originated not in this country, but in Ireland, where it existed many years ago under the name of Ribbonism. The organization was created for the purpose of resisting the actions of the landlords, or preventing them collecting their rents, and if one tenant would take the land from which another had been evicted for not paying his rent, the Ribbonmen maltreated the person who took such a place. At first they did not kill them, merely beat them, ducked them in ponds, and performed acts of that character. Those outrages were committed upon the landlords and bailiffs, and the constables who were intrusted with the collection of or making distress for rents, and when the members of the organization committed these outrages they were generally dressed as women, and hence became known as Mollie Maguires.

This organization thus founded in the old country, was brought here by persons emigrating from Ireland. In this country the organization is composed of what is known as the National Delegate and a President, residing in the city of New York. They have a State organization in each of the different States, a county organization in the respective counties, and divisions or lodges. The organization was created ostensibly for a beneficial purpose, and it was intended that its objects and purposes should appeal not only to the benevolence, but to the patriotism of its members; but, in fact, at least so far as this coal region is concerned, the organization is a band of cut throats and assassins, who have stopped at nothing for the purpose of carrying out their plans.

All of those defendants are members of that organization. John Kehoe occupied the position known as the county delegate, or the chief man in the county. James Roarity was the head of the Coaldale division or its body master. Dennis F. Canning was the county delegate of Northumberland County, or the chief of that county. Michael O'Brien was the body master at Mahanoy City. John Morris was a member of the organization but held no office. Christopher Donnelly was the county treasurer of this county. John Donohue, alias Yellow Jack, was the body master at Tuscarora. John Gibbons was simply a member of that organization, and Frank McHugh was the secretary of the division at Mahanoy City.

The body master was the head of a division. When an application was made, by any of the members, for a murder to be committed, a county convention was called, at which all the officers of the county were entitled to attend; that is, the officers belonging to the division, including the county secretary, county treasurer, and body masters and all the other division officers. These officers were composed of the body master, secretary, assistant secretary, treasurer, and a vice-president or vice body master, which although seldom exercised was yet provided for in their regulations.

There was, at one time, in Mahanoy City a disturbance at which one George Major, the chief burgess, was killed. Daniel Dougherty was arrested, indicted, tried, and acquitted of that murder. He was a member of the order. He belonged to a division near Mahanoy City. Some time after he was acquitted there was a convention held at Mahanoy City, at which John Kehoe presided. Michael O'Brien, Christopher Donnelly John Donohue, James Roarity, Dennis F. Canning, and Frank McHugh were present, and also one James McParlan. At that convention a complaint was received from Daniel Dougherty, that notwithstanding he had been acquitted of the crime of the murder of Major, an attempt had been made to assassinate him. The members of the convention went for Dougherty; he was brought into the room, and he told them that he had been shot at several times, and showed them his coat in which were the holes of the bullets, which he alleged had been fired at him. In the course of his narrative he told the convention that he thought if Jesse and William Major, and William M. Thomas, who was known as Bully Bill, were put out of the road, he would be allowed to live in peace. He then retired from the room, when a motion was made and it was resolved that the three men he had named should be killed. Dennis F. Canning, the county delegate of Northumberland County, said that if it was necessary he would find the men who would put the Majors out of the way. Christopher Donnelly said that that place would not answer; that he lived down near Mt. Laffee, and he thought that it was a very light job, and he could get men to commit the crime, and would go with them, if necessary, himself; and that it would not need any assistance from Northumberland County. Canning said that that was all right, but if they needed any assistance in the commission of the crime he would furnish the men to do it. Kehoe then told Roarity, the body master of Coaldale, O'Brien, the body master of the Mahanoy division, and McParlan, who belonged to the Shenandoah division, that the duty of furnishing the men to shoot Bully Bill devolved upon them, and that in his opinion the best plan to commit the murder would be to go to —— in broad daylight in the streets of Mahanoy City and shoot him down on the spot. O'Brien objected to that. He said that in his estimation that was not the proper way to commit the crime; that the plan he would suggest for carrying out this murder would be to obtain men from a distance and bring them to Mahanoy City; to have a place prepared for them to board with some member of the organization; to have their board paid out of the county funds of the organization, and then that they should lie in wait on the railroad between the colliery where Bully Bill worked and his residence, and catch him some time when he was going from the colliery to Mahanoy City, or from Mahanoy City to the colliery, and then shoot him down and kill him. This plan was agreed to, and Kehoe then instructed James McParlan to bring men from the Shenandoah division to do the job. McParlan went home to Shenandoah City, and there was a meeting called of his division. He told them what he had been instructed to do, and, at that time, John Gibbons, Thomas Hurley, and Michael Doyle agreed to go along with him to do the job. McParlan took them to Mahanoy City and there saw O'Brien, the body master, and told him there were too many soldiers picketed around there to do their work in safety; that one of their lives was worth a great deal more than a thousand such as Bully Bill's, and he did not think it was right to risk the danger, as the soldiers might arrest them. At a subsequent meeting of the division O'Brien communicated to the members as his own, the statement which McParlan had made to him, and they then agreed not to risk their lives, and decided that they had better go home, as they concluded that they were in danger of being arrested. They went home, and McParlan was taken sick, and, while he was sick, John Morris who had been up in Luzerne County, returned home, and, in the place of McParlan, he was placed upon the committee to kill Bully Bill.

The meeting of the organization at which the murder of Bully Bill had been decided upon was held on the 1st of June, 1875, and, on the morning of the 28th of June, very early in the morning, these four men, John Gibbons, John Morris, Thomas Hurley, and Michael Doyle, went to the colliery where William M. Thomas was working, for the purpose of committing the murder. When

they reached the colliery they found Mr. Thomas in the stable currying the horses. His business was that of a hostler, and he was at that time inside the stable, feeding the horses and preparing them for their work. These men waited outside for some time, expecting that Thomas would come out, but finding that he did not come out as soon as they expected, or growing impatient and fearing that a crowd of men would gather around on their way to work, they went inside the stable and commenced firing at their victim. Hurley and Gibbons both fired. Thomas was shot in the neck, I believe, and in the body. Two bullets struck him, but fortunately for these defendants as well as for Mr. Thomas, he was not killed. He sheltered himself from their firing as well as he could, behind the live stock in the stable, and thus saved his life. In their firing at him they killed a horse and a mule, and, I believe, wounded another mule. One of the animals that was shot fell down and Thomas fell with it, sheltered by its body. The noise of the firing together with the shouts of Thomas and another stable boss frightened off these defendants, but not before they believed they had killed him, from seeing him fall and the blood on his person; and, escaping from the scene of outrage, they believed that they would always be safe from detection.

It was a part of the plan of this organization, whenever they desired to commit murder, to select members who were strangers both to the person who was to be killed and the people of the locality where the crime was to be perpetrated. Those members who were selected were always to be unknown in that particular neighborhood, so that if they were observed, they would not be likely to be recognized again, especially if seen only once, and that for a short time.

But the members of this organization were unaware of one fact. They did not know that in their midst was a detective, placed there for the purpose of finding out who were the authors of these crimes, and, if possible, to prevent them. In the summer of 1873, after a long series of crimes had been committed in this county, it became evident to parties owning large interests in the coal regions, that all these crimes were being committed by an organization, and it was therefore determined that this organization should be exposed. Application was therefore made to Major Allan Pinkerton, the head of the National Detective Agency, in Chicago, and an arrangement was entered into with him, by which he agreed to furnish a detective, who should come into this county for the purpose of becoming a member of the organization, and exposing its secrets and its crimes. James McParlan was the man selected for this duty. He was sent into this county, came here a stranger, and, shortly after his arrival, went from place to place in the county to learn its geography. Starting at the lower end, Port Clinton, and visiting Auburn, Schuylkill Haven, Tremont, Pinegrove, Tower City, Pottsville, St. Clair, Girardville, Tamaqua, Shenandoah, and Mahanoy City, he became acquainted with the manners and customs of the people. In order to move successfully to carry out the design with which he had been sent here, he represented himself as a fugitive from justice, and, by assuming a criminal character, he readily won the estimation of the class of people whose doings he was to expose, and soon gained their confidence and obtained admission to their Order.

He was initiated as a member of the Order of Molly Maguires at Shenandoah, and two of these defendants, John Gibbons and John Morris, were members of the same division as himself, namely, the division of Shenandoah City.

In order that he might have access also to the county council, he had himself elected an officer of the division. He was made secretary, and as such became entitled to a seat in their county conventions. In that capacity he attended the convention at Mahanoy, and there met the parties whom I have named, and took part in their proceedings. Through it he had himself appointed a member of the committee to kill William M. Thomas, had notice sent him of the intended attack upon him, and saw that the party whom he took did not commit the crime. He, Mr. McParlan was prohibited from communicating with any one except Superintendent Benjamin Franklin, in Philadelphia. Afterward the National Detective Agency placed another officer, Captain Linden, in this county, and McParlan was permitted to communicate with him verbally, but he was obliged to make a report of his investigations every day, and send it to the agency in Philadelphia, so that they might know what was going on. These reports will be produced here, and if Mr. McParlan tells anything upon this stand that is not true, he can easily be contradicted by his reports which were made at the time. He communicated these facts last summer, and gave the names of all these parties, but there was one thing in the way of their arrest. McParlan came under a pledge that he should never be used as a witness. It was a distinct understanding with him that, while he should expose these criminals, and given all the information he could, he never should be used upon the witness-stand, because if he was, his life would be in constant danger wherever he went, and his influence as a detective would be almost entirely destroyed. Therefore the authorities, although they knew the names of these parties, were not able

to arrest them. But, fortunately for this county and for the peace of the community, McParlan was detected by the Mollie Maguires. They found out that he was a detective. They discovered who he was, and what he was, and what his business was in this county, and in order to save his life, he was obliged to leave. Then all reason for secrecy was gone. All reason why he should not be a witness was removed, and he consented that he would take the witness-stand, and the very day that he took this stand, these defendants were arrested and placed in jail.

McParlan will detail to you all the facts as I have detailed them. William M. Thomas recognized the two men who came into the stable and did the shooting, namely, John Gibbons and James Hurley. He fully recognized then, and swears to their identity. We will show to you that these men were not at work upon the day we have mentioned; we will show to you that these parties were in Mahanoy City at the time that we place them there; and we will show you such corroborative evidence that you cannot fail to believe that all these parties took part in this transaction as I have narrated.

You will notice that we do not allege that either John Kehoe, Michael O'Brien, Christopher Donnelly, John Donohue, James Roarity, Dennis F. Canning, or Frank McHugh were present or near when this attack was made upon William M. Thomas. They were not anywhere near, so far as we know, when it occurred; but in the eyes of the law, the Court will tell you, that if they agreed to it, if they counselled it, if they assisted in it, conspired to do it and promoted it, they are just as guilty as the parties who perpetrated the crime. Aye, even more so, for it was their brains that concocted the scheme, and it was the weaker tools who carried it out; and the leaders should be punished. The law holds them equally guilty with the parties who committed the assault itself, and if we prove to you the facts as I have said, the Court will tell you, if you believe the facts, that you should find them guilty in manner and form, all of them, as they stand indicted.

The Commonwealth's Evidence

James McParlan sworn and examined.

By Mr. Kaercher.

Q. What is your full name? A. James McParlan.

Q. What is your occupation? A. Detective.

Q. Connected with what agency? A. The National Detective Agency.

Q. Who is at the head of that agency? A. Major Allan Pinkerton, of Chicago.

Q. When did you first become a member of that agency? A. In the spring of 1872.

Q. At what place? A. Chicago, Illinois.

Q. Did you ever come into Schuylkill County? A. Yes, sir.

Q. When did you come? A. In October, 1873.

Q. Who sent you here? A. Major Allan Pinkerton.

Q. Did you receive any instructions from any one else except Mr. Pinkerton? A. Superintendent Franklin, of Philadelphia.

Q. Had you seen Mr. Franklin before you came here? A. Yes, sir.

Q. How long did you remain here? A. I remained until March, the 5th or 6th, 1876.

Q. Where did you go to when you first came to Schuylkill County? A. Port Clinton.

Q. Where did you stop there? A. I stopped with a man named Timmons.

Q. A hotel keeper? A. No, sir.

Q. How long did you remain at Port Clinton? A. I guess about one or two days; a day and a half, or something like that.

Q. Where did you go to from there? A. Auburn.

Q. How long did you remain at Auburn? A. A portion of a day.

Q. Where did you go to from there? A. Pinegrove.

Q. How long did you remain at Pinegrove? A. I remained until evening the same day.

Q. Where did you stop at Pinegrove? A. I did not stop at any place particularly.

Q. Where did you go to from there? A. Schuylkill Haven.

Q. Where did you stop there? A. The first night I was there I stopped at the Washington House, I believe; the following day I went to, I think, the Swan Hotel, on the main street.

Q. How long did you remain at Schuylkill Haven on that trip? A. About five days.

Q. Where did you go to from there? A. During the time I remained in this big suspension, Mack brought him down, and asked to take him along with him.

Q. On that your recollection is positive? A. Yes, sir.

Q. And you kept his time? A. Yes, sir.

By Mr. L'velle.

Q. Where is the memorandum? A. I have it at home.

Q. Then you do not have it now? A. No, sir.

Mr. Kaercher. The Commonwealth closes.

The Case for the Defendants

Opening of S. A. Garrett, Esq.

With submission to the Court, Gentlemen of the Jury: I shall have but a very few words to say in opening this case. The position the defence occupies is a very peculiar one. The defendants are placed here almost without any defence whatever. That the majority of these defendants attended a meeting of the Ancient Order of Hibernians on the 1st of June we cannot deny. What took place there it is impossible for us to prove to you. The Commonwealth in this case have arrested and charged with this crime every man who attended that meeting, with the exception of McParlan, who is their witness in this case, and a man by the name of Gavin, whom we have been unable to find. In taking this course, the mouths of all the parties who were present at that meeting are entirely closed, and the defendants are left without being able to prove anything in their behalf as to the proceedings of that meeting. The only thing we can do is to accept the evidence of McParlan, as it comes before us, in order to see whether his evidence is of such a character as can be relied upon by you for the conviction of these defendants.

In the first place, we shall attempt to prove to you that Mr. McParlan has contradicted himself from the very beginning of his story to the close. We shall show to you that he has not only contradicted himself upon this stand, but that his story is narrated here is not the same story, in a great many essential parts, that he narrated upon the habeas corpus hearing of this case. We shall show to you, and say to the court, and ask them so to charge you, that the testimony of McParlan shows that he was clearly an accomplice; that no matter what his object was, in coming into this county, no matter whether he was or was not a detective, if the testimony as detailed by himself and by others shows that he came here and took part in these crimes and helped to plan them, or in any way aided and abetted their perpetration, he is essentially an accomplice, and that upon his testimony a jury cannot convict unless it can be corroborated in every particular.

Mr. McParlan tells you that he went to see John Kehoe upon the 26th and 30th of May, 1875.

He admits that he spoke to him in regard to this meeting of the organization, and states that he went to Mahanoy City and told O'Brien, and that he notified a large number of parties as to the purposes and objects of the meeting and where it was to be held. He also states that he appeared in that meeting and agreed to what was done. He testified that he was appointed upon one of the committees; that after he left that convention he went to Shenandoah and notified the members of his lodge that they had to hold a meeting to carry out the purposes of this convention; that he told Gibbons, Monaghan, Darcy, and one or two others; and, that in pursuance of what he told them, this meeting on the 4th of June was held in the bush near Shenandoah. Although he did not call that meeting himself, as he testifies, and although he did not fix the place of meeting, yet he admits that he notified all these parties of the fact that there was to be a meeting held, and the purposes for which that meeting was called. He also testified in regard to that meeting that he attended it, and, if I remember correctly, stated to the members that its object was to carry out the programme which had been laid down at the Mahanoy convention, and that, thereupon, these parties agreed to go upon this mission of crime, and that he was selected and agreed to perform his portion of the duty which was assigned to him, and that in pursuance of the plan, he did go with these three men to Mahanoy for the purpose of assassinating William M. Thomas, and that he or O'Brien got up this story in regard to the military being there, and that this matter was the fact.

Just at this point I submit to you this proposition; that whether this man McParlan did or did not assist in the perpetration of this crime, he, nevertheless, went to that meeting when it was conceived; he helped to perfect the plan, and he went with the men on this mission of crime; and even if he did not take any part in the actual perpetration of the offence, there is not a scintilla of evidence to show that he adopted any means to prevent its commission. On the other hand, the evidence is clear that he was always first to advise and counsel outrages, see to their execution, and never in the slightest manner adopted any means for the prevention of the same. In this way be became the main instrument in the commission of all these crimes. During all this time he was careful that no crime which he proposed should be carried out; but his conduct and acts taken together show very clearly his character, and that these crimes in their boldness, arose from his example.

We shall show you that Mr. McParlan was not at John Kehoe's on the 26th day of June. We have already shown to you, by the cross-examination of the witnesses for the Commonwealth, that Dr. Carr and Dr. Sherman, whom he placed at Mr. Kehoe's on that day, although they were there and came through that bar-room, stated they did not remember having seen McParlan there at that time. We shall show you by other witnesses who were present at that time, in corroboration of the fact we have already established by the cross-examination of the witnesses for the Commonwealth, that McParlan was not there that day, and that Jack Kehoe, instead of being where McParlan placed him, in the sitting-room and kitchen, was the greater part of that time in his wife's bedchamber. We shall show you that Mr. McParlan, upon the former hearing of this case, instead of testifying that Jack Kehoe had stated the objects of this meeting as he told you yesterday, then said that Kehoe had stated those objects quite differently. He has told you that Kehoe told him that the Modocs appeared to be having things in their own way in Mahanoy City, and that it was time the Irishmen took things in their own hands, and that he proposed to call out all the Irishmen and arm them for the purpose of challenging these Modocs, and if they did not accept the challenge, to shoot them down anyhow. He also testified that when they reached the meeting, this man Dougherty, who was shot by the Majors, was called in, and that at that time the killing of the Majors and Thomas was conspired. At the hearing of the habeas corpus he told quite a different story. Instead of then stating that Kehoe stated the objects of the meeting to be to take up arms against the Modocs, and Dougherty coming in and telling his story in regard to these parties who had shot at him, he said that Kehoe told him that the object of that meeting was to take means for the killing of William M. Thomas and the Majors, but not one word about the Modocs. Not one word was said here yesterday about Kehoe saying anything definitely about Thomas and the Majors. McParlan stated nothing about the commission of this outrage upon Thomas and the Majors. He did not mention their names at all, or that Dougherty had come into the convention, or as to that being the time when the killing of these men was proposed; whereas, upon the former hearing, he stated that the meeting was called for the special purpose of getting those men put out of the way.

In his testimony yesterday, upon cross-examination, he stated that there were three committees appointed; that he selected a committee from his own branch; that Michael O'Brien was to select a committee from the Mahanoy branch; and James Roarity was to select a committee from the Coaldale branch. He told you that in pursuance of that arrangement his committee was selected, and when to Mahanoy City. He told you, as far as that is concerned, the same story which he told at the hearing of the habeas corpus; but yesterday, in addition, he stated that Roarity told him upon the 18th day of June, that he had brought a committee to Tamaqua, for the purpose of going to Tuscarora to kill the Majors. His testimony at the hearing of the habeas corpus was, that upon the 18th day of June he met James Roarity in Tamaqua, and that Roarity told him, not that he had brought his own committee there, but that Christopher Donnelly had brought a committee up there to kill the Majors, and that he had received word from Donohue that he was not ready, and that he should not proceed in the commission of that offence; but yesterday not a word was stated by him as to Donnelly bringing a committee up there, until McParlan was cross-examined, and the words which he uttered at the hearing of the habeas corpus were placed in his mouth. Then he remembered and told you that this was so, and that if he did not state anything about the Roarity committee going over he should have stated it, because the facts were plainly upon his mind.

That is precisely what we say. These facts plainly upon the mind of McParlan. They were there just as plainly two months ago as they are today, and Mr. McParlan, upon the hearing at the habeas corpus, was just as likely to tell the truth as, upon this stand, he was likely to tell us the truth yesterday; but upon that occasion he did not remember, and tell us that he did not say a word about Roarity going to Tamaqua, or about Roarity saying a word to him about it.

You are called upon here to render your verdict upon the evidence of McParlan, a man who came to this county in 1873 for the purpose, according to his own story, of detecting and exposing crimes. Let us see, therefore, exactly what Mr. McParlan has done. He came to this county in 1873, with the object, as he stated, and which I suppose we must glean from what he said, that there had been crimes perpetrated before then, which we all knew to be a fact, and that he was sent here on account of their commission. Mr. McParlan came here at that time, and we are called upon today, and we have been called upon on three or four occasions, not to try crimes that took place before the time of his advent into this county, not to try crimes that had taken place long before he became a member of the organization, but we are called upon to try crimes that have taken place since McParlan, by his own statement, came to this county, and was mainly an instrument in their commission. Not a crime has been brought before you; not a word has been said with regard to crimes that took place prior to the time that he came here. Not a word has been stated

in regard to his real object in coming here, but we find that McParlan, knowing that he was unable to accomplish the purpose for which he was sent here, in order to get out of his dilemma, worked up new cases, even if he took no important part in them himself. I think you will say that it is conclusive that after his coming into this county he worked up and proposed crimes, and after aiding and abetting the men who committed them, turned around and came here and testified against their authors; but not one single word has been said as to his real object, and not a syllable has been said in regard to any crime which was perpetrated prior to the time when he came here. All that he has told you was simply directed to what has been done since he became a member of the organization.

The next witness which the Commonwealth produced upon the stand was William M. Thomas, the man who was shot on the 28th of June. We shall show to you something in regard to the character of this man, and I think we shall show to you such a state of facts as will compel you to say that the testimony of Thomas is hardly worthy of belief. That Thomas was shot at there can be no doubt, but that there might have been hundreds of others at whom Thomas had shot, nobody can deny; because, if it becomes necessary, we shall prove to you that Thomas shot at other people just as indiscriminately as other people shot at him; and if there was one man who ever shot at Mr. Thomas, there were perhaps hundreds of others who thought their lives were worth just as much as his, and if they attempted to commit violence upon Mr. Thomas, they knew full well that he was just as likely to commit violence upon them. Mr. Thomas, in his testimony, attempted to identify some of these prisoners. He told you that he could not identify all of them, but he thought that he could identify two of them. Before that he had stated he could not identify one of them. What was his object in making that admission? He tells you that he told Mike O'Brien so, so that O'Brien should not tell these people, and they should not run away. I cannot conceive why it was necessary for Mr. Thomas at that time to play the detective, and attempt to mislead anybody. He did not tell you that he had any reason to believe that O'Brien had anything to do with this crime, or that O'Brien knew anything at all about the crime. Why then had he any reason to tell Mr. O'Brien anything at all about it. So far as Mr. O'Brien was concerned, why did not Thomas maintain silence? But the only reason which he gave for stating to O'Brien that he could not recognize any of these parties, was because he did not want these parties who had committed the outrage upon him to run away. Mr. Thomas says that at one time, he came from Tamaqua here, and visited the prison in Pottsville, and when here, he saw Thomas Hurley, who was in jail, charged with a serious crime, and made up his mind that Hurley was one of the men who shot him, and he so tells his story. He does not say that he recognized any of the other men, and repeats at different times, that he could not identify them; but he came at the hearing of the habeas corpus, knowing that these defendants were charged with this crime, in conjunction with Thomas Hurley, and he picked out one of these men as one of those who attempted to assassinate him. Yet, yesterday he swore to you that he had never seen this man Gibbons before, and that he had never seen him afterward.

We shall prove to you that Mr. Thomas did see this man Gibbons; that he did know Gibbons, and that he had often met Gibbons. We shall attempt to show you that shortly after the perpetration of this crime, Mr. Gibbons met Thomas in a drinking saloon in Ashland, and there conversed with him, and had half a dozen drinks with him; but that at that time Thomas never imagined that Gibbons was one of the parties who perpetrated this crime. Yet he came here and testifies that he identifies Gibbons, and that he knows that Gibbons was one of the men who shot at him, although he met him Gibbons a few weeks after the perpetration of the deed, and conversed with him, without even pretending to recognize him at all.

We shall further show that this man is a convict; that he has been brought into this court upon several occasions for crime; that he is a fugitive from justice; that he is recognized as a man of a very low character; that he has been a vagabond around the streets for months; and that he is a man upon whose testimony no reliance can be placed, and upon which these prisoners should not be convicted.

The next witness the commonwealth called upon the stand was Frank McHugh. The difficulty with McHugh's testimony, in itself, was that in his answers to almost every question which was asked him by the defence, he did not remember; but forgot a good many things that were stated by McParlan, which were ascribed to have been done by him. His answer was that he did not hear certain conversations, or that he must have been out of the room. Why is it? Is it not simply the fact that this man McHugh is charged with being concerned in the perpetration of the crime for which all these defendants are indicted? He is indicted jointly with these other defendants for this crime, and, looking out for himself and for his own safety in the future, he determined to go upon the stand. He very naturally thought that if he gave his testimony on

behalf of the commonwealth, his punishment would be light. He felt that going upon the stand, he would have to tell a story that would agree in some parts with McParlan's, or his testimony would do him no good, and as he did not dare to go upon the stand if promises were made to him by the commonwealth, he simply signified his willingness to become a witness, and to tell his story. Of course, he has had no conversation with the officers of the commonwealth, and, of course, they did not know what his story would be, but hearing the testimony of McParlan, he knew well that he must corroborate him in things which McParlan stated, or else his testimony would be valueless. In many essential particulars, his answer was always that he did not remember, or that he was not there when certain things occurred at that meeting in Mahanoy City.

Let us see, however, whether McHugh was not there at the meeting nearly all this time. We shall show to you, from the testimony of McParlan and McHugh, that there were several important things that Mr. McParlan testified to that McHugh says must have taken place while he was out of that room. McParlan tells you, however, that McHugh was there, and that before anything else took place it was suggested that McHugh should obtain writing materials in order to write out the minutes of the meeting; that that was the first thing that took place in that convention, and therefore Mr. McHugh must have been there at the beginning of the convention, and he remained there until its close, so that he must have been in that room all the time that these matters transpired, and if Dennis F. Canning volunteered, as Mr. McParlan says, to send men over from Northumberland County, if they wanted them for the commission of this crime, and Mr. McParlan heard it, and, if as he says, Mr. O'donnell heard it, then Frank McHugh must have heard it, because he was there from the beginning of the meeting to the end; and the only time he could not have heard it must have been when Dennis Canning and himself were engaged in conversation on one side of the room. I, therefore, take it that if that remark was made, McHugh must have heard it, because that was the only time that he was not in the body of the meeting; and, if he did not hear everything that was going on, it was when he was engaged at one side in a conversation with Canning.

We shall show to you, and ask the court to say to you, that McHugh, being an accomplice in this crime, his testimony needs corroboration, and that standing alone it is worth nothing at all. We shall argue to you in the closing of this case that both McParlan and McHugh are accomplices in this crime, and shall ask the court to charge that the testimony of one accomplice is worth as much as a dozen, and that if twelve accomplices should go upon that witness-stand and detail the same state of facts, a jury would not be able to convict upon their testimony, if uncorroborated.

But so far we have not seen a word of corroboration. Corroboration cannot be merely in the fact that McParlan came into this county as a detective, or that McParlan went to Jack Kehoe's, but there must be a corroboration as to the real and essential facts in the case. The only particle of corroboration of this story of McParlan's told upon this stand, has been the testimony of Thomas.

Upon the testimony of the witnesses the Commonwealth have rested their case, and in reply the defence has but little testimony to offer. In the first place, you must remember that every man who was present at that meeting, when this conspiracy is alleged to have been conceived, has been arrested. Their mouths are closed, and we cannot detail before you one single thing that there took place. No matter if nothing at all took place; if nothing was said in regard to these matters which the Commonwealth's witnesses have testified to; no matter how innocent the prisoners may be, they never can prove it.

The key is alone in the hands of McParlan and McHugh; they are accomplices, theirs is the only story we can take, and we are placed in such a position that our story is worth nothing. We shall present the few things that I have detailed before you in rebuttal of the testimony of the Commonwealth, and we shall further go on to show you that these men, prior to the commission of this alleged offence, were men of good character; that the majority of these men have lived and grown up in Schuylkill County, and that a great many of them have been well known here, and that until this charge was brought against them their characters were unimpeached and unimpeachable. We shall show you that Canning, the only man who lives outside of this county, is a man whose character is beyond reproach, and that not a word can be said against it. But in reply to this, the Commonwealth will say that these men are Mollie Maguires, and rest their case, believing that that accusation alone will be sufficient to convict them of this charge. If they were Mollie Maguires, or members of this Ancient Order of Hibernians, I cannot conceive why that should militate against them. The Ancient Order of Hibernians is a legal association. It claims your respect just as much as the Masons or the Independent Order of Odd Fellows. The society is chartered by the State of Pennsylvania, and the act of Assembly incorporating the Ancient Order of Hibernians was approved the 10th of May, 1871.

The objects of the Order as set forth in the charter are these:

"To promote friendship, unity, and true Christian charity among its members, and generally do all and singular the matters and things which shall be lawful, to the well-being and good management of the affairs of said association, and shall have and exercise all the rights, privileges, and immunities necessary for the purpose of corporation hereinafter stated, not inconsistent with this charter and the Constitution and laws of the United States and of this Commonwealth."

We shall also place in evidence the constitution of the Ancient Order of Hibernians, and we will show you that the Order not only possesses a constitution, but that it is lived up to. The object of the Order, as declared in the preamble of their constitution, is this:

"The members of this Order do declare that the intent and purpose of the Order is to promote friendship, unity, and true Christian charity among its members, by raising a stock, or supporting a fund of money, for maintaining the aged, sick, blind, and infirm members, and for no other purpose whatsoever."

The witness, McHugh, told you that he was one of the members of this organization for over a year, that all the time he was a member he never knew of any crime being considered, being proposed, or being carried out by the organization; and that the first time he ever heard of crime being mentioned in connection with the organization was at the meeting in Mahanoy City on the 1st day of June. I will almost venture to say that there is not a man in this organization in this county, or the adjoining county, who, today, can say that they ever heard of crime being spoken of in the organization, and I will go still further and say I believe that three years ago, before this man McParlan came into this county, there was not a man in the organization of the Ancient Order of Hibernians who had ever heard crime proposed or even spoken of in their councils. McParlan himself does not pretend to say that he has discovered the perpetrators of the crimes committed prior to his coming into this county, and, as he is now engaged in the prosecution of crimes which are alleged to have been committed since that time, I think it is fair to assume that even if he did not propose the commission of the crimes, he, at least, aided and abetted the men who are now on trial for these offences.

Then we say to you that these men being members of the Ancient Order of Hibernians, and the objects of this association being legal and just, the mere fact of the connection with the organization of those who proposed crimes does not make it criminal in its character, and the mere fact of this informal meeting of the organization which was not countenanced by it, at which crimes were spoken of or proposed, should not reflect upon the character of this organization and upon these men who stand indicted before you.

If we shall show you these facts as I have narrated them to you, we shall ask you to consider well before you render your verdict in the case. Consider the position which McParlan and McHugh occupy before you. Consider what McParlan came here to do, and what he has done. Consider the part which he has taken in the crimes of which these men are charged, and, if you make up your minds that he

was in any way connected with the commission of these offences or either aided or abetted them in the commission of this crime, we say to you that McParlan is an accomplice, and that his testimony is worth nothing, and that the testimony of McHugh and Mr. Thomas is not such testimony as corroborates him; and, therefore, under no law of the commonwealth of Pennsylvania could you render a verdict of guilty against these prisoners.

Source:

Charles Albright. *The Great Mollie Maguire Trials.. . .* Stenographically reported by R. A. West. Pottsville, PA: Chronicle Book and Job Rooms, 1876.

J ohn Doyle preceded the great wave of Irish immigrants who appeared on American shores in the wake of the 1840s potato famine. But though the latter sparked by far the greatest wave of Irish immigration, people from Ireland have been coming to America since William Ayers of Galway set sail with Christopher Columbus in 1492.

Certainly the harsh conditions under British rule at home had influenced many Irish to set sail for America in hopes of a better life. Britain's cruelty to the people of Ireland equaled any misfortunes the crown later visited on the peoples of colonies in Asia and Africa, and to many Irish in the 1700s and 1800s, it appeared that the rulers in London had set out to destroy their land.

Irish unrest spawned a revolt in 1798, led by the United Irishmen. The latter group had been founded in 1791 by Wolfe Tone (1763-98) and others, who sought to use age-old animosity between Britain and France to their advantage. Tone enlisted the help of the French revolutionary government, but Irish resistance was broken in the Battle of Vinegar Hill on June 21, 1798. Among the participants in the United Irishmen uprising was Doyle's father, who apparently fled to America in 1801.

By the time of his letter home to his Fanny and their son Ned, Doyle had already been in America for nearly four months, during which time he had formed a great many impressions of the new country. Clearly he had already heard many stories of America, not all of them good, before he even set sail: hence his reference to "this strange country, which is the grave of the reputations, the morals, and the lives of so many of our countrymen and countrywomen . . . ."

In Doyle's mind, at least before he left Ireland, America was a place of corruption; but by the end of his letter it is apparent that already during his short time in the country, he had discovered more of what America had to offer. His thoughts, as he indicates early in the letter, were understandably filled with feelings of longing for his wife and child, and he wonders at how easy the trip—and his separation from his family—had seemed to him before he actually went through with it.

Doyle conveys his feelings of homesickness in the lilting, poetic language for which many Irish writers are famous. His almost musical use of words—"Oh, how long the days, how cheerless and fatiguing the nights"—is particularly impressive given the fact that he was a tradesman, not a professional writer or scholar.

It is noteworthy that Doyle was a skilled worker. He makes reference to himself as a journeyman printer, meaning that he had passed through his apprenticeship but had not yet become a master of his trade. Given the fact that his father participated in Tone's Catholic rebellion, this suggests that Doyle was in the minority of Irish immigrants, since most skilled tradesmen were Protestants from Ulster, or Northern Ireland. The great mass of Catholics from the south would not arrive for three more decades.

Doyle must have felt that he himself had not arrived too soon, given the fact that he found a shortage of available work in New York City. He had gone there after a reunion with his father in Philadelphia, though it is not clear why he made the move since there were obviously jobs in the latter town. After a period of pounding the pavement in New York, Doyle was able to report to his wife that he had attacked his problems with the blend of inventiveness and high spirits that would come to characterize the Irish and other immigrant populations in the New World.

Having reported on his success as a seller of maps and pictures, Doyle returns to his feelings of apprehension about the new land. But in these later observations, his view is larger, taking in many of his fellow Irish immigrants. One wonders if he was thinking of himself when he wrote that "if emigrants [people leaving Ireland] knew beforehand what they have to suffer for about the first six months . . . they would never come here."

At the end of his letter, it is almost as though Doyle is giving himself a pep talk, reminding himself of the reasons why he came to America. In his adopted country, he could keep the money he earned—and presumably salt it away to pay for his wife and son to join him—rather than give it up to tax-collectors. Having come from a land where executions were a regular part of daily life, he closes by expressing amazement at the relatively few instances of capital punishment that occurred in America.

Originally published in Journal of the American Irish Historical Society, XII (1912), pp. 197-204.

LETTER FROM JOHN DOYLE, TO HIS WIFE IN IRELAND

January 25, 1818

Oh, how long the days, how cheerless and fatiguing the nights since I parted with my Fanny and my little angel. Sea sickness, nor the toils of the ocean, nor the starvation which I suffered, nor the constant apprehension of our crazy old vessel going to the bottom, for ten tedious weeks, could ever wear me to the pitch it has if my mind was easy about you. But when the recollection of you and of my little Ned rushes on my mind with a force irresistible, I am amazed and confounded to think of the coolness with which I used to calculate on parting with my little family even for a day, to come to this *strange* country, which is the grave of the reputations, the morals, and of the lives of so many of our countrymen and countrywomen . . .

We were safely landed in Philadelphia on the 7th of October and I had not so much as would pay my passage in a boat to take me ashore . . . I, however, contrived to get over, and . . .it was not long until I made out my father, whom I instantly knew, and no one could describe our feelings when I made myself known to him, and received his embraces, after an absence of seventeen years. [The father was a United Irish refugee of 1798].. . . The morning after landing I went to work to the printing . . . I think a journeyman printer's wages might be averaged at 7 1/2 dollars a week all the year round .. . . I worked in Philadelphia five and one-half weeks and saved 6 pounds, that is counting four dollars to the pound; in the currency of the United States the dollar is worth five shillings Irish . . . I found the printing and bookbinding overpowered with hands in New York. I remained idle for twelve days in consequence; when finding there was many out of employment like myself I determined to turn myself to something else, seeing that there was nothing to be got by idleness .. . . I was engaged by a bookseller to hawk maps for him at 7 dollars a week .. . . I now had about 60 dollars of my own saved . . . these I laid out in the purchase of pictures on New Year's Day, which I sell ever since. I am doing astonishingly well, thanks be to God, and was able on the 16th of this month to make a deposit of 100 dollars in the bank of the United States.

As yet it's only natural I should feel lonesome in this country, ninety-nine out of every hundred who come to it are at first disappointed . . .Still, it's a fine country and a much better place for a poor man than Ireland . . . and much as they grumble at first, after a while they never think of leaving it.. . . One thing I think is certain, that if emigrants knew beforehand what they have to suffer for about the first six months after leaving home in every respect, they would never come here. However, an enterprising man, desirous of advancing himself in the world, will despise everything for coming to this free country, where a man is allowed to thrive and flourish without having a penny taken out of his pocket by government; no visits from tax gatherers, constables or soldiers, every one at liberty to act and speak as he likes, provided he does not hurt another, to slander and damn government, abuse public men in their office to their faces, wear your hat in court and smoke a cigar while speaking to the judge as familiarly as if he was a common mechanic, hundreds go unpunished for crimes for which they would be surely hung in Ireland; in fact they are so tender of life in this country that a person should have a very great interest to get himself hanged for anything.

Source:

The Irish in America, 550-1972: A Chronology & Fact Book, compiled and edited by William D. Griffin. Dobbs Ferry, NY: Oceana Publications, 1973. pp. 39-40.

March 17 *continues to be one of the most important Irish holidays in America. The Irish American celebration of St. Patrick's Day at the turn of the twentieth century was typically a huge city party with a parade. The festivities boasted many non-Irish Americans who joined in to celebrate an ethnic tradition that was established as early as 1737.*

Saint Patrick is the patron saint of Ireland. He was a missionary, probably from Wales, who spread Christianity throughout Ireland in the fifth century. His lifework is revered by Catholic and Protestant Irish Americans through parades and public gatherings. In Ireland the day is celebrated in a more restrained and religious way, with greater attention to the spiritual significance of the feast. Celebrations in nineteenth century American similarly focused on a more spiritual aspect, including special church services and Mass, but parades have typically been a community event with marching bands and a certain amount of non-religious frivolity. Even in cities without a parade, many Americans wear green, the national color of Ireland, and wish each other the "luck of the Irish" during the day. It is considered good luck to carry a shamrock or a representation of the plant. The three-leaf shamrock, according to legend, was used by Saint Patrick as a visual to aid his explanation of the Trinity to the pagan Irish.

Because Irish immigrants of the nineteenth century tended to remain in urban centers like Boston, New York, San Francisco, Chicago, New Orleans and

Philadelphia, St. Patrick Day celebrations became city-wide events. From the beginning of a famine in Ireland in the mid-1840s until 1860, about 1.7 million Irish immigrated to the United States. This immigration wave added to the Irish population of four million that had immigrated from 1820 to 1900. In more recent times, from the 1980s and through 1999, an unprecedented influx of undocumented Irish immigrants has occurred. These immigrants are young, well-educated individuals seeking employment opportunities, frequently in Irish-owned businesses. While the statistics are not known, the estimated number of Irish immigrants is between 100,000 and 150,000. Today in America, 38,760,000 people claim Irish ancestry.

Thought to be the oldest observance in America, the Boston Charitable Irish Society held a celebration in 1737. It was organized by Protestant Irish. Boston, particularly in the South Boston districts, continues to hold great St. Patrick's Day celebrations. The largest and most famous parade is held in New York City, a tradition that began in 1762. St. Patrick's Day is a very special day at the Empire State Building because construction of this famous national and city landmark began on St. Patrick's Day of 1930. The New York parade was originally sponsored by the Friendly Sons of Saint Patrick. Sponsorship passed to the Ancient Order of Hibernians in 1838 and they continued as sponsors in 1999. The Ancient Order of Hibernians is a Catholic, Irish American Fraternal Organization founded in New York City on May 4, 1836. The Order traces its roots back to a parent organization, of the same name, which has existed in Ireland for over 300 years. However, while the organizations share a common thread, the North American A.O.H. is a separate and much larger organization that aids the newly arrived Irish, both socially, politically. The New York parade in 1999 could be seen on the Internet, broadcast live by EarthCams.

The author of Reflections on the St. Patrick's Day Orations who laments the "vulgar and trite" nature of the celebration in 1975 would likely be astonished at the community events of St. Patrick's Day in 1999. Parades are not the only visible element of American St. Patrick Day celebrations. Mayors of Chicago and Savannah, Georgia dye their city rivers green for the occasion. Foods and beer are also dyed in homes and at restaurants. In Ireland, West Virginia, the parade is only a part of an Irish Spring Festival, and that is also true for the South Bay St. Patrick Day Parade and festival in Hermosa Beach, California. Shamrock, Texas has a parade and the Miss Irish Rose Pageant. Saint Patrick's Day celebration has become as Americanized as the Irish Americans who brought the tradition to this country. One reason for the continued celebration is financial. Saint Patrick's Day in 1999 in Savannah Georgia brought in $108,000 for the Savannah Waterfront Association. The St. Patrick's Day parade was established in 1824 in Savannah as a way for Irish Americans to show their Irish pride. In1999, the parade lasted four hours and featured about 300 units (typically floats and marching bands) of Irish pride.

REFLECTIONS ON THE ST. PATRICK'S DAY PARADES

Although the St. Patrick's Day parade may be the largest ethnic spectacle in the United States, many Irish-Americans feel ambivalent about it. On the one hand, the green lines painted on the parkways and the green paper hats appear vulgar and trite in contrast to the joyous array of symbols in the Italian *festa* or the Spanish-speaking community's fiesta. What Irish-American does not feel anger at the sight of a donkey cart bearing "The World's Worst Irish Tenor" or a pudgy young woman in a green T-shirt inscribed "Erin Go Bra-less"? How many of us are not weary of hearing the strident sounds of "Sweet Rosie O'Grady" and "When Irish Eyes Are Smiling" lunge out at us from the crowded bars along the parade route? Every year on March 17 I want to swear off clay pipes and blackthorns.

But then I see in my mind's eye my grandfather in top hat and morning suit, adorned with a sash across his chest proclaiming that the County Galway was his ancestral home. He always marched with a unit of the Ancient Order of Hibernians like so many other AOH stalwarts who graced the parades in New York and Chicago and San Francisco 30 years ago. In Boston there are still memories of Mayor James Curley riding in the parade in a fur coat, piously shaking hands with priests and nuns along the way; of Grand Marshall Knocko McCormack (brother of former House Speaker John McCormack) heaving his 300 pounds onto a dray horse that hauled the ashcart for the City of Boston; of Up-Up Kelly, a Curley lieutenant, punctuating the mayor's St. Patrick's Day speech by jumping up every minute to applaud Curley's excoriation of the British and urging the audience to do likewise; of thirsty marchers thronging into P.J. Connelly's Bar for a "one and one" a half-glass of blended whiskey and a dime glass of draft beer for a chaser. In those days the St. Patrick's Day parade had style and verve, and gave you a sense that the Irish had come from the docks and the railroad construction gangs to win a measure of acceptance in America.

In the nineteenth century, the Irish in America had no ambivalence about their enthusiasm for St. Patrick's Day parades. By the late 1840's the annual turnout in New York had dramatically increased with the coming of the Great Famine emigrants. In 1846 the *New York Herald* reported that during the St. Patrick's Day Mass at St. Columba's Church on 25th Street, the Reverend Joseph Burke preached

on the life of the saint in the Irish language. The reporter commented: "The oration was all Greek to us; but to judge from the breathless silence which prevailed during its delivery, we saw that the audience was delighted with it." The New York press described the burgeoning parades of the 1850's and 1860's with increased detail. By 1870 the line of march looked like this: a platoon of policemen; the Sixty-Ninth Regiment; the Legion of St. Patrick; Men of Tipperary; 21 divisions of the Ancient Order of Hibernians; numerous parish benevolent societies and total abstinence units (e.g., "Father Mathew T.A.B. Society No. 2 of New York, 400 men" and "St. Bridget's R.C.T.A.B. Society, 1300 members"). Thirty-thousand men walked in the procession of 1870.

The parades of that day sometimes drew complaints from certain quarters. The *Irish Citizen* protested in 1868 that because so many German bands were hired, there weren't enough Irish airs in the parade:

We are aware that there are but a few Irish bands in the city, but if those who hire the German bands insisted on having Irish music . . . their demands would be attended to. We feel confient that nearly every man in the procession would prefer marching to one of the spirit-stirring airs with which they are familiar in the old land if only played by a fife and drum than to have their ears dinned with the *chef d'ouvres* of some foreign composer, which could never awaken a responsive throb in their hearts, or impart a spring to their step.

But generally the Irish-American press praised the manly bearing of the marchers and the enthusiasm of the spectators or pointed out parade highlights. In 1863 the *Metropolitan Record* told of a group of boys, 10 to 16 years old, who in green jackets and black pantaloons carried two banners. One was inscribed "The Temperance Cadets of the Visitation of the Blessed Virgin" and the other read: "All's Right; Dad's Sober." In 1871 the *Irish Citizen* described "a triumphal car" drawn by 10 white horses "covered completely with green drapery, fringed with gold and ornamented with mottoes in gold." Surmounting this car was a huge bust of Daniel O'Connell and seated in front of the bust a certain Mr. McClean "harp in hand, to represent the Irish minstrel." McClean was described as a man who stands six feet four in his stockings and is splendidly proportioned. Flowing white locks fell over his shoulders and on his head was a wreath of oak leaves, with acorns of gold. A long white plaited beard fell down on his breast. He wore a jacket and skirting, with a heavy cloak and drapery of saffron, trimmed with gold and green. About his waist was a red belt with a gold buckle. His tights were of saffron and his sandals scarlet. With golden bracelets, a large Tara brooch, set with jewels, and a small harp, which rested on his knee his attire was complete.

To the rear of the bust rested in *papier-mache* an ancient Irish wolfhound "as large as a colt," bearing the legend "Gentle When Stroked; Fierce When Provoked." The car was preceded by a six foot seven inch "Irish Chieftain," with "his log-haired, herculean retainers and trumpeters."

Source: Charles J. O'Fahey in *Ethnicity*, II, pp. 244-246.

*B*orn in 1939 in Detroit, Michigan, Tom Hayden became well-known as a political leftist in the 1960s. As a co-founder of Students for a Democratic Society, he helped to inspire the student activism and radicalism that defined that tumultuous decade. Later he was one of the Chicago Eight, a group of defendants tried in 1968 on conspiracy charges for protesting the Vietnam War outside the Democratic Convention. Two decades later, in 1992, Hayden's progressive platform transformed the one-time anti-establishment protester into a California state senator. It was during this decade that he also emerged as an activist in another kind of politics— that of ethnic identity, and in his case, Irishness.

"Notes of an Irish-American Son" was published shortly after the historic May 1998 peace accords between Great Britain and Northern Ireland. The accords marked the first modern breakthrough in the Anglo-Irish "Troubles," a conflict with 800-year old roots. Originally a conflict of nationalism, it became a religious struggle as well when the English established Protestantism as the official state religion, and Protestants moved in great numbers into formerly Catholic Ireland. The victory of British armies over the Irish in 1690 marked the beginning of even firmer domination, which led to the colonization of Ireland in the nineteenth century—and to a period of oppression, famine, and desperate emigration. Even following Irish independence in 1921, when Northern Ireland was made a Protestant protectorate, the conflict did not end, its bloody sectarian violence rehearsed relentlessly across decades.

While greeting the 1998 peace accords cautiously, Hayden is concerned with an aspect of the old conflict that is uniquely American. His subject is much closer to his birthplace in the Motor City than to his ancestors' on the Emerald Isle: he examines what has happened to the ethnic identity of the Irish immigrants as a result of fleeing British oppression and becoming Americans. His theme is assimilation, an idea familiar to immigrants in the late nineteenth and early twentieth century. Immigrants in those periods wanted very much to fit in, to belong, to be accepted as citizens of their new country. The late twentieth century idea of diversity would have seemed strange to these diverse peoples. Struggling against discrimination and open hostility to win respect and success, they tried hard to look, speak, and act like everyone else.

Hayden thinks the successful effort to assimilate has cost the Irish Americans an important part of their identity. The price of assimilation, he wrote, is amnesia. On a simple level, this amnesia is a forgetfulness about their origins and a lack of interest in the fate of their ancestral homeland. Growing up, he recalled, no one in *his household seemed to be able to explain how he had been named after a famous nineteenth century Irish nationalist. By the time he is an adult, neither his family nor friends can relate to his interest in his own Irishness. "My inheritance," he wrote, "was to be disinherited."*

Hayden believed the problem went much deeper than spotty historical memory. Citing the work of the twentieth century theorist Albert Memmi, who has written extensively about the ruinous psychological effects of colonization upon colonial subjects, Hayden argues that Irish Americans have learned to identify with their traditional oppressors, the English. Making this transformation possible is an Irish American establishment of political leaders, who, Hayden argued, have discarded their ancestral roots in order to appear respectable. Consequently, he accused them of having helped advance Anglo-American ties, with the result that British propaganda about "The Troubles" has dominated American political discourse—at the expense of Irish Catholics' point of view. He deemed this acquiescence by Irish American politicians a "long-lasting effect of colonialism."

Beyond his controversial article for The Nation, *Hayden has contributed other work toward what he considers a necessary renaissance of Irish-American identity. As a state senator, he introduced legislation to make study of the Irish famine part of the state schools' curricula. Among his seven books on political philosophy and history is* Irish Hunger: Personal Reflections on the Legacy of the Famine *(Roberts Rinehart, 1998), a collection of essays by prominent Irish-Americans which he edited.*

NOTES OF AN IRISH-AMERICAN SON

It has always been very curious to me how Irish sentiment sticks in this halfway house—how it continues to apparently hate the English and at the same time continues to imitate them, how it contrives to clamour for recognition as a distinct nationality and at the same time throws away with both hands what would make it so.

—Douglas Hyde, 1890

The current peace agreement in Northern Ireland has captured the world's attention. It momentarily clarifies the political nature of a crisis still defined by many people in terms of a stereotypical saga of the wild and savage Irish.

The agreement gives fresh hope to many that the 45 percent of people in Northern Ireland who define themselves as Irish nationalists will be assured of equality of treatment. The contradiction is that they will continue to live indefinitely in a colonial province of the United Kingdom dominat-

ed by a 55 percent pro-British population of Unionists. The irony is that nationalist majorities exist in thirty of thirty-two counties in Ireland as a whole, and in four of six Northern counties, yet the continued partition and gerrymandering props up a Unionist state in Ulster.

One of the key practical issues left unresolved is what to do with a 90 percent Unionist police force (the Royal Ulster Constabulary) that is profoundly distrusted among Catholics and nationalists, and a judiciary that was recently condemned by a United Nations report for menacing treatment of human rights lawyers.

If the promise of equal rights in democratic America still rings hollow, if racial violence continues to explode thirty years after Lyndon Johnson promised "we shall overcome," only a hallucinatory spin doctor would claim that the Irish agreement will deliver peace with justice anytime soon. But at the very least the Irish peace process of the past several years has begun to bring these political issues to the surface, and the nationalist mission of leaders like Gerry Adams and Martin McGuinness out of demonization and into rational focus.

Northern Ireland should be of continuing importance in America not only because of the loss of life (more than 3,200 have been killed in thirty years, the equivalent of half a million Americans) but also because of the grave and persistent human rights violations within the borders of the multicultural and democratic West, and because it is a model test of the peace process strategies that are a hallmark of U.S. post-cold war foreign policy.

A small minority of the American Irish, usually with familial ties to the island, remain ardent, almost unreconstructed, believers in a thirty-two-county republic. But there is little awareness of or interest in the fate of Ireland beyond those circles, even among progressives. In fact, being a progressive and an Irish-American can be disorienting—as I have discovered. The basic progressive agenda focuses on the plight of the urban poor, racism and sexism, educational reform, the environment and corporate power. In foreign affairs, progressives tend to focus on the military budget, the Middle East, South Africa, Central America and sometimes Bosnia but rarely Northern Ireland. My own Irish passion, going back thirty years, is considered by friends to be an understandable eccentricity, nothing more. They privately see Irish-Americans as mostly Reagan Democrats living in suburbs like Orange County, former immigrants ludicrously pursuing assimilation like the old comic-strip strivers Jiggs and Maggie or the chauvinistic racists of E.L. Doctorow's *Ragtime*.

I was raised in an Irish-American home in Detroit where assimilation was the uppermost priority. The price of assimilation and respectability was amnesia. Although my great-grandparents were victims of the Great Hunger of the 1840s, even though I was named Thomas Emmet Hayden IV after the radical Irish nationalist exile Thomas Emmet, my inheritance was to be disinherited. My parents knew nothing of this past, or nothing worth passing on. (When I asked my mother, "If I'm the fourth, who were the others?" she answered, "The first, the second and the third.")

In the sixties, "the Irish" meant to me the local police the F.B.I., Father Coughlin and Chicago's Mayor Daley, all symbols of the coercive hierarchies that were suffocating the spirit of change. In the classic style of the assimilated, I had learned not to know that the Irish also included Bobby Kennedy, the Berrigan brothers and the Catholic Worker movement. Then, in 1968, immediately after the Democratic convention confrontations, I was jolted by the television coverage of Irish men and women marching for civil rights in Derry, being beaten down and singing "We Shall Overcome." Perhaps because my inherited American identity had been so challenged by the experience of the sixties, I suddenly recognized those Irish demonstrators, including Gerry Adams, Martin McGuinness and Bernadette Devlin, as my own lost brothers and sisters.

Ever since, I have been trying to feel the Irishness of who I am personally and politically. I've journeyed to Ireland many times. I have written of the Famine generation, the million dead and 2 million forced to immigrate here. I have supported the nationalist struggle in the North and relished the liberalizing of art, music, film and politics in the South. My 84-year-old aunt in Milwaukee is puzzled by this. Reflecting my parents' attitude, she says, "When we were growing up you got no edge from being Irish."

Today, when all things Irish seem trendy, the Irish and Irish-Americans are over the worst of a long inferiority complex. Having already achieved the confidence that comes with assimilation—symbolized by the election of John F. Kennedy—the new generations of Irish-Americans are increasingly aware of the cultural and psychic emptiness that is the other side of the assimilation experience. Thus we can laugh and cry while reflecting on ourselves in films like *Good Will Hunting*, in the keening voice of Sinead O'Connor and in the dark, hilarious memoirs of Frank McCourt and novels of Roddy Doyle.

The limits of assimilation are depicted in *The Commitments*, a film about Dublin's music scene, when the Irish longhair blurts out, "We're the niggers of Europe," and when Gerry Adams and Martin McGuinness journey off to strategic meetings with anticolonial leaders like Nelson Mandela. Even suggesting an identity beyond "whiteness" is profoundly subversive of the stereotypes of the Irish as either (a) mindless religious fanatics (the I.R.A.) or (b) right-wing superpatriots (Patrick Buchanan).

The Irish became "white," in the analysis of historians like Noel Ignatiev and Theodore Allen, by obtaining white-skin privileges (such as the fight to vote) when they immigrated to America. As the process of assimilation continued in this century, many tended toward antiblack racism, defense of law and order, anti-Semitism, zealous support of the Vietnam War and backing of Vatican attitudes toward women and gays. Whether this rightward trend was due simply to white-skin privilege is open to question. A more compelling explanation is that the Irish, having internalized the shame of colonial subjugation, transferred the stereotypes used against them onto others.

In any event, the old stereotype of the Irish as incorrigible savages continues to cast a distorting shadow over the long struggle in Northern Ireland. For most Americans, the dominant image of Ulster is of a bloody tribal dispute between equally dogmatic religious factions whose ancient conflict is mediated by civilized British diplomats and peacekeepers. The pervasive assumption is that the North is part of Britain by legitimate entitlement. This leads to a false analogy with the U.S. civil rights struggle, in which the British are equivalent to the U.S. federal government. The difference is key: The U.S. government could require that the South live up to national policies, but the British cannot end the Britishness of their allies. The notion of Irish fanaticism is a convenient means of attributing the conflict to Irish character rather than to colonialist power structures that have been in place for 800 years.

This myth of a mindless Irish conflict mediated by the fair-minded British has been engineered by a smooth P.R. campaign. The British have a decided institutional advantage; until recently, Sinn Fein members like Gerry Adams were officially censored in all of Ireland, and the State Department denied them visas. Meanwhile, according to Andrew Wilson's *Irish-America and the Ulster Conflict* (1995), "the British secret service . . . began a campaign of disinformation aimed at discrediting the IRA," while "US law enforcement agencies began covert operations against all militant Irish-American groups." Britain's Information Service, with a forty-five-person staff, spent millions annually on everything from dinners with U.S. journalists to distribution of as many as 6,000 radio "news spots" to U.S. stations.

The British propaganda campaign, however, addressed U.S. media that were culturally receptive. In the defining years of 1971 and 1972, for example, *The New York Times* editorially endorsed the British policy of internment and even reported that the Derry demonstrators had provoked the British killing of thirteen Catholics on Bloody Sunday in 1972. *The Los Angeles Times* was more rhapsodic that year: "Whatever the past sins of the British government, London is trying, decently and honestly, to tip the scales to the side of peace and justice. It deserves the world's sympathy and understanding in that enterprise."

While these editorials were appearing, British interrogators were physically assaulting Irish prisoners—tying bags around their heads, plunging them into cold water and deafening them with white noise—and sharing intelligence information with loyalist death squads, all of which was condemned by Amnesty International and European human rights courts.

The conflict has never been granted status as a real war but instead is referred to as "the Troubles," a kind of eruption of flaws peculiar to the Irish character. Sinn Fein is still only "the political wing of the Irish Republican Army," as if it takes orders from hooded men in the back rooms of darkened pubs. I.R.A. volunteers are "Roman Catholic guerrillas," although the Vatican virtually excommunicates the I.R.A. British terminology rules the media: "Londonderry" is still used by the *Los Angeles Times* for a city whose own elected council has changed the name to Derry.

Behind the fog of daily distortion is a determined revisionism of Irish history. All that public school students learn of the Great Hunger in the current *Oxford History of the United States* is that Irish immigrants were "ambitious, or they wouldn't have made the big journey to the New World." The effect of this kind of rewrite is to separate groups like the I.R.A. from the roots of their rationale, thus rendering their behavior inexplicable and atavistic.

The Irish conflict is further distorted to service the "special relationship" between Washington and London. The Americans and British were allies through two world wars and a cold one, during which time Northern Ireland was considered a British "internal matter." The Irish-American lobby was frustrated by this situation until 1993, when the end of the cold war made Bill Clinton's engagement in the peace process possible. But Anglophile State Department and national security strategists still view Northern Ireland as merely a localized conflict with significance mainly for domestic American politics, and Clinton's most crucial global ally is British Prime Minister Tony Blair, not Irish Prime Minister Bertie Ahern and certainly not the leader of Northern Ireland's largest nationalist party, John Hume.

Irish-American politicians, themselves beneficiaries of the assimilation process, have striven for a respectable middle ground, distancing themselves from Gerry Adams and Sinn Fein until quite recently. The so-called "Four Horsemen" of Irish-American politics during the seventies and eighties (Senators Ted Kennedy and Daniel Patrick Moynihan, Speaker of the House Tip O'Neill and Governor Hugh Carey), while calling for civil rights in the North, saved most of their venom for attacks on anyone siding with Sinn Fein in America or Ireland.

There is no question that Sinn Fein's internal factionalism during the seventies and I.R.A. atrocities inflicted on innocent people gave moral reason for Irish-Americans to keep their distance or issue condemnations. But the question is, Why did the Irish-American establishment, while claiming a sentimental Irish heritage dating at least as far back as the armed 1916 Easter Rising, choose to demonize the I.R.A. instead of criticizing the conditions that were leading to nationalist violence? The answer, I believe, lies in the subtle, long-lasting effects of colonialism, especially dependency and the need for respectability.

> Just as many people avoid showing off their poor relations, the colonized in the throes of assimilation hides his past, his traditions, in fact all his origins which have become ignominious.. . . The first ambition of the colonized is to become equal to that splendid (colonial) model and to resemble him to the point of disappearing in him.

> —Albert Memmi,
> *The Colonizer and the Colonized*

For a recent example, consider the February breakfast meeting of Tony Blair with Irish-American politicians in Washington. Notes taken by Blair's secretary of the talk with Senators Kennedy, Moynihan and Christopher Dodd; Representatives Joseph Kennedy and Peter King; and others reflect an overall tone of cooperation. The Americans voiced concerns on issues like policing, but didn't challenge British hegemony. Blair treated his breakfast companions as collaborators in a common project and asked them to "keep up the pressure on Sinn Fein not to go back to violence," while urging that they give "comfort" and "understanding" to Unionist leader David Trimble, who had recently supported violent Orange marches in nationalist communities. Blair's request was akin to asking African-American leaders to keep the lid on the ghetto and have faith in the Republican Party. The notes conclude that "this was a notably successful occasion. The already benevolent mood of those present towards us was further strengthened by the open approach of the Prime Minister. . . Feedback from those present at the breakfast has been universally favorable."

The Irish establishment in the United States and Dublin is bound to a sentimental and cautious nationalism that denies the colonial legacy (the purest anti-colonial nationalism—that of Sinn Fein—has been on raw display in the North). That is why it seeks little more than better treatment for Catholics and nationalists in a North under British rule. The Irish Republic does not want to reawaken ghosts of the past by incorporating militant Northern nationalists or Unionists into its modem state. Most Irish-Americans, safely severed from their lowly and radical heritage, have made this identity adjustment as well.

Cutting off as many Irish and Irish-Americans as possible from their roots in oppression is crucial to managing the status quo on both sides of the Atlantic. Only after the full recovery of Irish memory—of being colonized, oppressed, starved, demonized and denied dignity and democracy—will the Irish of today end the lingering colonial occupation of not only Northern Ireland but, more important, the Irish mind.

Source:
The Nation, May 18, 1998. Vol. 266, no. 18. pp. 20-23.

IROQUOIS CONFEDERACY

In September of 1977, the Non-Governmental Organizations of the United Nations convened a conference in Geneva, Switzerland, on "Discrimination Against the Indigenous Populations of the Americas." Among those attending were many Indian delegates from North America, including Oren Lyons of the Iroquois people. His speech to the delegates, reprinted here, exemplifies Native Americans' belief in the equality of all living beings.

Lyons reminds his listeners that diversity exists not just among people, but among all creatures. Disrespect for another creature is the same as disrespect for another human being. By the same token, to think of "rights" as belonging only to human beings is to forget that "we are after all a mere part of the Creation.. . . we stand between the mountain and the ant, somewhere and only there." Lyons's argument is important for understanding opposition to diversity, which has played such a large role in the social and ecological life of North America. Many early settlers regarded wolves, wildcats, and other North American creatures as "waste" animals that had to be exterminated or "removed" before settlement could proceed. In the same way, people were regarded as "waste." Indians were "removed" and African Americans were discouraged from entering northern states by Black Laws.

I SEE NO SEAT FOR THE EAGLES

We Forget and We Consider Ourselves Superior, But We Are After All a Mere Part of the Creation

To the people of Geneva, the people, the Odinashonee, the Six Nations, the Chiefs, the Clan Mothers, the warriors, the men, the women, the children, send our greetings, and our good wishes of health and friendship to all of you. Of the Red brothers of the Western Hemisphere, of the two great turtle islands, a certain few of us have been given a short time and a great task to convince you that we too are human. And have rights. Our nations who have principles of justice and equality, who have respect for the natural world, on behalf of our mother the Earth and all the great elements we come here and we say they too have rights. The future generations, our children, our grandchildren, and their grandchildren are our concern. That they may have clean water to drink, that they may observe our four-footed brothers before they are extinct, that they may enjoy the elements that we are so fortunate to have and that serves us as human beings. The President of the United States of America has brought forth into the forum, of the international world, the issue of human rights. It affords us the opportunity at this time to present our position on the issue of human rights. It is strange indeed that we have to travel this far to the east, to the European continent to turn and speak to the President of the United States and ask him about our human rights. We are concerned. It is the future of not only our people, the Red people of the Western Hemisphere, but it is the future of yourselves that is at stake. We have been given principles by which to live, mutual respect, the understanding of the creation.

Power is not manifested in the human being. True power is in the Creator. If we continue to ignore the message by which we exist and we continue to destroy the source of our lives then our children will suffer. Whose responsibility then, who are we speaking to and who is listening? We would be remiss in our duty if we did not bring this in front of you. We apologize if it hurts. But the truth must be spoken. We were told in the beginning that we were not human. There are great arguments in the histories of many countries as to the humanness of the Red people of the Western Hemisphere. I must warn you that the Creator made us all equal with one another. And not only human beings, but all life is equal. The equality of our life is what you must understand and the principles by which you must continue on behalf of the future of this world. Economics and technology may assist you, but they will also destroy you if you do not use the principles of equality. Profit and loss will mean nothing to your future generations. We are here for a very short time and we have been given a very short time upon that clock of the wall to convince you, to make you listen, to understand, that we are concerned for you as well as for us. Our grandfather from the Hopi Nation this morning spoke a prayer on behalf of all the world, of your future and of ours. And it is with this spirit that we come here and we hope that the people and the nations from which we come and to which we will have to return and which we will have to face, whatever they may have in store for our speaking the truth on behalf of people, of the world, of the four-footed, of the winged, of the fish that swim. Someone must speak for them. I do not see a delegation for the four-footed. I see no seat for the eagles. We forget and we consider ourselves superior, but we are after all a mere part of the Creation. And we must continue to understand where we are. And we stand between the mountain and the ant, somewhere and only there, as part and parcel of the Creation. It is our responsibility, since we have been given the minds to take care of these things. The elements and the animals, and the birds, they live in a state of grace. They are absolute, they can do no wrong. It is only we, the two-leggeds, that can do this. And when we do this to our brothers, our own brothers, then we do the worst in the eyes of the Creator. There should be brotherhood, and the Haudenosaunee, Six Nations, the Iroquois, who were here fifty-three years ago to say the very same thing, the unity of spirit, of brotherhood. United Nations is nothing new to us. Our Confederacy is a thousand years old. The representation of the people is nothing new to us because that is who we represent. And so for this short time I would ask that you open your ears, that you open your hearts, that you open your minds and that you consider very seriously the future of the generations, of our children to come.

Source:

Delivered to the Non-Governmental Organizations of the United Nations convened in Geneva, Switzerland, on "Discrimination Against the Indigenous Populations of the Americas." 1977.

*T*he Mid-Winter Festival or White Dog Feast, celebrated annually by the Iroquois, honored the life-giving god Teharonhiawagon with burnt offerings of tobacco, and with the sacrifice of a white dog. Though the date of the ceremony is often given as January 15, in fact it was determined by lunar cycles and by a joint decision by the sachems, or chiefs, of the five Iroquois tribes: Mohawk, Oneida, Onondaga, Cayuga, and Seneca.

In any case, the ceremony took place in the middle of January, or about a month into winter, and its purpose was to call on the earth to renew itself. Peoples throughout the world have conducted similar renewal feasts: thus the Iroquois ritual can be seen on a continuum, for instance, with ancient Greek and Roman festivals honoring the fertility goddess Demeter/Ceres.

Traveler Joshua Clark, who witnessed the white dog ceremony in 1849, compared it to another Old World ritual: the designation of a scapegoat in the Jewish religion, as prescribed in Leviticus 16:6-10. But whereas the scapegoat symbolically carried the sins of the Jewish nation into the desert on his back, where the sins were gone forever, the sacrifice of the white dog did not bear the same clear-cut relation to sin and guilt as the Jewish ritual did.

Nonetheless, there are certain parallels between the Iroquois white dog ceremony and the sacrifice of lambs in the Bible. Most striking among these is the description offered by Harriet Maxwell Converse, who had lived among the Seneca tribe, of the white dog itself as being "spotless and free from all blemish." Similar words were used to describe the sacrificial lamb in the Old Testament, and later the character of Christ in making his sacrifice on the cross in the New Testament. Mrs. Converses's use of this language, however, may simply have been an outgrowth of the fact that she had apparently spent her adult life among the predominantly Christian society of upstate New York.

Most sacrificial rituals tend to involve domesticated rather than wild animals, since the killing of an animal that no one owns would not constitute a sacrifice. In this regard, an interesting characteristic of the Iroquois ceremony was its use of a dog rather than the types of animals favored in sacrificial rituals of peoples in Europe, Asia, or Africa. Typically the latter used sheep, goats, or cows; but prior to the arrival of Europeans in the New World, the only animal domesticated by Native Americans—with the exception of the llama, tamed by the Incas—were dogs.

As with Judaism and other religions, strict rules governed the killing of the white dog in order to ensure that no bones were broken and no blood shed in the course of its strangulation. Given the Iroquois practice of hanging the dead dog up publicly for five days, it is hard to imagine that the ceremony could take place at any time other than winter—and then in the cold climate of upstate New York—when the freezing of the body would prevent it from becoming a health hazard.

The white dog's presentation for sacrifice was surrounded with symbolism, the elders of the tribe placing a variety of talismans on its body. As with the Passover ceremony, when a rabbi relates how the angel of death took all the firstborn sons of Egypt in Moses's time, but spared the homes of Israelites with the blood of a lamb on their doorframe, an Iroquois priest explained the history of the white dog sacrifice.

In fact the white dog ceremony was imbued with a number of elements which would have been quite recent from the standpoint of an early observer such as Clark. The practice of firing rifles alongside the sacred procession, which commenced on the fifth day, obviously could not have been part of any ceremonies prior to the arrival of Europeans in America. Likewise the practice of bringing the procession past the remains of Handsome Lake, or Ga-ne-o-di-yo, was not an ancient one, since Handsome Lake himself was only born in about 1734.

In 1799, as missionaries were converting great numbers of Iroquois to Christianity, Handsome Lake was a man of some 65 years who had abused his body through years of rough living. Seemingly on his deathbed, he had a vision that inspired him to lead a revival of the Iroquois's traditional beliefs. These beliefs, in their reinvigorated form, came to be known as the New Religion.

The New Religion has remained a powerful feature of Iroquois life, but the white dog festival died out. Already at the time of Mrs. Converse's report, it had become a thing of the past, a fact no doubt troubling to Iroquois traditionalists of that era.

WHITE DOG FEAST AT THE ONONDAGA RESERVATION

This religious festival is usually 'called' during the first quarter of the moon in the month of January [1888]. It may be held on various days during that period, its special beginning being named by the sachems of each nation, and continues for six successive days, including in it various ceremonies nearly all the features of the Iroquois religion. In accordance with olden customs such feast was 'called' last week by the Onondagas on their reservation near Syracuse [New York].. . .

On the first day of the 'new year jubilee' a white dog is selected and strangled. It must be, by the law, 'spotless and free from all blemish;' they are careful not to shed its blood nor break its bones. It is decorated with ribbons and red paint, and ornamented with feathers, and the very pious, who are taught that with each gift to the sacrifice a blessing is bestowed, hang upon its body trinkets and beads of wampum. Thus decorated, it is fixed to a cross-pole and suspended by the neck about eight feet from the ground. There it hangs until the fifth day, when it is taken down and carried by 'faith keepers' to the council-house, and laid out upon a bench, while the fire of the altar is kindling, while a priest, making speeches over it, relates the antiquity of this institution of their fathers, and its importance and solemnity, finally enjoining the people to direct their thoughts to the Great Spirit, concluding with a prayer of thanks that the lives of so many have been spared through another year. On this occasion, at 'noon by the sun,' twelve young warriors who were stationed at the northern corner of the council-house, firing their rifles, announced the procession as formed. Headed by four 'faith keepers,' who bore the sacrifice, and who were followed by the priests and matrons, and the old and young people, the procession slowly moved toward the main council-house, under which the remains of the celebrated prophet Ga-ne-o-di-yo (Handsome

Lake) are buried. Passing through the building from the western to the eastern door outward, and around the council-house, reentering it at the eastern door, they laid the sacrifice on the altar; and, as the flames surrounded it, a basket containing tobacco was thrown on the fire, its smoke rising as incense, as the priest, in a loud voice invoking the Great Spirit, chanted as follows: 'Hail, hail, hail! Thou who has created all things, who ruleth all things, and who givest laws to thy creatures, listen to our words. We now obey thy commands. That which thou hast made is returning unto thee our words, which are faithful and true.'

This was followed by the 'great thanking address' (given by the priest and people). . .. This concluded the religious rite, after which the people dispersed in various directions, to reassemble in the afternoon, attending the exciting and peculiarly Indian 'snow snake' game. The fifth being a day devoted to religion, there were no dances. The 'great f[e]ather dance,' a religious one, was given the next afternoon, followed by the 'trotting,' 'berry,' 'fish,' and 'raccoon' dances. Previous to the sacrifice the 'cousin clans' were divided: the Wolf, Turtle, Snipe, and Bear sat in the new council-house, the Deer, Beaver, Eel, and Hawk were in the old council-house, from whence the procession formed. Sachem Ha-yu-wan-es (Daniel Lafort, Wolf), Oh-yah-do-ja-neh (Thomas Webster, Snipe), hereditary keeper of the wampum belts, were masters of the religious ceremonies in which about two hundred Indians participated.

Source:
Journal of American Folklore, I (1888), pp. 83-85.
Reprinted from an article by Harriet Maxwell Converse, an adoptive member of the Seneca tribe, in the *Elmira (New York) Telegram*, January 29, 1888.

The Iroquois games of chance, which W. M. Beauchamp (1830-1925) described collectively as "white and black," were already old when Beauchamp wrote his 1896 paper on the subject. The games had been described, Beauchamp noted, in the Jesuit Relations. The latter was the name for a series of reports from the leading missionary of the Jesuit sect in Québec to his superior, the Provincial of Paris, during the years from 1632 to 1673.

Beauchamp also observed that a Father Bruyas "alluded to one of [the games] in his Mohawk lexicon of radical words." Here the term radical means "fundamental," and apparently Bruyas was compiling a dictionary of all the root words in the Mohawk language. Undoubtedly this is the same Bruyas who, along with two other priests, gave Kateri Tekakwitha (1656-1680), the first Native American nun, her first instruction in Christianity.

Beauchamp's description of the two games seems rather complex, perhaps an outgrowth of the language of his time, but the rules themselves were fairly simple. In the first game—a variant of which, as he noted, was called Finger Shaker by the Onondagas—two contestants each received eight disks of bone or horn colored black on one side and white on the other. If one player had six or more of a certain color, he drew a certain amount of beans. The Onondaga variety of the game involved a series of ascending levels of matched buttons, each with a corresponding value in beans, designated as Bird, Pumpkin, and Field.

The other contest, sometimes called "the dish game," involved peach stones ground to the shape of disks and, once again, colored black on one side, white on the other. It, too, made use of beans as a way of awarding points, but contestants threw the peach disks like dice, using a wide, shallow bowl as a playing area. The Jesuit missionary St. Jean de Brébeuf (1593-1649; canonized 1930), who worked among the Hurons of what is now Canada and was later killed by the Iroquois, described the dish game in great detail.

Beauchamp noted that the games were public spectacles, attended with much excitement, but that they also had a religious character as well. In fact the mixture of sports or games with religious festivals or ceremonies is an old one: thus the Greek Olympics, which originated in 776 B.C. or before, was not primarily an athletic but a religious, as well as an artistic, festival. Closer to home for the Iroquois, there was the ancient ball game called tlachli, played by the Olmec and other peoples of Mesoamerica in the first millennium B.C.

The consequences of failure in tlachli were dire, with members of losing teams usually being sacrificed; by contrast, the Iroquois games were much more joyful events. They formed a significant part of the Mid-Winter Festival, or White Dog Feast, a celebration in which the Iroquois called on the earth to renew itself. Hence the designation of various teams for the dish game, in particular a contest between men and women which the Iroquois believed would determine the size of the corn in the harvest many months hence.

The dish game in particular seemed to be imbued with predictive qualities, according to the beliefs of the Iroquois. At one time, Beauchamp reported, it had been used as a form of divination, or study of physical material in order to determine what the future holds. Each piece in the game set had been associated with its own familiar spirit; but as Beauchamp went on to note, the game had come to have a more social than spiritual orientation.

Brébeuf, writing 260 years before, described the dish game as being "in great credit [i.e., high repute] in matters of medicine, especially if the sick man has *dreamed about it." Thus the members of a village—the Hurons, at least, typically played the game village against village—would bring a sick person on a blanket to the area where the game was to be played. Brébeuf also noted the intensity of enthusiasm that greeted the game: "The whole company crowds into one cabin, and arranges itself on the one side and the other, upon poles raised even to the top.... Both sides bet loudly and firmly."*

Bruyas, in his dictionary of "radical" words, found that the Mohawk word at-nén-ha, or fruit stone (i.e., pit) was the root of the infinitive twa-ten-na-wé-ron, "to play with the dish." Thanks to Bruyas, Brébeuf, and others—not to mention Beauchamp himself—a record of the Iroquois games was preserved; however, one early observer made the mistake of describing them as dice games. Though the Iroquois games and dice both involve chance and probability, there are at least as many differences between them as there are similarities.

GAMES AT THE WHITE DOG FEAST

Some Iroquois games have a high antiquity, having survived the test of time. Two forms of the game of white and black still exist, and there are frequent allusions to one of these in the Jesuit Relations, where it is termed that of the plate or dish. It excited the highest interest; for though it was of the simplest nature, nation played against nation, and village against village. From the floor to the ridgepole of the cabin the eager spectators looked at the two players, showing their sympathy by their cries.

Two forms of this simple game of chance remain, and perhaps there were never more than these. Father Bruyas alluded to one of them in his Mohawk lexicon of radical words, speaking of it as the game in which the women scatter fruit stones with the hand. This distinction of throwing remains, although disks of bone or horn are now used instead of the stones of fruit. L. H. Morgan described this as the game of deer buttons, called Gus-ga-e-sá-ta by the Senecas. They used eight circular buttons of deer horn, about an inch in diameter, and blackened on one side. These are about an eighth of an inch in thickness, and beveled to the edge. He said: "This was strictly a fireside game, although it was sometimes introduced as an amusement at the season of religious councils, the people dividing into tribes as usual, and betting upon the result." In public two played it at a time, with a succession of players. In private two or more played it on a blanket, on which they sat and threw. His counting differs at first sight from that which I received, but amounts to the same thing. Beans were used for the pool, and Morgan said that six white or black drew two, seven drew four, and all

white or black drew twenty. Less than six drew nothing, and the other player had his throw until he lost in turn.

Among the Onondagas now eight bones or stones are used, black on one side and white on the other. They term the game Ta-you-nyun-wát-hah, or Finger Shaker, and from one hundred to three hundred beans from the pool, as may be agreed. With them it is also a household game.

In playing this the pieces are raised in the hand and scattered, the desired result being indifferently white or black. Essentially, the counting does not differ from that given by Morgan. Two white or two black will have six of one color, and these count two beans, called O-yú-ah, or the Bird. The player proceeds until he loses, when his opponent takes his turn. Seven white or black gain four beans, called O-néo-sah, or Pumpkin. All white or all black gain twenty, called O-hén-tah, or a Field. These are all that draw anything, and we may indifferently say with the Onondagas, two white or black for the first, or six with the Senecas. The game is played singly or by partners, and there is no limit to the number. Usually there are three or four players.

In counting the gains there is a kind of ascending reduction; for as two birds make one pumpkin, only one bird can appear in the result. First come the twenties, then the fours, then the twos, which can occur but once. Thus we may say for twenty, Jo-han-tó-tah, you have one field, or more as the case may be. In the fours we can only say, Ki-yae-ne-you-sáh-ka, you have four pumpkins, for five would make a field. For two beans there is the simple announcement of O-yú-ah, Bird. There is often great excitement over this game.

The game of peach stones, much more commonly used and important, has a more public character, although I have it in an Indian parlor. In early days the stones of the wild plum were used, but now six peach stones are ground down to an elliptic flattened form, the opposite sides being black or white. This is the great game known as that of the dish nearly three centuries ago. The wooden owl which I used was eleven inches across the top and three inches deep, handsomely carved out of a hard knot. A beautiful small bowl which I saw elsewhere may have been used by children.

The six stones are place in Kah-óon-wah, the bowl, and thence the Onondagas term the game Ta-yune-oo-wáh-es, throwing the bowl to each other as they take it in turn. In public playing two players are on their knees at a time, holding the bowl between them. When I played, simply to learn the game, we sat in chairs, the bowl being on another chair between us. Beans are commonly used for counters, but we had plum stones. Many rules are settled according to agreement, but the pumpkin is left out, and the stones usually count five for a bird and six for a field. All white or all black is the highest throw, and five or six are the only winning points. In early days it would seem that all white or all black alone counted. The bowl is simply struck on the floor; and although the game is said to be sometimes intensely exciting, the scientific spirit restrained my enthusiasm. I was not playing for beans, but for information.

This ancient game is used at the New Year's or White Dog Feast among the Onondagas yet. Clan plays against clan, the Long House against the Short House, and, to foretell the harvest, the women play against the men. If the men win, the ears of corn will be long, like them; but if the women gain the game, they will be short, basing the results on the common proportion of the sexes.

Source:

Journal of American Folklore, IX (1896), pp. 269-270. From a paper on "Iroquois Games" by W. M. Beauchamp read at the annual reading of the American Association for the Advancement of Science in 1896.

ISRAELI AMERICANS

$\mathbf{O}$n May 14, 1948, the President of the United States granted the world's first recognition of the new Jewish nation of Israel, the first Jewish state in 2000 years, that came in to existence at midnight in Jerusalem which was 6 P.M. in Washington. President Harry S Truman signed the document at 6:11. When Truman had requested the officials papers from the Jewish Agency in Washington, the document arrived with the name of the country left blank because it had not been decided. "The State of Israel" is hand-written above the scratched out "Jewish State."

From the late nineteenth-century and throughout both world wars, Zionists campaigned for the formation of a Jewish homeland. Britain had received a special mandate over Palestine from the League of Nations after World War I with the understanding that an independent home for Jews in Palestine would be created. By 1947 Palestine was a major trouble spot in the British Empire, requiring some 100,000 troops and a huge maintenance budget. Hundreds of thousands of Jewish Holocaust survivors temporarily housed in displaced persons camps in Europe were clamoring to be settled in Palestine. International public opinion sided against British policy. President Truman pressured Britain to change its course in Palestine. Postwar Britain depended on American economic aid to reconstruct its war-torn economy.

On February 18, 1947, the British relinquished their mandate in Palestine and handed the problem to the United Nations, one of the international community's first tests in working together. On May 15, 1947, a special session of the UN General Assembly established the United Nations Special Committee on Palestine (UNSCOP), consisting of 11 members. The UNSCOP reported on August 31 that a majority supported the partition into separate Arab and Jewish states, a special international status for Jerusalem, and an economic union linking the three members. Backed by both the United States and the Soviet Union, the plan was adopted after two months of intense deliberations as the UN General Assembly Resolution of November 29, 1947. The League of Arab States Council, meeting in December 1947, said it would take whatever measures were required to prevent implementation of the resolution. Violence between Arabs and Jews mounted. Many Jewish centers, including Jerusalem, were besieged by the Arabs. In January 1948, President Truman, warned by the United States Department of State that a Jewish state was not viable, reversed himself on the issue of Palestine, agreeing to postpone partition and to transfer the Mandate to a trusteeship council.

President Truman released the recognition to the complete surprise of the American delegation at the United Nations. That delegation had just days before recommended on behalf of the United States that the proposed partition of Palestine creating a Jewish state, be abandoned. The two-sentence recognition resulted immediately in euphoric celebrations by Jewish Americans and by the American population as a whole. Americans were still stunned by discovering the true scope of the Nazis' extermination of Jews and favored the establishment of a Jewish homeland for the thousands of surviving but displaced Jews. Official U.S. recognition of the State of Israel climaxed a protracted effort by Jewish interest groups such as the American Zionist Emergency Council that had persuaded 33 state legislatures to pass resolutions favoring a Jewish sate in Palestine.

Support for a Jewish homeland was good politics in 1948. The United States also expected to benefit strategically from having from an ally in the Middle East. Political, humanitarian and foreign policy concerns pressured President Truman in deciding the Palestine issue. Harry S Truman had become president upon the sudden death of Franklin Roosevelt on April 12, 1945. Truman's presidential duties included meeting with Stalin and Churchill in July of 1945 to decide the shape and future of war-torn Europe, the decision to use the first atomic bomb in a bid to end the war in the Pacific in August of 1945, continued support of the new United Nations, and the Palestine question in 1948. Margaret Truman, in her book Where the Buck Stops revealed her father's circumstances in his words as:

> I'd recognized Israel immediately as a sovereign nation when the British left Palestine in 1948, and I did so against the advice of my own secretary of state, George Marshall, who was afraid that the Arabs wouldn't like it.

It is impossible to overestimate the value of U.S. recognition within the international community. In 1999, that recognition is still unsuccessfully sought by the Palestine Liberation Organization as well as by the Dalai Lama's Tibetan government in exile. From 1948 until the present, the United States continues to express a commitment to Israel's security and well-bing, and has devoted a considerable share of its world-wide economic and security assistance to Israel.

U.S. RECOGNITION OF THE NEW STATE OF ISRAEL

First Draft

This Government has been informed that a Jewish state has been proclaimed in Palestine, and recognition has been requested by the Government thereof.

The United States recognizes the provisional government as the de facto authority of the new Jewish state.

Harry S Truman

Approved May 14, 1948

6:11

Final Draft

This Government has been informed that a Jewish state has been proclaimed in Palestine, and recognition has been requested by the *provisional* Government thereof.

The United States recognizes the provisional government as the de facto authority of the new *state of Israel.*

Harry S Truman

Approved May 14, 1948

6:11

Source:

Electronic image of original document available from the National Archives and Records Administration's website at http://www.nara.gov/exhall/originals/ israel.html. Actual document kept at Harry S Truman Library in Independence, Missouri.

Children hold up an Israeli flag during the annual "Salute to Israel" parade along New York City's Fifth Avenue.

ITALIAN AMERICANS

*T*his oral history interview was given in New York in 1938, and gives a glimpse of how nicknames were established among Italian immigrants when they returned to Italy with their stories of America. Nicknames are an important element in the folklore of an ethnic group. The custom of taking a nickname has a long history in Italy. For example, the Italian Renaissance painter Michaelangelo Merisi (1571-1610) was nicknamed Caravaggio because he was born in the northern Italian town of Caravaggio. Italian nicknames were often derived from habits or events that came to characterize an individual to their community, as this document shows.

Italian immigrant Vincent Viola D'Atri recounts how his uncle was given the nickname "Shut Up" by his friends. His uncle was one of more than five million Italians who became Americans according to immigration records. The largest Italian immigration wave occurred between 1880 and 1920, involving immigrants who are mentioned in this document. Most of these Italians came from the southern Italian provinces of Abruzzi, Calabria, Basilicata (Lucania), Campania, and Apilia. By 1900, at least 100,000 Italians came to America each year, and in 1907 that number climbed to 285,731. In America, 90 percent of these immigrants settled in large cities. Most of the immigrants of this wave were men between the ages of 16 and 45 who came to earn enough money to return to Italy and prosper. Like Vincent's uncle, about half of this immigration wave returned to Italy. According to immigration records, 3.8 million Italians came to the United States between 1899 and 1924, and 2.1 million left the United States. Some Italians who left came back after their money ran out. After the turn of the century, immigrants were more inclined to remain in the United States, because more families immigrated.

New York was the destination of choice for 97 percent of these Italians immigrants. New York had the largest number of Italians and the most crowded neighborhoods. There were more Italians in New York by 1910 than there were in Florence, Venice and Genoa combined. Many immigrants rented apartments in hastily constructed tenement buildings that were routinely cited for housing violations. The Italian community below Fourteenth Street in New York was said to be mobile because immigrants moved every two or three months, shifting the community within New York. Vincent became a factory worker in New York. Most Italian immigrants found work in nearby clothing factories in the garment district, or construction jobs, or railroad or dock work. Housing communities were typically next to the place of employment.

NICKNAMES AND THEIR SOURCES— ITALY

STATE: NEW YORK

NAME OF WORKER: May Swenson

ADDRESS: 509 E. 79th St., Apt. 21, New York City

DATE: October 17, 1938

1. Date and time of interview: October 18, 2 to 4:30 PM

2. Place of interview: 2910 Avenue D, Brooklyn

3. Name and address of informant: Vincent Viola D'Atri 2910 Ave. D., Brooklyn

4. Name and address of person, if any, who put you in touch with informant: Mildred Shachter 2910 Avenue D., Brooklyn

5. Name and address of person, if any, accompanying you: None

6. Description of room, house, surroundings, etc.: Mr. D'Atri lives in bachelor quarters which he sublets from an Italian family at the above address.

FORM B: Personal History of Informant

1. Ancestry: Italian, both father and mother

2. Place and date of birth: Sara Cena, Italy, 1900. Moved to New York about 9 years ago.

3. Family: Two brothers, two sisters.

4. Places lived in, with dates:

5. Education, with dates: Public school in Italy. Private study of the English language, and night school in New York.

6. Occupations and accomplishments, with dates: Factory worker in machine industries; typewriters, sewing machines.

7. Special skills and interests: Interested in music; plays accordian and mouth-organ. Has written poetry and articles for American-Italian publications.

8. Community and religious activities:

9. Description of informant: Mr. Vincent Viola D'Atri is a short plump man, with smooth dark features, clean shaven, his glistening black hair parted on the side, and brushed in a semi-circle above his forehead. Very mellow, large brown eyes; full lips. His whole appearance and manner is reserved, polite, smiling, and his voice has a melodious lilt, emphasized by a heavy, but charming accent. While talking, he moves his plump little hands with agility; and when trying to think of a word that is slow in coming off the tip of his tongue, the thumb and forefinger of his left hand go to his brow; sporadic wrinkles appear in a sharp V over the bridge of his nose.

10. Other Points gained in interview: When I interviewed him, he was very neatly and modestly attired in a dark blue suit, white pin-stripes, pale blue-green shirt, and a silk, salmon-colored tie. He wore yellow oxfords, highly polished, with the toes coming to a perfect point.

FORM C: Text of Interview (Unedited)

This is really happen to an uncle of mine — Uncle Vincent, of which I am christened; he went from our little village (Sara Cena, Italy, 4,000 inhabitants) in the south of Italy, to America and stayed there five or six years, then he came back to Italy. This was some years ago; then when the people there living in the village welcomed back their neighbor who have been over in U.S., they were very friendly and curious and asking him about all that he had seen and done in his travels and in America. Naturally, in America they are very interested.

My Uncle had learned a slang of America: "Shut up!" And he said this word whenever he was talking of his experience, meaning you see, to impress with his new learning of the U.S. language, all his friends. He kept saying this word so much, and not ever what it meant, and his friends heard him, and soon they were calling him by that word, "Shut up." That is the way is often done in Italy, a man called by not his name, but other name of which he reminds by his speech, or something he is doing, or such like that. . .see? So my Uncle Vincent become "Shut up" and went after that in his town by that name.

****

There was another man I am knowing in Italy; he they call "Golden Chain". For why they call him that, "Golden Chain"? Because when coming from a big town in North, and after many years away, coming back to his village there, he have got wealthy and have brought a gold watch and chain hanging across his middle of his suit; the chain, a fine gold chain they seen hanging. The word, Golden Chain, in Italian it is "L'oro Giao". That what they call him "L'oro Giao". . .a man of the Golden Chain become his name there.

****

Well, you ask me now, I think of "Shep di Sciasciao"; he have of his christening the name "Joseph" an' live in Sciasciao. They call for short just "Shep". I tell you his story, and a song. This song like what you want: they put the words after many people sing; one put one word and one another, and it was stretched, so.

This man, "Shep", old man very wealthy, had beautiful daughter, only one daughter young an' nice. He was widow (widower) and the young boys they flock around his beautiful daughter. She very beautiful and very young, and father away in his shop, during day, and boys flock around her, court her. So her father, "Shep di Sciascao", he got mad, he tell daughter to be more careful. She say no; she like the boys; go more an' more to window, see young boys singing in garden; smile at that. Shep, he got mad, make anger with daughter, and after this they made a song in the village. All who know of this affair have much laughter, an' afterwards a song was sung around there, like this:

This evening, at three hours of night,
In this neighborhood will be fight
Shep di Sciasciao, he got mad
Against his daughter, he become full of rage.
An he got mad hard. From his bed he got up,
Went outside, in the porch of his house.
he hided himself behind the pillar
An' he start to throw plaster stone at one her lovers.
From inside the door, his slave of a daughter
　　answered:

"If you want a stone, then come and get it!"

The above was translated by informant from the following, in Italian:

Questa sera a ter ore di notte
In questo vicinato correranno botte
Shep di Sciasciao ci e adirato e contro
La piglia so l'epigliato
En ci e Adirato forte
Scende dal letto e vax davanti la prota.
En mitti dentro una garagogna e gittaon,
Calle rogna, e risponde la shiava
"Della piglia se vuoi, pietre aneni ti pigh!"

This song very funny; not funny in English. Yes, I can make better translation and write it you.

In the place where I live, this song was sung around; the young men [did something—transcript unclear] and considered very funny.

******

Another nickname was of an artisan shoemaker living in our village, but went away South America. Some time away. He came back; is friends they meet him; he have on eyeglasses. Never have they seen these thing, eyeglasses, in that village before. So ask, "What is it you got with your eyes underneath?" An man he tell, "It Cent-occhi: eyeglasses." After that, this man called by all his friends, "Signor Under-Eyes"!

Source:

Library of Congress. *American Life Histories: Manuscripts from the Federal Writers' Project, 1936-1940* from the American Memory website (http://memory.loc.gov/ammem/wpaintro/wpahome.html).

Italian American immigrants often turned to creative methods of self-employment in order to earn a living. Many operated food push carts in the crowed streets of New York. Others went from door-to-door, offering carpentry work, cleaning services, or any other skill for which they could be paid. In this oral history given by an Italian American woman, we learn about her struggle to support her family after her husband's death.

Melicenda derives her income from cooking for non-Italian Americans, toward whom she feels superior in culinary skills. "Italians know how to make their own Italian dinners. These are Americans," she explains. This attitude continues in the 1990s according to best-selling author Frances Mayes, who bought a home in Italy and wrote about her American Italian experiences in Under the Tuscan Sun *and* Bella Tuscany. *Mayes tells that Italians have begun a "Slow Foods" movement to encourage Italian culinary practices and foods thought to be endangered by American fast foods.*

Melicenda mentions that many of the Italian American women have pasta machines. Americans had already begun their love affair with time-saving conveniences, gismos and machines. Clarence Birdseye had invented frozen food in 1923, and the pop-up toaster had come along in 1927. By 1930, 60 percent of all household in the United States had radios. However, Melicenda did not use a pasta machine back in Italy and can't afford one in America. Pasta machines had already been around quite a while. Thomas Jefferson saw a macaroni or pasta machine while touring northern Italy in 1787. At the time, macaroni was a highly fashionable food in Paris, where Jefferson was stationed as minister to France. He later commissioned his secretary William Short to purchase a macaroni machine in Italy, but the machine was not very durable. Jefferson is credited with bringing the first macaroni machine to America in 1789, so they were hardly new in the 1940s when Melicenda is cooking for non-Italian Americans. As a matter of fact, the first industrial pasta factory in America was built in Brooklyn in 1848 by a Frenchman.

Melicenda observes that Americans had begun to ask for Italian food "in the last ten years" which would be the 1930s. Italian foods known to most Americans prior to World War II were the foods of southern Italy. Most of these are rich in tomato sauces and pasta-based, such as spaghetti and meatballs and pizza. In the second half of the twentieth century, the foods from northern Italy, where the diet was more frugal and basically vegetarian, became more popular. Dishes such as risotto (rice), polenta (corn), and pesto, the trademark sauce of Liguria made by pounding basil, garlic, and olive oil.

Melicenda serves wine with her dinners. The National Prohibition Act passed by the U.S. Congress in 1920 to make selling alcohol illegal had been repealed in 1933. Liquor control then became a state rather than a federal problem. Many communities voted to become "dry" meaning that the sale of alcoholic beverages was illegal. Apparently Melicenda lives in a dry community, because she fears the raids of local police and says of her sale of wine, "I know it's against the law."

ITALIAN FEED

Mari Tomasi {Men Against Granite}
Recorded in: Writers' Section Files
DATE: SEP 21 1940

The woman was sitting at the kitchen table feeding small pieces of meat, onion, garlic and spinach to a food grinder. She was well over fifty. As she spoke and worked, her long gold earrings bobbed and swung.

"I'm getting a dinner ready for a party of twelve people. All from Montpelier. Not Italians. Italians know how to make their own Italian dinners. These are Americans. In the winter I get about two orders a week for good-sized dinner parties. In the summer, not so many. They like to get out then in their cars and stop at different places to eat."

She had finished grinding the food. It was a soft brown-green mass[?]. This she seasoned with salt, pepper and crushed mint leaves.

"This is the filling for the *ravioli*," she said. "Always they want *ravioli* for their dinners, and some want spaghetti at the same meal. Me, I think it is foolish to have both at the same dinner. They're almost the same except that the *ravioli* are stuffed. But if that's what they want—me, I don't care. It means more money for me—"

She cleared the table and tacked a heavy white oilcloth over it. She rolled to a very thin sheet a rather stiff pastry made of eggs, flour and mashed boiled potatoes.

An Italian American family offers a toast during a celebration.

"I been doing this kind of work for ten years or so. Since my husband died. Quite a few women in Barre earn money this way."

"It's a funny thing—In Italy I was always too busy to think much of food. I lived in the Lake Como district up north. Our house was on a hill outside the city. My two sisters and me would go to the city every day to work in the mills. Silk mills. We were so hungry at noon we were satisfied with any kind of food. We carried our lunch with us. *Polenta* and cheese tasted as good to us then as chicken does today. We like good food, but we were always too busy and didn't have enough money to eat only the simple food. Over there it seems funny to be cooking meals for people who got no more money than me. It's in the last ten years that American people have been asking for Italian food."

The woman had finished rolling the pastry to a thin sheet. Now she cut it in diamond shapes about an inch wide.

"Many Italian women have machines to make these *raviolis*," she said. "I haven't got one. They're quite expensive and anyway, I'd rather make them by hand."

On each diamond of pastry she placed a teaspoonful of the ground food. she flapped the end of the pastry over this and pressed it to the lower half with a fork. The finished *ravioli* were V-shaped—like the flaps of envelopes. "They look better when they're made by machine," she said. "But they taste the same.

"We always made them this way in the old country, we never had any machines to help us. Our fingers were the machines. I never saw the machines until I came to this country. I came over when I was eighteen years old. I wasn't married then. I came over here to marry Pietro Bartoletti. I grew up with Pietro. I went to school with him. We were always good friends in the old country. He came over here to work in the sheds. Every month I got a letter from him. He told me how good the

An Italian American family dines outside. The family meal has been a traditional meeting place for Italian families and is the traditional centerpiece of the day.

granite business was. He asked me to marry him, so I wrote back *yes*. I came over here in August. I liked Barre. It didn't seem strange to me. We were married right away. And right away a great many people came to visit me. Italian people. Not many I know. But all Italian people from the north of Italy who spoke my Italian and lived the way I lived. I had no time to be lonesome.

"My Pietro, he worked in the sheds for fifteen years. Always he was *not* satisfied. Always he said some day he would find other work. But no other work he found. He stayed in the sheds until he died. He caught a bad cold one winter. The doctors, they all said his lungs were already weak. He couldn't stand the added sickness. He died."

The woman set down the rolling pin. She folded her arms and sighed. "Well, I was with four children, all young enough to be in school, so I said to myself: you got to earn some money, Melicenda. You got to earn a little money to add to the insurance money Pietro left. So I started to cook meals for

these American people. They like Italian food and they pay good money for it. It was work I could do at home, so I tried to get as many orders as I could.

"One Italian woman, a friend of mine, does the Italian cooking for one of the restaurants; but me, I don't want to bother with that. I got enough to do. I got one girl in her last year at high school. I got to keep the house for her.

"The other three children are married. The boy is in the printing business in Boston, and the two girls both live outside the State. They were both married before they were out of high school three years. I'm glad for them. They got nice homes and they are happy. I'm happy they didn't marry stone-cutters. Always with them it is worry, worry. Worry about their health; and worry about how many days a week they work. No matter how good looking a man is or how good he is, I never would say to a girl: marry him this stonecutter. No, less than twenty years I had with my Pietro. That is too little.

"The girls, they didn't like it when I started to get meals for Americans. They said, 'You are as good as they are, why do you get dinners for them?' They didn't understand much about money then. They didn't know that you have to work to make a living. They learned soon, soon. They worked three years after they were out of high school, they learned it took money to live. Libera, the youngest girl, doesn't mind. Some times she helps me wait on table. She even helps me get the meals, it's different now! People don't look down so much on how you earn your money. It's a good thing. Everybody's got to live one way or another.

"After Pietro died I had to figure a way to live. I said to myself: I have the house—small as it is, it's mine and all paid for. I have a little insurance money, but there are four children. I got to make that money stretch. So I began taking orders for dinners. And sometimes if the neighbors were sick—but not sick enough for real nurses—I took care of them. They liked someone who spoke their own tongue. I don't do much nursing now. It's different. Many Barre born Italian girls have graduated from our hospital. They know twenty times more about nursing than I do, and they speak Italian well enough to understand the patient.

It's a funny thing—In Italy I was always too busy to think much of food. I lived in the Lake Como district up north. Our house was on a hill outside the city. My two sisters and me would go to the city every day to work in the mills. Silk mills. We were so hungry at noon we were satisfied with any kind of food.

"I like to work like this—here in the house. I know where every pan is hung, where every spice is kept. Sometimes my customers want me to cook in their own homes. Well, I do not refuse, but I charge them more."

She had finished cutting and pressing together the last of the *ravioli*. She sprinkled them lightly with white cornmeal and placed them on a long board to harden.

The kitchen was small. Six plain, sturdy chairs and a heavy round table almost filled the room. A coal fire burned in the stove. Beside the pantry door was a doorstep of granite—a polished gray ball of granite.

The woman said, "My husband made that doorstep. I got two more upstairs. One I gave to my daughter in Massachusetts. Pietro used to take home odd pieces of granite that I could use around the house. I still have some thin, flat pieces—just grout—that I use in the fall when I make pickles. I put them on the cucumbers to hold them down in the brine. Once he made me a knob of granite, a little bigger than this—"the woman held up a clenched fist, "he made it smooth and put a handle on it. I used it to pound steak. One day the youngest boy took it out in the yard to hammer a nail in his cart. It split. I haven't got another one. I miss it.

"You want to see where my customers eat?" the woman asked. "Right in here."

The dining room was but little larger than the kitchen. The walls were covered with a golden brown paper almost the same shade as the oval table of oak. Afternoon sunlight spilled through the two windows, giving warmth to the bareness. The room was scrupulously clean.

Melicenda said, "I don't bother to fix the table pretty. I figure my customers come here to eat, not to look at my table. Oh, I fix the food fancy so it will look good to the eyes, too. And I give them plenty. That's what they pay for.

"I charge them $1.25 each. That isn't too much. First I serve them a big platter of stuffed celery, thin slices of *salami* and *mortadella*, ripe olives, and pickles. Then the *ravioli* with a rich tomato sauce. If they want spaghetti, too," the woman shrugged resigned shoulders, "Well, I give them the spaghetti as well. The little Italian rolls are good with *ravioli*. I don't make them myself. I buy them from the Italian baker down the street. Just before it's time to serve the dinner, I sprinkle them with milk and put them in the oven for a few minutes to heat them. Dessert, no. I never serve dessert. The *ravioli* are so rich that I make them a dish that will cut the richness. I give them a salad of lettuce, endive, tomato, onion, celery, mixed with vinegar and olive oil. I use the wine vinegar. It gives a better taste to the salad. With the dollar and a quarter dinner I serve just one glass of red wine. If they want more they got to pay for it.

"Tonight my customers will get here at seven o'clock. They won't leave until eleven. I know. They have been here before. It is a crowd of young people who work in offices in Montpelier. They will drink about five dollars worth of wine before they go home. Sometimes one or two of them bring a pint of their own whiskey. They want to drink it here. Well, I don't refuse. But it's not so much profit for me when they don't buy my wine.

"You know what happened to a friend of mine last summer? She is a woman my age, and she earns a living getting dinners like I do. She got a dinner for sixteen people. A fried chicken dinner she charges $1.50 for. Well, not one of those sixteen people bought wine. Not one glass. They drank whiskey they had brought with them. About half-past ten policemen, come in the house—three of them, to raid it. Well, they go down cellar and they find the same kind of whiskey that is on the table. They want to arrest the woman. She says no, that she hasn't sold any. Her customers, they all say no, too. Well, the police can't prove that she sold it. They don't do anything to her. But after that they watch her close. She doesn't do much business now. She's afraid to sell wine.

"Why don't the police leave us alone? We got to make a living. We hurt no one. I know it's against the law. But just the same it's an honest way to live. There are worse ways of making a living and the law says nothing about it. I never been raided, maybe some day I will. Then I will lose customers. I will have to be extra careful about the people I sell wine to."

Melicenda smiled. "Well, any time you want a good Italian feed, call me up. My name is in the telephone book. Just call Melicenda Bartoletti."

Source:

Library of Congress. *American Life Histories: Manuscripts from the Federal Writers' Project, 1936-1940* from the American Memory website (http://memory.loc.gov/ammem/wpaintro/wpahome.html).

*S*an Gennaro or St. Januarius, patron saint of Naples, died for his faith during the persecutions of the Emperor Diocletian. According to the legend, he was killed with a sword but only after miraculously surviving a fiery furnace and a den of wild beasts into which he was cast, and after converting many of his persecutors. Two vials believed to contain his congealed blood are preserved in the Cathedral of San Gennaro in Naples. The blood in these vials liquefy on the anniversary of his death. In New York, the festival is sponsored by a lay organization consisting mainly of Italian-Americans of Neapolitan origin, the Society of San Gennaro. Its setting is a half-mile stretch of Mulberry Street in the heart of Little Italy. The society's first festival took place in 1925, and the celebration runs from the thirteenth of September to the twenty-first.

FEAST OF SAN GENNARO IN LITTLE ITALY

In Little Italy tomorrow [September 13, 1980], the Feast of San Gennaro will offer the pageantry befitting "A festa 'e tutte 'e feste"— "the festival of all festivals," in the translation of the Society of San Gennaro.

As a marching band plays, the silver-and-brass bust of San Gennaro, the patron saint of Naples, will be borne along Mulberry Street, under the 42 arches with a million lights and past the 300 food and game booths.

Today and through Sept. 21, the half-mile stretch of Mulberrry Street will be awash with laughter, music and all varieties of Italian food, including sausages, peppers, clams, calzone, *zeppole*, and *sfogliatelli*.

In an age when street festivals have become as much a part of New York as open fie hydrants on a summer day, San Gennaro remains something special, the granddaddy of street affairs.

"Pople keep asking what's new about the festival," said Arthur Tisi, president of the Society of San Gennaro. "The answer is nothing is new about the festival. It is the same thing, the same tradition, the same cultural and religious activity."

Italian Americans wait in line to buy zeppole at the Scialo Brothers Bakery in Rhode Island.

And when all the other street festivals fade, Mr. Tisi insists, San Gennaro will remain.

"This is our 54th year," he said. "And we'll be here for another 54 years."

The fair stretches along Mulberry Street for 10 blocks, from Worth to Houston Streets, and continues from 9 A.M. to midnight each day. Las year, the 11-day event attracted three million people, who, the organizers say, consumed two million sausage heros alone. This year organizers expect nothing more and nothing less.. . .

At last night's official opening, the bust of the saint was carried from the storefront headquarters of the society at 140 Mulberry Street to the corner of Hester and Mulberry Streets, where it was placed in a temporary shrine. The parade tomorrow takes place at 3 P.M. and is the first of several to come.

A week from today, Sept. 19, on the traditional anniversary of San Gennaro's martyrdom in the year 305, there will be a parade with the relic of the saint. Bishop Lorenzo Graziano will participate.

The following day, Saturday, Sept. 20, there will be a celebration with more of a Mardi Gras Flavor, presided over by this year's queen of the festival, 17-year-old Kim Ianniello.

According to Mr. Tisi, each one of the queens has married within two years of her festival reign. Matrimony, in fact, is one of the goals of the event, said Mr. Tisi, who keeps a thick book of all the couples who met at San Gennaro festivals. Among those in the book is Mr. Tisi himself, who met his wife Marie at the 1966 festival.

Source:
New York Times, September 12, 1980.

Primarily a celebration by descendants of Italians from the vicinity of Naples, most notably observed in the Greenpoint section of Brooklyn, New York, for more than a century, this celebration combines the feast days of Our Lady of Mount Carmel on July 16 and St. Paulinus of Nola, a town near Naples, whose day is June 22 and who is the primary patron. St. Paulinus is said to have been an architect who built aqueducts and churches. When Vandals raided Nola and carried off a number of the townspeople into slavery, he offered himself as a substitute for the only son of a widow. Somehow he miraculously managed to obtain the freedom of all his fellow citizens. St. Paulinus was canonized in 431 A.D. The festival includes a mass, street fair, and reunions but its main feature is a procession that ends at the Church of Our Lady of Carmel in which bearers carry a giglio, a tower some six stories high weighing two tons, which is surmounted by a statue of the patron saint. Because June 22 is the summer solstice and because of the shape of giglio, there is speculation that a pagan fertility rite lies behind the holiday.

CARRYING THE GIGLIO

Each year, in Greenpoint, there are a hundred and twenty-eight lifters under the command of three capos [heads, chiefs]. There is the capo paranza [head of the company], the head capo. Under him are Capos No. 2 and No. 3. There is often an honorary capo from a previous year, and a godfather of the giglio [tower]: they do nothing more laborious than represent the past. There is also a singer, who, along with a ten-man brass-and-drum band, sits in front of the giglio on a giant platform and serenades the capos and their lifters. Each successive capo paranza has his trademark tune, his style of conducting the lift, and his favorite kind of lift. The repertoire is limited by the bulk of the object being carried. Mostly, the lifts are a matter of heaving the giglio aloft, then walking it forward and dropping it without anyone's getting hurt. The giglio rarely moves more than thirty yards in a given lift. Some capos ask the paranza [group, company] to bounce the giglio. Some like to see the giglio rotated through three hundred and sixty degrees. The lifters never know what a capo plans until he raises his cane of office in the air. The capo paranza deploys the cane much as a conductor does his baton. Certain capos carry the cane solemnly, projecting heartbreaking dolor. Certain capos pump the cane like a Giants cheerleader at the halftime break. Certain capos grunt and shout at the cane as if it were something alive. And certain capos invent a technique as they go along, drawing on the whim of the moment, the temperament of the music, the emotion they absorb from the paranza and the crowd.

Source:
New Yorker, June 4, 1990, pp. 81-82.